Signs of Reincarnation

Signs of Reincarnation

Exploring Beliefs, Cases, and Theory

James G. Matlock

Foreword by Jeffrey Mishlove

ROWMAN & LITTLEFIELD
Lanham • Boulder • New York • London

Published by Rowman & Littlefield
An imprint of The Rowman & Littlefield Publishing Group, Inc.
4501 Forbes Boulevard, Suite 200, Lanham, Maryland 20706
www.rowman.com

6 Tinworth Street, London SE11 5AL, United Kingdom

British Library Cataloguing in Publication Information Available

Library of Congress Cataloging-in-Publication Data
Names: Matlock, James G., 1954- author.
Title: Signs of reincarnation : exploring beliefs, cases, and theory / James G. Matlock ;
    foreword by Jeffrey Mishlove.
Description: Lanham : Rowman & Littlefield, [2019] | Includes bibliographical
    references and index.
Identifiers: LCCN 2019005826 (print) | LCCN 2019017045 (ebook) |
    ISBN 9781538124802 (electronic) | ISBN 9781538124819 (cloth : alk. paper) |
    ISBN 9781538124796 (pbk : alk. paper)
Subjects: LCSH: Reincarnation.
Classification: LCC BL515 (ebook) | LCC BL515 .M333 2019 (print) |
    DDC 133.901/35—dc23
LC record available at https://lccn.loc.gov/2019005826

♾™ The paper used in this publication meets the minimum requirements of American National Standard for Information Sciences—Permanence of Paper for Printed Library Materials, ANSI/NISO Z39.48-1992.

Printed in the United States of America

For Cristina

Contents

Foreword: A Tale of Two Theories: Reincarnation
  versus Archetypal Synchronistic Resonance (ASR),
  by Jeffrey Mishlove   ix

Preface   xvii

1 Introduction to the Study of Reincarnation Signs   1
What Is Reincarnation?   33
Challenge to Materialism   42

2 The Belief in Reincarnation   53
Signs, Beliefs, and Customs in Animistic Cultures   53
A Brief History of the Belief in Rebirth, West and East   63
Karma, God, and the Individual in Rebirth Theory   75

3 Research Methods and Interpretative Frames   87
Accounts of Past-Life Memory Recorded before 1960   87
Ian Stevenson's Field Research and Its Critics   98
Interpretative Frames for Reincarnation Cases   110

4 Child Studies: The Principal Signs of Reincarnation   123
Involuntary Memory of Previous Lives   123
Behavioral Identification with the Previous Person   136
Birthmarks and Other Physical Signs   148

5 Child Studies: Secondary Signs of Reincarnation   163
Signs of Discarnate Agency   163
Universal, Near-Universal, and Culture-Linked Patterns   177
The Psychological Impacts of Past-Life Memory   189

6 Past-Life Recall in Adulthood and Third-Party Reports **201**
Developmental Factors in Past-Life Memory Retrieval 201
Fantasy and Fact in Past-Life Regression under Hypnosis 213
The Contributions of Shamans, Psychics, and Mediums 223

7 The Process of Reincarnation **235**
Beyond Materialism 235
Personal Identity and Postmortem Survival 246
Reincarnation and Life 259

Afterword: Implications of Reincarnation Cases for Biology,
  by Michael Nahm 273

Glossary of Specialized and Technical Terms 289

References 309

Index 359

About the Author and Contributors 385

Foreword

A Tale of Two Theories

Reincarnation versus Archetypal
Synchronistic Resonance (ASR)

Jeffrey Mishlove

From the conventional, materialist point of view, a human life could be thought of as analogous to a piece of string. One end represents your birth. Then the string meanders around until you reach the other end—and your life is terminated. Once you leave this physical plane of existence, there is no more string. From the perspective of reincarnation as an empirical fact, life seems more like a circle or even a spiral. The string doesn't end with death. Nor does it begin with birth. In fact, reincarnation is sometimes likened to a wheel. Around and around we go, hopefully learning a bit more each time. Where the string begins and where it ends are questions subject to further inquiry.

The very idea of reincarnation, or rebirth, has powerful archetypal implications—far beyond the metaphoric differences between a piece of string and a spiral with no obvious beginning or end. It can shake one to one's core.

I remember quite distinctly the very first time I was introduced to this notion. I was a ten-year-old child, in the fourth grade, when my classmate presented a book report on Morey Bernstein's (1956) *The Search for Bridey Murphy*—an international best seller about a case of past-life hypnotic regression. At the moment I heard my classmate saying that this book explores the possibility that we have lived other lives before we were born, I felt an electrical shiver running up and down my spine. For me, moments like that seem to reflect a deep inner knowing or remembering.

To be clear, in spite of their importance to many individuals (including myself), neither past-life hypnotic regressions nor electrical shivers running up and down the spine are regarded as major signifiers of reincarnation in this book—based as it is on an analysis of the empirical data derived from a collection of more than seventeen hundred cases in which young children have reported veridical memories of previous lives.

Here, anthropologist Dr. James Matlock proposes that other "signs" do exist and have been known to both ancient and indigenous peoples throughout the world. Our modern, Western culture has lost this knowledge. But now, thanks to the diligent research of the late Dr. Ian Stevenson and the team that remains at the University of Virginia, along with a few others, this knowledge is being recovered. Matlock, an independent scholar associated with the Parapsychology Foundation, is at the forefront of that recovery process. To my knowledge, this book is unique. It bears the distinction of being the first college-level text to thoroughly review and evaluate the many empirical signs and pointers that relate to the ostensible process of reincarnation. It is interesting to note, for example, that over half of the time when children report memories of previous lives, those memories entail a violent death.

In order to understand the reincarnation process, it is helpful if we are willing to think of ourselves as reincarnation investigators. Matlock understands this because in the very first chapter he will be taking us along with him on a case study, visiting Bartlesville, Oklahoma. There we will come to know a young child, Rylann O'Bannion, born in 2008, who appears to have hazy yet uncanny memories concerning the tragic death of eleven-year-old Jennifer Schultz, who was sitting on a swing in the carport of her family's home in Kenner, Louisiana, just outside of New Orleans, speaking on the phone, when Pan Am Flight 759 faltered upon takeoff and crashed into the house.

Matlock will take us to the neighborhood where Jennifer Schultz was killed. He will even present a photo of the Schultz's ruined house on Fairway Street.

As I read through Matlock's manuscript, in preparation for writing this foreword, I could not help but notice a remarkable coincidence: I have been to that very location on Fairway Street in Kenner, Louisiana, before! Like many people, I suppose I am prone to push bizarre coincidences out of my mind. Nevertheless, my experience as a parapsychological investigator, as well as a psychotherapist with Jungian leanings, has shown me that the pursuit of such striking coincidences can lead to unexpected insights. The story of how my own life has surprisingly intersected (albeit only geographically) with Matlock's case investigation of Rylann O'Bannion's previous-life memories highlights, in this case, the difficulties faced by researchers, such as Matlock, who maintain that seemingly paranormal events are deserving of scientific investigation.

In 1983, I was hired by my late friend William Jennings, attorney for the International Airline Passengers Association, to organize a press conference in New Orleans in conjunction with the National Transportation Safety Board hearing about the tragic crash of Pan Am 759. The Association wished to promote the notion that the accident was caused not only by wind shear (the official explanation), but also by rain. The press conference was a success and was covered on national television. While on that trip, Jennings and I visited the crash site where Jennifer Schultz and 152 others lost their lives. That is the simple, prosaic basis for the coincidence. But, there is much more to the story that bears on the status of parapsychology as a legitimate scientific endeavor.

William Jennings was an unusual man, who had come into my life in a weird way. Years earlier, I received a phone call from him, out of the blue, introducing himself as "Captain Rainbow." He told me that he was the inventor of "Captain Rainbow's Laser Visors" and that he had plans to sell one to every person in China. He explained that the diffraction grating plastic visors turned everything into rainbow colors and that this had the effect of "opening up the chakras."

When I told my wife, Janelle, about this strange phone call, her response—to my admiration and delight—was "let's invite him over for lunch." That was the beginning of a friendship that lasted for decades. A few years later, in 1980, I received my doctoral degree in parapsychology from the University of California, Berkeley. To this day, my doctoral diploma remains the only one granted by an accredited university anywhere in the world that actually names the discipline of "Parapsychology." So, inevitably, I became a target for individuals who were hostile to the field. After graduating, I was publicly libeled in a major national magazine and found that—after a decade in graduate school—I was, essentially, unemployable in parapsychology (where few employment opportunities existed in the first place).

My friend William Jennings, who kept a statuette in his law office of Don Quixote on horseback jousting with a windmill, agreed to handle my defamation lawsuit on a contingency basis. Knowing of my desperate situation, he also helped me financially by providing this work opportunity in New Orleans. Looking back, I can say that I was fortunate to have been libeled. Amazingly, we eventually prevailed in our lawsuit. The financial settlement enabled me to enter the real estate market and accumulate the wealth that is now the basis of my retirement. But I can assure you that tireless and brave researchers such as Matlock have also had to confront the same social stigma that I once faced.

Attorney William Jennings loved coincidences and used to refer to them as "quinkydinks." The great Swiss psychiatrist Carl G. Jung (1973) developed his theory of "synchronicity," claiming that some coincidences had great psychological significance and could be very useful in furthering the therapeutic process. Jung and his colleague, Nobel laureate physicist Wolfgang Pauli, went further and maintained that human consciousness was able to interact in the physical world in a mysterious, "acausal" manner.

Driven by a series of personal experiences that I shall presently describe, I incorporated some of Jung's thinking into a related theory called "archetypal synchronistic resonance" (Mishlove & Engen, 2007) that I felt could account for certain ostensible signs of reincarnation appearing in my own life. This is where Matlock and I began to disagree.

When I first encountered Matlock's "Signs of Reincarnation" online course in 2014, I had a host of reasons why I thought we should be looking at alternatives to the reincarnation concept to account for the cases of childhood memories of past lives. For me, the notion of disembodied consciousness, for example, seemed like a contradiction in terms. It literally made no "sense." After all, disembodied points of awareness have no sensory organs. Furthermore, I had personally received psychic readings concerning my own previous incarnations about which I was quite dubious, albeit intrigued.

In the year 2000, Walter Semkiw, MD, learned that I owned the URL www.williamjames.com. I had secured that URL in the early days of the Internet because I then regarded (and still do regard) William James, who died in 1910, as an intellectual hero. He is widely acknowledged as the father of American psychology, an important philosopher in the American pragmatic tradition and, most importantly from my point of view, a pioneer in the field of psychical research (the field investigation discipline that preceded experimental parapsychology). Semkiw considered my strong admiration for William James as a sign of reincarnation and suggested to me that, perhaps, I had been William James in a past life. He also noted that my facial features resembled those of William James. Furthermore, he proposed that I test his hypothesis by seeing if individuals who were close colleagues, friends, and family members matched up in similar ways to persons known to have been close to William James.

I followed up on this idea and, to my surprise, was able to identify eight individuals close to me who bore some resemblance to friends and family members of William James. Semkiw then took this information to the trance channel Kevin Ryerson (also a friend and colleague of mine who once served with me as an officer of the California Society for Psychical Study), whose "spirit guide," Ahtun Re (ostensibly an ancient, Egyptian priest) offered his confirmation that each of my potential matches represented actual past-life identifications.

Later I participated in past-life hypnotic regression sessions conducted by Charles Tramont, MD, in which I attempted to recover memories of having been William James. (At one point, I had the thought that I was being called "Billiam." But I have never been able to find any reference to such an appellation accorded to William James.) During each session, I spontaneously awakened from the hypnotic state with stomach pains. Dr. Tramont took this as a sign that I was actually experiencing the bodily sensations of William James. However, considering that I already knew William James to have been a sickly man, I do not consider those symptoms as evidential of a past-life connection. For all I know, it was a question of diet and digestion.

The bottom line, for me, was that, as a researcher, I found the William James past-life identification unconvincing. However, at a personal level, it provided an opportunity for me to delve more deeply into the life of my intellectual hero. I gave Drs. Semkiw (2003) and Tramont (2008) permission to describe the William James reincarnation hypothesis in books they were writing—with the proviso that they also state that I, myself, do not accept that identification. Semkiw agreed, saying that "William James wouldn't have accepted it either," implying that he took my rejection of the identification as yet another sign of reincarnation (i.e., that we shared a certain scientific skepticism).

Kevin Ryerson's spirit guide, Ahtun Re, also made another past-life identification for me—as the ancient Roman philosopher, dramatist, and statesman Lucius Annaeus Seneca, that I have also *not* come to accept. This came about because of a videotaped hypnotic session that I had with Martin Rossman, MD, in the late 1980s. Dr. Rossman put me into a light trance state and asked me to contact my "inner healing advisor." I reported mental imagery of a man wearing a toga. Although I was hoping he would be the great Greek orator Demosthenes (as I wished to improve my public speaking abilities), the figure identified himself as "Seneca." I then asked the figure what he would recommend for me. He said, "Study my life."

This was the beginning of another intellectual exploration for me—studying a most fascinating character. Seneca was a Stoic philosopher, as well as a playwright, who, as personal tutor to the teenage emperor Nero, literally governed the Roman Empire for five years. Later in life, he was ordered by Nero to commit suicide. At the time, Seneca was at a dinner party with friends. He requested that he be allowed to make out his last will and testament. When that request was denied, he turned to his assembled friends and said, in effect, "I bequeath to you my life. Study my life" (Sorensen, 1976).

When I shared aspects of this exploration with my friend Kevin Ryerson, he provided me with a psychic reading in which "Ahtun Re" offered confirmation of Seneca as a past-life identification.

I thought very little more about this until the summer of 2005. At the time, I was in Spain, journeying to the city of Cordoba where, coincidentally, Seneca was born. It was then that I received an email from Brendan Engen, whom I did not know, saying that he had been told by a trance channel (who happened to be Kevin Ryerson, I later learned) that I was the reincarnation of Seneca, an individual with whom he, supposedly (also according to "Ahtun

Re") had been closely associated in a past life. This was the beginning of a fascinating email correspondence, in which I assured Brendan that I did not accept the past-life identification with Seneca—but was intrigued by the various coincidences involved (such as his email arriving just as I was embarking on a journey to the city of Seneca's birth). I told him that I suspected Jungian synchronicities were at play here. In fact, Brendan and I uncovered a series of unusual coincidences between us. This led to our joint authorship of the aforementioned paper, "Archetypal Synchronistic Resonance: A New Theory of Paranormal Experience."

In that paper, we suggested that the ASR dynamic could account for experiences that "can neither be accepted as literally construed nor dismissed as mere artifact or error" (Mishlove & Engen, 2007). In particular, we pointed to our own story involving an ostensible past-life connection. In our exuberance, we went so far as to claim in this paper that the ASR hypothesis could, in principle, account for the strong evidence of reincarnation developed through the investigations of Ian Stevenson (1974b, 1997a) and his colleagues. This is the point to which Matlock objected. He agreed that archetypal synchronistic resonance might well account for ostensible reincarnation experiences of adults, gathered through psychic readings and past-life regressions. However, he insisted it was not the best fit for the many hundreds of cases of young children's past-life memories—especially given their accompanying behavioral and physical symptoms.

The Signs of Reincarnation course that I took with Matlock in 2014 was very much akin to the process you will go through reading this book, chapter by chapter. The empirical data include many overlapping threads of evidence, or, as Matlock phrases it, "signs of reincarnation." When one takes all of this into account—personality factors, habits, phobias, birthmarks, talents, behavioral propensities, physical features, and, yes, dreams, synchronicities, and shamanistic perceptions—the ASR hypothesis is simply too much of a stretch, especially in comparison with the psychological dynamics of reincarnation that Matlock patiently explains in this book.

During the course, I raised many arguments in defense of the ASR position as well as other skeptical alternatives to reincarnation. Matlock very patiently walked me gently through the data, point by point, as he has done in this very book. By the completion of the course, I was convinced that Matlock's own interpretations, carefully honed over many years, offered the best interpretation of the empirical data. I told him so, naturally. In 2017, I invited him to Las Vegas, where we recorded, for the *New Thinking Allowed* YouTube channel, a series of twelve video conversations covering most of the same topics as this book. Once again, I repeated my conviction that his interpretation, and not ASR, offered the best fit to the data.

In theory, it is conceivable that the acausal connecting principle identified by Jung and Pauli could result in the manifestation of events that trick us into mistakenly accepting the reincarnation idea—because, after all, rebirth is such a powerful archetype. While I now believe that reincarnation itself is a more parsimonious theory for the type of data presented in this book, both the reincarnation and ASR theories require further elaboration—because they each presuppose a worldview vastly different than the materialist metaphysics that now dominates modern institutions. We are fortunate to live in an era in which, in spite of the social stigma, many brave scientists and brilliant scholars are addressing their professional time to this very problem.

Preface

From early in my life, I wanted to be a creative writer. I recall dictating stories to my mother before I was able to write them down myself. I held to the dream of making a living as a writer until well after I graduated from Emory University in 1977, although I struggled, as many would-be writers do, unable to bring in a satisfactory income.

At one point I decided to give up on fiction and went to my local library in Arlington, Virginia, to look for ideas for a nonfiction book. It was there that I first encountered works on reincarnation and past-life memory. I knew nothing about reincarnation, although I had noticed the theme of rebirth cropping up in short stories and novels and was intrigued by it. I did not see a general survey or introductory treatment of the subject, so decided that that was something I could write. This was no later than 1980. Ian Wilson's *Mind Out of Time? Reincarnation Investigated*, published in the United States by Doubleday in 1982 as *All in the Mind: Reincarnation, Hypnotic Regression, Stigmata, Multiple Personality, and Other Little-Understood Powers of the Mind* (I. Wilson, 1982), was not yet available.

I do not remember what book on reincarnation I read first. Probably it was on past-life regression. Quite possibly it was Dethlefsen's (1977) *Voices from Other Lives*, which impressed me greatly. I began a systematic study of regression accounts, noting the details of each on a set of index cards I still have in my possession today. I noticed books by Ian Stevenson, MD, in the stacks, but they were clearly of a different nature. I left them until I had completed my analysis of the regression material. When I finally picked them up, I was struck forcibly by the contrast between Stevenson and the regression therapists. Although the regression accounts had seemed convincing, few of the ostensible past-life memories were substantiated. Stevenson worked with young children who recalled earlier lives in the waking state. Many said enough about the lives for the people they were talking about to be traced, and it was then possible not only to verify the children's statements but to show correspondences in behavior and physical traits between the lives. Stevenson documented his cases carefully, for an academic audience, unlike the regression therapists, who wrote for the general public.

Stevenson's books did more than alter my appreciation of reincarnation research; they introduced me to academic parapsychology. By the time I left Emory, where I was taught Skinnerian operant conditioning in my experimental psychology classes, I was dissatisfied with the materialist understanding of human nature. I read widely in the New Age literature before taking up reincarnation. Stevenson directed my attention away not only from the regression therapists, but from New Age metaphysics altogether. Once I discovered that serious research was being done on the things that had come to interest me, there was no turning back. I subscribed to parapsychology journals and began to attend professional conferences.

My first Parapsychological Association meeting was held at Tufts University in August 1985. D. Scott Rogo had just published *The Search for Yesterday: A Critical Examination of the Evidence for Reincarnation* (Rogo, 1985). He was at the meeting also, and I obtained a copy of the book from him. It covered the full range of reincarnation accounts, including regressions as well as involuntary memories, and was the sort of book I had been preparing to write myself. Before the meeting was over, I had arranged to review it for the *Journal of the Society for Psychical Research.* That review (Matlock, 1986) was my first publication in parapsychology. I applauded Rogo for taking on the subject so comprehensively, but faulted him for writing in too popular a style. I concluded by saying that I hoped that someday there would be a more scholarly assessment of the evidence for reincarnation.

Four years later, I wrote a review of the research on past-life memory cases for the annual series, *Advances in Parapsychological Research* (Matlock, 1990b). My *Advances* review came out as I was beginning graduate studies in anthropology. For my MA thesis, I did a cross-cultural study of reincarnation beliefs in relation to social practices in tribal societies (Matlock, 1993), but my attention shifted to other concerns when I began working toward my PhD, which I completed in 2002. It was not until I was invited to do a historical review of Stevenson's classic *Twenty Cases Suggestive of Reincarnation* (Matlock, 2011) and then to teach a course on reincarnation in a contemplated new graduate program in parapsychology at Atlantic University that I returned to reincarnation in a major way. I left Atlantic when the parapsychology program was canceled but continued to develop the course and began to teach it online through the Alvarado Zingrone Institute for Research and Education in the spring of 2014. I offered it again in the spring of 2015, 2016, and 2017.

I had always intended to publish my course lectures as a book, but for one reason or another was unable to complete the project until now. I revised the lectures each year, bringing in new material and improving my expression of the old. In 2016, Erlendur Haraldsson asked me to coauthor a book about reincarnation with him (Haraldsson & Matlock, 2016). In 2017, I became a contributor to the web-based *Psi Encyclopedia*, sponsored by the SPR. These writings allowed me to address certain topics beyond the space I could devote to them in my lectures, and I added references to them where appropriate. The protracted composition process has resulted in a better end product, I believe. Nonetheless, I saw that the updating and revision could easily go on forever. I did not offer the course in 2018, so as to have time finally to finish this book.

The course is designed as an advanced-undergraduate or MA-level graduate seminar, with written lectures supplemented by readings from the scholarly literature. Participants are asked to read, then to discuss what they have read. The course is conducted on the Moodle platform, and I embrace the Moodle philosophy that we learn best in dialogue with each other. I aim to inform, but also to stimulate discussion. I explain my interpretation of the facts, but others may have different responses to them, depending on their own experiences and intellectual backgrounds. The course runs for fifteen weeks (a full semester).

This book includes revised versions of my course lectures, organized into seven chapters of three sections each. It draws upon and has application to several disciplines, including consciousness studies, memory studies, psychotherapy, and other branches of psychology; religious studies; anthropology; and philosophy, in addition to parapsychology. Its orientation, however, is parapsychological. I am chiefly interested in the nature of the evidence for reincarnation, the question of how good that evidence is, and, if it is satisfactory, how best to interpret it. Because beliefs about reincarnation provide the backdrop against which the evidence appears, I give some attention to beliefs, but I treat them differently than they are normally handled in the social sciences. I focus on the interaction between belief and experience rather than on beliefs as strictly intellectual data.

Chapter 1 opens with the report of an American reincarnation case. The case of Rylann O'Bannion was featured in the 2014 second season of the television series *Ghost Inside My Child* but has not previously been documented in print. It serves to introduce the type of material with which Stevensonian reincarnation research is concerned. We may say that Rylann's behaviors and veridical past-life memories suggest reincarnation, but what do we mean by this? There is no universally accepted understanding of what reincarnation is or how it works, so after presenting my report of Rylann's case, I supply operational definitions to assist with my appraisal of the evidence for reincarnation. The chapter concludes with a consideration of the challenge reincarnation cases present to the materialist conception of consciousness as a product of cerebral activity. The materialist position rules out any possibility of the survival of consciousness after physical death, but it is coming under increasing pressure from various directions, quite apart from parapsychology and research on postmortem survival.

In Chapter 2, I step back to examine beliefs in reincarnation and rebirth. I look at animistic tribal beliefs and related social practices cross-culturally, sketch the history of rebirth beliefs in the West and East, and show that rebirth eschatologies can be assigned to one of three categories according to the agency (karma, God, or the individual himself or herself) believed responsible for selecting the parents of the new life. In Chapter 3, I return attention to signs of reincarnation. There are accounts of past-life memory from many societies throughout history but it was not until the 1960s, with Stevenson's research, that the systematic study of reincarnation cases began. I address criticisms of Stevenson's work and discuss interpretive frameworks for the case data short of reincarnation.

In Chapters 4 and 5, I delve more deeply into the research findings and begin to develop a theory of reincarnation, based on those findings. In Chapter 6, I turn to the transition from child to adult forms of past-life memory, consider apparent memories of previous lives arising under hypnosis, and analyze the past-life identifications and readings of shamans, psychics, and mediums. In Chapter 7, the final chapter, I first review independent evidence of an interactional relationship between the mind and brain and the survival of consciousness after death, then take up philosophical concerns related to reincarnation, personal identity, and discarnate survival. I conclude with a summary of my theory of reincarnation. After this, Michael Nahm examines the implications of reincarnation cases for evolutionary biology in an afterword. Following the reference list is a glossary of specialized and technical terms employed in the book.

Nancy Zingrone asked me to develop the course for Atlantic University and provided a platform on which to offer it after we left Atlantic. My parents, Jack and Rebecca Matlock, and a friend, Rosie Jones, participated in a trial run of the course in 2013. Their feedback was invaluable in helping me prepare to take it live. I am also indebted to the participants in the 2014 inaugural offering, especially my colleagues Jeffrey Mishlove, Ohkado Masayuki, Vernon Neppe, and Guy Playfair. In later years, Antonia Mills, K. M. Wehrstein, Patricia Hofer, Patricia Stein, Shannon Haftner Adams, Mauricio Sierra Siegert, and the late Suitbert Ertel, in particular, contributed stimulating discussions and comments that helped me fine-tune my presentation.

K. M. Wehrstein took the course three times (in 2015, 2016, and 2017) and has followed this project with special interest. Jim B. Tucker, Edward

F. Kelly, Sami Yli-Karjanmaa, Stafford Betty, Kuldip Kumar Dhiman, Titus Rivas, and Iris Giesler read over selected lectures or book sections and supplied helpful critiques. Michael Nahm, Marjorie Woollacott, K. M. Wehrstein, and readers contacted by Rowman & Littlefield reviewed the manuscript in its late stages and provided additional critiques and suggestions.

I am very grateful to Rylann O'Bannion; her mother, Cindy; and father, Lonny, for allowing me to tell Rylann's story. Cindy O'Bannion has been a responsive informant from my first contact with her in 2014. I interviewed the O'Bannions in their Bartlesville, Oklahoma, home in August 2018, then, in September, traveled to Kenner, Louisiana, in order to corroborate Rylann's memories as fully as possible. I am indebted to Royd Anderson, producer of a documentary about the crash of Pan Am Flight 759, for assistance with my investigations in Kenner and after, and to Nikki Ryder and her mother, Lauri Apken, who acted as my main liaison with Jennifer Schultz's friends before I went to Kenner. In Kenner I interviewed Evelyn Pourciau, Ethel Koscho Pourciau, Christy Simon, Lauri Apken, Natalie Brassette, Theresa Bourgeois, and John Williams. After my return from Kenner, I made contact with Robert Barlsey, MD, the forensic dentist who identified the remains from the accident, among them those of Jennifer Schultz. The field research on this case was supported by the Society for Psychical Research (SPR).

My case report is illustrated by photographs taken by Cindy O'Bannion, Christy Simon, and John Williams, reproduced with their permission. Later on, I present the translation of a passage about an eighteenth-century Indian case made for Ian Stevenson and preserved at the Division of Personality Studies (DOPS) of the University of Virginia's Department of Psychiatry, used by permission of Jim Tucker.

Finally, I would like to acknowledge my daughter Cristina, to whom I am dedicating this book. Cristina began relating her past-life memories when she was three years old. As she grew older, I was able to discuss them with her and to try out some of my theoretical ideas, particularly about similarities and differences between present- and past-life memory. Cristina's input has had an important influence on my thinking about the problems I confront in the following pages.

Chapter 1

Introduction to the Study
of Reincarnation Signs

Pan American World Airways (Pan Am) Flight 759 was a regularly sched-
uled flight from Miami to San Diego, with stops in New Orleans and Las
Vegas. On July 9, 1982, the Boeing 727 left Miami and reached New Orleans
International Airport, in the suburb of Kenner, Louisiana, as expected. It was
raining that day and there were thunderstorms over the eastern side of the
airport, where the departure runway was. The airplane took off at 4:07 p.m.
into gusting and swirling winds. At an altitude of no more than 150 feet, it
encountered a microburst that introduced a sudden wind shear that in turn
imposed a downdraft and decreasing headwind. The plane struck the top of a
line of trees and flew on in an easterly direction before hitting other trees and
crashing into Kenner's Morningside Park subdivision a minute after takeoff
and less than a mile from the end of the runway. The resulting impact, explosion, and fire destroyed fifteen houses on three streets. All 145 people on
the plane died, and eight people on the ground were killed as well (National
Transportation Safety Board, 1983; That Day in Kenner, n.d.). At the time,
the accident was the third deadliest in U.S. aviation history (Twenty Worst
Aviation Disasters, n.d).

Witnesses to the crash said that the plane seemed to stall in the air then
rolled to the left after tearing the branch off an oak tree on Fairway Street.
The tip of the left wing hit the ground, plowing a ten-foot-long gash in the
earth and adjacent street pavement before there was an explosion and the
plane tumbled through the neighborhood, breaking apart, jet fuel spilling
from the ruptured tanks on its wings. The first houses affected were those of
the Weems and Schultz families opposite Evelyn Pourciau on Fairway Street.
E. V. Weems and his three sons had gone to a store, and so were spared, but
the Schultzes were not as lucky.

Eleven-year-old Jennifer, talking on the telephone in the carport, was the first of the fatalities on the ground. Her mother, Barbara; younger sister Rachael; and Rachael's friend, Lisa Baye, were in the house when it caught fire. They crawled out of the front door and ran across the street into Evelyn Pourciau's front yard, where they rolled in the wet grass to extinguish the flames engulfing their bodies. Evelyn rushed to the yard when she heard the explosion. She had never seen burned bodies before and did not know how to help, but as it turned out she did exactly the right thing: She brought wet sheets to cover her neighbors until ambulances arrived. Lisa died in the hospital ten hours afterward; Barbara and Rachael survived, although badly burned (Anderson, 2012; DeMers, 1982; and interviews in Kenner). The Schultzes later were awarded $10.9 million in damages, the largest individual settlement reached with Pan Am (Largest Award Yet, 1984).

Rylann O'Bannion was born on March 11, 2008, in Bartlesville, Oklahoma, the fourth and last child of her parents, Cindy and Lonny. Rylann quickly revealed herself to be an exceptional child. She was sleeping through the night within forty-eight hours of her birth. She was keenly observant and when the family went out, always attracted attention, especially from men. As she became mobile, she would go right up to any man who spoke to her. She was able to size up people quickly and was much more socially mature than her siblings had been at her age.

Rylann reached developmental milestones early and began speaking in full sentences between eighteen and twenty-four months, well before her siblings had. She quickly learned to count, and her pre-K and kindergarten teachers reported that she was good at math. She regularly tested several grade levels above her own in math and reading comprehension.

Unlike many young children, Rylann enjoyed doing chores and helping around the house. As she grew older and became aware of the value of money, she would ask for a quarter or a dollar in return. She would take the initiative in proposing chores, sometimes suggesting activities more suitable for an older child. This behavior carried over to outside the home. All of her teachers from daycare onward have raved about what a good helper Rylann is.

From the time she was able to do so, Rylann had the curious habit of opening drawers in the bathroom vanity. The vanity had three rows of drawers, the lowest close to the floor. She never took anything out of the drawers; she would just open them, look at what was inside, and shut them again. She did not do this in the kitchen, bedroom, or any other room except the bathroom.

Rylann was unafraid of anything except thunder and lightning, from which she recoiled. As she grew older, she would run to Cindy or call for her to come to her, seeking comfort and assurance, during thunderstorms. She changed in other ways as well. By twenty-four months, she was no longer sleeping through the night. She would awaken, go to her parents' room, and get in bed with Cindy. If Cindy put her back in her own bed after she had fallen asleep again, the same thing would happen.

Shortly after she started waking up during the night, Rylann began to sleepwalk. She did this with increasing frequency until she was about three years old, then steadily, five or six times a week. She never sleepwalked anywhere but her own house and always visited one of three places, depending on where Cindy happened to be. If Cindy was in bed, Rylann went directly to her side. If Cindy was in the living room, she went and stood by the door. If Cindy was working late on the computer, she went and stood by the couch. She never said a word on these occasions, waiting patiently for Cindy to notice her. She did not remember anything about these nocturnal excursions in the morning.

Rylann had straight hair, which she wore long, like her mother and older sisters. When she was young, it was strawberry blonde in color but gradually it darkened and the reddish tinge was not as evident by the time she was four or five. At ten, her hair is the same medium brown shade as her mother's and sisters', although in the sunlight it can appear auburn, as can Cindy's.

Early in her third year, Rylann began to complain that her hair touching her back hurt her back. She threw little fits about her hair touching her back. She did not say the hair tickled or itched her back, but that it "hurt" it. She began to complain that her clothing hurt her neck and wanted tags cut out of her shirts. This behavior persisted as she grew older. Every day when it was time to get dressed for school, Rylann threw fits about putting on shirts. She would throw very dramatic fits when changing shirts and would complain that the clothing hurt her back, neck, and shoulders. She would say that it felt like her skin was burning.

In the middle of May 2010, when Rylann was twenty-seven months old, Cindy had a friend take photographs of her and the rest of the family in the front and back yards of their house. She framed several of these photos and placed some around her home and others in her office at work. When Rylann visited the office for the first time a few weeks later, she noticed one of the pictures in particular. It shows her in an ivory dress with a green belt, holding a large white flower (Figure 1.1). She informed Cindy that she had been "bigger" in the picture. Each time she visited the office, two or three times a week, she would make a similar comment about being bigger in the picture. When Cindy asked what she meant, she would give her a look and walk away.

This went on for over a year, until July 2011, when Rylann was age three years and five months (forty-one months). It was her bedtime, and Cindy had read her a book and turned off the light. Rylann asked, "You know when I

Figure 1.1 Photograph of Rylann taken in O'Bannion backyard in Bartlesville, OK, on May 15, 2010, when she was 27 months old. *Source*: Courtesy of Cindy O'Bannion.

was bigger in that picture? I was nineteen in that picture. You know, how big Ashlen is." Ashlen, one of her older sisters, was nineteen at the time. Cindy asked, "Rylann, how were you nineteen in that picture when you were born only three years ago?" Rylann was quiet for a moment then said softly: "Mommy, I died. I was in our backyard. It was raining. I was alone but I wasn't scared. Then the rain shocked me." When Cindy asked what she meant, Rylann explained: "It was raining a lot. There was a loud noise, then the rain shocked me. I floated up to the sky then."

Maintaining her self-control, Cindy asked Rylann if there was anything else she recalled, but she said she was tired and wanted to sleep. Cindy immediately told Lonny about this new development. The O'Bannions are Catholic and had never before considered the possibility of reincarnation. They were not sure what to make of the idea but were not so dogmatic about the teachings of their faith to rule it out a priori. Rylann's claim of having died during a rainstorm might help to explain her fear of thunder and some of her other odd behaviors, Cindy reasoned; it had a certain appeal as an explanatory paradigm.

Over the next several weeks, always at bedtime, Rylann added new bits of memory. On the night following her revelation about having died, she told Cindy that the name Kevin sounded familiar to her. On other occasions she said that her family lived in a white house with a big front porch and that they owned a red car. She had worn dresses, of which she had nine.

During this period, Rylann also spoke about things that had happened in heaven after her death. There were many other children in heaven, and they played together. They were given lots of presents, but these were not toys like on Earth. When it was time to be born, you floated down from the sky to your new mother.

Rylann said that in heaven she had met God and Jesus, and also Cindy's mother, Sally, whom she at first referred to as "your mom." Sally had died in 1996, twelve and a half years before Rylann was born. When she returned to the subject a night or two later, Rylann called her "Grandma Sally," as she had been known in the family. Cindy had never mentioned her mother's name to Rylann or showed her a picture of her, yet Rylann described Grandma Sally correctly as "looking like us." Before Sally began dyeing her hair in later middle age, she had had the same medium brown hair and brown eyes as Cindy, Rylann, and her sisters. Rylann added that Grandma Sally had played with her. This was a characteristic behavior of Sally, who had enjoyed playing with her grandchildren.

Until July 2013, when she was five, Rylann related all of her memories to Cindy at bedtime. The first thing she said about them during the day was to her brother Lane, then eight, evidently in response to a television commercial neither of them now recalls. Cindy had just gone to the kitchen and did not see the commercial herself; if she heard it, she paid no attention. She heard Rylann say to Lane, "Not everyone comes back. You can choose to come back if you died before you were supposed to." Cindy walked back to the living room, in time to hear her add, "Most people only come back twice." With that, she was done talking, and returned to watching television. From this time on, she reported most of her memories during the day, usually out of the blue. Once she looked straight at Cindy and said, "I remember the name Jennifer."

At the beginning of September 2013, Cindy watched four episodes from the first season of the Lifetime television series *Ghost Inside My Child* with Rylann and Lane. She hoped that seeing other children who recalled previous lives would help Rylann deal with her memories. Rylann sat right beside Cindy and was in her arms or holding her hand the entire time. She was fascinated with the stories but did not like the way they were made to seem creepy and overly dramatic. She commented, "It's not a ghost inside of you. It's you, just different."

At one point, Lane asked Rylann if she thought she had lived in the United States or another country. She replied, "I think Canada. Canada sounds familiar." Within moments, however, she said, "Louisiana sounds familiar. It feels right." Rylann had mentioned Louisiana previously but had not said that was where she had lived. Cindy recalls trying to figure out what Canada and Louisiana had in common, other than some French heritage.

In February 2014, when Rylann was upset about her hair hurting her back, Cindy asked her if the sensation could be related to how she had died when she was bigger. Rylann instantly presented a wide-eyed, frightened look, covered her ears, stared down with her eyes closed, and said, "La, la, la, la. I don't want to talk about that! Don't talk about that!" It did not take her long to process the idea, however. On March 4, shortly before her sixth birthday, she walked into the bathroom where Cindy was combing Lane's hair before sending him off to school and asked what year Cindy was born. Cindy said 1971, but why did she want to know? Rylann said, "In my dream it sounds familiar. I was standing there in the yard and saw a plane crash." Cindy said, "In 1971, you saw a plane crash?" Rylann replied, "I don't know when, it's just familiar."

Two days later, during her lunch hour on March 6, 2014, Cindy searched online for plane crashes in 1971, in Canada, and finally in Louisiana. Nothing came up in connection to 1971 and nothing of relevance for Canada, but there were numerous pages about Pan Am 759 crashing in Kenner, Louisiana, on July 9, 1982. The first article Cindy read stated that the plane had gone down in a heavy thunderstorm, killing everyone on board, along with eight people on the ground. Among the latter was eleven-year-old Jennifer Schultz. The pieces started to fall into place: Rylann's talk about rain, thunder, Louisiana, and Jennifer, all made sense now. Moreover, if Jennifer Schultz was eleven in 1982, she had been born in 1971.

At first, Cindy said nothing to Rylann about what she had found. She did not want to feed her daughter information or influence her memories. Over the next few days, without prompting, Rylann said that she thought she had been standing by a tree or pole when the plane crashed, that she remembered a park, and also water near her house. She repeatedly mentioned the number nine, in various contexts. In late March, when she threw a fit about changing shirts, Cindy again asked if she thought there might be a connection between her behavior and the plane crash. This time Rylann said, "I don't know . . . maybe . . . did I catch on fire?" Cindy replied, "I don't know. Did you?" Rylann said, "I think I did." Following this exchange, her reaction to changing shirts improved and gradually her fits faded away.

On or around March 20, Cindy asked Rylann if she wanted to know if she had found out anything relating to her memories. Previously, Rylann had said she did not want to know, but this time she said yes. Cindy gave her an overview of what she had read online. Rylann's response was, "That matches everything I've told you." She added, "Canada sounds like Kenner." When Cindy went through the list of names of those who were killed, Rylann remarked, "I've said the name Jennifer before." Cindy agreed that she had. Rylann asked, "Was I Jennifer?" Cindy said that she did not know. Rylann was quiet for a few moments then said, "I think I was Jennifer."

On March 30, in the car on the way back from Lane's basketball tournament in Wichita, Kansas, Rylann suddenly asked, "Mom, do you want to see what the plane looked like?" The question did not immediately register with Cindy, but when it did, she said, "Sure." Lonny shot her a sideways glance from the driver's seat. Lane exclaimed, "Oh my gosh, what now?" Rylann drew a picture of a large airplane with a blue blob on its tail on her Nintendo 3DS handheld game console. Cindy was not familiar with the colors of Pan Am, which had ceased operation in 1991, but later learned that its logo was a blue-and-white circle.

On April 2, Cindy asked Rylann what she remembered about how the crash had happened. Rylann said that the plane's left side and wing had gone down first, a detail Cindy had omitted from her account of the accident, but did not want to talk further about it.

Rylann's story was one of two featured on the second season of *Ghost Inside My Child* (*GIMC*) in an episode entitled, "Wounded in Battle and Lightning Storm Rattle." The program aired on Saturday, September 20, 2014.

Cindy first emailed the *GIMC* producers on April 17, 2013, in response to an article about the series she had seen on the Internet. She told the producers that the O'Bannions were not interested in participating in the show but that she thought the things Rylann was saying might be of assistance to them. In summarizing Rylann's case to that point, Cindy drew on a journal she had been keeping since early August 2011. The journal unfortunately has been lost—Cindy had it hidden among work papers that have been shredded—but because it was a source for the narrative she provided the *GIMC* producers in April 2013, almost a year before Rylann recalled the plane crash, her emails allow Cindy and me to reconstruct the early timeline of events. Just as importantly, because Cindy kept the producers apprised of new developments, her emails furnish a record of the case as it unfolded between April 2013, and July 2014, after filming for Rylann's episode was complete.

On September 3, 2013, the day after watching the four *GIMC* episodes with Rylann and Lane, Cindy emailed the producers that Rylann remembered being a girl struck by lightning in her backyard, her interpretation at that point of what Rylann was saying. Early in 2014 she commented about Rylann's memories on a post on the *GIMC* Facebook page. A few minutes later, a producer messaged her to ask if she was willing to talk to them about being on the show. Cindy was still reluctant because she did not want Rylann or her family exposed to public scrutiny or for anyone to think they were crazy. As she reflected on the proposal, however, she decided that there was a reason for everything. She came to believe that their involvement would help provide closure for Rylann and she was inspired to tell the story as an aid to other parents of children with past-life memories, as she herself had been helped by viewing the episodes she had seen.

Rylann was hesitant at first but was talked into it by Lane, for whom it sounded like fun. She then became excited by the prospect of going to Kenner, thinking that it might evoke new memories. She repeatedly expressed interest in seeing pictures of Jennifer's family and friends, her house and neighborhood, and other things from her life, but was indifferent about meeting family members and friends in person because she feared they would have changed too much in the interim for her to recognize them. In the end, the producers arranged for her to meet Evelyn Pourciau, and she appears in the program.

Jennifer's mother was no longer living; she had died in 2010, Cindy learned from her online obituary (In Memory, 2010). The date of Barbara Schultz's death was not the only information Cindy gleaned from the obituary. She also discovered that Jennifer's middle name was Elizabeth, the same name she and Lonny had given to Rylann as a middle name. "Elizabeth" had not been a name they were considering, but it impressed itself on Cindy's mind and felt right for some reason. Her pregnancy with Rylann had been normal and uneventful, although it had come as surprise, because after Lane's birth, Lonny had had a vasectomy, and they were not expecting another child. Cindy and Lonny are sure of the date that Rylann was conceived—June 26, 2007—and where. It was on a business trip to San Diego. San Diego, Cindy later realized, was the final destination of Pan Am flight 759. June 26, she came to learn, had been Jennifer Schultz's birthday. Although Cindy could not see how these pieces fit together, each seemed to have a place in the larger puzzle, and each gave her the chills when she stumbled upon it.

In the lead-up to the filming in Bartlesville, the *GIMC* producers sent Cindy a DVD about the accident by history teacher and documentary filmmaker Royd Anderson (Anderson, 2012). Rylann had known the DVD was coming and was eager to watch it, thinking that it might prompt new memories. When Cindy told her it had arrived, she asked when she could see it, but Cindy said that she would watch it first. Rylann then asked, "What was that other girl's last name?" Confused, Cindy asked what girl she meant—what was her first name? Rylann replied, "I think it was Lisa." Lisa Baye was the six-year-old friend of Jennifer's sister Rachael, whose suffering and death have a prominent place in the documentary. After viewing it, Cindy decided not to allow Rylann to watch the video. The *GIMC* producers agreed and as of March 2019, Rylann still has not seen it.

Cindy cannot explain what made Rylann ask about Lisa Baye, unaware as she was of the circumstances of the crash beyond those of her memories, unless it was through an extrasensory apprehension of the documentary's contents. Rylann often made comments about sensing or feeling things she could not have known in a normal way. She predicted the winners of basketball and football games with good accuracy. There had been many little things that had made Cindy wonder about Rylann's extrasensory abilities, especially precognition.

GIMC spent two days with the O'Bannions in Bartlesville before taking them to Kenner. They were there on July 9, 2014, the thirty-second anniversary of the accident. The episode that aired in November of that year is mainly a reenactment that in places appears to be scripted. The presentation does not always follow the course of events described in written documents. Cindy is portrayed as having searched the Internet and found a Louisiana girl who died after having been struck by lightning in her yard in the 1940s, but emailed communications show that it was the producers, not Cindy, who made this identification. Cindy did not search the Internet before Rylann remembered the plane crash, because Rylann had said she preferred not to know anything about her previous life. Also, Rylann's pivotal revelation that she had died is depicted as coming while Cindy was reading her a book, not afterward while she was lying quietly in the dark. Lonny describes her reaction to thunder and lightning as more severe than it was in fact.

The segment showing Rylann and her family in Kenner is heavily edited and reveals little of Rylann's response to being in Jennifer's neighborhood or with Evelyn Pourciau. In a diner before going to the Morningside Park subdivision, Anderson spreads out a newspaper story about the crash that includes a photograph of Jennifer, identifying her for Rylann. The photograph shows a girl half-turned and smiling over her shoulder. Cindy remarks, "Wow, that picture of Jennifer—you give that same kind of little look, don't you?" Indeed, Cindy has several pictures of Rylann in exactly this pose. Rylann stares at the photograph. She smiles and nods, but says nothing.

Anderson tells Rylann that they will be going to Jennifer's neighborhood and will be meeting Evelyn Pourciau. On Jennifer's block, he asks Rylann, "Do you remember anything here?" She replies, "The neighborhood looks familiar." Anderson explains how the disaster unfolded and tells Rylann that Jennifer died in her carport. In footage that was not aired, he added that she was on the telephone at the time and Cindy asked if she perhaps had been talking with Kevin. Anderson replied that he had heard that it was a girl, but did not know her name, or how to reach her. While Anderson was talking, Rylann was staring at the oak tree hit by the plane, Cindy noticed. She kept near Cindy and was unusually quiet the entire day, although Cindy had the impression that she was paying close attention to everything around her

When Evelyn asks Rylann if she has been having memories about Jennifer, she replies confidently, "I was Jennifer," but this declaration was inserted in the editing. Rylann actually did not say anything in return. Evelyn tells the O'Bannions that she had been in the habit of giving Jennifer money for doing small chores. Jennifer would come and offer to rake leaves, wash dishes, vacuum, and so on, in exchange for pay. This much is included in the program, but Cindy's startled response, that Rylann from an early age had asked to do chores, was edited out.

The impact of Rylann's interaction with Evelyn is reduced by her knowing who Evelyn was before meeting her, and similarly, Evelyn's perception of Rylann must have been influenced by her knowing that Rylann claimed to have memories of Jennifer. Cindy recalls Evelyn saying that she could see similarities in their personalities and appearance, especially in the eyes. Rylann for her part felt unusually comfortable with Evelyn, although she did not speak to her. The rapport between them can be seen in the expression on Rylann's face as she gives Evelyn a hug at the conclusion of the aired segment. Recently, Rylann has said that when she met Evelyn, she recognized her voice.

The most significant event of the day occurred when the filming was over. Rylann needed to use the toilet, and Evelyn invited her into her house. Rylann walked in the door and through the kitchen to the bathroom without Evelyn having given her directions. Cindy followed her because Rylann was still wearing a microphone and she did not want it to fall off. When Cindy entered the bathroom, Rylann was staring at the vanity. She looked at Cindy and said, "I know this. I've been here before." When they emerged, Cindy told Evelyn about Rylann's reaction to the vanity, and Evelyn explained that Jennifer had had the habit of pulling drawers out of it. She never removed anything from the drawers; she only looked at what was inside, then closed them again. Cindy laughed and said that Rylann had been doing the same thing in their home since she was a young child.

When they returned home from Kenner, Cindy asked Rylann if she was happy they had gone there. Rylann said that she was glad they had gone, but did not want to talk about it. "I will tell you one thing though," she said. "I can still see in my mind that wing hitting the tree and scraping the street." Cindy did not recall having read or heard the detail about the plane's wing scraping the street but before turning in for the night, was able to confirm through a Google search that it had done so.

Cindy also asked Rylann if she knew with whom Jennifer was talking on the phone. Rylann replied that maybe it was Kevin. This is now thought to be incorrect. Jennifer knew boys named Kevin in her school and neighborhood, but she was not close to either of them. Kevin also was the name of her catechism instructor, whom Jennifer would be seeing for her regular class the following morning (Saturday) and most likely it was he that Rylann recalled. It is not yet known to whom Jennifer was speaking on the phone.

After the trip to Kenner, Rylann stopped sleepwalking for a full year and for a period thereafter did so only occasionally. She sleepwalked three or four times in July 2015, but between then and my visit to the O'Bannions in August 2018, only three or four more times. She still slept with Cindy but no longer needed to be right beside her and fell asleep on her own.

After the *GIMC* episode aired in September 2014, Cindy was contacted by Barbara Schultz's cousin, Toni Goldkamp. Toni approached the show's producers, who put her touch with Cindy. She and Cindy spoke on the phone in April 2015, and have stayed in touch via email. Toni lived in another state and met Jennifer only once, but she knew Barbara and her family well. Cindy learned from Toni that the Schultzes were Catholic. It occurred to her that that might help to explain why Rylann had always demonstrated such an interest in Catholic ritual and found it so easy to learn the catechism and prayers. At times, she seemed to know prayers without having been taught them.

Around her ninth birthday in March 2017, something was brought up in Rylann's class at school that made her think of the Pan Am 759 crash and the *GIMC* episode in which she had participated. This led her to mention the show to her teacher later that day. The teacher told her that she had heard about it from another teacher but not yet had the chance to watch it. Rylann decided to make a booklet of articles about the accident to inform her teacher and for the first time looked up material about the crash on the Internet. She produced her booklet and took it to her teacher, who returned it a day or two later, saying that Rylann's experiences were all very interesting and amazing.

As a result of her research and learning about the impact of the accident on Jennifer's family, Rylann became obsessively concerned about Rachael. She did not relate memories of Rachael but expressed concern for her every few days for several weeks. At around this time, Rachael's maternal grandmother died and she heard about the *GIMC* episode featuring Rylann. Rachael emailed Toni Goldkamp, who shared what she knew about Rylann from her contacts with Cindy. Toni also provided Rachael a link to the *GIMC* episode and Cindy's email address and telephone number. For both Toni and Cindy, the coincidental timing of Rylann's concern for Rachael and Rachael's reaching out to Toni seemed meaningful. As of March 2019, Rachael has not gotten in touch with Cindy, however, and I have not tried to contact her.

Not long after producing the booklet for her teacher, Rylann reminded Cindy that she had talked about seeing a tree and a pole before she died, adding the detail that the pole had wires, like a utility pole for a power line. Cindy was surprised, having assumed it was a pole supporting the carport roof. "I thought I told you. I think it was one of those electrical poles," Rylann said. Perhaps her memory was jogged by seeing a picture of power lines next to the tail section of the plane in Anderson's (2013) written account of the accident, which is posted online. However, there was a utility pole at the right corner of the Schultz's driveway and both this utility pole and the oak tree struck by the plane would have been in Jennifer's line of sight simultaneously from within the carport.

The Schultz and Weems houses have been replaced, but in September 2018, I emailed Cindy a photo taken from the driveway where the Schultz's carport had stood. The configuration of the oak tree and the utility pole reminded Cindy of a similar view of trees and a utility pole from the spot where Rylann was standing when the photograph of her in the ivory dress holding the white flower was snapped. That picture (Figure 1.1) was the only picture taken with Rylann in that location that day, perhaps the reason that it alone prompted her to tell Cindy that she was "bigger" every time she saw it. None of Jennifer's friends in Kenner to whom I showed the photograph saw anything in it related to Jennifer. Rylann's reaction to the picture was one of the biggest mysteries of the case until the photo I emailed Cindy suggested an unexpected solution.

I took the photograph from the driveway in Kenner in September 2018, more than thirty-six years after Jennifer died there, but except for the oak tree having grown substantially, I am advised that the view is similar to the one Jennifer would have had in 1982. The utility pole is in the same position at the right corner of the driveway now as it was then. The picture I sent reminded Cindy of a utility pole in her backyard and she suggested that it was not anything in the picture of her in the ivory dress itself, but rather her association of what she had been looking at when the picture was taken with what would have been a familiar sight for Jennifer, that drew memories of Jennifer into Rylann's conscious awareness. Cindy in turn sent me a picture taken from the position in which Rylann had been standing when the photograph was taken.

The name of the photographer for the Bartlesville photo shoot was Jennifer, and hearing it repeatedly that day could have been another factor in the past-life memory retrieval. I agree with Cindy that Rylann seems to have conflated the two images, of Jennifer's view from the carport and of her own backyard, past and present. Thus, she told Cindy in July 2011, that she was in "our backyard" when she died. As late as March 2014, when she first remembered the plane crash, she thought she had been in the yard, although this time she could have meant the Schultzes' yard. "I was standing there in the yard and saw a plane crash," she said. Rylann frequently mentioned trees and poles in connection with her memories of the crash. She definitely separated the images of the past and the present only after her visit to Kenner.

On June 26, 2016, when she was eight, Rylann saw an antique piano in a shop and became infatuated with it. She spoke about it daily for months and wanted her parents to buy it for her. Finally they purchased a smaller used piano of more recent vintage and gave it to her for her ninth birthday in March 2017. Rylann enjoys playing it but refuses lessons, saying she already knows how it is done. Rylann has never reported memories of Jennifer with a piano. The Schultzes did not own a piano, and whether Jennifer had a connection to one is unknown. Nonetheless, the fact that Rylann happened to see the piano on Jennifer's birthday, and remained fixated on it for so long, suggests to Cindy that a piano must have had some significance for Jennifer.

I became acquainted with Cindy when she joined the Signs of Reincarnation group I formed on Facebook on October 2, 2014. I posted announcements about the new group in other reincarnation groups on the platform; Cindy saw one of these announcements and immediately joined. She gave details about Rylann's memories in comments on the group page and in instant messaging and emails to my colleague Iris Giesler and me. Giesler and I planned to document the case in a journal paper, but since it was still active, we wanted to monitor it for new developments before writing it up.

After the decision was made to include Rylann's case in this book, I drove to Bartlesville to interview the O'Bannions. I was there for two days in August 2018. I interviewed Rylann and her parents and spoke more briefly to Lane. Rylann's elder sisters, Ashlen and Kayla, are now out of the home; they were not witnesses to anything except for Rylann's early behaviors, which are well attested by other members of the family, so I did not feel that it was necessary to contact them. I have confirmed what they witnessed from interviews conducted with them by others in December 2018, as I explain below.

Rylann continues to speak about her memories of Jennifer and the plane crash most frequently in March and April and in June and July of each year. On April 6, 2018, within a few days of turning ten, she reported for the first time the sense that she had been sitting on a swing in the carport while talking on the telephone. She described the memory of the swing to me again when I interviewed her in August. I had never heard of a swing in a carport and asked if it could have been in the yard, but she was certain it had been in the carport. She still had clear memories of sitting on the swing, talking on the telephone, when she saw the plane hit the oak tree and make the gash in the yard and street, she told me. This was the last thing she remembered having seen. She speculated that Jennifer had been electrocuted through the telephone line. The possibility of electrocution had not occurred to Cindy or to me, but sounded conceivable. I wondered what cause of death was given on Jennifer's death certificate or if there had been an autopsy performed on her body.

Rylann also told me that she had had nocturnal dreams about the plane crash, but in these dreams she saw it from a different perspective, standing in a yard by a tree rather than sitting on the swing in the carport. She could remember having had this dream three times as of the summer of 2018. The dream was always the same, with no variation. All her other memories had come to her in the waking state, although she sometimes loosely referred to them as dreams. In response to a question that came up later, she said that the image of the Pan Am plane in profile she had drawn on her Nintendo 3DS was derived in part from this dream. "I knew [how the plane looked in profile] because in my dream I was by a tree at the side. Also, when I drew it the logo just seemed right and it looked familiar."

Following my visit with the O'Bannions, Rylann suffered a relapse of her sleeping difficulties. Over the next three weeks, she awoke during the night twenty times. On five of these occasions, she sleepwalked. When sleepwalking, she either went to the living room or straight to Cindy's bed. She appeared to be in an agitated state, unlike previously. As soon as Cindy spoke to her, however, she became calm, climbed into her bed, and imme-diately returned to sleep. After three weeks, this phase passed and Rylann went back to sleeping through the night on her own. There were no daytime consequences of this waking and sleepwalking, and Rylann has reported no new memories of Jennifer in relation to it.

It became clear that I needed to go to Kenner to interview Evelyn Pour-ciau and others of Jennifer's friends and to see if I could obtain her autopsy report or death certificate. I wanted to try to confirm more of Rylann's memories about Jennifer's life and death and to see if I could correlate more of her idiosyncratic behavior with Jennifer. Cindy put me in touch with Royd Anderson, the documentary filmmaker, and those of Jennifer's contemporaries with whom she had made contact. Anderson helped con-nect me with Evelyn Pourciau. Iris Giesler emailed Toni Goldkamp on my behalf.

I spent three days in Kenner in September 2018. I drew the map in Figure 1.2 in order to better understand what had happened to Jennifer. It depicts the Schultz (5) and Weems (6) houses, across from the houses of Evelyn Pourciau (2), her sister-in-law Ruth Pourciau (3), and John Williams (4) on Fairway Street in Kenner. The map portrays the descent path of the doomed plane (A), indicating the locations of the oak tree (B) it struck in the yard next to Ruth Pourciau as it made contact with the ground before hitting the Schultz and Weems houses. Also marked are the utility pole (C) at the corner of the Schultz driveway and the Schultz carport (D) in which Rylann said Jennifer was sitting on the swing.

The map in Figure 1.3, based on a Google Earth image, provides a larger-scale view of the relevant parts of Kenner and Metairie, which borders Ken-ner to the east. A canal (7), possibly the water that Rylann recalled, runs along West Metairie Avenue two blocks from Jennifer's house. Through interviews and photographs, I can place Jennifer at two parks, Butch Duhe Playground (10) and Lafreniere Park (9). There are stores and other businesses along Airline Drive, a few blocks south of Jennifer's house. Jennifer went to John Clancy Elementary School (now the Clancy-Maggiore Elementary School for the Arts) (6). She attended Saturday catechism classes and Sunday services at Our Lady of Perpetual Help Church (11).

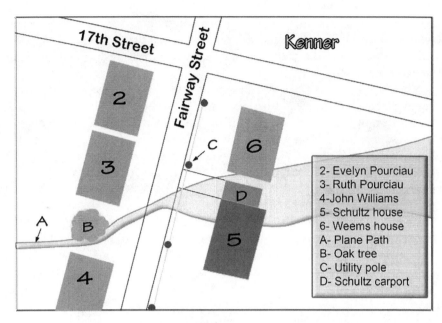

Figure 1.2 The Crash of Pan Am Flight 759 in Kenner, LA.

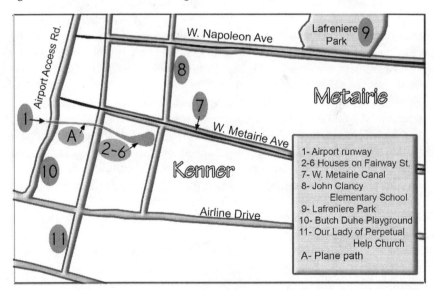

Figure 1.3 Sites of Importance to Jennifer Schultz in Kenner and Metairie, LA.

Ruth Pourciau and her husband (Evelyn's husband's brother) are now deceased, but I interviewed several other people in Kenner and Metairie. These included Evelyn Pourciau; Ethyl Koscho Pourciau, Ruth Pourciau's daughter-in-law; Jennifer's neighborhood friend Natalie Brassette; her school friend Christy Simon; as well as two friends from her church who had been taking catechism classes with her at the time of her death, Lauri Apken and Theresa Bourgeois. Because many of these people lived close to Jennifer, the social circles overlapped.

While in Kenner, I created a Facebook group where friends of Jennifer could exchange memories of her and stay in touch with Cindy. The following account of Jennifer in comparison to Rylann draws on my audio-recorded interviews; on more informal conversations and email exchanges with Royd Anderson, John Williams, and others; on photographs and information posted on Facebook; and on Jennifer's autopsy report, which I obtained from the Jefferson Parish Coroner's Office.

Jennifer Schultz was born on June 26, 1971, in Landstuhl, West Germany. The U.S. military operates a substantial medical facility at Landstuhl, and her father, Christopher, was assigned there during his time in the army. Upon discharge, he moved with his young family to Kenner, where Jennifer began kindergarten. Christopher Schultz worked at a men's shop in a mall; Barbara was a housewife who was home most of the day with Jennifer and Rachael, who was four years younger than Jennifer.

Jennifer was known as Jenny to her contemporaries but Jennifer to her elders. She had stunning red hair, which she wore long. Her friends remember her as having an outgoing personality. She was kind and generous, always ready to help others. She was self-confident and self-assertive. Her family was not well off, and she offered to do chores not only for Evelyn Pourciau but for others to earn spending money.

Evelyn Pourciau remembers Jennifer dressing well as a child. She appeared to be fashion conscious, and Evelyn told Cindy when she met the O'Bannions that she remembered thinking that Jennifer would be a model when she grew up because she cared about her appearance. During the summer, she would dress more informally, Evelyn told me, and neither she nor any of Jennifer's contemporaries recall her having a special liking for dresses. Evelyn thought it unlikely that she would have owned nine of them. In a photograph taken at a friend's birthday party in Lafreniere Park in February of the year she died (Figure 1.4), Jennifer is wearing an athletic sweatshirt. When she was young, Rylann wore dresses, but at ten she prefers sports attire similar to what Jennifer is wearing in the photograph.

At eleven, Jennifer was not yet showing a strong interest in boys, although like other girls her age, she was starting to take notice of them. She played with boys as well as girls from her neighborhood. One of her friends recalls her playing cabbage ball, a game similar to T-ball or softball that originated in the New Orleans area. Beginning when she was around four, Rylann enjoyed

Figure 1.4 Jennifer (center) at friend's birthday party in Lafreniere Park, Metairie, LA, in February 1982. *Source*: Courtesy of Christy Simon.

T-ball. She has continued to be athletic, and now plays softball, soccer, and volleyball competitively.

Jennifer's friends were not aware of any connection she might have to a piano. They could not remember hearing about her sleepwalking nor could they recall her demonstrating ESP. However, in a joint interview, three of them (Lauri Apken, Theresa Bourgeois, and Natalie Brassette) asked me if Rylann was good at crafts, because Jennifer had loved making crafts. She made crosses, which she gave away at Christmastime. Especially prized were yarn owls perched on sticks she had created for Lauri Apken and Theresa Bourgeois. Also, they told me, Evelyn Pourciau had a pet parrot and parrots were important to Jennifer for that reason. I later confirmed with Evelyn that she had indeed owned a parrot, of which Jennifer had been fond.

I told Jennifer's friends that I did not know if Rylann made crafts or liked parrots but that I was sure there were things about Rylann's personality that Cindy had not realized might be related to Jennifer and so had not relayed to me. As it turns out, Rylann greatly enjoys making crafts. She makes crosses and gives them away to her friends. She fashioned an owl from yarn and perched it on a stick. The similarity between Rylann's owl and Jennifer's is very meaningful to Lauri and Theresa, for whom it is among the more important signs of identification between them. Rylann's favorite animals are parrots and rabbits. She often draws parrots, Cindy told me. She sent me a photograph of a macaw Rylann had drawn on a folding fan.

In my interviews, I gave some attention to exactly where and how Jennifer died, because of conflicting reports. Royd Anderson told Rylann during the *GIMC* filming that Jennifer died "underneath her carport." In an Associated Press story featuring an interview with E. V. Weems (Foster, 1982), Jennifer is said to have died in the Weems carport. John DeMers (1982) says that Jennifer was "making a telephone call under a carport," without specifying whose.

In Kenner, I was shown newspaper clippings that stated that Jennifer had been on a porch swing at the time of her death. I did not recall reading about a swing before, so I did an online search using the word "swing" in connection to Jennifer Schultz and Pan Am Flight 759. I found that Barbara Schultz had referred to a swing during a trial deposition. The story reported Barbara as having said that Jennifer "was on the porch swing talking on the telephone when the jetliner roared through" (Witnesses Testify, 1984).

Some of Jennifer's friends also placed Jennifer on a porch swing. Rylann had insisted that Jennifer was on a swing in the carport. I could find no news stories, published online or not, that placed Jennifer on a swing in a carport. However, Evelyn Pourciau and Ethel Pourciau recalled there being a swing in the Schultz carport. When I went back over this issue, I was told that swings were common features of carports in Kenner in 1982. Typically, they were hung on the outer side of the carport, so that sitting in them, one was sheltered from the rain but could swing out into the sun. Walking around Jennifer's neighborhood, I found a porch swing hung in exactly this position in the carport of a house unaffected by the crash a block away from where the Schultz's house had stood.

Jennifer spent a lot of time on the carport swing, Evelyn Pourciau told me. She also said that the night before Rylann's arrival in 2014, she had dreamed about Jennifer on the carport swing, something she had not mentioned to the O'Bannions when she met them. She had told them that Jennifer had visited her in a dream, but had not given details. This is Cindy's recollection as well. Rylann could well be right that Jennifer was sitting on the carport swing while talking on the phone when she died, although this detail seems not to have been recorded anywhere in print and may not have been known to anyone in Kenner. I do not see how Rylann could have learned about it from any source other than her own memory.

The crash scene covered a large area, with most of the debris and bodies recovered from beyond Fairway Street. It was some time before Jennifer's body was located, and in the meanwhile there was uncertainty about what had happened to her. News accounts and the friends to whom I spoke differed on where they thought her body had been found and its condition upon recovery. Most thought it had been struck by the plane and flung into a yard or swimming pool beyond Fairway Street. One friend had heard that it was so badly fragmented that it could not be reconstructed, the only body from the crash site that could not be.

In Louisiana, death certificates are not public record documents, but autopsy reports are. The report on Jennifer's autopsy is brief. It says that her body was recovered from a carport. The Weems house, it turns out, did not have a driveway or carport, so this would have to have been the Schultz carport. The body was intact, with no major injuries apparent upon external examination. However, it "revealed 100% third degree body burns (charred body)." Notably, "The trachea contained no soot. No cherry pink discoloration of the blood or soft tissues was present." This indicates that Jennifer was not hit by the plane and that she was dead when the fire reached her. The plane must have passed over her as she lay on the carport floor. Her body was identified by physical appearance, confirmed through dental examination by Dr. Robert Barsley.

When Rylann first told Cindy that she had died, she said that she had heard a loud noise, then the rain had "shocked" her and she had "floated up to the sky." Evelyn Pourciau and neighbors who lived blocks away from the Schultz house recall hearing an explosion around the time of the crash. Evelyn was in her backyard when the plane first made contact with the ground and so cannot testify to the exact sequence of events, but it is possible to reconstruct them with confidence.

In the Morningside Park subdivision, telephone lines run along the same poles as electrical lines, a little below them for safety reasons. The electrical lines were uninsulated in 1982, I learned from Dr. Barsley. The plane ripped through the power and phone lines in front of the Schultz house and was still partially airborne when it struck the Schultz and Weems houses, demolishing the Schultzes's carport. At some point it began to cartwheel and traveled on for two more blocks before breaking up completely, so it must not have exploded at this point. More likely the explosion heard throughout the neighborhood was from the pole-hung fuse or a ground transformer, Dr. Barsley thinks. Evelyn Pourciau recalls jet fuel spilled on Fairway Street, even before the plane hit the power and phone lines. The fuel continued to spill out of the ruptured tanks and, despite the rain, ignited the fire that so badly burned Barbara, Rachael, and Lisa.

Figure 1.5 is a photograph of the crash site taken by John Williams, who lives in the house beyond Ruth Pourciau's former house on Fairway Street. John was not home at the time of the accident and I have not used him as a primary witness for this report, but I did talk with him. John shared this photograph, which he took the morning after the crash, before debris removal had begun. The path of destruction leads through the left side of the Schultz house

Figure 1.5   The Pan Am 759 crash site on Fairway Street the morning of July 10, 1982. The Schultz house is on the right. The left side of the house and carport were struck by the plane and destroyed. *Source:* Courtesy of John Williams.

and carport and the right side of the Weems house. Note that the Schultz house was brick. The door, which appears to be at the end of the house, was in the center. The utility pole at the corner of the driveway is out of the frame to the left. It was left standing, and the lines that ran across the street to Evelyn's, Ruth's, and John's houses were unaffected; these houses never lost power or telephone service. The Schultzes's Volkswagen station wagon, partially obscured by the truck, is pointed into the driveway. Both of the trees in the foreground of the photograph have since been removed.

In my interview with her at age ten, Rylann speculated that she had been electrocuted while talking on the telephone. Electrocutions over telephone lines during thunderstorms sometimes occur, and would have been possible had the uninsulated power line come into contact with the telephone line, but Jennifer might have received an electrical shock from a cloud-to-ground lightning strike on the aluminum frame of the carport, or the plane might have let off a static charge when it came in contact with the street or ground structures, Dr. Barlsey notes. Death by electrocution is not always apparent in autopsies but can show up as burns on the skin (Wick & Byard, 2009), which would have been erased by the fire that left Jennifer's body 100% charred. It is therefore possible that Jennifer did die of electrocution, although this cannot be confirmed, and it would have been possible for her to have been electrocuted in ways other than over the telephone line.

Astonishingly, Rylann's account of what happened to Jennifer is entirely consistent with the early phase of the crash and with her autopsy report, although these details were not known, or even surmised, by any living person, and so far as I can determine, nowhere have been suggested in print.

In October 2018, I was contacted by television producers about doing a documentary on children with past-life memories. I told them about Rylann's case and we talked about filming it. Although they ultimately decided not to carry through with the project, they flew me to Kenner on December 14 and 15, where I met with scouts for the planned production. We were joined for part of the time by Royd Anderson and spoke with Evelyn Pourciau and John Williams. This furnished the opportunity for me to go back over testimony from my previous visit, to ask follow-up questions, and to confirm and correct details of my understanding of events. From Kenner, the scouts flew to Bartlesville to interview the O'Bannion family, including Rylann's sisters, Ashlen and Kayla. Ashlen and Kayla spoke about having witnessed Rylann's early behaviors, which they had not understood at the time. The photograph of the ruined Schultz house taken by John Williams and presented in Figure 1.5 is reproduced from a high-resolution scan the scouts had made while we were in Kenner.

Table 1.1 provides a detailed timeline of events in the case, beginning with Jennifer's birth and death and Rylann's conception and birth. I have included

Table 1.1   Timeline of Events in the Case of Rylann O'Bannion

Witnesses

O'Bannion family: A = Ashlen; C = Cindy; K = Kayla; L = Lane; R = Rylann;
Y = Lonny

Jennifer Schultz and friends: EKP = Ethel Koscho Pourciau;
EP = Evelyn Pourciau; JS = Jennifer Schultz; LA= Lauri Apken;
TB = Theresa Bourgeois; TG = Toni Goldkamp

Other witnesses: JW = John Williams; RA = Royd Anderson; RB = Robert Barsley

Event and Witnesses	*Sources and Verifications of Correspondence to Jennifer Schultz*
June 26, 1971. JS born in Landstuhl, West Germany.	JS's autopsy report.
July 9, 1982. JS dies in Kenner, LA, in connection to crash of Pan Am Flight 759.	JS's autopsy report; various news reports; witness interviews.
June 26, 2007. R conceived in San Diego, CA, per C, Y.	San Diego was the final destination of Pan Am Flight 759.
March 11, 2008. R born in Bartlesville, OK, per R's birth certificate.	The interval between JS's death and R's birth is 312 mos. (25 yrs., 9 mos.).
B1. From c. Dec. 2008 (9 mos.). It becomes clear that R is drawn to men. Per C, Y, but witnessed by entire family; a source of humor in the family.	Appropriate for JS, who was considered a "daddy's girl" and who at 11 was beginning to notice boys, per EP and JS's friends. JS is believed to have been talking on a phone with a boy when she died.
B2. From c. March 2009 (12 mos.). As soon as she was able to help, R would ask to do chores. Once she had grasped the concept of money, from c. 30 mos., she would ask to be paid, per C.	Consistent with JS, per EP. JS would go around neighborhood, offering to do chores for people for pay. EP used to pay JS to do chores for her.
B3. From c. Sept. 2009 (18 mos.). R starts to be afraid of thunder and lightning, per C, Y, but noticed by entire family. When interviewed at 10, R said that thunder still "freaks me out a little."	Consistent with JS's death during a thunderstorm.
B4. From c. Feb. 2010 (before 24 mos.). From the time that R could pull a drawer open, she was opening and looking in the vanity drawers, per C.	EP says JS had a similar habit with her bathroom vanity.
B5. From c. Feb. 2010 (before 24 mos.). R starts to wake up during the night, per C.	Possibly a sign of trauma consistent with JS's death.
B6. From April–May 2010 (25 mos.). R starts to sleepwalk. Witnessed by C, Y, A, K.	None of JS's friends are aware that she sleepwalked. It may be a sign of trauma consistent with JS's death.
B7. From c. May 2010 (27 mos.). R starts to say that hair touching her back hurt her back. Witnessed by entire family. Persists until age 6.	A sign of trauma consistent with JS's death, particularly if the death was by electrocution.

Table 1.1

B8. From c. May 2010 (27 mos.). R wants tags cut out of shirts, saying they hurt her neck. This behavior began shortly before the picture in Fig. 1.1 was taken and continued to age 6, whenever R changed shirts. As she grew older, she would say that it felt like her skin was burning. Witnessed by entire family.	A sign of trauma consistent with JS's death, particularly if the death was by electrocution.

Photograph taken of Rylann in her backyard.

May 15, 2010 (27 mos.). Figure 1.1 taken of R in backyard of her house. The photograph is date-stamped 5/15/2010.	R's view of her yard when photo was taken included a utility pole and trees, similar to JS's view from the carport where she died.
S1. From June 2010 (28 mos.). In response to Fig. 1.1, R would tell C, "I was bigger in that picture." She said this every time she saw the photo in C's office, several times a week, for over a year.	JS was 11 when she died, so was bigger than R at 28 mos.
B9. From June–July 2010 (30 mos.). R starts having bad dreams at the rate of about 5 a year until she tells C that she recalls plane crash on Mar. 4, 2014 (S20), only occasionally thereafter. She never wants to talk with C about the dreams.	That these dreams are related to JS is suggested by the time frame in which they occurred.
S1b. July 2011 (3 yrs., 5 mos.; 41 mos.). At bedtime with lights out, R says to C, "You know when I was bigger in that picture? I was 19 in that picture. You know, how big Ashlen is." C tells Y about this and S2–S8 immediately afterward.	JS was 11 when she died, so was bigger than R at 28 mos.
S2. July 2011 (3 yrs.). Continuation of S1B. R says, "Mommy, I died."	Correct for JS, who died on July 9, 1982, per news stories, autopsy report.
S3. July 2011 (3 yrs.). Continuation of S2. "I was in our backyard."	Incorrect for JS, who was in the carport at the side of her house.
S4. July 2011 (3 yrs.). Continuation of S3. "It was raining."	Correct for JS, per NTSB report of Pan Am 759 crash, news reports, witnesses.
S5. July 2011 (3 yrs.). Continuation of S4. "I was all alone . . ."	Correct for JS, who was alone in the carport when she died.
S6. July 2011 (3 yrs.). Continuation of S5. ". . . but I wasn't scared."	Unverified but plausible for JS.
S7. July 2011 (3 yrs.). Continuation of S6. "Then the rain shocked me."	Unverified but plausible for JS. Autopsy report implies that she died before fire reached her.

(Continued)

Table 1.1 (Continued)

S8. July 2011 (3 yrs.). C responded to S7 by asking R if she meant there was thunder and lightning. R said yes, then explained, "There was a loud noise then the rain shocked me. I floated up to the sky then." Repetition of S4 and S7 with addition of the loud noise.	Plausible and partially verified for JS. EP, EKP, and other neighbors report hearing a loud sound at the time of the accident. The sound, like an explosion, seems to have been heard throughout the neighborhood. RA received the same impression from his interviews.
S9. July 2011 (3 yrs.). On the night following S1b–S8, also at bedtime, R tells C that she remembers the name Kevin. R does not mention Kevin again until S29.	Correct for JS, although unspecific. There were Kevins in her class at school, per DF, and in the neighborhood, per other friends. Kevin was also the name of JS's catechism teacher, per LA and TB, who took classes from him along with JS on Saturday mornings.
S10. July–Aug. 2011 (3 yrs.). One evening shortly after S9, also at bedtime, in response to C asking her if she wants to talk more about her memories, R adds that she lived in a white house with a big front porch. She said this only once.	Wrong for JS. The Schultz house was brick (Figure 1.5), with a small front porch, per EP. The Weems house next door was white clapboard, but did not have a large porch.
S11. July–Aug. 2011 (3 yrs.). In days and weeks following S9, also in response to C asking if she would like to share more of her memories R says that her family had a red car. Again, she said this only once.	Wrong for JS. No witnesses recalled the car being red. The parked VW station wagon in the Schultz driveway in Figure 1.5 is white. Chris Schultz normally rode the bus to work, per JW.
S12. July–Aug. 2011 (3 yrs.). Again in response to C's question, R says that she wore dresses. As with S10–S11, she said this only once.	Partially correct for JS, who did at times wear dresses, but in the summer mostly wore shorts and sports attire, per EP and friends, and as seen in Figure 1.4.
S13. July-Aug. 2011 (3 yrs.). She had nine dresses. Said in continuation of S12 and not repeated.	Unverified but improbable for JS, whose family was not well off, per EP.
July–Aug. 2011 (3 yrs.). Again at bedtime, R volunteers to C that she had met God and Jesus in heaven.	Unrelated to JS; unverified, although consistent with the intermission memories of other reincarnation case subjects.
July–Aug. 2011 (3 yrs.). Shortly after above, also at bedtime, R tells C that she knew Grandma Sally in heaven. R adds that Grandma Sally "looks like us" and that she played with her in heaven.	Unrelated to JS, but name, appearance, and the habit of playing with grandchildren are characteristic of C's mother, per C.

Table 1.1

Cindy first contacts GIMC producers on April 17, 2013.

S14. July 2013 (5 yrs.). During the day and out of the blue, R looks straight at C and tells her, "I remember the name Jennifer." C reports this in email to the GMC producers.	Correct for JS.

Cindy watches four GIMC episodes with Rylann and Lane.

S15. Sept. 2, 2013 (5 yrs.). L asks R where she thinks she lived before and she says, "I think Canada." Reported in email to GIMC producers.	Incorrect for JS, taken literally, although "Canada" might be a stand-in for "Kenner."
S16. Sept. 2, 2013 (5 yrs.). Immediately following S15, R adds, "Louisiana sounds familiar. It feels right." Reported in email to GIMC producers. C recalls that R had previously said that the name "Louisiana" sounded familiar but had not said that was where she was from.	Correct for JS.
S17. Sept. 2, 2013 (5 yrs.). C asks R if she could have been younger than 19 when she died, as she had said previously (S1B) and she says, "Maybe I wasn't 19, maybe I was 9. There's something about the number 9." She has mentioned and continues to mention the number 9 in various contexts.	JS was 11 when she died on July 9, 1982.
Feb. 2014 (5 yrs.). When C asks R if she thinks that her fits about changing shirts might be related to the way she died when she was bigger, R says, "La, la, la, la. I don't want to talk about that!"	The reaction would be consistent with JS, if it reflects a trauma related to her death.
S18. March 4, 2014 (5 yrs.). C is combing L's hair when R enters room and asks what year was C born. C says, "1971, but why?" R says, "In my dream it sounds familiar."	Correct for JS, who was born in 1971.
S19. March 4, 2014 (5 yrs.). Following on S17, R adds, "I was standing there in the yard and saw a plane crash." Reported in email to GIMC producers.	Partially correct for JS, who would have seen the plane crash from the carport, not the yard.

(Continued)

Table 1.1   (Continued)

During her lunch hour on March 6, 2014, Cindy finds report of Pan Am 759 crash on the Internet.

March 6, 2014. C learns from Barbara Schultz's online obituary that Elizabeth was Jennifer's middle name. Elizabeth was the middle name she and Y gave to R.

That Jennifer's middle name was indeed Elizabeth is confirmed by her autopsy report.

S20. March 6, 2014 (5 yrs.). At bedtime, C asks R about her "dream" of the plane crash, but R says she does not want to talk about it. C asks if she can tell her one more thing and R says that she thought she was near a tree or pole or behind a tree. She mentions trees and poles frequently thereafter.

JS was not behind a tree, but there was a utility pole at the corner of the driveway and the oak tree struck by the plane was across the street but in her line of sight from within the carport.

S21. March 6, 2014 (5 yrs.). At bedtime, R told C, "I remember something about a park." She says this repeatedly thereafter, always in connection with trying to remember more about JS's life.

Correct for JS, who visited and played in two parks, Butch Duhe Playground and Lafreniere Park (Fig. 1.2). She was at a birthday party in Lafreniere Park in February of the year she died.

S22. March 6, 2014 (5 yrs.). Following on S21. "I think there was water nearby too." This she also repeated regularly, usually in association with S21.

Correct for JS. A canal runs along W. Metairie Ave., two blocks north of the Schultz house (Fig. 1.2). JS would have crossed the canal to get to Lafreniere Park.

S23. Mid-March 2014 (5 yrs.). When C asked again whether her fits about changing shirts might be related to the way she died before, R said, "I don't know . . . maybe. . . . Did I catch on fire?" Reported to *GIMC* producers.

Correct for JS, whose body was 100% burned when recovered, per her autopsy report, but since the body was burned postmortem, the feeling of catching on fire might also refer to electrocution.

S24. c. March 20, 2014 (5 yrs.). When C reads R the names of victims of the Pan Am 759 crash, R says in response to Jennifer Schulz, "Was I Jennifer? I think I was Jennifer." Reported to *GIMC* producers.

Correct for JS.

B10. After above, R repeatedly expresses interest in seeing pictures of JS, her family, her house, the neighborhood, etc., thinking they might help to elicit more memories

Expresses identification with JS.

B11. March 30, 2014 (6 yrs.). In the car during the day, R draws image of plane, in profile, with large blue blob on its tail. Later she explains that she drew the plane in profile because that was the perspective from which she saw it in her dream. Drawing witnessed by C, L, Y.

Correct for Pan Am, whose logo was a blue-and-white circle, and therefore consistent with JS's death. Although JS would not have seen the plane in profile at the time of her death, she likely had seen Pan Am planes on other occasions.

Table 1.1

S25. April 2, 2014 (6 yrs.). At bedtime, C asks R if she remembers how the crash happened. R says that the plane's left side and wing went down first, but did not want to talk about it anymore.	Correct for Pan Am 759 crash in Kenner, so consistent with JS's death.
S26. April 27, 2014 (6 yrs.). R tells C that she remembers that her parents sometimes went to a grocery store near her house. Reported in email to *GIMC* producers.	Plausible for JS. There are stores along Airline Drive (US 61) a few blocks south of the Schultz house. Several news stories say the Weems family was spared because they had gone to a store.
S27. June 11, 2014 (6 yrs.). Upon learning that C has received a DVD of RA's documentary of the Pan Am 759 crash, R asks C what the name of the "other girl" was. C asks what other girl—what was her first name? R says she thinks it was Lisa. Reported in email to GIMC producers.	Correct for Lisa Baye, friend of JS's sister Rachael, whose suffering and death are featured prominently in RA's documentary (Anderson, 2012).

The O'Bannions visit Kenner with GIMC crew on July 9, 2014, 32nd anniversary of plane crash.

B12. July 9, 2014 (6 yrs.). C has several pictures of R in same pose as JS in photo in newspaper shown them by RA.	RA shows R picture of JS in newspaper. She is half-turned, looking over her shoulder and smiling.
B13. July 9, 2014 (6 yrs.). R seems to recognize EP. In *GIMC* episode, this is expressed in the apparent comfort level between R and EP. R later said she felt that EP seemed familiar to her and that she recognized her by her voice.	Appropriate for JS, who had been close to EP.
B14. July 9, 2014 (6 yrs.). R goes straight to the bathroom in EP's house without having been directed to it. When C reached her, she was staring at the vanity. She told C she thought she had been there before.	Appropriate for JS, who had often been in EP's house, where she visited the bathroom and pulled drawers out of the vanity.

The O'Bannions return to Oklahoma on July 11, 2014.

S28. July 11, 2014 (6 yrs.). In Kenner, the O'Bannions learned from RA that JS had been on the phone when she died and C brought up the possibility that it was with Kevin. On the evening of their return to Bartlesville, C asks R if she knows who JS was on the phone with and R replies that perhaps it was Kevin. This is the first time she mentioned Kevin since S9.	The identity of the person on the phone with JS is not yet known, but it is unlikely it was Kevin. The Kevin R referred to in S9 was most likely JS's catechism teacher.

(Continued)

Table 1.1   (Continued)

S29. July 11, 2014 (6 yrs.). C asks R if being in Kenner triggered any new memories. She said she did not want to talk about it, then added that she last thing she could remember having seen was the plane's wing hitting the street.	Plausible for JS. If JS died after the plane hit the ground but before it struck the power and phone lines and before her house caught fire, the last thing she would have seen was the plane's wing scraping Fairway Street.
B5b, B6b. July 11, 2014 (6 yrs.). R begins sleeping better, stops sleepwalking. She goes a full year without sleepwalking.	Consistent with JS and suggests a resolution of the remembered trauma of her death from having visited the site of her death.

GIMC *episode featuring Rylann airs on September 24, 2014.*

B15. April 2, 2015 (7 yrs.). C learns from TG that JS's family was Catholic and realizes that this might help to explain R's seeming familiarity with Catholic ritual. R finds it easy to learn Catholic prayers and the catechism, sometimes seems to know things without being taught them.	Consistent with JS. The Schultzes were observant Catholics and JS had been in catechism classes at the time of her death.
B6c. July 2015 (7 yrs.). After not sleepwalking for the year after visiting Kenner, C reports that R sleepwalked 3–4 times in July 2015, then ceased again. She sleepwalked 3–4 times more between then and August 2018.	R's memories of JS surface most often in April–May and June–July of each year. The resumption of R's sleepwalking came during one of the peak periods of her memories of JS.
B16. June 26, 2016 (8 yrs.). After seeing an older piano in an antique shop on JS's birthday, R becomes obsessed with wanting a piano until she is given one for her 9th birthday.	No connection has yet been established between JS and a piano.
March 2017 (9 yrs.). For the first time, R researches the Pan Am 759 crash in order to inform her 3rd-grade teacher about it. She produces a booklet of news stories downloaded from the Internet.	
B17. March–April 2017 (9 yrs.). Perhaps as a consequence of learning about what Rachael went through after the crash, R becomes very concerned about Rachael. R did not talk about memories of Rachael, but about her concern for her, every few days, for several weeks.	Expresses identification with JS.
S30. May 1, 2017 (9 yrs.). There was a utility pole in her field of vision when she died. Previously R had said she saw a pole, but for the first time she described this to C as the utility pole of a power line.	Correct for JS. There was a utility pole at the corner of the Schultz driveway that JS would have seen from within the carport.

Table 1.1

S31. From April 6, 2018 (10 yrs.). For the first time, R mentions sitting on a swing in the carport while she talked on the phone. She repeats this several times thereafter.	Plausible for JS. There was a swing in the Schultz carport according to EP and EKP. Her body was recovered from the carport, per her autopsy report.

I interview Rylann, Cindy, Lonny, and Lane in Bartlesville, OK, on August 13–14, 2018.

Aug. 13, 2018 (10 yrs.). In my interview with her, R stated that she recalls having three nocturnal dreams about JS. In the dream, she sees the crash from a different perspective than in her waking memories. She is in the yard and sees plane from side.	
S32. Aug. 13, 2018 (10 yrs.). In my interview with her, R speculated that she (JS) had been electrocuted while talking on the phone in the carport. This is the first time she mentioned electrocution, but it is consistent with S7.	Unverified, but possible. Electrocutions can occur over phone lines during thunderstorms and the uninsulated phone line in front of Schultz house was cut and could have come into contact with cut power line (Figure 1.5).
B5c, B6d. Aug. 14–Sept. 4, 2018 (10 yrs.). Relapse of waking up & sleepwalking. Over 3 weeks following my visit, R wakes up during 20 nights, sleepwalking in agitated state in 5, then returns to normal.	

I visit Kenner for three days, September 22–24, 2018, to interview Jennifer's friends and obtain her autopsy report.

B18. In response to my query, C reports that R likes to make crafts, including crosses, which she would give away. She made a yarn owl perched on a stick.	In my interviews with them, JS's friends asked whether R enjoyed making crafts, as had JS. JS made crosses to give to friends and owls on sticks for LA and TB.
B19. In response to my query, C reports that R's favorite animals are parrots and rabbits.	EP had a pet parrot of which JS was very fond, per EP. Whether rabbits had significance to JS is unknown.
Sept. 24, 2018. I obtain JS's autopsy report from the Jefferson Parish Coroner's Office. The report says that JS's body was recovered intact from a carport with 100% third-degree burns.	The autopsy report is significant because it corrects some impressions about the accident known and recalled by witnesses, yet is consistent with R's memories of JS's last moments.

(Continued)

Table 1.1   (Continued)

Oct. 10, 2018. RB suggests different ways
lightning might be conducted, mentions
aluminum frame.

Oct. 12, 2018. I learn in an email from
RB, whose father was an engineer and
district manager for the power company
for many years, that the phone lines
in the Morningside Park subdivision
were strung along the same poles as the
power lines and that the power lines
were uninsulated in 1982.

That phone lines ran on the same poles
as power lines and that both they and
the power lines were uninsulated in
1982 was confirmed with RA, but
has not yet been confirmed with Bell
South or the power company.

Oct. 12, 2018. In his email on this date,
RB suggested that the explosion heard
throughout the neighborhood was
from the pole-hung fuse or a ground
transformer.

*I return to Kenner on December 14 and 15, 2018, to meet with scouts for a planned
production featuring Rylann.*

Dec. 15, 2018. The scouts and I obtain a
photograph of the ruined Schultz house
taken by JW the morning of July 10,
1982, before debris removal had begun
or JS's body had been recovered.

The photograph (Figure 1.5) confirms
witness reports that the Schultz
house was brick and that their car
was white, not red. It also confirms
that the power and telephone lines
in front of the house were torn
down.

Dec. 15, 2018. JW tells me that the
utility pole at the corner of the Schultz
driveway did not come down when the
power and phone lines running in front
of the house were cut. Lines running
from that pole across the street to the
Pourciau and Williams houses were
unaffected and they did not lose power
or telephone service.

On December 16, production scouts interview O'Bannion family in Bartlesville.

Dec. 16, 2018 (10 yrs.). R tells the scouts
that when she met EP, she recognized
her voice. So far as C recalls, this is the
first time she said this.

Appropriate for JS, who knew EP well.

Dec. 16, 2018. Production scouts
interview A & K about what they
witnessed of R's early behavior,
confirming what C told me.

all items of significance so that the development of Rylann's memories of Jennifer Schultz can be appreciated in the context of other things going on around them. The table is modeled after the tables Ian Stevenson used to summarize his cases; it includes information on the witnesses to Rylann's statements and behaviors and the ways in which their correspondence to Jennifer Schultz was confirmed or not.

Rylann's statements and behaviors related to Jennifer are prefixed by "S" or "B." Rylann made thirty-two discrete statements about Jennifer's life and death, some in response to questions. Repetitious statements are counted only once, unless they introduce new elements. Statements referring to the intermission between lives are included in the table but are not given an "S" designation.

Of the thirty-two statements relating in some way to Jennifer, twenty-five are correct, substantially correct, or plausible. Eight are incorrect or implausible, but of these, only four are demonstrably false or highly unlikely. The four statements that are demonstrably false or highly unlikely are: S10, she lived in a white house with a big front porch (the Schultz house was brick and had a small front porch); S11, her family had a red car (the car was white); S13, she had nine dresses (undetermined, but thought by her friends to be improbable); and S28, maybe it was Kevin on the phone with Jennifer (thought to be wrong). Rylann made none of these four false statements more than once. She made S10, S11, and S13 in response to Cindy's asking if she remembered anything more about Jennifer. She made S28 after hearing Cindy and Royd Anderson discuss the possibility of it being Kevin on the phone with Jennifer.

Four other statements are incorrect if taken literally but may be attributable to mental distortions and confusions rather than to faulty memory. S3, she was in her backyard when she died, appears to be due to Rylann's conflation of her view of the O'Bannion backyard as she posed for her picture in the ivory dress with Jennifer's view from the carport. S19, she was standing in the yard when she saw a plane crash, is a near-repetition of S3 and may be explained in the same way. S20, she was near a tree or pole or hiding behind a tree, was often repeated, with variations. Although Jennifer was not near a tree when she died, trees and a utility pole would have figured prominently in her view from the carport. S15, she thought she might have lived in Canada, may be construed as correct if "Canada" is a stand-in for "Kenner."

The twenty-five correct or plausible statements range from ones that would be applicable to many people (e.g., S21, she remembered a park, and S26, her parents went to a grocery store near her house) to the highly specific and personal (S31, she was sitting on a swing in the carport while talking on a phone when she saw the plane coming toward her). S31 and S32, she had been electrocuted while talking on the phone, emerged only when she was

ten, providing a correction to her earlier claim to have seen the plane crash
while standing in her yard.

Reincarnation cases typically include not only episodic memories, but
behavioral signs correlated with the previous life recalled. Rylann's case is
rich in examples. There are several habitual patterns, such as B2, offers to
do chores, and B4, pulls drawers out of bathroom vanity, which appeared
before Rylann began to relate her episodic memories. Her fondness for making crafts and knowledge of Catholic ritual may be assigned to this category
as well. Closely related to habitual behaviors are personality traits. These are
more difficult to pin down than are habitual behaviors, but at the time she met
Rylann, Evelyn Pourciau told the O'Bannions that she believed that she could
see something of Jennifer in the way she acted.

Another large group of behaviors (e.g., B3, is afraid of thunder and lightning; B5, wakes up during the night) indicate extreme anxiety or stress.
Sleepwalking (B6) might be a behavioral carryover if Jennifer also sleepwalked (none of her friends had heard of her doing so, though), or it could
be another manifestation of extreme stress. Nothing in Rylann's early life
can account for these signs of trauma, which began to appear when she was
around twenty-four months old. They would, however, be appropriate for a
person who had suffered a sudden physical blow, such as an electrocution.
B7, starts to say that her hair touching her back hurt her back, and B8, complains that clothing hurt her neck and wanted tags cut out, sound as if they
could be related to a subliminal memory of being electrocuted. This impression becomes stronger when Rylann begins to say it feels as if her skin is
burning.

A few behaviors appear to derive from memory of Jennifer's life and the
people she knew (e.g., B10, the picture of the plane she drew; B12, the sense
of comfort with Evelyn; and most notably, B13, finding her way to the bathroom in Evelyn's house). Only one behavior, B15, the obsession with the
piano, cannot at present be associated with Jennifer.

Researchers have come to look for physical signs in addition to behavioral signs and episodic memories in cases like Rylann's. The most dramatic
physical signs appear when there has been a violent death and are expressed
as birthmarks or birth defects. Rylann has no birthmarks or birth defects, but
we would not expect to find them, if she died by electrocution before her body
was burned. Physical signs may also relate to features of core identity. Rylann
is approaching the same age Jennifer was at her death and Jennifer's friends
note a similarity in their physiques. Some believe they see a similarity in the
eyes. Another possible influence is in the color of the hair. Jennifer's hair was
red. Rylann's hair was strawberry blonde during her first years, especially
noticeable in photographs taken between the ages of two and five. We must
not make much of this possible influence, however. Rylann's hair certainly

was never as red as Jennifer's and after she was five it darkened until it is now of a shade similar to other members of her family.

WHAT IS REINCARNATION?

Rylann recalled many things about the life and death of Jennifer Schultz while in the waking state, not under hypnosis. She identified with Jennifer and recounted her memories from Jennifer's point of view. She displayed reactions that might be expected from someone who experienced what Jennifer must have experienced. When Evelyn Pourciau met Rylann, she believed she could see Jennifer in her looks and behavior. Rylann appeared to recognize Evelyn and walked through her house to the bathroom without having been directed to it.

Rylann's case is far from unique. Thousands like it have been reported from around the world. Although these cases have been studied systematically for almost sixty years (since 1961), they are little known outside a small group of specialist researchers and critics. They raise many questions I will address and try to answer in this book. They seem to suggest reincarnation, but to say that begs the first question that must be answered: What exactly is reincarnation? What is it that these cases suggest? We cannot go on to other questions until we have come to grips with this very basic one.

In the authoritative fifteen-volume Thomson Gale *Encyclopedia of Religion*, J. Bruce Long writes that "the doctrine of reincarnation concerns the rebirth of the soul or self in a series of physical or preternatural embodiments, which are customarily human or animal in nature but are in some instances divine, angelic, demonic, vegetative, or astrological (i.e., are associated with the sun, moon, stars, or planets)" (J. B. Long, 2005, p. 7676). This definition attempts to encompass the diverse ways reincarnation has been depicted in religious traditions, but it fails at the outset by stating that it involves "the rebirth of the soul or self," because Buddhism, for which rebirth is a central precept, denies the existence of a soul or self and holds that what passes between lives is a contentless stream of consciousness (Premasiri, 1996).

In a companion article in the same encyclopedia, R. J. Z. Werblowsky and Jan Bremmer treat reincarnation under the heading of "Transmigration." Transmigration, they say, "denotes the process by which, after death, either a spiritual or an ethereal, subtle, and thinly material part of the personality, leaves the body that it previously inhabited; it then 'migrates' to enter (i.e., is reborn in) another body, either human or animal, or another form of being, such as a plant or even an inanimate object" (Werblowsky & Bremmer, 2005, p. 9325). This definition is no better than Long's. Buddhism denies that personality passes between lives; to the extent that personality traits reappear, it is due to the persistence of their karmic underpinnings (Premasiri, 1996). Moreover, it is unclear how personality may be said to possess "an ethereal, subtle, and thinly material part." Perhaps Werblowsky and Bremmer mean that personality is conveyed from one embodiment to another in a subtle body of some sort, but this does not work with Theravada Buddhism, which denies that the consciousness stream is supported between embodiments by such a vehicle (Premasiri, 1996).

A better definition is required if what is wanted is something that covers the diversity of conceptions that may be brought under the heading of reincarnation or rebirth. However, that definition would have to be so broad that it would be of little assistance in deciding whether or not cases of reincarnation provide evidence for reincarnation, which is what is meant by saying that they suggest reincarnation. The cases might provide evidence for one type of reincarnation but not for other types, and it would be wrong to generalize from the specific type suggested by the data to assume that all types are equally likely to occur. Therefore, I propose to isolate the basic elements of the rebirth concept and to introduce a set of terms that will facilitate discussion of the reincarnation case data without reference to any particular system of belief. After analyzing the case material, I will return to belief systems and ask which, if any, receive empirical support, and to what extent.

The first step in this task is to look more closely at the variety of rebirth beliefs. There are important common denominators in the tenets of the Indic religions (Hinduism, Jainism, Buddhism, and Sikhism), despite significant differences between them. All affirm karma and have the goal of overcoming the rebirth cycle. Many scholarly writers on reincarnation (e.g., Burley, 2016; Garrett, 2005) take the Indic doctrine to be paradigmatic of rebirth beliefs, but belief systems outside the Indic sphere do not necessarily include these features.

Reincarnation ideas were prevalent in the circum-Mediterranean region in ancient times. Many Greeks and Romans believed in rebirth, as did some early Jews and members of groups that developed into modern-day heterodox Shia Islamic sects like the Druze of Lebanon, Syria, and Israel. Reincarnation is widely attested in indigenous tribal societies today, and this was doubtless true of the past. Cross-cultural studies have found rebirth beliefs of one sort or another in as many as 60% of small-scale societies. The beliefs have been reported in historical times from every inhabited continent and from most culture areas in all continents except Europe (W. D. Davis, 1971; Matlock, 1993; Somersan, 1981).

The animistic beliefs of tribal societies are the most divergent from Indic ideas and so deserve the closest scrutiny in delineating the parameters of the reincarnation concept. The term *animism* was introduced by Sir Edward

Burnett Tylor (1871) in his book *Primitive Culture*. Tylor identified Animism as the world's earliest religion, but it may be more accurate to think of animism, lowercase, as a worldview rather than as a religion. Animism is concerned with spirits, both human and nonhuman, and their interaction with embodied persons, although its details are worked out differently in different cultures.

Animistic souls and spirits are more complex entities than their counterparts in non-Buddhist Indic and Abrahamic religions (or in Anglo-American Spiritualism or the French Spiritism of Allan Kardec). Each language has its own words for spirit concepts, and there are rarely direct translations into English, but generally speaking, animistic peoples think of the soul as embodied spirit and the spirit as disembodied soul. In other words, they are the same thing, except that the soul is embodied and the spirit is not. Not only human beings, but other animals possess souls, and there are nature spirits of various kinds. Spirits of all kinds are consciously aware and may interact purposefully with the living. In this book I focus on human souls and spirits and their destinies, although these form only a part of the total animistic system (Hultkrantz, 1953; Matlock, 1993; Tylor, 1871).

From the animistic perspective, the soul is not confined to the body but may depart from it (as a spirit) in dreams and during illness (Hultkrantz, 1953; Matlock, 1993; Tylor, 1871). The soul inhabits or is in some way connected to the body during life, but that connection is severed by death. In some cultures the body is believed to be animated by multiple souls, each responsible for a different bodily function. At death, one of these souls (perhaps that associated with the breath) reincarnates, while others become ancestral spirits or simply cease to exist.

Where a person is thought to possess a single soul during life, this soul may divide or fragment at death. When this happens, most often there is a division into an ancestral spirit and a reincarnating spirit, but the spirit may also split three ways, one part staying with the corpse, another part traveling to the land of the dead, the third part reincarnating. Alternatively, the process may be thought of as a replication of the soul or spirit postmortem, allowing it to reincarnate and remain in the afterlife simultaneously (Matlock, 1993, pp. 66–67, 127–29). Åke Hultkrantz (1953) described these ideas and variants of them in North America. In African philosophy the idea of "partial reincarnation" has been mooted to explain how a person's spirit may be housed in an ancestral shrine at the same time as it is reborn (Majeed, 2012; Mbiti, 1989; Onyewuenyi, 2009).

In the animistic view, there need not be a one-to-one correspondence between the deceased and the reincarnate. More than a single soul may be associated with a body at one time (*concurrent reincarnation*). This idea is found in Africa as well as elsewhere (Matlock, 1993, pp. 61–62). Among the Eskimo and Inuit, names are thought to embody souls, and a person who bears more than one name is believed to possess more than one soul (Guemple, 1994). Some cultures recognize the possibility of soul transference beginning before death or concluding after birth (Matlock, 1993, p. 61). Others allow a spirit to return in multiple bodies simultaneously (*multiple simultaneous reincarnation* or simply *multiple reincarnation*) (Matlock, 1993, pp. 61–62). Concurrent and multiple reincarnation and the premortem initiation of reincarnation are recognized in Tibetan Buddhism, which has many animistic features (Calkowski, 2013; David-Neel, 1932/1965, p. 122). Concurrent and multiple reincarnation are possible also in the Kabbalist *gil-gul neshamot* (Hebrew, "cycle of souls"), at least under the Lurian regime of a multitiered soul (Trugman, 2008; Wexelman, 1999).

Ideas such as these last confound the attempt to supply a simple characterization of reincarnation. Nonetheless, as a core definition, we may say that *reincarnation* denotes the transfer of some aspect of a human being's life force to the body of another human being. This definition does not exclude concurrent and multiple reincarnation, and it allows for the premortem initiation of reincarnation and for continuous incarnation, but it is restricted to the rebirth of human beings as human beings. "Human being" might be replaced with "member of a species" so that the definition would read, "Reincarnation denotes the transfer of some aspect of the life force of a member of a species to the body of another member of the same species," but for present purposes, that is unnecessary. The important points are that reincarnation by this definition is confined to rebirth in species lines and that it refers specifically to the continuance of an entity's life force, or part of it.

Indic religions permit interspecies rebirth but many other systems do not, so it would be wise to keep intra- and interspecies rebirth separate terminologically as well as conceptually. I call the latter *transmigration*: *Transmigration* denotes the transfer of the life force of a human being to the body of a nonhuman animal or other nonhuman entity. The same term may refer to the transfer of the life force of nonhuman animal or other entity to a human being. The latter possibility is recognized by Theosophy, which denies that transmigration may proceed in the reverse direction, down the line of physical evolution (Blavatsky, 1989a, 1989b). The essential idea of transmigration is rebirth into a species other than the original one.

When it appears in animistic systems, transmigration usually is an end in itself, without a subsequent return to human form (Matlock, 1993), so we need a way of distinguishing between transmigration that does not lead back to human life and transmigration that is part of a human-other-human cycle. I refer to the human-other-human cycle by the Greek term *metempsychosis*, fitting because that was the classical Greek conception (as well as the Indic one): *Metempsychosis* denotes a rebirth cycle that includes one or more lives as a nonhuman animal (or other nonhuman entity) between human lives.

It will be good to have an umbrella term that signifies the common process of reincarnation, transmigration, and metempsychosis—that designates rebirth without making distinctions as to type—and I will call this simply *rebirth*: *Rebirth* denotes the process by which an entity's life force leaves it, usually at death, and becomes associated with another entity, generally before birth.

In this last definition, I introduce the qualifiers "usually at death" and "generally before birth" in order to allow for rebirth initiated before death and for the replacement of an entity's life force after birth, a possibility recognized in India and Tibet. *Parakaya pravesh* or *parakaya pravesha* is a Sanskrit and Hindi term that denotes the entry of a spirit (wandering soul) into a body after birth, displacing the soul with which the body was born. *Parakaya pravesh* (more properly, *parakayapravesh*) usually is glossed as "possession" and indeed it is a sort of possession, except that when it lasts until the person dies it amounts to a substitute or *replacement reincarnation*. In pre-Buddhist Tibet, an induced replacement reincarnation was an institutionalized part of the succession of rulers (Kingsley, 2010, pp. 137–38).

In my operational definition, metempsychosis subsumes Hindu conceptions, because Hindus, like Buddhists, allow humans to be reborn as other animals. More often, *reincarnation* is used in reference to Hinduism, which assumes a personal soul, and *rebirth* in reference to Buddhism, which denies a personal soul. My terminology is different and may be confusing for that reason. The essential thing to remember is that when I refer to reincarnation, I mean human-to-human rebirth. I use *transmigration* for the rebirth of humans as nonhuman animals or other forms; *metempsychosis* for a human-other-human cycle; and *rebirth* to designate the process of returning to life in a new body after death without making these distinctions.

Variations in the meanings of *rebirth* and *reincarnation* are not the only possible source of confusion. Some authors, especially in older writings, use *transmigration of souls* in the way I use *rebirth*. *Metempsychosis* and, more rarely, *metensomatosis* and *palingenesis*, may denote the same thing as *reincarnation* or *rebirth*. In reading, it is important to examine how these terms are deployed in a given text.

A brief comment on "life force" may be helpful at this juncture. In animism, the life force is typically associated with the breath or another bodily function, although it has roughly the meaning of soul, spirit, psyche, mind, or consciousness in English. Buddhism conceives of the life force as an aggregate of factors, the most important of which is consciousness (Becker, 1993a; Premasiri, 1996), but this consciousness is only what may be called *conscious awareness.* Belief systems that understand memory, personality, and so on, to be part of the life force of an entity do not imagine those attributes to be carried in conscious awareness. Rather, they implicitly recognize a duplex consciousness that has both conscious and subconscious strata, although the division may be realized only at death (Hultkrantz, 1953, p. 476). This conception is similar to F. W. H. Myers's (1903) portrayal of the mind as having both supraliminal and subliminal levels. Sigmund Freud, also, had the concept of a duplex consciousness, but for him the "unconscious" was the repository of forgotten memories and repressed conflicts, not the more creative and expansive subconscious assumed in animistic traditions and described by Myers.

In Hinduism, whose metaphysical concepts have become more extensively differentiated and elaborated than those of any other religion, the life force (prāna) may be distinguished from the soul (ātman or jīva). In his *Autobiography of a Yogi*, Yogananda says that the life force is "an expression of the *Aum* vibration of the omnipresent soul" (1998, p. 540). In some Hindu philosophical schools, the atman is said to be an emanation from God (Brahman), while the jiva is the personal soul that incarnates. In Advaita Vedanta, it is the atman that incarnates (M. N. Prasad, 1999). The atman, jiva, and prana are closely linked, and it does not seem necessary to make these distinctions here. The essential idea of reincarnation cross-culturally is of a life force that animates a living entity and survives death, returning to animate another entity when it is reborn. The experiencer or "owner" (Sorabji, 2006) of the consciousness stream may be termed the *self.*

Now, concerning karma, the great moral law of cause and effect of Hinduism and Buddhism (and of Jainism and Sikhism): Karma is considered moral because it is thought to derive from one's own actions. Good deeds produce positive karma; bad deeds result in negative karma. Even when moral values are removed from consideration, as in some Indian philosophical commentaries, karma is thought of as an external force that determines not only where and to whom one is reborn but much of what befalls one in life. Theosophy adopted the traditional moral concept of karma and tied it tightly to reincarnation, to the point that one is thought to be inconceivable without the other (Blavatsky, 1889a, 1889b). However, there is nothing about reincarnation that logically entails karma as a juridical force external to the individual. Non-Indic rebirth eschatologies make no reference to karma in this sense (Matlock, 1993; Obeyesekere, 2002), so it may be omitted from an operational definition of reincarnation.

Interestingly, modern Westerners appear to be reimagining karma. For many Westerners today, karma involves no more than the transfer of psychological traits and perhaps conflicts from one life to another. Europeans who take up Hinduism or Buddhism often subscribe to this revisionist idea, which is more compatible with Western values of self-determination and progress than is the Eastern one (Walter & Waterhouse, 2001). Some Asians resident in the West (e.g., Tigunait, 1997) also espouse this psychological conception of karma. Because it avoids the moral dimension and situates responsibility with the thoughts and actions of an individual, this version of karma is not karma in the classic sense and deserves a different name. I call it *processual karma*, in contrast to *juridical karma*. Processual karma entails the carrying over from life to life of memory, emotions, behavioral dispositions, and other attributes that inform personality. Processual karma may involve self-judgment, but it derives from a force internal rather than external to the actor.

Another concept central to Indic traditions but missing from animistic ones is the idea of liberation from the cycle of births and deaths (saṃsāra). In some Hindu philosophical schools, liberation (mokṣa) is attained when after many lives an individual soul is reabsorbed into the blissful supreme consciousness from which it arose. In Buddhism, the individual frees himself from the karmic cycle and achieves Nirvana when he has surmounted all emotional attachments to the world of the flesh. Indic societies have been called life-negating, in trying to avoid rebirth. Animistic societies, by contrast are life-affirming, in welcoming reincarnation. Under animism, the reincarnation cycle may in principle go on forever, but limits are sometimes placed on the number of returns, after which an individual's spirit is thought to pass out of existence or to be absorbed into the pool of ancestral spirits (Matlock, 1993, p. 62).

There are other variations in how reincarnation is thought to operate. Buddhism stipulates that rebirth occurs at conception. Jains expect there to be no interval between death and rebirth, the soul passing at once into an entity conceived or coming into being at the moment of death, but Druze hold that upon death the soul passes immediately into a human baby then being born. Many of these variations are in conflict; they cannot all be correct. In addition to examining the case data for indications of which type of rebirth receives the most empirical support, I will be looking for evidence of juridical karma and other subsidiary features of the process.

Scholars have proposed many places for the origin of the belief in rebirth. In antiquity, the Greeks followed Herodotus (*History of Herodotus* II.123) in supposing that it came from Egypt. Thomas McEvilley (2013) maintained that it traveled from Greece to India. Alexander Alexakis (2001) was in good company in pointing to India as its homeland. M. L. West (1971) expanded the ancestral region to include Persia, a view echoed by Walter Burkert (1972, p. 165), who called rebirth beliefs "Indo-Iranian."

Arnold Toynbee (1959, p. 55) speculated that both Greek and Indian rebirth beliefs originated on the "Great Eurasian Steppe," which would push them back to Proto-Indo-European society. This view was shared by Mitra Ara (2008, p. 78), who, however, explained rebirth as a variant of ideas about what happened after death that included bodily resurrection and regeneration as alternate possibilities. Peter Kingsley (2010, p. 147) proposed that the reincarnation idea originated in Tibet and Mongolia and spread from there to Greece, India, and northwest North America. This would provide a link to tribal societies, but Kingsley did not seem to appreciate how widespread reincarnation beliefs are among indigenous peoples. Indeed, none of these proposals account for the global distribution of animistic reincarnation beliefs.

Ara argued that the notion of rebirth was inspired by the awareness of otherness and opposition in nature—"day and night, earth and sky, water and fire, man and woman, sacred and profane, life and death, life here and life hereafter." Rebirth and its transformations expressed human concerns "which arise from hopes and fears within a given time and place" (Ara, 2008, p. 78). Some variant of this view is common in the social sciences, which tend to treat soul and spirit concepts as mental constructs. The early twentieth-century French sociologist Émile Durkheim (1912/1965) supposed that reincarnation and spirit beliefs were inspired by human social organization. "A society has all that is necessary to arouse the sensation of the divine in minds, merely by the power that it has over them; for to its members it is what a god is to his worshippers," he declared in *The Elementary Forms of the Religious Life* (1965, pp. 236–37).

In *Primitive Culture*, Tylor advanced a radically different, experience-centered proposal. Tylor wrote before the advent of modern anthropology and based his portrayal of animism on the reports of travelers, missionaries, and colonial administrators. In these sources he found many mentions of apparitions, dreams in which human figures appeared, what today are called out-of-body and near-death experiences, and mediumistic trance, in connection with beliefs about life after death, and he argued that these experiences had suggested the idea of postmortem survival to indigenous peoples. Similarly, Tylor thought that reincarnation was a conclusion drawn from phenomena such as the dreams of expectant mothers, birthmarks on newborn babies, and the telltale behaviors of toddlers. Once established, Tylor supposed, the soul concept was generalized from humans to nonhuman animals and to wholly imaginary spirit beings. Some cultures extended the soul concept to plants, to features of the landscape, to natural forces, even to words and names (Tylor, 1871).

I think Tylor was on to something important. One can readily appreciate how apparitions, near-death experiences, and so forth, might have suggested postmortem survival to people long ago, because these experiences have a similar significance for many people today. In fact, Tylor's ideas were influenced by his contact with Victorian Spiritualism, which he perceived to be a "survival and revival" of animistic thinking and practices (Stocking, 1971). Similarly, the signs of reincarnation Tylor identified would quite naturally be interpreted as evidence of the return of a spirit in a new body, especially when, as sometimes happens, children claim to remember previous lives.

Many anthropologists dislike animism because of its association with an evolutionary scheme of human social development propounded by Tylor, but animistic thinking has nothing to do with an evolutionary framework imposed on these societies. The attribution, in some societies, of spirit to all manner of inanimate objects and forces has created the impression that animism denotes an indiscriminate anthropomorphizing of the natural world, but these more extreme traits are by no means universal features of animism as represented in the ethnographic record (Matlock, 1993, 1995). Durkheim (1912/1965) ridiculed animism as the assertion that the spirit concept derived from dreams alone, but this is a perversion of Tylor's insight that animistic beliefs have an empirical basis.

Many scholars from outside anthropology appear to be confused about the relationship between animism and shamanism. Shushan (2009, p. 33) observed that it was unlikely that certain prehistoric civilizations (Old and Middle Kingdom Egypt, Sumer, Vedic India, pre-Buddhist China, pre-Columbian Mesoamerica) were shaped by shamanic practices that were part of a common cultural substrate. This seems true enough, but animism as a worldview could have and probably did inform all early civilizations. Raymond Martin and John Barresi (2006, p. 11) thought that ideas about the soul that influenced Pythagoras and Plato and through Plato much of subsequent Western thought might have arisen from the "dark heart of shamanism." However, shamanism and animism are by no means the same. A shaman is a "magico-religious practitioner" whose business it is to interact with the spirit world (Winkelman, 1992). The shamanic outlook is animistic, but animism is a more general attitude and has a more widespread presence than does shamanism. Shamanism rests on animism, but animism does not depend on shamanism.

Because the animistic conception of souls, spirits, and their reincarnation is empirically grounded, animistic ideas provide a suitable starting point and touchstone for discussion of the reincarnation case data. From the animistic perspective, the distinction between souls and spirits is a transformational one (a soul is embodied; a spirit is not), and the soul/spirit may be equated with psyche, mind, or consciousness, an entity's life force. The life force of a disembodied spirit is continuous with the life force of an embodied being. In animism, there is no essential difference between the consciousness of human and nonhuman entities, which consequently may interact with one another and with human beings, either directly, as apparitions or in dreams, or indirectly, through shamans and other intermediaries.

Reincarnation in animistic systems involves neither juridical karma nor liberation from a cycle of births and deaths, but simply the return of the life force (consciousness stream) of a deceased human being to the body of a living human being or beings. Continuities of personality, behavior, interests, skills, and so forth, are recognized, but the notion that the conditions of life are contingent upon the moral qualities of actions in previous lives is not even considered.

I follow Tylor (1871) in thinking that reincarnation was a conclusion drawn from signs such as a woman's pregnancy dreams, an infant's birthmarks, and a child's behaviors, which frequently are cited in association with the belief (Matlock, 1993). This means that the belief in reincarnation may be very old and that it may have more than a single geographical source. There is no reason to assume that it originated in one place, such as India, and spread from there. What India exported to the rest of the world were philosophical elaborations on the rebirth idea, notably juridical karma, not the concept of rebirth or reincarnation per se.

CHALLENGE TO MATERIALISM

Reincarnation likely was originally—and in contemporary indigenous societies still is—assigned to the provinces of psychology and biology rather than religion. It had a solidly empirical basis in the signs Tylor (1871) identified. The idea was divorced from empiricism and became philosophically elaborated in India, Greece, and elsewhere. It entered into religious systems, and that is what our modern Western culture has inherited. But although reincarnation typically is considered a religious belief in academia and in our wider society today, it need not be treated that way. By taking an experience-centered approach and examining cases of past-life memory and other signs of reincarnation, I aim to focus attention on the evidential dimensions of the problem. Could reincarnation be not merely a belief of a good many of the world's peoples, but a reality for some or even all of us? Is there evidence to support this straightforward conclusion from cases like Rylann's?

A reincarnation interpretation of the case phenomena encounters obstacles that go beyond the resistance one might expect from a religious bias against the idea in the Western world. Our modern psychological and biological sciences have no place for a mind that can exist independently of the body and thus rule out at the start any possibility of postmortem survival, much less of reincarnation. However, modern science is rooted in a seventeenth-century, Newtonian understanding of how the world works. In the twentieth century, quantum mechanics brought a radically new perspective. Newtonian or classical mechanics is now known to provide only an approximate account of events at the macroscopic level of physical reality and to be altogether unsuited to describing interactions at the deeper subatomic or quantum level. Along with this new outlook has come a new way of thinking about consciousness and its engagement with the material world.

There is no agreement about the place of consciousness in quantum theory. The experimental findings are open to multiple interpretations (Atmanspacher, 2011). Nonetheless, several great physicists have held that consciousness is the wellspring of physical reality. Max Planck, one of the founders of quantum mechanics, told *The Observer* newspaper of London (on January 25, 1931): "I regard matter as derivative from consciousness. We cannot get behind consciousness. Everything that we talk about, everything that we regard as existing, postulates consciousness." Planck and other early quantum theorists adopted an idealist view of consciousness as primary and matter as secondary to it. They suggested that consciousness influences outcomes at the quantum level and plays a role in how physical reality manifests on an ongoing basis.

Henry Stapp of Berkeley's Lawrence Livermore National Laboratory concurs and goes further, attributing cognitive functions such as attention, intention, and will to consciousness (Stapp, 1999), which he presumes to interact with the brain while existing independently of it (Stapp, 2005). Moreover, Stapp (2009) pointed out, if consciousness is separate from physical (read biological) systems, it could in principle survive bodily death. In his most recent statement on the topic, he said that allowing for reincarnation would require only minor tweaking of the mathematical formalisms and would leave most of the quantum mechanical model of mind/brain interaction untouched (Stapp, 2015, p. 181). Elsewhere he has said, "Rational science-based opinion on this question [of the survival of consciousness after bodily death] must be based on the content and quality of the empirical data, not on a presumed incompatibility of such phenomena with our contemporary understanding of the workings of nature" (2009, p. 9). The door is open to a parapsychological appraisal of the reincarnation case data.

The parapsychological approach belongs to the sciences rather than to the humanities and an important part of it is theory building and hypothesis testing. The term *theory* is sometimes used to denote a well-established theory and *hypothesis* to refer to a theoretical construct that has not been established through testing or is not widely accepted. Michael Sudduth (2016), for instance, writes about "the survival hypothesis" and "the reincarnation hypothesis." This usage, common in philosophy and religious studies, creates ambiguity in the meaning of *hypothesis*, which is employed both in the sense of an unestablished theory and the means by which that theory is evaluated. I prefer to use *theory* in the sense of a construct or set of principles that explain

something, as is the practice in psychology (and anthropology, my professional field). I use *hypothesis* to indicate a proposition that is derived from a
theory and used to test it.

A good theory is one that explains many or all things under its purview,
yet is open to falsification. Good theories can be tested and determined to be
right or wrong (can, in other words, be confirmed or falsified). As hypotheses
are tested and accepted, they add to the presumptive validity of the theory
from which they are derived. When a theory has been well confirmed, it
is considered established. An established theory can be very productive in
generating additional research. Hypotheses derived from the theory continue
to be tested and if confirmed make it stronger and stronger. The stronger the
theory gets, the harder it becomes for a rival theory to gain ground against
it. All scientific knowledge comes from theories that have been tested and
confirmed but in principle are subject to revision or replacement when better
theories come along.

There is as yet no widely accepted theory of reincarnation. The operational,
working definition I have given hardly amounts to one either, although it
provides a start toward developing a theory. Conceptualizing what reincarnates as a duplex stream of consciousness that carries forward memories,
behavioral dispositions, and other aspects of personality through death to
the union with a new body is an improvement over the nebulous "soul." The
restriction to human-to-human rebirth narrows the scope of what must be
explained. These postulates help construct what may be called an interpretive
framework or interpretive frame and create the space in which to develop a
theory. If appropriate, I will bring in transmigration and metempsychosis later
to create a general theory of rebirth, but I will begin with reincarnation, as I
have defined it.

To be successful, a theory of reincarnation must not only handle the evidence better than rival theories do; it must not conflict with current knowledge in biology and psychology or any other field. Quantum mechanics has
been successful as a theory in part because it does not require abandoning
classical mechanics but only shows the latter's representation of physical
reality to be incomplete (Rosenblum & Kuttner, 2011; Stapp, 2011). Similarly, a successful theory of reincarnation must assimilate the case data into
the accepted findings of psychology and biology without asking that any of
those findings be set aside. Some findings may need to be reinterpreted, but
that is different from throwing them out.

Chief among the alternative theories of reincarnation signs is the fantasy theory, which considers all apparent memories of previous lives to be fantasies.
In a sense, the fantasy theory is a hypothesis derived from broader materialist
theories of consciousness, perception, and memory as derivatives of cerebral

activity, but it itself has generated hypotheses that have been tested by cognitive psychologists concerned with false memory, the apparent recollection of events that did not actually occur (e.g., McNally, 2012; Meyersburg, Bogdan, Gallo, & McNally, 2009).

This research typically involves laboratory-based tasks such as memorization of word lists whose application to real life is unclear. Moreover, the supposed past-life memories examined in these studies are mostly induced under hypnosis with adults and differ phenomenologically and evidentially from children's involuntary past-life memories. This immingling of hypnotically induced and spontaneously occurring memories of previous lives is common in materialist research (Meyersburg, Carson, Mathis, & McNally, 2014; Spanos, 1996), but I believe it is a mistake. There are enough differences between involuntary and hypnotically induced memories of previous lives for these categories of experience to be kept separate analytically. Almost all serious research on reincarnation has been done with what in parapsychology are called spontaneous cases, so I will be dealing primarily with them.

Most of the scholarly work on reincarnation in anthropology, philosophy, and even, perhaps surprisingly, religious studies, adheres to the fantasy theory as well. Our social sciences developed in the late nineteenth century when materialism was at its height and have not made the transition to a postmaterialist appreciation of nature and man (Nadeau & Kafatos, 1999). They take for granted that the mind is a product of the brain and consider the postmortem survival and reincarnation of consciousness to be impossible in principle.

In recent years there have been attempts to bring lived experience into cognitive science (E. Thompson, 2007, 2015; Varela, E. Thompson, & Rosch, 2016), but this enactive approach treats experience in the abstract and resists taking it seriously. Evan Thompson (2015, p. 290) writes off Stevenson's case studies as "anecdotal" and thus beyond the bounds of scientific inquiry. Jesse Bering (2006a, 2006b, 2012) pays more attention to experience in his "cognitive science of religion," but he regards the sense of God and perception of spirits to be effluences of the brain that provided humanity an evolutionary advantage early on, but which no longer serve a useful purpose and must be relinquished.

Of particular interest in the cognitive science of religion is the work of Claire White, who has investigated why similar signs are interpreted as suggestive of reincarnation cross-culturally (White, 2009, 2015a, 2015b, 2016, 2017; White, R. Kelly, & Nichols, 2016). White ignores the possibility that different people reach the same conclusion because they perceive the same truth and looks for patterns in cognitive processing that are independent of culture. Reincarnation identifications are sometimes made on the basis of very slender and easily contestable evidence. Not infrequently, signs run counter to the beliefs promoted by a culture or taught in the religion to which its members adhere. A better understanding of why people interpret certain signs as indicative of reincarnation, even when cultural support and strong evidence are lacking, is important, but I have to wonder how far the reduction to neural operations takes us.

The experience-centered approach anticipated by Tylor (1871), elaborated by David Hufford (1982), and embraced by Whitley Strieber and Jeffrey Kripal (2016) and by Gregory Shushan (2018), focuses on events sometimes dismissed as anecdotal. As Shushan (2018, pp. 227–28) notes, this approach is as compatible with a materialist as with a survivalist orientation. Although he recognized that beliefs about souls and spirits in indigenous societies were founded on observation and experience, Tylor (1871) thought of this as an example of primitive logic that Victorian civilization had come to see through. Strieber and Kripal (2016) attempt to move past mind/brain reductionism, but their choice of subject (UFO abductions) is not the best with which to explore ontological issues and Kripal favors mythologizing as the explanation for the entire range of "super natural" experience. Elsewhere, Kripal (2010, p. 254) proposes that "paranormal" and "anomalous" experiences (again adverting to ufology) be treated as sacred phenomena, to be confronted on their own terms and not evaluated scientifically.

The experience-centered approach has sometimes been used to question materialist assumptions. Hufford (1982) held that cross-cultural similarities in Old Hag and kindred phenomena pointed to a reality that could not be reduced to culture, and by implication to mind/brain identity, but his material was not suited to what I believe presents the greatest challenge to the fantasy theory—the veridicality (factualness) of some anomalous experiences. Near-death experiences provide more opportunity to grapple with veridicality, and Shushan (2018) notes veridical elements when they appear, but his main interest lies in exploring the ways culture impacts experience, not with judging how far experience may be taken as support for a theory of postmortem survival.

Parapsychology is obsessed with veridicality, and spontaneous case studies challenge the fantasy theory (and by extension materialism) more directly than any other experience-centered approach. A veridical spontaneous case cannot rightly be called a fantasy—whatever it is, it is not a fantasy—and labeling an investigated case "anecdotal" is a rhetorical effort to minimize the threat to materialist orthodoxy. Similarly, casting academic parapsychology into the trash bin of "pseudoscience" (as many critics do) is an attempt to reduce the threat posed by the discipline.

That threat becomes acute when a reincarnation case is "solved," when the person whose life is recalled (the "previous personality," in Stevenson's terminology; the *previous person* in mine) is identified. Solved cases, such as Rylann's, take veridicality to the next level; they involve not just a few verified facts but a sufficient number of verified facts to allow a researcher to conclude that one specific previous person, and no other, matches the case subject's memories.

Critics have responded to solved reincarnation cases by alleging memory distortions among witnesses, methodological flaws in investigations, and the sloppy reporting of findings (Angel, 2015; Augustine, 2015; P. Edwards, 1996; Lester, 2005, 2015; Shermer, 2018). They ascribe apparent veridicality to a "subjective illusion of significance" (Angel, 2015). Many adopt some form of what I call the *psychosocial theory*, which dismisses veridical phenomena and portrays cases as developing from a combination of psychological and social factors in accordance with culturally mandated beliefs in rebirth.

Psychiatrist Eugene Brody (1979) embraced the psychosocial position in a review of one of Stevenson's volumes of case reports. Brody argued that a child's past-life memory claims reflected a compromised relationship between mother and child that began in early infancy. A child's frequent crying and "feeding difficulties" signaled "partially repressed impulses, wishes or ideas," the expression of needs not met (Brody, 1979, p. 78). A mother, in her attempt to come to terms with her perceived inadequacies at parenting, turned to her culture's belief in reincarnation for support. That belief shaped the way she treated her child and was conveyed to him, so that he grew up imagining that he had lived before. The child might be acting out "unconscious fantasies of its parents," his behavior might reflect "disguised identification with some important figure," or it could be "a mode of unconscious conflict resolution" (Brody, 1979, pp. 78–79).

There is reason to take parental shaping of children's behavior (*parental guidance*) seriously. Experimental work has shown that false memories may be implanted by suggestion and young children are especially susceptible to this possibility (Bruck & Ceci, 1999). Social construction enters to some extent into the development and reporting of all reincarnation cases, and some claimed identifications have proven to be self-delusions or fabrications (Stevenson, Pasricha, & Samararatne, 1988).

In some tribal societies, previous lives are believed to have passed in the same lineage or clan. There are strong cultural reasons for this, because reincarnation within the descent group is required for a child to inherit the name (and with it a significant element of the identity) of the previous person and so be in a position to reprise his role in society. Family connections between the case subject and previous person make it hard for investigators to rule out the possibility that a child has learned the information he imparts from someone in his family or social circle. By no means are all cases veridical to any great extent. When veridicality is weak or lacking, it is easy to overinterpret phenomena and come to questionable conclusions regarding them (Steven-son, Pasricha, & Samararatne, 1998).

Even when memories are verified and a case is solved, memories come a year or more after pregnancy dreams, birthmarks, and an infant's nonverbal behaviors, which may have suggested a past-life identity and set up the potential for cuing. Social construction does not necessarily explain all facets of a given case, but investigators must always be on the lookout for it. In order to reduce the possibility of social construction to a minimum, Stevenson preferred to study cases in which the two families were unknown to each other before a child began to relate his memories. Although unusual in tribal societies, *stranger cases* are common in other societies, and therefore Stevenson worked mainly in these other societies.

The psychosocial theory has generated several testable hypotheses, all of which have been falsified. A central assumption of the theory and common skeptical charge is that cases come only from places where reincarnation is endorsed by the mainstream culture, but this overlooks the many Western cases that have been reported since the early twentieth century (Muller, 1970; Stevenson, 2003; Tucker, 2013; and of course Rylann). The psychosocial theory also fails to confront the fact that Asian cases frequently depart from cultural ideals.

The Druze believe that one is reborn immediately upon death, with no lapse of time between death and reincarnation. In Stevenson's Druze cases, however, the median interval was eight months. To explain the discrepancy, the Druze posit brief intermediate lives that are not recalled, thus bringing their beliefs into line with their cases, although Stevenson was aware of no evidence for these intermediate lives (1980, pp. 9–10). The psychosocial theory attributes similarities in cases to diffusion of knowledge about them (Chari, 1987), yet David Barker and Satwant Pasricha (1979) found that information about cases rarely traveled far. They also discovered that many cases had unique characteristics that could not be explained on the diffusion hypothesis. Pasricha (1990b) determined that Indians unfamiliar with cases held unrealistic expectations about them. Respondents to her survey thought that subjects would begin and cease speaking about previous lives later than most children actually do.

Pasricha (1992) examined the possibility of parental guidance in relation to nineteen Indian cases she and Barker collected but judged it untenable partly because, in stranger cases, the details of the previous life were unknown to the parents while the case was unfolding. Antonia Mills (1990, 2003) studied twenty-six Indian cases with differences of religion (Hinduism and Sunni Islam) between the child and the previous person and asked why parents would impose a different religious identity on their children. Coming at the issue from a different angle, Stevenson and Narender Chadha (1990) described the techniques many Asian parents use to keep their children from speaking about previous lives. If the cases are responses to parental guidance, why do many Asian parents attempt to suppress them once they have brought them into being?

Children who claim to remember having lived before are rare. We do not know exactly how rare, because Barker and Pasricha's (1979) survey is the only one to have been reported. Barker and Pasricha covered a development block in Uttar Pradesh, India, a region with a relatively high incidence of reported cases, and arrived at an estimate of about one case per 550 people. Reincarnation cases may be more common among the Druze than any other group in the world (Stevenson, 1980, p. 8), but until proper surveys are done with them and others, we cannot be certain.

Because involuntary past-life memories are rare, researchers seldom learn about them before the previous person has been identified and are left to document what has already transpired, sometimes years in the past. This allows critics to allege that the lapse of time has permitted selective recall and other errors to creep in. Sometimes, however, a child's statements are recorded in writing before the previous person is identified. Sybo Schouten and Stevenson (1998) compared cases with and without records made before verifications and discovered that more statements were recorded, yet the percentage of correct statements was just as high in cases with prior written records as in cases without them. It appears that cases are not enhanced with the passage of time, but on the contrary become weaker, as facts are forgotten (a conclusion reached by Stevenson & Keil, 2000, as well).

Rylann's case adds to the small number of solved stranger cases with written records made before the previous person's identity was known. Cindy had been in email correspondence with the *GIMC* producers for a full year before Rylann recalled the plane crash, the memory of which led to her identification with Jennifer Schultz. How confident can we be in that identification, though?

Some of Rylann's memories are so general they could apply to many people. Her memories of her house being near water and going to a park are like that. She recalled the names Kevin, Jennifer, and Lisa, but these are common names and could be coincidental also. She was wrong about some things, such as the color of her house and the family car. At first, she talked as if she thought she had died in her yard after having been struck by lightning. Only after being told by Royd Anderson that Jennifer died in her carport while talking on the telephone did she start to remember having died in the carport while talking on the telephone. When asked to whom she had been talking, she guessed that it was Kevin, when in fact it more likely was someone she did not remember. She may not have been talking on the phone at all.

When she told Cindy that her death had something to do with a plane crash, Rylann was not sure of the year or where it was. She thought it might have been in either Canada or Louisiana and it was only after Cindy ascertained that Pan Am Flight 759 had crashed in Kenner, Louisiana, that the determination was made that she had been Jennifer Schultz. From then on, all that Rylann said could have been influenced by what Cindy read online. Cindy could have mentioned things to her that she forgot having said, but Rylann remembered and related as her memories. Rylann might not consciously recall having heard these things. However, she was six by this time and could have snuck to the computer to look up the crash without Cindy knowing about it. She later admitted to doing research online and even compiled a booklet of news reports about the accident. Everything Rylann said and did during and after the trip to Kenner must be discounted because Royd Anderson told her in advance that he was taking her to Jennifer's old neighborhood and that she would be meeting Evelyn Pourciau, Jennifer's neighbor and friend.

This would be a typical skeptical reading of Rylann's case. A parapsychologist might take note of Rylann's ESP abilities and wonder how much of her apparent memories was acquired by psi, the term parapsychologists use as a cover term for ESP and psychokinesis (PK), or mind-over-matter. If extrasensory awareness of the contents of Anderson's documentary (Anderson, 2012) is the correct explanation for her reference to Lisa Baye, why could Rylann not have used psi to learn other things about Jennifer and the plane crash? Rylann appears to have a talent for precognition, so perhaps her "memories" were really precognitions of what she learned when she went to Kenner or when she read about the crash online. It is not inconceivable that the entire story entered Rylann's subconscious at one time early on, then presented itself to her conscious awareness as memories piecemeal over the years. This possibility receives support from the discovery that the configuration of the utility pole and trees in what would have been Jennifer's final view was similar to what Rylann was looking at when the picture of her in the ivory dress was taken.

Is there any reason not to adopt one of these scenarios as the proper explanation for what at first blush appear to be Rylann's memories of Jennifer's life and death? I would say yes, there are quite a few. First of all, Rylann was correct about many items and not all of her statements concerned items either she or Cindy could have read online or elsewhere. That makes a psi interpretation of them less likely. Some of her statements could be related to Jennifer coincidentally but we must ask how many seeming coincidences may occur before we decide that, taken together, they point to something beyond coincidence.

Most importantly, Rylann was right about the swing in the carport and her memories of electrocution are consistent with Jennifer's autopsy report and details of the plane crash. It is hard to imagine what the psi source for this information would have been, unless a retrocognitive tapping into Jennifer's view on the verge of her death plus a clairvoyant perception of the plane breaking the power and telephone lines, but this stretches credulity beyond the point that any but the most committed anti-survival parapsychologist would be comfortable going.

There is also Rylann's behavioral identification with Jennifer. Skeptical parapsychologists and parapsychologically sensitive philosophers downplay or ignore reported behavioral correspondences between a case subject and an identified previous person or else claim (with Braude, 2003) that the behaviors could have been shaped by psi impressions, when there is no independent evidence that complex behaviors can be acquired via psi. Other critics attribute children's behaviors to parental guidance, but this rationale becomes strained when parents are not aware of the behavioral patterns in the previous persons they supposedly are helping to instill in their children. Rylann's parents were Catholic and had given no serious thought to the possibility of reincarnation before Rylann told Cindy that she had died before. By this time, Rylann was already displaying habitual behaviors and post-traumatic symptoms consistent with Jennifer Schultz and her death by electrocution.

Normally in science when a theory has been repeatedly refuted it is considered falsified and is abandoned. This has not happened with the psychosocial theory of past-life memory claims, perhaps because the studies that have assessed it are not widely known, but more likely because the possibility of reincarnation challenges not only the psychosocial and fantasy theories but their well-established parent theories of consciousness, perception, and memory as products of cerebral activity and because researchers have no way of explaining how reincarnation would operate in biological terms. There is not yet a reincarnation theory to test, and researchers have been attempting to falsify theories (the psychosocial and fantasy theories, along with their well-established parent theories) without offering an alternative in their place.

Stephen Hales (2001) made this point and there is justice to it. We do need a proper theory of reincarnation to set against other possibilities. I think Hales underestimates the evidence for survival and reincarnation, though. Like Brody (1979) and others (Angel, 2015; Augustine & Fishman, 2015), he is convinced that survival is highly unlikely, because of its conflicts with materialism. Those who assume this stance are what David Ray Griffin (1997) called paradigmatic as opposed to data-led thinkers. Data-led thinkers let evidence inform how they see the world, but paradigmatic thinkers must have their fundamental assumptions addressed before they will attend to evidence that challenges their convictions. Hales (2001), Keith Augustine and Yonatan Fishman (2015), and Michael Sudduth (2016) underplay the weaknesses of the materialist position, thereby overestimating its ability to counter the survival and reincarnation data (Almeder, 2001; Matlock, 2016a, 2016b, 2016c).

For their part, several data-led philosophers (Almeder, 1992; Griffin, 1997; Grosso, 2004; Lund, 2009; Preuss, 1989) and at least one scholar of religion (Becker, 1993b) have concluded that reincarnation is a plausible interpretation of the evidence. For Robert Almeder (1996, p. 512), it has become "irrational" to deny that reincarnation occurs. I would not put it that way. The denial is entirely rational within a materialist frame of reference. However, materialism has been known to provide only an approximation of macroscopic physical processes and to be restricted in its application for more than a century now and cannot be used to rule out the possibility of postmortem survival and reincarnation a priori. Our judgment must be based on evidence, and that is where signs come in. Signs of the sort represented in Rylann's case provide empirical evidence supporting not only a belief in reincarnation but, potentially, the reality of reincarnation, and are the basis of the theory I propose in this book.

Scientific paradigms change when faced with data for which they cannot account, and they can change rapidly, as generations of workers committed to certain positions pass from the scene (T. S. Kuhn, 1962). Science has seen many paradigm shifts in its history. The scientific revolution accompanying the appreciation that the Earth revolves around the sun is a well-known example. The change in perspective brought to physics by quantum mechanics is another. Materialism is coming under increasing pressure from various directions (e.g., Kastrup, 2014; E. F. Kelly, Crabtree, & Marshall, 2015; Koons & Bealer, 2010), and I believe we are on the brink of another great seismic shift in science. The study of reincarnation signs may contribute to this shift and help to provoke a radical change in our thinking about what makes us human, with implications for how we understand personhood and an array of other issues not only in psychology and biology, but in anthropology, religious studies, and philosophy as well.

Chapter 2

The Belief in Reincarnation

Much remains to be said about rebirth beliefs around the world and over time. In this chapter, I begin with animistic cultures and show how in them, not only is the belief in reincarnation supported by signs such as pregnancy dreams and birthmarks, the belief in turn inspires mortuary, naming, and other customs designed to facilitate and acknowledge the return of the deceased to the social order. This integration of reincarnation into the social fabric is characteristic of indigenous cultures, many of them small-scale tribal societies, but it is absent from the larger and more complex societies that developed into the nation-states of the modern world. I examine this shift in the cultural valuation of reincarnation through the history of the belief in rebirth among Indo-European language speakers and their neighbors in the West and the East. Lastly, I explore ideas about the ways new parents (and new life circumstances) are determined, according to different belief systems. Many of these ideas are reflected in the reincarnation cases I take up in later chapters, and it is essential to start off with a good understanding of them.

SIGNS, BELIEFS, AND CUSTOMS
IN ANIMISTIC CULTURES

I will illustrate the relation between signs and reincarnation beliefs and the connection between reincarnation beliefs and institutionalized practices first with the Tlingit Indians of the southeastern Alaskan panhandle, then with other indigenous peoples around the world, and finally with formal cross-cultural studies I conducted in the early 1990s (Matlock, 1993, 1995).

The Tlingit have lived in the same region since at least 500 BCE, hunting, fishing, and gathering nuts and berries. They are matrilineal, meaning that they reckon kinship solely through their mothers. Family lines or lineages are grouped into clans and clans into larger divisions called moieties, the largest kinship group of Tlingit society. People belong to their mother's moiety and marry members of their father's moiety. The Tlingit are ranked between aristocracy and commoners and live in sedentary villages. In the past, they cremated their dead, but with conversion to Christianity in the nineteenth century, many communities began to bury instead. Cremation or burial traditionally was marked by a communal feast. This was followed a year later by a more substantial feast, which marked the end of the mortuary cycle for the deceased individual (de Laguna, 1972; Kan, 1989).

The first comprehensive study of Tlingit culture was conducted by the Russian Orthodox priest Ioann (Ivan) Veniaminov, who lived in Alaska from 1824 to 1867, initially on the Aleutian Islands and later among the Tlingit, whose language he learned. After Alaska was purchased by the United States in 1867, American anthropologists began to visit the Tlingit and to write about them. Most descriptions refer to coastal communities, but the most extensive ethnography, that of Frederica de Laguna (1972), relates to the inland Yakutat of the 1950s. Ian Stevenson studied Tlingit reincarnation beliefs and cases in the 1960s (Stevenson, 1966a). He reported seven of the forty-three Tlingit cases he investigated in his first volume of case reports, the now-classic *Twenty Cases Suggestive of Reincarnation* (Stevenson, 1966b, 1974b).

The Tlingit told inquirers they had learned about the afterlife from people who almost died but revived, as well as from children who recalled events from the intermission between death and reincarnation (Matlock, 2017). John Swanton (1908, p. 461) collected one such narrative early in the twentieth century. A man died but found it so hard to walk up to heaven that he returned to life. He told his people that he needed moccasins and gloves as protection from bushes and devil's clubs along the way. They provided him with those garments and gave him a knife so that he could defend himself against wolves and bears. They put red paint on his face and eagle down in his hair. He advised them to sing songs to lead the deceased to their destination and told them that spirits could communicate with them only through a crackling fire. The crackling meant that the spirits were hungry and should be fed by throwing food into the fire. Then he died again and this time did not revive. He had returned only to let his people know how to treat the dead.

A more recent account collected by de Laguna (1972, pp. 767–68) tells of 'Askadut who, after dying of smallpox, attended (as a spirit) a feast in his honor. He tried to comfort his widow and children but they could not hear him. When he spoke they heard only the crackling fire. He felt hungry but was unable to eat until his relatives threw food into the flames. He accompanied his family to the funeral pyre and tried to follow them home afterward but something held him back. After a while he began to think of the land of the dead and to walk there, but found it hard going because he had stayed too long at the pyre. He came to a river and called to spirits he saw on the opposite bank to come for him. They did not hear him until he became tired and yawned, then they sent a canoe to fetch him. On the other side of the river he encountered many spirits, some long dead, others recently deceased. Among the latter was a paternal aunt who advised him to return to the living and helped him back across the river. There he settled by a tree on the bank and went to sleep. He slept for nine days, during which time the bank caved in little by little. When he awoke the water was almost at his feet but he found himself unable to move. After a while he fell into the water and then heard someone say, "He's born already!"

A Tlingit might declare his intention to reincarnate in a certain family before dying and seemingly bring this off (de Laguna, 1972, pp. 778–79; also Dall, 1870, p. 423; Stevenson 1966a, 1974b; Veniaminov, 1840, p. 58). Planned reincarnations figure in ten of the forty-three Tlingit cases studied by Stevenson (1966a, p. 240). Spirits might make their intentions known in pregnancy dreams (de Laguna, 1972, pp. 755, 768; Stevenson, 1966a, 1974b; Veniaminov, 1840, p. 58), which Stevenson appropriately christened "announcing dreams." There were announcing dreams in twenty of Stevenson's Tlingit cases (Stevenson, 1966a, p. 237). Expectant mothers or others sometimes saw apparitions in the same role (de Laguna, 1972, p. 774).

All Tlingit children were thought to be the reincarnations of deceased persons and a newborn was checked for identifying physical marks (Jones, 1914, p. 234; Swanton, 1908, p. 463; Veniaminov, 1840, p. 58). Birthmarks figured in twenty-four of Stevenson's cases, with some cases having more than one (Stevenson, 1966a). Six of the seven Tlingit cases in *Twenty Cases* (Stevenson, 1974b) feature birthmarks. Birthmarks were especially important if there had not been planned returns or announcing dreams. 'Askadut was recognized by a mark on the baby's foot (de Laguna, 1972, p. 768). George Emmons (whose fieldwork was conducted in the 1910s and 1920s) heard about a child born with marks on the ears, in places earrings had been worn (1991, p. 288). Birth defects, also, might provide clues. A child born with a missing soft palate was thought to be the reincarnation of a man whose tonsils had rotted away (de Laguna, 1972, pp. 779–80).

Identifications might be based on behaviors as well. The reborn 'Askadut was said to have reached out to 'Askadut's widow with a smile but refused to nurse from his mother, who had been 'Askadut's sister (de Laguna, 1972, p. 768). As children grew older, they might provide additional evidence of remembering people, places, articles, and events from earlier lives. When they became able to talk, they sometimes addressed people with the kin terms the previous person had used with them and were called by reciprocal terms in return (de Laguna, 1972, p. 778).

Children sometimes made remarks that suggested or confirmed their identities. Swanton related a story he heard throughout the Tlingit territory of a man who was killed in a battle and spent some time in the land of the dead before being reborn. As a young child, when he heard someone talking about this battle, he began to cry and would not stop. Asked why, he said that if only they had obeyed him (that is, the person he felt himself to have been) and let the tide go out before attacking, they would have won, and from this the people knew who he was, or had been (Swanton, 1908, p. 463).

Children who spoke about having lived before were expected to stop doing so after a few years and parents might discourage such talk by an older child, worried that its mind was still in its past life or in the land of the dead (Kan, 1989, pp. 109–10). The father of one of Stevenson's case subjects sought to discourage him from speaking of his memories because of warnings from "old folks" about the dangers of doing so (Stevenson, 1974b, p. 234). By the time they reached adolescence, children's memories of the previous lives were expected to have faded entirely, although the children continued to be identified with the previous person through adulthood (Kan, 1989, pp. 109–10).

A newborn had to be properly identified in order to be given the name it had held before, but because names were lineage property, reincarnation needed to be in the correct lineage to begin with. Ideally a spirit reincarnated in the family of the "nearest relative" in the deceased's matriline. Judging by signs and "alleged instances," the ideal was realized most of the time (de Laguna, 1972, p. 777). In Stevenson's data, the case subject and previous person were related on the father's side in only five cases (1966a, p. 232). Returns on the father's side presented a problem because they were in the wrong moiety. The same English name might be given to a baby but the Tlingit name could not be, so the reincarnation could not be completely acknowledged and socially recognized (de Laguna, 1972, pp. 780–81).

If there were no signs to go by, a name was simply bestowed, and this called the designated spirit to take up residence in the child (de Laguna, 1972, p. 782). Naming contrary to signs was permitted and might be done if signs suggested the presence of an unwanted spirit. One child was given a distinguished chief's name even though a birthmark indicated that he was one of the chief's nephews (de Laguna, 1972, p. 714). De Laguna was told that the chief "is still alive. But he didn't choose his mother. They just named the boy" (1972, p. 782). This naming strategy could succeed only if the spirit to be replaced acquiesced. A wrongly named child might become sick and have to be renamed to keep it alive (Kan, 1989, p. 72).

Occasionally signs suggested that the same spirit had returned in more than one child, and in these instances all children involved would be named after the same person. In one instance, or set of instances, of multiple reincarnation, a man told several of his nieces that he did not want to return to any of them because they had bad tempers. He asked them not to name their children after him and said he would go to a more distant relative instead, because she was quiet and her husband was a good hunter. When this woman soon thereafter gave birth to a boy, she named him for the man. A short time later one of the nieces he did not want as a mother bore a boy and gave him another of his names. The man was recognized as reincarnated in both children and when the first child died, the second was called by both names (de Laguna, 1972, pp. 778–79).

Two spirits sometimes fought over a body, and these tussles might result in twin births, the Tlingit believed (de Laguna, 1972, p. 779). In exceptional cases, the names of two different persons might be given to one child. De Laguna's informants were uncertain whether the bearer of two names possessed two souls (de Laguna, 1972, pp. 779–80), although she provided an account that implied that it might. A man with two names announced before his death that he would be reborn in two children, borne by different women. He stated further that he would be recognized by a birthmark on the forehead, resembling his own birthmark, which was thought to be derived from an earlier life in which he had died in battle. After his death, two boys were born to different relatives, two months apart. They were very similar (in appearance or in personality or both is not clear), "like one boy," although only one had a birthmark on his forehead. The boys were friends as well as kin and became very close (de Laguna, 1972, p. 780).

Tlingit multiple naming practices might have begun as responses to demographic fluctuations (Matlock, 1990a, p. 13). Hereditary names could not be allowed to die. If there were too few or too many people to take names, adjustments were required. By giving more than one name to an individual or the same name to different individuals, the names (and associated spirits) were kept in circulation, no matter how the size of the population changed. Still, names (and spirits) could and did expire. A woman who belonged to a line that was dying out told de Laguna that when she died, she would "die out of this world for good" because there was not an appropriate person to whom she could return and no one to give her back her hereditary name (de Laguna, 1972, p. 781).

In the proper course of affairs, naming was the first step in the reintegration of a reincarnate into Tlingit society. A child was expected to grow up to inherit other names, privileges, and statuses possessed by his namesake. Because these assets were lineage, clan, and moiety property, a person could have again what he had before only if he made a suitable reincarnation and was given back his old name (Matlock, 1990a).

A similar constellation of signs, beliefs, and naming practices appears in other North American native cultures (Jefferson, 2008; Mills & Slobodin, 1994). Stevenson studied reincarnation among several Alaskan and British Columbian groups besides the Tlingit. One of these was the Haida, another matrilineal people, who live north of the Tlingit on the Northwest Coast (Stevenson, 1975b). Stevenson found that the Haida, like the Tlingit, used signs that included announcing dreams, birthmarks, and behaviors to ascertain children's past identities, so that they could be given their former names. Older children might confirm their identities by relating memories of events or recognizing people, places, or articles from their previous lives. The Haida thought that they could decide on their new mothers in advance of death and sometimes expressed the desire for a change in physical appearance in their next lives. They also believed in the possibility of reincarnating in multiple individuals at once.

Anthropologist Antonia Mills (1988a, 1988b, 1994a, 1994c, 2001, 2010; Mills & Champion, 1996) documented reincarnation-related signs, beliefs, and customs among the Wet'suwet'en (Bulkley River Carrier) and the neighboring Gitxsan. The latter are kin to the Tsimshian peoples who live farther down the Northwest Coast from the Haida and the Tlingit. The Wet'suwet'en and the Gitxsan employ announcing dreams and birthmarks in identifying a child with a deceased relative. They give the child the same name he had in his past life, which allows him to grow up to take possession of the articles and rights he owned before. High-status individuals have their ears pierced for earrings, and some children are born with pierced-ear birthmarks that identify them as reincarnations of members of the nobility (Mills, 1994c). When signs are absent, the Wet'suwet'en may consult "Indian doctors" in making past-life identifications (Mills, 1988a). The Gitxsan, although not the Wet'suwet'en, recognize the possibility of multiple reincarnation (Mills, 1988b, 2001, 2010).

Similar reincarnation-related signs, beliefs, and naming practices have been reported from other parts of the world. The Igbo of Nigeria look to birthmarks and behaviors to determine who a child was in his previous life, then name him accordingly. When there are no signs to go by, an oracle is consulted. A correct identification is imperative, because an Igbo needs to observe the same taboos from life to life, lest he fall ill. A wrongly named child must be renamed before he will recover. Stevenson (1985) was told that some Igbo believed it possible to plan one's reincarnation before dying and to initiate one's reincarnation before death. Some thought it possible to reincarnate in multiple bodies simultaneously.

The Yukaghir of northeastern Siberia provide another example of this complex. Some Yukaghir let it known to which families they plan to return before they die, pregnant women may experience announcing dreams, and there may be idiosyncratic behaviors and other postnatal signs revealing past-life identity. Children are given the name, or at least the nickname, of their recognized previous incarnations. If child is wrongly named, his soul will feel offended; it will dislike him and work against him all his life. Yukaghir usually reincarnate in the same family, usually in a child or grandchild, but there is no rule about this. Rane Willerslev heard of a boy who as a toddler told his mother his name was not Igor, but Tompúla. She did not recognize the name Tompúla, but an elderly relative told her that this was the nickname of her maternal great-grandfather. When she began calling her son Tompúla, he became "much more cheerful and much less offensive" (Willerslev, 2007, p. 51).

The Beng of the Ivory Coast present a variation on the custom of naming children after the persons of whom they are believed to be the reincarnations. Like other people around the world, the Beng are concerned to name their children correctly, but the name may be that by which they were called by during the intermission between lives, not their previous lives. Diviners are consulted for assistance in selecting the right name, which must be called before a child will emerge from the womb. All Beng are believed to be the reincarnations of ancestors, although only a few people know who they used to be. If a family member dies on the day a child is born, it is clear who the child was before, but for many children identification has to wait until it is revealed through their behaviors, Alma Gottlieb (2004) was informed.

Naming practices are not the only reincarnation-related practice in animistic cultures. In some societies, there are rules regarding whom one should or should not marry that, in conjunction with expectations of reincarnation in the line of descent, appear to be designed to reunite the same couples life after life (Matlock, 1993, pp. 109–14). Reincarnation is implicated in certain mortuary practices as well (Matlock, 1993, pp. 84–91).

In many societies, bodies (especially those of infants and young children) are buried in the floor or environs of the house, along village paths, or other shared spaces, to facilitate the return of the deceased's spirit in his family or community. Conversely, a person whose return is not desired might be buried at a crossroads. The Igbo bury the corpses of unwanted persons facedown, directing their spirits away from the land of the living (Stevenson, 1985, p. 17). Clan-based societies may have clan cemeteries, which help to reconstitute the clans in death; because reincarnation emerges from these postmortem lineages, proper burial helps to ensure proper rebirth (Bloch, 1982; Bradbury, 1965). In some societies, bodies may be disinterred and reburied after a period, generally a year. Secondary burial among the Igbo augments the status of the deceased and positions his spirit to make a good reincarnation (Stevenson, 1985, p. 16). Kan (1989, p. 42) said that the mortuary feast the Tlingit held a year after the funeral served to commemorate the ghost of the deceased settling into the graveyard; the arrival of the ancestral spirit in the land of the dead; and the return of the reincarnating spirit to a matrilineal relative.

Recognized reincarnations are not always as closely aligned with cultural ideals as they reportedly are for the Tlingit. Among the Tsimshian peoples studied by Christopher Roth, hereditary names follow a prescribed track but the pattern of recognized reincarnations does not conform to it (2008, pp. 67–68). In some societies, such as the Beaver, Dene Tha, and Kutchin first nations of the Canadian subarctic, announcing dreams, birthmarks, behaviors, and the recognitions of people and articles help to determine the past-life identities of children, but identifications do not lead to the children being given their former names (Goulet, 1994; Mills, 1988b; Slobodin, 1994). The same is true of the Buryat of Mongolia (Empson, 2007, 2011). Even without the naming convention, identifying children with predecessors through signs acknowledges their reincarnation, affirms the circulation of individuals through a given population, and promotes social cohesion (Empson, 2007, 2011; Gottlieb, 2004; Mills, 1988b).

Comparative anthropology can be a tricky business. It is easy to see the patterns one wishes to see and to overlook cultural elements that do not meet one's expectations. In order to overcome these tendencies and to evaluate my theory that, in animistic cultures, certain customs developed in response to reincarnation beliefs, I undertook a formal cross-cultural study using a randomly chosen thirty-culture subsample of the sixty-culture Probability Sample of the Human Relations Area Files (HRAF) (Matlock, 1993). The sixty cultures of the HRAF Probability Sample are small-scale indigenous societies selected from different "culture clusters" that are known or presumed to have no recent historical connection with one another. Sample societies are considered statistically independent, and sophisticated studies may be conducted with them.

My theory that reincarnation inspired certain customs was based on Tylor's insight that, in animistic societies, soul and spirit concepts and reincarnation beliefs were conclusions drawn from observations and experiences. If that was true, the beliefs could have come first, with customary practices following them. Anthropologists who had worked in societies with reincarnation beliefs had suggested that naming, mortuary rituals, and other practices were related to reincarnation, but they had examined these associations cross-culturally only in a comparative fashion.

Earlier cross-cultural studies involving spirit beliefs and reincarnation (W. D. Davis, 1971; Somersan, 1981, 1984; Swanson, 1960) assumed that the beliefs were symbolic constructs and searched for social and economic factors related to them. The studies lumped together all types of rebirth beliefs and used rebirth (calling it reincarnation) as a dependent variable, with social and economic factors as independent variables. In statistical tests, an independent variable is used to predict the value of a dependent variable. Thus, the statistical procedure of these studies underscored the theoretical assumption that spirit and reincarnation beliefs developed in response to social and economic structures, not the other way around. Although two studies (Somersan, 1981, 1984; Swanson, 1960) found statistically significant relationships between spirit and rebirth beliefs and cultural variables, these findings were not confirmed in replication (W. D. Davis, 1971; Matlock, 1995), so they could have appeared by chance.

In my study, I made reincarnation the independent variable, and used naming, mortuary rituals, and other customary practices as dependent variables. I employed the operational definitions of reincarnation, transmigration, metempsychosis, and rebirth I introduced in Chapter 1. Coding different types of rebirth belief independently allowed me to examine the relationship between reincarnation, transmigration, and metempsychosis and to assess whether they could legitimately be grouped together, as W. D. Davis (1971) and Semra Somersan (1981, 1984) had done. If my theory that reincarnation inspired certain customary practices was correct, then reincarnation, but not transmigration, should be associated with the practices, because reincarnation, but not transmigration, entailed a return to human society.

Fifteen of the thirty societies in my sample had reincarnation beliefs and twelve had transmigration beliefs, but the same societies did not always have both. Reincarnation and transmigration appeared together in eight societies, but the relationship between these beliefs was nonsignificant ($p = .165$) (Matlock, 1993, pp. 129–30). Metempsychosis beliefs were present only in four societies within the Indic sphere (Matlock, 1993, pp. 181–82). When I repeated my tests of the relationship between reincarnation beliefs and customary practices using rebirth rather than reincarnation as the independent variable, the strength of the association between beliefs and practices went down (Matlock, 1993, pp. 175–77), confirming my prediction that the practices developed in expectation or recognition of the return of the deceased to the social order, because that would not have been possible had he been born a nonhuman animal.

Signs such as dreams, birthmarks, behaviors, and children's memories of previous lives were reported in six (40%) of the fifteen societies with reincarnation beliefs in my sample—the Ojibwa, a North American Indian tribe; the Lapps, a Scandinavian people; the Trobrianders, from Papua New Guinea; the Toradja, from Indonesia; the Bush Negroes, from Surinam; and the Central Thai. Many older accounts of reincarnation in small-scale societies contain few details about the belief or related customs, anthropologists having taken little interest in them. Signs are reported so regularly in societies whose reincarnation beliefs have been well described, we may justifiably wonder whether their absence in the descriptions of other societies with reincarnation beliefs is due to underreporting by the ethnographers. Regardless, it is an axiom of anthropology that the more widespread a trait is, the older it is likely to be. The wide geographical distribution of the same reincarnation signs adds to the impression that the signs, interpreted as indications of reincarnation, played a role in originating the belief.

I found that children were named after ancestors significantly more often in societies with reincarnation beliefs than in societies without them ($p <$ .05) (Matlock, 1993, pp. 149–50). Signs or tests were used to assign names in many of these societies. Unfortunately, my thirty-culture sample was too small to detect statistical relationships between reincarnation beliefs and many of the customs I examined, but I did find a significant relationship between the beliefs and several common customs. Reincarnation beliefs were related to what anthropologists call cross-cousin marriage ($p = $ .05) (Matlock, 1993, p. 158), to clans ($p = $ .009) (Matlock, 1993, pp. 155–57), and to inheritance in lines of descent rather than of filiation ($p = $ .009) (Matlock, 1993, pp. 159–61). Contrasted in this way, descent refers to a spiritual bond between non-adjacent generations (such as between grandparents and grandchildren) and filiation to the blood bond between adjacent generations. In animistic cultures with reincarnation beliefs, property generally passes not from a man to his children, but from a man to his descendants in a later generation (typically his grandchildren), in whom he is expected to be reborn. The Tlingit, it seems, are not the only people who try to reincarnate in a way that allows them to have again what they had before.

Unlike the cross-cultural studies using reincarnation as a dependent variable, none of whose significant findings have been replicated, I confirmed the association between reincarnation beliefs and clans in a study using a sample structurally parallel to the sixty-culture HRAF Probability Sample (Matlock, 1995, pp. 170–72). This and the consistency of my cross-cultural findings with my other work in this area (Matlock, 1990a, 1994) gives me confidence that I am right that certain widespread customs developed as a result of a belief in reincarnation based on signs such as announcing dreams, birthmarks, behaviors, and recognitions of people, places, and articles from previous lives.

I must leave these problems here. I moved away from this line of research in the mid-1990s and never returned to it. Nonetheless, making the belief in reincarnation an independent variable and using it to predict the presence of customary practices turned out to be much more productive than treating the belief in rebirth as a dependent variable, with social and economic factors as independent variables. Both Tylor's theory that reincarnation beliefs were empirically grounded and my theory that reincarnation beliefs inspired practices intended to promote and acknowledge the return of the deceased to the social order were supported in my 1993 study and other work. This outcome is contrary to what cultural-constructionist theorists of religion like Durkheim would have us suppose, and it is very different from what we find in the industrialized world today, where spirit beliefs exist without any connection to institutionalized practices outside of religious observance. The closest parallel is to be found in Tibet, where recognizing successive reincarnations in order to pass on status and possessions became a preoccupation of the Buddhist elite beginning in the fourteenth century (Gamble, 2018).

A BRIEF HISTORY OF THE BELIEF IN REBIRTH, WEST AND EAST

Mitra Ara (2008) identified rebirth as one variant of an eschatology that included regeneration and resurrection as alternative ideas of what happened after death in Proto-Indo-European tradition. Proto-Indo-European society was most likely centered in what is now eastern Ukraine (Anthony, 2007). Afterlife beliefs might well have varied among communities at early stages of separation from an original common society. Differences in the religious beliefs and practices of Indo-European speaking peoples show up during the historical period, certainly. However, eventually rebirth beliefs of one sort or another appear in societies across the geographical spectrum, from Ireland to India.

Reincarnation belief among the Celts of Ireland, Britain, and France was noted first by Julius Caesar in *De Bello Gallico* (*Gallic Wars*), where he observed that, "by this tenet [they] are in a great degree excited to valor, the fear of death being disregarded" (*Gallic Wars* 6.14, trans. McDevitte & Bohn). Celtic reincarnation beliefs have been documented more recently by W. Y. Evans-Wentz (1911/2007, pp. 365–80) and by Myles Dillon and Nora K. Chadwick (2003, pp. 152–53). Rebirth beliefs are attested for northern Germanic peoples as well (Davidson, 1943). They figure in the thirteenth-century Icelandic *Poetic Edda*, where two of the main characters are reincarnated (Larrington, 2014). However, in the following discussion I will focus on rebirth beliefs in India and in the circum-Mediterranean region.

It is unclear whether the ancient Egyptians believed in reincarnation. Most modern scholars have concluded that the Egyptians believed in a resurrection of the body in the afterlife rather than rebirth in another living body. Winifred Blackman (1927) discovered reincarnation beliefs and related practices among the Fellahin, a tribal people of Upper Egypt, at the beginning of the twentieth century. Blackman considered these beliefs and practices to be survivals from earlier times. It may be, as James Bonwick (1878, p. 82) suggested, that resurrection was the "popular" view and reincarnation the "esoteric" teaching (or the opposite) in the Egyptian heartland in pharaonic times. If the ancient Egyptians did believe in bodily resurrection in the afterlife, they would not have been alone in their region and era. We find resurrection as a form of survival alternative to rebirth among the Zoroastrians and Jews as well during the last centuries before the emergence of Christianity (Boyce, 2001).

In Greek antiquity, the person most closely associated with rebirth was Pythagoras, who lived from about 570 to about 495 BCE. Pythagoras is thought to have visited Egypt and other places around the Mediterranean before settling in Croton, on the coast of what was then Magna Graecia (greater Greece) and is now southern Italy, around 530 BCE. There he founded a community where he taught mathematics and cosmology and seems to have promoted a daily regimen that included the retrieval of past-life memories through contemplation.

Pythagoras favored oral instruction and left no writings; texts attributed to him have turned out to be forgeries. His first biographies were not written until centuries after his death, when much about his life had been converted to legend, so it is exceedingly difficult to determine exactly what he said and did (Burkert, 1972; Kahn, 2001). In the ancient sources, he is depicted as a flamboyant figure who dressed in white trousers and tunic rather than the conventional Greek cloak, sported a golden thigh (about which no details have survived), and wore a golden crown. He is said to have been a miracle worker, healer, and prophet; sometimes he is likened to a shaman (Burkert, 1972; Kahn, 2001; Kingsley, 1995, 2010). According to Aristotle (388–322 BCE), he claimed to be an incarnation of the god Apollo (Kingsley, 2010, p. 120).

From the start, there has been uncertainty over the source of Pythagoras's ideas about rebirth. He may have borrowed the concept from Pherecydes of Syros (c. 580–c. 520 BCE), the first Greek known to have taught reincarnation (Schibli, 1990). Another possibility is that he drew inspiration from Orphism, whose roots go back centuries before his time. By Pythagoras's day, Orphism had developed a myth of the dismemberment and reconstitution (regeneration) of Dionysius (Johnston, 2013, pp. 73–80), but this is a very different type of rebirth than the recycling of consciousness promoted by Pherecydes and Pythagoras. References to a personal rebirth in later Orphic hymns may have appeared under the influence of Pythagoreanism, rather than the reverse (Alderink, 1981; Burkert, 1972; Kingsley, 1995).

It is generally assumed that Herodotus had Pythagoras in mind when he wrote in 440 BCE that metempsychosis had been introduced into Greece from Egypt by persons he knew but would not name (perhaps because they were his contemporaries). Herodotus stated that the Egyptian doctrine affirmed that "when the body dies, the soul enters into another creature which chances then to be coming to the birth, and when it has gone the round of all the creatures of land and sea and of the air, it enters again into a human body as it comes to the birth; and that it makes this round in a period of three thousand years" (*History of Herodotus* II.123, trans. Macaulay), but these ideas do not sound Egyptian. Franz Cumont (1922, p. 177) thought it "infinitely probable" that they came from India, but they do not sound Indian either.

Peter Kingsley thought that the idea of reincarnation originated "far away in the East" of Greece, in the distant hinterlands of Tibet and Mongolia (2010, p. 40). He pointed to a Mongol shaman named Abaris who is said to have made contact with Pythagoras and afterward spent some years wandering around Greece. Abaris carried with him a golden arrow, which, legend has it, he presented to Pythagoras. In *The Pythagorean Way of Life,* Iamblichus (245–325 CE) stated that Abaris recognized Pythagoras as an incarnation of Apollo "both from the noble marks he observed in him and from the proofs of identity revealed to him in advance," along the way to Croton (Kingsley, 2010, pp. 41, 118). Abaris, too, was regarded as an incarnation of Apollo, so that in gifting the arrow, Abaris was acting on the basis of a felt affinity, "two bodies but only one being, like recognizing like" (Kingsley, 2010, p. 48).

I have a different take on this. Perhaps because they have not been acquainted with the widespread reports of reincarnation signs, scholars from antiquity to the present have not fully appreciated the significance of Pythagoras's past-life memories. There are varying accounts of these, but the most reliable source may be the earliest, a no-longer-extant manuscript by Heraclides of Pontus (387–312 BC) cited by Diogenes Laertius (180–240 AD) in his *Lives of Eminent Philosophers.*

Heraclides recorded that Pythagoras remembered having been Aethalides, son of the god Hermes in human form. Hermes offered Aethalides any gift except immortality, and he chose to retain memory of his experiences through successive lives and deaths. He was reborn as Euphorbus, a Greek hero from the Trojan War whose death at the hand of Menelaus is portrayed by Homer in the *Iliad* (XVII.9–50). As Euphorbus, he recalled his life as Aethalides as well as an intermediate period spent as plants and animals and in Hades. When Euphorbus died, his soul passed into Hermotimus. Hermotimus recalled having been Aethalides and Euphorbus, and upon a visit to the temple of Apollo at Branchidae, recognized the shield Euphorbus had held when he was slain five hundred years earlier. When Hermotimus died, he became Pyrrhus, a fisherman of Delos, and remembered having been first Aethalides, then Euphorbus, then Hermotimus. When Pyrrhus died, he became Pythagoras, and still remembered everything that had passed before (Diogenes Laertius, *Lives of Eminent Philosophers,* VIII.1.4–5).

The discrepancy between being Apollo incarnated and starting off as a son of Hermes is not the only variation in the legend of Pythagoras. Other sources give other series of lives, although all include Euphorbus, which may explain why some ancient authorities mention only Euphorbus as a previous life of Pythagoras (Burkert, 1972, pp. 139–40). Some later sources also have Pythagoras rather than Hermotimus recognize Euphorbus's shield. Moreover, they place this event in different temples. Heraclides said that Pythagoras recognized the shield at the temple of Apollo at Branchidae, but Ovid said that this occurred at the temple of Juno at Argos (*Metamorphoses* XV.161), and Porphyry that it was at a temple dedicated to Argive Hera in Mycenae (*Life of Pythagoras*, 26).

The only constants are that Pythagoras remembered a past life or lives and at some point in his series of lives recognized Euphorbus's shield in a temple. Although the facts cannot be established with certainty, it seems entirely possible that Pythagoras did have some past-life memory, and that that is what impelled him to travel and to seek out authorities on rebirth. On this reading, Pythagoras's convictions about rebirth arose from his own experiences, not from Pherecydes or from contact with the south, east, or north of Greece. Kingsley (2010, pp. 118, 127) stressed the recognition of the shield as a feature of Tibetan and Mongolian tradition, evidently unaware that recognitions of articles from past lives are important signs of reincarnation cross-culturally.

Pherecydes is reputed to be the first Greek to proclaim the soul's immortality in general, not only its reincarnation. In Homer's time (800s–700s BCE), an individual's psyche was thought to leave his body at death and repair to Hades, where it "could only be perceived as the dreary, feeble life of a gibbering shade," a pale reflection of its earthly existence (Schibli, 1990, pp. 106–7). For the Homeric poets, souls remained immured in Hades for eternity, but Pherecydes provided for all but the vilest murderers to return to a new body after a few years. Pythagoras by all accounts developed a more pervasive dualism of body and soul as well as a provision for escaping the rebirth cycle. Like Homer and Pherecydes, he envisioned an afterworld in Hades, but he encouraged ascetic and dietary practices designed to help souls purify themselves and so grow ever closer to the divine in their nature, overcoming the pull to rebirth (Burkert, 1972; Schibli, 1990).

The poems of Pindar (c. 522–c. 443 BCE) were commissioned to honor people and commemorate events. Portions of two of Pindar's odes dealing with reincarnation have survived, one because Plato quoted from it in the *Meno*. In this ode, Pindar portrays souls as paying for their sins in Hades before reincarnation. After eight years, souls are reborn on Earth as "noble kings / And the swift in strength and greatest in wisdom," heroes forevermore (*Meno*, 81b–c, trans. Guthrie). The second Pindaric ode referencing reincarnation, *Olympian 2*, was written for the tyrant Theron of Acragas, Sicily, in honor of his Olympic victory in 467 BCE. In lines 55–75 Pindar says that those who have committed crimes against Zeus will be judged and will serve their time in Hades, but those who have avoided wrongdoing for three successive lives will be released from the rebirth cycle and permitted to retire to the Island of the Blessed, where they will reside with the gods.

Empedocles (c. 490–430 BCE), born in Acragas, was a young man when Pindar composed his ode for Theron. His views on rebirth more closely resemble those described by Herodotus than do the ideas of any other Greek philosopher. Empedocles distinguished the psyche, which was associated with a body and perished with it, from the daemon, which survived death and was reborn in a succession of other bodies (Wright, 1995). He maintained that daemons had their home with the gods in the heavens, but those which embraced Strife rather than Love fell into incarnations on Earth. There they were born "as all kinds of mortal forms" for "three times countless years" before they could rejoin the gods (Fr. 107/115, trans. Wright; this last phrase is given as "thrice ten thousand years" by Kirk, Raven & Schofield, 2007, p. 315). Empedocles believed that he had lived before as a boy and a girl, a laurel bush and a bird, and a mute fish in the sea (Fr. 108/117), but in his present life, he had transcended the rebirth cycle and traveled among the people as an immortal god (Fr. 102/112).

The Greek philosopher whose reflections on rebirth have had the greatest influence on Western thought is Plato (c. 424–347 BCE). Plato does not address rebirth in his early dialogues but it is an important theme of his middle and late periods. He seems to have become acquainted with the concept on a visit to Magna Graecia midway through his career. He borrowed ideas from his predecessors, but developed them in his own way, exploring them through the words of the characters in his dialogues.

In the dialogue that bears his name, Timaeus, echoing Empedocles, explains that God created humans with two souls. One He made out of the matter from which He fashioned the universe; this soul was preexistent of the flesh and immortal. The other soul was created along with the physical body and perished along with it (*Timaeus*, 34b–c; 41c–d; 69c–d). In an earlier dialogue, Socrates recognizes only one soul per person. This soul, he says, is ungenerated, having been in existence before the creation of the universe (*Phaedrus*, 245c–246a). He likens it to a pair of winged horses hitched to a chariot. Winged souls reside with the gods but some souls have lost their wings and adopted the flesh. The soul is freed from the body at death to be judged and may be sent to Hades to do penance for one thousand years before resuming corporeal life. Most souls require ten such cycles (ten thousand years) before they can regain their wings and return to the gods (*Phaedrus*, 246a–249c).

In the *Republic* (X.615a), Socrates again mentions the thousand-year interval between lives. Before being reborn, souls are judged by the gods, and may choose to be nonhuman animals in their next lives, according to their temperaments. Socrates describes the judgment and selection of new bodies in detail in the Myth of Er (*Republic* X.614b–621), which has the structure of a near-death experience. Er appeared to die, but his body never decomposed, and after twelve days he revived on his funeral pyre, sent back to life, he said, to describe what he had witnessed in the spiritual realm. He had seen souls of the deceased judged and dispatched either to Elysium or to Hades. Other souls, returning from these places, were permitted to select their next lives from an array of possibilities, then were made to drink from the River of Forgetfulness (Lethe) to wipe clean their memories before assuming their new bodies.

Timaeus describes how human souls are associated with stars (*Timaeus*, 41d). He asserts that a soul that has conducted itself righteously while in the flesh rejoins its native star at death, while one which did not acquit itself well during its embodied life becomes a woman in its next incarnation. If the soul continues to transgress in that life, in its next life it will become "some brute who resembled him in the evil nature which he had acquired" (*Timaeus*, 42b–c, trans. B. Jowett).

Recent advances in archaeology and linguistics have shown that when the Sanskrit-speaking ancestors of the Hindus arrived in the vicinity of the Indian subcontinent in the middle of the second millennium BCE, they joined a vibrant Indus Valley Civilization (Witzel, 1999). This covered part of present-day southeastern Afghanistan, western Pakistan, and northwestern India between about 3000 and 1900 BCE, making it contemporaneous with ancient Egypt and Mesopotamia. Although it was probably multiethnic and multilinguistic, the dominant language of the Indus Valley Civilization most likely was Munda. There was substantial trade between it and Mesopotamia. In fact, the Indus Valley Civilization and the Sumerian Empire, which was part of the Mesopotamian, may have had a common origin (Southworth, 2005; Witzel, 1999).

A fair amount is known about early Hindu religious beliefs and practices from the Rig Veda (Ṛgveda), a book of hymns written in Sanskrit around 1500 to 1300 BCE. The hymns were transmitted orally before being written down, and linguists have been able to isolate several verbal strata in them. The earliest stratum points to an origin in Central Asia, after the breakup of the Proto-Indo-European linguistic and cultural group (Anthony, 2007, pp. 452–56; G. Thompson, n.d.). There are a substantial number of Munda loan words in a later stratum. Munda loans appear also in three later Vedas composed between 1000 and 500 BCE, after the collapse of the Indus Valley Civilization, when the Hindus moved southeast farther into what is now

India. Dravidian loans are found only in the later Vedas (Witzel, 1999), indicating a relatively late contact with Dravidian speakers, but this meeting was by all appearances revolutionary.

Karma is a Sanskrit word meaning "action." It is used in the Vedas in the sense of ritual action, but without connection to rebirth. Most scholars agree that rebirth does not enter until the first of the Vedic commentaries called the Upanishads, thought to have been composed sometime in the 600s BCE, about the time contact was made with the Dravidians. Anthropologists had suspected that Hindu rebirth beliefs were borrowed from indigenous Indian tribes (Fürer-Haimendorf, 1953; Obeyesekere, 1980), but their sudden appearance in the Upanishads was unexplained until the recent archaeological and linguistic work. G. W. Beck (1996) argued that the rebirth idea was an outgrowth of earlier practices of ancestor worship, but that it was adopted from the Dravidians or other indigenous peoples now seems more likely.

Two paths are open to Brahmins, we are told in the Upanishads, one leading to the heavens and absorption in the godhead, the other to repeated cycles of birth and death on Earth (*Brihadaranyaka Upanishad*, 6.2.1–16, especially 6.2.16). The same teaching is presented in the later *Chandogya Upanishad* (5.10), with the addition of the following: "Those whose conduct has been good, will quickly obtain some good birth. . . . But those whose conduct has been evil, will quickly attain an evil birth, the birth of a dog, or a hog, or a Kandala [Chandala, an outcaste or Untouchable]" (5.10.7, trans. unknown).

These last verses introduce the idea that the circumstances of one's rebirth depend on the moral nature of one's actions, the essence of juridical karma. Rebirth as a nonhuman animal is a penalty for evil deeds. There is no postmortem judgment or rebirth in a form consistent with one's character, as with the Greeks, only an automatic assignment to a new birth based on one's conduct in life. This idea is not animistic and is not found among the Dravidians or other Indian tribal peoples (Fürer-Haimendorf, 1953; Obeyesekere, 1980, 2002; Parkin, 1988, 1992). The concept of rebirth may have been acquired from the Dravidians, but its association with juridical karma seems to have been entirely a product of the Indian religious mind.

The karma doctrine developed gradually and in dialectic with Buddhism and Jainism from about 500 BCE (Krishan, 1997; O'Flaherty, 1980a). Two centuries later Buddhist monks and adepts began to move out along the Silk Road, proselytizing and converting peoples to the south and east (Foltz, 2010). Buddhism reached what is now Sri Lanka (formerly Ceylon), Myanmar (Burma), and Thailand in the third century BCE. It is thought to have reached China around the same time, but Tibet and Japan not until the seventh and eighth centuries CE. It was banished from India for political reasons in the thirteenth century and today has only a small presence there, surrounding the Dalai Lama in exile from Tibet.

Because monks adapted their teachings to indigenous beliefs and practices, Buddhism developed differently in each place it became established (Becker, 1993a; Skilton, 2003). The many varieties of Buddhism are customarily grouped into three branches: Theravada, which spread to the south and east of India, to Sri Lanka, Myanmar, and Thailand; Mahayana, which spread to the north and east, to China and Japan; and Vajrayana (a type of tantric or esoteric Buddhism), which developed in Tibet (Pilgrim, 1996; Premasiri, 1996; Thondup, 2005).

Buddhist monasteries were built in the eastern Persian Empire (largely Afghanistan) and Buddhist ideology influenced Manichaeism, centered in what is now Iran, in the third century CE (Bulliet, 1976). However, Indian ideas had little impact on Greece. We must assume that the Greeks were familiar with them, especially after Alexander the Great reached India in 326 BCE, established colonies there, and opened a branch of the Silk Road to the Mediterranean (Foltz, 2010). Several Greek thinkers expressed interest in Indian philosophy and even traveled to India to study it at firsthand. Greek rebirth concepts, however, show little movement in the direction of the Indian and, significantly, the Greeks never adopted the karma doctrine (Obeyesekere, 2002). The idea that the gods judged the soul after death and that rebirth occurred after penance had been paid made juridical karma superfluous as an ethical theory.

Interest in rebirth declined in Greece after Plato but made a comeback in first-century BCE Rome (Cumont, 1922). Several Latin writers of the time showed that they accepted reincarnation as a fact of life. In his essay *On Old Age*, Cicero (106–43 BCE) embraced an argument of Plato's: "It is a strong proof of men knowing most things from birth, that when mere children they grasp innumerable facts, with such speed as to show that they are not then taking them in for the first time, but are remembering and recalling them" (*On Old Age* 21, trans. Shuckburgh). Virgil (70–19 BCE) drew on the Myth of Er for inspiration:

But, when a thousand rolling years are past,
(So long their punishments and penance last,)
Whole droves of minds are, by the driving god,
Compell'd to drink the deep Lethaean flood,
In large forgetful draughts to steep the cares
Of their past labours, and their irksome years,
That, unrememb'ring of its former pain,
The soul may suffer mortal flesh again.
(Virgil, *The Aeneid*, Book 6, lines 1000–1008; trans. Dryden)

Plutarch (45–127 CE) quoted Heraclitus of Ephesus (387–312 BCE): "Living and dead are potentially the same thing, and so too waking and sleeping, and young and old; for the latter revert to the former, and the former in turn to the latter" (*Consolatio ad Apollonium* 10, trans. Babbitt). Roman rebirth beliefs vied with traditional ideas of the afterlife in a subterranean inferno and it is not known how widely held they were among the general populace (Cumont, 1922). Possibly the situation was much like it is in Western countries today, with a few prominent defenders and a good many adherents to some rebirth doctrine, yet the dominant posture was one of doubt.

The first of the Neoplatonists whose work has come down to us, Plotinus (c. 204–270), rejected bodily resurrection in favor of rebirth (*Enneads* III.6.6). He acknowledged that some people believe they may be reborn as animals as a result of "sin" (*Enneads* I.1.11, trans. MacKenna & Page) but followed Plato in teaching that one is reborn in a form consistent with one's character (*Enneads* III.4.2; *Enneads* VI.7.6–7). When transmigration occurs, a human soul "does not enter directly into the brute," but only affects it from the outside (*Enneads* I.1.11, trans. MacKenna & Page). The idea that a rational human soul cannot enter the body of an irrational animal was promoted also by Plotinus's student Porphyry (c. 234–c. 305), who, if he did not rule out metempsychosis altogether, stopped just short of it (A. Smith, 1984).

The influence of the Neoplatonists extended beyond the Roman Empire to the east and helped to shape the ideologies of several small ethnic groups, including the Alevis in Turkey and the Alawis, Ismailis, Nosairis, and Yezidis in Syria and Iraq, eventually taking in the Druze of modern Lebanon, Syria, and Israel (Besterman, 1968b; Obeyesekere, 2002, pp. 311–14; Stevenson, 1980, pp. 3–16, 177–82). All except the Yezidis accepted Islam late in the sixth century and landed on the Shia side of the schism that divided Islam after the death of Muhammad in the seventh century. The Druze separated from the Ismailis in the eleventh century. The reincarnation beliefs of these sects set them apart from orthodox Shia Muslims and from Sunni Muslims (Bennett, 2006; Halabi & Horenczyk, 2019).

The influence of Porphyry's student Iamblichus, a Syrian, shows in the rejection of transmigration and metempsychosis, at least by the Druze (Bennett, 2006; Stevenson, 1980, pp. 4–6). The Alevi and perhaps others of the heterodox Shia sects may be more open to transmigration (Besterman, 1968b), but according to Ian Stevenson, who studied Druze and Alevi reincarnation beliefs as well as cases, "all ideas of this type among the Alevis seem to me crudely developed, and I found nothing like the concepts of karma of the Hindus and Buddhists" (1980, p. 186). Druze ideas on this score depart even further from the Indic ones (Stevenson, 1980, pp. 6–7). Gananath Obeyesekere (2002, pp. 314–15) went back over the main source material and concurred with Stevenson's conclusions on these matters.

Neither the Druze nor the Alevi allow for changes of sex between lives (Stevenson, 1980, pp. 3, 185). According to Theodore Besterman (1968b, p.

6), as late as 1915 some Nosairis believed that women did not have souls, which would have precluded them from reincarnation. If this was once a common belief among the heterodox Shia sects, the admission of female souls to the system could have led to the idea of reincarnation along gender lines, as one finds today (Stevenson, 1980). In any event, there is no provision of early escape from the cycle of death and rebirth for either sex. The reincarnation cycle ends for everyone on the Day of Judgment, when God considers the conduct of all their lives in toto before sending souls to heaven or hell for the balance of time.

The status of Jewish reincarnation beliefs during the early centuries of the Common Era is less clear. Dina Ripsman Eylon (2003) found no unambiguous evidence of rebirth beliefs in early Jewish Gnosticism and mysticism. Sources sometimes taken to refer to reincarnation can just as well—and often more forthrightly—be read as alluding to resurrection after death or preexistence without prior incarnation before birth, rather than rebirth.

Jews of the last centuries BCE and the first centuries CE were organized into three sects, the Sadducees, Pharisees, and Essenes. In *Antiquities of the Jews* (XV.10.4.13), the historian Flavius Josephus (37–100 CE) wrote that the Essenes "live the same kind of life as do those whom the Greeks call Pythagoreans," but that does not mean that their beliefs were Pythagorean also. In *The Wars of the Jews* (*The Jewish War*), Josephus explained that for the Essenes, "souls are immortal . . . and are united to their bodies as to prisons, into which they are drawn by a certain natural enticement; but that when they are set free from the bonds of the flesh, they then, as released from a long bondage, rejoice and mount upward" (II.8.11, trans. Whiston). This indicates preexistence and postmortem survival, but not necessarily reincarnation.

Josephus reported that the Pharisees "say that all souls are incorruptible, but that the souls of good men only are removed into other bodies,—but that the souls of bad men are subject to eternal punishment" (*Wars of the Jews* II.8.14, trans. Whiston). Many scholars have taken this as a reference to reincarnation, although some (e.g., Cohn-Sherbok, 1991, p. 191) insist that Josephus means bodily resurrection. If reincarnation is intended, there is a twist: Only the righteous are reborn; the wicked are destined to spend their remaining days in hell.

The first-century Hellenistic Jew, Philo of Alexandria (25 BCE–50 CE), held that perfected souls escaped the rebirth cycle, whereas the imperfect were reborn (Yli-Karjanmaa, 2015, p. 158). Philo's view is consistent with Greco-Roman thinking, but opposite the situation described by Josephus, if he is talking about reincarnation. Reincarnation beliefs in Jewish culture become more visible over time. Reincarnation was endorsed by the eighth-century Karaite movement, and in the ninth century, the philosopher and theologian Saadia (Saadya, Saadiah) addressed it in his *Book of Beliefs and Opinions* (VI.8). Saadia said that he had encountered Jews who believed in reincarnation and some who believed in transmigration or metempsychosis, then refuted their views (Saadia Gaon, 1989, pp. 259–63).

Reincarnation reached prominence in the twelfth-century *Bahir* and the thirteenth-century *Zohar*. The *Bahir*, now recognized as the seminal work of the Kabbalah, is popularly attributed to the first-century Rabbi Nehunia ben HaKana (Kaplan, 1979). Reincarnation is portrayed as punishment for wrongdoing (e.g., see *Bahir*, paragraph 184). Italian kabbalists of the fifteenth century considered various types of rebirth (Ogren, 2009). In the sixteenth century, the Kabbalist Yitzchak (Isaac) Luria (1534–1572) introduced a novel variation in his *Gate of Reincarnations*, recorded after his death by his protégé, the rabbi Chaim Vital (Luria, 2015). For Luria, a soul is comprised of several levels that may combine with the soul levels of other individuals during embodiment and may progress independently toward "rectification." The Lurian conception has become dominant in Hasidic thinking and nowadays is presented as the general Jewish idea of reincarnation (Pinson, 1999; Wexelman, 1999; Winkler, 1996).

There are intriguing parallels between Jewish reincarnation beliefs and the beliefs of the heterodox Shia sects that suggest some connection between them. Avraham Trugman (2008, p. 24), who adheres to the Lurian position, says that God judges souls at the conclusion of all their incarnations rather than at the end of each. Trugman (2008, p. 15) allows for immediate rebirth, at least for sages. In traditional Jewish mysticism, women did not reincarnate (Pinson, 1999, pp. 171–76; Trugman, 2008, p. 105), although exceptions might be made under certain circumstances (Winkler, 1996, p. 35). In other respects, there are differences between the Jewish beliefs and the beliefs of the heterodox Shia sects, but on these points (judgment when the reincarnation cycle has reached its conclusion, immediate rebirth, and no reincarnation for women) the correspondences are remarkable, the more so because these tenets do not appear in any other system known to me. They may be very ancient, involving influences from before the conversion to Islam by the Shia sects.

Rebirth ideas were so much a part of the intellectual climate of Jesus's day that it is hard to believe that he was not familiar with them, but his position on the subject is uncertain. There are passages in the New Testament that can be read as allusions to reincarnation on the part of Jesus's disciples (MacGregor, 1978), but these passages could refer to preexistence without prior incarnation rather than to reincarnation (Hamerton-Kelly, 1973). There was considerable controversy over this even in antiquity (Trumbower, 2016). We must remember that the Christian Gospels were not recorded contemporaneously with the events they describe. They were reworked before being compiled in the form that has come down to us, and it is possible that more explicit references to reincarnation were removed from the Bible early on. In any event, both preexistence and reincarnation, as well as resurrection, were major ideas in the circum-Mediterranean region in the centuries immediately before and after Jesus.

Several Christian Gnostics of the second century, including Carpocrates (d. 138), Basilides (who taught from 117 to 138), and Valentinus (100–160), espoused reincarnation (DeConick, 2016; Layton, 1989; A. P. Smith, 2015b). The belief was almost certainly current throughout the Levant at this time, as evidenced by the energy other writers invested in disputing it. Justin Martyr (100–165) discussed reincarnation in his *Dialogue with Trypho* (4–6), then moved on to other concerns without offering any real arguments against it, but Theophilus of Antioch (d. c. 181), Irenaeus of Lyons (d. 202), Tertullian of Carthage (160–222), and Marcus Minucius Felix (d. 260) were clearer in their condemnation of the idea (H. Chadwick, 1984; Trumbower, 2016).

From the third century onward, much of the Christian invective was aimed at Origen (185–254), who, like Clement of Alexandria (150–215), was more interested in the possibility that the soul preexisted conception than that it reincarnated after death. In 325, Roman Emperor Constantine the Great (274–337) convened the First Council of Nicaea for the purpose of resolving disagreements over Christian doctrine and deciding what books should be included in the New Testament. The Council ruled against reincarnation, and Constantine set about a concerted rewriting of Church history, so that the thoughts of early fathers who had favored reincarnation were expunged from the record (Layton, 1989). At the Second Council of Constantinople (the Fifth Ecumenical Council of the Church) in 553, Origen's speculations about preexistence were declared to be heretical (MacGregor, 1978, pp. 48–62). Christianity asserted that God created souls for each body at its conception and affirmed bodily resurrection rather than reincarnation after death.

After the Edict of Milan legalized Christian worship in the Roman Empire in 313, Christianity was carried through Europe and into England by soldiers and settlers. Now that it was aligned with the state, it had what it needed to suppress contrary opinions. This was often achieved through violence, the Christians behaving toward others as they had been treated during the early centuries of persecution, leading, in the Middle Ages, to the Crusades and the Inquisition. These policies were expressed in the thirteenth-century extirpation of the Cathars (Albigenses), a group with roots in Christian Gnosticism (A. P. Smith, 2015a).

Reincarnation beliefs were driven underground but managed to survive in some areas. Alexander Alexakis (2001) documents their persistence in lands dominated by the Eastern Church, after the separation of Roman Catholicism from Greek and Russian Orthodoxy in the eleventh century. In Western Europe, reincarnation popped up periodically in philosophical and literary works (Givens, 2010; Head & Cranston, 1967; Kurth-Voigt, 1999). Reincarnation beliefs made their way to the American colonies and the United States beginning in the sixteenth century (L. Irwin, 2017a, 2017b). By the later twentieth century, American culture had reworked the old ideas into a new synthesis and had begun to integrate them into a New Age metaphysics (DeConick, 2016; L. Irwin, 2017a, 2017b).

KARMA, GOD, AND THE INDIVIDUAL IN REBIRTH THEORY

An important problem facing any system of reincarnation (or more generally, rebirth) beliefs is accounting for the selection of parents for the next life. Why is a person reborn in the family and under the circumstances he is? What may be termed the *selection problem* has been resolved in three different ways—by stipulating that one's karma is the determining factor; by asserting that God makes or shapes the decision; by assigning responsibility directly to the individual. These solutions overlap to some extent, but fundamentally they are different and have different implications for the human condition. They are closely connected to an array of other issues, including the question of what it is that reincarnates; the nature of discarnate existence during the intermission; and ethical concerns about inequalities at birth. These are large topics and I can do no more than organize and introduce them here. Later we will see what the reincarnation case data have to contribute to the discussion about them.

I have noted the appearance of the karma doctrine in the *Chandogya Upanishad* (V.10.7), where it is said: "Those whose conduct has been good, will quickly obtain some good birth. . . . But those whose conduct has been evil, will quickly attain an evil birth, the birth of a dog, or a hog, or a Kandala" (trans. unknown). Reichenbach (1990, pp. 190–95) quotes other passages about karma from the Upanishads. In all of them, one's conduct in life is said to dictate the nature of one's rebirth. As Hindu thought on the subject matured, God was brought into the picture, so that many philosophical schools came to maintain that God mediated karma. I will return to Hindu ideas later, but first I want to examine juridical karma in a generalized sense and to look at its place in atheistic Buddhism and Theosophy.

Juridical karma is portrayed as a moral law of cause and effect, of action and reaction. A similar notion is expressed in the biblical maxim "as you sow, so shall you reap," although most Christians do not expect the results to manifest in subsequent lives on Earth. Not all actions have karmic entailments, only those with ethical significance performed with conscious intent (Krishan, 1997; Reichenbach, 1990). Karma may flow also from one's thoughts and intentions, especially if they are to do harm or to act in a malicious manner. Good deeds and intentions count in one's favor; evil deeds and intentions count against one. All one's merits and demerits feed into and alter the karma one has amassed over countless lives. One is at the mercy of one's karma, yet one also is its master, because through one's good deeds one may improve one's prospects for the future. For this reason, karma is not synonymous with fate, nor does it imply predestination.

Although the Buddha did not invent the idea of karma, he accepted it as part of his account of human suffering. As he approached enlightenment, the Buddha realized that human beings possessed no enduring essence that might be called a "soul." Rather, a person's consciousness underwent constant change, both physical and mental, from birth until death. Emotional attachments drove a person's consciousness to return to embodiment and suffering after death, but they did so as a result of its karmic tendencies, which helped give rise to a new person as a candle's flame serves to light a new wick. The new person inherited its predecessor's karma but was only in that limited sense its continuation (Becker, 1993a; McDermott, 1980; Premasiri, 1996). The Buddha became aware of over five hundred of his previous lives (related in the Jakata Tales: Appleton, 2010) through the extrasensory faculty of retrocognition in his meditative state, not through memory of them (Becker, 1993a, p. 7).

Buddhists consider the human being to be composed of five aggregates (*khandhās*): form, feelings, perceptions, predispositions, and consciousness, the last conceptualized as a contentless stream of conscious awareness (Becker, 1993a; McDermott, 1980; Premasiri, 1996). The last four of these aggregates constitute a person's mental faculties, collectively called a *gandhabba* (Pali; Sanskrit, *gandharva*). Karma (*kamma* in Pali) directs the gandhabba to a couple engaged in sexual intercourse and rebirth is effected at conception, the gandhabba mixing with the father's semen and the mother's menstrual blood (or ovum, in modern thinking) to create the new person (Becker, 1993a; McDermott, 1980; Premasiri, 1996). In Tibetan Buddhism, this mixing is expected to occur around seven weeks (forty-six days) after death (Nahm, 2011b; Thondup, 2005).

Early Buddhism recognized four realms of existence: human, nonhuman animal, hell, and heaven. Later, hell became subdivided into hell proper and hungry ghosts, and heaven into god and demi-god, so that today it is more common to encounter the doctrine of six realms (Appleton, 2014; Becker, 1993a). One's destiny is determined by one's karma, with clear expectations associated with rebirth in each realm. Naomi Appleton (2014) analyzed stories from the early Buddhist literature of India that show how this works.

Extreme violence, killing fellow humans, and eating meat land one in hell; deception, lying, and swindling lead to being reborn a nonhuman animal; goodness, humility, and compassion toward others result in a human birth; and an ascetic life with its austerities brings rebirth as a god or demigod.

The accrual of good and bad karma through thought and action applies mainly to births as human beings, although often one must spend considerable time in other realms to extinguish one's bad karma before being reborn in human form. The human life is the pivotal one, the one in which it is easiest to accrue good karma, and the only one from which it is possible to escape the rebirth cycle. Buddhism allows for a change of sex between lives, but to go from male to female is considered a demotion, a consequence of less than sterling thoughts and behavior. In order to free oneself from all attachments to the material world and achieve Nirvana, one must be born a human male (Appleton, 2014; Becker, 1993a; McDermott, 1980). In the Vajrayana (tantric) Buddhism of Tibet, there is no release from the rebirth cycle, although more advanced adepts have greater control over it (Gamble, 2018; Thondup, 2005).

The Buddha seems to have thought of the gandhabba as having no postmortem existence until it became the potentiality for the next life. Carl Becker (1993a, p. 16) suggests that he thought of the process in psychic terms, as bridging space and time without the need for spatiotemporal continuity. However, the logical preference for a consciousness stream persisting from death to conception was apparent even in the Buddha's day and quickly became the canonical position (Becker, 1993a; Premasiri, 1996).

Theravada Buddhism retains the idea of a dynamic stream of consciousness as a constituent of the gandhabba (Premasiri, 1996), but as Buddhism moved beyond India to the north and west, into China and Tibet and later into Japan, the gandhabba concept changed. In the Mahayana Buddhism of China and Japan and in the Vajrayana Buddhism of Tibet, the gandhabba came to be a quasi-physical or subtle vehicle that supported the consciousness stream in its intermediate state between death and rebirth (Becker, 1993a; Gamble, 2018); in Tibet, it might also inhabit relics during that period (Zivkovic, 2014). The consciousness stream was credited with experiences, including interaction with other spirit beings, and with the ability to exercise extrasensory perception and psychokinetic agency (Becker, 1993a; Rinbochay & Hopkins, 1980; Thondup, 2005), faculties denied the gandhabba in Theravada Buddhism (Premasiri, 1996). Past-life memories were expected to come in meditation to adepts nearing enlightenment, as they had for the Buddha, and were suspect when they appeared spontaneously to regular people.

A limited degree of personal agency is sanctioned within the karmic framework. Thoughts at the time of death are said to influence where one is reborn, but this is because the dying person's state of mind "summarizes the total balance sheet of good and evil deeds performed during a given lifetime" (Becker, 1993a, p. 13). In Tibetan Buddhism, the individual is able to make choices during the bardo (intermission) period (Thondup, 2005). Advanced adepts state their intentions and may even initiate their reincarnations before death (Gamble, 2018). The *Tibetan Book of the Dead* is designed to be read to a deceased individual as a guide to avoiding rebirth. Still, for all except advanced adepts, karma determines whose womb the gandhabba enters if the individual fails to avert rebirth (Evans-Wentz, 1957, p. 175; Rinbochay & Hopkins, 1980, pp. 58–59; Thondup, 2005, p. 8). This is the *karmic solution* to the selection problem.

The karmic solution was adopted by Theosophy and through Theosophy has had a major impact on Western, especially American, ideas about reincarnation (Irwin, 2017a, 2017b; R. S. Ellwood, 1996). The Theosophical Society was founded in 1875 in New York City by the Russian-American Helena Blavatsky. Until then, American thinking about reincarnation had been shaped mainly by Western esoteric traditions, which made do without karma (Irwin, 2017a, 2017b). In 1877, Blavatsky published *Isis Unveiled: A Master-Key to the Mysteries of Ancient and Modern Science and Theology*, which merged Indic with Gnostic and Kabbalistic sources and embraced karma along with reincarnation.

In recognition of its Eastern influences, Blavatsky moved the Theosophical Society's headquarters to Madras (Chennai), India, in 1882. After her death nine years later, the Indian office separated from its American branches, but the movement has survived, and Theosophical centers continue to operate in both India and the United States (R. S. Ellwood, 1996; Irwin, 2017a, 2017b; Neufeldt, 1986).

In *Isis Unveiled* and subsequent writings, Blavatsky presented reincarnation as a "cycle of necessity," part of a general pattern of renewal that characterized all of nature. She called that which reincarnated a "monad" or "ego." Monads spun off from a Universal Mind and cycled through mineral, plant, and nonhuman animal lives before coming into possession of a human body. Although Blavatsky allowed for transmigration from lower to higher physical forms, she rejected metempsychosis. Once it had attained human status, a monad was reborn only as a human or higher being, continuing its climb up the evolutionary ladder on a long pilgrimage back to its source (Blavatsky, 1886, 1988b, 1889a, 1889b; see also R. S. Ellwood, 1996, and Neufeldt, 1986).

At death, an individual's "lower three vehicles"—its physical body, astral body, and personal ego—ceased to function. The monad's remaining spiritual components found themselves in an "astral locality" called Kama-loka, "the Hades of the ancients," where they underwent further purification. Eventually the cleansed monad was admitted to Devachan, a blissful place where its "spiritual ego"—its permanent essence—had all its wishes fulfilled. After a period of convalescence in Devachan lasting from one thousand to three thousand years, a monad became re-affiliated with a physical body, though not necessarily on Earth (Blavatsky, 1886, 1889a, 1889b).

Rebirth on the same planet twice in a row was "a violation of the laws of harmony of nature" and happened "only when [nature], seeking to restore its disturbed equilibrium, violently throws back into Earth-like the astral monad which had been tossed out of the cycle of necessity by crime or accident" (Blavatsky, 1877, vol. 1, p. 351). Also allowed to reincarnate again on Earth were the souls of persons who had been aborted, were congenital idiots, or who had died before the age of reason, whose situations likewise had subverted their life's purpose and who therefore were given another opportunity for spiritual advancement (Blavatsky, 1877, vol. 1, p. 351). For these categories of persons, reincarnation followed immediately upon death (Blavatsky, 1889b).

In Section 8 of *The Key to Theosophy* (Blavatsky, 1889a), Blavatsky was at pains to explain why individuals were held responsible for their past actions through karmic penalties if they did not recall their previous lives. Although the memory of a personal ego was limited to a particular embodiment, memories of past lives were retained by the spiritual ego. Memories might make their way into the personal ego's conscious awareness when the brain's defenses were lowered, as in altered states and dreams (Blavatsky, 1888a). Because the spiritual ego remembered, even though the personal ego did not, it was fair for karma to reward and punish the embodied person for things he did not consciously recall.

Blavatsky portrayed karma as driving the cycle of necessity, although as a moral law of retribution aimed at restoring balance and harmony to the natural order, it was applicable to human beings only. Nonhuman animals and other beings that could not be held responsible for their actions were subject to a complementary "principle of compensation" (Blavatsky 1889a).

Because in Theosophy, karma acts in support of the cycle of necessity, Blavatsky's concept is different from the Indic one (R. S. Ellwood, 1996, pp. 192–93). Theosophists do not think of karma as a force that traps people in a world of suffering but rather "associate karma and reincarnation with the concepts of evolution and progress, as the means by which consciousness comes into self-realization" (Algeo, 1987, pp. 6–7, cited by R. S. Ellwood, 1996, p. 195).

Blavatksy's karma is less subtle than the Buddhist version. Although invariably just, its impact is said to be more directly and immediately felt and physically expressed. By way of illustration, Blavatsky presented the parable of a Prussian king who slit the throat of a witch who tried to warn him about the consequences of his murderous excesses, then millennia later was reborn as a prince who contracted a painful throat disease that left him unable to speak (Blavatsky, 1888a). Although clearly related to Indic juridical karma, Theosophy's karma is different enough to be given its own name. I will follow Stevenson (2001 and elsewhere) in referring to it as *retributive karma*, employing the adjective Blavatsky (1889a) used to describe it.

The *theistic solution* to the selection problem grants God a role in deciding on the rebirth parents. In some systems, He superintends the workings of karma, whereas in others He assigns the new parents directly, delegates the responsibility to other spirit entities, or establishes the conditions under which the individual soul or spirit makes the choice of where and to whom to return.

Hinduism exemplifies the first of these variants. As might be expected from the world's oldest living religion, Hinduism is extraordinarily diverse. In its observance, it is highly ritualistic, but its written texts have garnered considerable exegesis, often with disagreements among commentators. Most Hindu philosophical schools agree on the preeminence of God (Brahman, Krishna, Shiva, Vishnu) yet also recognize a panoply of lesser figures operating under God's direction. The different schools agree on the existence of an eternal self or soul, called the atman (ātman) or jiva (jīva), which is independent of the physical body, although they differ on the relationship between it and God. According to Advaita Vedanta, Brahman is present in the atman, and embodied persons must lose the illusion that they are separate from Brahman in order to transcend the rebirth cycle (A. Sharma, 1990; Prabhavananda, 1979).

Because they consider the soul to have an existence separate from the physical body, most Hindu schools allow the soul to attach itself to a new body at any point during gestation, not only at conception. In rare cases, the soul with which a body is born may be replaced by another soul after birth (*parakaya pravesh*). The soul may pass into nonhuman animals and take on nonmaterial forms, rebirths considered, as in Buddhism, to be karmic sequelae to evil thoughts or deeds. Regular people and not only advanced meditators may remember previous lives. The Sanskrit term *jati gyanam* denotes the memory of previous lives and the word *jatismara*, one who recalls a previous life. Patajali refers to past-life memory in his *Yoga Sutras* (III.18), thought to date to the first centuries CE, and there are several references to it in the earlier *Mahābhārata* (Kuldip Dhiman, personal communication).

God's role in the rebirth process is understood, if not always acknowledged (Krishan, 1997). The Brahma or Vedanta Sutras (III.2.38–42) deal with it, and in the *Bhagavad-Gita* it is said: "The Supreme Lord is situated in everyone's heart, O Arjuna, and is directing the wanderings of all living entities, who are seated as on a machine, made of the material energy" (*Bhagavad-Gita* 18:61, trans. Bhagavan Sri Krishna), and: "Those who are envious and mischievous, who are the lowest among men, I perpetually cast into the ocean of material existence, into various demoniac species of life" (*Bhagavad-Gita* 16:19, trans. Bhagavan Sri Krishna).

According to Charles Keyes (1983, p. 15), many Hindus believe that God writes one's destiny on one's forehead in invisible lettering at birth, and several of the ethnographers in Keyes and Valentine Daniel's (1983) *Karma: An Anthropological Inquiry* describe headwriting in modern Indian societies. Brenda Beck (1983) analyzes a story from a drama based on the *Mahābhārata*, an epic poem. A barren woman consults a soothsayer (Shiva in disguise), who reveals that her headwriting says that she is to be childless for seven more lives. The soothsayer prescribes a lengthy penance that includes a series of seven symbolic deaths and rebirths. The woman completes this penance and is rewarded with a wish to be granted by Shiva. She asks for two sons as strong as great elephants. Shiva has his underlings retrieve suitable souls from a heavenly storage area and insert their life-seeds in a lemon, which the woman is instructed to eat, and she thereby conceives and bears twins. Shiva later sends Yama (the lord of death) to collect these two souls again, and so God is shown to rule over both birth and death.

As this drama suggests, the inclusion of God in the equation allows Hindus to imagine karma rather differently than Buddhists and Theosophists. One's karmic lot is ameliorable through entreaties to God. One may appeal to God to have certain persons reborn in one's family or to obtain specific attributes in one's child. Additionally, Hinduism allows for the ritual transfer of karma to other persons (especially spouses and children) and to spirits of the dead (O'Flaherty, 1980b, pp. 28–37), practices that go back to the ancient Vedic tradition (O'Flaherty, 1980a, pp. xiii–xvi) and may have preceded the pairing of karma with rebirth (O'Flaherty, 1980b, p. 3). Interestingly, both Theravada and Mahayana Buddhists sometimes engage in rites of merit transfer that are inconsistent with Buddhist dogma and probably are survivals of pre-Buddhist ancestor worship (Appleton, 2014, pp. 129–35; Becker, 1993a, pp. 47–48; Obeyesekere, 2002, pp. 138–39).

Indian thinkers such as Shankara (Śankara), the eighth-century philosopher credited with consolidating the teachings of the Advaita school of Vedanta, argued that God arranges events so that a person's experiences match the merit or demerit flowing from his actions (Potter, 1980, p. 258). Similar arguments are made by Swami Bhaktivedanta, a devotee of Vishnu and adherent to Vaishnavism, which originated in the last centuries BCE and first centuries CE (Baird, 1986). Bhaktivedanta avers that karma is expressed through the body, which reaps its harvest. Death usually entails being in trance for seven months, after which one awakens, ideally in the womb. There are 8,400,000 species of life into which one's karma may direct one, although because the laws of the material world and of karma are under God's jurisdiction, he has it in his power to adjust their workings.

According to Swami Bhaktivedanta, some transgressions cannot be forgiven. If one kills animals for food, rather than for ritual sacrifice, one will become an animal in one's next life. Persons with unrestrained sexual appetites will be reborn as animals to fulfill their animalistic propensities. One should make the best of one's years in a human body to properly worship the Lord. "If one wastes one's human years in sense gratification, one will transmigrate in the next life to the body of an animal such as a dog, cat, or hog. One may even take the form of a tree" (Baird, 1986, p. 285).

For fuller consideration of God's management of karma in Hinduism, see Yuvraj Krishan (1997). For examination of the related logical issues, see Bruce Reichenbach (1990). For a larger perspective, see J. B. Long (1980), who discusses conflicting presentations of divine, karmic, and human agency even in texts as basic to Hinduism as the *Bhagavad-Gita* and the *Mahābhārata*.

The "life readings" of Edgar Cayce provide an example of the theistic solution involving karma in the Western context. Cayce, a Kentucky-born psychic, began reading the previous lives of clients in 1923 after meeting Arthur Lammers, a businessman interested in esoterica. Lammers requested an astrology reading and Cayce obliged, although previously he had confined himself to the diagnosis of illness and the prescription of remedies (Cerminara, 1950; Stearn, 1967; Sugrue, 1942).

The astrology reading for Lammers concluded with the revelation that he had been a monk in a previous life. Reincarnation was alien to Cayce's fundamentalist Christian upbringing and he resisted it at first, but under Lammers's guidance came to accept it and karma as manifestations of God's will (Langley, 1967; I. C. Sharma, 1975; Stearn, 1989). In his life readings, Cayce described series of four or five lives, related through karmic bonds. A typical sequence was: "Atlantis, Egypt, Rome, the Crusades period, and the early [American] Colonial Period" (Cerminara, 1950, p. 43). Another was: "Atlantis, Egypt, Rome, France in the time of Louis XIV, XV, or XVI, and the American Civil War" (Cerminara, 1950, p. 43).

As J. Gordon Melton (1994) demonstrated, Cayce's life readings have a strongly Theosophical slant. Not only are the reported lives exclusively human, Atlantis and Egypt are preeminent in the Theosophical rendering of human history. Cayce's intermissions were not as long as Blavatsky envisioned, but by 1923, opinion about the length of the intermission had changed. Irving Cooper, a leading exponent of Theosophy early in the twentieth century, asserted that it had been shown "by actual investigation" (the nature of which he left unspecified) to range from five to 2,300 years, with an average of 500 years (Cooper, 1920, p. 55).

Cayce said that he learned about his clients' previous lives sometimes straight from their minds and sometimes from the Akashic Records (Cerminara, 1950, p. 44). Cayce seems to have been the first to utilize the Akashic Records for this purpose, but the concept is Theosophical. From classical times until the later nineteenth century, the universe was thought to be suffused by a material ether. In *Isis Unveiled*, Blavatsky explained that "akasa" is a Sanskrit word that means sky and "the all-pervading ether" (1877, vol. 1., p. 139n). In *The Secret Doctrine*, she informed readers that "Akâsa" was equivalent to the "primordial Æther" (1888b, vol. 1, p. 76) that "pervades all things" (1888b, vol. 1, p. 343) and that it is "objectively eternal" (1888b, vol. 1, p. 635). Blavatsky wrote before the 1887 Michelson-Morley experiment called into doubt the existence of a physical substance consuming the vacuum of space, so may be excused for her language; not so her successors.

C. W. Leadbeater introduced the "âkâshic records" in his book *Clairvoyance*, first published in 1899 with a second edition in 1903. He says, "Every object is undoubtedly throwing off radiations in all directions, and it is precisely in this way, though on a higher plane, that the âkâshic records seem to be formed" (Leadbeater, 1903a, p. 60) by producing indelible impressions on the ether. Because they were imprinted on a physical substrate, the âkâshic records could be accessed clairvoyantly. Leadbeater professed to learn from them about the origin of the cosmos and the Earth and about the development of human civilization through Lemuria, Atlantis, and ancient Egypt. Edgar Cayce took the next step, turning to the Records for the details of his clients' previous lives. Thanks to Cayce's popularization of the concept, the idea of the Akashic Records as a store of information about past lives has become ingrained in New Age metaphysics (Taylor, 2016; Wetzel, 2009).

In some cultures, one finds the idea that God alone designates new parents for a reincarnating soul. This is true of the heterodox Shia sects, for instance. God sends the soul of a deceased person immediately into the body of a baby at its birth, with no interval between lives (Stevenson, 1980, p. 186). For the Hasidim, God allows the righteous to remain in his presence, condemns the wicked to eternal damnation, and sends the remainder (or their appropriate soul levels) to new lives, during which they have another chance to better themselves. According to one school, all souls were created by God at the inception of the world and are working off defects acquired during their first embodied lives, whereas according to another, all are descended from Adam and are redeeming his sins (Pinson, 1999; Trugman, 2008).

The Spiritism of Allan Kardec (the penname of a Frenchman, Hippolyte Léon Denizard Rivail) is a Western example of the theistic solution sans karma. Spiritism is a loose set of doctrines communicated by spirits through mediums, compiled and commented upon by Kardec (1986, 1996, 2003), whose works furnish its principal texts. Spiritist doctrine affirms that one is reborn in a variety of religious and ethnic groups and economic situations and as both sexes, in order to grow through a variety of experiences. God points one in the direction of one's new birth and may select it for one, although one may state one's preference and have it granted. Spiritism regards human suffering not as karmic payback but as divine retribution for misdeeds in earlier lives.

Kardec's commentaries draw on Mesmerism, the positivism of Auguste Comte, the utopian philosophy of Charles Fourier, and the Christian mysticism of Emanuel Swedenborg (Hess, 1991, pp. 72–75; L. L. Sharp, 2006, pp. 8–10). Spiritism referred to the beliefs of the ancient Gauls (a Celtic people) as evidence that reincarnation was not alien to France (L. L. Sharp, 2006, p. 10). The acceptance of reincarnation sets Spiritism apart from Anglo-American Spiritualism, which was strong in Great Britain and the United States during the same period (Irwin, 2017a, 2017b). Alexander Aksakof (1875) traced the origin of the reincarnation teachings of Spiritism to a single medium with whom Kardec sat in the 1850s. Although Spiritism has had little impact on the English-speaking world and has dropped in influence in France, it continues to be important in Brazil (Hess, 1994; Stevenson, 1974b).

Sometimes God delegates to his subordinates the authority to appoint new parents. In Plato's *Republic* (X.614b–621d), Er tells of seeing souls assembled in a meadow awaiting rebirth. A prophet places patterns of all kinds of lives on the ground and institutes a lottery that determines the order in which souls may select among them. Some souls choose hastily and regret their choice. Others take their time and make better decisions. However, in general, the lives chosen are consistent with the characters and habits the souls have developed in earlier embodiments.

In the weakest form of the theistic solution, God goes no further than setting up the conditions in which the choice of parents is made. In the *Laws*, Plato has the Athenian explain that God "designed the rule which prescribes what kind of character should be set to dwell in what kind of position and in what regions," but the choice is up to the individual and the individual typically follows his deep-seated habits. "For according to the trend of our desires and the nature of our souls, each one of us generally becomes of a corresponding character" (*Laws* X.904b–c, trans. Bury).

I will term the third solution to the selection problem the *elective solution*. The elective solution assigns responsibility for the choice of parents directly to the individual. The elective solution is associated most closely with animistic belief systems and with a New Age reincarnation mythos.

In animistic societies, a person may decide on his next parents before he dies. In one of the ten Tlingit cases of planned reincarnation investigated by Stevenson, a fisherman named William George repeatedly told his favorite son that "if there is anything to this rebirth business" he would return to him as his son. He added that he would be known by the same two birthmarks he then had. Immediately after William's death, his daughter-in-law became pregnant, and when born, her child was found to have birthmarks in the two places William George had indicated. The boy was recognized as his grandfather come back and christened William George, Jr. (Stevenson, 1974b, pp. 231–33).

Planned reincarnations are reported from Indic cultures less frequently than from animistic ones. Hindus may express their wish to be reborn in certain families (generally their own), but they expect this to come about through the intercession of God or the instrumentality of karma, not via their own agency. Tibetan adepts often declare where they will be reborn, though they are thought to have overcome their karmic ties and to be returning to the world of their own volition. These masters rarely state exactly to whom they will be reborn, but only give general guidance on where to look for them (Gamble, 2018; Mackenzie, 1996; Wangdu, Gould, & Richardson, 2000). The animist, on the other hand, states precisely where he intends to go.

In animistic cultures, the choice of parents may be made during the intermission period and communicated to the mother-to-be. Upon death the spirit is freed from the body but retains its ability to think and to act on the world. Thus, whether or not a person has stated his intention in advance, his spirit may let his will be known by appearing as an apparition, a poltergeist, a mediumistic communicator, or most commonly, through an announcing dream.

Individual initiative is prized in American culture, and perhaps for that reason the idea that the deceased choose their parents for the next go-round is strong in the New Age reincarnation mythos. The selection is presumed to be made during the intermission and is said to accompany planning for the upcoming life, during which goals for spiritual advancement are set.

One of the principal thought leaders in this part of the metaphysics is hypnotherapist Michael Newton. Newton produced two hugely successful books (M. Newton, 1996, 2000) that purported to reveal what happens after death, based on hypnotic sessions he led. The soul of the newly deceased, Newton claimed, passes through a tunnel into light. There it is met by soul mates, spirit guides, and loved ones who have gone before it. After a while, these entities pull away and the soul is led to an "orientation station." Anguished souls that cannot accept their bodily deaths and the souls of people who engaged in "criminal abnormalities" are separated out and sent for rehabilitation, but the rest are debriefed and treated to a "shower of healing" before being drawn or led on to a "staging area." From there they are escorted or "projected" to their appropriate "soul cluster groups," to be with souls with whom they have associated on countless previous occasions. Before reincarnation, souls go before a spirit tribunal, where they are made to evaluate how well they met the goals they set for their last lives and to formulate goals for their next.

Life planning before reincarnation raises the question as to why one would choose to be born into a disadvantaged family or with a physical handicap. Newton's answer—an answer typical of New Age metaphysics—is that the soul elects to experience different situations in order to further its spiritual growth. New Agers not infrequently blame karma for life's vicissitudes, even while they credit the individual with selecting his parents. For many followers, karma has features more akin to processual than to juridical or retributive karma. Processual karma is a psychological force that carries forward an individual's personality and personal conflicts. Processual karma may come back to bite the individual, but it operates from within him, not on him from without.

These are the solutions to the selection problem that have been proposed by different traditions. According to the karmic solution, the parents (and circumstances) of one's next incarnation are determined by one's karma. According to the theistic solution, God mediates karma, makes the decision outright, or at a minimum, establishes the conditions under which the decision is made. The elective solution places the decision in the hands of the individual. Granted some overlap between these solutions, as in God's mediation of karma, they are fundamentally different and contradictory.

So what should we believe? How might reincarnation work? The best way to reach an answer, I suggest, is to examine cases of past-life memory and their associated signs carefully, following the data without constraint from any preconceived ideas about how reincarnation operates. I aim to develop a theory that makes sense of the case data in the wider context of scientific knowledge, not merely to demonstrate the likelihood of reincarnation's occurrence in a generalized sense. Before we can take up the research findings, however, we need a deeper acquaintance with research methodology and an appreciation of interpretive frames for the data, apart from reincarnation.

Chapter 3

Research Methods and Interpretative Frames

For the parapsychologist, the most significant signs of reincarnation are veridical past-life memories such as Rylann's, but this area of investigation is relatively new. Psychical research, the forerunner of parapsychology, was focused on apparitions and mediumship as evidence for postmortem survival from the founding of the Society for Psychical Research (SPR) in London in 1882, but took little interest in reincarnation until Ian Stevenson published a review article of past-life memory claims in 1960. The accounts Stevenson summarized in that article have numerous similarities to the cases he began to study in 1961, suggesting considerable stability in the expression of reincarnation-related phenomena over space and time. In the first section of this chapter, I present a series of these early reports of past-life memory. In the second section, I describe Stevenson's research methodology, still the standard for reincarnation case studies, and address the criticisms it has received. In the third section, I cover interpretive approaches to the case data, short of reincarnation. This chapter finishes preparing the way for consideration of post–1960 research findings, which I undertake starting in Chapter 4.

ACCOUNTS OF PAST-LIFE MEMORY RECORDED BEFORE 1960

In places where reincarnation is accepted as a fact of life, it is easy for announcing dreams, birthmarks, and behaviors to be overinterpreted in identifying a child with a forebearer. There is less room for overinterpretation when a toddler relates memories of an earlier life, especially when these memories refer to people the parents do not know. Children's past-life memories typically appear along with other signs of reincarnation and form a recognizable complex or syndrome I call the *rebirth syndrome*. More than individual signs taken in isolation, it is their persistent co-occurrence in the rebirth syndrome that puts pressure on the psychosocial theory's assumption that social construction is an adequate explanation for all reincarnation cases.

The past-life memories of Pythagoras, described in Chapter 2, are the first to enter the historical record. A few centuries later, the Neopythagorean Apollonius of Tyana (c. 15–c. 100 CE) said that he remembered having been an Egyptian ship's pilot who had an encounter with pirates on the Mediterranean Sea (Philostratus, Apollonius of Tyana, III.23–24). It is not known if Pythagoras and Apollonius recalled their previous lives from childhood or if their memories came to them in adulthood. The earliest clear accounts of children's past-life memories were culled by Dutch sinologist J. J. M. De Groot (1901, pp. 143–55) from Chinese documents of the first millennium CE.

The oldest of De Groot's accounts date to the Tsin dynasty (post–265 CE). De Groot looked for but found no similar narratives in earlier records (1901, p. 143). I give one of his twelve accounts below. I summarized others in an article for the *Psi Encyclopedia* (Matlock, 2017, July; see also Paton, 1921).

> In the district of Fu-yang, in Siang-chen, there was a Buddhist monk, Yuen-kao by name, who lived in the Chi-leh monastery, and whose lay surname was Chao. The son of his elder brother had a previous existence as a child of the Ma family, which lived with him in the same village. This child died in the last year of the Ching kwan period (A.D. 649). When on the point of breathing its last, it looked around, and said to its mother: "I, your child, have connections with Chao Tsung's family; I shall become his grandson after my death." That mother, discrediting the words she heard, made a black spot on the child's right elbow. And the wife of Chao dreamed of that child coming to her with the words, "I must become your descendent"; on which she became pregnant. Her vision closely resembled that son of the Ma family, and on her giving birth to him, the black spot was found on his body in the same place. When three years old, he went into the house of Ma, without anyone showing him the way thither, and there he declared that it was his "former dwelling." (De Groot, 1901, p. 144)

Note the planned reincarnation, suggesting an animistic survival in a Buddhist culture, and the mother's announcing dream. The child's birthmark is what has come to be called an *experimental birthmark* because it was apparently stimulated by an intentional marking of the previous person's body (Matlock, 2017, June; Tucker & Keil, 2013).

British folklorist Gerald Willoughby-Meade (1928) ran across another early Chinese account, this with a purported communication between the deceased and living members of his family during the intermission and a reincarnation decision that must be ratified by an underworld official:

> A book from the eighth century A.D. tells how Ku Huang lost his only son at the age of seventeen. The boy's soul hovered about in an uncertain state without leaving the house. Ku gave way to bitter sorrow, and wrote a verse in which he lamented that he was seventy years old, and would soon have to enter the grave also. The boy's soul, hearing his father recite the verse he had written, was suddenly heard to say, in a human voice, "I will again become a son in the Ku family." Presently the soul felt that it was being seized and sent before an Official of the Underworld, who ordered it to be reborn as a child in the Ku household. Then the soul became insensible and after a little while, opening its eyes, it recognized its home and its relations, but remembered no details of its former life as a son of Ku. When the reincarnated son was seven years old, however, an elder brother jokingly gave him a slap, so he retorted, "I am *your* elder brother. Why do you slap me?" Thereupon he gave a complete history, without any mistake, of his former seventeen years of life as a son of the family. (Willoughby-Meade, 1928, pp. 76–77; italics in original)

Past-life memories from India are referenced in the *Vishnu Purana*, of unknown but likely early date (Walker, 1888, p. 39); in the *Yoga Vasistha*, a Vedic commentary thought to have been composed between the eleventh and fourteenth centuries (O'Flaherty, 1980a, p. xxi); and in the sixteenth-century *Rámáyana* of Tulsi Das (Growse, 1937, p. 652).

Stevenson (1974b, 2001) drew attention to an Indian case examined by the Muslim Emperor Aurangzeb (1618–1707) at the end of the seventeenth century. This may be the first reincarnation case to be examined by independent observers, and its importance should not be underestimated. The translation presented below was made for Stevenson from an eighteenth-century Urdu book that took it from an earlier Persian text, *Khulusat-ut-Tawarikh*, by Munshi Subhan Rai. A copy of the Urdu and the translation are preserved along with related correspondence at the University of Virginia. Another translation of the same passage is given by Rawat and Rivas (2007, pp. 26–27).

> In the 40th year of the reign of the emperor [1699], there was a village headman named Rawat Subharam in Village Bhakar. He had an old enmity with another person, who after overpowering him, wounded him in the back and in the root of his ear. Due to these injuries Rawat (mentioned above) died. A few months later a son was born to his son-in-law named Ramdas. This boy had a mark at the back as well as the root of his ear. News spread that Rawat Sukharam, who had died after being injured, had reincarnated and was born again. And this boy, when he was able to communicate, said that he was Rawat Sukharam. He gave the correct address and other information which were verified and found correct.

When the emperor heard about this strange incident, he called the child to his court and personally satisfied himself about these facts. (Typescript on file at the University of Virginia, reproduced by permission of Jim B. Tucker)

The Japanese case of Katsugoro began to develop in 1823 and quickly became famous in Japan. Katsugoro and his family were interviewed by several different investigators, although as with the case probed by Aurangzeb, apparently none took the trouble to seek out the previous family (Bolitho, 2002). I have drawn my presentation of the case from its first English-language rendering, by Lafcadio Hearn (1897, pp. 267–90).

Katsugoro was eight when he asked his elder sister if she could remember her previous life. She said she could not, but she told their parents what Katsugoro had said and they questioned him about it in the presence of his grandmother. The following excerpts come from an interview with the grandmother, Tsuya (Katsugoro himself being too shy to speak to the investigator), but there are signed statements from others as well, lodged with the local Buddhist temple. The documents were copied by a collector of odd tales, from whom they passed to another collector, in whose possession they were when translated for Hearn.

After hesitation, Katsugorō said,—"I will tell you everything. I used to be the son of Kyūbei San of Hodokubo, and the name of my mother then was O-Shidzu-San. When I was five years old, Kyūbei San died; and there came in his place a man called Hanshirō San, who loved me very much. But in the following year, when I was six years old, I died of smallpox. In the third year after that I entered my mother's honorable womb, and was born again." (Hearn, 1897, p. 284)

Katsugoro told Tsuya that he had remembered more until he was four, but his memories had faded somewhat since then. His name had been Tozo, he said. He pleaded so insistently to be taken to Hodokubo to visit Kyubei's tomb and Tozo's former home that finally Tsuya took him there.

Tsuya went with Katsugorō to Hodokubo; and when they entered the village she pointed to the nearer dwellings, and asked the boy, "Which house is it?—is it this house or that one?" "No," answered Katsugorō, "it is further on—much further,"—and he hurried before her. Reaching a certain dwelling at last, he cried, "This is the house!"—and ran in, without waiting for his grandmother. Tsuya followed him in, and asked the people there what was the name of the owner of the house. "Hanshirō," one of them answered. She asked the name of Hanshirō's wife. "Shidzu," was the reply. Then she asked whether there had ever been a son named Tōzō born in that house. "Yes," was the answer; "but that boy died thirteen years ago, when he was six years old." (Hearn, 1897, pp. 284–85)

Tsuya confirmed that Tozo had died of smallpox. Katsugoro asked about some things that had changed since Tozo's death, which convinced Tozo's family that he was their son reborn. Tsuya and Katsugoro returned home, but Katsugoro was allowed to visit Tozo's family and Kyubei's grave on several subsequent occasions (Hearn, 1897, pp. 285–86).

The distinction between an investigated case and uninvestigated account is so important that I will acknowledge it formally. By *case* I mean a set of events that have been investigated or closely observed. An uninvestigated *account* is a story or anecdote about whose reliability we can say nothing. We can have greater confidence that events have been described accurately in cases, but accounts are not worthless. This is true especially of those recorded before 1960, which provide an opportunity to test the psychosocial theory's proposition that their reporting is shaped by the expectations of a culture's belief system by checking for patterns in narratives collected in far-flung places over a lengthy span of time.

Basic elements of the rebirth syndrome—young children with accurate memories of earlier lives, recognitions of articles owned by deceased persons, and birthmarks linked to scars on the bodies of those persons— appear again in a series of Burmese cases that Harold Fielding-Hall included in *The Soul of a People* (1898, pp. 335–53), published a year after Hearn's rendition of Katsugoro's case. Here is one of Fielding-Hall's cases. I summarized two others for the *Psi Encyclopedia* (Matlock, 2017, July).

> I met a little girl not long ago, a wee little maiden of about seven years old, and she told me about her former life when she was a man. Her name was Maung Mon, she said, and she used to work the dolls in a travelling marionette show. It was through her knowledge and partiality for marionettes that it was first suspected, her parents told me, whom she had been in her former life. She could even as a sucking-child manipulate the strings of a marionette-doll. But the actual discovery came when she was about four years old, and she recognized a certain marionette booth and dolls as her own. She knew all about them, knew the name of each doll, and even some of the words they used to say in the plays. "I was married four times," she told me. "Two wives died, one I divorced; one was living when I died and is living still. I loved her very much indeed. The one I divorced was a dreadful woman. See," pointing to a scar on her shoulder, "this was given me once in a quarrel. She took up a chopper and cut me like this. Then I divorced her. She had a dreadful temper."
>
> It was immensely quaint to hear the little thing discoursing like this. The mark was a birth-mark, and I was assured that it corresponded exactly with one that had been given to the man by his wife in just such a quarrel as the little girl described. (Fielding-Hall, 1898, pp. 348–49)

Physician and longtime resident in Syria John Wortabet (1860) related the following account he heard from the Syrian Druze. This was the first detailed account of the rebirth syndrome to be published in English and perhaps for that reason, was passed over by writers on reincarnation (e.g., Walker, 1888) until after other similar accounts had appeared.

> A child, five years old, in Djebel el A'ala, complained of the life of poverty which his parents led, and alleged that he had been a rich man of Damascus; that on his death he was born in another place, but had lived only six months; that he was born again among his present friends; and desired to be carried to that city [Damascus]. He was taken there by his relatives; and on the way astonished them by his correct knowledge of the names of the different places they passed. On reaching the city he led the way through various streets to a house which he said had been his own. He knocked, and called the woman of the house by her name; and on being admitted told her that he had been her husband, and asked about the welfare of their several children, relatives, and acquaintances whom he had left. The Druses of the place soon met to inquire into the truth of the matter. The boy gave them a full account of his past life among them, of the names of his acquaintances, the property which he had possessed, and the debts which he had left. All was found to be strictly true, except for a small sum which he said a certain weaver owed him. The man was called, and on the claim being mentioned to him, he acknowledged it, pleading his poverty for not having paid it to the children of the deceased. The child then asked the woman who had been his wife, whether she had found a sum of money which he had hid in the cellar; and on her replying in the negative, he went directly to the place, dug up the treasure, and counted it before them. The money was found to be of exactly the amount and kind of specie which he had specified. His wife and children, who had become considerably older than himself, then gave him some money, and he returned with his new friends to his mountain home. (Wortabet, 1860, pp. 308–9n)

The ability to find one's way around places and to recognize people from a past life are recurrent features of the rebirth syndrome. So too is locating valuables hidden in the previous life (Matlock, 2017, October-b). Wortabet said he heard of many other accounts of past-life memory from the Syrian Druze, but this is the only one he shared. A Lebanese Druze account from the same period was related by Colonel Charles Henry Churchill. Upon hearing sudden gunfire, a schoolboy stopped his ears with his fingers "and displayed symptoms of alarm." Asked why, he said he had been murdered in his previous life (Churchill, 1853, p. 171n).

Western psychical research inspired investigations of reincarnation claims in India beginning in the 1920s (Rawat & Rivas, 2007, pp. 29–31). A paper by R. B. S. Sunderlal (1924) reported four cases he investigated appeared in the French *Revue Métapsychique*. Records in the archives of the American Society for Psychical Research (ASPR) show that this article was originally submitted to the ASPR's *Journal,* but that the editors were skeptical of the cases because they were not familiar with others of their type and so rejected it for publication there (Matlock, 2011, p. 810n13).

K. K. N. Sahay (1927) investigated both sides of several cases and reported seven in a booklet published in India. Except for summaries of some of the cases by Francis Yeats-Brown (1936), Sahay's booklet went unnoticed until it was acquired some years later by Ian Stevenson. Stevenson and Satwant Pasricha (Pasricha & Stevenson, 1987) reinvestigated several of the cases, and Stevenson (1975a) published extensive reports of two of them. One of the less complicated concerns a boy named Sunder Lal, the youngest son of a compounder (mixer of medicines) recently retired from Kamalpur Hospital. Sahay quoted the boy's father as testifying:

> When this boy was 2 years and six months old and began to speak with ease, he began to resent being called Sunder Lal and wanted to be called Hanne Lal. The baby gave his name as Hanne Lal, resident of Fyazabad, Mohalla Katra Phuta. He gave his caste as Lala. He said he had two children and a wife. When he was asked how he came from Fyazabad he said that when his body was thrown into the Sarju river and his present mother was bathing he came along with her. The Railway station is very near the compounder's quarter at Kamalpur. This baby was often brought back by passersby who found him going towards the station. On being asked he said he wanted to take the train for reaching his home at Fyazabad. He remembered the story until he was four or five years old. (Sahay, 1927, p. 16)

Sunder Lal's father had done nothing to verify his son's memories, but Sahay's investigations revealed that there had indeed been a man named Hanne Lal who lived in Fyazabad. He had died of plague some fourteen or fifteen months before Sunder Lal's birth. Hanne Lal's wife, son, and daughter had left him during his illness. Not wanting to touch his corpse to cremate it, the people of Fyazabad had thrown it into the Sarju River, where Sunder Lal's mother happened to be bathing (Sahay, 1927, p. 18).

Another Indian case, the case of Shanti Devi Mathur, produced a stir in Western esoteric circles in the middle years of the twentieth century. Manly Palmer Hall (1946, pp. 147–54) devoted a chapter to it in his *Reincarnation: The Cycle of Necessity*. The case was studied most extensively by Swedish journalist Sture Lönnerstrand in the 1950s (Lönnerstrand, 1998). K. S. Rawat (Rawat & Rivas, 2005, 2007) was the last person to interview Shanti Devi.

Shanti Devi was born in Delhi in 1926. When she was about three years old, she began to talk about a life in Muttra, a town about eighty miles away from her home. She said her name had been Lugdi Devi and that she had been married to a cloth merchant, whose name she at first declined to give. Eventually she was persuaded to tell her school headmaster that it was Kedar Nath. She and Kedar Nath had lived on Chaubey Street in Muttra, she said. She had died ten days after giving birth to a son. The headmaster addressed a letter to Kedar Nath Chaubey in Muttra, giving details of the things Shanti Devi had said and inquiring whether they fit any known person. The response was in the affirmative. Kedar Nath Chaubey replied that all Shanti Devi had said was correct for his late wife Lugdi Devi. When members of the Chaubey family visited Shanti Devi in Delhi, she recognized them by name.

A government committee was appointed to witness Shanti Devi's first trip to Muttra in November 1935 (Gupta, Sharma, & Mathur, 1936). In that town, she showed the way to Lugdi Devi's home and recognized other people from her life. She knew her away around the Chaubey house and asked about money she (Lugdi Devi) had buried in a room there. A cavity was discovered beneath the floor in the spot she indicated, but it was empty. Later, Kedar Nath confessed that he had found and removed the money after Lugdi Devi's death (Lönnerstrand, 1998).

The first significant European reincarnation case is that of Alexandrina (Alessandrina, Alexandrine) Samonà, investigated and reported at length by Charles Lancelin (1922, pp. 312–63) following initial descriptions by the girl's father, a physician of Palermo, in Italian medical journals in 1911. Stevenson (2003, pp. 23–27) and Ralph Shirley (1936, pp. 43–52) provide the most comprehensive treatments of the case in English.

Alexandrina's elder sister Alessandrina died of meningitis on March 15, 1910, when she was five years old. Three days later, her mother Adèle dreamed that Alessandrina came to her and told her not to grieve, that she had not left her and would be returning as her child. Three days after that, Adèle had the same dream again. She knew nothing about reincarnation at the time, but a friend suggested that that is what the dreams portended, and gave her a book to read. Adèle had had an operation related to a miscarriage and doubted that she could become pregnant again. But the signs continued. One morning the family heard knocks on the door and opened it, thinking they had a visitor, but no one was there. After this, they tried to contact Alessandrina through mediumistic séances. At the first séance, a communicator identifying herself as Alessandrina said that she had made the knocks and again reassured the distraught Adèle that she would be returning to her. In a later séance, she said she would be back before Christmas of that year and that she would not be alone. In April Adèle realized that she was pregnant, in August her doctor confirmed that she was carrying twins, and in the afternoon of November 22, 1910, she gave birth (Lancelin, 1922, pp. 312–15).

Lancelin (1922) included photographs of the twins and of Alessandrina. The twins were strikingly different in appearance but one of them so closely resembled Alessandrina that she was given the same name. I will call the second Alessandrina Alexandrina, the Anglicized spelling by which she has become known in English. Alexandrina shared with Alessandrina several physical traits and medical problems—in particular, hyperemia (engorgement) of the left eye, seborrhea (inflammation) of the right ear, and a slight asymmetry of the face. (I have taken the translations of the medical terms from Stevenson, 2003, p. 25.)

As she grew older, Alexandrina behaved in many ways like Alessandrina. She would spend hours folding and smoothing clothes, placing them in good order on a chair or a chest, and preferred playing with other children rather than with toys. She was generally calm, although she had a phobia of loud noises and disliked cheese. In all these traits (and others) she resembled Alessandrina but differed from her twin sister, Maria-Pace. Alexandrina also was left-handed, like Alessandrina, but unlike Maria-Pace and other members of her family (Lancelin, 1922, pp. 325–28). The climax of the case came when the twins were about nine. Alexandrina's father described the event in a letter to Lancelin:

Two years ago [i.e., around 1920], we were talking about an upcoming excursion to Monreale. As you know, there is in Monreale the most splendid Norman church in the world. My wife said to the girls: "In Monreale, you'll see things you've never seen before." [Alexandrina] responded: "But mother, I know Monreale; I've already seen it." My wife told her that she had never been to Monreale. But the girl replied: "But yes! I have been there! Don't you remember that there is a big church, with a huge man with his arms outstretched, on the roof?" She gestured with her arms. "And don't you remember that we went with a woman who had horns and that we met little red priests?"

We were not aware of having spoken about Monreale with the girls; in any event, Maria-Pace was not acquainted with it. We admit that someone else in the family may have talked about the large church with the [statue of the] Savior above the main door; but we were unable to think of the woman with the horns or of the red priests. Then suddenly my wife recalled that the last time we had gone to Monreale, with little [Alessandrina] before her death, we had taken with us a woman of our acquaintance who had come from the provinces to consult with the doctors of Palermo regarding substantial protuberances on her forehead; and that, on leaving the church, we had encountered a group of young Greek Orthodox priests who wore blue robes decorated with red. We remembered furthermore that all of these details had made a great impression on little [Alessandrina]. (Lancelin, 1922, pp. 362–63; my translation)

We might wish to downplay this case were it the only one of its kind, yet it is far from unique, and there is the rub. Not only does it have many points in common with rebirth syndrome accounts and cases from other parts of the world, other Western cases were reported after it, at first mostly in French.

Albert de Rochas is well known for his pioneering exploration of hypnotic age regression to previous lives, but perhaps because *Les vies successives* (Rochas, 1911) has not been translated into English, it is not generally realized that the regressions comprise only a small portion of the book. Rochas provided a wide-ranging discussion that included a review of spontaneous cases of past-life memory from a variety of sources, including Fielding-Hall (1898). In 1924, Gabriel Delanne, a follower of Allan Kardec, released another general study of reincarnation. In addition to children's past-life memories, Delanne covered accounts of child prodigies, adult déjà vu experiences, and retrocognition, as well as announcements of reincarnation in mediumistic communications. Again, no doubt because his book has not been translated, it has had little impact on the English-speaking world.

Shirley (1936) produced the first well-rounded analysis of the evidence for reincarnation in English. He discussed the strengths and weaknesses of automatic writing, age regression under hypnosis, and involuntary memories, including many of those assembled by the French writers. Yeats-Brown (1936) summarized many of the same cases. The following year, Arthur Osborn (1937) treated reincarnation as an aspect of the human experience in *The Superphysical*. Osborn included descriptions of several British cases, gathered in response to his own surveys. These cases are less evidential than those presented by Shirley and Yeats-Brown, but they give a sense of the quotidian ground from which the better cases spring.

Manly Palmer Hall (1946) and George Brownell (1949) also drew attention to reincarnation accounts and cases in Great Britain and the United States during this period, but Anglo-American psychical research ignored them, as it had the earlier contributions. This may be because official Anglo-American Spiritualism, unlike the French Spiritism of Allan Kardec, had no place for the belief (Alvarado, 2003, pp. 83–84). That mediums on opposite sides of the Atlantic held such divergent views on what happened after death struck many (e.g., Sudre, 1930) as suspicious. Another possibility, suggested by D. Scott Rogo (1985, pp. 17–18), is that the SPR's lack of interest in reincarnation stemmed from its promotion by Theosophy and the SPR's dislike of Helena Blavatsky, whom they had investigated and determined to be a fraud (Hodgson, Netherclift, & Sidgwick, 1885).

An additional factor is that in the 1930s, concern with spontaneous cases and postmortem survival was on the decline as parapsychology shifted toward a preoccupation with the experimental detection of psi abilities, modeled on J. B. Rhine's work with card guessing and dice throwing at Duke University (Mauskopf & McVaugh, 1980). In the 1950s, reincarnation was brought to the public's attention through the past-life readings of Edgar Cayce (made famous by Gina Cerminara, 1950, 1957) and the age regression of Virginia Tighe, documented by Morey Bernstein (1956) in his best-selling *The Search for Bridey Murphy*. Parapsychology continued to look the other way, however, until 1960, when Ian Stevenson (1960a, 1960b) published his two-part paper, "The Evidence for Survival from Claimed Memories of Former Incarnations," in the *Journal of the American Society for Psychical Research*.

In the first part of this paper, Stevenson reported having found forty-four accounts (among them a few investigated cases) of people, mostly children, who had made verified claims of having lived before. They came from thirteen countries, including India (the cases of Sunderlal, Sahay, and others), Burma (Fielding-Hall's accounts), Italy (Alexandrina Samona), Belgium, Greece, Cuba, Mauritius, Japan (Katsugoro), Syria (Wortabet's Druze account), France, England, Canada, and the continental United States. Stevenson was not then familiar with the Chinese accounts of De Groot (1901) and Willoughby-Meade (1928).

Apart from one set of memories that arose in dreams and another under hypnosis, all came in the waking state. The subjects of the forty-four accounts were about equally divided between males and females. Of the twenty-five accounts in which age of the subject was given or could be deduced, twenty-two occurred to children under ten; in eight accounts, the subjects were three or younger. In thirty-eight accounts, the previous person was a member of the same sex as the subject; in six, the previous person was of the opposite sex. The families of the subject and the previous person were strangers in thirty-nine accounts; they were related in five (Stevenson, 1960a, pp. 62–63).

The subjects' memories differed in quantity and in character. Usually the name of the previous person was recalled, as was the place the previous person had lived. In several instances, when taken back to that place, the child showed the way around unassisted. In addition to recalling people and places, he might recall events in which the previous person had been involved. Especially notable was that the subjects recalled places and people as they were at the time the previous persons lived, not as they were at the time the memory was reported (Stevenson, 1960a, p. 64). In twenty-eight of the forty-four accounts, the subjects were not related to the previous persons and knew nothing about them, yet made six or more correct statements about their lives.

Stevenson (1960b) discussed ways that further research might be done on reincarnation. He considered hypnosis and psychoactive drugs to be promising research tools, although he believed that all past-life memories, no matter how they arose, deserved more careful scrutiny than they had received. He thought work with children was especially important, because it was easier to rule out the possibility that children had learned things about the previous lives by reading or hearing about them. He proposed looking at the use of languages apparently acquired in previous lives, the topic of a regression case he was to report a few years later (Stevenson, 1974c), but he does not appear to have anticipated the program of study for which he was to become known.

IAN STEVENSON'S FIELD RESEARCH
AND ITS CRITICS

Ian Stevenson was born in Montreal, Canada, in 1918. He graduated from McGill University with a medical degree in 1943, but for health reasons relocated to Phoenix, Arizona, for his residency and internships. His specialty at that time was internal medicine. He secured a fellowship in biochemistry but was repelled by killing rats in order to dissect their kidneys and decided to go into psychosomatic medicine instead. When this failed to develop as he had anticipated, he made another move, into psychiatry. Stevenson was critical of Freudian dogma concerning sexuality and the origins of personality in infancy, however, and probably in part because he was making a name for himself as an unconventional thinker, was hired by the University of Virginia as a tenured chairman of its Department of Psychiatry in 1957, before he had turned forty (E. W. Kelly, 2013; Stevenson, 1989).

Stevenson's mother owned books on a wide range of topics, including Theosophy, of which she was an adherent. Stevenson read many of these books as a child. Through them, he became acquainted with reincarnation, which he found congenial, but he regarded Theosophy as a religion—"a potted version of Buddhism," he called it (Stevenson, 1989)—and because he could not see a way of approaching reincarnation scientifically, took no interest in it when he was young. His childhood reading opened his mind to non-materialistic ways of thinking about the world and human nature, though, and as he continued his search for answers to questions about the roots of personality and individual difference, he was drawn to parapsychology. He joined the professional Parapsychological Association at its formation in 1957, the same year he went to the University of Virginia. He resumed his reading on "paranormal" topics, leading to his 1960 review of past-life memory accounts (Stevenson, 1989, 2006).

A grant from the Parapsychology Foundation made it possible for Stevenson to go to India and Ceylon (Sri Lanka) on his first tour of investigation in the summer of 1961. He went with leads to a few new reincarnation cases and learned about several more on his trip. Later, with the support of Chester Carlson, the multi-millionaire inventor of the Xerox process, he traveled to Lebanon, Brazil, and Alaska, and returned to India and Ceylon for further research (Stevenson, 2006). By the mid-1960s he was familiar with two hundred cases, of which he selected a representative sample for *Twenty Cases Suggestive of Reincarnation* (Stevenson, 1966b, 1974b).

His direct acquaintance with reincarnation cases convinced Stevenson that he had stumbled onto something of great importance and he redirected his energies accordingly. Carlson's continuing support made it possible for him to resign as chairman of the Department of Psychiatry and to set up a research division, the Division of Parapsychology (later the Division of Personality Studies, currently the Division of Perceptual Studies [DOPS]), within the department. Carlson provided funding for an endowed chair and upon his death in 1968 left the University of Virginia a $1,000,000 bequest in further-ance of parapsychological investigations there (Stevenson, 2006). Although Stevenson concentrated on reincarnation, he and his colleagues also studied trance mediumship, near-death experiences, and other phenomena, mostly but not exclusively bearing on the survival of personality after death.

Stevenson quickly extended his investigations to countries and cultures beyond those that contributed to *Twenty Cases*. These included European countries and the contiguous United States, as well as Burma, Thailand, Tur-key (the Alevi), and Nigeria (the Igbo). He examined a few cases in depth but collected basic data on many others in order to search for patterns across large groups of cases. Initially Stevenson focused on a subject's statements to the exclusion of other signs. He was slow to appreciate the significance of behaviors and physical traits but devoted increasing attention to these in publications after *Twenty Cases* (Stevenson, 2006).

Like Sahay, Stevenson modeled his research methods on those of the early SPR personnel, whose pioneering field studies emphasized interviews with firsthand witnesses to a phenomenon (such as an apparition) and the col-lection of supporting written documentation (Gurney, Myers, & Podmore, 1886; Sidgwick, Sidgwick, & Johnson, 1894). The SPR investigators were very concerned about malobservation and the fallibility of human memory. Ideally a subject described an experience in writing before it was confirmed, but this ideal was seldom realized. It was the same with the majority of Ste-venson's reincarnation cases. Usually the previous person had been identified and the child had met the previous family before Stevenson learned about the case and he had to establish what had already transpired. He did this by inter-viewing as many firsthand witnesses on both sides of the case as he could, allowing them to recount what they recalled without prompting, then going down a checklist of features common to the cases. He reinterviewed wit-nesses over a period of years to check for consistency and consulted medical, police, and court records when they were available. From the start, he col-laborated with persons native to, or intimately familiar with, the cultures in question. These collaborators acted as interpreters and collected information for him before and after he went into the field (Stevenson, 1974b, pp. 4–11).

* * *

Stevenson not only developed a new methodology for investigating reincarnation cases, he set a new standard for reporting them. Most of the accounts and cases he reviewed in his 1960 paper were brief summaries of events. In *Twenty Cases* and later volumes of what he came to call cases of the reincarnation type (1974b, 1975a, 1977a, 1980, 1983b, 1997a, 2003), Stevenson fully documented what he had done and how he reached his conclusions. Many of his reports ran to twenty or more pages. After summarizing a case, he listed his informants, gave a short biography of the previous person, discussed connections between the present and previous families, and considered the statements and behaviors of the case subject related to the previous life. There were tables of statements, behaviors, and other features, with indications of which witness had contributed which and if and how the item was verified as relating to the previous life. The reports concluded with observations on the subjects' development during the period he had him under observation. The care with which he handled his research and write-ups is one of the hallmarks of Stevenson's work and a major reason for the attention it has received.

At first, Stevenson labored alone with the small cadre of assistants he trained to help him in the field. Many were academic professionals like K. S. Rawat and Satwant Pasricha, who went on to investigate and publish cases of their own. Other early collaborators included Francis Story in Burma and Thailand, Jamuna Prasad in India, Godwin Samararatne in Sri Lanka, and Reşat Bayer in Turkey. Brazilian researcher Hernani Andrade worked independently using the same methods (Andrade, 1988, 2010a, 2010b). Then, in 1984, Stevenson met anthropologist Antonia Mills.

Mills was acquainted with the reincarnation beliefs and accounts of the Beaver Indians of British Columbia, but she had not studied cases before meeting Stevenson. He trained her and underwrote her further research with the Beaver, Gitxsan, and Wet'suwet'en, reported in 1988 (Mills, 1988a, 1988b). In 1987 and 1988 he sent her to India to see if she could "replicate" his findings by coming to similar conclusions regarding new cases similar to the ones he had reported (Mills, 1989), part of a larger project that included psychologists Erlendur Haraldsson and Jürgen Keil (Mills, Haraldsson, & Keil, 1994). Child psychiatrist Jim B. Tucker joined Stevenson's staff in 1999 and has come to specialize in Western cases (Tucker, 2013). Tucker has since succeeded Stevenson as head of DOPS.

Stevenson died in 2007, but Pasricha, Rawat, Mills, Haraldsson, Keil, and Tucker have continued the field research, Pasricha and Rawat in India; Mills in India and Canada; Haraldsson in Sri Lanka and Lebanon; Keil in Turkey, Thailand, and Burma; Tucker principally in the United States. Additional contributions have come from Dutch philosopher Titus Rivas, Japanese linguist Ohkado Masayuki, and others (notably Mary Rose Barrington, Kuldip Dhiman, Dieter Hassler, Tricia Robertson, and K. M. Wehrstein). I have been concerned mainly with armchair analysis (Matlock, 1989, 1990b, 2017; Matlock & Giesler-Petersen, 2016) but in recent years have begun to investigate cases also (Haraldsson & Matlock, 2016; Matlock, 2015). Rylann's is my most significant case to date.

In recent years, a fair number of reports and self-reports, mainly of Western cases, have appeared in publications for the general reader. These reports vary in quality but all contribute to the larger literature on the rebirth syndrome. I will consider them where appropriate, although they do not constitute my main source material. Fortunately, two of the most significant cases—those of James Leininger and Jenny Cockell—have been followed up by the research community. James Leininger recalled being a U.S. Navy fighter pilot downed near Iwo Jima during World War II. His case was solved and reported by his parents (Leininger & Leininger, with Gross, 2009), then investigated and documented by Jim Tucker (2013, 2016). Jenny Cockell (1994) wrote about her successful efforts to verify her memories of having been Mary Sutton, an Irish woman who died of an illness, leaving several young children behind. Mary Rose Barrington (2002) went back over Cockell's research and found it to be correctly reported.

Several cases have been published in popular books by lay researchers. Journalist Vicki Mackenzie (1988, 1996) described Western (Canadian and European) children with past-life memories who have been officially recognized as Tibetan masters reborn. The most significant work of this kind is that of Peter and Mary Harrison (P. Harrison & M. Harrison, 1991), who contributed twenty-six (mostly unsolved) British child cases. Although important in demonstrating that cases of this type occur in Great Britain, the latter collection is a good example of why we should prefer academic reports. Commendably, the Harrisons interviewed the children's parents (and sometimes researched the children's memories), but they do not give any indication of when the cases occurred or how long after the main events the interviews took place.

More commonly in popular writing, one finds uninvestigated accounts that are little better in quality than those that appeared before 1960. Carol Bowman (1997, 2001) described the past-life memories of her two children and presented accounts collected in response to media appeals in the United States. Many are quite interesting and it is a pity that Bowman chose not to do follow-up interviews, because interviews often bring out additional details and sometimes reveal weaknesses in seemingly strong cases that lead them to be set aside. Peter and Elizabeth Fenwick (Fenwick & Fenwick, 1999) recorded a lengthy series of adult memories (which tend to be less substantial than children's) from a British survey of past-life memories, but again, they neglected to follow them up for additional details or evaluation.

Involuntary memories involving historical figures are unusual in the academic literature, but some have been self-reported in books for the general reader. A. J. Stewart (Stewart, 1978) had a lifelong affection for Scotland and fragmentary memories of a sixteenth-century life there that she came to identify with Scottish King James IV. Jeffrey Keene (Keene, 2003) related how he became convinced that he was the reincarnation of Confederate general John B. Gordon. Neither of these cases has been vetted by the academic community, but I tentatively accept them as legitimate, barring revelations that would undermine them. Christian Haupt identified himself as Lou Gehrig, the major league baseball player of the 1920s and 1930s, and revealed himself to be what can only be described as a child prodigy in baseball (Byrd, 2017). Jim Tucker looked into this case, but was not convinced by the identification with Gehrig, however.

There is also Barbro Karlén, a Swedish woman who identifies herself as Anne Frank reborn. At ten, Karlén led her parents through Amsterdam to the Frank house, remarked that the front of the house had changed, and noticed that some photographs that had hung on the wall of the attic room in which the family had hidden were no longer there. Her apparent memories of death in a concentration camp persisted into adulthood (Karlén, 2000). Karlén's story should not be read uncritically. Her book is written as a novel. Some of her statements do not fit the historical facts (Rivas, 2001, p. 2), and she has at least five rivals in her claim to Frank's memories (Gershom, 1999). The only people who would be able to corroborate her childhood experiences, her parents, are now deceased.

Neuroscientist Norm Shealy believes he is the reincarnation of phrenologist John Elliotson (Semkiw, 2003, pp. 355–56). Dianne Seaman is convinced she lived before as Margaret Mitchell and authored *Gone with the Wind* (Semkiw, 2003, pp. 59–65). Unfortunately, these claims have never been investigated properly and are difficult to assess. They are described by Walter Semkiw in his book *Return of the Revolutionaries* (2003), which purports to show that prominent figures of American Revolutionary War days have returned to positions of leadership in the modern world. Semkiw's method is to look for facial resemblances in photographs, search for correspondences in handwriting and personal interest, then confirm his identifications through consultation with psychic Kevin Ryerson. He does not conduct interviews, and his subjects rarely give direct evidence of having lived before. Semkiw's research style contrasts sharply with Stevenson's, and I will give little attention to his work in this book.

Reincarnation challenges Western cultural and religious values and conflicts with the materialist paradigm of the West's psychological and biological sciences, so it should come as no surprise that method and procedure are the first things queried by those who find the possibility too outlandish to countenance. We know that reincarnation cannot occur, according to this way of thinking, so there must be something wrong with the evidence advanced for it, and that starts (and often ends) with the way cases are investigated.

Many critics who take this position identify themselves as "skeptics." These skeptics have been merciless in their attacks on Stevenson's methodology, although seldom do they demonstrate more than a superficial acquaintance with it. Michael Shermer (2018, p. 100) maintains that "one need not read deep in the literature" to see that the identification of a previous person in a reincarnation case is due to "*patternicity*—the tendency to find meaningful patterns in both meaningful and random noise" (his emphasis). However, it is clear that Shermer has concluded this precisely because he has not read deeply in the literature. A reincarnation interpretation of the cases is founded on the veridical nature of the memories, behaviors, and physical signs, but rather than confronting this veridicality, Shermer and other skeptics ignore it or try to explain it away.

Skeptical philosopher Leonard Angel (2015) charges that Stevenson and his colleagues "have not even attempted to show that there is anything that needs to be explained" in the cases they have studied. "One should try to determine whether the sorts of correspondences found between a living person's verbal memory claims and the facts about a purportedly reincarnated deceased person defy chance expectations. If they do, there is something that needs to be explained. But if they don't, then there is nothing to be explained" (Angel, 2015, pp. 575–76).

Angel (2015) would like to see "controlled experimental work" designed to rule out what he calls the "subjective illusion of significance." He (Angel, 2008, 2015) illustrates the concept of subjective illusion of significance by alleging to have found no fewer than twenty-one facts about Stevenson mentioned in his obituary in the *New York Times* (Fox, 2007) that are true for him as well as for Stevenson: Both were born in Montreal, both attended McGill, both were married twice, and so forth. Some of the correspondences are not as exact as Angel would have them, though. He says that both he and Stevenson have a sister and a brother, but Stevenson had a sister and two brothers (E. W. Kelly, 2013, p. 2). He says that both he and Stevenson have published four books, but Stevenson published fifteen books (E. W. Kelly, 2013, p. 391).

The "controlled experimental work" Angel (2008, 2015) has in mind would contrast results of the sort of comparison he made between Stevenson and himself (X cases) with the results of comparisons of a case subject's statements and facts about the deceased person identified as his predecessor (Y cases). One would have shown that there was something to be explained only if (a) blind judges rated the correspondences of X cases "at least as good as" the correspondences of Y cases and (b) the judges tended "to ask for special explanations of the correspondences" of Y cases more often than of X cases (Angel, 2015, p. 576).

Angel (2015, pp. 579–80) identifies sundry deficiencies in Stevenson's (1997a) *Reincarnation and Biology*, emphasizing his difficulties in negotiating this massive work. He had trouble locating a case report even on consulting the index, he says, because "there one finds thirty-three instances of the name of the case to look up" (Angel, 2015, p. 649). This is true, but most of those citations are to figures and tables, marked with the suffixes *f* and *t*. Only one entry, "300–323" (Stevenson, 1997a, vol. 2, p. 2217), is to a range of pages, and it should not have been hard for Angel to deduce that that was the citation to the case report.

A second "problem" is that "one finds strange gaps in the build-up of supposed evidence" (Angel, 2015, p. 579). For instance, Angel alleges, Chanai Choomalaiwong is listed in Table 15.1 (Stevenson, 1997a, vol. 1, pp. 1132–34) as having birthmarks that lie within five centimeters of the locations of wounds on the person whose life he recalled, yet the case report (Stevenson, 1997a, vol. 1, pp. 300–323) does not mention that the birthmarks are located within five centimeters of the wounds.

Actually, Stevenson's (1997a) Table 15.1 is a listing of cases with two or more birthmarks in the same places as wounds and does not include information on how close the correspondences are. Stevenson was trying to make the point that the likelihood of the correspondence between wounds and birthmarks being due to chance is much reduced when more than one birthmark is involved (1997a, vol. 1, p. 1131). His discussion about Chanai's birthmarks being within five centimeters of the corresponding wounds (1997a, vol. 1, p. 1135) is incidental to this point. Angel states that "no evidence is presented for either of those two 5 cm square area matches" (2015, p. 580), but this too is incorrect. Stevenson discussed the birthmarks in detail and said that one of them "approximately corresponds" to a wound to the previous person (Stevenson, 1997a, vol. 1, p. 319); he also (pp. 305–6) provided testimony about the location of the wounds. Angel's (2002) review of *Reincarnation and Biology* contains many misrepresentations of this sort.

A third "problem" with *Reincarnation and Biology*, according to Angel, is that "there are numerous little—but serious—errors throughout the book" (2015, p. 579). One is that Stevenson "incorrectly claims that he has done a satisfactory probability analysis" concerning the likelihood of a birthmark to correspond in location to a wound by dividing the human body into grids of ten centimeter squares (Stevenson, 1997a, vol. 1, p. 1135). Angel (2015, p. 580) would prefer that Stevenson had used the radial distance from a mark as a measure and asserts that by this standard a birthmark has a 1/26 rather than a 1/160 chance of being in the same place as a wound. Angel does not explain how he reaches this figure, and I will not pretend to understand. Regardless of what the true probability is, I cannot see that it matters as much as Angel thinks it does. There are hundreds of cases with striking correspondences between birthmarks and scars of one sort or another and the matches are not only of location but also of appearance (Stevenson, 1993, 1997a, 1997b). In many cases, there are multiple birthmarks matching multiple scars. The probability that all of these correspondences are due to chance seems to me vanishingly small.

Another example of a "little" but "serious" error is supposed to be Stevenson's use of "backwards reasoning" from birthmarks to wounds. Angel (2002) made this issue the centerpiece of his book review and returns to it in Angel (2015, p. 580), where he takes as an example the case of Tali Sowaid of Lebanon (Stevenson, 1997a, vol. 1, pp. 362–81). Tali recalled having been a man who was shot through the tongue, and when Stevenson examined Tali, he found hyperpigmented macules (small dark spots) that could have been birthmarks on either side of his jaw at approximately the locations the bullet had entered and exited the previous person's face. These marks were not noticed by Tali's parents at birth, and Stevenson discussed what might have produced them. He predicted their presence on the basis of his research, in which wounds very often have corresponding birthmarks, and concluded that this was the most likely explanation for Tali's spots (Stevenson, 1997a, vol. 1, pp. 379–80).

For Angel (2002, 2015), this is unacceptable procedure. He says, "What legitimated his backward reasoning? Not much, it seems" (2015, p. 580). How about the other 214 cases in the book? Do they not provide a basis for Stevenson's reasoning? Angel implies that the birthmarks helped to identify the previous person, whereas the identification was made first, thanks to Tali's memory claims and behaviors consistent with them. Stevenson predicted Tali's birthmarks from knowledge of the previous person's wounds, which were documented in a medical report (Stevenson, 1997a, vol. 1, p. 368). What he referred to as reasoning "backward from birthmarks to wounds" in two cases (one of which was Tali's) is not the prediction of wounds, but an attempt to explain why the larger of two birthmarks represented the bullet's entry rather than exit wound, contrary to what is usually seen. This can occur when a weapon is discharged at close range, which is plausible but not definite in the cases in question (Stevenson, 1997a, vol. 1, p. 932).

Angel (2015, pp. 580–82) next reprises his remarks on Stevenson's Lebanese Druze case of Imad Elawar, investigated in 1964 and reported in *Twenty Cases* (Stevenson, 1966b, 1974b). Angel first published his appraisal of this case in 1994 (Angel, 1994a, 1994b), when, as Julio Barros (2004) noted, it was already thirty years old. Angel (1994a, 1994b, 2015) is mainly concerned with arguing that Stevenson's identification of the previous person is uncertain. The case was not solved when Stevenson reached it, and Imad's parents, in an effort to make sense of what he was saying, had strung his statements together in a manner that turned out to be mistaken.

Angel (2015, p. 581) makes much of the fact that the statement, "His name was Bouhamzy and he lived in the village of Khriby" (Stevenson, 1974b, p. 286), omits Bouhamzy's first name, Ibrahim. The reason, however, is clear: Imad seems never to have mentioned the name Ibrahim. Because Imad's parents wrongly inferred Bouhamzy's given name from other names Imad gave, Angel regards Stevenson's presentation as "suspicious," suggesting "after-the-fact selection of information" (2015, p. 651). What should be a strength of the case—the written record made before verifications—becomes problematic for Angel, who believes that Stevenson is selecting which information to credit and which not.

In a careful reanalysis of Imad's early statements, Barros (2004) showed that they alone are sufficient to identify Ibrahim Bouhamzy as the person Imad remembered having been and supported Stevenson's interpretation of the case over Angel's. Barros was not uncritical of Stevenson's investigation and reporting but believed that allowance should be made for it being one of the first cases Stevenson investigated and the first he was able to solve himself. Angel (2015) cites Barros's (2004) paper without acknowledging his divergent opinions about the case.

When he wrote his analysis of the Imad Elawar case in 1994, Angel seemed unaware that Stevenson produced anything after *Twenty Cases* and falsely stated that Stevenson began his field research in the 1950s and concluded it in the 1970s. He thought that the first edition of Stevenson's monograph did not bear the title *Twenty Cases Suggestive of Reincarnation* (1994b, pp. 273–74). These errors would be inconsequential and not worth noting were it not that Angel seizes upon every deficiency he perceives in Stevenson's writings and that his criticisms have been held up as among the most incisive of skeptical commentaries on Stevenson (e.g., by Shermer, 2018, p. 101, and Evan Thompson, 2015, p. 290).

The first extended critique of Stevenson's work was made in a private report prepared for him by a research assistant, Champe Ransom, in 1972. D. Scott Rogo learned about this critique secondhand and exposed it in his book, *The Search for Yesterday* (Rogo, 1985). Rogo's remarks were picked up by skeptical philosopher Paul Edwards and used, along with a summary statement from Ransom, in his *Reincarnation: A Critical Examination* (P. Edwards, 1996). The "Ransom Report" since has become a staple of the skeptical response to Stevenson. It has never been published in full, but an abbreviated version has now appeared, and we can see more exactly what it involves.

Ransom (2015) summarizes thirteen of his original eighteen points, most of which concern not research methods, but the way the cases were reported in the first edition of *Twenty Cases*. For instance, "[O]ften the case reports are lacking in the details of when the statements (of a subject or witness) were made and in what context and to whom" (Ransom, 2015, p. 640). Other points turn on hypotheticals, for example, "Leading questions may have been used" (Ransom, 2015, p. 641). Ransom raises some serious concerns, including subtle distortions of memory over time, the need for interpreters in the majority of cases, and the practice of spending only brief periods with witnesses. However, these and many other potential pitfalls were acknowledged and addressed by Stevenson in the Introduction to *Twenty Cases* (1966b), so it cannot be said that he was unaware of them before they were brought to his attention. Furthermore, especially after the initial phase of his research, Stevenson employed trained colleagues as interpreters. These colleagues were coinvestigators (and frequently coauthors of journal papers) who investigated cases before Stevenson's arrival and after his departure. In addition, there might be written records of various kinds. The little time that Stevenson personally spent with his subjects was not the limit of his involvement in their cases.

Ransom (2015) adds that after he presented his critique to Stevenson, he asked to see the files on solved cases with written records made before verifications and was provided eleven of them. He found that seven were "seriously flawed in some respect" and that "the other four had the merits and weaknesses of the typical rebirth case and were not particularly impressive" (Ransom, 2015, p. 644). This, again, is hardly surprising or damning. Stevenson himself was the first to comment on the variable quality of the cases in his collection (1966b, p. 2).

The force of Ransom's critique is reduced further by its generality. It would have been more helpful had he cited places in the book where the deficiencies appeared. In this, Rogo's (1985) critique is superior. Drawing on four additional volumes of case reports Stevenson had published by 1983, Rogo centered his attention on four cases in which he had detected problems. The first of these was the Alevi case of Mounzer Haïdar (Stevenson, 1980). In investigating this case, Stevenson first sketched the location of a birthmark on the right side of the subject's abdomen. When he subsequently interviewed the previous person's mother, he asked her where the previous person had been shot, and she pointed to the right side of her abdomen. Stevenson then showed her his sketch and the woman said that the wound was in the place marked. This indicated to Rogo that Stevenson sometimes led his witnesses, because he did not ask the woman to sketch the place the bullet had entered her son's body before showing her his sketch (1985, p. 73).

Another case criticized by Rogo is the South Indian case of Mallika Aroumougam (Stevenson, 1974b). For Rogo (1985, p. 73) this case revealed that Stevenson "sometimes deletes important information when writing his reports" because he did not mention that the subject's father and grandfather had publicly refuted a reincarnation interpretation of the case or that he had used one informant (the previous person's brother-in-law) as an interpreter to interview another informant (the subject's father) without stating clearly that he had done so. Stevenson (1986b, p. 235) granted that the investigation and reporting could have been better handled but observed that inasmuch as neither Mallika's father nor grandfather were witness to any of her statements or behaviors relating to the previous life, their opinions were irrelevant in judging the facts of the case.

Rogo's other complaints are similarly insignificant (Matlock, 1990b, pp. 248–50), and he allowed (1985, p. 77) that they were all "very trivial." Another of Stevenson's early critics, Ian Wilson (1982), raised the question of whether Stevenson could have been fooled by his subjects and informants. He acknowledged that Stevenson was sensitive to this possibility, but considered that he had been too quick to dismiss dissident witnesses. Dissident witnesses appear in few of Stevenson's cases, however, and Wilson (1982, p. 23) was forced to admit that there were "considerable numbers of his cases where such an interpretation cannot be justified."

As inconsequential as they are, the criticisms of Rogo (1985) and Wilson (1982) are routinely referenced by skeptics (e.g., Augustine, 2015; Edwards, 1996). For a consideration of critical and skeptical commentary on Stevenson before 1990, see my review of reincarnation research published that year (Matlock, 1990b, pp. 238–55). For an overview of criticisms to date, see the introductory article on reincarnation I wrote for the *Psi Encyclopedia* (Matlock, 2018, August). As I remark in the latter piece, the skeptical charges against Stevenson fail not because they are altogether without foundation, but because they are exaggerated and overgeneralized and do not address the full scope of his methodology and research findings.

Some critics have suggested ways to improve reincarnation research methodology. Although potentially helpful, these suggestions, also, have tended to miss the mark. Vitor Visoni (2010) faulted Keil for interviewing the Alevi family of Kemal Atasoy only once (Keil & Tucker, 2005), but as Keil and Tucker (2010) noted in their reply to him, this was a private case, confined to Kemal's family, and the information Keil obtained from his single set of interviews was sufficient for him to solve the case. The reason for reinterviewing witnesses is to check on the reliability of memories, but that was not necessary in this case. Visoni (2010) also recommended videotaping all interviews in a given case. With the greater ease of video recording, it may well become part of research protocols. Mills (2003, 2004, 2006) employed videotape to good effect in India. However, recording interviews can have an adverse impact on informants not comfortable with the technology (Keil & Tucker, 2010), and in Islamic societies such as the Alevi, video cannot be used most of the time, because of the religious prohibition against representing the human image in art or capturing it on film.

Jonathan Edelmann and William Bernet (2007) outlined an elaborate research protocol, which for Evan Thompson (2015, p. 290) shows that it is "possible in principle to investigate claims of past-life memories using scientific methods." Edelmann and Bernet's project would proceed in four phases, employing three separate teams of field investigators. In the first phase, one team would interview the child with the past-life memories, getting him to make at least twenty specific statements about the previous life. In the second phase, a different team would interview the child's parents, collecting as much background information about the child as possible. In the third phase, a third team would collect data about the previous person and data about a second, unrelated (control) person, without knowing anything about what the child or his parents had said. In the fourth phase, the project director, who had not been involved in any of the interviews, would collate the data and see if the child's statements matched the previous person better than the control and write up the report.

Edelmann and Bernet (2007) suggested that verification of a child's statements be done by researchers other than the investigators who interviewed the child and his family and that the latter be blind to the findings of the former. However, given that it is on the basis of the child's statements that the previous person is identified, it is hard to understand how he could be located without knowledge of what the child has said. One may question also the requirement that all information come directly from the child, rather than from people who heard him speak about the previous life, and that at least twenty statements be compiled. Children never claim complete, unfettered access to their past-life memories, and it is unrealistic to expect them to be able and willing to share everything with strangers on demand. Moreover, many children are no longer talking about the previous lives when their cases are investigated.

Similarly impractical is the requirement that the third team collect data from and about the previous person and his environment without knowing anything about what the case subject has said. The team would need to collect a tremendous amount of information to have any chance of evaluating all of a subject's statements. A better idea would be to furnish the team with a list of items to be checked (including not just statements, but behaviors, physical marks, etc.) with decoy items mixed in with actual items, but not telling the team which were which. The same list could be assessed against a control child without past-life memories and the results compared. This could be done whether or not the case had been solved by the child's family before the investigation began. This simpler procedure would be easier to repeat in order to build up a sizeable sample of cases for statistical analysis, as Edelmann and Bernet (2007) would like to see. It might also be helpful to begin with a survey, as Pasricha (1993) did with near-death experiences in South India and Haraldsson (2012b) did with apparitions in Iceland.

INTERPRETATIVE FRAMES FOR
REINCARNATION CASES

A favorite tactic of skeptics unfamiliar or insufficiently familiar with the case data is to contrive a straw man conception of reincarnation to rough up (Almeder, 1997). This is what Paul Edwards (1996) did in *Reincarnation: A Critical Examination*, which Shermer (2018, p. 102) pronounced "still the best work on the topic." Edwards never explained what reincarnation meant to him, although his arguments appear to be aimed at Theosophy. He assumes that reincarnation entails human-to-human rebirth, astral bodies during the intermission, and retributive (rather than juridical) karma. He cites Helena Blavatsky, Annie Besant, and Irving Cooper repeatedly. Edwards claims to dispense with reincarnation, but all he has done is marshal arguments against the Theosophical version.

Shermer (2018) constructs his own straw man, or straw men, at which he flails. "If reincarnation is real," he says, "it means that souls in search of new bodies are migrating primarily in and around the Indian subcontinent" (2018, p. 98). A deeper familiarity with the literature would have benefited him here. Individuals native to the Indian subcontinent do tend to recall previous lives in that region, but Druze recall previous lives in the Middle East, Alevi recall previous lives in Turkey, and Americans recall previous lives in the United States. Shermer's "geography problem" is a nonproblem.

Shermer, like Edwards, assumes that karma and reincarnation go hand in glove. Despite variations in "details about what, exactly, reincarnates, when, where, and why," reincarnation for Shermer implies a cycle "that involves an ethical/justice component of karma . . . based on cumulative virtues and vices" (2018, p. 98). By associating reincarnation with karma, Shermer assumes that when he questions karma, he is questioning reincarnation, but as the many belief systems in which karma plays no role attest, there is no necessary linkage between reincarnation and karma.

Edwards (1996) and Shermer (2018) both evoke the Christian Church Father Tertullian, another critic who created a straw man depiction of rein-carnation to assail. In his polemic *De Anima* (*On the Soul*, chaps. 28–35),

Tertullian observed that although it is manifest that the dead are formed from the living, it does not follow therefrom that the living are formed from the dead. Tertullian appears to be speaking to Plato, who had Socrates make the opposite argument in the *Phaedo* (16) and the *Phaedrus* (77c). If the dead were reborn in the living, Tertullian continued, there should be a constant number of people on Earth, but then how is population growth to be explained? What about multiple births, such as of twins? Why do people die at different stages of life, yet always return as infants? If reincarnation were a fact, would not people retain their character from one life to the next? But in that case, why was Pythagoras so different from Euphorbus and the other men he was supposed to have been?

Tertullian's logic exposes his concept of an immutable personal soul and other presuppositions. Apparently he assumed that personality is static: A reincarnated person should be an exact replica of the deceased person of whom he is the continuation and there should be no personality change from one life to the next. Only if the soul is indivisible and immutable can one assume that character must be eternally unchanging. If one adopts the Buddhist notion of anattā (no-self), then personal identity does not persist after death, much less into the next life, which is something entirely new.

Tertullian evidently believed that reincarnation implies a fixed number of souls, each of which returns to a new body after a fixed interval. He seems to have been the first to raise the population growth objection to reincarnation, something that continues to excite skeptics (Edwards, 1996, pp. 226–33; Shermer, 2018, pp. 98–99). There are, however, several replies to it. If the length of the intermission is not fixed, simply shortening it would allow for population increase, even granting the same total number of souls in circulation (Bishai, 2000). Need the number of souls be fixed, though? Perhaps Vedanta is right that new souls spin off from the godhead as required, there could be something to the idea of preexistence without prior incarnation, the Lurian notion of a soul composed of multiple levels reincarnating independently could be valid, Theosophy could be correct that souls are promoted up the evolutionary line, or animism could have the answer and spirits may replicate at will.

Skeptics sometimes allege that reincarnation cases are fraudulently produced, although they do not back up their allegations with anything but surmise. Stevenson occasionally encountered cases of journalistic fraud. He first learned of many cases through news reports and had his assistants follow them up. In three instances in India, they were unable to do so, and Stevenson concluded that the stories were most likely fabricated by their authors (Stevenson, Pasricha, & Samararatne, 1988, p. 29). Another report not substantiated by inquiries in the field concerns a Druze boy on the Golan Heights who was said to have recognized his past-life murderer and shown where his body was buried (Haraldsson & Matlock, 2016, pp. 256–58). The most extravagant example is a story that appeared in *Fate* magazine in 1968 about an Israeli boy who claimed to remember having been King David of biblical times. The story was backed by several named authorities, none of whom existed; when the fraud was exposed, *Fate* printed a retraction and canceled pending contributions from the author (Stevenson, Pasricha, & Samararatne, 1988, pp. 26–29).

If accounts are not fraudulently produced, perhaps they are figments of the imaginations of people invested in the belief in reincarnation. So indeed they appear to be in some instances. Stevenson, Pasricha, and Samararatne (1988, pp. 3–7) described a Buddhist monk from Sri Lanka who believed that his cousin had been reborn in northern India, traveled there, and convinced himself on very slender evidence that he had found the appropriate child. The villagers played along, hoping for some advantage for themselves. In another Sri Lankan case described by Stevenson, Pasricha, and Samararatne (1988, pp. 7–10), a miserly and oppressive landowner was shot and killed by one of his employees. A few years later a child born into a poor family on one of his estates began to say that he had been this landowner but now recognized that his laborers were poorly paid and should be better compensated—or so the story went. Stevenson's team was unable to locate any such child and he came to think that if there had been a child who claimed past-life memories, they had been distorted and built up into a case that conformed to Buddhist expectations of karmic demotion and moral recompense.

Rivas (1991) recounted his efforts to confirm a Dutch man's self-identification with a child who perished aboard the *Titanic*. The man remembered a partial name that he had connected to a child on the passenger manifest, but upon investigation, none of his apparent memories matched either this child or the conditions on the ship. Rivas concluded that it was all a "complex fantasy," based in part on the man's childhood experiences in traveling from the Dutch East Indies (Indonesia) to the Netherlands aboard ship. Unwarranted conclusions were drawn also in the case of Carl Edon, an English boy who recalled being a Nazi pilot killed during an attack on Britain during World War II, when his plane crashed into the window of a building (P. Harrison & M. Harrison, 1991, pp. 41–46; Stevenson, 2003, pp. 67–74). Carl's family came to believe that they had identified the person Carl talked about, even though this man was the bombardier rather than the pilot, his name was not the one Carl gave, his plane was not of the type Carl specified, and it had struck a barrage balloon rather than a building (Haraldsson & Matlock, 2016, pp. 258–60).

Cases that cannot be ascribed to fraud or fantasy require a more sophisticated explanation. For many critics, it is obvious that parents must have shaped their children's memories and behaviors (Augustine, 2015; Edwards, 1996). Indeed, parental guidance has been demonstrated in a few cases. A Turkish Alevi man whose wife was pregnant dreamed that President John F. Kennedy came to him and said he wanted to be reborn in his family. This was in November 1965, two years to the month after Kennedy's assassination. Soon after the apparent announcing dream, a son was born and named Kenedi. Kenedi had a birthmark on his shoulder, which was thought to be where Kennedy was shot (in fact he was hit in the neck, not the shoulder). Kenedi was told that he was Kennedy's reincarnation and came to believe it, although as a young child he never spoke about Kennedy or gave other evidence of recalling Kennedy's life (Stevenson, Pasricha, & Samararatne, 1988, pp. 22–26).

In another case, an Indian child said that he had been murdered by Nathu Ram. This was interpreted by his parents as referring to Nathu Ram Godse, the assassin of Mahatma Gandhi, and on this basis the child was taken to be Mahatma Gandhi reborn. The identification seemed to be confirmed by a birthmark on his chest, close to where Gandhi had been shot. The boy grew up believing he had been Gandhi but did not begin to claim memories of his life until he was twelve or thirteen, around the time that a teacher caught him reading a book about Gandhi in his school library. An official Indian inquiry put no credence in the case (Stevenson, Pasricha, & Samararatne, 1988, pp. 10–15).

These examples of parental guidance involve very slight cases, with no childhood memories or impersonations of deceased individuals. They show how easy it is to over-interpret signs like announcing dreams and birthmarks. Social constructions can enter at later stages of a case as well, especially at the point at which a child's past-life identity is verified in a meeting with the previous person's family. In many societies, special emphasis is placed on the child's ability to recognize people, places, and things, and he is subjected to recognition tests. So strong is the expectation that children will prove their identities in this way, when they are unable to, the previous families may not accept them as reincarnations of deceased loved ones. Keil (2010b, p. 83) described an instructive Turkish (probably Alevi) case of this sort.

If not properly handled, recognition tests can produce ambiguous or misleading results that weaken or altogether vitiate their evidential value, even though they may be taken as certain proofs by the people involved. Mills (2003) demonstrated this in an analysis of a videotaped series of such tests. Although Sakte Lal, a thirty-month-old boy, made a few spontaneous recognitions on tape, more often he was either mistaken or led to the correct answer by onlookers. Despite the obvious coaching, he was judged to have passed the tests, and his past-life identity was confirmed. Mills commented on the emotional involvement of all concerned and said that Sakte Lal was consistently addressed as if he were the reincarnation of the previous person, reinforcing the identification.

A child may relate many memories about the previous life before meeting the previous family. Indeed, it is on the basis of what he has said that the previous family is tracked down. The psychosocial theory presumes that the child's statements, or some of them, are coincidentally matched to a deceased person. Statements inconsistent with the designated life are forgotten and permitted to drop out of the narrative, while new information learned about the previous person is brought in to flesh out the past-life identity. Sakte Lal mispronounced some crucial names when he first spoke them. He said he had been named Avari rather than Itwari, that Avari had been murdered by Vishnu rather than Kishnu, and that he was from Amalpur rather than Jamalpur (Mills, 2003, pp. 76–77). His mispronunciations might have been baby talk, but a less charitable view would be that the social construction of his case began with a reinterpretation of the names to make them fit a locally well-known event, as the murder was.

When veridical memories are involved, assumptions of parental guidance and other sorts of social construction become difficult to sustain. Marwan Dwairy (2006) adopted the psychosocial perspective in a study of reincarnation among the Israeli Druze. He forced his cases to fit his theoretical model, ignoring examples in his own report of children's unprompted veridical statements and recognitions. We must not approach these cases naively, but we do no service to science if we refuse to remove our own cultural blinders.

A case that has received considerable play in skeptical circles is that of Rakesh Gaur, investigated and reported by Satwant Pasricha and David Barker (Pasricha & Barker, 1981). Rakesh, who was five when he first started talking about the previous life, said several things that were incorrect for the person with whom he came to be identified. He wrongly named the section of town in which that person had lived, wrongly named his wife, and described his house as unbaked brick not served by electricity when in reality it was made of baked brick and was electrified. Major informants differed on whether Rakesh named the previous person or not. Barker believed that after Bithal Das was proposed as the best candidate, the adults involved adjusted Rakesh's statements to make them fit the life of Bithal Das. What before the identification was a lack of consensus about what Rakesh had said became uniformity after the identification had been made.

Barker's analysis has a flaw, however. As he acknowledged himself, it does not explain Rakesh's recognition of a bus driver from Bithal Das's hometown, Tonk (Pasricha & Barker, 1981, p. 398). Not only did Rakesh recognize this man, he convinced him that he was the reincarnation of Bithal Das and the man told Bithal Das's family about him before Rakesh and his father first went to Tonk in an attempt to find someone matching Rakesh's memories. Pasricha (Pasricha & Barker, 1981, pp. 400–401) noted other things Rakesh got right. Bithal Das had been a member of the carpenter caste, as Rakesh said he was, and he had died of electrocution, as Rakesh stated. Rakesh said he had hidden money in "his" house, which was true for Bithal Das. Bithal Das had owned two houses, the older of which was made of unbaked brick and lacked electricity, and both were used by his family during his life. Although the name Rakesh gave for his past-life wife was not that of Bithal Das's wife, it was the name of another woman Bithal Das had known.

When asked what he had been called "before," Rakesh gave a name by which he, Rakesh, had been called previously, evidently misunderstanding the question. He made a few outright mistakes, such as wrongly identifying the place Bithal Das died, but on the whole his early statements applied to Bithal Das much better than Barker allowed. Barker's interpretation of this case has nevertheless been picked up by skeptics (e.g., P. Edwards, 1996, pp. 263–64) who make no mention of Pasricha's counterarguments in her joint paper with Barker (Pasricha & Barker, 1981) or her later findings and opinions about the case (Pasricha, 1983). Even if Rakesh did not mention the name Bithal Das, his statements before he first went to Tonk would have been sufficient to associate him with Bithal Das (Pasricha, 1983). K. S. Rawat (1979) independently investigated this case and his conclusions agree with Pasricha's.

The cases of Sakte Lal and Rakesh Gaur demonstrate how messy the process of verifying a child's past-life memories can be and how easily social construction enters into that process. One reason Rakesh's case was difficult to solve was that his father misconstrued his statement that he had died of electrocution to mean that he had been an electrician in his previous life. Before going to Tonk he wrote to the Electricity Board there about an employee named Bithal Das but because the Electricity Board had never had an employee by that name, his inquiry led nowhere (Pasricha & Barker, 1981, p. 389).

A similar thing happened in the case of Imad Elawar (Stevenson, 1974b, pp. 274–320). Imad spoke about a beautiful woman named Jamileh and about an accident in which a man died after being run over by a truck. His parents thought he was saying he had been that man and that Jamileh had been his wife, but the totality of his statements pointed to the unmarried Ibrahim Bouhamzy, whose girlfriend had been named Jamileh and whose cousin and good friend had died following a truck accident such as that Imad described. In these two cases, parents not only did not impose the past-life identity that was ultimately determined to be the correct one, by their misinterpretations they actually impeded that identification.

It may seem that our only recourse is to accept reincarnation as the best interpretation of cases for which fraud, delusion, and social construction can be ruled out, but we are not there yet. L. E. Rhine (1966), C. T. K. Chari (1967), Stephen Braude (2003), Jürgen Keil (2010b), Michael Sudduth (2016), and others have suggested that children with past-life memories might have learned about the previous lives via psi. Stevenson (1974b, pp. 343–48) gave some attention to this possibility but pointed out that if this was the answer, it was odd that the children rarely exhibited ESP in other contexts (1974b, pp. 353–54), and moreover, that ESP alone could not account for the children's behavioral identifications with the previous persons (1974b, pp. 360–65). The behavioral identifications often are very striking. In addition to mannerisms, habits, and skills characteristic of the previous persons, children may employ familiar forms of address in speaking with people from the previous lives and may display appropriate emotional responses to those people.

This state of affairs brought Stevenson to consider ESP plus personation, the dramatic portrayal of another person, as appears in some cases of mediumship, but he drew attention to an essential difference between the latter and the reincarnation cases (1974b, pp. 361–65). Children who speak about previous lives identify with the people they claim to have been so fully that they use the first person in describing their memories, unlike in mediumistic personation.

Braude (2003, p. 24) contended that an extreme form of ESP he called "super-psi" (1979b, 1992) might be available to case subjects through altered states of consciousness, notwithstanding the fact that few children show outward signs of entering altered states in connection with their memories. Braude's concept of super-psi is an updating of the "super-ESP" introduced by Hornell Hart (1959) and elaborated by Alan Gauld (1961). Hart and Gauld employed the term to designate a hypothetical extreme form of ESP used by parapsychologically oriented skeptics to dispense with evidence for postmortem survival from apparitions and mediumistic communications, but Braude defended the concept on philosophical grounds.

It is important to appreciate the distinction between *psi* and *super-psi*. *Psi* may be defined as the transfer of information between two minds (telepathy), the acquisition of information from a physical source (clairvoyance), or direct impact on the material world (psychokinesis [PK]), in a single step by a single mind. The former two processes may be designated *psi (ESP)* and the third *psi (PK)* when it is necessary to differentiate between them. There is a great deal of evidence for these capabilities from spontaneous cases and laboratory experiments (J. C. Carpenter, 2012; H. J. Irwin & Watt, 2007; Radin, 2006, 2009). Super-psi is sometimes regarded as no more than an unusually extensive psi, the possibility of which cannot be ruled out (Braude, 1979b, 1992, 2003). Super-psi imagined as unrestrictedly extensive psi presents a challenge to the survival interpretation of many mental mediumship and apparition cases. However, the super-psi required to explain reincarnation cases would have to be not only unusually extensive, but unusually complex, well beyond capabilities for which there is independent evidence.

When applied to reincarnation cases, super-psi quickly becomes mired in what Braude (2003) called "crippling complexity," complications so dense and convoluted they defy all plausibility. Nonetheless, Braude (2003, p. 306) ended his book on survival and reincarnation with the conclusion that the evidence "at best . . . justifies the belief that some individuals survive for a limited time" in a discarnate state, apparently without reincarnating. Recently, Braude (2017, p. 157) has said that he "continues to stand tentatively on the side of the survivalist," but he does not explain whether this extends to the reincarnation material. Meanwhile, he has continued to produce works (Braude, 2009, 2013) defending a super-psi interpretation of survival phenomena, without drawing the distinction between an extensive and complex hypothetical ability.

Sudduth (2013, 2016) would like to do away with the term *super-psi* and subsume the concept under the heading of "living agent psi," but he is forced to acknowledge the need for a subcategory that covers unusually complex psi. He proposes to call this "robust living agent psi" (Sudduth, 2016, p. 282)—but why need we substitute an awkward new term for one with a long history in psychical research and parapsychology? I will continue to use the term *super-psi*, specifying that I mean a complex super-psi, not merely an extensive one. To be precise, super-psi, for me, is the acquisition of information in more than a single step, often requiring the integration of information from multiple sources, sometimes accompanied by psychokinetic actions on human bodies or on the material world in addition to the acquisition of information.

Ervin Laszlo (2007, 2009; Laszlo & Peake, 2014) has been promoting the idea that past-life memories are drawn (by psi or super-psi) from a sub-quantum store of information something like the Akashic Records of Theosophy. Another argument considers past-life memories to be based on archetypal images in a Jungian collective unconscious (Mishlove & Engen, 2007; Woolger, 1997). A third proposal comes from Rupert Sheldrake, who thinks his concept of morphic resonance (1982, 1988, 2009) might explain past-life memory without presuming that the rememberer is the reincarnation of the remembered (1988, p. 221). These concepts are more appropriate to past-life regressions under hypnosis and to the past-life readings of psychics than to veridical rebirth syndrome accounts and reincarnation cases. I will have more to say about them when I consider regressions and past-life readings in Chapter 6.

With his concept of retroprehensive inclusion, David Ray Griffin (1997) expanded on the usual understanding of super-psi in an attempt to explain behavioral signs in mediumship, apparition, and reincarnation cases.

Retroprehensive inclusion involves reaching back retrocognitively to the lives of deceased persons and incorporating their identities in one's own. Griffin (1997, pp. 197–207) considered that this construct had some utility in regard to apparitions and mediumistic communications, but when he brought it to bear on reincarnation cases, he found that although it fared better than other varieties of super-psi, it encountered formidable obstacles. Griffin rejected retroprehensive inclusion as unworkable and came down in favor of a reincarnation interpretation of the cases.

I am sometimes asked if genetic memory could account for the reincarnation case data. Recent work (Dias & Ressler, 2014; Klosin et al., 2017) has shown that environmental stresses on worms and mice can influence epigenetic factors not only of the individuals exposed to the stimuli, but of their offspring, influencing the behavior of subsequent generations. These findings suggest to some that genetic memory may be the explanation for what appears to be memory of previous lives, but when considered in relation to cases, it is clear that it cannot be. The sorts of memories that have been found to be transmitted genetically are behaviors that might assist a species to adapt to environmental change but do not include autobiographical memories. Moreover, even if it were possible to pass on autobiographical memories, genetic memory would not apply to cases in which there was no biological relationship between lives, nor could it account for memories of persons who died without leaving progeny or of events (such as deaths) that occurred after the last children were conceived.

Others wonder whether spirit possession might account for reincarnation cases. I do not mean demonic possession, as conceived by the Catholic Church, but temporary possession of the body by a spirit of the animistic sort (as proposed, e.g., by Tenhaeff, 1972, pp. 104–6). Possession could account for the behavioral as well as the informational aspects of reincarnation cases, but unless it were sporadic it would not explain the occasional upwelling of images many children (and adults) experience. Nor could possession account for birthmarks or other physical signs (Stevenson, 1974b, pp. 374–82).

In my interview with her, Cindy O'Bannion suggested another possibility in relation to Jennifer and Rylann. Although she appreciates the logic of reincarnation as an explanation for Rylann's experiences, Cindy wonders whether, rather than Jennifer's spirit being reincarnated in Rylann, Jennifer's memories and personality somehow became transferred to Rylann's spirit during the intermission. This would mean that their spirits were independent but also would require that Rylann's spirit came into existence in some unspecified way and preexisted Rylann's birth. Although we might not want to discard this possibility, it is more complicated than a mind that outlasts death and continues on until its affiliation with a new physical body.

Some parapsychologists have tried to dispose of the reincarnation case data without evoking super-psi. Several theorists have drawn on variations of Whately Carington's psychon theory for this purpose. Carington (1945) conceived of the mind as a network of images and sense data (psychons) held together by associative linkages that under certain circumstances interfaced with other sets of associative linkages. Carington was mainly concerned with explaining telepathy, but by allowing psychon systems to outlast the dissolution of the physical body, he thought he could explain apparitions, mediumistic communications, and other survival phenomena as well. Gardner Murphy (1973) applied Carington's model to Stevenson's reincarnation cases (for Stevenson's reply, see Stevenson, 1973a), after which John Hick (1976), W. G. Roll (1982), and D. Scott Rogo (1985) adopted similar positions.

Although they differ in detail, these proposals all follow Carington in assuming that at death the psyche collapses into its constituent parts and that a case subject is responsible for reeling in the psychons or equivalent particles related to the previous person (Matlock, 1990b, p. 253). I will take Roll (1982) as an example. In Roll's view, the personality fragments at death, there no longer being a physical body to hold it together. The fragments remain associated with places or people dear to the previous person, and a child coming into contact with one of these places or people retrieves information from the fragments through a psychometry-like process.

In support of this theory, Roll (1982, 1983) noted that in many reincarnation cases there are what Stevenson called psychic (psychological) or geographical factors, that is, there are either personal links between the people of the two lives or someone related to the child came near to where the previous person died. Roll analyzed the seven published cases with written records made before verifications that were available at the time he wrote and discovered that there were "personal or local connections" in four of the seven (Matlock, 1990b, p. 246). He called this a confirmation of his theory, but is it? The proportion of exceptional cases is hardly negligible and, moreover, geographical factors do not relate to the child, but to the child's parents or other relatives or friends. Any information gained through these links would not have come directly to the child, but rather would have been transmitted to him through a psychic conduit of some sort, a nice example of super-psi.

Jürgen Keil (2010b) made a proposal that deserves special consideration because it is informed by fieldwork. Keil granted that some of Stevenson's cases might best be interpreted as reincarnation but thought that was not true of those he had investigated. He proposed the existence of "thought bundles" that might be "emitted" during "the last phase of life" and "may then independently persist for periods of time and may occasionally be absorbed by a very young child who is not as yet encapsulated within his or her own personality"

(2010b, p. 96). Thought bundles would not include memories of an entire life, but only of its more prominent episodes, producing the fragmentary recollections characteristic of past-life memory.

Keil said that thought bundles "do not usually reflect any significant personality characteristics" (2010b, p. 91), yet many reincarnation case subjects display quite profound personality traits corresponding to the persons whose lives they recall. Moreover, Keil's concept cannot account for cases in which subjects are older when they begin to relate their memories or cases with apparent memories of the intermission between lives, which suggest a high level of psychological functioning at that time (Nahm & Hassler, 2011; for Keil's reply, see Keil, 2011).

Keil (2010b, p. 82) appealed to maternal impression to explain birthmarks and other congenital abnormalities connected to a previous person. Maternal impression is the influence of a mother's thoughts and feelings on her baby in utero, a possibility for which there is some evidence (Stevenson, 1992). However, unless the mother was acquainted with the previous person's circumstances, she would have had to have become aware of them through psi. And unless the fetus absorbed the thought bundle while in her womb, she would have had to have precognized that her child would eventually come into contact with it, taking us well into the realm of super-psi.

Braude's (2003, p. 181) super-psi explanation for birthmarks in reincarnation cases fares no better. After they see the birthmarks on a newborn, members of its family reach out via psi to find a deceased person with bodily features matching those marks, acquire information about that life, and pass it on psychically to the child, shaping his behaviors in the process. Alternatively, a member of the previous person's family psychically locates a child with the appropriate birthmarks, then transfers data about the previous person to him or her.

I have now considered all the major interpretive frames for rebirth syndrome accounts and reincarnation cases alternative to personal survival and reincarnation and found all wanting as explanations of at least the better cases. This places us in the uncomfortable position of having either to denigrate the investigators who have concluded that reincarnation is the best interpretation of the cases they have studied or to agree with them. Our Western culture has not prepared us for this quandary.

In the words of Eugene Brody (1979, p. 73), "the problem lies less in the quality of the data Stevenson adduces to support his point than in the body of knowledge and theory which must be abandoned or radically modified in order to accept it." The demonstration by Henry Stapp (2009) that personal survival is compatible with quantum theory and his statement (2015, p. 181) that reincarnation requires only minor revision of the mathematical formalisms of quantum mechanics suggest that quantum biology may have an easier time with the data than conventional biology does, but we are still in need of a sound theory. Where does memory reside, if not in the brain? How are memories, habitual behaviors, traumatic reactions, and physical traits conveyed from one life to another? What does it mean to be reincarnated, when we have different physical bodies, and therefore are different people, in different lives? In Chapter 4 I begin tackling these questions and developing theories of reincarnation and past-life memory, not through abstract theorizing, but in relation to the case material.

Chapter 4

Child Studies

The Principal Signs of Reincarnation

Having looked at beliefs in and about rebirth and examined research methods and interpretative frames for reincarnation cases, we are ready to take up research findings. Earlier, I stressed that more than individual signs taken in isolation, it is their co-occurrence in the rebirth syndrome that demands accounting from the psychosocial theory. Nonetheless, in studying the case material it will be helpful to consider the different classes of signs separately. In the present chapter I first discuss autobiographical memories of previous lives and the statements and recognitions that flow from them, then the behavioral aspects of the cases, and after that the physical aspects. These three classes cover the principal signs of reincarnation in the cases.

INVOLUNTARY MEMORY OF PREVIOUS LIVES

Henry Stapp (1999, 2005, 2009, 2011, 2015) has written extensively about consciousness in relation to quantum mechanics. His point of departure is the standard, or orthodox, version of quantum theory, which means that his position is more conservative than those that involve string theory, many worlds, implicate orders, and the like (Stapp, 2011). Essentially, Stapp follows the founders of quantum mechanics in holding that consciousness stands apart from the physical order and yet is required to make the physical order work properly. The founders reached this conclusion because the only way they could explain the outcomes of certain experiments was to imagine the experimenter's consciousness terminating random quantum processes (in technical terms, collapsing state vectors) at the appropriate times.

Taking my lead from Stapp (2009, 2015), and consistent with the propositions I introduced in Chapter 1, I suggest that consciousness is what survives bodily death and reincarnates. I consider *mind, psyche, spirit,* and *soul* to be roughly equivalent to *consciousness.* The differences in the meanings of these terms are less important than their common dimension, in my estimation, so that making distinctions between them would be more confusing than helpful in working out the problems before us. Moreover, like Myers (1903), I think of consciousness as duplex, consisting of a subconscious along with conscious awareness. I consider the subconscious to be the repository and source of all of our memories, dispositions, desires, drives, and so forth. As I see it, our subconscious gives rise to much of our motivation and creativity and helps to maintain our personalities over time.

Most children display no recognizable behavioral or physical signs of reincarnation, much less do they say that they remember having lived before. Even when they have imaged memories of previous lives, these may not be extensive. In the case of Alexandrina Samona (Lancelin, 1922; Stevenson, 2003), the deceased Alessandrina expressed her intention to return through announcing dreams, poltergeist raps, and mediumistic messages, yet Alexandrina spoke about only a single event, the excursion to Monreale. Her memory apparently was triggered by her mother's announcement of their upcoming excursion to that town and this suggests something very significant—that memory of past lives is in principle no different from memory of present lives. Just as the memory of past events in our present lives may be jogged by association with things we see and hear, so too are memories of previous lives.

Not infrequently, chance encounters with people or places connected to past lives trigger memories of those lives. The stimuli may be auditory or olfactory as well as visual. Rani Saxena recognized a man by his voice (Stevenson, 2001, pp. 188–89). Sujith Lakmal Jayaratne, who recalled having been an alcoholic, knew that a man had been drinking arrack, a distilled liquor, by his smell (Stevenson, 1977a, p. 171). Sometimes the trigger appears to be the contrast between the past and present lives, as when a child tells his mother that his "other mother" or his "wife" is prettier than she is or invidiously compares his family's economic circumstances with those of his previous life.

In many cases there are no apparent cues for the initial memories, but that does not mean that there was not some stimulus of which we are unaware. The stimuli may be very subtle. His father's taking him to an aircraft museum at twenty-two months likely was responsible for the early onset of James Leininger's memories of James Huston. James Leininger was born in April 1998 (Leininger & Leininger, with Gross, 2009, p. 8). He visited the museum in February 2000 (p. 19), and a month later made his first statement related to Huston, the identification of a "dwop tank" on a toy airplane (p. 16). In May, he began to have nightmares about being shot down (p. 3) and only after that did he start to talk about his memories of Huston's life and death. This timeline was confirmed by Tucker (2013, 2016).

At first, it seemed that Rylann's memories were prompted by the photograph of her in the ivory dress holding the large white flower, whereas the cue most likely was not the photograph itself, but the association of the photograph with the memory of Jennifer Schultz's view from the carport in Kenner, Louisiana, which Rylann conflated with the view she had of her yard in Bartlesville, Oklahoma, when the picture was taken. It took a year for memories of Jennifer's death to become clear enough in Rylann's mind for her to tell Cindy that she had died, but the incubation process seems to have begun during the photo shoot in Bartlesville, if not before.

Past-life memories are not always triggered in any obvious way, and younger children seem to be less in need of cues than older children are. An appreciable number of case subjects start talking about previous lives as soon as they begin to speak, which suggests that they had memories before they were able to articulate them. Cueing becomes more obvious as children age (Matlock, 1989).

When she was three years old, my daughter Cristina talked about having lived before. Her first comments came in response to a motorcycle she saw. We were driving and had stopped at a traffic light, the motorcycle ahead of us. Cristina asked, "Daddy, do you like to ride on *motos*?" *Moto* is short for *motocicleta*, the Spanish word for motorcycle. Cristina's mother is Peruvian, and we were raising her to be bilingual.

"No, I don't," I confessed. "They scare me."

"You have to hold on real tight," she said, earnestly.

"Honey, when did you ride on a motorcycle?" I asked. "Was it in Lima?" Cristina had gone with her mother to Peru every winter and we had not been together continuously.

"No," she said. "It was a long time ago. Before I came to you and Mommy."

The traffic started to move again and I had a left turn to make. I was thankful that we were almost to the mall that was our destination that day. I asked Cristina if she remembered anything else about the earlier life and she said that she recalled a pink house, which seemed to amuse her. "It was all pink. The outside was pink. The roof was pink. Everything was pink."

This left me even more stunned. I was acquainted with two pink houses. One was near my sister-in-law's home in Bethesda, Maryland, and we had driven by it frequently. The other was part of a small farmstead Cristina's mother and I had seen while driving up Interstate 81 on the way to the D.C.

area about a year before Cristina was conceived. The main house was pink, all the outbuildings were pink, and the wooden perimeter fence was pink as well. The oddity of this farm had made a great impression on us and we had talked about it for weeks. That this pink farm was the likelier candidate for the site of Cristina's memories became clear later, when she volunteered that the pink house was part of a farm.

Most children who speak about previous lives begin to do so between the ages of two and five years, although some may start as early as eighteen months. The median age at onset in Stevenson's case collection varies by culture, from about thirty-six months in Sri Lanka, Turkey, and Lebanon, to about forty-three months in his nontribal American cases (Stevenson, 2001, pp. 105–6). This is largely consistent with accounts collected before 1960, although the median age is lower in the more recent and better-documented cases. Of the twenty-five accounts in which the age of the subject was given or could be deduced in the pre-1960 series, twenty-two occurred to children under ten, and eight to children three years or younger (Stevenson, 1960a).

Cristina was at exactly the right age to begin expressing her memories, but although riding on the motorcycle was the first she talked about, it plainly was not her earliest. She was unable to tell me how long she had been thinking about the pink farm. I suspect she waited until she had made sense of that and other images in her mind before giving voice to them. At three, she might have realized that people do not normally talk about past lives, but she would not have known how unusual such memories are. No doubt they seemed entirely natural to her.

Cristina reached the conclusion that she was remembering a past life on her own, without any suggestion from her mother or me. I was not concerned with reincarnation during this period, and Cristina would never have heard me talk about it. Her mother is sure she never said anything about it around Cristina either, and we do not think she could have been exposed to the concept elsewhere in the United States or in Peru. She watched *Dora the Explorer* and *SpongeBob SquarePants* videos in preference to television programs. She evidently was guided by a sense of psychological continuity with the person whose life she recalled. She was entirely content in her present life, but she also felt that she had been another person before. For a few months after the motorcycle incident, she came to me from time to time to relate other memories, invariably prefacing her accounts with, "I want to tell you a story about myself."

Stevenson noted that children vary in the extent of their identification with the previous person and immersion in the previous life. Many children separate the two lives, signaling their distance from the past with such phrases as, "When I was big . . ." Others use the present tense, saying things like, "I have a wife and two sons," and seem to imagine the other life as running concurrently with their own. Children may demand to be called by the name of the previous person, even to the point of refusing to respond to their own name. They may weep as they relate scenes from the previous life or angrily denounce the people who brought it to an end. Some have trouble comprehending what has happened to them. Celal Kapan, a Turkish boy, was thoroughly confused to find himself in a child's body. He recalled having been a man who had fallen asleep in the hold of a ship while it was being loaded. A crane operator who did not know he was there had dropped a heavy oil drum on him, killing him instantly (Stevenson, 2001, pp. 106–8).

Most children talk about their memories in the waking state with no noticeable alteration of consciousness, as did Cristina, Rylann, and all but two of the forty-four subjects of the pre-1960 accounts. A few children become abstracted from their immediate surroundings and may even appear to be in a partial trance. Some talk to themselves about the previous life. Some speak about it more when they are about to fall asleep or soon after waking (Stevenson, 2001, p. 108). Mills (1994b) reported three cases of American and Canadian children whose memories surfaced in nightmares. Altered states, including dreams, are more strongly involved in the memories of older children and adults, and I will address this topic again when I consider developmental factors in past-life memory retrieval in Chapter 6.

Children's past-life memories are largely of people, places, or events of importance to the previous person—the type of autobiographical memory Endel Tulving (1972, 1985) called "episodic." They may be quite trivial. One of Cristina's memories was of drinking hot chocolate while she sat and watched snow fall, something she said she used to like to do. She came from playing to tell me this one day in May and I have no idea what could have elicited the memory. She had never seen snow in her present life and had never drunk hot chocolate.

The previous persons are of various ages and may be of the sex opposite to, or of a religious affiliation or ethnic background other than, the child. Some children have a lot to say about the previous life, whereas others say little or repeat the same few things over and over. Many speak about the previous life for years, but some say all or most of what they have to say in a short period of time. Cristina talked about the pink farm periodically for about six months, then stopped.

A few children recall events from long before the previous person's death. Lalitha Abeyawardena (Stevenson, 1977a) recalled an event from twenty-two years before and Sujith Lakmal Jayaratne (Stevenson, 1977a) an event from twenty-five years before the deaths of their respective previous persons. Long-term memories such as these likely had considerable emotional significance to the previous persons (Stevenson, 2001, p. 282n18) and may have been rehearsed over and over in their minds. They fit within what memory researchers call the "reminiscence bump" (Conway, 2005) related to the prime years of life.

In general, however, children's past-life memories predominantly concern the last year, month, and days of the previous life, demonstrating a recency effect common in memory of the present life. Nearly 75% of Stevenson's subjects described how the previous lives ended. They were especially likely to do so when death was violent (Stevenson, 2001, p. 110). One of Cristina's stories concerned "her" death, which may have been accidental. One evening she went out for a walk in the snow, she said. She could not recall exactly what happened, but, "I went to sleep, and when I woke up, I started walking. I walked and walked and walked and walked and walked and walked and walked, then I saw you and Mommy were looking for a baby, so I came to you."

Cristina said that she had been wearing a pink flowered shirt or blouse when she went out for her last walk and was convinced that she had brought it with her to her present life. She took me through our house and had me open locked closets and cabinets until she found some hand-me-downs that her mother had relegated to rags and placed under the bathroom sink. One of these had a pattern similar to the one she had described and she handled it uncertainly before deciding that this was the top she had brought with her. She then returned it carefully to the pile of discarded garments. On one later occasion she had me again unlock the cabinet so that she could see "her" shirt.

I have now recounted all of the memories Cristina related to me when she was three. Her case remains unsolved. Partly because I did not want to risk drawing out her memories further when she was young, we never tried to confirm them by visiting the farm her mother and I saw from the highway, and it may now be too late. The last time I drove that way the site had been converted into a KOA campground. Cristina's apparent memories could be fantasies, despite her conviction that they were real. This is true of unsolved cases in general (Cook, Pasricha, Samararatne, Maung, & Stevenson, 1983a), but the same cannot be said of the many solved cases on record, such as Rylann's, and the remarkable Indian case of Swarnlata Mishra (Stevenson, 1974b).

Swarnlata was between three and three and a half, traveling with her father, a school inspector, through Katni, a town unknown to her, when suddenly she asked their driver to turn down a street she said led to "her" house. The driver ignored her and kept going, but this event sparked Swarnlata's recollections and she subsequently said many things about the previous life. Two years later her family moved to another town, where she first performed unusual songs and dances she had had no opportunity to learn. After another five years, the family moved again. Swarnlata continued to talk about the previous life, mostly to her siblings, several of whom had their own past-life memories. Among other things, she said that her name had been Biya Pathak and that the Pathak house in Katni was white with black doors, that it was near railroad tracks and lime furnaces, and that there was a school behind it. She said Biya had been married and had two sons, whom she named.

Swarnlata was ten when she learned that a woman from Katni was visiting her town and asked to meet her. She recognized the woman as someone Biya had known, and through this woman Swarnlata's family confirmed some of the things she had been saying. Her father then wrote down others of her statements, including details of the house and its surroundings, and gave these notes to an Indian investigator. The investigator went to Katni and, solely with the help of Swarnlata's description, located the Pathak house. The Pathaks had had a daughter named Biya who had lived with her marital family in another town near Katni but had died of a heart attack at age forty in 1939, nine years before Swarnlata was born. Not long after the investigator's report, members of Biya's birth and marital families came to meet Swarnlata and she recognized several of them, despite attempts to mislead her. Shortly after this, she was taken to visit the two families in their homes. There she recognized other people and things and commented on changes made after Biya's death.

Most children's past-life memories are involuntary, often of the emotionally charged "flashbulb" type, brief yet durable memories of events (Brown & Kulik, 1982), but lack context. Children vary in their ability to answer questions concerning the lives they remember. Swarnlata's access to Biya's memories was unusually extensive. She recalled different places and groups of people, Biya's marital as well as natal families and friends. She made her many recognitions quickly and without prompting. She claimed also to have fragmentary memories of another life, which she placed between Biya's and her own. She assigned her songs and dances to this intermediate life, in a region that is now part of Bangladesh. Although the performances were authenticated and details of the geography she described were plausible, the previous person, Kamlesh, could not be traced. Assuming this intermediate life did occur, at death Kamlesh would have returned to the region in which she had lived as Biya. Perhaps being in the environs of Katni helped to stimulate Swarnlata's memories of Biya's life, even though it was not her most recent one.

Memory as normally experienced is a constructive activity that includes errors as a matter of course (Cohen & Conway, 2008; Hyman & Loftus, 1998). Most solved reincarnation cases are solved on the basis of information provided by the subjects, but their memories are not infallible.

Although children often talk about how they died, this is a topic about which they frequently make mistakes. Rakesh Gaur was wrong about where the previous person died (although not about the cause of death). Swarnlata said Biya died of throat disease, but although Biya had had trouble with her throat in her final months, it was her heart attack that was fatal (Stevenson, 1974b, p. 74). James Leininger said he died when his Corsair was shot down, but although James Huston had flown and tested Corsairs for the U.S. Navy, the plane in which he was killed was an FM–2 Wildcat (Leininger & Leininger, with Gross, 2009, pp. 198, 241).

Mistakes are common also with verbal past-life memories, such as names of people and places. Swarnlata said that the head of Biya's family was Hira Lal Pathak, fusing the names of Biya's father, Chhikori Lal Pathak, and her eldest brother, Hari Prasad Pathak, the head of the family when Biya died (Stevenson, 1974b, p. 72). Ryan Hammons said "Senator Five" rather than "Senator Ives" (Hammons, 2017; Tucker, 2013). Rylann said "Canada" instead of "Kenner." Many mistakes are in pronunciation, particularly when children are very young, and may be affected by developmental factors. Sakte Lal said Avari rather than Itwari, Vishnu rather than Kishnu, and Amalpur rather than Jamalpur (Mills, 2003, pp. 76–77). Sujith Lakmal Jayaratne at first said "Golokana" rather than "Gorakana" and "lollia" instead of "lorry" (Stevenson, 1977a, p. 268).

On average, 20 to 25% of children's memories about the previous life in solved cases are wrong in one way or another. This holds true whether or not the statements were recorded in writing before they were checked. In their comparison of Indian and Sri Lankan cases with and without written records made before verifications, Schouten and Stevenson (1998) found that 76.7% of statements in cases with written records and 78.4% of statements in cases without written records were correct for the previous person, even though significantly more statements were recorded per subject in written-record cases (25.5 vs. 18.5, $p < .01$).

Another type of error in past-life memory stems from a confusion of images in the case subject's mind. Imad Elawar (Stevenson, 1974b) seems to have partially merged the image of the truck accident that led to the death of Ibrahim Bouhamzy's cousin and friend with that of a bus accident in which Ibrahim himself was involved and Sujith Lakmal Jayaratne (Stevenson, 1977a), like Rakesh Gaur (Pasricha & Barker, 1981), confused memories of different houses. At first, Swarnlata did not distinguish her memories of Kamlesh and Biya. She gave her previous name as Kamlesh and only later (although before her memories were investigated and confirmed) placed Kamlesh in the intermediate life. Swarnlata's self-correction is not unlike Rylann's experience in separating the sight of her yard in Bartlesville from her mental image of Jennifer's view from the carport. Ryan Hammons, also, sometimes confused events from his past and present lives (Kean, 2017, pp. 75–76).

In their comparison of solved and unsolved cases in six countries, Emily Cook, Satwant Pasricha, Godwin Samararatne, Win Maung, and Stevenson (1983b) found that the proportion of solved cases varied from a high of 92% (thirty-five) of thirty-eight cases in Thailand to a low of 20% (sixteen) of seventy-nine nontribal cases in the United States. Sri Lanka had the second-lowest percentage of solved cases, 32% (thirty-seven of 117). The figures for the other three countries were: 80% (185) of 230 cases in Burma, 79% (ninety-nine) of 126 cases in Lebanon, and 77% (204) of 266 cases in India.

The failure of Sri Lankan children to state personal names and their tendency to get them wrong when they do state them may be related to the disinclination to use personal names among Sinhalese Buddhists (Stevenson, 1980, p. 9). If a person is not accustomed to using names, it should not be surprising that a child who has inherited his memories has trouble recalling them.

With unsolved cases, we cannot know the extent to which children's statements are true or false. Cristina's case is relatively undeveloped, but many unsolved cases are as rich as solved cases (Cook et al., 1983a). In a comparison of Indian and nontribal American cases, solved and unsolved combined, Stevenson (1983a) found that although the cases of both countries included a median number of fourteen statements about the previous life, the mean number of statements in the American cases was 23.3 and the mean number of statements in the Indian cases was 18.2. This difference was not significant, even though American cases were solved significantly less often than Indian ones ($p < .001$).

Structurally, also, unsolved cases closely resemble solved cases. Children began speaking of the previous life at about the same age and mentioned the manner of death (natural or violent) with high frequency in both groups, but they gave the previous person's name significantly less often ($p = .00001$) and described a violent death significantly more often ($p < .00001$) in unsolved cases than in solved ones (Cook et al., 1983b). This was true of American cases in particular. Indian subjects gave the name of the previous person in 169 (75%) of 225 cases, but American subjects mentioned the name in only twenty-seven (34%) of seventy-nine cases ($p < .001$) (Stevenson, 1983a). Because violent death is associated with a high rate of error and the failure to remember names contributes to the solvability of cases, these factors may be as or more critical than fantasy in explaining why many cases remain unsolved.

Children stopped speaking about their past-life memories earlier in unsolved cases, at seventy as opposed to ninety months (at six rather than seven and a half years) ($p < .00001$) in the data analyzed by Cook et al. (1983b), perhaps because they did not become as emotionally invested in their memories and did not have the social reinforcement that comes from having them verified. Past-life memories usually begin to fade by middle childhood, but often they do not disappear entirely (Haraldsson, 2008; Haraldsson & Abu-Izzeddin, 2012).

Mainstream memory researchers classify episodic memories as "declarative" or "explicit" because one is consciously aware of them. Other types of declarative memory are semantic memory, spatial memory, and recognition memory. Although episodic memories predominate in past-life memory, case subjects (particularly younger ones) demonstrate the other types of declarative memory too.

Semantic memory is memory for items of a general nature, such as facts about politics or geography, as opposed to personal events. Names and words are considered semantic if they do not have a personal connection. The majority of verbal memories in past-life memory are of personal names, which are episodic rather than semantic, but semantic memories are sometimes reported. Spatial memory is more common in reincarnation cases than is sematic memory. Many children are credited with finding their way to the previous person's house, as Katsugoro (Hearn, 1897) and Wortabet's (1860) Druze boy did. Rylann exhibited spatial memory when she found the way to the bathroom in Evelyn Pourciau's house unassisted.

Many case subjects demonstrate recognition memory. Wortabet's (1860) Druze boy and Swarnlata (Stevenson, 1974b) were said to have recognized many people from their previous lives. Such recognitions rarely are made under controlled conditions, and we may rightly wonder about social influences on them, as Mills (2003) showed had occurred with Sakte Lal. However, a Sri Lankan girl, Gnanatilleka Baddewithana, whose case Stevenson (1974a) documented in *Twenty Cases*, made several recognitions under the supervision of a researcher, H. H. S. Nissanka (2001), who was the first to investigate her case. Recognitions that are made spontaneously or that are accompanied by unsolicited additional information also deserve credit (Stevenson, 2001, pp. 113–14).

Children may fail to recognize people or places that have changed substantially since the previous person's death (Stevenson, 2001, pp. 277–78n8). Often they are more successful with photographs taken during the previous person's life. Ryan Hammons's recognition of his previous person in a photograph led to solving his case (Hammons, 2017; Tucker, 2013). The older children are, the harder time they have with recognitions. Rakesh Gaur recognized the bus driver when he was four, but at five failed to recognize other people or to find his way to Bithal Das's house in Tonk (Pasricha & Barker,

1981). Mills (2004) reports a case in which a boy who was not taken to meet the previous family until he was thirteen made no recognitions of either people or places, despite having made many veridical statements recorded in writing before verifications when he was younger.

The only type of declarative memory seemingly absent from past-life memory is what Conway (2005) termed *autobiographical knowledge*. Autobiographical knowledge supplies the "big picture" context for understanding episodic memories. Its lack is only partially compensated by what I call *autobiographical impression*, an intuitive awareness of events surrounding an episodic memory. Autobiographical impressions sometimes arise on their own, without relation to episodic memories, but they do not provide a schema for understanding memories within the flow of an entire life, as autobiographical knowledge does. The absence of autobiographical knowledge in past-life memory contributes substantially to the difficulty of identifying the persons case subjects believe themselves to have been and means that past-life memory should be regarded as a restricted form of autobiographical memory.

Materialist neuroscientists assume that memory traces are stored in the brain, although they have never been able to explain how this is accomplished (Braude, 2006; Gauld, 2007). Recently Takashi Kitamura et al. (2017) claimed to find evidence that long-term memories are consolidated in the neocortex, but this would not allow for learning by more primitive organisms. Tal Shomrat and Michael Levin (2013) trained planarian flatworms to find a food source then cut off their heads and allowed them to regenerate. The worms with regenerated heads were faster to the food than were worms that had not been trained. Shomrat and Levin interpreted this as indicating that memories migrated out of the old head into the trunk of the body then returned to the new head, but it may be that the memories were never in the head at all and that what was lost when the head was removed was the means of retrieving them. Even more suggestive is a study by Chris Reid et al. (2014) with slime mold, which lacks a brain and nervous system, yet is capable of learning.

It may be surprising to think of memory as registered in the subconscious part of the mind, but the idea has a good deal going for it. During near-death experiences, the brain is shut down or effectively off-line, yet memories may be formed then and retrieved later, after the experiencer has recovered (J. Long & P. Perry, 2010; van Lommel, 2010). Similarly, children's intermission memories (Matlock, 2017, May; P. Sharma & Tucker, 2004), some of which are veridical (Matlock & Giesler-Petersen, 2016), would be possible only if they were not encoded in and retrieved from neural structures. Other phenomena suggestive of postmortem survival, such as apparitions and mediumistic communications, likewise often imply memory formation, storage, and retrieval in a discarnate state.

I do not assume that memories are preserved in the subconscious exactly, like bits on a computer hard drive. Braude (2006) argued against trace theories of memory, by which he meant "mechanistic" processes of faithful reproduction. I agree with him about that, although I do not think we need conclude, as he did, that memories therefore are not stored anywhere at all (but, rather, perhaps, are retrocognitively recalled from our earlier mental states). It may be preferable to think of memories as imperfectly mirrored representations that are susceptible to psychological processes during their registration, storage, and retrieval in and from the subconscious (Cohen & Conway, 2008). This would account for memories' notoriously imprecise and flexible nature and for their emotional associations (compare Broughton, 2006a, 2006b, who sees a nexus between memory, emotion, and psi).

The psychosocial theory is hard-pressed to account for the features of past-life memory I have reviewed. Its usual strategy is to cherry-pick the data with which it wants to deal, ignoring the rest. This may be seen in the loud critical response to the James Leininger case. James's visit to the aircraft museum at twenty-two months is said to have allowed him to learn all the facts he later narrated (Skeptico, 2005), when his knowledge of Huston's life and death went well beyond what he could have picked up at the museum (see Leininger & Leininger, with Gross, 2009; Tucker, 2013, 2016).

I should acknowledge that the Skeptico (2005) blog was written in response to an episode of ABC's *Primetime Thursday* that first aired in 2004, before James's parents' book (Leininger & Leininger, with Gross, 2009) was written. However, the Skeptico post continues to be cited as an authority and later online critiques show no familiarity with either the book or Tucker's investigation of the case. Tucker called the aircraft museum and learned that the Corsair on display had been acquired only around 2003, as a replacement for one that had crashed at an airshow in 1999, six months before James's visit (2013, p. 69). There was no Corsair on display when James was at the museum, as skeptics (e.g., Shermer, 2018, p. 105) have assumed, so James's memories could not have been triggered by a Corsair he saw there, nor could that have been the reason that he said he died in a Corsair.

For Shermer (2018, p. 105), the timeline of events "strongly suggests a causal vector of childhood fantasy, not reincarnation." He reaches this conclusion because he thinks that James's statements and behaviors were influenced by his visit to the flight museum and watching a video about the Blue Angels his father bought for him there, shaped further by his parents' convictions about reincarnation that were suggested to them by his mother's mother and researcher Carol Bowman. Shermer does not acknowledge that James related many specific veridical memories of James Huston before Huston was identified as the person James was talking about; indeed, it is the specificity of his memories that allowed James's father to identify Huston as their referent (Tucker, 2013, 2016).

Psi (of the regular as well as the super variety) poses more of a theoretical challenge to reincarnation as an explanation of veridical past-life memory than does social construction, and I need to say something more about it. In Chapter 3, I noted that children with past-life memories rarely have been reported to have psi (regular psi) abilities, but Rylann and a few others have been.

Most of the subjects with talents in this direction have demonstrated them exclusively in relation to the previous person's family and friends. Swarnlata Mishra (Stevenson, 1974b, p. 90), Gnanatilleka Baddewithana (Stevenson, 1974b, pp. 142, 146–47), Shamlinie Prema (Stevenson, 1977a, pp. 38–40), Nirankar Bhatnagar (Stevenson, 1997a, vol. 1, pp. 243–44), Sunita Khandel-wal (Stevenson, 1997a, vol. 1, p. 486), Einar Jonsson (Stevenson, 2003, p. 132), and Reena Kulshreshtha (Mills, 1989, pp. 145–46) are like this. Marta Lorenz (Stevenson, 1974b, pp. 201–2) exhibited psi (ESP) both in connection with her previous life and her present life. Although psychic links to people from previous lives could be read as support for the idea that all the information about the previous lives that these subjects reported was gained via psi, because spontaneous psi often manifests between people who are on intimate terms (Feather, with Schmicker, 2005; L. E. Rhine, 1981; Stevenson, 1970b), such psychic links are consistent with genuine past-life memory.

A few children have been credited with ESP that was not directed toward the previous person's family and friends. Rylann is one example, Ryan Ham-mons another (Tucker, 2013, pp. 113–16). Rakesh Gaur (Pasricha & Barker, 1981, p. 406) exhibited ESP, but we are told nothing about it. Marta Lorenz (Stevenson, 1974b) may be the only case subject to have exhibited ESP directed toward people of the previous life as well as more generally, but the person whose life she recalled also had ESP abilities, so it looks as if Marta's talents could be a carry-over of a psychological trait. None of Jennifer Schultz's friends remembered Jennifer having psi experiences, so that seems unlikely in Rylann's case. We do not know if either Bithal Das, the previous person of Rakesh Gaur, or Marty Martin, the previous person of Ryan Ham-mons, demonstrated psi, but the issue is not of great importance, because it is hard to see how psi could account for subjects' declarative memories anyway.

Past-life memory bears more resemblance to present-life memory than it does to psi. Psi-interpretation advocates must explain why case subjects' psi is so closely focused on particular people and is expressed in the form of personal memories. Psi does not normally act that way. Psi casts its net more widely and percipients do not confuse its catch with memories. Spontaneous psi tends to look to the present and future rather than to the past (J. C. Carpenter, 2013; Feather, with Schmicker, 2005; L. E. Rhine, 1981). Credible instances of retrocognition have been reported (G. F. Ellwood, 1971; Murphy, 1967), but there are not many of them.

There is no reason that cueing should be so apparent, that there should be such a pronounced recency effect, that children should have an easier time recognizing people in old photographs than they do people or places that have changed substantially since the previous person's death, or notice and comment on changes since the previous person's death, if they were exercising psi. Further, the mistakes that case subjects make suggest memory more than psi: It is hard to understand why children should make more errors when deaths were violent if they were employing psi, nor would one expect to find unsolved cases, if psi were at play. Super-psi is of course another matter because it can be endowed with whatever qualities its proponents wish, but I find it strange that the super-psi required to account for cases of past-life memory would operate so very differently from regular psi.

BEHAVIORAL IDENTIFICATION
WITH THE PREVIOUS PERSON

Many super-psi enthusiasts presume that all they must explain is how the subject of a reincarnation case can gain knowledge of deceased persons and their environments. However, case subjects identify with deceased persons not only through their words, but also through their behaviors. Although he was slow to recognize the significance of this personation, Stevenson came to believe that it was more important as a sign of reincarnation than was veridical memory of people and events from previous lives (Stevenson, 2006).

I will defer my discussion of phobias and post-traumatic symptoms such as those Rylann displayed to my treatment of mental health issues in Chapter 5 and in the present chapter will concentrate on the reappearance of habitual behavior patterns, emotional bonds, and other personality traits. These may appear before a child starts speaking about the previous life, sometimes before he is able to put his memories into words. One of the most striking of Rylann's behaviors that in retrospect can be linked to Jennifer Schultz is pulling out the drawers of the bathroom vanity. She began to do this as soon as she was able to, but like Jennifer in Evelyn Pourciau's house, only looked at what was inside the drawers and never removed anything from them. Rylann went on to demonstrate many other patterns of behavior reminiscent of Jennifer, including asking to do chores, liking to make crafts, and engaging in sports. Any one of these might be coincidental by itself, but taken together they leave the impression of a deeper connection.

The Tlingit watch how infants behave for clues to their past identities. If a baby refuses its mother's breast, this suggests that it had been its mother's brother or another relative for whom suckling would be inappropriate (de Laguna, 1972). As they grow older, children may express their memories in their play. Stevenson (2000b) looked at unusual play in 278 cases of which he had published reports. He excluded cases in which play had a model in the children's families. Slightly less than a quarter (sixty-six or 23.7%) of the children in his sample had engaged in play for which he could find no model in their present lives. In each of the twenty-two solved cases in the sample, the play corresponded to the previous life. Most often it mimicked the previous person's vocation or avocation. A few subjects named their dolls or other playthings after their past-life children. Subjects who recalled having been members of the opposite sex engaged in play typical of the opposite sex. Sometimes, the play reenacted the previous person's death.

For older children, behavioral memories may extend beyond play to include a variety of deportments and demeanors. Sujith Lakmal Jayaratne (Stevenson, 1997a) was eight months old when his mother chanced to mention the word "lorry" (truck) in his presence. He quickly drank his milk, which she had been trying to get him to do. The word "lorry" had the same effect on later occasions and was the only way she could get him to drink his milk when he resisted doing so. Later, Sujith said that he had been killed when he was hit by a lorry while crossing a busy highway. It turned out that the person whose life he recalled, Sammy Fernando, had been a bootlegger of arrack and an alcoholic. On the day of his death, he had gone home roaring drunk and quarreled with his wife, who had taken off down the road, as she regularly did when he was in this state. He had started after her but had stopped in a shop for cigarettes. The accident had occurred when he emerged, still quite inebriated.

Sujith would ask for arrack and when given carbonated water would sit with his legs drawn up in the posture assumed by Sammy when drinking and afterward would belch, wipe his mouth, and wander about as if tipsy. He requested foods preferred by regular arrack drinkers. He offered "arrack" to Sammy's drinking partners when they visited him. Sammy Fernando had been a good singer and dancer and Sujith enjoyed these activities. He also had something of Sammy's temper and was quick to violence. On one occasion he pummeled his mother with his fists, explaining that that is how the police conduct interrogations. Sammy had had many run-ins with the law, and Sujith would hide whenever he saw policemen (Stevenson, 1977a).

The strongest behavioral signs appear when children begin to relate their memories early (as Sujith did) or when the previous person died in the prime of life (like Sammy), but some of the most pronounced occur when there is a difference of caste, religion, ethnicity, or sex between the previous person and the case subject (Matlock, 2017, October-a).

Although caste distinctions have largely disappeared in Indian cities, they persist in the villages, where many reincarnation cases develop. Swaran Lata (not to be confused with Swarnlata Mishra) was born into a high-caste Brahmin family but recalled the life of a Sweeper, an Untouchable (Chandala), the lowest class in the Indian social scheme. It is the job of Sweepers to sweep streets and clean public latrines and Swaran Lata enjoyed washing diapers and tidying up after her younger siblings. She was dirty in her personal hygiene, to the point that her hair became infested with lice and had to be cut short; she wanted to eat pork, surprising to her vegetarian family; and she resisted going to school, on the ground that Sweepers did not attend school (Pasricha & Stevenson, 1977). Stevenson (2000b, p. 564) described similar behaviors in another Sweeper born into a Brahmin family.

Swaran Lata's actions may be contrasted with those of Gopal Gupta, who claimed to be a Brahmin, although his family were Banias, members of the merchant caste. Gopal first spoke about the Brahmin life in an outburst when asked to remove a glass used by a guest in his home. Thereafter he frequently asserted the superiority he felt by refusing to do housework (for which he had servants, he said). He would not touch eating utensils used by anyone but his father and would not drink milk from a cup anyone else had used, his father included. He preferred foods favored by Brahmins to those eaten by his family (Stevenson, 1975a). Other intercaste cases with strong behavioral features include Jasbir Jat (Stevenson, 1974a) and Veer Singh (Stevenson, 1975a). For years both refused food not prepared in the Brahmin style.

Mills (1990, pp. 180–83) described the unusual behaviors of twenty-six Hindu or Sunni Muslim Indian children who recalled having belonged to the other religion in their previous lives. Some of the Hindu children asked their vegetarian parents to serve them meat. One asked for semia (a noodle dish eaten by Muslims in northern India) and eggs, others for Muslim food on Muslim holidays. Several engaged in namaz, the Muslim prayer in which the worshiper kneels and bows facing Mecca. One boy performed namaz before he could speak. A girl of about thirty months said namaz for her sick father and for some time thereafter performed the ritual at 5:00 a.m. and 9:00 p.m. each day. Conversely, Muslim children who recalled lives as Hindus refused to eat beef and fish. They resisted Muslim religious practices and wished to enact Hindu rites. Other interreligious cases with strong behavioral features include Pushpa and Ram Prakash (Pasricha & Stevenson, 1977), Gamani Jaysena and Wijanama Kithsiri (Stevenson, 1977a), and Sandika Tharanga (Haraldsson & Samararatne, 1999). Yonassan Gershom (1992) heard from numerous American Gentiles who had episodic memories or behaviors consistent with European Jews killed during the Holocaust, although all these accounts were unsolved.

Bongkuch Promsin, a Thai boy, remembered the life of a Laotian youth who was murdered at eighteen (Stevenson, 1983b). As a young child, Bongkuch was given to "attacks of adulthood." He said he had been born in 1936, the year of the previous person's birth, and gave his age as eighteen. He asked to be shaved following a haircut, brushed his teeth like an adult (children of his family did not regularly brush their teeth), insisted on wearing a loincloth while bathing at the village well (as did adults), and sat with adults rather than playing with other children. He was sexually aggressive toward adolescent girls, whose breasts he tried to fondle. One female houseguest left abruptly after he visited her during the night. Bongkuch also displayed Laotian behavioral traits that were out of place in his family. He washed his hands by immersion in a bowl rather than running water over them and ate with his hands rather than with a spoon. He craved Laotian foods and disliked dishes served by his mother. When asked to account for himself, he said, "I am not Thai. I am Laotian."

Ma Tin Aung Myo was one of several Burmese children who claimed to have been Japanese soldiers killed in Burma during World War II (Stevenson & Keil, 2005). Hers is a sex-change as well as interethnic case, but unlike the cases of Sujith Lakmal Jayaratne and Bongkuch Promsin, it is unsolved. Ma Tin Aung Myo had a phobia of airplanes, fearing that she would be shot by them. On cloudy days she would become depressed and cry, saying that she was pining for Japan. She disliked the hot climate of Burma and its spicy food but fancied sweet foods and fish, especially semi-raw fish, which the Burmese do not eat (Stevenson, 1977b, 1983b).

Ma Tin Aung Myo also displayed a pronounced gender dysphoria. She played with boys rather than with girls, and particularly enjoyed playing at being a soldier. She refused to wear girls' clothes and when her school insisted that she dress as a girl, she dropped out. Although she modified some of her behavior in her later teens and came to accept life in Burma, she never adjusted to her gender role and in her twenties began to live openly with another woman (Stevenson, 1977b, 1983b). Although common in sex-change cases, gender nonconformity does not appear in cases in which the previous person was of the same sex as the subject (Pehlivanova, Janke, Lee, & Tucker, 2018).

Stevenson (1983b) called Ma Tin Aung Myo's an "international case," but he used the same term for cases in which the previous person died in a country other than that where the subject was born (Stevenson, 1997a, vol. 1, p. 188). I prefer to limit *international case* to the latter sense and to use *interethnic case* when the previous person and the subject are of different ethnicities, regardless of whether or not the past life death occurred in the case subject's native country. In my terminology, James Leininger's case is international but not interethnic and Ma Tin Aung Myo's case is interethnic but not international.

Among the most interesting interethnic cases are those of Asian children, such as Ma Win Myint and B. B. Saxena, who recall being Englishmen or

Americans (Stevenson, 1997a, vol. 2). B. B. Saxena gave his name as Arthur and said he had died during a war that was taken to be World War I. He liked to play European games such as leapfrog and hopscotch and to eat with a fork, knife, and spoon. He wanted to wear shirts, shorts, and shoes, and he complained about the hot weather in India. He liked to play at being a soldier and would march around giving the commands "Left, right" and "March" in English, a language not spoken by his family. He would pretend that a stick was a gun and asked to be given a gun. His case was never solved, although a British man resident in India was convinced that he was the reincarnation of his brother, who had been killed in World War I, and tried to adopt him (Stevenson, 1997a, vol. 2, pp. 1768, 1770–72). If Arthur died in Europe, as represented in B. B. Saxena's memories, this case would be both international and interethnic.

As the behavioral correspondences between the child subjects and the persons they claim to have been pile up, it becomes harder and harder to understand how social construction, with or without psi, could account for them. The difficulty is especially great when it comes to skillful behavior. Skills are perfected through repetition and cannot be acquired merely through observation or the amassing of information. If skills cannot be attained through learning alone, but require practice to make perfect, there is little reason to think that they could be mastered through psi.

Paulo Lorenz, a Brazilian boy who claimed to be his deceased sister reborn, spontaneously demonstrated how to thread and use her sewing machine when he was less than four years old (Stevenson, 1974a). Other children who exhibited unlearned skills possessed by the persons whose lives they recalled include Corliss Chotkin, Jr. (Stevenson, 1974a), who had a way with boat engines, and Bishen Chand Kapoor (Stevenson, 1975a), who could play tabla drums. A young girl in a Finnish case described by Karl Müller (Muller, 1970, pp. 68–70) performed the Charleston, a dance unfamiliar to her but known to the child she remembered having been. Swarnlata Mishra's (Stevenson, 1974a) Bengali dances provide a probable additional example, although they belong to her unsolved intermediate life.

Unlearned skills of this order shade, almost imperceptibly, into those of child prodigies. Tucker (2013, pp. 130–35) contributed the case of a boy who from age two showed a particular interest in and talent for golf and later identified himself with 1920s golfing great Bobby Jones. The boy recognized Jones and some of his friends in photographs, although he did not otherwise have much to say about his life. Another example is Christian Haupt, who identified himself as Lou Gehrig reborn and excelled at baseball from an early age (Byrd, 2017). There are also a few examples of artistic skills in painting or writing apparently carrying over, but these behavioral prodigies are different from mental prodigies, such as math prodigies. The latter display a different sort of talent, which may have a different basis. To date no prodigies in math or other purely cognitive skills have been reported to have past-life memories.

Language is an especially important type of skill that involves not only accumulating vocabulary and mastering grammatical rules but developing the mechanics of speech production. It is speech production that results in varying accents across regions where the same language is spoken. There is also a social dimension to language; speakers of any given language often may employ different registers in different contexts.

Stevenson (1974c) assigned the name *xenoglossy* (an anglicization of *xénoglossie*, coined by Charles Richet, 1905–1907) to the use of language not acquired by normal means. Richet (1905–1907) gave examples of xenoglossy in automatic writing. Xenoglossy has been reported in spoken mediumship also (Stevenson, 1974c). Although some instances of purported xenoglossy have been traced to cryptomnesia (source amnesia) or have turned out to be artificial languages invented by the speakers, not all can be dispensed with so easily (Stevenson, 1974c).

Stevenson (1974c) distinguished between *recitative xenoglossy* and *responsive xenoglossy*. Recitative xenoglossy is the use of unlearned language in a rote, uncomprehending fashion. Responsive xenoglossy is the ability to understand and converse intelligibly in an unlearned language. Spontaneous cases of past-life memory supply examples of both recitative and responsive xenoglossy. In addition, spontaneous cases furnish examples of a variety of unconscious influences on speech production that I have termed *passive xenoglossy* (Haraldsson & Matlock, 2016, pp. 239–40).

Stevenson documented what he believed to be Swedish responsive xenoglossy (1974c) and German responsive xenoglossy (1984) in regressions under hypnosis. I treat these cases in Chapter 6, when I take up the regression material. Xenoglossy in involuntary past-life memory has received less attention than that appearing in regressions, although in many ways it is more interesting and arguably is more important (Matlock, 2017, August).

Swarnlata's Bengali songs are an example of recitative xenoglossy. Swarnlata did not understand the words she sang. She repeated them by rote and could not sing them except when she performed the dances with which they were associated. However, she pronounced them well enough for them to be written down by a native Bengali speaker and identified as the lyrics of Bengali folk tunes (Stevenson, 1974b, pp. 82–86). B. B. Saxena's "Left, right" and "March" were likely recitative also, inasmuch as there is no evidence that he had a broader command of English. Other children who have used recitative xenoglossy are Sri Lankan boys who recalled lives as Buddhist monks and chanted stanzas in Pali, the otherwise-extinct Buddhist ritual language (Haraldsson & Samararatne, 1999).

Subjects of interethnic cases often speak at least a few words in a language unfamiliar to their parents. This speech appears to be more than recitative but it is unclear to what extent it is responsive. Murvet Dissiz, an Alevi girl who recalled a previous life in Istanbul (Durant, 1968, pp. 74–79), and Mehmet Arikdal, an Alevi boy who said he had lived in Adana (Keil, 1991, p. 48), first spoke Turkish rather than Arabic, the language of their families. Andrade (1988; summarized by Playfair, 2006) reported Brazilian cases with German and Italian xenoglossy, both unsolved international cases with alleged previous persons who died in Europe during World War II. Gustavo's first words were German, and as he grew older he showed an unusual affinity for Germany, such as cheering its soccer team during matches (Playfair, 2006, pp. 68–69). Simone spoke Italian with some fluency and might have spoken it responsively had there been an Italian speaker around to converse with her (Playfair, 2006, pp. 59–60).

Bongkuch Promsin referred to certain fruits and vegetables with words his mother did not use but came to find out were Laotian. Bongkuch spoke Laotian with the previous person's family and friends, although his ability to converse was never tested formally and may have been limited (Stevenson, 1983b, pp. 129–31). Subashini Gunasekera (Stevenson & Samararatne, 1988) employed words and phrases that were not used by her family, but were appropriate to the girl whose life she recalled, including calling her father by the same term that that girl had used in addressing her own father. Kumkum Verma (Stevenson, 1975a) likewise used dialectical expressions appropriate to the previous person of her case.

Ma Tin Aung Myo and other Burmese children who remembered lives as Japanese soldiers spoke a strange language, presumably Japanese, when they were young, but because there were no Japanese speakers remaining in their area when they grew up, there was no one there to identify it (Stevenson & Keil, 2005). The same children were slow to learn Burmese, a phenomenon Stevenson (2001, p. 127) dubbed *glossophobia*. Nawal Daw, a Lebanese Druze girl with glossophobia, refused to speak Arabic until she was five and instead chattered away in a language incomprehensible to her parents. Nawal had an affinity for Indian culture and once when she saw some Sikh tourists she ran to them and appeared to her parents to carry on a conversation with them in their language (Stevenson, 1974c, p. 17). Brownell (1949, pp. 44–47) described another example of glossophobia.

Glossophobia is a type of passive xenoglossy. There are several other types. Cross-sex behavior may be expressed in the manner of speaking, the latter especially noticeable in languages that mark gender (Stevenson, 2001, pp. 120, 188–89). Children whose previous persons hail from different parts of the same linguistic sphere may speak with the appropriate regional accents. Keil (2010a) described an Alevi girl who at three years spoke both Turkish and Arabic with accents different from her family, but appropriate to the teenager she recalled having been. Pasricha (2001b, p. 45) described an Indian boy who spoke with an accent different from others in his family (including his twin brother) but like that of the previous person's family. Bongkuch spoke Thai with a Laotian accent (Stevenson, 1983b, pp. 129–30).

Some children, like Ashok Kumar Shakya, start to speak their native languages unusually early. Ashok Kumar's mother noted that he at first spoke clearly in an adult fashion, then at five years began talking falteringly in the manner of a child his age (Mills, 1989, p. 148). Imad Elawar had no trouble learning French, which his previous person had spoken (Stevenson, 1974b, p. 305). Stephen Stein read a Spanish place name from a map when a toddler and as an adult corrected his mother's pronunciation, although he never learned the language formally (Haraldsson & Matlock, 2016, pp. 242–43). Bishen Chand Kapoor, who recalled the life of a person fluent in Urdu, was said to have been able to read that language before he was taught it (Stevenson, 1975a, p. 199). Anagarika Govinda (1966, pp. 131–36) recounted meeting a four-year-old Burmese boy who remembered being a Buddhist monk and was able to read Pali, despite coming from an illiterate family. Ohkado (2013) reported a Japanese child who recalled a life in Scotland and wrote his name and some words in English.

Differences between identical or monozygotic twins reared together present another problem for the psychosocial theory. Fraternal or dizygotic twins, who develop from separate eggs, are no more similar than any two siblings, but monozygotic twins, formed from a single egg, share the same genetic material. According to the materialist theory of human biology, monozygotic twins should behave in very similar ways, especially if they are brought up together and shaped by the same environmental factors. Researchers have offered various explanations for differences, including varying micro-environments in the womb or parents favoring one twin over the other (Stevenson, 2001, pp. 191–92). In any event, monozygotic twins with memories of previous lives are often markedly different, in line with the persons whose lives they recall. The differences may be physical as well as behavioral, but at present I am concerned only with the behaviors.

Gillian and Jennifer Pollock (Stevenson, 1997a, 2003; I. Wilson, 1982) are monozygotic British twins. They remembered the lives of their sisters, Joanna and Jacqueline, who were killed together by a crazed driver who deliberately ran them down from behind as they walked along a street. Gillian recalled the life of Joanna, who had been eleven when she died, and Jennifer the life of Jacqueline, who had been six. Jennifer was dependent on Gillian, as Jacqueline had been on Joanna. She held pencils in her fist to write, as had Jacqueline, whereas Gillian wrote normally, as had Joanna. Gillian gave the general impression of being more mature than Jennifer. She was more independent, more generous, and liked to author plays and act in them wearing costumes, as had Joanna.

Another pair of monozygotic twins who exhibited strong behavioral differences are Indika and Kakshappa Ishwara of Sri Lanka (Stevenson, 1997a, vol. 2, pp. 1970–2000). Indika was a quiet, bookish boy who did well at school; Kakshappa was active, tough, and resisted going to school. Indika was religious and liked to visit a Buddhist temple; Kakshappa was indifferent to religion. Indika enjoyed eating chili peppers more than Kakshappa did. These differences corresponded to the personalities of the persons the boys recalled having been.

Alexandrina and Maria-Pace Samona were strikingly different in behavior as well as appearance, but we do not know that they were monozygotic (Stevenson, 2003). For more extensive discussion of twins with past-life memories, see Pasricha (2008, pp. 379–96) and Stevenson (1997a, vol. 2, pp. 1931–2062; 2001, pp. 189–94).

Behavioral memories may be evoked when a child meets the previous person's family and friends (Stevenson, 2001, p. 115). The child may act as a parent toward the previous person's children and a spouse toward the previous person's spouse, displaying either affection or distance, as appropriate. Gopal Gupta was friendly toward the previous person's sister but cool and indifferent toward his wife, with whom the previous person had not been on good terms (Stevenson, 1975a, pp. 97–99). Keil (1991, pp. 45–46) described how a two-year-old Thai boy, upon meeting two men who had been employees of the person whose life he recalled, presented himself as a boss, standing with his hands clasped behind his back. He called the men by their nicknames and addressed them as inferiors (using a particular linguistic form) in their dialect, which he understood and spoke with them.

If the previous families accept the children as the reincarnations of their loved ones, old ties may be revived and behavioral memories given reason to persist. Reena Kulshreshtha (Mills, 1989) entered into an unusually close relationship with the previous person's husband, Shyam Babu Yadev. Shyam Babu's wife of fifteen years had died at thirty from an allergic reaction to an injection she had been given in a hospital, nineteen months before Reena was born. When she was about three years old, Reena recognized Shyam Babu and thereafter repeatedly asked her parents to invite him to special events hosted by her family. He attended ten such events, at which Reena would serve him food and tea then retire, as a proper Hindu wife would do.

Reena requested gifts from Shyam Babu and also sent to him gifts in keeping with a marital relationship. On one occasion, she asked him for material to make a long dress, then insisted that her parents provide her with a sweater and a baby bonnet to send to him in return. She stopped wanting to visit him after learning that he had remarried, although she continued to have him invited to functions at her home. Shyam Babu attended these affairs without bringing his second wife, out of regard for Reena's feelings. When she was about seven, he decided to withdraw, yet he accepted an invitation as late as 1989, when Reena was thirteen. When she saw him enter the room where she was dining, she stopped eating and retired, as she had done when she was younger (Mills, 1989, p. 146).

How are we to account for these behavioral signs of reincarnation? They may be grouped into two classes. In one class are behaviors with a strong emotional component, including deep-seated attachments, temperaments, and other dispositions. These are called "affective" (Titchener, 1895) or "emotional" (Buchanan, 2008) memories in mainstream memory research. I will refer to them as *emotional memories*. In the other class are motor and language skills and habitual actions, which Tulving (1985) termed *procedural memories*. (Vocabulary is classified as semantic memory, but language performance is learned and perfected through regular use, hence a type of procedural memory.) Emotional and procedural memory are the two classes of implicit memory, so called because it remains unconscious, in contrast to declarative (explicit) memory. Emotional memories become explicit when we become aware of them, but I will treat them in their implicit dimension. Again, we see that past-life memory can be analyzed using the same concepts employed in relation to memory of the present life.

Case subjects may voice concern for the previous person's children, assert their ownership of the previous person's property, bear grievances against his or her murderers, and assert their identification with him or her in ways other than those I have discussed. Like other kinds of behavioral memories, emotional memories related to previous lives may be expressed before children start talking about their episodic memories and they may outlast them (Stevenson, 2001, pp. 119–20). Usually they recede eventually, yet like episodic memories, they may persist into adulthood.

Mills (2006, pp. 144–46) cited two cases of young adults with continuing attachment to the spouses of the previous lives. One was Reena Kulshreshtha, who at twenty-eight retained no episodic memories but continued to be in love with Shyam Babu Yadev and had refused a marriage arranged for her when she was twenty-three. The other was a young man unhappy in his arranged marriage because he was still infatuated with his past-life wife, a woman then seventy years old. Stevenson (1997a, vol. 1, p. 213) reported a Burmese case whose subject, at eighteen, upon hearing that his past-life wife had been widowed by her second husband, sought her out and married her.

Procedural past-life memories have less associated emotion and are per-formed automatically, as are procedural memories from the present life. To a greater extent than episodic memories, they are associated with altered states that Stevenson at one point (1977a, p. 271n11) compared to deliria, and they may be accompanied by noticeable changes in case subjects. Ste-venson (1997a, vol. 2, pp. 1882–990) described distinctive postures, gait, handedness, and other muscular habits and involuntary actions in subjects that accord with the practices of the persons whose lives they recalled. Tomo, the Japanese boy studied by Ohkado (2013), normally was right-handed but became left-handed when he peeled garlic, as he claimed to have done in his Scottish life.

Procedural past-life memories may be cued by the sight of people, places, and things, just as episodic past-life memories may be. Rylann's pulling out the drawers in the bathroom vanity is an example. The Harrisons described an English girl who mechanically took up a baby vest, bunched it up, and used it to dust furniture, and who when she first saw a boarded-up fireplace, made as if to shovel out the hearth (P. Harrison & M. Harrison, 1991, pp. 116–17). Procedural past-life memories may persist for years, outlasting episodic past-life memories, although they, too, usually disappear over time. By the time she was twenty-eight, Swaran Lata had lost her memories of being a Sweeper. She had matured into a charming young woman and had been married for eight years (Pasricha, 2001b, p. 48).

It is hard to imagine how parental imposition of identity or other social construction could account for these behavioral signs. It is equally difficult to explain them in terms of psi or super-psi (Almeder, 1992; Lund, 2009; Stevenson, 1974a, 2001). Few critics and skeptics have even attempted to do so. Braude thinks that the acquisition of skills is not beyond super-psi but does not try to explain how this would work in reincarnation cases. Instead, he minimizes the evidence for skills in the cases (2003, p. 179).

Emotional memories pose as much of a problem for psi as procedural memories do. Why and how does the information acquired via psi produce extreme involvement in the previous life and strong identification with the previous person? It was to deal with this aspect of the cases that Stevenson (1974a, pp. 343–73) considered personation along with ESP, and this is a large part of the reason Griffin (1997) developed his theory of retroprehensive inclusion. Keil's (2010b) thought bundles might help here, if they included emotional as well as imaged and verbal content. Thought bundles face quite a few hurdles in connection with reincarnation cases, though. I have already mentioned several and will now add another.

Keil said that thought bundles entered the wombs of pregnant women or the minds of young children who came near the "objects, localities, people, or situations" (2010b, p. 98) to which they were attached. This could explain Swarnlata Mishra's memories, because she began talking about Katni when passing through that town (Stevenson, 1974b), but it will not do for many other cases, including two Keil himself investigated: Kemal Atasoy (Keil & Tucker, 2005), who had never visited Istanbul, five hundred miles away from where the previous person lived; and M. C. (Keil, 2010a), who at age three recalled the life of a teenager accidently shot at a wedding celebration in a village neither she nor her parents visited until she was seventeen.

If we dismiss psychosocial propositions as well as thought bundles and super-psi as explanations for behavioral past-life memories, we are left with a real puzzle. It is not very satisfying to say that if behavioral signs cannot be explained in one of these ways, they must be due to reincarnation, unless we can say *how* they are due to reincarnation. Emotional memories might be carried in the subconscious along with episodic and semantic memories, but the same cannot be said of procedural memories. Something besides a memory recorded in consciousness, something somatic, would seem to be involved in procedural memories, and the body in which the behaviors was trained and perfected has been left behind.

Significantly, different types of memory are handled in different ways by the brain. Episodic and semantic memories are associated with the hippocampus, whereas emotional memories are affiliated with the amygdala (Eichenbaum & Cohen, 2001; LaBar & Cabeza, 2006). Both the hippocampus and the amygdala are regions of the medial temporal lobe. Responsibility for procedural memory is distributed throughout the brain, and rather than considering it a distinct memory system, it may be better to think of it as reflecting "a general principle of plasticity within neural processing circuits that leads to adaptive reshaping of function to match experience" (Reber, 2013, p. 2027). That is to say, procedural learning and memory are supported by labile neural pathways. Although they are susceptible to change over time, they have a physical substrate.

The question, then, is, how does this physical substrate get transferred to a new body? I think it happens via the reincarnating mind. If habitual and skillful behaviors wear neural pathways through the brain, they could be replicated in a new brain if a mind were to lay down the appropriate pathways in the course of reincarnating. This would mean that procedural past-life memories originate in the subconscious like other sorts of memories, but with the added step that the reincarnating mind impresses them on the new brain.

The reincarnating mind could accomplish this feat through psi (PK) (Haraldsson & Matlock, 2016, p. 272). The psychokinesis I am proposing is in no manner super-psi; it need be no more extensive or complex than that involved in what parapsychologists call "direct mental action on living systems" (DMILS), which includes what is known popularly as psychic healing

(Braud, 2003; Schlitz & Braud, 1997), or that suggested by many cases of mind/brain interaction, such as the placebo effect and psychosomatic illness (E. W. Kelly, 2007b).

This must be only one element in a larger picture, though. When they meet certain people and recognize them, case subjects recall how to behave with them and act appropriately, as did the boy who responded to his previous person's employees as a boss (Keil, 1991). Places may evoke a similar set of responses. When he was twenty-one, Ashok Kumar Shakya told Antonia Mills that his memories had not faded but that he avoided going to the previous village because when he went there he "became" the previous person (Mills, 2006, p. 146). Apparently all types of past-life memory are linked in the subconscious mind, so that they may be retrieved together. Paul Reber (2013, pp. 2038–39) reached a similar conclusion regarding different types of present-life memory.

I wonder if emotional memories play a mediating role here. If I am right that the reproduction of procedural memories is the mind's doing, then what the mind chooses (perhaps unconsciously) to reproduce may be those things to which it feels the greatest emotional attachment. This is consistent with my theory that memory is stored in the subconscious and would mean that all memories are implicit at their core, the difference being that declarative memories present themselves to conscious awareness, whereas the implicit may remain unconscious even when they are expressed behaviorally or somatically.

BIRTHMARKS AND OTHER PHYSICAL SIGNS

Many people have some sort of birthmark or birth defect. Some birthmarks, such as those associated with neurofibromatosis, are known to have genetic links, and others are thought to be produced by conditions in the womb and during birth. However, nothing is known about the genesis of the majority. The same is true regarding the locations of birthmarks on the body and of the causes of most birth defects. Although the mechanism by which reincarnation might be involved in the creation of birthmarks and congenital malformations is by no means obvious, it would be unwise to discard, without due consideration, the possibility that reincarnation might contribute to them (Stevenson, 1993, 1997a, 1997b).

Birthmarks are an important part of the rebirth syndrome. They are one of the signs Tylor (1871) thought inspired the belief in reincarnation, and they figure in several of the pre-1960 accounts reviewed by Stevenson (1960a). Initially Stevenson paid little attention to them, however. It was the Tlingit who first brought their significance home to him (Stevenson, 1966a) and he began to devote special attention to the topic. He described six Tlingit cases with birthmarks in *Twenty Cases* (Stevenson, 1974b) but held most of those he studied until he could present a large group together.

In 1993 Stevenson summarized his findings concerning the relation of birthmarks to mortal wounds (Stevenson, 1993). Four years later he published his two-volume *Reincarnation and Biology* (Stevenson, 1997a), which presents 225 cases with birthmarks and congenital physical abnormalities connected to previous lives, many illustrated by photographs. Stevenson put out a single-volume abridgement of this monograph (Stevenson, 1997b) at the same time, but I refer to the complete work here. I also draw on contributions from other authors, when they help to elucidate the complex issues arising from this material.

The exactness of correspondence in the locations of wounds and birthmarks, which preoccupied Angel (2002) in his review *of Reincarnation and Biology*, is an overblown problem, because the wounds were inflicted on one body and the birthmarks appear on another body of much smaller size. One cannot measure with any precision how close birthmarks are to where wounds were. The correspondence can only be approximate, in relation to anatomical landmarks, and by this standard, the resemblance between wounds and birthmarks is usually quite remarkable. Moreover, birthmarks often appear in association with episodic memories and behavioral signs. Birthmarks may help to match a case subject to a previous person but they are only one facet of a case.

Stevenson and his colleagues sought police and medical records to support their interviews and observations of physical anomalies. They could not always obtain written records and some that they did obtain omitted relevant details, but in most instances, the records accorded well with a case subject's physical traits. Stevenson found a good concordance in location between wounds and birthmarks in forty-three (88%) of forty-nine cases for which documents provided adequate data for comparison (1997a, vol. 1, p. 1087). Reincarnation cases with birthmarks or birth defects backed by written documents have been described by Mills (1989), Haraldsson (2000b), and Pasricha, Keil, Tucker, and Stevenson (2005), in addition to Stevenson (1997a).

The likelihood that concordances in location between wounds and birthmarks are due to chance is much reduced when there are multiple birthmarks matching wounds. Stevenson (1997a, vol. 1, pp. 1132–34) listed thirty-three cases with two or more birthmarks. In six of these cases, there were two birthmarks corresponding to the entry and exit wounds of gunshots. A Tsimshian native boy, Alan Gamble, recalled having been his father's adoptive brother, who had accidently shot himself in the hand with a twelve-gauge shotgun for which he was reaching (Stevenson, 1997a, vol. 1, pp. 382–87). The shot entered the palm of Alan's uncle's left hand and exited through his left wrist, producing wounds described in a death registry Stevenson inspected. Alan had one birthmark on his left palm and a second on the back of his left wrist, in the places the projectile had entered and exited his uncle's hand.

With birth defects, there can be little question about the correspondence in location to wounds. Lekh Pal Jatav (Stevenson, 1997a, vol. 2, pp. 1186–99), who recalled the life of a toddler who lost the ends of the fingers of his right hand after sticking it in a fodder-chopping machine, was born missing the ends of the fingers of his right hand. Semïh Tutşmuş (Stevenson, 1997a, vol. 2, pp. 1382–403), who recalled having been shot in the right ear at close range, was born with severe microtia of the right ear (the pinna was much reduced in size, as if it had been cut off).

There does not seem to be a way of predicting which wounds will lead to birthmarks and which to birth defects. Moreover, a given type of wound may correspond to different types of birthmarks, a given type of birthmark may correspond to different types of wounds, and when there are multiple birthmarks, all need not be of the same type (Stevenson, 1997a). Psychosocial theorists can claim that the resemblance between a wound and a birth defect is coincidental, and super-psi enthusiasts may claim that the mother learned about an injury of which she was consciously unaware through psi and was so moved by it that she unconsciously impressed the baby in her womb with the same injury (maternal impression), but how likely are these propositions to account for the resemblance between wounds and birth defects in hundreds of cases in which there are also episodic memories and behavioral signs?

Dermatologists recognize several kinds of birthmarks, some more common than others. The most common are salmon patches ("stork bites" or "angel kisses"), café au lait spots, and small nevi (moles). Although frequently seen in newborns, salmon patches and café au lait spots do not figure in any documented reincarnation cases. Congenital dermal melanocytosis ("Mongolian blue spots") and hemangiomas do not appear either. Birthmarks in reincarnation cases are exclusively other sorts of melanocytic and vascular nevi (Stevenson, 1993, 1997a).

Melanocytic nevi result from the accumulation of melanin. They are most often brown or black (hyperpigmented, darker than the surrounding skin), but they may be the same color as the surrounding skin or hypopigmented (lighter than the surrounding skin). Most melanocytic nevi lie flat against the skin, but some are raised or sunken in relation to it; some are hairy. Vascular nevi result from concentrations of blood vessels and tend to be pink, purple, or reddish in color. Most vascular nevi are substantially larger and more irregular in shape than are melanocytic nevi.

Small, flat melanocytic nevi occur but are unusual in reincarnation cases. Most reincarnation-related birthmarks are elevated or depressed in relation to the surrounding skin. Some are puckered, markedly elongated, or have other unusual features, such as abnormal pigmentation (Stevenson, 1997a, vol. 1, p. 180). Often they resemble the scars of healed wounds or other lesions. Ravi Shankar Gupta, an Indian boy, recalled having his throat slit. He was born with a linear mark resembling the scar of a knife wound across the front of his neck. When Stevenson inspected this birthmark in 1964 it was about five centimeters long and five millimeters wide. It was hyperpigmented and stippled, much like the scar of a healed knife wound (Stevenson, 1974b, 1997a).

Alan Gamble's two birthmarks were different in appearance. The one in the palm of his hand was small, only about three millimeters long and one millimeter wide. It was slightly depressed, but its pigmentation was no different from the surrounding skin. The birthmark on the back of his wrist was roundish, about eight millimeters in diameter, and of a dark purple-red color (Stevenson, 1997, vol. 1, pp. 382–87). The difference between these birthmarks conformed to the difference between the entry and exit wounds of the gunshot documented in the death registry. As always with the exception of shots fired at very short range, the entry wound was smaller than the exit wound.

Surprisingly, some marks are open at birth and bleed or otherwise discharge (see the index to *Reincarnation and Biology*, vol. 2, p. 2259, under "Pathology of birthmarks and birth defects at birth"). The affected area may heal within a few days or weeks or it may fester for years, requiring medical attention. Pasricha, Keil, Tucker, and Stevenson (2005, pp. 370–74) described an Indian boy born with severely malformed fingers and toes that bled and became chronically infected, one finger so frequently that his parents had it amputated. The boy claimed to have been a dacoit, a bandit, who had been set upon, tortured, and murdered by his comrades, but Stevenson's team was unable to identify a specific previous person and this case remains unsolved.

Many birthmarks changed in appearance during the years Stevenson had them under observation, and his photographs show these progressive alterations (e.g., 1997a, vol. 1, pp. 900–901). Birthmarks may shift in relation to other anatomical features as children grow. Most birthmarks vanish by the time episodic memories fade (ages five to eight years), but some persist longer and a few become larger and more pigmented rather than disappearing (Stevenson, 1997a, vol. 1, pp. 881–82). Ravi Shankar's birthmark moved farther up his neck, shortened, faded, and lost its stippling appearance, but never disappeared entirely (Stevenson, 1997a, vol. 1, pp. 909–10).

Postmortem reports sometimes show that there were more wounds on a previous person's body than a case subject has birthmarks (Stevenson, 1997a, pp.

1105–6). Stevenson (1997a, vol. 1, pp. 1104–10) speculated that the wounds (resulting from accident or murder) for which there were corresponding birthmarks were made before the previous person lost consciousness, whereas those not reproduced on the subject's body were made when the previous person was unaware. This conjecture seems plausible as a general rule, but birthmarks may reflect wounds received *after* death as well as before.

Stevenson (1997a) described two cases in which birthmarks matched postmortem injuries to a body. In one of these, the birthmark corresponded to a wound made during a postmortem examination (Stevenson, 1997a, vol. 1, p. 361). In the other, the birthmark corresponded to an injury made by a gravedigger's shovel (Stevenson, 1997a, vol. 1, p. 1126). Keil (1991, pp. 37–38) reported the case of a Burmese girl who had a birthmark on her thigh in the place the previous person's corpse was pierced by a stick used to push it into its tomb. I. C. Onyewuenyi (2009, pp. 21–22) described a baby born in his Igbo family with birthmarks resembling stitch marks on her chest, matching marks from an operation performed postmortem on her paternal aunt in order to remove a "bag of cough" so that when she reincarnated she would not be afflicted with the respiratory illness from which she died.

Although the majority of birthmarks in reincarnation cases commemorate wounds, wounds are not their only model. Mills (1994c) described ear-piercing as a status marker on the Northwest Coast, where Gitxsan and other native children may have birthmarks on the lobes or helixes of their ears. Stevenson (1997a, vol. 2, pp. 589–633) reported a series of cases with earring birthmarks. Tattoos and many other lesions may also reappear as birthmarks. Sergeant Phoh of Thailand had "protective" tattoos (for supernatural defense) on his hands and feet, and the boy who recalled his life was born with similar tattoo-like marks on his hands and feet (Story, 1975, pp. 168–72). The index to *Reincarnation and Biology* lists adhesive tape marks, disfigurements caused by leprosy, lip biting just before death, rope marks, spilled medicine, styes, and ulcers, among the many items replicated in birthmarks.

A considerable number of rebirth syndrome accounts and reincarnation cases have physical signs. Stevenson found birthmarks or birth defects in 309 (35%) of 895 solved cases from the nine societies that contributed the majority of cases to his collection (Stevenson, 1997a, vol. 1, p. 1093). Unsolved cases frequently implicate violent death (Cook et al., 1983b) and may have a higher incidence of physical signs than solved cases have. Birthmarks are an important feature of "silent cases" (those without past-life memories; Keil, 1996) and are especially common in tribal cultures (Matlock, 1993; Matlock & Mills, 1994).

As common as they are, however, physical signs do not figure in the majority of reincarnation cases, even those in which the previous person was fatally wounded. Of thirty-four cases in which snakebite was known or alleged (by a subject) to be the cause of death, birthmarks were present in only fourteen (41%) (Stevenson, 1997a, vol. 1, pp. 1091–92). Stevenson did not say what percentage of all his violent-death cases have physical signs, but he implied that it is comparable. Why should this be?

Long intermissions appear not to inhibit birthmarks and birth defects (Stevenson, 1997a, vol. 1, pp. 1100–1102). The intermission in the Sri Lankan case of Wijeratne lasted eighteen and a half years, much longer than in most Asian cases (Stevenson, 1974b, 1997a). Fewer birthmarks and birth defects are reported when intermissions are less than nine months long (Stevenson, 2001, p. 120), but a short intermission is not necessarily an impediment to them either.

Stevenson (1997a, vol. 1, p. 1095) listed twenty-one cases of birthmarks or birth defects in cases with intermissions of under nine months. In three of these cases, the intermission lasted no more than two weeks. It was eleven to fourteen days in a case in which a child with a birthmark on his thumb recalled having been bitten on the thumb by a snake (Stevenson, 1997a, vol. 1, pp. 745–59). It was five to seven days in a case in which a boy born with a meningocele (an open area with meninges exposed) on the back of his head recalled the life of a man who had been killed by a blow to the head (Stevenson, 1997a, vol. 2, pp. 1442–54) and two days in the case of a boy born with a bleeding sore under his chin and a birthmark on the crown of his head, corresponding to the entry and exit wounds of the gunshot by which the previous person suicided (Stevenson, 1997a, vol. 1, pp. 728–45).

Notably, however, these cases with brief intermissions have only birthmarks or minor birth defects. No major birth defects (e.g., missing or badly deformed limbs) have been reported in cases with intermissions of less than six months, which suggests that the stage of embryonic or fetal development may be a factor in their expression. The most severe birth defect in a case under nine months in length (a stunted forearm and missing hand) figured in the Haida case of Bruce Peck, whose intermission was seven months long (Stevenson, 1997a, vol. 2, pp. 1361–66).

Birthmarks may not appear when there are intermediate lives that are not well recalled (Stevenson, 1997a, vol. 1, pp. 1096–1100), yet physical signs sometimes recur in successive lives under circumstances that rule out genetic transmission. A Burmese girl, Ma Khin Nyein, recalled two previous lives, in the earlier of which she was a monk who was deep in meditation when his monastery caught fire. Both the intermediate previous person and Ma Khin Nyein suffered from severe ichthyosis (plaque psoriasis), which she attributed to the monk's having been burnt to death. Ma Khin Nyein was distantly related to the intermediate previous person (he was her mother's second cousin), but neither she nor this boy were related to the monk who died in the fire (Stevenson, 1997a, vol. 2, pp. 1706–15).

Recurrent birthmarks have been reported in other cases (Stevenson, 1997a, vol. 2, p. 2240). There are cases with recurrent birth defects also. In one, a boy was born with a deformed ear resembling the deformed ear with which the previous person was born and on this basis was accepted by the previous family as the reincarnation of their son (Stevenson, 1997a, vol. 2, pp. 1410–24). A recurrent left-sided cleft lip figures in a Tlingit case (Stevenson, 1997a, vol. 2, pp. 1475–82). The Gitxsan (Mills, 1988b, p. 35) and Nisga'a (Mills et al., 2011, p. 91) have contributed other examples of birthmarks and birth defects manifesting in successive lives.

Both birthmarks and birth defects may be planned before death. I have already mentioned the case of William George, a Tlingit man who told his favorite son and daughter-in-law that he would try to come back as their son, adding that he could be recognized by birthmarks like the two pigmented moles he then had. After his death, his daughter-in-law became pregnant and in due course gave birth to a son who bore pigmented moles in the same places (Stevenson, 1974b, p. 232). Another Tlingit man, Corliss Chotkin said that he would be known by birthmarks matching surgical scars he had by his nose and on his back, and Corliss Chotkin, Jr., had such birthmarks (Stevenson, 1974b, pp. 259–60). Bruce Peck was identified as the reincarnation of his paternal grandfather, a fisherman who was so tired of having to throw out and pull in nets that he declared before he died that he would return without a hand so he would not have to work so hard the next time around (Stevenson, 1997a, pp. 1361–66).

In Burma, experimental birthmarks may correspond to marks made on the body of a dying person (Stevenson, 1997a, vol. 1, pp. 803–75; Tucker & Keil, 2013). More commonly, they correspond to marks on a cadaver. Experimental birthmarks have been reported throughout eastern Asia, east from India to Japan, and south from Mongolia to Burma and Thailand, in both contemporary and historical accounts and cases (Matlock, 2017, June). Rebecca Empson (2007, 2011) found cadaver marking to be common among the Buryat of Mongolia. Two of the first-millennium Chinese cases described by De Groot (1901) have experimental birthmarks. Ohkado (2017, p. 564) cited several Japanese cases, one as early as 1661. The substance used in the marking varies. In Japan, it is often sumi ink (Ohkado, 2017), whereas in Burma, it is typically soot from the bottom of a cooking pot (Tucker & Keil, 2013). In an unusual Burmese case, friends of a young woman who were preparing her body for cremation used red lipstick to mark the nape of her neck and the girl recognized as her reincarnation was born with a red mark (an area of erythema) on the nape of her neck (Stevenson, 1997a, vol. 1, pp. 840–41).

Occasionally, experimental birthmarks reappear in successive lives. Stevenson (1997a, vol. 1, p. 867) reported the case of a youth who was marked on his back after his death. A boy with a corresponding mark was born to another family in the same village, but died in infancy. The mark then reappeared on a girl, the subject of the case. She recalled the life of the youth, though not of the infant, yet felt drawn to the infant's family and was adopted by them. Experimental birthmarks are nearly always flat hyperpigmented nevi, unlike other kinds of birthmarks in reincarnation cases (Stevenson, 1997a, vol. 1, p. 804).

Birth defects, also, may be purposefully induced. Throughout West Africa one finds the belief in "repeater children" who are born again and again to the same parents, only to die by early childhood each time (Collomb, 1973; Edelstein, 1986; Stevenson, 1985, 1997a). Repeater children are believed to be members of a spirit band who have taken an oath to die young as a torment to their parents, and afflicted families may have several children die in a row. Repeater children, however, are thought to be a vain bunch and an individual may be kept from dying if his body is defaced, making him unattractive to his fellows.

While this basic belief is widespread, different tribes favor different parts of the body for mutilation. Among the Igbo, a segment of a little finger or toe usually is removed, whereas among the Serer of Senegal an ear is more likely to be cut. Generally this is done to young children suspected of being repeater children (because several siblings have predeceased them) but the dead also may be disfigured. Children born with missing parts of fingers, toes, ears, etc., are presumed to have been marked in their previous lives or after their deaths and are considered unlikely to die prematurely in their present lives. Stevenson (1997a, vol. 2, pp. 1625–51) reported examples (with photographs) from Nigeria and Senegal.

Birthmarks and birth defects are not the only physical signs of reincarnation. Some children suffer from internal diseases related to the life they remember (Stevenson, 1997a, vol. 2, pp. 1655–721). Alexandrina Samona shared several physical traits (hyperemia of the left eye, seborrhea of the right ear, facial asymmetry) with the deceased Alessandrina (Lancelin, 1922; Stevenson, 2003). Marta Lorenz (Stevenson, 1974b), who recalled having been a woman who died of pulmonary tuberculosis, was plagued with upper respiratory infections. Norman Despers (Stevenson, 1974b), whose eyesight was poor, remembered incidents from the life of his grandfather, who had been blind for the last four years of his life. See Stevenson (1997a, vol. 2, pp. 1657–61) for a table listing twenty cases with internal diseases related to previous lives.

Children may suffer from afflictions associated with the previous person's manner of death. A case similar to that of Ma Khin Nyein, the girl with the severe ichthyosis (Stevenson, 1997a), is that of the Burmese boy Maung Yin Maung. Maung Yin Maung recalled being a man who died in fiery plane crash. At birth his skin was unusually red and covered by small vesicles, from some of which a fluid oozed. After about a month, his skin "shed flakes," became entirely normal, and remained so (Stevenson, 1983b, p. 292). Tali Sowaid, the Lebanese boy who recalled having been shot through the tongue, was late to start talking and then had trouble articulating certain sounds, especially those that required raising the tongue to the roof of the mouth (Stevenson, 1997a, vol. 1, pp. 380–81). DG, an American boy who remembered being a policeman who died after being shot in the chest, had significant congenital heart disease (Pasricha, Keil, Tucker, & Stevenson, 2005, pp. 379–81; also, Tucker, 2005, pp. 52–55, and Tucker, 2013, pp. 1–17, under the name Patrick Christenson).

I have learned of three cases with seizures and neurological issues that may be correlated with damage to the previous person's head. When he was three, Stephen Stein recognized the Alamo as the place he had died as a Mexican soldier. He told his mother that he had fallen to the ground in front of the compound (Haraldsson & Matlock, 2016, pp. 240–44). Around the same time, he began to complain about headaches, and at thirty-four still suffers from chronic retinal migraines, some of long duration. When he was thirty, he had a drop seizure and lost all motor function below his neck for several hours, resulting in his being hospitalized in a neurology ward for five days. Doctors were unable to locate the source of the problem; one attributed it to "a complicated migraine." Although other members of his family experience migraines, Stephen is the only one to have regular retinal migraines, the only one who has poor vision, and the only one who has experienced a seizure. His case is unsolved, so we cannot be sure, but his symptoms suggest that the soldier was killed by a shot to the head. I have studied the other two cases with seizures less well. One involves apparent memories of suicide by a shot to the head, the other execution in an electric chair.

Some physical signs relate to what may be regarded as aspects of the previous person's core identity. We are moving further now into areas for which there is comparatively little data, not because the phenomena are rare but because Stevenson and his colleagues were slow to start inquiring about them. Researchers are only beginning to appreciate the extent to which reincarnation may be expressed physically.

Stevenson (1997a, vol. 2, p. 1664) described a girl, identified as being the reincarnation of a woman who died on the eve of the start of her regular menstrual period, who was born bleeding from the vagina. Many of the most pronounced congruities appear in interethnic and sex-change cases. Among them are similarities of physique, facial structure, eye shape, skin color, and other physical traits between a person and the child who remembers his life.

Hindu boys who recall lives as Muslim men may be born without fore-skins—circumcision being a Muslim practice, but not a Hindu one (Pasricha, 1998, pp. 287–88; Rawat & Rivas, 2007, p. 163; Stevenson, 1997a, vol. 2, pp. 1621–23). The Burmese children who recalled being Japanese soldiers had Japanese facial characteristics (Ohkado, 2014; Stevenson, 1997a, vol. 1, pp. 1913–15). Asian children who claim to have been Englishmen or Americans, such as B. B. Saxena, are often physically larger than other children in their families, have eyes of the European shape, and in their complexion are virtual if not actual albinos (Stevenson, 1997a, vol. 2, pp. 1757–846; Weird Story, 1907). Girls who remember being boys or men may be of relatively large stature and their menarche may be delayed (Stevenson, 1997a, vol. 2, pp. 1663, 1873). Ma Tin Aung Myo's menarche did not begin until she was fifteen, almost two years later than the mean for Burma (Stevenson, 1983b, p. 235).

Equally striking are physical differences between monozygotic twins. Gillian and Jennifer Pollock closely resembled each other when young, but only Jennifer had birthmarks. One matched a scar Jacqueline had had, the result of an accident when she was three (three years before her death) and another was a mole on her waist where Jacqueline had had a mole (Stevenson, 1997a, vol. 2, pp. 2045, 2053–56). Gillian for her part had a peculiar splay-footed gait in which she resembled Joanne but not Jennifer or Jacqueline (Stevenson, 1997a, vol. 2, p. 1893). The Sri Lankan twins Indika and Kakshappa Ishwara weighed the same at birth but their faces were different and Indika quickly became taller than Kakshappa. In addition, Indika (but not Kakshappa) had a nasal polyp at the site the person whose life he recalled had had a tracheal tube inserted in the week before his death (Stevenson, 1997a, vol. 2, pp. 1995–97).

Some children have commented on the feeling that their bodies were smaller than they used to be and one felt himself to be in a large body as he walked along the road to the village in which the previous person had lived (Stevenson, 1997a, vol. 2, p. 2092). Other children have complained about phantom pain at the site of birthmarks that commemorate the place the previous person was fatally wounded. In a case I have studied, a Guatemalan woman experienced a recurring pain on the back of her left flank whenever someone came near her with a knife. She had a diamond-shaped birthmark in that place, where her great-uncle had been ambushed and stabbed, but she had no waking memories of his life. Andrade (1988, pp. 170–205; summarized in Playfair, 2006, pp. 70–71) described a Brazilian boy he calls Rogerio who even as a teenager (when Andrade met him) used a cane and walked with a limp due to a sharp pain in his leg, where his previous person had suffered a fatal snakebite.

* * *

When birthmarks are the only sign of reincarnation, they can easily lead to hasty and false identifications (Keil, 1996; Stevenson, Pasricha, & Samararatne, 1988), but social construction seems forced as a blanket explanation for physical signs, especially when we consider that there are supporting documents in some cases and that birthmarks may be planned before death or (apparently) stimulated by marking cadavers. Super-psi can account for physical signs by involving maternal impressions but models of that sort become mired in ever more crippling complexity. Even so, it is not immediately apparent how reincarnation could result in birthmarks and other congenital abnormalities.

At the conclusion of *Reincarnation and Biology*, Stevenson proposed that memories, behaviors, and form were conveyed from one life to another via a "psychophore," his version of a subtle or astral body. The "astral body" is a quasi-physical "subtle body" that is supposed to be aligned with the physical body during life. It is said to separate from the physical body at death and to continue existence in a discarnate state until its union with a new physical body. The term comes from Theosophy (Besant, 1892) and is in general use in New Age metaphysics, but similar ideas are found in many religious and esoteric traditions.

A psychophore (which means "soul bearing") would support consciousness, but would also carry the residues of physical scars (such as wounds) and act as a "template" for a new physical body (Stevenson, 1997a, vol. 2, p. 2084). The psychophore would help shape an embryo or fetus through a field effect when it moved into "topical alignment" with the new body's physical features (Stevenson, 1997a, vol. 2, pp. 2086–88). Stevenson broached this idea first in a journal paper (1974a) and returned to it in *Children Who Remember Previous Lives* (2001, pp. 234, 251), where he speculated at greater length about the reincarnation process.

I think the psychophore is a superfluous concept. Stevenson (1997a) devoted 146 pages (two of the first three chapters) of *Reincarnation and Biology* to showing how mental imagery may affect the physical body, for example, in stigmata and maternal impressions. Similar but more inclusive arguments regarding the mind's ability to influence its body physically are made in literature reviews by E. W. Kelly (2007b) and Mario Beauregard (2012b) and by Henry Stapp (2011, pp. 145–52). Throughout *Reincarnation and Biology* Stevenson referred to psychic influences in the production of birthmarks and birth defects. He apparently thought that the reincarnating mind operated on its body through mental fields in the psychophore (Stevenson, 2001, p. 251), but if a mind can affect its physical body in this fashion, why could it not do so independently of a psychophore?

Earlier I suggested that procedural memories might be conveyed from one body to another through the actions of a reincarnating mind and the same possibility exists with physical signs. Melanocytic birthmarks could be created by stimulating melanin production and vascular birthmarks by impacting the formation and concentration of blood vessels. Birth defects, internal diseases, and other physical traits would require either altering the body's genetic blueprint or modifying its tissues, but it is noteworthy that major birth defects are not seen when gestation is further than six months advanced at the arrival of a reincarnating mind, because the new body is essentially formed by the end of the first trimester of pregnancy. The "template" in this alternative view is not a psychophore, but a baby's developing body, which the reincarnating mind in effect customizes for the life ahead.

If the reincarnating mind is responsible for the production of physical signs, psychological factors would naturally play a role, making it easier to understand why birthmarks and birth defects appear under a variety of conditions, but not invariably under any single one. I do not think that a mind's effect on a baby's body would have to be conscious and deliberate, in relation to either behavioral or physical signs. The psi influence would flow out of the subconscious and we may presume that any such psychokinetic actions could be unconsciously as well as consciously activated.

Nonetheless, it would seem that what is registered in the subconscious is informed to a large extent by waking experience. A shock to an organism severe enough to cause death might well render a surviving mind unaware (at least temporarily), which would explain why the initial blows only of a series of fatal blows are reflected in birthmarks and birth defects. If, on the other hand, a surviving mind were to retain or regain awareness after death, it could take note of postmortem wounds and marks and reproduce them on its new body during gestation. Other variations in the expression of physical signs appear to be a function of the meaning and emotional salience of the stimuli for them, returning us to the possibility of a mediating role for emotional memories.

I imagine the reincarnating mind's influence starting as a psychic obsession and proceeding gradually to a possession of the body in the womb. In parapsychology, obsession is the overshadowing influence on a living person by a spirit, short of outright possession (see Hyslop, 1909; Muller, 1970, pp. 193–207; and Stevenson, 2003, pp. 235–46, for examples of obsession). By possession, I do not mean that the reincarnating mind replaces a spirit already in the body (with which perhaps it was conceived), merely that it becomes affiliated with the body. I am suggesting that the body in utero does not have its own mind (consciousness, spirit, soul) before an incarnating (or reincarnating) mind takes possession of it.

Note that retributive karma has no place in this model. Retributive karma is the Theosophical variety of karma, but it matches the popular Asian conception more closely than does the juridical karma expounded in philosophical commentaries on religious texts. The Theosophical idea that retributive karma assists individuals in their spiritual growth is absent from the Asian perspective, but the Asian popular view agrees that karma may be expressed physically. If retributive karma were a genuine force, we would expect to see its effects in physical signs. But reincarnation cases show the opposite of what retributive karma predicts. Rather than a killer being cursed with the deformities he has inflicted on his victim (Blavatsky, 1888a), it is his victim who bears the scars.

Retributive karma was suggested by Stevenson's informants in only four cases (Stevenson 1997a, vol. 2, p. 1372). Two of these cases, both from Burma, have not been described at any length, and I can say nothing more about them, but the other two can be interpreted according to my theory just as well. Ma Khin Ma Gi (Stevenson, 1997a, vol. 2, pp. 2000–2007) said that defects of her arm and leg were due to her having hunted and mistreated animals in her previous life. If the previous person had felt guilty about this behavior, could her reincarnating mind not have created the defects in the belief that they were the appropriate karmic payback? The other case is the Sri Lankan case of Wijeratne (Stevenson, 1974b, 1997a), who was born with a badly stunted right arm. Wijeratne recalled having killed his bride when she tried to renege on her marriage commitment to him. He believed that his defect was his karmic due for having used his right arm to wield the knife, but could the defect not have been produced by Wijeratne's reincarnating mind itself?

Karma was evoked in two of Stevenson's sex-change cases. When she was twenty-two, Ma Tin Aung Myo conjectured that she was reborn as a woman because she had misbehaved as the Japanese soldier. This is the usual Burmese explanation for what are considered karmic demotions, and we would be right to be suspicious of it. As a child, Ma Tin Aung Myo gave a different answer to this question. She said she had become a girl because the soldier had been shot in the groin (Stevenson, 1983b, p. 239). Rani Saxena, who recalled the life of a male lawyer who had "selfishly exploited women," said that God had put her in a female body so that she could experience what it was like to be a woman (Stevenson, 2001, p. 186). In both of these cases, also, is it not possible that the reincarnating mind was responsible for the effect?

Retributive karma begins to look more like a cultural construct than a theoretically useful concept, a suggestion supported by two other cases. Ma Khin Nyein's ichthyosis was widely believed to be the consequence of having set fire to the monastery in a previous life, not to having been burnt to death in it, as the previous person claimed to recall (Stevenson, 1997a, vol. 2, pp. 1710–11n). Süleyman Zeytun (Stevenson, 1980) was born deaf and dumb. All who knew him or were familiar with his case attributed his inability to hear and speak to misdeeds in a life anterior to the one he seemed to remember, which everyone agreed had been exemplary. However, congenital deaf-mutism has known genetic causes, and Süleyman's younger sister also was born deaf-mute. Is karma after all no more than a convenient fiction, as philosopher Eliot Deutsch (1973) and skeptics Michael Shermer (2018) and Paul Edwards (1996) would have it? I return to this question in Chapter 5.

Chapter 5

Child Studies

Secondary Signs of Reincarnation

Episodic memories with their related statements and recognitions, behavioral identifications, and congenital physical abnormalities are the three major classes of signs suggestive of reincarnation, but they are not the only signs. Many cases include announcing dreams and a subject's memories of the intermission period, which suggest a discarnate agency operating between lives. Another important class of sign is patterns across the entire dataset of cases. It is hard to understand how either psychosocial propositions or psi could produce these patterns, which show up cross-culturally as well within cultures over time. Finally, there are signs such as phobias and other post-traumatic reactions of case subjects. These emotional responses are consistent with past-life memory, but it is unclear how they would be shaped by parental guidance or acquired by psi.

SIGNS OF DISCARNATE AGENCY

Animism takes the postmortem survival of consciousness and the possibility of interaction between the dead and the living as givens (Tylor, 1871). The material I have reviewed to this point provides some support for this perspective. Stevenson (1966a, 1974b) described Tlingit announcing dreams, which figure in some pre-1960 accounts. In the first-millennium Chinese account of the Chao boy, his mother "dreamed of that child coming to her with the words, 'I must become your descendent'; on which she became pregnant" (De Groot, 1901, p. 144). Alexandrina Samona's mother repeatedly dreamed that Alessandrina said she was returning to her. Alexandrina's family heard raps on the door and received messages through a medium from a communicator identifying herself as Alessandrina (Lancelin, 1922; Stevenson, 2003).

In the eighth-century Chinese account from Willoughby-Meade, the youth's spirit is portrayed as hanging around his house after his death. It hears his father lament his loss and the family hears a voice say, "I will again become a son in the Ku family," after which his mother becomes pregnant and gives birth to a boy who grows up to recall the youth's life (1928, p. 76). Rylann said that she had met God, Jesus, and Cindy's mother in heaven, and Cristina told me that she had seen that her mother and I were "looking for a baby" and so had come to us.

More than the usual degree of caution is called for in interpreting this material. It is subjective and as such is more amenable to the impacts of culture than are objectively observable behaviors and birthmarks. Indeed, there are indications that many of these experiences are culturally influenced. Nevertheless, some are intersubjective, in the strong sense of being shared by two or more minds. A good number are veridical. There are cross-cultural consistencies in structure and content. It would be wrong to dismiss what children say they remember about the intermission as no more than creative imagining without a proper hearing. As with everything to do with parapsychological research, we must examine the data carefully before reaching even tentative conclusions.

I have argued that procedural memories and physical signs of reincarnation may be explained as the products of a mind acting on its body during gestation in the womb. This presumes that the mind survived the death of its former body, and if that is so, we should not be surprised to find signs of discarnate agency during the intermission between lives. Signs of discarnate agency provide support for my theory of the reincarnation process. They also return us to the selection problem, the question of how the rebirth parents are chosen. If a discarnate mind retains its will and its ability to act on the world, does that mean the elective solution is the only plausible solution? Might the karmic and theistic solutions play roles also? That more may be involved in reincarnation than personal choice is suggested by Willoughby-Meade's (1928) account in which the youth's spirit has to have its intention ratified by an underworld official before it can return to his family.

Announcing dreams were among the signs Tylor (1871) identified as the basis of the belief in reincarnation. It is easy to see how people could have reached this conclusion, because the dreams seem to depict the spirit of a deceased person asserting his intention (or less commonly, requesting permission) to be reborn to a particular woman, generally (but not necessarily) the dreamer.

Ma Tin Aung Myo's mother on three occasions while she was pregnant dreamed of a stocky Japanese man wearing short pants and no shirt who said that he would come stay (reincarnate) with her. Eight years had passed since the Japanese occupation of Burma had ended, but she recognized the man as an army cook who had been encamped near her house. She had traded and discussed foods and cooking techniques with him. She had not known that he had died—much less how he had died—so Ma Tin Aung Myo's statement that he had been killed by strafing from an aircraft could not be confirmed, nor could her claim that the man was shirtless and wearing shorts at the time of his death (Stevenson, 1983b).

Stevenson recorded announcing dreams in all the countries in which he investigated cases (2001, p. 99), although in different numbers. They occur frequently among the Burmese, the Alevi, and the Tlingit and other tribal peoples of northwestern North America, but they are rare among the Igbo and the Druze and in Sri Lanka. In India they have been reported only in association with cases with a family relationship (Stevenson, 2001, p. 175). The character of the dreams varies by culture. Many Burmese announcing dreams depict the spirit as a petitioner, requesting permission rather than stating his intention to be reborn (Ma Tin Aung Myo's mother's dream was exceptional in this regard), whereas Tlingit dreams frequently have symbolic elements.

There are cultural variations in the timing of the dreams as well. In Burma they tend to occur before conception (Ma Tin Aung Myo's mother's dream was again anomalous), whereas in the Pacific Northwest they most often come in the final months of pregnancy or shortly before birth (Stevenson, 2001, p. 99). Among the Druze, they may come before the previous person dies (Stevenson, 1980, pp. 11–12) or after a child is born (Stevenson, 1980, pp. 236, 255–56; 1997a, pp. 272, 594, 677, 1603–4).

Closely related to announcing dreams are departure dreams, in which members of a deceased person's family dream that he tells them where to find him reborn. Pasricha, Keil, Tucker, and Stevenson (2005, p. 378) reported an Alevi example in which the previous person's mother and brothers were led by a dream to the child's house soon after his birth but were not permitted to see him. They did not confirm his identity until years later, when he was talking about the previous life.

Departure dreams are much less common than announcing dreams, and unlike announcing dreams, most occur postnatally. Of seventeen departure dreams I have found recorded in the literature, twelve occurred postnatally (Mills, 1988b, p. 40; Pasricha, Keil, Tucker, & Stevenson, 2005, p. 378; Stevenson, 1997a, vol. 1, pp. 267, 671, 750, 1114; 1997a, vol. 2, pp. 1446, 1700–1701, 1718; 2001, p. 100 [3 instances]) and only five antenatally (Rawat & Rivas, 2007, p. 116 [2 instances]; Stevenson, 1983b, p. 281; 1997a, vol. 2, pp. 1405, 1603). In some departure dreams, the reincarnated individual complains (to the previous family) about his present circumstances (Stevenson, 2001, p. 100).

Most rebirth announcements are delivered in dreams but they may come in mediumistic communications (Nahm & Hassler, 2011, p. 312) and they may be conveyed by apparitions perceived in the waking state (Matlock, 2018, January). Apparitions typically are visual but may be partly or exclusively auditory, olfactory, tactile, or, at least in principle, gustatory (Green & McCreery, 1975; Haraldsson, 2012b). The figures that appear in announcing and departure dreams technically are apparitions, but generally the term *apparition* denotes a waking experience.

Visual apparitions were sighted between death and reincarnation in nine cases Stevenson investigated (Stevenson, 1997a, vol. 2, p. 2091). Visual apparitions also figure in the early twentieth-century Italian case of Blanche Battista (Stevenson, 2003), the Indian case of Harsh Vardham (B. Prasad, 1967), and the Brazilian case of Karen (Playfair, 2011, p. 165). Jean-Guy Goulet (1998) described visual apparitions of spirits seeking reincarnation among the Dene Tha. Mills (1988b, pp. 51–52n10) documented visual and tactile apparitions interpreted as rebirth announcements by the Beaver.

Willoughby-Meade's (1928) Chinese account is not the only one with an auditory apparition. Muller (1970, p. 69) mentions an auditory announcement in a Finnish case. Andrade (2010b) tells of a Brazilian woman who heard a familiar voice and turned to see a curtain billowing but no one there. Later she discovered that the voice's possessor (a priest she had known) had been killed in a highway accident around the same time and her next child recalled events from his life. Leadbeater (1903b, pp. 411–12) described an American case in which a pregnant woman heard the voice and saw the apparition of a woman who said she was reincarnating as her child.

Occasionally apparitions in reincarnation accounts and cases are intersubjective or reciprocal. Children say they remember "sending" dreams or meeting their present parents, who report parallel experiences. Maung Yin Maung recalled that after dying when his light plane crashed, he had wandered about as a spirit, approaching his brother's home just as someone exited the outhouse. It was his sister-in-law, and he walked toward her, halting when he felt he could go no further. She saw his apparition and spoke to him, telling him that he could "stay" with them if he wished. Later that night he visited her in her sleep. His mother and sister showed up, asking him to return with them, but he told them he would stay with his brother and sister-in-law. The sister-in-law (Maung Yin Maung's mother) recalled seeing the apparition and inviting him to stay with them and also having had a dream in which the deceased man appeared along with his (still-living) mother and sister (Stevenson, 1983b, pp. 280–81).

Rebirth announcements are a regular feature of the rebirth syndrome. They suggest a discarnate presence communicating with the dreamer or percipient and when they convey veridical information or are intersubjective they are not easily dismissed as fantasies. Another way reincarnating spirits may communicate with their mothers-to-be is by influencing their activities, particularly their desires for certain foods. Pregnancy cravings that turn out to be for foods favored by the persons whose lives children later recall have been reported in several cases (Stevenson, 2001, pp. 197–99, 298n28). Bongkuch Promsin's mother experienced a strong craving for soup with noodles and tamarinds, a craving experienced by the previous person's mother during her pregnancy as well. The previous person had been fond of noodles and Bongkuch particularly liked soup with noodles, which he sought out whenever he went to a town at which he could obtain the dish (Stevenson, 1983b, pp. 128–29).

Skeptic David Lester (2005, pp. 151, 153, 207, 208; 2015, p. 706) makes much of what he believes is the absence of memories of the intermission, yet Rylann and Cristina are far from the only children who have talked about it.

Veer Singh, an Indian boy who recalled the life of a four-year-old who had died after an illness, said that during an eleven-year intermission he had resided in a peepal (Bodhi or bo) tree (a sacred fig tree) in the yard of his former family. He knew that the family had purchased a camel and had been engaged in lawsuits and he stated the names of (and later recognized) two children born after "his" death. He said that he had left his tree to accompany a brother and others when they departed the compound alone and that he had notified his mother about this in a dream. His mother recalled having had such a dream, after which she had confronted the boy in question and secured a confession from him (Stevenson, 1975b, pp. 328–29).

Once, Veer said, he had become annoyed with two women swinging from a branch of his tree and caused the plank on which they were seated to break. This incident, also, had occurred in reality (Stevenson, 1975b, p. 329). This may be the only example of confirmed psychokinesis or "poltergeist" activity during the intermission recalled by a case subject. A Burmese boy, Maung Tinn Sein (Stevenson, 1997a, vol. 1, p. 183), claimed that he had thrown stones at passersby, including the man who became his father, but these incidents could not be verified. The mothers of the previous persons in a German case reported by Hassler (2013) and a Japanese case reported by Ohkado (2016) observed poltergeist activity they believed was connected to their deceased sons, but the boys who recalled their lives did not remember having done these things. Alexandrina Samona did not recall producing the raps on the door her family heard, although when Alessandrina first communicated at a séance she said that she had made them (Lancelin, 1922; Stevenson, 2003).

Poonam Sharma and Jim Tucker (2004) found intermission memories in 217 (20%) of 1,107 cases in the DOPS collection and compared cases with and without them. On the whole, the two groups were closely similar, but children with intermission memories made significantly more verified statements about a past life than did children whose memories did not include the intermission ($p < .001$). They were also more likely to recall more than one previous life ($p = .002$). These findings suggest that children who remember the intermission have unusually strong memories. There are no data on whether they are more suggestible or fantasy prone than children who do not recall the intermission, but we do know that children with past-life memories in general are no more suggestible than their peers (Haraldsson, 2003; Haraldsson, Fowler, & Periyannanpillai, 2000). Thus there is no good reason to reject out of hand what children say about the intermission, although much of it is unverifiable and must be assessed indirectly.

From an analysis of thirty-five Burmese reincarnation cases, Sharma and Tucker (2004) identified three stages of the intermission experience: a transitional stage following death (during which the funeral may be witnessed), a "stable" stage in some fixed location (recall Veer Singh's peepal tree), and a stage during which new parents are selected. Iris Giesler and I confirmed the validity of this scheme in a cross-cultural sample of eighty-five published cases with intermission memories from seven Asian and five Western countries (Matlock & Giesler-Petersen, 2016). For some subjects, the three stages are followed by a fourth, life in the womb, and a fifth, events surrounding birth (Ohkado, 2015). Few intermission memories include more than three of the five stages, but together they outline the structure of the intermission experience (Matlock, 2017, May; Matlock & Giesler-Petersen, 2016).

The first two stages of the intermission experience have much in common with the near-death experience (NDE), especially the non-Western NDE, which is a stripped-down version of the typical modern Western one (Kellehear, 1996, 2008; Shushan, 2018). Western and non-Western NDEs share the same basic structure, but features such as a life review and passing through a dark tunnel toward a bright light occur rarely in non-Western NDEs. Darkness and light seldom figure in intermission memories, either (Purnima Ekanayake, whose case was reported by Haraldsson, 2000a, is a rare exception).

NDEs, like intermission memories, may include encounters with spirits (Greyson, 2010b; E. W. Kelly, 2001), but whereas in NDEs these spirits tell the NDEr that his time has not yet come and send him back to his body, in intermission experiences they welcome the deceased in death and may lead him on to rebirth (Matlock, 2017, May; Nahm, 2011a). Significantly, Giesler and I discovered veridical perceptions of the material world reported in all five stages of the intermission experience, another indicator that the children's memories of the intermission may be more than fantasies (Matlock & Giesler-Petersen, 2016). Veridical perceptions (presumably via clairvoyance) occur in all stages of the NDE as well (Holden, 2009; Rivas, Dirven, & Smit, 2016).

The guides or assisting spirits in intermission memories are often experienced as God or a surrogate. Many Westerners (like Rylann) identify them as Jesus or angels, whereas in India they are usually someone working with Yama (the Lord of Death), and in Buddhist countries they are figures in white or yellow monks' robes. Katsugoro said that he was led to his house by a figure who resembled a tutelary deity of the Japanese Shinto religion (Bolitho, 2002). Deceased family members may appear in intermission experiences as well, although they are mentioned less often than religious figures.

Many elements of the intermission experience are attributable to culturally derived expectations. In this respect, intermission memories resemble the transcendental stage of NDEs. There is a cross-culturally common structure, but the details of the experience vary from place to place, from person to person (Matlock, 2017, May; Matlock & Giesler-Petersen, 2016). Similarly, although descriptions of the "bardo" in the writings of different Tibetan Buddhist schools are said to be based on the experiences of practitioners who returned from this realm, the descriptions vary in line with the expectations of the schools' meditation practices (Nahm, 2011b).

In cultures influenced by Theravada Buddhism, intermission existence may be envisioned as rebirth in non-human form. E. W. Davis (2008) gave a nice example from the Khmer of Cambodia. A girl recalled that between her human lives she had been a tree spirit. It was always light where she was, with no alternation of day and night. If she felt hungry she had only to imagine what food she desired and immediately it floated to her side. She avoided humans and if her tree was about to be felled, she moved to another. One day her tree spirit mother told her that it was time to be reborn as a human being. Leaving her treetop and her forest, she came upon her present human mother harvesting rice, entered her body, and was reborn to her.

This account illustrates an important characteristic of Asian intermission memories: They are more likely to depict the intermission as passing on Earth than in the heavens. Giesler and I found a highly significant ($p < .000001$) difference between Asian and Western intermission memories in the depiction of a "terrestrial" vs. "heavenly" Stage 2 environment (Matlock & Giesler-Petersen, 2016). Tribal cases and accounts also depict the intermission environment as terrestrial or subterranean rather than heavenly (Matlock, 2017; Shushan, 2018). When terrestrial, the environment is typically in a land of the dead located across a river or past the end of the world.

It may be best to think of postmortem existence as an alteration in the state of mind rather than as a change of location (Tucker, 2013, p. 195). Differences in postmortem experiences can then be seen as reflections of individual and cultural expectations, at least in part. There are intriguing similarities in these experiences beyond a common structure. Although spirit figures encountered during the intermission are perceived differently in different cultures, the roles of Gatekeeper, Escort (or Guide), and Entity in Charge appear over and over again (Matlock, 2017; Matlock & Giesler-Petersen, 2016). Animism may be right that nonhuman spirits have the same ontological status as human streams of consciousness. This would mean that nonhuman spirits are objectively real, although they are subjectively perceived by the discarnate mind, in terms that are familiar to the experiencer (Matlock, 2017).

Some children credit their ability to recall previous lives to not having eaten something they were offered during the intermission (Matlock, 1990b, p. 205). The "fruit of forgetfulness" recalls drinking from the River Lethe in the Myth of Er (Plato, *Republic* X.613–21). In a Vietnamese account, the food is a soup that the spirit avoids consuming by slipping it to his dog, which had been killed along with him (Le Quang Hu'o'ng, 1972). Eating these foods is not invariably effective in inducing amnesia, however. Ampan Petcherat (Stevenson, 1983b, p. 68) and Santosh Sukla (Stevenson, 1997, vol. 1, p. 556) said they ate foods offered to them during the intermission, yet they recalled their previous lives anyway.

Many children with memories of the intermission have nothing to say about how they came to be with their parents (Stage 3 of the experience). Veer Singh did not explain how, after eleven years in the peepal tree, he came to be reincarnated in a lower-caste family (Jat rather than Brahmin) in a neighboring village (Stevenson, 1975b). Other children do talk about it, though. About half (forty-two of eighty-five) of the subjects in Giesler's and my sample described how the connection to the new parents was made (Matlock & Giesler-Petersen, 2016). With few exceptions, the process may be classified under one of two headings, "elective" or "assisted."

In *elective reincarnation*, a spirit selects its parents without assistance. An American boy, Bobby Hodges, told his mother that he had wanted to be born to an aunt but was forced out by a miscarriage induced by his then-twin brother and when he tried again, found the womb already occupied. Bobby's aunt indeed had been carrying twins but suffered a double miscarriage and soon thereafter became pregnant with Bobby's cousin, circumstances unknown to Bobby when he related these things to his mother at age four (Tucker, 2005, pp. 164–67; also Bowman, 2001, pp. 169–79, under the name Sam).

James Leininger told his parents he had found them when they were vacationing in Hawaii. James accurately described their dinner on the beach and the hotel in which they stayed, although he was not conceived for another five weeks, after they returned to the mainland, and was born in San Francisco (Leininger & Leininger, with Gross, 2009, pp. 153–54). Carol Bowman (2001, pp. 129–60) recounted other examples of spirits choosing their parents, often ones they had had before. She observed that the very non-randomness of family connections between past and present lives implied a conscious decision by a spirit about where it would go. Discarnate agency is suggested by the patterns of suicide cases (Haraldsson & Matlock, 2016, pp. 252–53) and international cases (Haraldsson & Matlock, 2016, pp. 232–35) also. It is very striking in cases of twins with past-life memories (Stevenson, 1997a, vol. 2, pp. 1931–2062). In thirty-four (86%) of forty twin pairs studied by Stevenson, the previous persons had a "verified or claimed close relationship" (1997a, vol. 2, p. 1932); in each (100%) of the thirty-one cases in which both twins had verified past-life memories, the previous persons were acquainted (Stevenson, 1997a, vol. 2, p. 1937).

In *assisted reincarnation*, a spirit either has help in deciding when and where to be reborn or the decision is made for it. The ratification by an underworld official in Willoughby-Meade's (1928) account is unusual and looks as if it was inspired by Chinese bureaucracy. More commonly, assisting spirits push a spirit toward reincarnation, as did the Cambodian tree spirit whose mother suggested it was time for her to be reborn to a human mother (E. W. Davis, 2008). John Rhodes, an English boy, said that God prompted him to choose his father and he selected a boy who had pretended to go on playing his violin after its strings snapped during a performance—something his father had done in school, well before meeting his mother (Muller, 1970, p. 66). A Dutch boy, Kees, said that he had not wanted to return to human life but had been spurred on by an angel (Rivas, 2003, p. 530).

Sometimes in assisted reincarnation, a spirit entity makes all the arrangements. Three English children described by the Harrisons said that the decision of when and where to reincarnate was made for them (P. Harrison & M. Harrison, 1991, pp. 72, 104, 141). In Asian cases the decision-maker often is a man dressed in white or yellow. In the case of a Burmese Buddhist monk, the Ven. Sayadaw U Sobhana, a man in white not only arranged for the reincarnation but appeared in an announcing dream to the mother-to-be and in a departure dream to the previous person's widow (Stevenson, 1983b, p. 245; Story, 1975, pp. 197–98).

Stevenson (2001, pp. 236–44) took a different approach to explaining why a person is born into a particular family. He identified two factors as of special importance, a geographical factor and a psychic or psychological factor. Both may be expressed variously.

The geographical factor may, as with Ma Tin Aung Myo and other Burmese children who recalled lives as Japanese soldiers (Stevenson & Keil, 2005), mean that the previous person died near to where the child who inherits his memories is born. In other cases, one of the parents comes near the previous person's body. This occurred in Sahay's (1927) case of Sunder

Lal, who recalled his previous body being thrown into the river in which his mother was bathing. In a similar case from Sri Lanka, Thusitha Silva's mother was two months' pregnant when she bathed in a river near to where the girl whose life Thusitha recalled had drowned (Stevenson & Samararatne, 1988, p. 224). In Hassler's (2013) German case, a young man run down by a car died in the arms of the woman who became his new mother.

Not only family ties but bonds of affection or animosity between the previous person and the child's mother or other family members may serve as psychological factors. We see this in Hassler's (2013) case, in Ma Tin Aung Myo's mother's friendship with the Japanese army cook (Stevenson, 1983b), and in Andrade's (2010b) case of the priest killed in the automobile accident who is reborn as the son of the woman he once knew. Animosity is a factor in the Druze case of Zouheir Chaar (Stevenson, 1980), who recalled having been a man who had quarreled with his mother over water rights and constantly berated her for stealing water from him.

Geographical and psychological factors provide indirect support for elective reincarnation and for the elective solution to the selection problem. Rebirth announcements through dreams, as waking apparitions, in poltergeist activity, and in mediumistic messages likewise depict the spirit in control. If this indirect evidence is considered along with instances of reincarnation planned before death and memories of choosing parents during the intermission, elective reincarnation is easily the most commonly attested manner of selecting the rebirth parents. Elective reincarnation provides strong evidence of discarnate agency, consistent with my model of the reincarnation process.

It is noteworthy, however, that although spirits of the deceased may choose their new parents, there is in the spontaneous cases no indication of the more detailed life planning commonly envisaged in the New Age reincarnation mythos. Children do not say they chose their life circumstances in order to advance their spiritual growth. The draw to the parents typically has an emotional element, but it is limited to that. Nor have children talked about spirit tribunals, waiting with soul groups, or other features of the intermission period portrayed by Michael Newton (1996, 2000). Two of Ohkado's (2016) subjects recalled having spent some time in a "reflection room" after their deaths, the only example of a life review in the spontaneous reincarnation cases. Some subjects say they remained alone, some remember interacting with other spirits or with living persons, a few were assigned tasks to carry out, but for the most part postmortem existence is depicted in involuntary intermission memories as biding time until reincarnation.

Involuntary intermission memories provide only marginal support for the theistic solution to the selection problem and then only if the nonhuman spirits (the men in white, angels, etc.) in assisted reincarnation are considered

God's surrogates. One of the recurring roles of spirits in intermission memories is what Giesler and I (Matlock & Giesler-Petersen, 2016) called the Entity in Charge. Sometimes the Entity in Charge is a deity figure, but this entity is not usually the one who assigns the new parents.

Another difficulty facing the theistic solution is the fact that none of the reported experiences are veridical and rarely are they intersubjective (the man-in-white in both announcing and departure dreams in the case of the Ven. Sayadaw U Sobhana, Stevenson, 1983b, is unique in the case literature). We have no way of assessing the credibility of these memories, unlike those related to elective reincarnation, for which there are many converging lines of support. Perhaps the theistic solution lies in the background and acts as a default, becoming activated when decisions are not made within an appropriate time, but this suggestion is wholly conjectural.

Involuntary memories of the intermission provide no support at all for the karmic solution to the selection problem. For juridical karma to be operative, the decisions of discarnate actors (in elective reincarnation) or nonhuman spirits (in assisted reincarnation) would have to be constrained by karmic laws, and there is nothing to suggest that they are. This negative conclusion comes on top of the concerns about retributive karma I raised in Chapter 4 and the problems for karma do not end with it. There is no good evidence of juridical karma operating in the lives of children with past-life memories (Stevenson, 2001, pp. 251–54; Tucker, 2005, pp. 221–22). There is no discernable relationship between conduct in one life and the social or economic circumstances of the next. Saints are reborn into no better conditions than sinners.

Karma theorists reply to such objections that karma may derive not only from the life recalled, usually one's immediately previous life, but from an anterior life or lives (see Appleton, 2014, pp. 8–13, for an exceptionally clear articulation of this position). This claim is incontrovertible because although case subjects sometimes remember multiple lives, rarely has it been possible to identify the previous persons in more than one of them. Hence, even when there are memories of multiple lives, it is possible that researchers have missed something of relevance. But even if karma routinely skips over all remembered lives and flows exclusively from unremembered earlier lives, it is refuted by discarnate agency. If karma dictated where they were reborn, spirits would have no decisions to make between lives, nor would psychological and geographical factors come into play in determining rebirth, except coincidentally. And yet these factors are important in many cases.

According to Buddhism, Theosophy, and some theories of the reincarnation process (e.g., the Biological Organizing Model of Andrade, 2011), the incoming soul or consciousness stream joins egg and sperm at conception to initiate a new life. However, many cases have intermissions of less than nine months and with the Haida, Alevi, and Druze these short intermissions are in the majority (Stevenson, 1986a, p. 212). A few Druze cases come close to the cultural ideal of immediate rebirth (Stevenson, 1980, p. 9). Stevenson heard of three Druze NDEs in which subjects felt themselves transported to locations where women were giving birth but recovered in their own bodies and the babies were stillborn (1980, p. 12). An English case similar to these last is reprinted from a newspaper account by George Brownell (1949, pp. 15–17) and by Emily Cook, Bruce Greyson, and Stevenson (1998, pp. 387–88).

Then there are the cases in which a reincarnating spirit joins a body after birth. Stevenson referred to these as "anomalous-date" cases, or alternatively as instances of parakaya pravesh or its usual English gloss, possession. When he first wrote about this phenomenon, in *Twenty Cases*, Stevenson judged these cases to be "intermediate" in form between possession and reincarnation (Stevenson, 1974b, p. 374). By *Reincarnation and Biology*, he had come to consider them clear examples of possession but was uncertain about how to classify cases with intermissions of under nine months. He thought it a matter of taste whether one termed cases of the latter group reincarnation or possession (Stevenson, 1997a, vol. 1, p. 1142).

This classificatory problem arose for Stevenson because he thought of the psychophore as providing a "template" for a new body. He was unable to explain what happened to the psychophore when it joined a body during gestation or exactly how it acted as a template when the body's formative process was already underway. The problem is easily resolved, though, by dispensing with the psychophore and instead adopting the proposition that a consciousness stream takes possession of a body, then acts upon it to produce the desired physical effects.

The term *possession* may be confusing here, because it is commonly used in parapsychology to denote transient and short-term forms of possession, such as mediumistic or demonic possession, in which the body's original spirit is not permanently displaced. I think it is preferable to define *possession* simply as the occupation of a body by a spirit. Reincarnation then may be understood to be a state of long-term possession by its nature. Reincarnational possession generally begins before birth, but in anomalous-date cases its inception is postnatal. I propose that *possession* be reserved for transient or short-term forms of possession (as in mediumistic possession or the thirteen-week possession of Lurancy Vennum: Stevens, 1887) and use *reincarnation* to signify long-term or permanent states of possession. Long-term possession beginning after birth may be termed *postnatal reincarnation*.

I know of ten cases of postnatal reincarnation described in the parapsychological literature. In nine of these ten cases, the reincarnating spirit definitely or presumably replaced a spirit already associated with the body. I call these latter cases *postnatal replacement reincarnation* (Matlock, 2017, March). The single case of postnatal reincarnation that is not also replacement reincarnation is that of the Ven. Chaokhun Rajsuthajarn of Thailand (Stevenson, 1983b). The previous person of his case, his mother's brother, died about eighteen hours after Rajsuthajarn was born, but he had been semicomatose for a week, during which time he felt himself leave his body and follow his mother around. His mind did not become closely associated with Rajsuthajarn's body until after his birth, but there is no indication that he displaced another spirit in doing so. This case closely resembles accounts of premortem initiation of reincarnation in which the previous person was moribund when reincarnation occurred (Calkowski, 2013; Stevenson, 1985, p. 18).

Postnatal replacement reincarnation is suggested more strongly in nine other cases. An unnamed Indian child whose case has not yet been reported fully (Stevenson, 1974b, p. 376) was four and a half days old, a Turkish child (Keil, 2010b, p. 93) was fifteen to eighteen days old, and the German Ruprecht Schulz (Stevenson, 2003, pp. 210–22) was five weeks old, when their previous persons died. The reincarnation was not immediate in any of these cases, but the intermissions were no more than two or three months long. A Thai boy, Juta, was four months old when his uncle was killed in an accident and eight months old when he assumed his uncle's identity following a serious illness (Tucker, 2013, pp. 23–25). An Indian boy, Sudhakar Misra (Pasricha, 1990a, pp. 104–7), was less than three years old, and an Indian boy, Jasbir Jat (Stevenson, 1974b, pp. 34–52), was about three and a half, when they too sickened, seemed to die, but recovered, claiming to be other people who had died not long before. Another Indian girl of about three appeared in good health when she went through a similar change, although she fell ill afterward (Stevenson, 1997a, vol. 1, p. 1068).

In two cases, the subject was much older when the replacement occurred. Iris Farczády was fifteen (Barrington, 2005) and a practicing medium when she underwent a radical change. She lost the ability to understand and converse in Hungarian and started speaking Spanish, identifying herself as a cleaning woman from Madrid named Lucía Altarez de Salvio (Barrington, Mulacz, & Rivas, 2005; Tabori, 1951). Sumitra Singh seemed to die when she was about seventeen then revived with a distinctly different personality, identifying herself as Shiva, a married woman who had been murdered by her in-laws two months prior (Dayal, 1988; Mills & Dhiman, 2011; Stevenson, Pasricha, & McClean-Rice, 1989). Other accounts of replacement in the teenage years have been reported in non-parapsychological sources; one is Vietnamese (Chau, 2011), the other Chinese (Willoughby-Meade, 1928, pp. 6–7). The oldest subject reported to have undergone this transformation was a thirty-year-old Chinese woman (Willoughby-Meade, 1928, p. 9). For more on these and other replacement reincarnation accounts, see Matlock (2017, March).

Most postnatal replacement cases begin with accidents or illness, often severe illness. A person appears to die, then revives unexpectedly, claiming to be someone who died not long before. Researchers have little insight into how or why replacement occurs, although none of the cases suggest that the original possessor was forced out of its body. Iris Farczády said that she (Lucía) had been happily floating in space after her death, and had no idea how she came to supplant the original Iris (Barrington, Mulacz, & Rivas, 2005). After reviving, Jasbir Jat said that he had been led to Jasbir's body by a holy man (Stevenson, 1974b, p. 47). Shiva said that Yama had allowed her return to life in Sumitra's body, but for another seven years only (Dayal, 1988). Sumitra lived another thirteen years, according to a follow-up study by Mills and Dhiman (2011).

Postnatal replacement cases do not usually have physical signs related to the previous person, although they may. Tucker (2013, p. 24) says that after Juta took on his uncle's personality at seven-to-eight months, three marks in the places his uncle had started to have a tattoo done appeared on his arm. These marks continued to be visible until he was five years old, after which they faded. Behavioral signs, among them procedural memories, appear regularly in replacement cases. Sumitra, for instance, was able to write much more proficiently after Shiva took over and her handwriting began to resemble Shiva's (Mills & Dhiman, 2011). With Lucía's arrival, Iris Farczády began to sing Spanish songs and show off her flamenco dancing (Barrington, Mulacz, & Rivas, 2005).

It is possible that some cases with intermissions of under nine months are prenatal (rather than postnatal) replacement cases. In *I Saw a Light and Came Here* (Haraldsson & Matlock, 2016, pp. 194–95), I suggested this as the best explanation for the case of Toran (Titu) Singh (Mills, 1989), which features two sets of birthmarks. Titu's birth date is not certain, but the most likely possibility is three months after the murder of Suresh Verme. Suresh was shot in the head, and Titu had a birthmark on his forehead and a bony protrusion by his left ear, marking the bullet's entry and exit points, per his autopsy report. However, Titu also had three other, smaller birthmarks on the back of his head, unrelated to Suresh, which might be connected to a spirit Suresh replaced in Titu's body. Interestingly, Titu's mother had a normal pregnancy until her last trimester, but suddenly fell ill and remained sick throughout that period.

Replacement reincarnation is sometimes confused with what are popularly called walk-ins (e.g., by Semkiw, n.d.-a), but there are significant differences. In their original formulation by Ruth Montgomery (1979), walk-ins were said to be spiritually advanced beings that take over human bodies. Walk-ins are said to enter after the teen years with the permission of the walk-out; subsequent personality changes may develop over time but do not involve a complete loss of memory of the present life (Jaymes, 2017; Y. Perry, 2013).

No walk-ins have been investigated by the parapsychology community and their evidential status is uncertain (Matlock, 2017, March).

In their main features replacement cases resemble other reincarnation cases, and they may be more common than is realized. I know of several similar cases that remain unpublished, have appeared in non-academic venues (with correspondingly poor documentation), or about which there are unresolved questions (Matlock, 2017, March). For discussions of the replacement phenomenon from different theoretical perspectives, see Almeder (1992, pp. 143–50), Braude (2003, pp. 198–207), Keil (2010b, p. 93), Nahm (2011a, p. 464), and Nahm and Hassler (2011, pp. 309–10).

UNIVERSAL, NEAR-UNIVERSAL, AND CULTURE-LINKED PATTERNS

Early in his field research, Stevenson realized that he was learning about far more past-life memory claims than he had the time and resources to investigate thoroughly and decided on a two-pronged strategy: He would study a few cases intensively and collect basic data on as many others as he could in order to search for patterns across large groups of cases. He carried out the latter part of this project in a series of journal papers (Stevenson, 1966a, 1970a, 1971, 1973b, 1975a, 1983a, 1986a), culminating in 1986 with profiles of ten cultures in a paper concerned primarily with the Igbo. Other authors since have contributed information on other countries and cultures. Mills (1988a) provided statistics from her work with the Beaver, Gitxsan, and Wet'suwet'en of British Columbia. Richard Slobodin (1994) added data on the Eastern Kutchin (Gwich'in) of Canada's Northwest Territories. Most recently, I supplied figures for Brazil, based on the published work of Stevenson and Andrade (Haraldsson & Matlock, 2016, pp. 219–27).

Most of these data pertain to cases investigated between 1960 and 1985, the years that Stevenson was most active in the field. Andrade's investigations in Brazil were conducted during the same period as Stevenson's. Slobodin's fieldwork began earlier, in 1938, and concluded in 1968 (Slobodin, 1994). Mills's (1988a) numbers refer to investigations between 1984 and 1987. Cases studied later, principally by Mills, Haraldsson, Keil, Tucker, and Ohkado are not included in the data summarized in Tables 5.1, 5.2, and 5.3.

The cultural profiles are supplemented by studies of correlations between variables by Cook et al. (1983b), Narender Chadha and Stevenson (1988), Stevenson and Chadha (1990), Matlock (1989), Tucker (2000), and Sharma and Tucker (2004), as well as by within-culture cross-historical comparisons from Pasricha and Stevenson (1979, 1986), Keil and Stevenson (1999), Stevenson and Keil (2000), and Stevenson and Haraldsson (2003). Stevenson

(2001) and Tucker (2013) reported the results of additional analyses employing the DOPS database.

This statistical work is an important complement to reports of single cases and furnishes the opportunity to explore further the ways culture shapes experience that I began with my discussion of announcing dreams and intermission memories. The pattern analyses have revealed several universal, near-universal, and culture-linked case features (Matlock, 1990b, and 2017, February). Although skeptics like to assert that the culture-linked features support the psychosocial theory, the issues, as usual, are more complicated than they acknowledge.

Among the universal or near-universal features of reincarnation cases are the signs—announcing dreams, birthmarks, behaviors, and claims to remember having lived before—that characterize the rebirth syndrome. Some additional universal or near-universal features relate to the case subject, whereas others concern the previous person.

Boys outnumber girls as subjects in Stevenson's collection by a two-to-one margin (63% to 37%) overall. The disproportionate number of boys is sometimes taken to be a universal feature of the cases, and indeed there is an imbalance between the sexes in most cultures, but in Sri Lanka girls slightly outnumber boys (51% to 49%) (Stevenson, 1986a). The early age (two to five years) at which most children who speak about previous lives begin to do so, and the later age (five to eight years) at which most cease are universal features of the cases (Matlock, 1990b; Stevenson, 2001). Stimuli to the memories are more obvious with older children (Matlock, 1989). The social statuses of the case subject and previous person have not been compared across cultures in a rigorous way. However, it is apparent that usually the case subject and previous person are of the same ethnic, religious, and social group. There are exceptions, such as the Hindu/Muslim cases documented by Mills (1990), but they are in the minority everywhere.

Several other universal or near-universal case features relate to the previous person. Chief among these are the sex of the previous person, his manner of death and age at death, and whether or not he died leaving unfinished business.

Previous persons, like case subjects, are predominantly male. Since in the majority of cases there is no change of sex, this is not surprising, but as it turns out, the same pattern shows up in sex-change cases. In Stevenson's collection, three times as many girls claimed to have been boys or men than boys claimed to have been girls or women (Stevenson, 2001, p. 294n15).

Most children remember having died close to where they were born. Long-distance cases (with distances greater than fifty kilometers, or thirty-one miles, from the place of death to the place of birth) occur in larger countries like India and the United States, but cases that cross international boundaries are atypical, and solved international cases are rare. I know of only fourteen of them. In all fourteen, one can discern a motive for going abroad, suggesting that reincarnating internationally requires focus and intention on the part of the reincarnating mind (Haraldsson & Matlock, 2016, pp. 232–35).

Children everywhere are likely to recall how the previous person died, especially when the death was violent, and there are a disproportionate number of violent deaths in the cases of all cultures (Matlock, 1990b; Stevenson, 2001). Violent deaths—by accident, murder, suicide, during war, and so on—figured in 51% of solved cases and were claimed in 61% of unsolved cases in 1983 (Cook et al., 1983, p. 121). There was some variance in the proportion of violent death cross-culturally, but the number of violent death cases in all cultures was much higher than the incidence of violent death in the general population (Stevenson, 2001, p. 165).

Chadha and Stevenson (1988) examined length of intermission and age of first speaking about a previous life in relation to manner of death, natural or violent, in 326 cases from eight cultures and found violent death to be significantly associated with both variables: Violent-death cases had shorter intermissions than did natural-death cases ($p < .01$) and children with memories of violent deaths began to speak about them at a younger age than did children who recalled natural deaths ($p < .01$).

Intermissions are particularly short when death is by suicide. In a sample of ten solved suicide cases, I found the median intermission length to be three months (Haraldsson & Matlock, 2016, p. 253). The mean intermission length for these ten cases is twelve months, well under the 46.5-month mean that Chadha and Stevenson (1988) found for violent death cases in the DOPS collection. Ohkado (2016) reported a Japanese suicide case with an intermission of seven years and eight months. With this case included, the median intermission for solved suicide cases in the reincarnation studies literature is four months and the mean is 19.2 months.

Suicide cases also reveal a strong tendency to be associated with reincarnation in the same family or among friends. Of the eleven solved cases (including that reported by Ohkado, 2016), ten have family connections between the previous persons and the case subjects, and in the exceptional case, the previous person was the best friend of the case subject's father (Haraldsson & Matlock, 2016, pp. 252–53). This suggests that the self-killing gave the discarnate mind a degree of control lacking in other types of violent death, perhaps because the death was not sudden or unexpected, imposed against its will.

In a series of tests restricted to Indian cases, Stevenson and Chadha (1990) found age at death to be lower in violent-death cases than in natural-death cases, but the difference was not significant. Keil and Stevenson (1999) and Stevenson and Haraldsson (2003) found both a high incidence of violent death and a relatively early age at death among the Alevi and Druze, respectively. Because violent deaths are premature deaths, an earlier age at death in violent-death cases is not surprising. What is more interesting is that in natural-death cases, also, deaths tend to come at much younger ages than in the general population.

As of 2013, the median age at death in natural-death cases in the DOPS database was thirty-five years. In 25% of natural-death cases, the previous person was under fifteen. The younger the previous person was when death came, the more likely his life was to be recalled later (Tucker, 2013, pp. 200–202). Premature deaths—by violence or illness—are lives cut short and might produce the sense of things left undone, an effect Stevenson termed "unfinished" or "continuing business." He noted some sort of continuing business in the great majority of his cases (Stevenson, 2001, p. 212).

On other variables, there is pronounced cultural patterning. Length of intermission, calculated as time between the previous person's death and the case subject's birth, is one of these. In 2001 Stevenson wrote that with the exception of cases of replacement reincarnation and a "small number of outliers," all the cases in his collection had intermissions of less than three years. In a series of 616 cases, the median length was fifteen months (Stevenson, 2001, p. 120). The median varied across cultures, however, as shown in data from the 1980s (Table 5.1). It was four months among the Haida ($N = 17$) and eight months among the Druze ($N = 79$) but thirty-four months among the Igbo

Table 5.1   Median Intermission Length in Fifteen Countries or Cultures

Country or culture	Median intermission length (in months)	N
Haida*	4	17
Druze*	8	79
Alevi*	8.5	64
Beaver**	12	16
India*	12	170
Gitxsan**	16	22
Sri Lanka*	16	35
Thailand*	18	33
Burma (Myanmar)*	21	125
Tlingit*	24	41
Igbo*	34	35
Eastern Kutchin***	36	35
Brazil****	69	7
United States (nontribal)*	141	25
Wet'suwet'en **	180	16

Sources: *Stevenson (1986a); **Mills (1994b); ***Slobodin (1994); ****Haraldsson & Matlock (2016).

(N = 35) and 141 months (almost twelve years) in nontribal American cases (N = 25). It was relatively long also in Brazil and for the Wet'suwet'en.

Another variable on which there is distinct cultural patterning is the relationship between the previous person and the child's family. Cases may be grouped into three categories: family cases, acquaintance cases, and stranger cases, where family cases include all those with known genetic or marriage relationships between the previous person and the case subject. In tribal societies, family relationships include kinship structures such as lineages or clans. In 702 solved cases from ten cultures (not including the Beaver, Gitxsan, Wet'suwet'en, and Kutchin), the previous and present families were related in 42% of cases, otherwise acquainted in 31% of cases, and unknown to each other in 23% of cases. The only country or culture in which there were more stranger cases than family and acquaintance cases combined was Sri Lanka, where 52% of the cases were stranger cases (Table 5.2).

At the other extreme are animistic tribal cultures, including the Igbo and the native peoples of Alaska and western Canada, where there were few or no stranger cases. The 2% of Igbo stranger cases is represented by a single case, an "enemy" case involving a man from a different tribe who was killed in Igbo territory and became reincarnated among them (Stevenson, 1986a). In fact, the great majority of tribal cases were family cases. Some 96% of

Table 5.2 Percentage of Family, Acquaintance, and Stranger Cases in Fifteen Countries or Cultures

Country or culture	% of family cases	% of acquaintance cases	% of stranger cases	N
India*	16	41	43	183
Sri Lanka*	19	29	52	31
Druze*	24	46	30	80
Alevi*	29	54	17	63
Eastern Kutchin**	48	52	0	40
Burma (Myanmar)*	54	31	15	154
Brazil***	58	28	14	7
Thailand*	69	9	22	32
Haida*	87	13	0	23
Igbo*	92	6	2	53
U.S. (nontribal)*	94	6	0	16
Tlingit*	96	4	0	67
Beaver****	100	0	0	23
Gitxsan****	100[a]	0	0	67
Wet'suwet'en ****	100[a]	0	0	43

Sources: *Stevenson (1986a); **Slobodin (1994); ***Haraldsson & Matlock (2016); ****Mills (1994b).

Stevenson's Tlingit cases had family or lineage connections and all of Mills's Beaver, Gitxsan, and Wet'suwet'en cases did (Mills, 1994b). The Eastern Kutchin are an exception. Slobodin (1994) used different categories in reporting numbers for them, but it appears that the subjects and previous persons were related in twenty-seven (61%) of forty-four cases. Several of Slobodin's accounts (they do not seem to be fully investigated cases; most are historical anecdotes) involve non-Kutchin who happened to die on Kutchin lands and include persons with whom the Kutchin were acquainted, such as a runaway slave, a Japanese trapper, and two White men, as well as members of other indigenous groups.

Ohkado has found a large number of family cases in Japan. Of eight spontaneous cases he has studied, six had family connections (Ohkado, 2016, 2017) and two (Ohkado, 2012, 2013) were unsolved international cases. Ohkado has also studied an unsolved Japanese regression case suggesting a previous life in Nepal (Ohkado & Okamoto, 2014). Katsugoro (Hearn, 1897), it appears, was unusual in recalling the life of an unrelated person in Japan.

The most outstanding culture-linked feature of reincarnation cases is sex change between lives. In several cultures, there are no reported cases of sex change, but in Burma, as of 1986, 33% of cases were of this type. Among the Dene Tha, the figure is 44% (Goulet, 1994). The Eastern Kutchin traditionally expected to change sex from one life to another. On a brief visit in 1977, Stevenson found six (86%) of seven of Kutchin cases involved a change

Table 5.3   Percentage of Sex-Change Cases in Fifteen Countries or Cultures

Country or culture	Percentage of sex-change cases	N
Alevi*	0	133
Druze*	0	77
Haida*	0	24
Tlingit*	0	65
Wet'suwet'en **	0	46
Gitxsan**	1	67
India*	3	261
Sri Lanka*	12	114
Beaver**	13	23
Thailand*	13	32
U.S.*	15	60
Igbo*	18	56
Brazil***	28	7
Burma (Myanmar)*	33	154
Eastern Kutchin***	50	44

Sources: *Stevenson (1986a); **Mills (1994b); ***Haraldsson & Matlock (2016); **** Slobodin (1994).

of sex (1983b, p. 218n13), but Slobodin (1994) reported a 50% rate for his largely historical and anecdotal sample (Table 5.3). There are more female than male subjects of sex-change cases in most cultures. In Stevenson's non-tribal American cases, fourteen of fifteen children who remembered the life of a person of the opposite sex was a girl. Only among the Igbo did an equal number of boys and girls say they were a member of the opposite sex before (Stevenson, 2001, pp. 177–78). A similar disparity was found by Karl Müller (Muller, 1970, p. 131) with his sample of mostly Western cases. It is especially striking given the disproportionate number of male subjects in most cultures and underscores the predominance of male previous persons in reincarnation cases.

Pasricha and Stevenson (1987) compared Indian cases whose subjects were born before 1936 (first reported in the 1920s and 1930s and reinvestigated by them later) with cases with subjects born in 1965 or after. They found statistically significant differences on only five of fifty-four variables, revealing remarkable stability in the main features of Indian cases over time. This finding is consistent with an earlier study (Pasricha & Stevenson, 1979) in which the same authors compared cases they had investigated independently of each other and found significant differences on twelve of fifty-six variables, most having to do with the greater thoroughness of investigation by Stevenson. Keil and Stevenson (1999) likewise found that Alevi cases they had studied independently about twenty years apart were strongly similar, with the exception that the earlier ones had been more thoroughly investigated by Stevenson. Stevenson and Haraldsson (2003) reached a similar conclusion regarding Lebanese Druze cases they investigated independently.

Whether universal or culture-linked, or cross-historical, the patterns across reincarnation cases clearly are non-random. The psychosocial theory ignores the universal and near-universal patterns and seeks to explain the culture-linked patterns as responses to culturally sanctioned beliefs. That is, it presumes that beliefs about the reincarnation process determine how the cases develop and are reported. Let us evaluate this hypothesis by examining case features in relation to belief, culture by culture.

The great majority of Stevenson's Indian cases are Hindu, with some Sunni Muslim and a few Jain and Sikh. Unfortunately, Stevenson ignored the religious (and ethnic) affiliations of subjects in his statistical analyses, lumping together all cases from a given country. It is risky to take "country" as a proxy for "culture," especially in a nation as diverse as India, yet we have no choice but to examine Indian case features in relation to Hindu beliefs. Most Hindus do not have a firm expectation about the length of the intermission, but allow rebirth to occur at any point during gestation or even (as in parakaya pravesh or replacement reincarnation) after birth. The median intermission of 170 Indian cases was twelve months as of 1986 (Table 5.1). Hindus attribute the selection of the new parents to God and karma and do not normally expect the previous and present families to be acquainted or related, although the possibility is not ruled out. A relatively high percentage (43%) of Indian cases were stranger cases and a low percentage (16%) were family cases (Table 5.2). Announcing dreams in Indian cases occurred almost exclusively in family cases (Stevenson, 2001, p. 175). Hinduism does not forbid changing sex between lives, and 3% of Indian cases involved a change of sex (Table 5.3).

India is the only country in Stevenson's collection to have a marked disparity in socioeconomic circumstances between the previous person and the case subject (Matlock, 1990b, pp. 227–28). In two-thirds of the Indian cases, the previous persons lived in better socioeconomic circumstances than the subject. This disparity was said by Ian Wilson (1982, pp. 21–22) to be due to subjects imagining better lives for themselves in the past and therefore to provide evidence that the memories were no more than fantasies. Wilson's argument has been embraced by many skeptics (among them Edwards, 1996, p. 260, and Lester, 2005, p. 127), but in terms of the karma theory central to Indian culture, rebirth in poorer circumstances would indicate a demotion into the present life, not something a child would be likely to claim and certainly not something his parents would encourage (Stevenson, 2001, pp. 251–53).

Most of Stevenson's Sri Lankan cases developed among the Sinhalese, who adhere to the Theravada branch of Buddhism. Buddhism asserts that rebirth occurs at conception and expects intermissions to last at least nine months. The median intermission length of thirty-five Sri Lankan cases was sixteen months (Table 5.1). The relatively high percentage (52%) of stranger cases and relatively low percentage (19%) of family cases (Table 5.2) accords with the expectation that karma will determine the circumstances of the next life. Buddhism allows for a change of sex between lives, and 12% of Sri Lankan cases were sex-change cases (Table 5.3).

Announcing dreams were rare in Sri Lanka, consistent with the Theravada belief that there is no awareness during the intermission period (Stevenson, 2001, p. 175). They were common in Burma, where Theravada Buddhism is syncretized with animism to a notable extent (Brac de la Perrière, 2015; Spiro, 1982), but the majority came before conception (Stevenson, 1983b, p. 215), in line with the Buddhist idea that rebirth occurs at conception. Animistic influences may account for the high percentage (54%) of Burmese family cases in Stevenson's collection. Another 31% of Burmese cases were acquaintance cases and only 15% were stranger cases (Table 5.2). The median intermission length of Burmese cases was twenty-one months (Table 5.1). About a third (33%) of Burmese cases involved a change of sex (Table 5.3).

Stevenson's Lebanese cases were, with rare exceptions, from the Druze, whose distinctive beliefs likewise are reflected in their cases. The Druze maintain that reincarnation occurs immediately upon death, the spirit passing at once into the body of a child being born, and the eight-month median intermission in Stevenson's Druze cases is much shorter than in Buddhist cultures (Table 5.1). The Druze believe that God decides on the family into which one reincarnates, and as of 1986, 30% of Druze cases were stranger cases, 46% were acquaintance cases, and 24% had a family relationship (Table 5.2). The Druze hold that one cannot change sex between lives and Stevenson heard of no Druze sex-change cases (Table 5.3). Announcing dreams are rarely reported from the Druze, and when reported tend to be either premortem or postnatal, consistent with the expectation of immediate rebirth after death (Stevenson, 2001, p. 175).

Although the commonalities in animistic spirit beliefs allow them to be classed together as a type, each culture has its own expectations about the reincarnation process. Reincarnation within family lines is the ideal in lineal societies such as the Tlingit and Igbo, but whereas cases fall predominantly on the mother's side among the matrilineal Tlingit, they fall on the father's side among the patrilineal Igbo (Stevenson, 1986a). The Beaver and Eastern Kutchin, on the other hand, have a bilateral or cognatic social organization, and their cases show no tendency to cluster on one side or another (Mills, 1988b; Slobodin, 1994). The coastal Tlingit and the Gitxsan say that it is impossible to change sex between lives and have few or no sex-change cases. The Wet'suwet'en and Haida do not deny the possibility of changing sex between lives but have no reported sex-change cases (Table 5.3; Matlock, 1990b, pp. 226–27).

I know of no beliefs that would predict the wide variation in intermission length in animistic cultures, with medians ranging from four months in Haida cases to 180 months in Wet'suwet'en cases (Table 5.1). Mills (1988a, p. 397) suggested that the unusually long Wet'suwet'en median may be due to the inclusion of identifications made by "Indian doctors" (shamans). Among the Tlingit and other animistic peoples, announcing dreams occur during gestation, generally shortly before birth, although they are rare among the Igbo (Stevenson, 2001, p. 175).

Relatively few nontribal American cases are solved. As of 1983 (Cook et al. 1983b), 92% of Stevenson's Thai cases, 80% of his Burmese cases, 79% of his Lebanese (Druze) cases, and 77% of his Indian cases were solved, yet only 20% of his American cases were solved. All but one of Stevenson's sixteen solved American cases were family cases (Table 5.2) and in this exceptional case the previous person was a close friend of the mother (Stevenson, 1983a).

Little has been reported about most of these cases. Stevenson did not complete a planned book on nontribal American cases before his death in 2007. In *Children Who Remember Previous Lives*, he provided summaries of only two solved American cases, those of Susan Eastland and Michael Wright. Susan Eastland's is a family case and Michael Wright's is an acquaintance case. Two other solved American family cases have been reported since 2001, by Pasricha, Keil, Tucker, and Stevenson (2005) and Tucker (2005, 2013). I reported a solved American acquaintance case, the case of Cruz Moscinski (Haraldsson & Matlock, 2016). The longest intermission of these five cases is twelve years, in the case of Patrick Christenson (Tucker, 2005, 2013), but since this is the median given by Stevenson (1986a) for his American cases, there must be in the files a great number of unpublished American family cases with longer intermissions.

Since 1990, a few solved American stranger cases with child subjects have appeared. James Leininger (Leininger & Leininger, with Gross, 2009) is one, and Tucker (2013) reported three others (the cases of Ryan Hammons, Lee, and Hunter). With Rylann O'Bannion I have added a fourth. The shortest intermission of these four cases is Rylann's twenty-six years; the longest may be Ryan Hammons's forty years (Haraldsson & Matlock, 2016, p. 215). The median intermission length of these four American stranger cases is around thirty years. There is some uncertainty because the lengths of the intermissions for Lee and Hunter are not given by Tucker (2013), but clearly the intermissions of American stranger cases are a good deal longer than those of most American family and acquaintance cases.

Similar patterns are evident in solved European child cases. All are family and acquaintance cases, with a range of intermission lengths from seven days (in the case of Einar Jonsson, an Icelandic boy: Stevenson, 2003) to nineteen years (in the case of Ditta Larusdottir, an Icelandic girl: Stevenson, 2003). When combined with the family and acquaintance cases, the median intermission for published solved European cases is twenty-four months, considerably shorter than the median of American child cases, but longer than the median of sixteen months for all cases in the DOPS database (Tucker, 2013, p. 200).

American and European cases differ from Asian and tribal cases not only in intermission length but intermission distance (distance from the place the previous person died to the place the case subject was born). Although systematic figures on intermission distance cross-culturally are not available, it appears that long-distance cases (in which the birthplace was more than fifty kilometers or thirty-one miles from the site of death) are more common in Western than in Asian and tribal societies. Moreover, both Western and Asian international cases and accounts often have a European connection. Andrade (1988; Playfair, 2006, 2011) studied two Brazilian children besides

Karen (Yvonne Ehrlich) who recalled previous lives in Europe. Some Asian international cases, for example, B. B. Saxena (Stevenson, 1997a) and Tomo (Ohkado, 2013), have European previous persons. The exceptions are few. Three unsolved accounts portray previous lives in India (Gadit, 2009; Ohkado, 2012; Stevenson, 1974b, p. 17). Africa was the apparent site of the previous life in two unsolved European cases (P. Harrison & M. Harrison, 1991, pp. 53–57; Stevenson, 2003, pp. 114–26).

Longer intermissions would allow spirits of the deceased to meet loved ones at their deaths, a Western expectation not shared by the rest of the world. Longer intermission lengths and distances in Western accounts and cases also are consistent with the notion that intermissions are long and lives widely spaced geographically, characteristic of Western beliefs about reincarnation expressed in systems such as Theosophy and Spiritism and in some respects going back to the ancient Greeks. These features would result in greater contrast between past and present lives, presenting fewer cues to recall, which might help to explain why Western cases are comparatively rare and why those that are known are so much more difficult to solve than are Asian cases.

At first glance, there may seem to be a fair amount in the culture-linked patterns to support psychosocial theorists' contention that the cases are contrived responses to ideas about reincarnation in a given culture, but this assumption does not stand up to scrutiny. Most obviously, the psychosocial theory has trouble explaining universal and near-universal patterns in the cases. It does not have an explanation for cases among people who reject belief in reincarnation, such as Sunni Muslims in India (Mills, 1990) and Christian Europeans (Stevenson, 2003), nor why they occur in some belief contexts but not in others that are very similar (Pasricha, 2001a). Moreover, even where local beliefs are reflected in cases, the correspondences are not nearly as close as the psychosocial position supposes. The median intermission of six to eight months in Druze cases is less than all other cultures except the Haida, but it is far from immediate rebirth.

In earlier writings (Matlock, 1990b, 2011) I observed that many of the cultural influences on reincarnation cases have a ready explanation if we acknowledge that beliefs are diathanatic (a useful word, meaning "able to survive death," first used by Stevenson in *Reincarnation and Biology*, 1997a, vol. 2, p. 2074) and may influence a discarnate mind. Stevenson (2001, p. 180) made the same point. People are apt to adopt opinions and precepts prevailing in their cultures and religions, and if their minds survive the demise of their bodies, it should not be surprising that those opinions and precepts persist and help to determine what is experienced in the postmortem state. This may be why there are such strong cultural influences on descriptions of discarnate existence (Matlock, 2017; Matlock & Giesler-Petersen, 2016), and it may help to explain decisions about reincarnation made postmortem. If a person is convinced that sex-change is impossible, he might not be inclined to change sex in his next life. If he is sure that reincarnation occurs at conception, he might choose a woman who has not yet become pregnant to be his new mother. If he believes he must reincarnate in his father's line, that might be where he chooses to go.

Interethnic cases sometimes have features that differ from the expectations of the subjects' families, exactly what we should see if reincarnating spirits held variant ideas and the spirits' ideas were determinative. The announcing dreams experienced by Ma Tin Aung Myo's mother were exceptional in two respects for Burmese announcing dreams: They occurred during pregnancy rather than before, and the army cook informed her mother of his intention to be reborn to her rather than asking if he might be (Stevenson, 1983b). In another Burmese interethnic (and international) case, Ma Min Myint's mother had an unusual announcing dream, with an unrealistic scene blending into an announcement in which an English friend who died in London declared that he was coming back to her, bringing his luggage with him (Stevenson, 1997a, vol. 2, p. 1754).

Although the cases of the Burmese children who recall being Japanese soldiers are unsolved, we know approximately when the soldiers died and intermission lengths can be estimated. They are much longer than usual for Burma, having a median of 129 months (10.8 years) as opposed to twenty-one months (1.7 years) (Stevenson & Keil, 2005, p. 175). The intermission was unusually brief—if not immediate—in the account of a British functionary who died and was reborn in Burma in the early 1900s (Weird Story, 1907).

We see something similar in two cases of Alevi children who recalled the lives of ethnic Turks from Istanbul, five hundred miles away from their hometowns. Not only is this distance unusually great for Turkish cases, most of which develop among the Alevi, the intermissions were much longer than the eight-and-a-half-month median for Alevi cases (Table 5.1). Kemal Atasoy recalled the life of a man who had died fifty years before his birth (Keil & Tucker, 2005). Like Kemal, Murvet Dissiz remembered the name of the person she believed she had been, but Stevenson and his Turkish assistant Reşat Bayer found no evidence of her existence during the ten years of records they were able to search (Durant, 1968, pp. 74–79).

The idea that culturally prescribed beliefs may influence discarnate actors receives further support from two additional cases. When Nai Chook, a Thai boy, met the mother of the person whose life he recalled, she asked him why he had not been reborn to her. He explained that it was because of the sacred thread. The sacred thread is part of a Buddhist ceremony following a death. Monks chant and hold a thread, which is passed around to all present, who cut off sections and tie them to their wrists. The remainder of the thread is hung around the house to deter spirits, hence Nai Chook's reluctance to enter. He waited outside for his mother, but she did not emerge. He went to the well thinking she would go there, but his present mother appeared instead, and he got into the basket she was carrying. When she stopped by a canal on her way home, he jumped into the water. As soon as she drank, he lost awareness, coming to as her child (Story, 1975, pp. 193–94).

Stevenson (1997a, vol. 1, pp. 1634–40) describes a case (the case of Cordelia Ekouroume) in which an Igbo medicine man whose sister had been threatened with death dispatched the offender by witchcraft. The woman later died of natural causes and was reborn in her brother's family (as identified by an oracle), but died again after a year. Enraged that she had not lived longer after what he had done for her, the man chopped the fingers and toes off the infant's corpse and hung them, along with some "medicines," in a bag in his house. This ritual was intended to banish her spirit from his family. The medicine man also bound the corpse's legs together, to prevent her spirit from walking. For eleven years his action had the desired effect, but a new wife, unaware of what he had done, cut down the bag, breaking the spell, and her next child (she had already delivered three healthy babies) was born with several malformed digits (both fingers and toes) and with a deep constriction ring on the lower left leg, where the infant's corpse had been bound.

THE PSYCHOLOGICAL IMPACTS
OF PAST-LIFE MEMORY

I think it is time to let go of the idea that reincarnation entails karma in either the retributive or juridical sense, but that does not mean that I see no influence of past lives on present ones. On the contrary, reincarnation cases provide abundant illustrations of the past impinging on the present, but through the carryover of psychological traits and burdens, not the strictures of a moral law imposed on a person from without. It would make sense that we would see signs of such "processual karma" if what passes from life to life is a continuous stream of consciousness which is duplex in its nature because the subconscious would preserve the memory, behavioral dispositions, elements of personality, and so on, that comprise a person's identity. It would make sense also that this subconscious content brought over from a previous life would remain latent in the present life unless and until it was drawn forth by some precipitating event, and then it might intrude upon conscious awareness and/or be expressed behaviorally.

In Chapter 4, I described how case subjects identify with the people whose lives they recall through their behaviors as well as through their words, but I left until this chapter a discussion of the psychological impacts past-life memories have on case subjects. The impacts may be negative as well as positive and can be hard not only for the subjects but also for their families and friends to handle. Rylann's case is a good example of how deaths can affect the psyche and lead to behavioral difficulties that have all the earmarks of post-traumatic stress disorder, even before memories enter conscious awareness. However, this is only one of the ways past-life memories may affect children.

Skeptics come at this topic from a very different position than I do. Because they believe that the mind cannot survive death, skeptics explain the problem behaviors of some case subjects as reactions to their home environments. They assume that a child's genetic makeup coupled with his upbringing—nature and nurture—is sufficient to explain everything about him. Eugene Brody (1979) elaborated the parental guidance scenario from a psychoanalytic perspective. Stephen Braude (1995, 2003) called for intensive studies of family dynamics in reincarnation cases. Some critics have gone a step further and presumed to see signs of mental illness in the children. Ian Wilson (1982) compared past-life memory to multiple personality disorder (MPD), now officially called dissociative identity disorder (DID). C. T. K. Chari (1967, p. 220) charged that the "patchy memories" of reincarnation cases resembled the disordered memories seen in some psychopathologies.

Erlendur Haraldsson (1995) rephrased these presumptions as testable hypotheses: Children with past-life memories have disturbed relationships with their parents, live in social isolation from their siblings and peers, are highly suggestible and attention-seeking, lead rich fantasy lives, and have dissociative tendencies. These psychological and behavioral traits can be identified through questionnaires, and Haraldsson and others have administered batteries of tests to case subjects and their caregivers, sometimes also to their teachers, in Sri Lanka, Lebanon, India, and the United States. Let us see what these studies tell us.

Haraldsson (1995) compared twenty-three Sri Lankan children (aged seven to thirteen years) whose cases had been studied either by himself or Stevenson to a control group of children who had not claimed to have past-life memories, matched by sex, age, and neighborhood. The subjects included eight boys and fifteen girls. Haraldsson administered the Gudjonsson Suggestibility Scale, the Raven Progressive Matrices, and the Peabody Picture Vocabulary Test to the children and the Child Behavior Checklist to an adult in the home (usually the mother) and to a teacher.

Haraldsson (1995) found that children with past-life memories (target children) were no more suggestible and no more given to confabulation than their peers (control children) were, but that they had greater verbal skills, better memory test scores, and performed better in school than their peers did. Parents of target children rated them higher on several items in the Child Behavior Checklist, but their teachers did not. Their teachers, in fact, judged them to be socially more mature, getting along with other children significantly ($p < .05$) better than their peers. Haraldsson (1997) confirmed these findings with a slightly larger sample ($N = 30$).

Haraldsson (1995, 1997) at first included no good measure of dissociation but rectified this in a later Sri Lankan study with twenty-seven pairs of children aged five to ten years (Haraldsson, Fowler, & Periyannanpillai, 2000). The sample included fourteen pairs of boys and thirteen pairs of girls who had not been included in the earlier studies. This third study found that children who claimed past-life memories had greater dissociative tendencies (e.g., rapid changes in personality and frequent daydreams) than their peers did, but they scored no higher on social isolation, suggestibility, or attention-seeking.

There were no signs of disturbed relationships with parents, as assessed by the Family Questionnaire, although as in the earlier studies, target children were considered by their caretakers to talk too much and to be more argumentative, more tense, more highly strung, more anxious and fearful, and more obsessional and perfectionistic than were control children. Contrary to Haraldsson's earlier findings, there was no difference in cognitive abilities, although target children performed significantly ($p < .01$) better in school than did their peers, and when the samples of the three Sri Lankan studies were combined, the difference in the scores on the cognitive measures was significant overall (Haraldsson, 2003, p. 57).

In order to evaluate the cross-cultural validity of these results, Haraldsson (2003) turned to the Lebanese Druze. This study included thirty pairs of children, aged six to fourteen years. There were nineteen pairs of boys and eleven pairs of girls. Of the children with past-life memories, seven were still spontaneously talking about the past life, eighteen would do so if asked, and five had lost all their childhood memories. Haraldsson employed many of the same instruments as before, with the addition of the Dream Questionnaire. He found that children with past-life memories daydreamed more and had more dissociative tendencies but were no more suggestible than their peers, did not confabulate more than their peers, and did not live in social isolation. They did not differ from their peers in their vocabulary or memory, nor in how hard they worked, how appropriately they behaved, or how happy they were. They received higher scores on attention-seeking, though, and when Haraldsson examined the pooled results of the Sri Lankan studies on this item, he discovered a significant association on this variable as well (2003, p. 60).

Mills (2003) tested fifteen American children with imaginary playmates and fifteen Indian children with past-life memories, aged three to five years, together with controls in both countries. She found that children in both groups started talking about their experiences at thirty months (two and a half years) and stopped talking about them between seventy and ninety months (six to seven and a half years). Although she found no significant differences between the target and control groups, children in both target groups were notably less suggestible than their peers, but they (in contrast to what Haraldsson found in Sri Lanka and Lebanon) scored more poorly on cognitive measures and performed less well in school. In a later study, Mills (2006) submitted the Tellegen Absorption Scale to thirty-one Indian young adults who as children had claimed to recall previous lives and to thirty-one control subjects who had not asserted past-life memories. The target group scored significantly ($p < .05$) higher than the control group, indicating a greater capacity to immerse themselves in their mental imagery.

Jim Tucker and F. Don Nidiffer (2014) examined the psychological functioning of fifteen American preschoolers, aged three to six years, who had spoken or were speaking about previous lives. Most of the lives were of strangers and the cases were unsolved but in four cases there were family connections and the previous persons were recognized. The children were assessed on the Stanford-Binet Intelligence Scale and the Children's Apperception Test, while their parents completed the Survey Form of the Vineland Adaptive Behavior Scales, the Child Behavior Checklist, the Child Dissociative Checklist, and the Family Questionnaire. The children's scores were compared to statistical norms rather than to matched controls. Scores on the Stanford-Binet scale were greater than one standard deviation above the mean. On the Vineland Adaptive Behavior Scales, the children scored significantly above average in daily living skills, motor skills, and on the composite score. There was no distinct patterning on the Family Questionnaire. The Child Behavior Checklist averages were all in the normal range, and all but two children obtained low scores on the Child Dissociative Checklist, meaning that they revealed no tendencies toward dissociation.

These studies vary in their methodology and all have small sample sizes but none provide support for the suppositions of the psychosocial theory as advanced by Brody (1979), Braude (2003), and others. There are no signs of disturbed relationships with parents or of other interpersonal conflicts that could explain why the children feel the need to invent past lives. Nor is there evidence that the children are more suggestible or fantasy-prone than their peers or that they are socially isolated. Indeed, several studies have suggested the opposite, that children with past-life memories are more mature, socially adjusted, and intelligent than other children. The problem behaviors reported for some children could be consequences of their memories rather than causes of them.

Haraldsson (1997, p. 331) says that subjects of solved cases were significantly ($p = .03$) less suggestible than subjects of unsolved cases in Sri Lanka, an intriguing finding, should it hold up cross-culturally. In addition to comparing solved and unsolved cases, it would be good to see comparisons of children who recall natural deaths with those who recall violent deaths and to differentiate between those who are still actively speaking of a past life and those who are not. Children typically cease speaking about their memories around the time they start school, so some of the difference in the evaluations of parents and teachers on the Child Behavior Checklist could be attributable to the age of the child at the time he was evaluated. In one study (Haraldsson, 1995), the teachers were interviewed almost eighteen months after the families. It may be that although some children with past-life memories face behavioral challenges, these recede as the memories fade or become better managed, leaving longer-term benefits.

Children received high problem scores on the Child Behavior Checklist in Sri Lanka and Lebanon but not in the United States, perhaps because of the relatively high proportion of violent-death cases in the former countries. Some 76% of Sri Lankan children and 77% of Lebanese children claimed to recall sudden or violent deaths, and these memories could have acted as stressors leading to the excessive attention-seeking and other behavioral deficits (Haraldsson, 2003, p. 64). Indeed, Sri Lankan and Lebanese children (combined) who recalled violent deaths had significantly ($p = .03$) higher problem scores than did children who recalled natural deaths (Haraldsson, 2012a, p. 228).

Memories of sudden and violent death may help to explain the elevated scores on measures of dissociation in Sri Lanka and Lebanon. The level recorded for Sri Lanka is comparable to that reported for sexually abused American girls, although Haraldsson saw no evidence of abuse or neglect and the scores were well below those of American MPD/DID patients (Haraldsson, 2003, pp. 63–64). The general profile is comparable to that of children at risk for developing schizophrenia later in life (Haraldsson, 2003, p. 64), but only one of Stevenson's subjects (Wijeratne) was diagnosed with schizophrenia and his illness stemmed not from memories of the previous person's death but from the guilt he felt about the murder he recalled having committed (Stevenson, 1974b, 1997a). A similar symptomology, consistent with "a non-pathological dissociative response to stress," is seen with near-death experiencers (Greyson, 2000).

Another class of stress-related behaviors are phobias that cannot be explained by reference to incidents in the child's present life but which correspond to people, places, or articles related to the previous person's death. Phobias differ from other behavioral memories in that they do not mimic behaviors exhibited by the previous persons but instead constitute the emotional reactions one might expect him to have displayed, had he lived rather than died.

Jennifer Schultz died during a thunderstorm and Rylann became anxious during thunderstorms. She told me when I interviewed her at age ten that they still made her uncomfortable and a little fearful. Rylann has never had a fear of planes or of flying, only of thunder and lightning.

Phobias are common in reincarnation cases. In a series of 387 cases examined by Cook et al. (1983b), 141 (36%) included phobias. The phobias occurred (with varying frequency) in the cases of all cultures and they occurred with about equal frequency in solved and unsolved cases. However, they were nearly always associated with violent death, known or alleged. In a series of 240 Indian cases, phobias were reported in fifty-three (39%) of the 135 cases in which the previous person's death was violent but in only three (3%) of the 105 cases in which it was natural (Stevenson, 1983a).

Phobias often are most pronounced when associated with strong episodic memories but they may appear before a child is able to express his memories in words—as they did with Rylann—and they may appear in silent cases. Derek Pitnov, a Tlingit boy, was identified by a diamond-shaped birthmark on his abdomen as the reincarnation of a warrior who had died in a spear fight sixty-five years before his birth. From childhood he showed a marked fear of knives, bayonets, and spears, although he never spoke about a previous life (Stevenson, 1974b). As this case suggests, not only may phobias appear without conscious awareness of the event to which they relate, they may be generalized as well as specific. Ravi Shankar Gupta, who recalled having his throat slit by a barber and a washerman, was afraid of all barbers and washermen (Stevenson, 1974b). Phobias generally fade along with episodic past-life memories, but some outlast them, even continuing into middle adulthood (Haraldsson & Abu-Izzeddin, 2012). Stevenson (1990) discussed phobias in reincarnation cases in greater detail (see also Stevenson, 2001, pp. 182–84).

For some children, painful memories arise in nightmares. James Leininger (Leininger & Leininger, with Gross, 2009) is a famous example. Mills (1994b) described three unsolved cases of American and Canadian children troubled by nightmares that seemed to be connected to earlier lives.

Recollections of having been a member of a different religion, caste, or ethnic group, or of the opposite sex, are of a different order (they do not flow from memories of the previous person's death), but may be just as troubling to a young child trying to find his place in the world. The assumption of the psychosocial theory that these past-life identities are somehow foisted upon the child by his parents fails not only to explain why the parents would induce these alternate identities, but why the children should invest so much emotion in them.

The most intense conflicts emerge in sex-change cases, unsurprising because self-identity is closely tied to gender. A previous life as the opposite sex is recognized as a possible explanation for gender dysphoria in Indic (Stevenson, 1977b, 1977c, 2000a; Tucker & Keil, 2001) as well as animistic (Goulet, 1996, 1997; Mills, 2014) cultures. This apparently is a minority view among contemporary American gays (Kear, 1999), although reportedly it is common among those in the LGBTQ community who believe in reincarnation.

In the majority of sex-change cases that involve cross-dressing or other gender nonconformity in young children, this lessens and dissipates as the children age. Examples include Gnanatilleka Baddewithana (Stevenson, 1974b), Ampan Petcherat (Stevenson, 1983a), Erin Jackson (Stevenson, 2001), and Jacira da Silva (Andrade, 2010a). Occasionally there is a more lasting gender dysphoria. Paulo Lorenz recalled the life of a sister who had killed herself, having stated her wish to be male the next time around. Paulo identified strongly with his sister as a child, and even though he became heterosexual in adulthood, continued to be notably effeminate and never married. At forty-three, he took his own life (Stevenson, 1974b). Ma Tin Aung Myo lost most of her memories of the Japanese army cook by her late teens but never adjusted to a female gender role and in her twenties became an open lesbian (Stevenson, 1977c, 1983b). Will, an American who identifies as a straight man in a woman's body and is legally married to a woman, is another example of gender dysphoria in childhood persisting into adulthood (Wehrstein, 2019).

Although the fading of past-life memories by age eight is considered a universal feature of reincarnation cases because it occurs cross-culturally, the memories may last through late childhood and even into adulthood. In a study of Sri Lankan adults who as children spoke about previous lives, Haraldsson (2008) discovered that sixteen (38%) of forty-two still possessed some of their memories. Haraldsson and Majd Abu-Izzeddin (2012) found that twenty-four (86%) of twenty-eight Lebanese subjects did so. The difference between these findings may stem from cultural factors. Relatively few Sri Lankan cases are solved, most likely due to the Sinhalese disinclination to use personal names and the failure of many children to recall them (Stevenson, 1977a), and children stop speaking of previous lives much earlier when cases remain unsolved (Cook et al., 1983b).

If retention of at least some memories is common with those who have them when young, it may be wrong to assume that when children cease speaking about their memories spontaneously, they have forgotten them. My daughter Cristina stopped relating her memories of the pink farm after a few months when she was three. I assumed that they had faded and let the matter drop. I did not bring up the subject again until she was eleven, but when I asked her if she remembered anything of what she had said when she was younger, she told me that she did. At that time all were recurring memories she had had since early childhood, but the following year she recalled what she thought was something new: painting at an easel before a window on the farmhouse's second floor. She was certain that the windows opened out, rather than up, and that they were not far to the right of a fireplace. Rylann first spoke about being on the carport swing when she was ten. Haraldsson and Abu-Izzeddin (2012) note that some of their Lebanese subjects likewise reported memories they had not mentioned in childhood.

Memory management is a critical issue for those who recall previous lives. Children like Cristina and Rylann carry a double identity. They feel themselves to have been other people before, yet they must adapt to their present lives as the people they are now. Most children, even those who experience difficulties when young, learn to manage their memories as they grow older and come to lead well-adjusted and productive lives as adults (Haraldsson, 2008; Stevenson, 2001). In Lebanon, Haraldsson and Abu-Izzeddin (2012) found that fifteen (53%) of twenty-eight subjects evaluated their memories as beneficial, although only four would wish their children to have their own past-life memories. Mills (2006; also Mills, 2004, p. 632) found in a follow-up study of her case subjects in India that most subjects felt that their memories had been "helpful" and eighteen (64%) of twenty-eight said that they would like their children to remember a previous life. Nonetheless, some of Mills's subjects felt that their memories had interfered with their education or with the establishment of mature relationships. The relatively poor school performance captured in Mills's (2003) psychological study may be due to the interference of the past-life memories.

The reaction of a child's parents to his memories is another potential source of difficulty. Many parents attempt to keep their children from talking about their past-life memories. Suppression measures are widespread for reasons that range from the belief that children are making up stories (in cultures without reincarnation beliefs) to the folk myth that children with such memories die young, fear of reprisals from people the children name as the previous persons' murderers, and worry that the previous families will take the children away (in cultures with reincarnation beliefs). Indian parents tried to suppress their children's memories in twenty-nine (41%) of sixty-nine cases studied by Stevenson and Chadha (1990).

In Cambodia, and no doubt in other Buddhist countries, past-life memories are expected to surface in meditation as a person nears enlightenment and are a cause of concern when they occur to young children. Behavioral memories are considered detrimental karmic influences and parents take steps such as having the child consume unfertilized birds' eggs in order to induce amnesia for the past life (E. W. Davis, 2015). In southern China, children may be fed carp soup to make them forget their past-life memories (Southern Weekly, 2015).

Most known suppression attempts are unsuccessful. E. W. Davis (2015) described a Khmer girl who retained her memories at age ten, when he interviewed her, despite her parents' best efforts to rid her of them. Tucker and Keil (2001) described a Thai boy who claimed to remember the life of his grandmother. The boy cross-dressed, wore his mother's earrings and lipstick, preferred to play with girls, and disliked boys' games, traits in which he persisted despite complaints from both parents and attempts by his father to make him more masculine. Sometimes the suppression efforts backfire on the parents, as happened with Ravi Shankar Gupta (Stevenson, 1974b). Ravi Shankar's father, fearful that the past-life parents would try to take him away, beat him severely to get him to stop talking about the previous life, but this succeeded only in making the boy afraid of his father and he continued to relate his memories to others.

Stevenson and Chadha (1990) found no statistically significant relationship between suppression and the duration of a child's speaking about a past life in India. This is probably true elsewhere as well. Even when they succeed in getting a child to stop talking about his memories, suppression measures may not make the images disappear from his conscious awareness. The Ven. Chaokhun Rajsuthajarn (Stevenson, 1983b) desisted from his claims to have been his mother's brother when he tired of his family's attempts to make him forget that life, yet his memories remained clear in his mind when Stevenson interviewed him at sixty-one.

In a study of maternal attitudes in India, Pasricha (2011a) compared initial reactions of mothers to their children's claims to remember previous lives to attitudes after the case was solved and the previous family and other outsiders had become involved in their lives. Of 292 cases for which data on initial attitudes were available, Pasricha judged 21% of mothers to be encouraging, 51% to be neutral, and 28% to be discouraging. Follow-up information was available for 136 subsequently solved cases. The "encouraging" rating increased slightly, but the "discouraging" rating much more so, to 43%, as many mothers shifted from neutrality to discouragement and began acting to make their children forget the previous lives out of fear of losing their children to the previous families.

Some children experience the trauma of being rejected by the families they remember. Dolon Champa Mitra (Stevenson, 1975a) recalled the previous family fondly and showed the way to their house, but was rejected by the mother, who could not understand why her son had not reincarnated in the family and why he was now a girl rather than a boy. Many previous families reject children who cannot pass recognition tests to their satisfaction, even if other signs support their claims. In Western cases, past lives may lie in the more remote past and circumstances have changed so much that the previous families cannot be traced, even if their houses are located, leaving the children despondent (e.g., Cameron, as reported by Robertson, 2013, and Tucker, 2013).

In Western societies the lack of acceptance of past-life memories can create problems for parents and children alike. Many parents of children who speak of previous lives and deaths have never taken the possibility of reincarnation seriously and do not know how to respond to what they hear. Some are able to allow their opinions to change and provide support as required, but not all can. No doubt the majority of Western parents maintain a dismissive attitude. When my three-year-old nephew began to talk about having lived in Chicago, a city to which he had never been, my sister passed it off by saying that he had not been talking long and frequently got his pronouns and tenses mixed up. I could not get her to write down anything he said about the Chicago life and after a few years, he forgot about it.

There would seem to be no lasting harm from most cases of this nature. If parents feel challenged in their beliefs, though, they can react negatively, and this can have more detrimental effects. I have heard from a woman whose memories began to surface at an early age but were ridiculed by her secular humanist mother. When she was not quite three, she chanced to see a picture she believed depicted herself in the life she recalled. She excitedly showed this to her mother, who responded by locking her out-of-doors on a winter day. Not surprisingly, she did not speak of her memories again, but began to draw the scenes of realistically gruesome pre-firearms battles and other events she saw in her mind. She remembers drawing hundreds of pictures, all but two of which her mother destroyed. Gradually her imaged memories receded, but corollary interests persisted. Strong feelings of shame and guilt, along with the sense that she was in some way bad or crazy, stayed with her into middle adulthood before she came to appreciate that her childhood drawings and related lifelong concerns derived from memories of an earlier life.

The many documented cases of past-life memory with psychological impacts in the present life suggest that mental health professionals would do well to consider the possibility that some of their clients' conflicts are rooted in previous existences (Mills, 1994b; Pasricha, 2011b; Stevenson, 2000a). Materialist clinicians tend to assume that reincarnation beliefs are pathological in themselves, although the beliefs may be thought to say something about the relation of cultural and religious precepts to psychological disturbance (Daie, Witztum, & Rabinowitz, 1992; Iancu, Spivak, Mester, & Weizman, 1988; Spivak, Iancu, Daie, & Weizman, 1995).

Julio Peres (2012) made the point that accepting reincarnation is not necessary for treatment to be effective, so long as the patient's values are respected. A. A. Gadit (2009) viewed past-life memories as fantasies, although his treatment included assuring his child patient (a Sunni Muslim boy whose visit to India evoked memories that caused him considerable angst) that there was no doubt about their genuineness. J. R. T. Davidson et al. (2005) held that beliefs in karma and reincarnation helped Americans cope with trauma, although they did not themselves believe that the trauma emanated from previous lives.

Some Western clinicians have portrayed reincarnation beliefs as socially useful. Roland Littlewood (2001) argued that identifying young children as the returns of deceased persons replaced prolonged mourning among the Lebanese Druze. Eli Somer et al. (2011) found that reincarnation beliefs provided comfort to Israeli Druze parents of youth killed in combat. See Peres et al. (2005) and Peres et al. (2007) for additional thoughts on this subject.

Not all children have negative experiences with their past-life memories. Cristina did not. She talked about her memories of the pink farm matter-of-factly, never with distress, or even nostalgia. For many children, however, past-life memories can be as much a curse as a blessing. In the end, the memories may confer scholastic or other advantages, but getting there is not always easy. Rylann no longer throws fits when changing shirts, rarely sleepwalks, and sleeps well on her own, but for several years she behaved as if she were badly traumatized. Her family's patience must have been severely tried, particularly before they began to form an idea of what might be causing her to act in these ways.

Positive past-life memories can create confusions and conflicts when a child recalls having been an elder (perhaps a parent) to his elders and parents. When the previous and present families are unknown to each other before a child is recognized as the return of a deceased loved one, social and psychological adjustments are required on both sides (Bennett, 2006). Persisting emotional bonds may lead to problems over the long term, as they did for Reena Kulshreshtha (Mills, 1989). Reena's love for Shyam Babu Yadev lasted well after her episodic memories had faded, preventing her from forming attachments to other men. Chanai Choomalaiwong (Stevenson, 1997a, vol. 1, pp. 300–323), whom Stevenson last saw at eighteen, in his forties came to wish he no longer had his past-life memories and attachments to the previous family. He stopped going to see them, so that he could get on with living in the present (Haraldsson & Matlock, 2016, p. 127). Rajiv Khanna (Dhiman, 2002, Jan. 12) also found himself torn between his previous and present families.

It should not be surprising that past-life experience may impact subjects behaviorally, even when they have no conscious memories. Depth psychology has understood this dynamic for more than a century in relation to memories of our present lives, and mainstream memory researchers have recently come to the same realization. Martin Conway remarks, "The suggestion that episodic memories arising from everyday experience may have enduring nonconscious effects is particularly interesting and points to a new and potentially important direction for future autobiographical memory research" (2005, p. 596). My suggestion that past-life experiences may have an unconscious effect on us is only an extension of known psychological processes to include past as well as present lives.

Perhaps the most impressive thing about past-life memory is how personal it is. Episodic, emotional, and procedural memories are unified by an identification with, and a sense of psychological continuity with, a deceased person. This is apparent in both solved and unsolved cases. If we did not expect to find it with reincarnation, we should have. The psychosocial theory, for its part, is ill-equipped to account for the strength of the identifications, even with the assistance of super-psi. As Stevenson, Pasricha, and Samararatne (1988) showed, parental imposition of identity can occur, but when it does, it is not accompanied by the feeling of being one with a predecessor.

Why do only a few people remember previous lives? I believe we have built-in defenses against consciously remembering who we were or exactly what happened to us before. Our psyches block knowledge of the past so that we may get on with living in the present (Haraldsson & Matlock, 2016, pp. 262–63). I have seen it asked, How can we learn from our mistakes, if we do not remember having made them? This question assumes that reincarnation is about personal betterment, a very Western preoccupation. Reincarnation may not be about personal betterment, so much as about adaptation to circumstance. The question to be asked may not be, Why do we not remember our previous lives?, but rather, Why do some people remember some things, especially when the things they remember are troubling to them? What purpose does past-life memory serve? The answer varies from person to person, but often it seems to have to do with psychological needs of the previous person and to express unresolved issues carried over into the present life, an expression of processual karma (Haraldsson & Matlock, 2016, p. 263).

Chapter 6

Past-Life Recall in Adulthood
and Third-Party Reports

The reincarnation cases of adults are weaker than those of children in the variety of signs they include, in how extensively memories penetrate into conscious awareness, and in overall evidential value. Many fewer adult than child cases are veridical, much less solved. In the first section of this chapter, I show how these differences are attributable to developmental changes that make it more difficult for past-life memories to penetrate into conscious awareness and behavioral expression as case subjects age. In the second section, I take up apparent past-life memories arising under hypnosis. Regression memories reveal a much greater degree of distortion than do involuntary past-life memories. I argue that this is due to psychological blocks to recall when attempts are made to induce memories, rather than allowing them to surface spontaneously. In the concluding section, I turn to the past-life identifications and readings of psychic practitioners such as shamans, psychics, and mediums. Psychic practitioners sometimes are able to retrieve information from the minds of their clients that the clients cannot access for themselves. They cannot accomplish this, however, if the clients' subconscious resistance is too strong.

DEVELOPMENTAL FACTORS IN
PAST-LIFE MEMORY RETRIEVAL

The past-life memories of adults have received little attention from researchers, who have concentrated on children's memories largely for evidential reasons. Not only are adult past-life memories much less elaborate than children's, it is much easier to demonstrate that children have not been exposed to the things they talk about through books, magazines, films, or television than it is with adults. One of the few researchers to have taken an interest in adults' past-life memories, writer D. Scott Rogo (1985, 1986, 1991), held them to be qualitatively different from children's memories, but I believe he was wrong about that. The involuntary past-life memories of children and adults look different at first glance but can be seen as related if viewed along a developmental continuum (Matlock, 1988a, 1988b, 1989).

Adult past-life memories may be defined as those occurring to subjects ten years or older, although this is an arbitrary dividing line. There is no definite break between child and adult forms of past-life memory. We can trace the changes in relation to three variables: the strength of penetration of episodic memories into conscious awareness with related behavioral and physical signs; the presence of triggers or cues, especially for the initial memories; and the state of consciousness in which the memories emerge. The younger the subject when he first speaks about the previous life, the stronger and more varied the signs are likely to be, the less likely the memories are to be notice-ably cued, and the less likely they are to involve altered states of conscious-ness. The first and second of these relationships receive statistical support from Tucker (2000) and Matlock (1989), respectively. The third has not yet been assessed formally but can be demonstrated impressionistically and may be taken as a prediction from the theory of past-life memory I elaborate in this chapter.

Very young children may express their past-life memories somatically. Alan Gamble was only forty-eight hours old when his arm began to swell below the place a tourniquet had been tied on his uncle's arm to stanch the bleed-ing from the wound in his hand (Stevenson, 1997a). Before she could speak coherently, Nadine Mann's throat became red and swollen when she tried to describe her memory of being strangled and drowned by her past-life husband (Haraldsson & Abu-Izzeddin, 2004). Some children have displayed phobic reactions before they could put their memories into words (Stevenson, 1990). From her birth onward, Shamlinie Prema violently resisted being bathed and from six months had a marked fear of buses. When she could talk, she described having been forced by a bus off a road into a paddy field, where she drowned (Stevenson, 1977a).

Bishen Chand Kapoor, whose case was first studied by Sahay (1927) and later by Stevenson (1975a), made his first reference to a previous life at ten months. This was the word "Pilvit" or "Pilivit," corresponding to Pilibhit, a town fifty kilometers from where he lived. As his speech improved, he gradu-ally filled in his memories of a life in Pilibhit as a man named Laxmi Narain. Besides having extensive episodic memories, Bishen Chand was sexually precocious, wanted to eat meat, and was discovered surreptitiously drinking alcohol. He had a taste for finery, evinced an unusually keen interest in kite flying, and could play tablas without instruction. He spoke occasional words in Urdu (foreign to his family) and reportedly was able to read that language without being taught it. He also suffered from a chronic eye infection.

Bishen Chand was five and a half years old when he came to Sahay's attention. He had not been to Pilibhit and his case was not yet solved. Sahay recorded many of his statements and persuaded his father to take him to Pilibhit to see if they could be verified. In Pilibhit, Bishen Chand recognized places and people and correctly answered questions put to him about Laxmi Narain, who had died (of illness) two years before he was born. Bishen Chand led the way to a room in which gold coins had been hidden by Laxmi Narain's father, in a location unknown to his mother or others. Laxmi Narain had inherited a small fortune and was inclined toward debauchery. He ate meat, drank alcohol to excess, spent time with prostitutes, liked to fly kites and to play musical instruments. He had been able to read and write Urdu. He also had an eye infection, for which he had been treated with an Ayurvedic ointment that was found to be successful with Bishen Chand as well.

Bishen Chand's case includes a variety of episodic, procedural, and emotional memories along with physical signs and is among the most developed (and evidentially strongest) reincarnation cases on record. Several other unusually well-developed cases involve children who gave some indication of remembering a previous life before their second birthday (Tucker, 2000). Half of Stevenson's subjects were under three years old when they first spoke of the previous life (Cook et al., 1983b). When children are over three when they begin to relate their memories, they report fewer episodic memories and their behavioral and physical signs are weaker or absent. Ryan Hammons (Hammons, 2017; Kean, 2017; Tucker, 2013) is an exception to this rule, but Ryan had chronic problems with his adenoids that made it difficult for him to hear. He did not speak in complete sentences until he was four years old but then began talking incessantly about the previous life he recalled (Haraldsson & Matlock, 2016, p. 215).

When Mallika Aroumougam was an infant, her family moved to a new town where they rented the ground floor of their landlord's house (Stevenson, 1974b). Mallika became strongly attached to the landlord's wife but gave no indication of remembering a past life until she was nearly four and for the first time visited the rooms upstairs. There she noticed some embroidered cushions and declared that she had made them. In reality, they had been made by the woman's deceased sister, Devi. Mallika began to spend as much time in the landlord's apartment as she could. She recognized other things and people related to Devi and behaved in ways reminiscent of her but made no comments that were not cued in some fashion.

As a young child, Suleyman Andary (Stevenson, 1980) had some vague memories of having lived before. He said he had resided in the village of

Gharife, where he had had an olive press. At the age of five or six, he said some names in his sleep. When asked about them the following morning, he explained that they belonged to the children of his past life. However, fuller memories did not begin to come to him until he was eleven, provoked by an incident with his grandmother.

When this woman visited his home and asked to borrow a religious book, Suleyman refused to let her have it. Pressed to explain why, he suddenly recalled that in the previous life he had not allowed religious books to leave his house. After this he made an effort to remember more about the former life and succeeded in bringing forth new details. Among these were the name of the previous person, Abdallah Abu Hamdan, and that he had been the mayor of Gharife. When he was thirteen, Suleyman was taken to Gharife and there led the way to Hamdan's house and made additional statements as well as recognitions of people and places. His imaged and verbal memories were not strong, nor were his behavioral memories. Although Suleyman liked to carry himself like the important adult he believed he had been and was more interested in religion than were his family and peers, he did not display the specific behavioral signs many younger case subjects do.

In an appreciable number of other cases, memories emerging in later childhood or adulthood were preceded in early childhood or infancy by hints or outright claims of having lived before. In his childhood, Ruprecht Schulz (Stevenson, 2003) had the habit of gesturing with his hand as if he were shooting himself in the head but said nothing about a previous life. As an adult he had déjà vu experiences when traveling but it was not until he was in his fifties that distinct memories came to him.

Ruprecht was in a position of withdrawing account books from a wall safe night after night. Each time he did this he had the feeling that he had been in the same situation before. Finally he asked himself what exactly was the earlier situation. He then saw images of a man he felt was himself in a past life, dressed in formal attire as if he had come from a celebration of some kind. The man went to a wall safe, took out account books, and examined them. Seeing that he was ruined, he produced a gun and shot himself in the temple. Ruprecht noted these details in his diary and set about verifying them, eventually identifying the man he recalled and solving his own case.

Memories that arise in early childhood, even partially, may lie close to conscious awareness, making them relatively easy to retrieve later in life. Other adult cases with childhood precursors include Giuseppe Costa (Stevenson, 2003), Laure Reynaud (Stevenson, 2003), George Neidhart (Stevenson, 2003), A. J. Stewart (Stewart, 1978), Jenny Cockell (Cockell, 1994, 2017), Jeffrey Keene (Keene, 2003), Angela Grubbs (Grubbs, 2006), Yael

Shahar (ben Malka & Shahar, 2015), Stéphane Allix (Allix, 2017), and Will (Wehrstein, 2019).

Wehrstein (2019) claims that Will is an exception to the rule that past-life memories penetrate less fully in adulthood than in childhood. "Will's remembering appears to be more typically childlike in that it has strong penetrance, is accompanied by supporting behavioural and physical signs, is mostly not cued, and mostly arises during the normal waking state" (Wehrstein, 2019, p. 2). However, "Will feels that he always had memories, but did not recognize them as such at first and so had no notion of the source of the images and scenes in his mind until around the age of 18, when he learned about reincarnation" (Wehrstein, 2019, p. 3). Perhaps it would be better to think of Will as a child who retained past-life memories into adulthood than as a subject whose past-life memories arose principally in adulthood, although the previous person in the life Wehrstein describes was not identified until Will was an adult. Looked at in this way, the apparent anomalies of his case disappear.

Frederick Lenz (1979) collected 127 accounts of adult past-life memory in the United States and categorized them according to their triggers and states of consciousness in which they arose. Lenz made no attempt to verify the accounts and most are unsolved. He claimed that they had features, such as a bright light and dark tunnel, consistent with the near-death experience then recently described by Raymond Moody (1975), although few of the accounts he reported actually demonstrate these features. Rogo (1985) collected another series of adult past-life memories in an effort to verify Lenz's findings. There were no NDE-like features in Rogo's series, but the accounts showed the same triggers in roughly the same proportions as in Lenz's series, so Lenz's analysis of factors in adult past-life memory retrieval was supported. Other collections of adult past-life memories (Fenwick & Fenwick, 1999; Gershom, 1992, 1996; Jacobson, 1974; Muller, 1970; Osborn, 1937; Rivas, 1998; Shirley, 1936; Tenhaeff, 1972) leave the same impression.

Some kind of cue to the past-life remembrances, as Lenz called them, were involved in seventy-nine (62%) of the accounts. In nine accounts, the remembrances were brought on by hearing a piece of music, seeing a painting, or coming into contact with an object thought to be associated with the previous life. In twenty-eight accounts, the remembrances were triggered by visits to a city, town, or other place (including in three the place where the previous person was felt to have died). The largest group of remembrances, no fewer than forty-two, were responses to people the rememberer believed he had known in a previous life, or to people whose previous persons his previous person had known. This last factor is interesting, especially given its frequency. Nils Jacobson (1974, pp. 182–88) described a Swedish case that may have been evoked in this way, and Karl Müller (Muller, 1970, pp. 117–20) provided other examples. Unfortunately, although it may make sense psychologically, it is hard to see how the impression could be verified without knowing the past-life identities of both individuals.

Adults seldom report unstimulated or uncued memories in the waking state. Lenz (1979) heard about only thirteen such cases (10% of the total). Unprompted adult memories are more likely to arise in dreams or other altered states of consciousness. Of Lenz's 127 accounts, nineteen (15%) involved dreams. Children also sometimes dream about past lives, but whereas children's dreams often accompany memories in the waking state (Mills, 1994b; Stevenson, 1997a, vol. 2, pp. 1386–87n; Stevenson, 2001, p. 281n13), the past-life dreams of adults may be all there is to a case. Some of the apparent Holocaust memories that Yonassan Gershom (1992, 1996) collected surfaced in dreams, and dreams figure in other collections of adult past-life memories (Fenwick & Fenwick, 1999; Muller, 1970; Rogo, 1985).

Past-life memories may also arise unbidden during meditation. Lenz's (1979) collection includes seventeen accounts (13% of the total) related to prayer or meditation. Stevenson (1983b) reported the case of a Thai woman, Pratomwan Inthanu, who at twenty while meditating recovered fragments of two lives that ended in infancy. Her memories surfaced quickly, as images, sense impressions, and voice-overs that gave the names of people and places related to each life. She traveled to the specified locations, where she recognized people, found her way around unaided, answered test questions, and acted in other ways like younger subjects, but her episodic memories were relatively weak. She had no behavioral memories of these earlier lives and her body expressed no physical signs of them. Allix (2017) self-reported a French case of verified past-life memories arising during meditation. As a child, he experienced nightmares related to the earlier life, and in retrospect he connected certain emotional memories and personality traits to that life, but none penetrated as strongly as they typically do with young children.

Other altered states, not represented in Lenz's collection, may also be conducive to involuntary past-life memory retrieval. Children sometimes recall things when they are sick (Stevenson, 1997a, pp. 194n, 696n), especially during febrile illness (Stevenson, 2001, p. 53). Severe stress and mental illness have been known to release past-life memories in adults (Muller, 1970, pp. 126–28). George Neidhart (Neidhart, 1956; Stevenson, 2003) had some slight memories as a child but was in his twenties, in precarious economic circumstances and tormented by religious doubts, when he experienced a series of waking visions with associated names that pointed to an earlier life in medieval Germany. Pasricha (Pasricha, 1990a, pp. 109–12; Pasricha, Murthy, & Murthy, 1979) reported the case of a schizophrenic Indian man who on one occasion while in his psychosis recalled occurrences in the life of his maternal grandfather. Past-life memories may also appear under the influence of psychotropic drugs such as LSD (Grof, 1985, 2009; Rogo, 1985, 1991).

Some children (e.g., Parmod Sharma in Stevenson, 1974b; Indika Guneratne in Stevenson, 1977a) have a tendency to become immersed in their memories, but dissociative episodes with children are rare. Many adult past-life memories reveal a greater detachment. Adults often see images passing before them, as if they are watching a movie (Lenz, 1979; Rogo, 1985). They sometimes see themselves from the outside, in observer perspective, as Ruprecht Schulz did (Stevenson, 2003).

Occasionally there is a more extreme dissociation. Krishnanand (1968, pp. 102–11) tells of witnessing a ten-year-old Indian boy without a history of seizures convulse and fall to the ground following a lecture on the virtues of right living. While in trance, the boy led the way to what he said was his home, recognized the woman who came to the door as his wife, and answered questions sufficient to convince her of his identity. He indicated the place where the man had secreted some money. When the woman left to get refreshments for her visitors, the boy emerged from his trance without any awareness of what he had said and done.

Rogo held that children experience their past-life memories no differently from the memories of their present lives but that adults' past-life memories arise in "special states of mind radically different from waking consciousness" (1991, p. 15). However, past-life memories may appear during normal waking, dream, and altered states of awareness in children as well as adults. The main difference lies in the relative frequency of these states, not in any absolute difference in the way past-life memories are expressed in childhood versus adulthood.

Factors on the side of the case subject are not the only ones implicated in past-life memory retrieval. The previous person's concerns and mental qualities are important as well (Haraldsson & Matlock, 2016, pp. 264–65). This is not surprising, if the previous person's consciousness stream is continuous with the case subject's, because in significant respects the previous person has become the case subject and the previous person's needs have become the case subject's needs. This is why the circumstances of the previous person's death may be reflected in a case subject's phobias and other post-traumatic symptoms.

Stevenson (2001, p. 212) noted that in the majority of his cases, there were indications of ongoing or unfinished business carried over from the previous life. A premature death from murder, accident, or illness might produce a sense of incompleteness, but many cases have more specific types of unfinished business, such as a desire to tell widows where valuables are hidden, a wish to collect or repay debts, or a yearning to return to children left behind.

The emotional quality of these more specific types of unfinished business is clear. A. C. Holland and E. A. Kensinger (2010) stressed the importance of emotional factors in present-life memory formation and retrieval. Once again, memory of past lives seems not to be very different from the memory of present lives.

The emotional dynamic is apparent in Krishnanand's (1968) case if we allow that the determination of the previous person to show his widow where he had hidden money was strong enough to cause a dissociation that permitted the memory to surface in the conscious awareness of the boy (who, incidentally, was primed for its reception by the lecture he heard). The determination originated with the previous person, but the impulse toward its expression arose within the boy. Likewise, Laxmi Narain may have carried with him the need to communicate where his father's gold was hidden and this could have helped encourage the early emergence of memories of his life in Bishen Chand Kapoor (Sahay, 1927; Stevenson, 1975a). Margot Klausner (1975, pp. 121–22) described a similar case from the Lebanese Druze. For other examples, see Matlock (2017, October-b).

Another factor in past-life memory retrieval appears to be the previous person's quality of mind. This goes beyond the state of mind at death, as emphasized in Hinduism and Buddhism; it refers to a general mental conditioning. Iris Giesler searched the published record for cases of death by natural processes in old age. She found ten cases in which natural deaths (deaths other than by accident or murder) came at age sixty or later and noted that in six of these ten cases, the previous persons were devout or pious Buddhists. This accords with Stevenson's observation (2001, p. 214) that the previous persons in several of the natural-death cases in his collection were unusually spiritual.

Many of the previous persons in Giesler's sample were practiced in meditation (which in Asian cultures, from which the majority of the cases came, typically accompanies spiritual practices). Some previous persons who died at younger ages also were assiduous meditators. The Ven. Chaokhun Rajsuthajarn's uncle had meditated regularly before his death at forty-five (Stevenson, 1983b). Exceptionally good and exceptionally poor memory on the part of the previous person may promote or inhibit past-life memory retrieval as well (Stevenson, 2001, p. 213), and there may be other mental traits with similar effects yet to be identified. There is some evidence that alcohol intoxication at death may militate against the appearance of birthmarks and other physical signs (Stevenson, 1997a, vol. 1, p. 1102).

The previous person's emotional needs and mental qualities seem to be factors in past-life memory retrieval with both adults and children, but they are more apparent with children, especially very young children. The appearance of behavioral memories before imaged memories in some cases suggests that children's episodic memories sometimes may be delayed in breaking into conscious awareness. Some children may have imaged memories before they are able to talk about them, as was almost certainly true of Ryan Hammons (Haraldsson & Matlock, 2016, p. 215).

Interestingly, some young children give the appearance of relating their memories under greater psychological pressure than is evident with older children and adults. Varying pressure from within the psyche to get out memories of a previous life could explain why memory triggers become more apparent when case subjects are older when they first start speaking of the previous lives. I suspect, though, that past-life memories arising at whatever age express a need of some sort. With adults, this may be a need for resolution of emotional conflicts carried forward from the past, a kind of unfinished business of the psyche, and after the initial triggering the memories may flow freely.

The past-life memories of adults differ from those of children not only in being less detailed, but in being less accurate (Stevenson, 2001, pp. 49–52). There are now over seventeen hundred solved child cases on record (Mills & Tucker, 2015, p. 318), but only about a dozen solved adult cases, counting those with memories that began in childhood but did not became fully expressed until adulthood. Stevenson's choice of case to investigate was dictated not by the age of the subject but by evidential strength, and he came across many fewer adult cases that justified his time and resources.

In many adult cases, the identity of the previous person appears to be blocked. Edward Ryall had memories of a past life from childhood but was in his seventies when he wrote them down (Ryall, 1974). His story includes semantic memories of time and place that give it a superficial plausibility, yet none of the named persons appear in historical records (Stevenson, 2003). Mrs. Smith (Guirdham, 1970) experienced richly veridical dreams of the Cathars, but the central figures of her story could not be identified. Angela Grubbs (2006) is highly unusual in being able to solve a case based solely on dreams.

A considerable part of the difference in the quality of child and adult accounts and cases may be ascribed to developmental factors. It may be harder for past-life memories to surface in the minds of adults, and a resistance to accurate recall is more apparent with adults. Memory is motivated (Conway, 2005), which is to say that it is susceptible to unconscious manipulation. Conway notes that memory distortions frequently are "attempts to avoid change to the self, and ultimately to goals" (2005, p. 599). Similarly, I believe that distortions in past-life memory assist the psyche in masking past-life identities. With older children and adults there are more pronounced distortions than in the memories of younger children. Distortions are especially evident in dreams.

Som Pit Honcharoen (Stevenson, 1997a) recalled the life of a man who was stabbed to death at a festival by a woman to whom he had made unwelcome sexual advances. As a young child he described what happened accurately in his waking state but between the ages of ten and twenty-eight he had a recurrent dream in which he came close to being stabbed at a festival by a man. Paul Von Ward (2008, pp. 27–28) described a recurrent dream in which a car falling from a cliff into the sea represented an aircraft crash into the sea. James Kent (2003) dreamed he was with a wounded Confederate general when they were captured by Union troops. He was able to identify the general and confirm his injury with documents from the National Archives, but there is no record of the general ever having been taken prisoner. Another example comes from the Guatemalan woman who experienced phantom pain at the site of a birthmark on the back of her left flank. Inquiries in her family led to her learning that her great-uncle had been ambushed and stabbed in this spot by a machete, but before she found this out she had a dream about being stabbed by a machete in a bar.

Many people who remember past lives feel themselves to have been transported to earlier times with personalities, attitudes, and emotional reactions different from their present lives. These experiences carry the stamp of authenticity, but unfortunately, they cannot be trusted unless they can be verified. Studies have shown that confidence in memory accuracy can be as high with false memories as with genuine ones (Barclay & Welman, 1986), even in subjects with highly superior autobiographical memory (Patihis et al., 2013).

I believe that all memories, from past lives no less than from present lives, are valid, in the sense that all express a psychological truth, but there is a difference between psychological validity and factual validity. Past-life memories may have good psychological validity but lack factual validity. There is individual variation, of course. Most people remember nothing about previous lives, while others remember something, and a few quite a lot. Some people recall multiple past lives well enough for more than one to be solved (Wehrstein, 2019). Nonetheless, the patterns in past-life remembering are consistent and clear. The strength of the penetration of the memories and their overall accuracy declines as children age and it is rare for subjects over ten to recall things in as much detail and with as much accuracy as young children do, even when they have retained some memories from childhood. Much work remains to be done with adult cases—especially solved adult cases—but it seems unlikely that additional cases will appreciably alter these conclusions.

Claims to remember the lives of famous people call for special comment. Famous people certainly can expect to reincarnate like everyone else, so famous past life (FPL) claims should not be dismissed summarily. I consider a few FPL reports to be credible (Keene, 2003; Stewart, 1978; Tucker, 2013, pp. 120–37). However, adults are much more likely than children to claim previous lives as famous people. Famous people also are much more likely than others to have their lives recalled by more than one person. Probably in the majority of these instances the identification is due to no more than wishful thinking and pattern matching, the search for a life that fits the fragmentary memories that have come to conscious awareness—what Angel (2015) terms the "subjective illusion of significance."

Few adult past-life memories have been subjected to the scrutiny routinely given those of children. The adult case that has received the greatest attention is the extraordinary case of Uttara Huddar, better known by the name of the previous person, Sharada (Akolkar, 1992; Pasricha, 1990a; Stevenson, 1984).

Unlike most cases of past-life memory, the Sharada case involves dissociative episodes, and it is unique in the extent of the dissociation involved. Sharada emerged not once, as in Krishnanand's (1968) case, but numerous times beginning in 1974, for periods of one to forty-three days. When she was in control, Sharada spoke an archaic regional dialect of Bengali, a language largely unknown to Uttara even in its standard contemporary form. She interacted with Uttara's family, to whom she believed her husband had entrusted her when he left on a trip, but was confused by modern life and behaved as if she were living in Bengal in the first third of the nineteenth century. The last thing she remembered was being bitten on her right toe by a snake when she was seven months' pregnant. She gave the names of her husband and several members of his family. The family was traced and several of the names found listed in a private genealogy, in the relations that Sharada assigned to them, but because the genealogy is restricted to the male line, Sharada's name and those of her female relatives do not appear on it. The case remains officially unsolved for this reason. If it were a solved case, the intermission would be around 107 years.

The Sharada case's unusual features have engendered much confusion. Almeder (1992) interprets it as a case of possession, but that was not the opinion of its investigators (Akolkar, 1992; Stevenson, 1984; Stevenson & Pasricha, 1980). Uttara was thirty-two when Sharada first appeared, but her emergence was preceded by developments similar to those in children's reincarnation cases. Uttara's mother repeatedly dreamed that she was bitten on her right toe by a cobra while she was pregnant with her and as a young child Uttara had a phobia of snakes. Uttara also had dreams that might have been of Sharada, although she never experienced waking images that could be related to a previous life and never claimed to remember one.

Sharada began to appear at a time when Uttara was in emotional distress, having been rejected by a childhood friend she had expected to marry. She had entered an ashram, run by a man (called Dr. Joshi by Stevenson, Dr. Z by Akolkar) to whom she felt strongly drawn. As part of her treatment she was meditating, and it was during meditation that she began to be aware of Sharada. The dissociative episodes began when Uttara happened to encounter Dr. Joshi dining in his private rooms with another woman (Stevenson, 1984, pp. 74, 105).

Sharada identified Dr. Joshi as her husband reborn. Dr. Joshi himself had no memories of a previous life, and there is no way of knowing whether Sharada was right or wrong about that. Regardless, the emotional reaction to finding the man she regarded as the reincarnation of her husband with another woman helps to explain why Sharada emerged when she did. She emerged in the way she did thanks to Uttara's age, I think, but that is only part of the explanation. Women who die leaving young children are among those with unfinished business and Sharada was close to term, already having had two miscarriages. She was evidently much in love with her husband and had every reason to want to prolong her life, which was cut short abruptly.

The Sharada case resembles MPD/DID more than possession and has much to teach us about past-life memory storage and retrieval. Sharada responded appropriately in her strange new situation, although she was in many ways stuck in the past, unable to get beyond her habitual actions, and she never seemed to grasp what had happened to her. Uttara and Sharada were amnesic about each other's activities, but there was evidence of communication between them that suggested a mutual awareness at a subconscious level (Stevenson, 1984, pp. 115–18). By the early 1980s there were indications that their personalities were beginning to merge (Stevenson, 1984, pp. 152–53), although Sharada continued to break through occasionally after that (Tucker, 2013, p. 28).

Uttara was in a psychologically vulnerable state when she met Dr. Joshi, whose presence seems to have been the catalyst that brought the memories of Sharada to conscious awareness. If Sharada shows us Uttara in a previous life, then memories laid down in the subconscious are vastly more extensive than standard reincarnation cases would have us suppose. But this case is not altogether exceptional. Uttara's past-life memories were much stronger than would be expected at her age, probably due to the dissociative state in which they were expressed, but in their nature they are no different from the memories of younger subjects.

Braude (1995, 2003) focused on Uttara's psychology while ignoring Sharada's. He supposed that Uttara invented the Sharada personality in response to the rejection by her friend and as a compensation for an unhappy life. He contended that Sharada's detailed knowledge of Bengali geography and customs was retrieved by Uttara through a "motivated psi" or super-psi in her altered state of mind. Griffin (1997) accepted Braude's portrayal of the case and discussed the issue of motivation in relation to retroprehensive inclusion. Sharada, Griffin suggested, was an alternate personality of Uttara, who reached out psychically to locate a deceased person who fulfilled her deepest psychological needs (1997, pp. 180–83). Sudduth (2016, p. 130), too, adopted the alternate personality interpretation.

This insistence on looking at Uttara's psychology without taking Sharada's psychology into account is born of a refusal to accept that Sharada could represent Uttara in a previous life, but if Sharada is reincarnated in Uttara, she is a part of Uttara. Sharada's psychological needs have become Uttara's. We can say that Sharada is an alternate personality of Uttara if we wish, but she is that by virtue of having been Uttara herself in an earlier life. This interpretation explains Uttara's knowledge of Bengal, its people, and its language without recourse to super-psi and provides a logical rationale for Sharada's restriction of focus to a particular place and time.

Linguist Sarah Thomason (1996) acknowledged that Sharada spoke Bengali mostly in full, grammatically correct sentences, but thought that Uttara's lessons in reading contemporary Bengali and her study of Sanskrit, an extinct language, were sufficient to explain Sharada's speaking in the archaic regional dialect she did. Thomason emphasized the conclusions of a linguist who listened to a short recording of Sharada's speech but ignored the opinions of native Bengali speakers who spent hours conversing with her. Braude (2003, pp. 114–27) did not dispute Uttara's linguistic proficiency but argued that not only "knowledge that" but "knowledge how" (skills, including language skills) might be acquired by super-psi, although he could not explain how this would be possible, or muster any data in its support. The assertion of a possibility on philosophical grounds does not make it plausible in practice. Thomason and Braude give the impression of searching for facts to support their preconceptions of this exceptional case rather than examining it in its complexity and with open minds.

FANTASY AND FACT IN PAST-LIFE REGRESSION UNDER HYPNOSIS

Many people can be hypnotized and brought to experience—often very dramatically—scenes that seem to depict earlier lives. The technique by which this is accomplished is known as age regression or, nowadays, past-life regression (PLR). The hypnotist guides the subject back through the years until he reaches his birth, then suggests that he go back further still, until other images come to mind. Alternatively, the hypnotist may direct the subject to go to the source of his traumas or conflicts, with the understanding that these may lie in previous lives. Regression has become a popular method of accessing past-life memories, but can it be trusted? How does the information retrieved under hypnosis compare to that which surfaces involuntarily in the waking state or dreams? Is hypnosis a useful clinical tool?

Dieter Hassler (2015) reviewed the long history of past-life memories arising under hypnosis or similar altered states of consciousness. The first person known to have conducted age regression as such was French physiologist Charles Richet in 1883, but he took his subject back only to age six (C. W. Perry, Laurence, D'Eon, & Tallent, 1988, p. 128). A few years later psychical researcher Albert de Rochas discovered that he could regress people beyond birth and thought that he had found a controlled way of studying reincarnation. Rochas reported his experiments first in the *Revue d'hypnotisme* in 1896 (Rochas, 1896) and described them in his books *Les états profonds de l'hypnose* (Rochas, 1904) and *Les vies successives* (Rochas, 1911). He followed up his regressions by checking the names and other information given in them but was unable to confirm the existence of any of the people his subjects identified as their previous persons, and many of the details of the lives they recounted were anachronistic or wildly improbable (Ducasse, 1961, pp. 271–74).

Regression studies continued, but with little notice until the 1950s. Early in that decade, British psychiatrist Sir Alexander Cannon produced *The Power Within* (Cannon, 1953), which summarized one thousand sessions and sought to show how later lives were impacted by earlier ones. Around the same time, Morey Bernstein, a Pueblo, Colorado, businessman and amateur hypnotist, regressed a woman he called Ruth Simmons (later identified as Virginia Tighe). Bernstein published the story in a newspaper serial in 1954, then two years later in a book, *The Search for Bridey Murphy* (Bernstein, 1956), which quickly became a number one national best seller. The success of Bernstein's book was due in part to some of Tighe's description of a nineteenth-century life in Ireland having been confirmed by investigations there, but when a rival newspaper claimed to locate the origin of Tighe's memories in her own past, the public turned on Bridey as quickly as it had fallen for her.

Skeptics, uninformed critics (Gravitz, 2002; Spanos, 1996), and even some reincarnation advocates (Iverson, 1976; Knight, 1995) continue to assert that the Bridey Murphy case was debunked, although the charges were discredited as soon as they were made. It was alleged, for instance, that Virginia Tighe could have picked up things about Bridey's life from an Irish aunt with whom she had lived in her childhood. But this aunt, albeit of Irish extraction, had been born in New York and spent most of her life in Chicago. She had never visited Ireland, and Tighe had gotten to know her when she came to live with her family when she (Tighe) was eighteen (Bernstein, 1965; Ducasse, 1961, pp. 276–99). *The Search for Bridey Murphy* was reissued in 1965 (Bernstein, 1965) with fifty pages of new material that discussed the controversy and reported the results of additional research in Ireland, but the damage to the reputation of the case was by then irreparable.

Professional hypnotherapists, fearing that their field was being diminished, were quick to react to the first edition of Bernstein's book. Milton Kline (1956) rushed out an edited volume that explained the apparent past-life content of some regressions as responses to the hypnotist's suggestions or as imagined memories masking repressed conflicts. E. S. Zolik (1958, 1962) described how the past-life regression of a young man related to unresolved present-life tensions with his grandfather. But some clinicians adopted a different stance. Denys Kelsey, the husband of far-memory novelist Joan Grant, started using hypnosis and age regression to help patients in a military hospital as early as 1948 and sometime later (he does not tell us exactly when) discovered that he could induce them to go back beyond their births to the sources of their traumas in earlier lives (Kelsey & Grant, 1967).

Kelsey accepted the induced memories as genuine without attempting to validate them. Other therapists (Dethlefsen, 1977; Fiore, 1978; Netherton & Shiffrin, 1978) took up past-life therapy in the 1970s and followed suit. Thorwald Dethlefsen (1977) believed that the dramatic force with which the ostensible memories were acted out warranted their authenticity. Edith Fiore (1978) and Morris Netherton and Nancy Shiffrin (1978) concluded that because their clients were helped by the regressions, the images that came to their minds represented real events. Helen Wambach (1978) regressed over one thousand people in a series of small groups and claimed, among other things, that because the reported lives were of average people and included a roughly equal number of males and females, she had good internal evidence of their truth. However, Wambach made no effort to verify any of the individual memories and identified no specific persons as the persons her subjects recalled having been.

The popularity of past-life therapy has not receded since the 1970s. New practitioners appeared in the 1980s (Goldberg, 1982; B. L. Weiss, 1988), the 1990s (TenDam, 1990; M. Newton, 1996), and the first decade of the present century (Freedman, 2002; Tomlinson, 2006), to cite only a few of the more influential. Starting with a book by Jungian analyst Roger Woolger (1987) that emphasized the value of the apparent memories to individuation (self-realization), sidestepping the evidential question, the field divided. Clinicians adopted Woolger's transpersonal model, while other practitioners debated the ontological status of the hypnotic productions and followed Wambach in trying to probe the reincarnation process (Knight, 1995, 1997; Lucas, 2007; Saunders, 2004).

Past-life therapy may help to resolve conflicts originating in earlier lives, but the claim of past-life therapy to be unusually successful should be accepted with caution. Hassler (2015) examined 291 regressions in which a cure was asserted. Follow-ups were reported in 44% of instances, but rarely more than a few weeks after the sessions concluded. No long-term follow-up studies of regression cures have been reported, nor have there been formal comparisons with standard psychotherapeutic procedures (Mills & Tucker, 2013, p. 308), so we cannot be sure that the apparent cures are lasting or that the technique really is superior to other approaches, as many of its champions (e.g., Woolger, 1987) would have us believe.

Moreover, even if regression therapy were more successful than other forms of psychotherapy, we would not be able to conclude that the lives recalled necessarily transpired as experienced under hypnosis. Past-life therapy could succeed if patients were subconsciously reworking memories in ways that allowed them to relieve anxieties without revealing what actually happened, permitting the psyche to process troubling issues without confronting them directly (Booth, 2007). Psychological validity does not necessarily equal factual validity.

Woolger (1987, p. 89) tells us that "the hypnotherapist . . . actively directs and helps rework stories, images and fixed ideas that arise from the unconscious in trance states" through his questions. This interactive role can be an effective therapeutic approach, but it has no place in research, because of the role suggestion plays in the proceedings. The mere suggestion of recalling a previous life is sufficient to make a person imagine one. Authors in Kline (1956) made this point, and it has been confirmed in laboratory tests by Robert Baker (1982), Nicholas Spanos et al. (1991), Y. D. Pyun and T. J. Kim (2009), and Pyun (2015). Ian Wilson (1982) noted that hypnotists who believed that intermissions would be centuries-long had subjects who reported lengthy periods between lives, whereas those who believed intermissions would be short had subjects whose intermissions were relatively brief. Instruction merely to go back to the source of trauma is no guarantee that things that come up under hypnosis are true in all details either.

Additional questions have been raised about past-life regression in comparison to spontaneous recollections in the waking state. Lyn Saunders found hypnotically induced and involuntary memories of previous lives were phenomenologically similar, but subjects with involuntary memories were significantly ($p < .001$) more likely to feel that they had benefited from them (2004, p. 102). Positive aftereffects often follow near-death experiences (Long & P. Perry, 2010) and apparition sightings (Arcangel, 2005, pp. 283–88) as well, yet Kellye Woods and Imants Barušs (2004) found that college students who envisioned past lives during guided imagery came away with no greater sense of well-being than those who did not experience such imagery.

Elke Geraerts (2012) determined that among girls reporting childhood sexual abuse, memories surfacing in the waking state were more likely to be real than those elicited under hypnosis. Involuntary intermission memories are more similar to NDEs than to regression accounts in their depiction of postmortem consciousness (Matlock & Giesler-Petersen, 2016; Sharma & Tucker, 2004). Some mediumistic messengers describe dying in terms very similar to NDEs (Carter, 2012, pp. 291–300), but many people undergoing regression do not. Whereas NDErs feel themselves to maintain continuity of identity with their bodies and selves, regressed subjects frequently report a shift of awareness with a change in personality (Wade, 1998, pp. 40–45).

One of the rationales for using hypnosis to access memories of previous lives is the idea that hypnosis enhances memory, but experiments by Jane Dwyan and Kenneth Bowers (1983) and by Stephen J. Lynn et al. (1997) have called this assumption into question (see also Spanos, 1996, pp. 57–68). Memories retrieved in age regression within a subject's present life are liable to distortion and confabulation (C. W. Perry, Laurence, D'Eon, & Tallant, 1988), and we should expect the same with past-life memories. Indeed, Peter Moss and Joe Keeton (1979) detected fantasy intrusions in several of Keeton's regressions. Stevenson (1994; 2001, pp. 43–47) gave other examples of fantasy intrusions and comments on the "foolish implausibilities" that often are introduced under hypnosis. Testimony based on hypnosis is not admitted into courts of law for these reasons.

If clinicians have been concerned with verity at all, they have tended to see it as an issue distinct from therapeutic efficacy (Booth, 2007). Efforts at verification have been left to other practitioners, but their investigations have turned up problems of various kinds (Bettis, 1998; R. James, 1995; Marriot, 1984). Spanos et al. (1991) solicited names, dates, and other verifiable data in one of their tests, but their regressed subjects could not name the leader of the country in which they found themselves, nor did they know whether the country was at war or peace at the time. Jonathan Venn (1986) studied a series of regressions intensively and discovered that he was able to corroborate information through archival records in the United States, where his subject resided, but not information he had to check in materials housed overseas, in France.

At the same time as it fails as a memory enhancer, hypnosis may allow forgotten information to enter conscious awareness with the appearance of genuine memory, a phenomenon known as source amnesia or cryptomnesia (Baker, 1992). Cryptomnesia is not restricted to hypnosis (Stevenson, 1983c), but it is well documented with present-life age regression (C. W. Perry et al., 1988), so again, it is no surprise to encounter it with past-life regression. Melvin Harris (1986a, 1986b) traced the sources of two of British hypnotist Arnall Bloxham's regressions (Iverson, 1976) to historical novels, Ian Wilson (1982) implicated cryptomnesia in one of Joe Keeton's (P. Moss & Keeton,

1979), and Rob Nanninga (2008) showed it to be involved in one of Peter Ramster's (Ramster, 1990). E. S. Zolik (1958) and Reima Kampman and Reijo Hirvenoja (1978) regressed their subjects to past lives, then hypnotized them again and asked where they had gotten their information for their historical portrayals. The subjects said that it was from stories they had heard, books they had read, or things that had happened to them in their present lives, but did not refer to previous existences.

Occasionally some information given in regressions checks out, but as with successful regression therapy, we must not overinterpret this to mean that the named individuals necessarily lived in the past. *Soul of Nyria* (Praed, 1931) has the distinction of being the first regression account to include extensive veridical content. Nyria represented herself as a Roman slave girl and gave many obscure but verified details of life in ancient Rome, but her existence could not be confirmed by historical records. Bridey Murphy (or Virginia Tighe as Bridey Murphy) mentioned, among other things, the names of shop owners in Belfast during the period Bridey said she lived and knew the names of places that did not appear on maps. Bridey gave a plausible account of her life, with none of the absurdities that mar run-of-the-mill regressions, but no one called Bridey or Brian Murphy (her supposed husband) could be traced (Bernstein, 1956, 1965; Ducasse, 1961, p. 282). The same pattern of veridical information alongside unverifiable past-life identities appears in the accounts of Henry Blythe (1957), Jess Stearn (1968), Linda Tarazi (1990, 1997), Marge Rieder (1993, 1996), and others (Iverson, 1976; P. Moss & Keeton, 1979; Rogo, 1985). I call this tendency for some information to check out while the identity of the previous person is obscured "the Bridey Murphy effect." It is much more apparent with regressions under hypnosis than with involuntary past-life memories, unsolved cases notwithstanding.

Not uncommonly, regressed subjects speak in accents or use archaic or foreign words, examples of passive or recitative xenoglossy. Bridey Murphy spoke with an Irish brogue and used Irish vernacular, such as requesting a "linen" (rather than a handkerchief) when Virginia Tighe sneezed (Bernstein, 1956, 1965). Responsive xenoglossy under hypnosis is rare. Stevenson studied two apparent examples, the Swedish xenoglossy of Jensen (Stevenson, 1974a) and the German xenoglossy of Gretchen (Jay, 1977; Stevenson, 1984). Even a limited amount of responsive xenoglossy in past-life regression would be significant, if it could be demonstrated conclusively. Stevenson believed that he had done this, but the evidence is not strong enough to convince critics like linguist Sarah Thomason (Thomason, 1984, 1987), who would like to see a more fully developed deployment of the foreign language.

Ohkado Masayuki and Okamoto Satoshi (Ohkado & Okamoto, 2014) described a Japanese regression case with Nepalese xenoglossy. The limited vocabulary and limited yet evidently responsive command of the language is similar to Jensen and Gretchen. Some aspects of the purported past life were veridical, but as with Jensen and Gretchen and the great majority of regressions, the previous person could not be traced. The ostensible xenoglossy in regression cases is weaker than that in children's spontaneous cases (Chapter 4; Matlock, 2017, August) and much inferior to that demonstrated by Uttara Huddar (Akolkar, 1992; Stevenson, 1984). Xenoglossy in drug-induced past-life memories (Rogo 1991, pp. 26–27), for instance the Chilean case described by Claudio Naranjo (1973), similarly is much weaker than in spontaneous cases.

I consider it unlikely that anyone named Bridey Murphy ever existed. This does not mean that there is nothing to her story, which may well be rooted in Tighe's subconscious memories of a life near Belfast in the second half of the nineteenth century. It is hard to explain the veridical aspects of her narrative otherwise (unless they were acquired by psi, a possibility to which I shall return). In their mixture of fact and fantasy, regression cases like Tighe's recall unsolved adult cases such as Edward Ryall (Ryall, 1974; Stevenson, 2003) and Mrs. Smith (Guirdham, 1970), but with a heightened obfuscation of identity made possible by the hypnotic state.

In contrast to those who experience past-life memories in the waking state or dreams, subjects under hypnosis commonly name the persons they used to be and may say precisely when they lived (e.g., 1863 BC: B. L. Weiss, 1988, p. 27). These facts ought to make their cases easier to solve, but they seldom do. When regression cases are solved, moreover, key elements sometimes turn out to be wrong.

In the celebrated case of Indianapolis police detective Robert Snow (Snow, 1999), who was able to solve his own case by identifying a painting he saw himself working on, the names he gave under hypnosis for his previous person and his wife were incorrect. While regressed, George Field recalled a life in the small town of Jefferson, North Carolina, around the time of the Civil War, and accurately answered questions put to him by a local historian—but after the case was publicized, the previous person's great-niece let it be known that several of Field's statements about the family were confused (Steiger & L. G. Williams, 1976, pp. 11–55). Jenny Cockell had a recurring childhood nightmare of being run over by a truck, but under hypnosis imagined the death was due to illness. The regression brought up enough details about Charles Savage for Cockell to locate his death certificate, which confirmed not only his existence, but his dying in a way consistent with her dreams rather than the regression (Cockell, 2008, p. 270).

Brownell (1949, pp. 55–56), Rogo (1985, pp. 108–12), and Colin Wilson (1987, pp. 195–97) provided shorter accounts of solved regression experiences with no mention of related involuntary memories. Involuntary memories are associated with many solved regression cases, though. Usually they precede the regressions, although they may follow them, as they did for Snow (1999) and Stephen Sakellarios (Sakellarios, 2011). Three of Saunders's six regression subjects reported having past-life "dreams and impressions" from childhood (2004, p. 99). Among them was William Barnes, who published his own account (Barnes, 2000). Martin Heald (Heald, 1997) and Douglas Edwards (O'Sullivan, 1998), along with Ray Bryant, Stuart McAllister, and Lyndi Clement (S. Carpenter, 1995), also had involuntary memories of previous lives before being regressed to the same lives and confirming their previous identities.

Bruce Goldberg (1994) reported the case of a woman with nightmares of being murdered and a phobia of things touching her neck who regressed to numerous lives in which she was involved in romantic triangles similar to the one in which she was entangled in her present life. It seems not to have occurred to Goldberg that all these triangles with their similar denouements might represent transformations of the same traumatic events. Repeatedly experiencing these events under hypnosis eventually allowed his patient to free herself from the pattern, at which point she regressed to the life of a Grace Loveless Doze, the details of whose life and death Goldberg found matched those described under hypnosis. Notably, names and other key details emerged not in answer to Goldberg's questions, but spontaneously, in unguarded talk.

Regressions aligned with involuntary memories suggest that hypnosis may sometimes tap in to the same stream as waking and dream recollections of previous lives, but regression is not always successful in eliciting new information. Bruce Whittier (1996) had a series of dreams related to a death during the Holocaust, then regressed to what apparently was the same life. An antique clock confiscated by the Nazis, closely resembling one featured both in the dreams and the regressions, was later found, but because Whittier did not recall his previous name, his past-life identity could not be confirmed. Monica O'Hara-Keeton (1996) had childhood memories and recalled a name related to the same life she relived under hypnosis, but although her regressions included veridical elements, and were followed by waking recognitions, the previous person could not be traced and the name she recalled spontaneously may have been incorrect somehow. Stevenson tried unsuccessfully to use hypnosis with thirteen children who spoke about previous lives (2001, p. 47).

Thelma Freedman (2002, p. 40) suggested that "stories" emerging from deep trance were more likely to be truthful, and she could be right. People vary in their capacity to be hypnotized and in the depth of trance they can reach (Kampman, 1976; Kampman & Hirvenoja, 1978; Spanos et al., 1991).

More deeply hypnotized subjects have less self-awareness, rationality, voluntary control, and memory for their experiences than those who enter a lighter trance (Cardeña, 2005), and these things have been reported in the better regression cases. Unfortunately, Freedman offers nothing to back up her hypothesis.

The fifteen cases discussed above (eleven with associated involuntary memories and four without) represent roughly half of the solved regression cases known to me. Several of the others involve famous people or seem rather too good to be true. Hassler (2015, vol. 2, pp. 933–35) lists twenty-six solved regressions, including some I have excluded for these reasons. No doubt others have escaped the notice of both Hassler and me, but nonetheless, it is apparent that there are many fewer solved regression cases than there are solved spontaneous cases. To this observation I may add that solved regression cases are on the whole much weaker evidentially than spontaneous cases, at least those of children. Errors appear in involuntary as well as induced memories, but with regressions the errors are more obviously strategic, more clearly aimed at making it difficult to identify the previous person.

Not only are there only a few regressions with identified previous persons, those few have not been studied with the same care as children's involuntary past-life memories. The seventeen hundred or so well-investigated, solved spontaneous cases provide the basis for my theoretical speculations about reincarnation. We cannot be as confident with uninvestigated and unverified past-life regressions, but this has not deterred efforts to generalize about them. Michael Newton (1996, 2006) called his regressions "case studies" and presented his findings as if they were the results of a scientific research project, but he made no effort to verify anything his clients said, other than to cross-reference the transcripts of their sessions.

Regression therapists tend to agree that "souls" set goals for themselves in advance of rebirth, a common idea in the New Age reincarnation mythos. However, although many children have said that they chose one or both of their parents, there is little indication of more extensive life planning in involuntary intermission memories. Furthermore, important patterns in the spontaneous cases do not appear in regressions. Regressed subjects do not describe psychological or geographical links between lives that would explain why one life follows another where and with whom it does. I know of no published regressions to lives among relatives, as in the spontaneous cases. International returns come up routinely in regressions, but are unusual in involuntary memories surfacing in either childhood or adulthood (Matlock, 2017, May).

From time to time one encounters the claim that because there are comparatively few spontaneous cases, it would be foolish to rely on them for insights into how reincarnation works. Because regressions can be produced on demand, the argument goes, they are more likely to provide accurate information (e.g., Woolger, 1987, pp. 68–70). However, it is very hard to justify this position, and the opposite is more likely true.

Regressions are similar to adult spontaneous cases in their evidential weaknesses, but I think for a different reason. The weaknesses of adult involuntary memories result from developmental factors, but regression memories are compromised because they are induced and meet resistance from the psyche. The subconscious mind reacts to the effort to elicit the memories by creating distortions, even when a subject consciously wishes to remember. On occasion, past-life memories surface spontaneously under hypnosis, and there is some evidence that these memories are more credible than those that are evoked through suggestion (Rogo, 1991). Goldberg's (1994) case of the woman who spontaneously recalled details of the life of Grace Loveless Doze after her therapy was complete serves to make my point.

I believe that this way of understanding regressions makes the best sense of the data, but there are other ideas about the source of past-life memory with different implications about reliability. Perhaps the most widespread, both among the general public and parapsychologists, supposes that past-life memories are drawn from a cosmic storage place such as the Akashic Records or a subquantum Akashic field (Laszlo, 2007, 2009). David Loye (2009) and Stanislav Grof (2009) interpret experiences that might be considered past-life memories in terms of Laszlo's theory.

Under this paradigm, information would be retrieved from the Akashic Records or the Akashic field via psi. The evidential weaknesses of induced past-life memories mean that it is easier to conceive of these experiences as products of the imagination, enriched as required by psi acquisitions, the more so when one considers that hypnosis and other altered states are psi-conducive (E. F. Kelly & Locke, 2010). But with them another problem moves to the fore, and that is the question of why a given person, and only that person, zeroes in on a particular life. Why is there a one-to-one correspondence between the remembered and the rememberer? What kind of mechanism precludes retrieving information that has already been accessed by someone else, unless the previous person was famous? There are many reports of adult involuntary memories and regressions related to the likes of Marilyn Monroe and Nicholas Romanoff, for instance.

Another idea, favored by many Jungian-trained regression therapists, is that past-life memories spring from the collective unconscious. Jung followed Freud in thinking of the personal unconscious as including content that had been forgotten or repressed, but beyond that he thought there was a collective unconscious, shared by all humanity. The collective unconscious, Jung believed, contained symbolic constructs called "archetypes"—mother, father, birth, death, et cetera—whose meaning was expressed differently in different cultures (Jung, 1959/1981). Woolger assigned past-life memories to the personal unconscious but believed that compulsions and trauma patterns were drawn from the collective or, as he termed it, transpersonal unconscious (1987, p. 119). Elise Wardle (2009, 2015) treated genocide as an archetype and interpreted past-life memories of the Holocaust from both regressions and involuntary memories as derived from it.

Involuntary and induced past-life memories differ in their level of authenticity and their evidential value, and it may be that something like archetypes comes into play in some induced memories (Booth, 1998). In any event, we would do well to keep involuntary and induced past-life memories separate conceptually and analytically. We should not generalize from one class to the other, assuming either that because apparent memories emerging under hypnosis often are quite dubious, involuntary memories are also, or that because we have some fine and convincing spontaneous cases, we can suspend our credulity in relation to the hypnotic and other induced productions.

THE CONTRIBUTIONS OF SHAMANS, PSYCHICS, AND MEDIUMS

No announcing dreams heralded the birth of Jeffery, a Wet'suwet'en boy described by Mills (1988a, 2010), nor were there birthmarks or other signs indicating who he had been in his previous life. His parents consulted a medicine man who held him in his arms and identified him as the reincarnation of his mother's brother Will. Will had died six years earlier after being kicked in the stomach and head by a horse he was harnessing. Jeffery gave no hint of remembering anything about Will's life until he was five years old, when his grandparents took him for the first time to the camp at which Will had died. While there, he began to say his name was not Jeffery, but Will, and to recount incidents at the camp in which Will had been involved. He began to dream about Will and continued dreaming about him into adulthood.

When signs of past-life identity are absent or a child is sick, tribal parents may seek the opinions of shamans or similar psychic practitioners (Gottlieb, 2004; Mills, 1988a; Stevenson, 1985). It would appear that the declarations of these practitioners are accepted unreservedly, but we know little about this practice. It is mentioned only incidentally in case reports, probably because those researching reincarnation claims do not put as much stock in psychic identifications (as we may broadly term them) as do members of the societies they are studying. Not only is there an important difference between remembering a past life oneself and being told by someone else that one has lived before, but the identifications may serve as starting points for the social construction of more developed cases. Jeffery's grandparents would have known that he was supposed to have been Will and would have been aware that they were taking him to the place where Will had died. They could have suggested to Jeffery that he had been Will, thus leading him to fabricate memories of Will's life. At a minimum, this possibility must be considered before cases like Jeffery's can be counted as serious evidence for reincarnation.

Not only shamans but psychics and mediums may contribute information about the previous lives of their clients. Past-life readings have become very popular, rivaling regressions under hypnosis for insights into reincarnation lineages. In addition, mediums sometimes deliver messages from spirits on their way to reincarnation. Examining past-life readings and reincarnation-related communications through mediums takes us into questions about the sources of the information acquired by psychic practitioners and the modes of interchange between living and deceased actors, critical issues in understanding the nature of postmortem existence leading to reincarnation.

In the tribal societies of North America, psychic identifications have been reported mainly on the Northwest Coast and bordering regions and among the Eskimo and Inuit in the Arctic and Subarctic (Matlock & Mills, 1994). Mills learned of seven cases of psychic identification (out of thirteen recognized rebirths) among the Wet'suwet'en, three (out of three) among the Gitxsan, and one (out of twenty-three) among the Beaver (1988a, p. 392). Wet'suwet'en, Gitxsan, and Beaver medicine men take pride in understanding the language of infants (Mills, 1988a, p. 405) and combine this facility with signs in making their identifications. Wet'suwet'en and Beaver practitioners may take their cues from announcing dreams (Mills, 1988a, p. 396). Their Haida counterparts historically referred to announcing dreams as well (C. Harrison, 1925, pp. 112–13), but announcing dreams now occur more often among the general population (Stevenson, 1975b, p. 374).

Psychic identifications have been reported from other parts of the world also and I believe are more widespread than the published data suggest. The Igbo normally take a child to an oracle for identification and naming when it is about a month old, but parents may go earlier if a baby is ill or is suspected of being a repeater child (Stevenson, 1985). Igbo oracles typically recite names until the infant gives some sign that it has heard the one by which it was called in its previous life, although if birthmarks are present they may provide clues. In one of Stevenson's Igbo cases (1997a, vol. 1, p. 585), a child born with a hairless, circular area on her head fell sick and her parents consulted an oracle, fearing that she had been wrongly named. The oracle informed them that she was the reincarnation of her father's mother, who had had an annular lesion on her head from carrying heavy loads there all of her life. The child was renamed, recovered, and when she was older, said a few things that suggested that she had inherited her grandmother's memories.

Practices such as these are not confined to tribal societies. When she was two months old, Hair Kam Kanya of Thailand (Stevenson, 1983b) became unwell and would not stop crying. Her parents took her to a medium who identified her as the reincarnation of her mother's sister. He advised that she be adopted by her mother's niece, who he said was the reincarnation of her mother's mother, thus placing her back in a mother-daughter relationship based on the past-life identities. A ceremonial adoption was performed and Hair Kam returned to normal, although she continued to reside with her parents. A few years later she went to live with, and then was formally adopted by, a nephew of her mother, a son of the woman the medium had identified as her previous person. Hair Kam was unusually at ease with this man and while in his care began to relate memories of the life of his mother.

Determining past-life identities is only one of the contributions psychic practitioners may make in relation to reincarnation. In *My Land and My People* the Dalai Lama tells us that it is a Tibetan custom to consult lamas and sometimes oracles after deaths but before funerals. When his younger brother died at two years, an oracle advised his parents not to bury the body but to mark it with butter and to preserve it, because the boy would be reborn to them. His parents did as suggested and his mother soon became pregnant with another boy, who, when born, was found to have a pale mark at the spot the butter had been smeared on his deceased brother (Dalai Lama, 1962, p. 53). The Dalai Lama himself was located partly with the help of oracles (Wangdu, Gould, & Richardson, 2000), a common Tibetan technique for finding reborn lamas (Gamble, 2018). Mackenzie (1988, pp. 96–97) described the signs that followed the death of a beloved master, Lama Yeshe, enabling his reincarnation to be traced to a Spanish Buddhist retreat.

When bereaved sitters tried to contact the spirit of her previous person, Marta Lorenz (Stevenson, 1974a) manifested but told them she had already reincarnated (although she did not say where) and asked them not to "call me up" again (Stevenson, 1980, p. 256). Several mediums have relayed rebirth announcements from spirits planning to reincarnate or from other persons with knowledge of such plans. These cases, all with veridical information, have been reported from Europe (Muller, 1970, pp. 233–34; Stevenson, 2003, pp. 24–25), Brazil (Andrade, 2010a; Playfair, 2011, pp. 167, 167–68), India (B. Prasad, 1967), and Burma (Stevenson, 1997a, pp. 827–31).

Occasionally birthmarks or physical abnormalities are announced through mediums. Stevenson (2003, pp. 42–44) described a classic French case first reported by Maurice Delarrey (1955) of veridical communications through a Ouija board from a spirit who stated when and to whom he would be reborn, adding that the child could be recognized as his return by a protruding right ear. For other mediumistic cases with predictions of physical signs, see Muller (1970, p. 190) and Stevenson (1997a, vol. 1, pp. 793–802).

Sometimes mediums put through spirits who claim to have known sitters or the mediums themselves in previous lives. Frederick Bligh Bond, whose archaeological digging at England's famed Glastonbury Abbey was guided by automatic writing from the spirits of monks who resided there (S. A. Schwartz, 1978, pp. 1–56), was told in a mediumistic message from one of these monks that he had known Bond when Bond lived at Glastonbury in a former life (Bond, 1924). In another well-known case, a medium named Rosemary was said to reproduce words in ancient Egyptian dictated to her by the spirit of a woman she had known in pharaonic times (Hulme & Wood, 1936; see discussion by Ducasse, 1961, pp. 248–56). Most cases of this kind contain little that can be checked and nothing that corresponds to spontaneous phenomena. An exception is an account from French astronomer Camille Flammarion (summarized in Muller, 1970, p. 231), in which an incident in the life of the previous person identified by the medium accorded with a recurring nightmare Flammarion had suffered from childhood.

A Japanese Buddhist clairvoyant, Seiya Kiriyama, reported on his efforts to help people with psychological complaints (Kiriyama, 2000). In several instances, he located the sources of the problem in past-life connections. Kiriyama's are all silent adult cases, but some have veridical elements. One involves a past life in China, unsolved but supported by a birthmark of which Kiriyama was unaware until after he had made the identification. Another case, in which Kiriyama was able to identify the individuals involved, concerns an apparent suicide in the Philippines of a Japanese man and his Filipino lover and her rebirth in Japan into the family of the man who had tried to separate them.

In Brazil, where the confluence of Kardecian Spiritism and West African tribal beliefs and practices has resulted in a popular culture that takes a spirit world for granted, reincarnation is widely accepted and mediums may be enlisted in a novel type of therapy. Stanley Krippner (1987, 1991) described how alters in MPD/DID cases might be diagnosed as past-life personalities, requiring integration with the presenting personalities. Mediums were employed to dialogue with the past-life alters and so facilitate the integration. Adam Crabtree (1985), also, considered the possibility of a connection between past-life personalities and MPD/DID alters.

How do shamans, mediums, and other psychic practitioners communicate with spirits and determine past-life identities? For many parapsychologists, the answer is psi, but most of them mean psi (or some variety of super-psi) exclusively on the side of the living. Why should psi abilities be restricted to embodied minds, though? If consciousness survives the body's demise, it seems likely that psi would be available to discarnate actors as well. In fact, psi may be an intrinsic property of consciousness and belong primarily to the discarnate state. When embodied, we have alternative physical means of communication, and these take precedence. From this perspective, mediums and other psychic practitioners are people who have fewer constraints on psi than the rest of us, so it would not be surprising if they were able to pick up things from discarnate as well as incarnate minds.

Psychic identifications are different from mediumistic communications, because they are initiated by the practitioner rather than by (ostensibly at least) the discarnate agent. Many practitioners join parapsychologists in thinking they are fetching past-life information from the Akashic Records or a subquantum Akashic field. I believe this notion derives from the failure to conceive of memory as registered in the subconscious mind. Without that concept, even if the survival of consciousness is accepted, information about the past must come from somewhere other than from a mind, and the common designation for that somewhere is the Akashic Records. However, if memories reside in the subconscious, psychic practitioners would be able to retrieve them from either incarnate or discarnate minds via psi, just as they would any other content, willfully directed to them or not.

Ken Llewelyn (1991) self-reported an instructive case in which he was told by a South African medium that in his last life he had flown a Dornier fighter-bomber in the German Luftwaffe but was shot down over Kent, England, in 1942. The medium gave his name as Paul Friedrich von Rueben and said that he had been decapitated in the crash. She saw him examining a photograph of his wife and two young sons before the plane came under fire. Death in an aircraft downing brought meaning to the urge to bail out that Llewelyn had experienced when flying with the British Royal Air Force early in his career. The feeling was so strong that it had caused him to withdraw from pilot training. Llewelyn returned to England, fully expecting to verify what the medium had told him, but discovered that although there had been a crash in Penshurst, Kent, during World War II, it was in 1940, the plane was not a Dornier, and the pilot was not named Paul Friedrich von Rueben.

Other sensitives adduced additional information, much of it conflicting. One placed the crash near Norfolk in the east of England instead of in Kent, which is in the south. Then Llewelyn's uncle told him that while on patrol around Norfolk in 1942, he had come upon the headless body of man in a Luftwaffe uniform at a crash site. Nearby in the debris was a photograph of a woman and two boys. He had taken the body in his arms and cradled it until it was carted away for burial. The pilot's name was not Paul Friedrich von Rueben, but the date fit, the plane was a Dornier, the pilot had been decapitated, and the photograph his uncle had found matched the medium's description of the picture she had seen the man perusing before the plane was hit. It may seem that Llewelyn at last had what he needed to trace the pilot's surviving family, but by this time he had lost confidence in the psychic process and did not attempt to follow up the case in Germany.

Llewelyn (1991) tried regression under hypnosis in an effort to expand upon the mediumistic testimony but although he apparently relived the last moments of the pilot's life, no new information emerged. Martin Heald (1997) had a different experience. After being told by an aura reader about a past life that seemed to correspond to images that had surfaced in dreams, he underwent regression and brought out new details that allowed him to solve his case. Stephen Sakellarios (2015) devised an innovative method of comparing psychic readings and regressions, then testing them against his involuntary memories and intuitions. When the information retrieved by different means agreed, he felt he had more reason to believe it correct than if he were to rely on any single approach. Indeed the approaches should agree, if I am correct that all are drawing on the contents of the subconscious.

Two psychics told Llewelyn that his mind was too conflicted to read and that the answers would come to him in time. This sounds like a cop-out but could be an honest appraisal of what they encountered in their mind-reading attempts. The South African medium was wrong about the name of the pilot; however, names of previous persons are often wrong in regression cases and may not be recalled in spontaneous cases. The location the medium gave as the crash site, Kent, was wrong. This might have been her mistake, but it looks like it could have been a motivated error by Llewelyn's subconscious mind, designed to deflect attention from the real site of his death in the previous life.

Karl Müller (Muller, 1970, p. 91) observed that sensitives consulted by Laurence Temple (Temple, 1970) related nothing that was not expressed in his childhood dreams. Besides confirming the content of John East's dreams and his sense that he had known his wife in an earlier life, a medium told him that his wife and he had been together many times before (East, 1960). While this may or may not be true, I have cited examples of veridical contributions from psychic practitioners which went beyond what their clients knew consciously.

Sometimes, psychic practitioners seem to be better at retrieving information from the minds of others than those others can access for themselves through regression. I believe this is because psychic practitioners can bypass defenses put up under hypnosis and other induced states of consciousness, but as Llewelyn's case shows, they cannot succeed if the subconscious resistance is too strong. In a similar occurrence, Kevin Ryerson told Ken Alexander that he could not perceive whom his recurrent dreams were about, but gave him clues that allowed him to identify that person (Von Ward, 2008, pp. 27–28).

* * *

There are many pitfalls in dealing with psychic material. Special care must be exercised in interpreting mediumistic communications. Most messages relayed by mediums have no veridical basis and the source of those that are veridical is notoriously uncertain. The information could come from spirits or it could be retrieved telepathically or clairvoyantly from living minds or written documents, if not through the "cold reading" of sitters (Larsen, 2015; Roe & Roxburgh, 2013). Cold reading is a technique, or set of techniques, used by mentalist stage magicians—and critics assume mediums and other psychic practitioners—to draw out facts by making their audience think that they know more than they do.

A medium's spirit controls and the discarnate entities put through by channelers may be no more than secondary personalities of the practitioner, and some "psychic" productions are without doubt wholly imaginary. A classic example of a medium claiming dubious past lives is Hélène Smith, who asserted that she had lived before as Marie Antoinette, an Indian princess, and an inhabitant of Mars (Flournoy, 1963). J. A. Hill (1929) examined a series of automatically written scripts in which communicators purported to be successive reincarnations of a man in love with previous incarnations of the automatist.

With psychic identifications, practitioners may misconstrue the images and impressions that enter their minds. As a child, Jeffrey Keene played at being a soldier, but he was an adult when he had an experience at the Civil War battlefield at Antietam (Sharpsburg), which he later associated with Confederate General John B. Gordon. Before he had made the connection, a palm reader told him that he had died at Antietam after having been shot several times. Keene had the sense that he had not died then and challenged the palm reader. Keene was right: Gordon survived the wounds he received at Antietam. So the mistake was not Keene's, but the palm reader's (Keene, 2003). It is rarely possible to pinpoint the origin of errors in this way, but that does not mean that the same thing does not happen often.

The most pervasive distortions of past-life data occur when psychic practitioners are influenced by preconceptions about the reincarnation process. There is no better example than Edgar Cayce, whose "life readings" were strongly colored by Theosophical notions introduced to him by Arthur Lammers (Melton, 1994). Perhaps because of the conceptual overlay, Cayce's life readings were considerably less successful than his health readings (Ducasse, 1961, pp. 274–75). Much that Cayce said, especially about earlier lives, either cannot be substantiated or is unlikely to have occurred as he depicted.

One of Cayce's more interesting life readings is a departure from his usual pattern. It is a reading for a fifteen-day-old girl he identified as the return of suffragist and temperance advocate Frances Willard (Furst, 1971). Gina Cerminara (1950, pp. 38–39; 1963, p. 47) noted other readings in which the previous person was found to have existed but added (1963, p. 69) that Cayce's identifications sometimes had been proven wrong. C. J. Ducasse was unable to confirm the existence of the Frenchman Cayce identified as his previous person (1961, p. 275n2). Stephan Schwartz (1978, pp. 165–97) tried to reconcile Cayce's Egyptian material with what is accepted by Egyptologists but could do so only by assuming that Cayce's dates were off by tens of millennia and that he used different names for some personages.

Despite their failings, Cayce's life readings and the philosophy they express have been hugely influential in Western popular culture and New Age metaphysics. They are the unacknowledged model for many contemporary past-life readings, which take retributive karma and intermissions long in both time and distance for granted and accept the Akashic Records as a reliable font of information about past lives (e.g., Wetzel, 2009).

Another Cayce legacy is the tendency of past-life readers to produce lengthy series of lives, stretching far into prehistory. Although the majority of people who remember past lives involuntarily recall only one previous life, an appreciable minority say they remember incidents from multiple lives. Some children have reported memories of two or three (Stevenson, 2001, pp. 218–19). A Sri Lankan boy, Warnasiri Adikari (Stevenson, 1977a), claimed memories of four, one as a hare. However, from informal contacts and posts on Facebook and in Internet forums, I have the impression that adults are more likely than children to recall multiple lives.

Two adult subjects have been able to solve two sets of memories. One is Pratomwan Inthanu (Stevenson, 1983a), whose memories came during meditation when she was twenty. The other is Jenny Cockell (1994, 2017), who had memories of both lives from childhood but solved the cases in adulthood. Cockell (2008) came close to verifying a third set of memories, but was unable to confirm all their details and identify a previous person by name. K. M. Wehrstein (2019) reports that Will recalls thirty past lives, in four of which it has been possible to identify the previous person, although this publication—the first of a planned series—describes only Will's most recent solved life as Nazi Wilhelm Emmerich.

In most involuntarily recalled series, one life is remembered in greater detail than the others, and it alone is verified. Usually this solved life is the most recent one, although it may be the penultimate one (as it was for Swarnlata Mishra, reported in Stevenson, 1974b, and Wehrstein's Will, who has fragmentary memories of a life between Emmerich and his present life). With Pratomwan Inthanu (Stevenson, 1983b) and Jenny Cockell (Cockell, 1994, 2017), the two verified lives were the two most recent lives.

Psychic identifications and past-life readings reveal a similar pattern. Jeffrey Keene dreamed of a life after General Gordon, but only vaguely, and that life remains unverified. It was picked up by some of the sensitives he consulted, but not by all of them (Keene, 2003). Psychic identifications almost always relate to the most recent life, and when series are given in past-life readings, only the most recent life checks out. This consistency across spontaneous, regression, and psychic cases is to be expected if psychic practitioners are accessing the minds of their clients, but it leaves unanswered the question of why the most recent life or lives are more likely to be corroborated than earlier ones.

Perhaps it is a matter of not being able to confirm facts far removed in time. This is sometimes given as the reason for the large number of FPL identifications, because it is easier to find supporting evidence for them in the historical record. Certainly it is more difficult to establish the accuracy of memories of ancient lives, and veridical content can and does appear in unsolved cases. However, we should not assume that if some items are correct, everything that is remembered is correct, because there is the possibility of confabulation and other unconscious means of disguise. Nor can we assume that because we can show some things to be true, a given case is confirmable, if only we had what we needed to document the rest. Moreover, if one life in a series is solved, this does not mean that the details of all the other lives are equally reliable.

For most people with past-life memories, their minds may not preserve memories of more than one or two lives in enough detail for their past identities to be confirmed, although they might retain fragmentary memories of traumatic or otherwise emotionally salient events. Present-life memory is pruned in this way, and why should past-life memory be different? For Brazilian Spiritism, past-life personalities resemble MPD/DID alters in the subconscious mind (Krippner, 1991). From this perspective, past personalities lie within all of us, affecting us with their unresolved conflicts, but as their concerns are dealt with, they recede and become integrated with our present personalities. This model receives support from the case of Uttara Huddar, in which there was some merger of Sharada's personality with Uttara's (Stevenson, 1984). Time, it seems, is not a concern for the subconscious, which works on principles of affinity. Memories of any period may rise into conscious awareness if they meet some need. Wehrstein's (2019) Will is not the only adult to report memories of several past lives—only the first to be well studied and reported in print—and it may be that the multiple lives these subjects recall likewise serve a purpose for their psyches.

The work of Walter Semkiw introduces another set of issues. Semkiw (2003, 2011a, 2011b) places great reliance on sensitives, especially Kevin Ryerson, in making past-life identifications and in confirming ones he himself has made through photographic comparison, analysis of literary style, and the

discernment of synchronistic patterns. Semkiw does not interview his subjects to determine if there are related spontaneous experiences or behaviors
that might lend his identifications weight. Moreover, his handling of Ryerson
is parapsychologically (and more generally, scientifically) wanting. Rather
than keeping Ryerson blind to the identifications he has made, Semkiw asks
Ryerson (more exactly, the entity Ahtun Re, speaking through Ryerson)
simply to tell him whether they are right or wrong (Semkiw, 2011a, p. 261).
Under these conditions, Ahtun Re's pronouncements hardly qualify as independent corroborations, and it is of little consequence that they confirm 85%
of Semkiw's identifications.

Semkiw has never published in a peer-reviewed journal but his ideas have
had a notable impact on popular conceptions of reincarnation. Semkiw likely
is responsible for the widespread idea that facial features endure from life
to life and for the fad of side-to-side photographs in support of matches. He
asserts that Stevenson spent too much time studying birthmarks as opposed
to faces (Semkiw, 2011a, p. 41). However, facial features cannot be used in
the diagnostic way that Semkiw uses them, especially when both previous
and present persons are from the same ethnic group, as they are in most of
Semkiw's cases. Facial similarities between past and present are more significant in interethnic cases (Ohkado, 2014) or when there is something peculiar
about them, such as the healed wound on General Gordon's cheek represented as a birthmark on Jeffrey Keene's (Keene, 2003). Moreover, facial and
other physical signs are not invariably present. In a case I studied, there is no
physical resemblance between the subject and previous person, despite evidence that the previous person was the subject's grandfather (Haraldsson &
Matlock, 2016, pp. 209–14; Matlock, 2015). The comparison of faces alone
can lead to false negatives as well as false positives.

To be sure, Semkiw does not stop with faces. He compares the writing
styles of the identified previous and present persons, and he scours biographies for commonalities in interest and achievement, as well as for parallels
in life events. By this means, he has associated Abigail Adams with Marianne
Williamson, Kate Fox with John Edward, D. D. Home with Uri Geller, Sir
William Crookes with David Bohm, Peyton Randolph with Bill Clinton,
Horatio Gates with Al Gore, Daniel Morgan with George W. Bush, James
Wilson with Oprah Winfrey, and so on. Richard Salva (2006) employed
similar criteria in making the identification of Abraham Lincoln with Charles
Lindbergh. Curiously, Semkiw designated someone else as Lincoln's reincar-
nation and Ryerson ratified that match (Semkiw, 2011a, p. 393).

Meaningful coincidences—synchronicities—are key for both Semkiw
(2003, 2011a, 2011b) and Salva (2006). Synchronicities are a vital part
of popular and New Age theorizing about reincarnation, so the concept
is important to understand. Synchronicity as portrayed by Jung (1973) is

the expression of contents of the collective unconscious in our conscious awareness or objective physical reality. Jung believed that certain apparently unconnected events are united at a deep level of consciousness that is consciously unknowable to us. Because we do not appreciate how they are related, we experience these events as coincidences, and yet we feel them to be meaningful in some ineffable way. To count as synchronistic, the coincidences should be consequential to the experiencer, not just to a researcher. Coincidences of having lived in or passed through the same place, or of having things happen on or around the same day of the year, are of supreme import for Semkiw, but since he does not interview his subjects, he does not know whether they hold any special meaning for them. It is easy to rack up any number of such coincidences by chance, as Angel (2015) points out, and they betoken little by themselves.

Psychologists Jeffrey Mishlove (whom Semkiw, 2003, has identified as the reincarnation of William James and the Greek Stoic philosopher Seneca) and Brendan Engen (said to have been a colleague of Seneca) drew on Jungian concepts in their theory of Archetypal Synchronistic Resonance (ASR) (Mishlove & Engen, 2007). The ASR model emphasizes the hidden nexus of meaning underlying seemingly disparate events and may have some utility in explaining unverified past-life memories, past-life regressions, and past-life readings that tap in to a client's mind if these relate to deep psychological processes and psychic connections between people rather than to the memory of previous lives. The model can accommodate veridical information obtained through psi, but I cannot see that it has application to solved reincarnation cases, particularly the more developed cases, which seem to be explained more satisfactorily in terms of memory. ASR represents a sophisticated use of Jungian concepts very different from Semkiw and Salva, but it has not had the impact they have had on the New Age scene.

Chapter 7

The Process of Reincarnation

Reincarnation cases do not stand alone in suggesting that the mind has an existence apart from the body. I begin this last chapter with an examination of other evidence of mind/body interaction and postmortem survival, then return to and refine my theory of the reincarnation process. In the final section, I summarize my "processual soul" theory, constructed from the case data, and compare it to the rebirth concepts promoted by animism, the world religions, Theosophy, and New Age metaphysics.

BEYOND MATERIALISM

In the seventeenth century, Sir Isaac Newton assumed that God created both minds and bodies. Although he differed from his near-contemporary René Descartes in the attributes he assigned to them, and avoided Cartesian substance dualism in favor of a type of panpsychism, Newton, like Descartes, understood minds and bodies to be distinct but interactive (Gorham, 2011). By the nineteenth century, God had been banished from physics and an unmitigated materialism had taken hold. Mind, or consciousness, was reconceptualized as a product of the brain. Ironically, this shift was brought about by Newton's major work, *Philosophiæ Naturalis Principia Mathematica* (*Mathematical Principles of Natural Philosophy*), which he published in Latin in 1687 with further editions in 1713 and 1726. The first English translation appeared in 1729.

Newton (1687, 1729) showed that everything in the cosmos, from the interaction of particles on Earth to the movement of the planets through the heavens, could be explained on the same mechanical principles. Newton's model laid the foundation of modern science and proved its practical worth during the Industrial Revolution. Matter and energy came to be seen as the fundamental constituents of a billiard-ball universe. They came together in predictable ways, and in principle, if you knew enough about how a process began, you knew how it would end. By the close of the nineteenth century it seemed to physicists that their science had little left to learn and they had every expectation that the few remaining problems would be resolved within the same deterministic framework (Herbert, 1993; Rosenblum & Kuttner, 2011).

They were wrong. The solutions to the outstanding issues (among them how light behaved) led at the beginning of the twentieth century to the realization that Newtonian mechanics gave only an approximate description of interactions at the macroscopic level and failed utterly when applied to a deeper, more fundamental level of physical reality. The rules of this deeper level, the quantum level, became stranger the more closely they were examined through experiment after experiment, confirming and extending theoretical speculations. Processes at the quantum level can only be described in terms of statistical probabilities. As odd as it may seem, the universe we inhabit is now known to be probabilistic at its core. There is no way to predict how things will turn out, except in terms of their statistical likelihood.

According to the most widely accepted (standard or orthodox) version of quantum theory, worked out by mathematician John von Neumann with extensions by physicists Shinichiro Tomonaga and Julian Schwinger, consciousness not only stands apart from physical reality, it is instrumental in the creation of physical reality (Stapp, 2005, 2011). An experiment's results depend on how the experiment is arranged and all physical aspects of the experimental setup, including the experimenter's body and brain along with the apparatus, are part of the same quantum system. The experimenter's mind alone lies outside the system, and therefore it must be responsible for the choices that lead to one possible outcome being selected over the rest.

Modern adherents to the brain-production model of consciousness (e.g., Baars, 1997; Churchland, 1986; Dennett, 1982; Searle, 1997; Sperry, 1980) differ in their ideas about how this is achieved, but all are sure that it is so, despite being unable to specify how. They subscribe to what philosopher Karl Popper (Popper & Eccles, 1977) aptly styled "promissory materialism"—the conviction that every currently intractable problem will succumb eventually to a materialist explanation, in essence a denial of the lessons of quantum mechanics.

Physicist Henry Stapp (1999, 2005, 2011, 2015), by contrast, espouses an interactionism that permits the mind to act directly on quantum processes in the brain and to play a key role in quantum biology (J. M. Schwartz, Stapp, & Beauregard, 2005). In his 2015 publication, Stapp brings in psi, which I believe plays a crucial role in providing mind with a non-physical (extrasensory) mode of perception and communication as well as a means of operating on the quantum domain. A strong argument can be made for mind/brain interaction and the postmortem survival of consciousness independent of the reincarnation case data. In the following discussion, I explore the relationship between mind and brain and trace the transition from life to death, through death and back to life, looking at evidence of the mind's ability to influence its body, terminal lucidity, near-death experiences, apparitions, mediumistic communications, and prebirth memories.

Emily Kelly (E. W. Kelly, 2007b) reviewed the literature related to what she called "psychophysiological influence," the mind's impact on its body. In *Anatomy of an Illness* Norman Cousins (1979) described how he used laughter to cure himself of ankylosing spondylitis (an inflammatory disease that can cause spinal vertebrae to fuse), but conscious intent is not required for the mind to affect the body. Emotional states alone can precipitate changes, and the bereaved may die within days of a spouse's passing (E. W. Kelly, 2007b, p. 124). Placebos (typically inactive sugar pills) are routinely used as controls in clinical trials of new drugs, but problems develop when they turn out to be as beneficial as the real thing, as seems to be happening with increasing frequency (Beauregard, 2012a; E. W. Kelly, 2007b). The "placebo effect" is attributable to the belief that one's health will improve if one takes the placebo, not realizing that it is inert. Effective faith healing also may be assisted by expectation (E. W. Kelly, 2007b, pp. 132–39), as may death following cursing or hexing (E. W. Kelly, 2007b, pp. 124–27).

It is hard to understand how the mind could have such influences on the body if it were no more than a byproduct of neural activity, and there is more. In false pregnancies, women who mistakenly believe they are enceinte stop menstruating and display other appropriate symptoms (E. W. Kelly, 2007b, pp. 149–52). For centuries, there have been reports of hair or skin suddenly turning white in stressful situations (E. W. Kelly, 2007b, pp. 148–49; Nahm, Navarini, & E. W. Kelly, 2013). Even more dramatic are stigmata, marks (accompanied sometimes by bleeding) that appear on the hands and feet of devout Christians, corresponding to wounds Jesus is presumed to have suffered on the cross (E. W. Kelly, 2007b, pp. 152–56; Stevenson, 1997a, vol. 1, pp. 34–53). Hypnotists have induced a variety of physical changes through suggestion, among them breast enlargement, changes in frequency and duration of the menses, and in heart rate, anesthesia of specific parts of the body, even the formation of blisters (Stevenson, 1997a, vol. 1, pp. 56–68). The recollection of past traumas, such as beatings by a parent, may be accompanied by wheals and other scars (Stevenson, 1997a, vol. 1, pp. 68–75).

In recent years functional magnetic resonance imaging (fMRI) has been used to examine how the brain behaves under various conditions. Studies have shown different regions lighting up when different tasks are performed. For materialist neuroscientists, the results provide clues as to where and how consciousness is generated, but as Kelly (E. W. Kelly, 2007b, p. 117) points out, correlation is not causation, and what really is being observed may be places where consciousness interfaces with the brain. That is how non-materialist neuroscientists interpret their fMRI findings. Jesse Edwards et al. (2012) considered neurobiological correlates of mindfulness and meditation. Mario Beauregard (Beauregard & O'Leary, 2008) reported distinctive patterns of neural activity in Carmelite nuns engaged in contemplative prayer. Elsewhere, Beauregard (2007) discussed what has been learned from neuro-imaging studies of emotional self-regulation, psychotherapy, and the placebo effect.

Some of the most interesting recent work concerns neuroplasticity, the ability of the brain to adapt to circumstance. Neuroplasticity had long been acknowledged for infants and children through their teens, but it was thought that the adult brain was hard-wired and could not be altered. Not only is it now clear that the adult brain, too, is malleable, it is apparent that it can change in response to the mind's will. Psychiatrist Jeffrey Schwartz demonstrated this in the 1990s with his innovative treatment of obsessive-compulsive disorder (OCD). Rather than taking patients through desensitization procedures, then the usual practice, he had them concentrate on changing their behavior. By comparing brain scans taken before and after therapy, Schwartz was able to show that the effort to modify behavior had created new neural pathways, altering the brain's structure (J. M. Schwartz, Gulliford, Stier, & Thienemann, 2005; J. M. Schwartz, Stapp, & Beauregard, 2004). *Neuroplasticity* has become something of a buzzword, with a plethora of self-help books proposing ways to take advantage of it. For overviews of the scientific data written for the general reader, see books by Beauregard (2012a, pp. 65–88), Norman Doidge (2006), and Jeffrey Schwartz and Sharon Begley (2002).

Traumatic brain injury can put patients in minimally conscious or persistent vegetative states that last for years, yet patients may be responsive under certain conditions (Coleman & Owen, 2009; Monti et al., 2010). Adrian Owen et al. (2006) described how a woman who was left in a persistent vegetative state by an automobile accident was able to communicate with researchers by thinking thoughts—walking about her house for *yes*, playing tennis for *no*—that caused neurons in different parts of her brain to fire. She not only heard the researchers' instructions and questions but responded to them appropriately. More recently, Owen (2017, pp. 207–25) described a patient in a persistent vegetative state who showed almost no brain activity during examination in an fMRI scanner but after his unexpected recovery remembered everything that had gone on at that time.

Owen (2017) was of the opinion that consciousness arises somehow from the brain's gray matter. Michael Nahm, David Rousseau, and Bruce Greyson (2017) assembled numerous other reports in which the condition of the brain did not seem to correspond to the patient's mental faculties and reached a different conclusion: Consciousness, it seemed to them, may persist unaltered when the brain is badly hurt, contrary to the materialist assumption that an intact brain is required for the production of consciousness.

Non-materialist medical researchers like Sam Parnia believe that the brain acts not only as a receiver of consciousness but as its filter or modulator. Parnia (2013, pp. 204–10) implicated the neurotransmitter dopamine in this process and noted that drugs that address dopamine deficiencies have restored awareness in comatose patients (2013, pp. 211–15). A similar awakening occurs spontaneously to some seriously ill people as they near death. In the days or hours before they expire, they experience one or more periods of sudden mental clarity during which they recognize and converse with loved ones, often for the first time in years. Nahm and Greyson (2009) documented this phenomenon, which they called terminal lucidity, in people suffering from chronic schizophrenia and other dementias.

Nahm (2012) and Nahm, Greyson, E. W. Kelly, and Haraldsson (2012) collected examples of terminal lucidity in connection with brain abscesses, tumors, strokes, meningitis, and affective disorders. Autopsies revealed damage to the brain extensive enough to have made it impossible for consciousness to manifest according to the brain-production theory, and materialists do not have a good explanation for what happens in these cases. The best skeptics Keith Augustine and Yonatan Fishman (2015, pp. 249–50) can manage is the suggestion that the reports were retrospectively embellished.

As death approaches, people not afflicted by organic brain disease may experience alterations of consciousness in which they see apparitions of deceased persons (Barrett, 1926; Osis, 1961; Osis & Haraldsson, 2012). Karlis Osis (1961) reported that 40% of dying patients in a New York survey of deathbed experiences saw apparitions, as compared to only 4% of the general population. Frances Power Cobbe (1882, pp. 254–63) and Bruce Greyson (2010b) assembled collections of deathbed visions in which percipients were not aware that the people they saw were dead (so-called Peak in Darien experiences). Deathbed visions usually are experienced by the dying person alone, but occasionally they are intersubjective, with others in the room sharing in them as well (Barrett, 1926; Moody & P. Perry, 2010). Deathbed visions are similar in the United States and India, although in India religious figures predominate over relatives and friends (Osis & Haraldsson, 2012).

People who have deathbed visions typically die shortly thereafter, not to be revived (Greyson, 2010b), but new techniques are allowing physicians to bring more people back from death, after longer periods, than ever before. Although their hearts have stopped and their brains have shut down due to the lack of blood flow, awareness returns if and when patients are resuscitated and their brains are reactivated. It has become clear that death is a process that takes hours to complete, as organs fail one after the other, but, if the organs are still viable, is to a large extent reversible with timely intervention (Parnia, 2013).

About 12 to 18% of people who survive cardiac arrest report having had the sense that they (or their minds) separated from their bodies and traveled to another realm, where they interacted with spirits, often of deceased loved ones, then returned to their bodies and awoke in them (Greyson, 2010a). These are what are called near-death experiences, although they do not occur only near death. In one study that checked medical records to see how close to death NDErs actually came, only 45% were judged to have had life-threatening illnesses or injuries. Some 82.5% of patients believed themselves to have been near death, however, so a conviction that death is imminent may be a more important trigger than the threat of death as such (Stevenson, Cook, & McClean-Rice, 1989–1990).

Rarely, NDE-like phenomena appear when there is no threat of death at all. A Mohawk man in Syracuse, New York, told me about an NDE that seems to have been prompted by no more than his obsessive concern for his mother, then recently deceased. He saw her during the experience; she reassured him that she was okay and told him he should return to his body. Interestingly, his wife awoke at the same time and thought that he had died. This account is entirely anecdotal, however, because I have only the testimony of the man. I was unable to interview his wife, from whom he had since divorced.

A variety of materialistic explanations for the NDE have been advanced, but all fall short of explaining the totality of the experience (Greyson, 2010a; E. W. Kelly, Greyson, & E. F. Kelly, 2007; Parnia, 2007). Three culture-independent features pose particular challenges to the idea that consciousness is produced by the brain. One is an extreme mental clarity during the experience. An analysis of a large series of hospital-centered NDEs at the University of Virginia found that 45% of NDErs said their thinking had been "clearer than usual" and another 40% said it had been "as clear as usual." A large majority also said their thinking had been as or faster than usual and as or more logical than usual (E. W. Kelly, Greyson, & E. F. Kelly, 2007, p. 386n16). Another study found that patients who were close to death were more likely than those who were not to report an enhanced perception of light and more acute cognitive processing (Owens, Cook, & Stevenson, 1990).

Secondly, some NDErs (as many as 24% in a prospective study by van Lommel, Wees, Meyers, & Elfferich, 2001) remember seeing themselves from the outside, often from above. A few claim to have observed things in the operating room or elsewhere while they were "out" of their bodies, perceptions that turn out to be veridical (Holden, 2009; Rivas, Dirven & Smit, 2016).

Thirdly, there are the spirits of deceased people many NDErs say they met while out of their bodies. In a series of 665 NDEs, 138 (21%) included an encounter with a spirit (Greyson, 2010b, p. 161). NDErs who come close to dying are significantly more likely to encounter spirits than are NDErs whose life is not genuinely threatened. Among 130 NDErs who came close to dying, twenty-eight (22%) encountered spirits, whereas among 107 NDErs who were not near death, only nine (8%) encountered spirits ($p < .01$) (E. W. Kelly, 2001, p. 236). Like apparitions seen from the deathbed, the spirits may represent people the NDErs do not realize are dead (Greyson, 2010b) or only recognize from photographs afterward (Alexander, 2012). Spirit encounters are one of the strongest cross-cultural features of NDEs (Kellehear, 1996; Shushan, 2018), although there are clear cultural impacts in the way the entities are perceived (Matlock, 2017; Matlock & Giesler-Petersen, 2016).

Apparitions that greet people on their deathbeds and spirits encountered during NDEs demonstrate memory and purpose in showing themselves when and to whom they do. The same may be said of "crisis apparitions," which appear at or around the time of death, usually to loved ones or close friends in distant places (Gurney, Myers, & Podmore, 1886). Crisis apparitions were more common in the days before email and cell phones, but they continue to be reported (Arcangel, 2005; Haraldsson, 2012b). Apparitions of persons dead for longer periods also may convey veridical information (Lang, 1897, pp. 133–86; Green & McCreery, 1975, pp. 75–79), and we should not forget apparitions that announce their intention to seek rebirth, either in the waking state (Goulet, 1998) or nocturnal dreams (Stevenson, 1982). Apparitions of all types may be perceived by more than one person, either collectively or intersubjectively, on a single occasion, or serially, on separate occasions (Hart & Hart, 1932–1933; Moody & P. Perry, 2010). Not only do many apparitions seem to have unfinished business to conduct, many represent people who died violently, and a good majority are male (Haraldsson, 2009; Stevenson, 1982). The similarity of these features to features of reincarnation cases is intriguing and may not be coincidental.

In mediumship also we see (at least in the better cases) indications of the persistence of personality and of purpose (Gauld, 1982). These qualities are on display in the most interesting recent case of trance mediumship, a chess game played between a deceased Hungarian grandmaster, Géza Maróczy, ostensibly dictating moves through the medium, and the living Russian grandmaster Victor Korchnoi (Eisenbeiss & Hassler, 2006). Maróczy was at the height of his fame in the 1920s and died in 1951. The game began in 1985 and went for forty-seven moves before Korchnoi prevailed in 1993. The "Maróczy" communicator played in an old-fashioned style appropriate to Maróczy in life. He controlled the endgame in a manner common in the early twentieth century, and at one point Korchnoi was afraid he might lose.

In addition to dictating the chess moves, "Maróczy" presented himself like Maróczy and gave a good deal of correct personal information about the life of Maróczy and other chess players of his day. In a careful analysis of the moves "Maróczy" made, Vernon Neppe (2007) concluded that the skill they demonstrated, along with other knowledge and behaviors displayed by "Maróczy," supported a survival interpretation of the case. Other commentators (Braude, 2013; May & Marwaha, n.d.) have thought that the medium would have been able to achieve these things by the exercise of his psi alone, although as always with super-psi propositions, it is difficult to understand how the psi of a living agent (the medium, in this case) could account for all the elements on display.

Super-psi has to stretch also to explain communicators—so-called drop-in communicators—who appear at séances unbidden and are unknown to the medium and sitters, yet provide evidence of earlier embodied existences (Andrade, 2010c; Haraldsson & Stevenson, 1975a, 1975b; Ravaldini, Biondi, & Stevenson, 1990).

In an Icelandic case described by Haraldsson and Stevenson (1975b), a communicator dropped in at a regular séance of the medium Hafsteinn Björnsson. At first, he would not give his name, but later he said that he was Runolfur Runolfsson, who went by the name Runki. He told the sitters that one night after drinking heavily he had decided to walk home along the beach. He had fallen asleep and the waves had washed him out to sea. His body was later recovered and buried, but without one leg, and he wanted his missing leg. More than a year after Runki's initial appearance, a new sitter joined the group. Runki showed up and declared that the new sitter had his leg in his house. The sitter knew nothing about a leg in his house, but indeed a human femur was discovered in one of the walls. (It was a custom in Iceland, as in other parts of Europe, to place a bone in a wall of a new house, as a talisman.) The leg was retrieved and buried, and with his unfinished business resolved, Runki relaxed. He continued to attend the group and became one of Björnsson's regular controls.

An unusual number of mediumistic communicators, many with verified identities, met unexpected or violent deaths. One-third of the communicators manifesting through Leonora Piper died violently, and two-thirds of those manifesting through Björnsson did so (Haraldsson, 2009, p. 114).

* * *

From mediumistic communications I pass to prebirth memories. The term *prebirth memory* is sometimes used in reference to any memory of prenatal existence but it seems preferable to restrict it to memories of prenatal existence that do not involve memories of previous lives or deaths. In this usage, prebirth memories cover only stages 2 through 5 of the intermission experience.

An astonishing 45% of Japanese schoolchildren in one survey said they had prebirth memories (Ikegawa, 2005; Ohkado & Ikegawa, 2014). In the United States similar accounts have been published mostly in books intended for wide circulation (e.g., Carman & Carman, 2013; Hallett, 2002; Hinze, 1995) but they deserve serious study. Materialist biology contends that fetal brains are not well-enough developed to support episodic memory formation and allows for fetal learning only in terms of habituation (Dirix, Nijuis, Jongsma, & Hornstra, 2009; Hepper, 1996), yet in prebirth memories children sometimes recount veridical perceptions of their parents and their external environments during the intrauterine period and before (Ohkado & Ikegawa, 2014; Rivas, Carman, Carman, & Dirven, 2015).

Western children with prebirth memories frequently tell of interactions with God, Jesus, or angels, and they often describe choosing their parents, prominent features of intermission memories (Matlock & Giesler-Petersen, 2016). Some mothers of children with prebirth memories have announcing dreams or feel themselves to be in spiritual contact with their children. Memories of being in the womb and of birth (stages 4 and 5 of the intermission experience) are more common with prebirth memories than with intermission memories, although they have been reported occasionally with intermission memories also (Matlock, 2017, May; Matlock & Giesler-Petersen, 2016).

For some analysts, prebirth memories suggest the possibility of preexistence without prior incarnation. This inference would be more convincing if the experiences included strong memories of all but the first stage of the intermission, but many reported prebirth memories are much weaker phenomenologically and evidentially than intermission memories. As matters now stand, it is probably best to regard prebirth memories not as a category distinct from intermission memories but as situations in which only the later parts of an interlife experience are recalled.

At the turn of the nineteenth century, William James (1898/1960) and F. W. H. Myers (1903) returned to the idea that the brain transmits consciousness rather than producing it. Both understood consciousness to include subconscious processing at one end of a spectrum and the opening into mystical states at the other. Unfortunately, their concepts were eclipsed by Freud's psychoanalysis, and this elicited a reaction from psychologist John Watson (E. F. Kelly, 2007).

Watson took the position that human behavior could be explained entirely as a response to environmental stimuli, without reference to consciousness, much less the subconscious. This way of thinking was embraced and extended in the operant conditioning of B. F. Skinner, which dominated American psychology through the 1960s and was still taught in the psychology department of Emory University when I was an undergraduate there in the early 1970s. Behaviorism was replaced by cognitive psychology, which brought consciousness back to respectability, although in a materialist guise. Gradually, however, attention has been returning to transmission models of consciousness, and the possibility that mind and brain are independent but interactive is once more being taken seriously (E. F. Kelly & Presti, 2015).

The dualist interactionism of Henry Stapp (1999, 2005, 2009, 2015) is very important theoretically. If Stapp is right, attention, intention, and will are intrinsic properties of consciousness and play key roles in mind/brain interactions. Stapp, Schwartz, and Beauregard (2005) argue that quantum physics must be used in analyzing cerebral dynamics in order to elucidate the structural features of ion channels critical to synaptic functioning. Quantum physics implies for them an independent consciousness with the attributes Stapp has indicated. They are of the opinion that the mind governs how the brain operates, not the other way around; and that this explains how intention and will become involved in neuroplasticity and in the mind's ability to influence the body generally.

The same properties could give mind a place in the making of physical reality, due to the probabilistic nature of quantum interactions. The interests of mind might bias otherwise random processes, making some outcomes more likely than others. It appears as if objective reality is constructed to allow mind to have an input, and, furthermore, that nothing in the cosmos happens without cause. Stapp calls this the "principle of sufficient reason": "nothing should happen without a sufficient reason for that particular thing to happen" (2015, p. 186). The "sufficient reason" may be determined by an "observer's choice" or by "nature's choice," the two agencies that enter into standard quantum calculations.

The idea that the mind can influence physical and biological systems has received a fair amount of experimental support. Parapsychological studies have shown the effects of intention on the output of random number generators (Radin, 2006, 2009; Radin & Nelson, 1989) and on biological organisms, including human bodies (Braud, 2003; Schlitz & Braud, 1997). These effects come under the heading of psi (PK), as do larger-scale actions such as table-tipping, raps, levitations, and other phenomena in physical mediumship (Braude, 1979a, 2007; Haraldsson & Gissurarson, 2015; Mishlove, 2000) and poltergeist activity that has been observed with and without embodied agents (Roll, 1972; Stevenson, 1972).

Other considerations tilt the balance even further toward the reality of mind/brain interaction and postmortem survival. It is not a trivial matter that violent death, unfinished business, and a preponderance of male actors figure in apparition, mediumship, and reincarnation cases, nor is it insignificant that veridical memories of previous lives, of the intermission, of the intrauterine months, and of being born are reported by some of the same children (Matlock, 2017, May).

With all the evidence now available of the mind's ability to function in a discarnate state and of its interactive relationship with the brain while embodied, why is the survivalist perspective still so strongly resisted by the materialist scientific mainstream? Why, for that matter, is materialism still mainstream rather than marginalized?

Part of the answer is that mind/brain identity continues to be a productive conceptual framework, and there is a lot of data that can be interpreted in its favor (M. Martin & Augustine, 2015). In the transmission theory of mind/brain relations, the brain sometimes is likened to a radio or television set, consciousness to the electromagnetic waves these receivers decode, but this is misleadingly simplistic. The quality of our conscious experience is affected by exogenous factors, including food and drink and other substances we ingest, and the impairment of brain functioning leads to the lessening or loss of the connection to awareness.

Moreover, it has become clear that our brains are involved in much besides determining how we experience consciousness. There is a substantial and growing literature on the neurobiology of emotions, with profound clinical implications (Heilman & Velenstein, 2011; Phillips, 2003), and advances have been made in appreciating neurobiological influences on personality traits more generally (Nardi, 2011; Yarkoni, 2013). For non-materialist researchers, correlation does not equal causation and mind/brain interactions are a two-way street (E. W. Kelly, 2007b), but the materialist model allows adherents to assume that the brain alone is involved in generating the observed effects.

Another part of the reason for the continuing resistance to mind/brain interaction is that the majority of scientists are not acquainted with the relevant data. They have not taken the time to examine them because they assume that there is nothing to them and they have been told by prominent authorities that there is nothing to them. The authorities who are most vocal in dismissing the evidence for mind/brain interaction are in many instances the skeptics of reincarnation whose arguments I have aired and addressed and they have approached the mind/brain interaction data in the same way they have approached the postmortem survival and reincarnation data: by ignoring some findings and distorting others. Moreover, they give every appearance of not being well versed in the literature they are disparaging (Matlock, 2016b, 2016c).

In his book, *Why You Are Not Your Brain, and Other Lessons from the Biology of Consciousness*, Alva Noë (2009) lays out many of the problems with the mind/brain identity thesis. Conscious experience, Noë thinks, arises from engagement with the external world, not from neural activity. Several neuroscientists (Beauregard, 2012a; Woollacott, 2015), biologists (Lanza, with Berman, 2009), and psychologists (Baruš & Mossbridge, 2017; Tart, 2009) have questioned the mind/brain identity thesis also. Philosophers (e.g., Göcke, 2012; Koons & Bealer, 2010) and others (e.g., Kastrup, 2014, 2015) have raised questions about materialism more generally. The various issues are explored in depth by Edward Kelly and his colleagues in *Irreducible Mind* (E. F. Kelly et al., 2007) and *Beyond Physicalism* (E. F. Kelly, Crabtree, & Marshall, 2015).

Augustine and Fishman (2015) maintain that the materialist position has so much going for it that it should be given the presumption of truth. They introduce a Bayesian analysis in which they assign much more weight to the mind/brain identity thesis than to the possibility of mind/brain interaction. The outcome of a Bayesian analysis is heavily dependent on how one weights the factors that go into it. By assigning the weights as they do, Augustine and Fishman ensure that the mind/brain identity thesis emerges the winner. However, the mere fact that there are serious questions about the mind/brain identity thesis reduces the weight that may in fairness be allotted to it, and if all the evidence in favor of mind/brain interaction is taken into account as well, the outcome of a Bayesian analysis looks very different (Matlock, 2016b, 2016c). Sudduth (2016) undertakes a similar Bayesian analysis that fails for the same reason (Matlock, 2016a).

I will mention one other position on the postmortem survival of consciousness. Douglas Stokes (2007, 2014) contends that because the brain is so heavily involved in personality formation, consciousness can survive bodily death only in a pure form, without any subconscious content or continuing conscious awareness. This rather Buddhist conception of survival is belied by the case data. Mediumship, apparition, and reincarnation cases suggest the persistence after death of personality, emotion, memory, cognitive ability, and the exercise of free will. I think it would be better to acknowledge the brain's role in making us who we are but insist that there is more to the story. It would be foolish to deny the evidence of the brain's contribution to our makeup, but it is equally silly to ignore the data that show that that is not all that we are.

PERSONAL IDENTITY AND POSTMORTEM SURVIVAL

Any venture in theory building can benefit from consideration of the attendant philosophical issues. In this section I examine philosophical debates about personal identity, personal survival, and the nature of postmortem states of consciousness, with the goal of reaching a better understanding of how reincarnation works. My discussion is securely anchored in the case data but ultimately moves beyond them in ways I have not done previously.

Braude (2005) contrasted metaphysical (ontological) and epistemological approaches to personal identity in relation to postmortem survival. The metaphysical questions concern what makes a person the same over time, despite changes in appearance, physiology, psychology, and so on. The epistemological questions are the practical ones of how one decides whether someone one meets is the same as someone one knows or once knew. Philosophers often ask these questions about living people, but they become more acute in connection to postmortem survival and reincarnation. What is it that survives death and reincarnates? What criteria do we use to identify a surviving individual with a deceased person? Is this sufficient basis on which to conclude that the surviving individual is the same as the deceased person? If not, what does it mean to say that that person has survived or reincarnated? After addressing these questions, I tackle the problem of disembodied survival (survival unsupported by a subtle body) and explain how I conceive the reincarnation process to function.

I have given my answer to the first question, "What is it that survives death and reincarnates?" I think that what is commonly called the "soul" is best thought of as a stream of consciousness. I see no essential difference between consciousness, mind, psyche, soul, and spirit. I imagine a duplex consciousness consisting of a subconscious along with conscious awareness. This last idea is important, because the subconscious is what conveys memory, personality, behavioral dispositions, and other aspects of personal identity from one embodiment to the next.

When the role of consciousness in quantum mechanics has been considered (e.g., by Atmanspacher, 2011, and Stapp, 2011), it has been limited to conscious awareness. Studies of altered states have concentrated on various sorts of conscious awareness to the neglect of the subconscious. David Chalmers (1996) and many other philosophers have concentrated on conscious awareness as well. In recent years, a good deal of attention has been given by psychologists and philosophers to what Evan Thompson (2007, p. 12) called the "cognitive unconscious"—unconscious perception, implicit learning, and implicit memory. Chalmers (2010) reviewed this work and suggested ways to further it, including exploring the neural correlates of unconscious processing.

This cognitive approach to the unconscious is limited to the processing of perceptual information and does not envision a subconscious that records memories and supports the range of personality traits involved in postmortem survival and reincarnation. Clinical psychologists and psychiatrists have a broader notion of the subconscious, although most embrace some form of Freud's conception of the unconscious as a repository of repressed thoughts and concerns. I use the term *subconscious* in order to avoid association with the psychoanalytic view and because I think that *subconscious* better represents the relationship between the two strata of mind, as F. W. H. Myers's cognate terms *subliminal* and *supraliminal* do.

Myers thought of the subliminal and supraliminal levels of mind as separated by a "threshold" or "limen" across which content moves, "so that what was once below the surface may for a time, or permanently, rise above it" (1903, vol. 1, p. 15). Myers (1903) considered a wide range of psychological and parapsychological phenomena, from dreams to secondary (multiple) personality to mediumship and apparitions. He showed how all participate in the subliminal stratum of mind but on occasion press themselves, though perhaps only partially and temporarily, over the threshold into the supraliminal (E. W. Kelly, 2007a). He arranged his examples on a continuum that suggested a unified mind survives bodily death (Cook, 1994). Myers wrote before cases of past-life memory were well known and so did not allow for reincarnation, but neither did he rule out its possibility.

It think it unlikely that a consciousness stream would lose its structure upon becoming discarnate and we may imagine it to possess both subliminal and supraliminal strata, just as it did when embodied. In addition to preserving memory and personality traits, the subconscious is where psi (ESP) inputs are processed and whence psi (PK) operations are initiated. Psi would provide a discarnate mind the means of perceiving and interacting with other discarnate minds, embodied persons, and the material world, but these interactions need not differ in any significant respect from those of embodied minds. Contrary to the claims of Braude (2009, 2013) and Sudduth (2009, 2016), I see no reason discarnate psi processes need involve super-psi, so granting psi capabilities to disembodied actors does not oblige survival theorists to credit the supposed super-psi of embodied actors.

Survival researchers and commentators have long noted that the fragmentary presentation of mediumistic messages and the dumbed-down appearance of apparitions suggest the survival of something less than an intact personality (Broad, 1962; Ducasse, 1961; Gauld, 1982). From my perspective, this apparent diminution is more illusory than real, a by-product of the nature of psi communication between disembodied and embodied minds and information processing at the subliminal level of mind, where inputs may be transformed before presentation to conscious awareness (Marshall, 2015, pp. 304–401; Price, 1995). Some subconscious content may be expected to move into conscious awareness of a discarnate mind spontaneously, as happens with embodied minds, while other content remains latent in the

subliminal until brought into play through psi interactions with other disembodied or embodied agents. Even without external stimuli and subjective
experience at the level of awareness, however, an individual's subconscious
may be expected to maintain its memories and personality intact throughout
the period we call death.

These metaphysical concerns bear on the epistemological ones and hence
on the second question posed above, "What criteria do we use to identify a
surviving individual with a deceased person?"

Philosophers are divided over whether memory or physical features are
more important in recognizing someone we know. Terence Penelhum (1970)
argued that identity was so closely tied to the physical body that the notion of
disembodied existence made no sense. After examining an array of survival
evidence, R. W. K. Paterson (1995) concluded not only that postmortem
survival was likely, but that identification of a surviving personality might
be made on the basis of several different criteria, not all physical. There can
be no doubt that Paterson was right. A physical likeness acts as an aid to
identification of many apparitions, but is unavailable with mediumistic messages. Sitters judge whether a mediumistic communicator is who he says he
is principally on the basis of how well he seems to remember the life of the
person he claims to have been, but with trance mediumship they may take
other factors into consideration, including the timbre of the medium's voice
if the communicator speaks through her, her mannerisms when doing so, et
cetera (Broad, 1962; Ducasse, 1961; Gauld, 1982).

Now, I do not think we want to say that because some percipients and sitters can identify discarnate actors with previously living persons, the discarnate actors and the previously living persons are one and the same. Obviously
they are not, because the discarnate actors are no longer embodied. So bodies
do count for something. Bodies are not required for identification and thus are
not essential to establishing identity, but they are fundamental to persons. A
person for me is embodied consciousness, hence my term *previous person* in
place of Stevenson's *previous personality*. I realize that I am defining *person*
differently from the way most philosophers and many laypeople do, but that
cannot be helped. The distinction between the physical and psychological
aspects of personhood is crucial. A person's mind survives death, carrying his
sense of self along with the dispositions and memories that undergird his personality, although he as a physical entity ceases to exist when his body dies.

A critical problem is determining to what extent personality is fixed postmortem and to what extent it is capable of change. If personality formation
were wholly dependent on the brain and the mind were to survive death, we
would expect to see a persisting personality pattern but no developmental
change in the discarnate state. Yet some mediumistic cases provide evidence

of postmortem developmental change (Broad, 1962; Gauld, 1982). Runki Runolfsson (Haraldsson & Stevenson, 1975b) relaxed once his missing leg was retrieved and properly buried. A related issue is postmortem cognition. If the brain were exclusively responsible for cognition, there should be no evidence of postmortem reasoning and decision-making, yet there is a substantial amount of such evidence, from intermission memories, announcing dreams, and mediumistic communications. The chess-playing of the "Maróczy" communicator (Eisenbeiss & Hassler, 2006) provides a mediumistic example.

A few philosophers (e.g., Ayer, 1963; Nayak, 1976; Quinton, 1975) have used reincarnation scenarios to discuss whether memory is sufficient for third parties to identify a living person with a deceased person. No single factor is involved in making such determinations in real life. Memory and recognition tests may be important, at times may be considered decisive, but the lack of a memory claim does not render identification impossible. In silent cases, identifications may be made on the basis of signs like birthmarks and announcing dreams (Keil, 1996).

Other philosophers have considered past-life memory and what personal identity means from the first-person perspective. In a chapter added to the second edition of his *Essay Concerning Human Understanding*, John Locke used the recollection of previous lives in his argument that memory was essential for personal identity. Citing the example of a mayor of Queenborough, who believed he had lived before as Socrates, Locke held that if the mayor had memories of Socrates's life, he could be considered one with Socrates, but otherwise not (Locke, 1694/1975, pp. 43–44).

A. J. Ayer wrote, "If a person who is physically identified as living at a later time [has] the ostensible memories and character of a person who is physically identified as living at an earlier time, they are to be counted as one person and not two" (1963, p. 127). This surely depends on what a "person" is and Ayer probably did not mean anything more than that the previous and present persons are to be regarded as numerically the same. That is problematical, though, because the previous and present persons each embody features not found in the other. Ayer would have done better to distinguish between persons and personalities, as I do.

Derek Parfit (1984, pp. 227–28) admitted that if there were evidence for veridical past-life memory, it would constitute evidence for reincarnation, but he asserted that there was no evidence of this kind, whereas there was, he believed, good evidence for the reductionist view that memory and personality were produced by the brain. In a footnote, he referred to a passage from C. D. Broad (1925/1949) that dealt with mediumship and postmortem survival, acknowledging that if some "credible person" were to claim to have better evidence for survival, "his claim should not be simply ignored" (Parfit, 1984,

p. 517n23). There was credible evidence already in 1925 and 1949. Since then more has been introduced and, in addition, the reincarnation data have come in. Much of this work was available to Parfit in 1984, but evidently he was not acquainted with it.

There would seem to be no reason reincarnation might not proceed in the absence of conscious memories (McTaggart, 1906; Rivas, 2012), although Griffin (1997, p. 186) believes that only people who remember previous lives have lived before. Whereas Locke claimed that whether or not there was continuity of consciousness, personal identity depended on memory, Griffin apparently assumes that unless there are past-life memories, there is no continuity of consciousness and hence no reincarnation.

Griffin's assumption does not allow for behavioral or physical signs in silent cases. Moreover, because it is possible that a person without past-life memories in childhood will experience them spontaneously or through regression, or have a psychic access them, in adulthood, one would not be able to say until a person's life was over whether or not his spirit was reincarnated. Griffin must explain the absence of past-life memories as due to a preexistent spirit incarnated for the first time or else suppose that a person's spirit came into being along with his body. For me, the assumption that reincarnation is a routine affair makes better sense of the data (and is philosophically sounder) than does the assumption that it is not. I explain the absence of past-life memories as due to unconscious blocks against remembering what happened before. The memories are preserved in the subconscious but do not make their way into conscious awareness (Haraldsson & Matlock, 2016, pp. 262–63).

An interesting phenomenon to consider in this regard is replacement reincarnation (Chapter 5; Matlock, 2017, March). Unlike in MPD/DID, in replacement reincarnation there is not an alternation of control by different personalities or sub-personalities. Rather, one spirit leaves and another takes its place, the replacing spirit having no memories of, and no feeling of connection to, the body's previous possessor. Replacement reincarnation would appear to be decisive proof that bodies are neither necessary nor sufficient for the establishment of personal identity, either of the first-person or third-person variety.

Now to the question, "What does it mean to say that a person has survived or reincarnated?" People who identify a child as the reincarnation of a deceased person do not mean that he is the same person as before. They recognize that he is a different person, with something of the personality, behavior, or physical features of the previous person. They—and we—may say that he is the reincarnation of the previous person without implying that he is that person returned in all particulars. It is not the person as such who has survived, but his sense of self and his personality, the constituent parts of which are carried in the subconscious part of his mind.

When reincarnation occurs, the mind comes into association with a new body, and this requires a reset of conscious awareness. The new body has its own brain, which will develop along its own trajectory, affecting the reincarnated mind along the way. While in the womb, the mind has the opportunity to customize its body. It is at this stage that birthmarks and other physical signs are impressed on the body, and neural pathways that convey practiced behaviors and skill sets are laid down in the brain. As a child matures, first in the womb and then postnatally, his brain comes to exercise more and more control over the supraliminal stratum of his mind and less and less of the previous life passes up from the subliminal.

Stevenson (2001, p. 109, and elsewhere) noted that past-life memories seem to become buried under memories of the present life as children age. Past-life personalities become more difficult to access over time. One interpretation of this finding is that past-life memories become walled off from the present-life personality, as in MPD/DID. This possibility receives some support from the case of Uttara Huddar or Sharada (Akolkar, 1992; Stevenson, 1984) and is suggested also by the Brazilian Spiritist therapy described by Krippner (1991). I am not sure that the past-life-personalities-as-alters model does full justice to the evidence, however. Those who remember previous lives experience their memories as from a single, continuous consciousness stream. Episodic past-life memories present in a fragmentary way, as do memories of the present life, but without the autobiographical knowledge required to place them in their proper sequence, they can seem arbitrary and random.

There is no question that personality traits may carry over from life to life. In a study with the DOPS database, a statistically significant similarity ($p < .01$) was found between previous persons and case subjects on each of six dispositional traits on which they were compared, confirming what we see in the casual inspection of case reports. The six traits were attachment to wealth; criminal behavior or tendencies; generosity or philanthropy; experience in meditation; participation in religious observance; and saintly character (Tucker, 2013, pp. 209–10). Nonetheless, it is clear that reincarnation is not about the replication of a complete identity in a new person, but about the persistence of a conscious stream and the influence of a previous personality on the present personality.

Braude (2003, p. 298) considered "implausible" the idea that the personality of a deceased individual survived for a time in a discarnate state, then went through a gradual transformation after reincarnating, but is this gradual change not something we all experience in the course of a single life? Would it not be natural for the process to be accelerated after a discarnate mind takes possession of a new physical body? We are different persons in each life, but something of our previous personalities is retained in our present ones. The degree of influence varies from person to person, and over time. It appears to be correlated to some extent with emotional needs, derived from either the previous life or the present one, sometimes from both, and may be most evident with people who show signs of remembering things from an early age. But always it involves bringing the past into the present, so the present is never something entirely new.

I will now take up the problem of disembodied survival—that is, the problem of whether the mind may exist apart from not only a physical body but from a quasi-material subtle body too (Flew, 1972; Penelhum, 1970). As Broad (1958/1976) observed, most people speak as if they imagine postmortem survival in a quasi-material spiritual form. Thanks to Theosophy, the most familiar term for this form is the astral body. The advantages to survival in an astral body over disembodied survival in a strict sense are said to be several— an astral body would contain the disparate parts of a personality, which otherwise would go their separate ways; it would serve as the locus of thought, perception, and action via psi; and it would provide a basis for socializing in the afterlife. Antony Flew (1972) considered an astral body indispensable to postmortem survival.

Broad (1958/1976; 1962) referred to what I am calling the consciousness stream, the Ψ-component (psi-component) of an individual. Broad considered how dispositions to feel and behave in certain ways are associated with a Ψ-component and with it survive bodily death, but he could not accept that these traits could remain integrated in the discarnate state without the support of an astral body (1962, p. 425). J. M. O. Wheatley (1979) agreed and compared Broad's "minded astral body" to Stevenson's (1974a, pp. 406–7) "intermediate 'non-physical body'," which would carry mental images and the imprints of wounds from one life to the next, a forerunner of the concept he (Stevenson, 1997a, vol. 2, pp. 2083–92) later elaborated as the psychophore.

Stevenson's (1974a, 1997a, 2001) psychophore and the psychoplasm of Von Ward (2008) rely on hypothetical processes and require considerable tweaking of the well-established account of genetics in sexual reproduction, a situation I avoid by having the reincarnating mind introduce alterations to the genetically engineered body directly, via psychokinesis. However, if my theory demands less of an adjustment to standard biology, by dispensing with a subtle body between lives it entails a strict disembodied survival and encounters the objections that Flew (1972) and others have raised. These objections can be met, I believe, if we turn away from substance dualism and adopt a Whiteheadian process metaphysics, as advocated by Griffin (1997), Eric Weiss (2012, 2015), and E. F. Kelly (2015b).

* * *

At this point, I must step back and say something about substance dualism versus substance monism and explain how the difference between them affects the conception of what survives death and reincarnates. Substance dualisms, such as that associated with René Descartes (1641/2000), assert that the mental and the physical are fundamentally distinct; they have always existed independently and will always exist independently of one another. The Cartesian mind or Ego undergoes experiences but is eternal, indivisible, and unchanging. There are two kinds of substance monism, the physical and the mental, associated with materialism and idealism. Materialism claims that matter is the foundation of all that exists, hence mind is generated by the brain. Idealism is the diametrically opposed position that everything is ultimately mental, which since the advent of quantum mechanics has come to mean that consciousness existed prior to material reality and is responsible for the creation of material reality.

In *Process and Reality*, first published in 1929, Alfred North Whitehead (1978) developed a "philosophy of organism" consistent with the principles of quantum mechanics as it was then beginning to be formulated. Whitehead rejected substance dualism in favor of idealism. For him, an organism was composed of a multiplicity of hierarchically arranged systems, or "societies," each with its own stream of experience and memory. The same organizational principles applied to nonliving complex societies such as rocks as to living societies, with the exception that living societies took an active role in interactions with their environments (Whitehead, 1978, p. 102).

According to Whitehead (1978), the experience of societies at all levels was composed of a series of discrete events, "occasions" or "actual occasions." Actual occasions were linked in a chain through a "concrescence" (growing together), propelled by a "craving for existence" he called a "creative advance." Whitehead's process model is evolutionary without being teleological. It emphasizes psychological continuity and, importantly for the present discussion, the concatenation of actual occasions ensures the coherence of an experiential stream, a stream of consciousness, without the need for a subtle body to support it.

Whitehead (1978, p. 186) held that actual occasions were initiated by "physical feelings," each with its corresponding "conceptual feeling" in the unconscious (subconscious). Conscious awareness arose through an integration of physical and conceptual feelings, but memories of past conceptual feelings were retained in the unconscious, providing a context for conscious awareness. Whenever there was conscious awareness, there was a corresponding "conceptual function" in the unconscious (1978, p. 242–43). I go further than this and, following Myers (1903), grant the subconscious its own psychological dynamics, but the basic premise is the same: Conscious awareness is (in philosophy's evocative phrase) parasitic upon the subconscious.

Whitehead believed that an individual's experiential stream survived his death, resulting in a sort of "objective immortality," but he seems to have thought of mental activity as having ceased then (1978, p. 351). Had he considered the evidence for discarnate agency assembled by psychical research, Whitehead might have reached a different conclusion. Thanks to psi perceptions and interactions, I see no reason that the concrescence of actual occasions should end at death, and with this amendment, Whitehead's process metaphysics allows for the survival of personality, discarnate agency, and elective reincarnation. In allowing for personal survival, this extension of Whitehead's metaphysics meets the objection of Rivas (2005) that the process position is "impersonalist" because it amounts to the Buddhist doctrine of anattā or no-self.

As I envision it, an experiential stream persists with its identity intact until its reincarnation. At that point, at the subliminal level the stream continues unimpeded, but at the supraliminal level there is a decisive break brought about by the engagement with the new body and brain. We begin each life with a tabula rasa, a blank slate, onto which the past impresses itself through involuntary memories and unconscious influence on our behavior. Autobiographical knowledge of the past is lost, or at least pushed deep into the subconscious mind, when the connection is made to the new brain.

My revised process model acknowledges the discontinuity of conscious awareness between lives while asserting the subconscious continuity of self over successive lives. I will name it the Processual Soul model or theory. It is very different from the Cartesian Ego model, which is concerned with conscious awareness, makes no provision for the subconscious, and has the same unchanging essence incarnating life after life. It is also different from the MPD/DID alter model, which envisions a group of personalities keeping company in a single mind.

My processual soul theory differs from Cartesian substance dualism not only in making allowance for the subconscious and in positing ongoing change in the surviving and reincarnating mind. Descartes (1641/2000) held that while disembodied, the immaterial thinking substance or Ego was unextended and unlocalized in space, but I cannot understand how there can be interactions between disembodied and embodied minds unless they coexist in the same spatiotemporal coordinate system (Matlock, 2016b, p. 196).

Some case reports explicitly locate discarnate minds and embodied persons in the same place at the same time. Communicators may claim to be standing beside their mediums when their voices are heard (Haraldsson & Gissuarson, 2015). There are numerous cases of persons who feel themselves traveling out-of-body to distant locations, where they are seen as apparitions (so-called reciprocal apparitions) (Hart & Hart, 1932–1933; Rivas, Dirven, and Smit,

2016, pp. 157–70; Robertson, 2015, pp. 91–92). Dying persons may see deceased loved ones in their rooms (Barrett, 1926; Cobbe, 1882; Osis & Haraldsson, 2012). In relating intermission memories, it is common to hear subjects tell of seeing their parents-to-be. In Asian cases, subjects talk as if they were physically near them on the ground (Matlock & Giesler-Petersen, 2016).

If the discarnate consciousness stream is localized, perhaps it has extension also. Stevenson (1997a, vol. 2, pp. 2089–91) used apparitions in his argument for a psychophore, but not all visual apparitions have recognizable shapes (Green & McCreery, 1975). Rather than direct representations of the psychophore or subtle body, apparitions are more likely to be mental creations of the percipient, constructed from psi impressions received by the subconscious mind and presented to conscious awareness as if they were something apprehended by the eyes (Gauld, 1982; Myers, 1903; Tyrrell, 1953/1973). The discarnate agent's mind might very well be extended in space near to the percipient's embodied mind. Conscious awareness need not be extended, but I think of the subconscious as a non-physical matrix that records, stores, and manages information, which means that it would be extended as well as localized.

Eric Weiss's (2012, 2015) Transpersonal Process Metaphysics takes Whitehead (1978) as a starting point, as I do, but Weiss and I differ in how we develop our proposals. Weiss acknowledges that memory may be unconscious as well as conscious (2012, p. 258) but he does not embrace the subconscious fully and therefore has trouble explaining the transmission of personality traits between lives. Early in his chapter on reincarnation he opines that "the personality that survives bodily death is itself mortal, and [except in Stevenson's cases] dies before any reincarnation takes place" (2012, p. 253). Later on he imagines a superintending essence he calls the "soul," defined as "some entity other than personality that somehow holds memories of past lives and is, rather than the personality itself, the entity that reincarnates" (2012, p. 270). However, apparitions and mediumistic communications do not suggest a radical separation of memory and personality postmortem, and it is not obvious why there should be a difference between survival leading to reincarnation and survival that does not (or has not yet) done so.

Jim Tucker (2013, 2014) understands postmortem consciousness to be continuous with the consciousness of embodied life, as I do. He suggests that both postmortem existence and embodied life are tantamount to dreams; when one reincarnates, one continues with the dream one left off at death. However, Tucker thinks that the past life dream "ends" in late childhood, when amnesia for the previous life sets in, whereas I place the resetting at conception, when the consciousness stream takes possession of a new physical body and begins interacting with a new brain. Also, I do not accept that there is amnesia for past lives at the subliminal level of mind, only at the supraliminal.

The processual soul theory recognizes a dualism of mind and body, but its dualism is a type of idealist property dualism rather than substance dualism. There is only one substance, and that is consciousness. Material things, including bodies, are, ultimately, creations of consciousness, I believe. Entities at all levels in a biological system have experiences and retain memories of them, but in addition, the biological system is animated by a stream of consciousness that takes possession of it, normally during gestation. An idealist mind/body dualism overcomes the problem of how mind and body can interact if they are composed of fundamentally different substances (Griffin, 1997, 1998), one of the common objections to Cartesian substance dualism (Kim, 2015).

Whitehead was trained as a mathematician and wrote *Process and Reality* in response to early quantum theory (Epperson, 2004). He wanted to show not only that it was possible to describe mental processes in a manner analogous to the quantum order but that similar processes unfold at all levels of an organism. His account has qualities of idealism, which assigns consciousness the principal role in the making of reality; panpsychism, which considers all elements of nature to possess some degree of consciousness or feeling; and panentheism, which views God as immanent in everything. Unsurprisingly, Stapp (1979, 2011) is a fan of Whitehead, although like Griffin (1997), E. F. Kelly (2015b), and me, he understands cognitive functioning to persist beyond death.

Similar concepts appear in animism and are a feature of most schools of Hinduism. Panpsychism has a long history in Western thought, although not all thinkers have framed it in the same way (Brüntrup & Jaskolla, 2017; Skrbina, 2005). Like E. F. Kelly (2015b), I favor the panexperientialism of Griffin (1997, 1998). Griffin observes that mind differs from brain cells "in degree" but not "in kind" (1997, pp. 129–30). He follows Whitehead (1978) in differentiating levels of organization in a given entity, stressing the contrast between the animate and the inanimate. There is a difference between individual molecules, each of which may be said to have some type of experience (and memory for past experiences), their aggregation in a rock or telephone, and in larger composite entities that share a collective experience. Interaction between mind and the aggregation of cells in the brain and body, Griffin says, take place through psi.

I am concerned with a slightly different problem than Whitehead and Griffin. Whitehead (1978) did not allow for personal survival or reincarnation, so did not consider the relationship between an organism's body consciousness and the stream of consciousness that takes possession of the organism. Because Griffin (1997, pp. 146–48) recognized reincarnation for some individuals only, and apparently only for human beings, he did not address this issue either. But the problem is central to the processual soul theory. I will not attempt to work out how the incoming consciousness stream interfaces with the body consciousness of an organism, except to stipulate that it is accomplished via psi, mostly likely at the quantum level (cf. Mørch, 2014, for other ideas), but I have some thoughts about consciousness in relation to biological evolution.

To suggest that entities (or "societies," in Whitehead's terminology) of all kinds and at all levels have experiences is not to allege that all are consciously aware. From the perspective of idealism, consciousness has been a part of the universe since its inception, but that does not mean that it has not become differentiated and specialized over time (P. Ellis, 2011; Nagel, 2012). In the beginning, consciousness may have been amorphous and undifferentiated, sensual but not sentient. This sort of consciousness may still be with us in the background of the universe, but over time it has evolved into many different forms. Under a panpsychist regime, evolution has a drive toward increasing complexity, and it is this that led to the creation of life out of insentient matter. Johnjoe McFadden (2000) explored how the differentiation could have begun, with reference to quantum mechanics. Although for Thomas Nagel (2012) the drive toward increasing complexity is goal-oriented, it need not be conceived that way.

The consciousness stream that animates biological organisms developed separately from their bodies, but in concert with them, I think. Consciousness as we experience it I imagine to have emerged in the course of development of biological life, each species associated with its own characteristic type of consciousness. The process of reincarnation began with life and death. As soon as there was death, there was reincarnation; reincarnation is a basic condition of all life. A corollary proposition is that our minds and our brains have evolved in tandem, to work together. Reincarnation could have played a key part in this process, conserving psychic "energy" and helping to guide physical evolution.

It follows from these speculations that all minds in existence today can trace their lineages back to a period when there was no separation between them. There is another possibility, and that is that consciousness streams spring from the primordial background consciousness as required. These newly emerged streams of consciousness might be called *stem souls*, souls (consciousness streams) that are not yet specialized to work with any particular species or type of entity. If consciousness streams blend back into the background consciousness when no longer needed, this would answer the question of what happens to the minds of those species that die out before they have time to evolve into other forms. Alternatively, stem souls might already be in existence, awaiting their turn for specialization or embodiment. Some stem souls might develop into nonhuman spirits. Stem souls would be consistent with the notion of preexistence without prior incarnation and would help to solve the population increase problem that has dogged reincarnation theory for so long. The available case data do not allow me to do more than raise these possibilities, and I will not take a stand on them. I place them in the record for consideration, no more.

REINCARNATION AND LIFE

The workings of reincarnation are often presumed to lie in metaphysical obscurity. In reality, as I have tried to show, the process is probably fairly simple, at least in outline. The stream of consciousness that animates a body during life continues into death, and persists through death, until it becomes associated with (possesses) another body, generally one not yet born. The consciousness stream is composed of both subliminal and supraliminal strata, the former bearing memories and various traits we may subsume under the heading of personality, the latter representing conscious awareness. Once in possession of its new body, the reincarnating mind customizes it by adding behavioral and physical effects through psychokinetic operations on its genome, brain, and underlying physiology. At the level of conscious awareness, there is a reset, as the mind begins to interact with its new body and brain. Amnesia sets in, the subconscious blocking conscious memory of the past in what it considers to be its own best interests. The influence of the past is expressed behaviorally, however, and at times the subconscious permits memories to erupt into conscious awareness.

This, in brief, is my processual soul theory. Its details must be worked out, but as presently formulated, it explains the genesis of the major classes of reincarnation signs—the past-life memories, behaviors, and physical features—and predicts others. If the consciousness stream continues into death more or less unimpaired, as it must if it is to have the hypothesized effects on its new body, we would expect to see evidence of other postmortem activities, and we do, in the form of announcing dreams, apparitions, and mediumistic communications during the intermission period (Matlock, 2018, January). Also, inasmuch as psi is a capability of embodied minds, we would expect to see it exercised by disembodied minds, and we do. Not only is psi implicated in announcing dreams, apparitions, and mediumistic communications, case subjects with intermission memories frequently describe veridical perceptions of the material world and sometimes recall performing actions that were witnessed by embodied persons (Matlock, 2017, May).

The processual soul theory introduces no new explanatory concepts and requires no great concessions from biology and psychology, although it does oblige us to think about some things in new ways. Chief among these is the nature of the subconscious and its relation to conscious awareness, but I cannot claim credit for this insight. I have not added appreciably to the concept of the subliminal and supraliminal strata of mind proposed by Myers (1903). Broad (1962), Whitehead (1978), Stapp (1999, 2009, 2015), and of course Stevenson (especially 1997a) have had significant influences on my thinking as well. I can trace most of my ideas to one or another of these five authors, although I differ from all of them in some respects.

The resetting of conscious awareness with each embodiment acknowledges the contributions brain physiology makes to personality development in each life. This is the "nature" part of the "nature versus nurture" debate in psychology. Another part of what makes us different in each life is that we grow up at different times and in different places (even if our new lives are lived close to where our old ones were)—the "nurture" part of the debate. The processual soul theory denies the role of neither nature nor nurture but posits a third stream of influence, derived from previous lives, on the formation of personality and the conduct of behavior.

Materialist critics will no doubt object that not only am I am assuming something they consider absurd, that the mind has an existence apart from the body, I am introducing an unknown and equally controversial factor in psi, then assigning it an essential theoretical role. First of all, I reject the characterization of psi as an unknown. Psi has been demonstrated and explored in life and lab for well over a century (J. C. Carpenter, 2012; H. J. Irwin & Watt, 2007; Radin, 2006, 2009). We may not understand the mechanism of psi, but neither do we understand the mechanism of gravity, yet we agree on its effects. Moreover, psi need not be accepted by materialist science for me to employ it in my theory. Many theories require new constructs. My theory requires psi, and if the concept were not already known, I would have to invent it. It is all the better for my theory that the psi concept already exists and is backed by considerable evidence to boot.

It is ironic that having taken pains to show that past-life memories and other reincarnation signs cannot be explained by reference to what Sudduth (2013, 2016) calls living agent psi, in the end I propose that psi plays an important role in the reincarnation process. I do not mean any sort of super-psi, of course, but the regular, simple psi (PK) of a mind newly in possession of a physical body, no different in principle from what is involved in the placebo effect or other self-influence by any person.

The processual soul theory is in line with the working definition of reincarnation I introduced in Chapter 1. Like that definition, the theory is restricted to the rebirth of human beings as human beings. This began as an operational definition of reincarnation I used to explore the nature of rebirth beliefs cross-culturally (Matlock, 1993), long before I contemplated the course that led to this book. The notion of a duplex stream of consciousness was derived from the traditions of depth psychology (Ellenberger, 1970) and the thinking of Myers (1903), an approach to which, again, I was committed before beginning work on my course lectures.

To be sure, I was familiar with the reincarnation case material and could see how these postulates applied to it, but I worked out the processual soul theory in writing my lectures, following the data. The theory is grounded in data rather than in any a priori considerations. I did not begin with a theory of reincarnation and go looking for evidence to support it; rather, I let the evidence guide the development of the theory. The result is an empirically based statement about what reincarnation is and how it works that can serve as the starting point for further discussion and theory building.

The belief in reincarnation originated as a conclusion drawn from observation and experience, I think, but it became elaborated and refined in different ways in the belief systems of different cultures. Some of the differences in belief are reflected in cases, e.g., the presence or absence in a given culture of cases with a change of sex between lives. The processual soul theory explains these differences as a consequence of beliefs held in life carried over into death, influencing postmortem decisions by discarnate actors. Significantly, however, although there are clear cultural impacts on some aspects of cases, the cases are not entirely culturally conditioned. There are limits to the cultural shaping, perhaps because some beliefs, for example, those concerning karma, depart too far from the way reincarnation works for an internal influence to be effective. In these situations, the cultural variance appears in how cases are perceived, not in how they manifest.

The religion whose portrayal of reincarnation (or more accurately, rebirth) is most in conflict with data and theory is Buddhism, especially Theravada Buddhism. This is interesting, because the Buddhist notion of an everchanging consciousness stream proceeding from life to life is akin to the continuing-yet-changing consciousness stream of the processual soul theory. However, because it focuses on conscious awareness and neglects the subconscious, Buddhism cannot explain how personality can outlast death and therefore denies that it can. Buddhism affirms that each embodiment of a consciousness stream is determined by karma acquired during past embodiments; that humans may be reborn as nonhuman animals, nonhuman animals as humans; and that rebirth occurs at conception. In Tibetan Buddhism, the period from death to conception is said to be around forty-six days. None of these tenets are supported by the reincarnation case data.

The different Hindu schools do better when confronted with the case data, because they provide for the persistence of personality across lives and do not have an expectation about when, exactly, reincarnation occurs. However, in all varieties of Hinduism, the popular as well as the philosophically elaborated, considerable emphasis is placed on karma as the determiner of life circumstances and metempsychosis is assumed.

I have not yet explained the processual soul theory's position on transmigration and metempsychosis or commented on the evidence for animal lives. The theory suggests that reincarnation is most likely to proceed in species lines or between species that are closely related genetically, less likely or impossible between species that are not closely related. The rationale is that a consciousness stream will be unable to work effectively with a biological system that is very different from the one to which it is adapted. I suppose that species that are able to interbreed and produce viable offspring most likely possess an interoperable consciousness, others not. The processual soul theory postulates that nonhuman animals reincarnate in their own species lines and transmigration between species is a rare event, if it happens at all.

The case data are consistent with this aspect of the processual soul theory. There is some suggestive evidence for the reincarnation of cats and dogs in species lines (D. Ellis, 2003; Meyer, 2008), but no good evidence for transmigration between humans and nonhuman animals or of nonhuman animals across species lines. Stevenson heard claims to remember lives as nonhuman animals only in South Asia and even there less often than the belief in metempsychosis would lead one to expect (2001, p. 209). Moreover, the claims, when made, typically lacked supporting detail, as with Warnasiri Adikari's assertion that he had once been a hare (Stevenson, 1977a).

Tucker (2013, pp. 38–40) related a peculiar Thai story of a boy born with ichthyosis who purportedly claimed that he could remember having been a python, identified the man who had killed the snake, and gave a veridical account of the killing. Francis Story looked into this story, but because he left no written report, we do not know what his opinion about it was. Given how extreme an outlier it is, it would be wise to regard it as no more than a folk tale. Interested readers will find other accounts of transmigration and metempsychosis in Besterman (1968a, 1968b), De Groot (1901, pp. 154–55), Dhiman (2002, Dec. 28), Fielding-Hall (1898, pp. 342–44), and Stevenson (1975b, p. 372; 1983, p. 167; 1997a, p. 811). None of the alleged instances recounted by these authors are as developed as the one investigated by Story. Some do not involve claims to remember having been nonhuman animals but are interpretations of events by observers.

The Druze and Alevi for the most part do not allow for transmigration and have at best crudely developed ideas of karma, but they have other beliefs that are reflected in their cases. They deem it impossible to change sex between lives, and no sex-change cases have been found among the Druze and few among the Alevi. The Druze believe that a dying person is immediately reincarnated in a child born at that moment; although no cases of immediate rebirth are known, the median intermission in Stevenson's Druze cases was eight months, shorter than in all other cultures except the Haida (Stevenson, 1986a). The Druze believe that Druze are always reborn as a Druze; interethnic cases are rare among them, but two international cases (Suzanne Ghanem and Wael Kiwan) feature Druze who died in the United States but were reborn in Lebanon (Haraldsson & Matlock, 2016, p. 230). The cases of the Druze and Alevi provide good examples of how a culture's religious precepts become reflected in its cases, through influences of a reincarnating mind acting on the cases from within.

Theosophy had a major impact on Western, especially American, ideas about reincarnation in the late nineteenth and early twentieth century and continues to influence the New Age reincarnation mythos, but much of its dogma is contravened by the case data. Intermissions between lives are generally a few months or years, rarely hundreds of years, and no categories of death lead to immediate reincarnation. The return is usually in the same geographical region, not a foreign country, and so far as is known, never another planet. Cases not only do not provide evidence for retributive karma, the victims rather than the perpetrators of crimes experience their consequences.

Theosophy imagines spiritual growth to be the purpose and driver of reincarnation, a prominent feature of the New Age reincarnation mythos. The mythos asserts that before reincarnating, souls set goals for themselves and choose parents and life circumstances to assist in their spiritual advancement. At the conclusion of each life, when they return "home," souls assess for themselves how well they achieved the goals they set before incarnating (M. Newton, 1996, 2000).

The spontaneous case data provide little reason to think that reincarnation facilitates personal or spiritual growth across lives. Children who recall having been religious persons may be unusually pious in childhood, although there is no guarantee that this will last into adulthood. Duminda Ratnayake, one of the Sri Lankan boys who identified himself as a monk and recited stanzas in Pali (Haraldsson & Samararatne, 1999), entered a monastery when he was old enough to do so, then at twenty-one disrobed and took up computer science (Haraldsson & Matlock, 2016, p. 33). Life planning is a regular theme in American prebirth memories (e.g., Carman & Carman, 2013; Dyer & Garnes, 2015), but not in Japanese (Ohkado & Ikegawa, 2014) or Beng (Gottlieb, 2004). Life planning is consistent with Western ideals but makes little sense in cultures where karma is thought to dictate the circumstances of one's rebirth or in cultures that assign the decision to God. If it occurs at all, life planning may be a culturally and personally determined rather than universal feature of reincarnation.

Another important element of the New Age reincarnation mythos is the idea that we reincarnate in soul groups and have soul mates with whom we reunite life after life. Spontaneous cases provide little support for either concept and although this may be due to limitations in the data, it seems more likely that soul groups and soul mates are artifacts of the tendency to reincarnate in the same region and among the same people than that intersecting lives are intentionally arranged in the discarnate state before reincarnation. Arthur Guirdham (1974, 1976) portrayed what he believed was the reincarnation of a group of individuals across a series of lives but his evidence is flimsy, consisting largely of perceived synchronicities of various kinds. Marge Rieder (1993, 1996) reported a group of regressions that many New Age followers hold up as evidence for reincarnating soul groups, but, despite her best efforts, she was unable to substantiate any of the lives portrayed under hypnosis.

Ohkado (2016) described four boys who said they had met during the intermission and made a pact to reincarnate together, but there is no indication that they knew each other from earlier lives. Alessandrina Samona said in a mediumistic communication that she had met someone during the intermission and would be bringing her along as her twin (Lancelin, 1922; Stevenson, 2003), but again, there was no suggestion of a prior acquaintance. There is more evidence for couples reincarnating in the same family as twins than separately, in a manner that would allow them to be reunited as a couple. Sivanthie and Sheromie Hettiaratchi were Sri Lankan twin girls who recalled having been male insurgents who had been gay lovers (Stevenson (1997a, vol. 2, pp. 1940–70). Fielding-Hall (1898, pp. 339–41) described Burmese twin boys, Maung Gyi and Maung Ngè, who recalled having been a married couple. The only subjects so far reported who recalled lives as a married couple and reincarnated in different families are İsmail Altınkılıç and Cevriye Bayrı of Turkey (Stevenson, 1983b), but although İsmail felt fondly about Cevriye, she wanted nothing to do with him.

Many adherents to the New Age reincarnation mythos believe that a sure way to ascertain past-life identities is through facial resemblance. Perhaps following the lead of Walter Semkiw, picture comparisons have become commonplace, if not de rigueur, on the Internet and in social media. However, although there is sometimes a degree of facial resemblance between previous and present persons, it is not always apparent, and when apparent, could have a genetic basis or be attributable to chance.

The processual soul theory does not rule out the possibility of a psychological driver toward spiritual as well as physical advancement over the long term. I worry, though, that this picture of spiritual progress is too human-centered. The evolutionary impulse seems to me to encourage a radiation of form and function rather than a determined effort to reach a certain end, and I am uncomfortable with the implication that humanity is in the vanguard of spiritual development.

In general, animism fares better in a match-up with the case data than the world religions, Theosophy, and New Age metaphysics do. Animism takes personal survival for granted and presumes that the deceased can interact with the living. Animism does not subscribe to juridical or retributive karma, by and large does not accept the possibility of transmigration, and makes no assumptions about the length of the intermission between lives. However, there are in animism other constructs—multiple simultaneous reincarnation (multiple reincarnation), concurrent reincarnation, and continuous incarnation—for which there is scant evidence. These constructs are of some theoretical interest, nevertheless, so I will examine them in relation to the processual soul theory. I want to show that they are more easily handled by my theory than by its chief rival, Cartesian substance dualism.

In concurrent reincarnation, two or more spirits coexist in a body from birth until death. The belief in concurrent reincarnation is found in more easterly Canadian Inuit communities in association with the Inuit belief that names embody souls (Guemple, 1994; Matlock & Mills, 1994). A child is given the name of a deceased person within a few days of his passing, and persons with the same name are thought to share a spiritual substance. At least among the Inuit of the Belcher Islands in Hudson Bay, children may also be named after living people, providing for the substance's continuous embodiment (Guemple, 1994).

I mentioned a Tlingit example of concurrent reincarnation in Chapter 2. A man who had been given two hereditary names and was thought to possess two souls announced that he would free them to go their separate ways after his death, and two boys born subsequently were taken to be the reincarnations of these two souls (de Laguna, 1972, pp. 779–80). Unfortunately, de Laguna (1972) gave no details about the man's experience of living with the two souls. She did not say whether he had memories of two previous persons or was identified with both of them behaviorally. In Tibet, where the animistic influence on Buddhism is pronounced, one encounters other varieties of concurrent reincarnation and continuous incarnation. Marcia Calkowski (2013) presented a series of accounts of lamas and other advanced adepts who chose to reincarnate before their bodies failed, some joining bodies already possessed by other spirits.

Concurrent reincarnation and continuous incarnation would be permitted under the processual soul theory—they would represent possession by multiple consciousness streams—but could be expressed in one of two ways. One possibility is alternating control, as in MPD/DID. The other possibility is that the consciousness streams merge at the subliminal level and share a supraliminal awareness. Continuous incarnation is best conceptualized in terms of the latter, because it is usually associated with concurrent reincarnation (Inuit children are assigned multiple names, each with a spiritual substance attached). Calkowski was told by a Tibetan yogi whose personality changed following a continuous incarnation that the changes were due to the second consciousness stream having been "absorbed" into his (2013, p. 347).

Multiple reincarnation involves the return of one person's consciousness in two or more bodies at the same time. Beliefs in multiple reincarnation have been reported from the Canadian arctic and subarctic, the Northwest Coast of North America, West and Central Africa, Burma, and Tibet (Matlock, 1993, p. 62; Stevenson, 2001, p. 300n1). Multiple reincarnation may be conceptualized as either soul replication or soul splitting. Stevenson noted that the Igbo believe that "different qualities of character, and even different physical traits of the discarnate person, may become expressed in several reincarnations of that person. For example, a person's strong physique may be embodied in one later-born child, while his tendency to stutter may appear in another" (1985, p. 18).

Mills (1988b, 2001, 2010) described three instances from the Gitxsan. Jean Slade announced before she died that she would return multiple times, and by 2010 twelve girls had been identified as her come-backs (Mills, 2010, p. 182). The identifications in these and in Mills's other examples were made on the basis of announcing dreams, distinctive behaviors, or apparent recognitions. None of the children claimed to remember anything concerning the lives of the people with whom they were identified. Jean Slade was reportedly seen in a near-death experience while she was said to have reincarnated multiply (Mills, 2001, p. 318), in keeping with the animistic belief in the persistence of consciousness and identity in the afterlife at the same time that another part (or version) of the consciousness stream has reincarnated.

In Tibet, advanced adepts are believed capable of generating "bodies" associated with the physical form, speech, and mind, "emanations" from which may reincarnate separately (Berzin, 1996; Gamble, 2018). The lama who was retrospectively recognized as the first Dalai Lama is said to have incarnated in several persons, the most important of whom became the second Dalai Lama (Rahul, 1995, p. 20). Multiple reincarnations may not only be planned but, reportedly, executed before death. Calkowski (2013, p. 345) heard about a woman who at thirty announced that she would reincarnate in five different bodies, all of which had been born by the time she died fifteen years later. None of these five people claimed to have memories of the woman's life, however.

Occasionally one encounters claims by two people to recall the same previous life in other cultures (Keil, 2010b, pp. 92–93, in connection with the Turkish Alevi; Stemman, 1998, in connection with the Lebanese Druze), but these cases are so poorly described that the claims cannot be evaluated. Stevenson's (1974a) Druze case of Imad Elawar is sometimes referenced in this context, based on W. G. Roll's (1977, 1984) depiction of it as one of "merged and divided" rebirth. Roll reached this conclusion because Imad recalled witnessing an accident that had befallen Ibrahim Bouhamzy's cousin, whose apparent reincarnation also recalled the accident. However, the children's recollections were from their respective vantage points. Since there was no overlap in the rest of their memories, there is no reason to regard memories of the accident as other than independent perspectives on the same event (Griffin, 1997, pp. 186–92; Matlock, 1992; Stevenson, 1984).

On his website, Walter Semkiw lists several cases he says represent "split incarnations" or "parallel lives." Most are spontaneous child cases, investigated by Stevenson and his colleagues, that involve postnatal or replacement reincarnation or have intermissions under nine months in length. The only case that depicts simultaneous lives is a mediumistic one original to Semkiw. The medium, in consultation with the Akashic Records, identified Penney Peirce as the reincarnation of two different people whose lives overlapped by twenty-six years (Semkiw, n.d.-b). There is no independent support for either identification, apart from coincidences perceived by Semkiw as meaningful, and no reason to take this case seriously as an instance of "soul splitting."

The best candidates (such as they are) for multiple reincarnation come from the Gitxsan (Mills, 1988b, 2001, 2010), whose multiple come-backs are conceived in terms not of soul splitting but of soul replication. Soul replication is consistent with the notion that spirits may persist in the afterlife with their identities intact even while they reincarnate; both ideas presume multiple copies of the same mind. The processual soul theory could accommodate either soul splitting or soul replication, although the latter concept strikes me as logically more satisfactory. Soul splitting implies a division of the soul's attributes, and could not be carried out indefinitely, whereas soul replication might be. Cartesian substance dualism, on the other hand, assumes a unitary and unchanging Ego or soul (Almeder, 2012; Rivas, 2005); a Cartesian Ego would be unable either to divide or replicate.

Concurrent and multiple reincarnation and continuous incarnation may seem so unlikely that we need not take them seriously, but we should not discard the testimony about them before considering evidence from a very different direction—organ transplant recipients who adopt the emotional sets, personality traits, and food preferences of their donors, without knowing who they are or anything about their lives (Joshi, 2011; Lock, 2002, pp. 323, 327, 343; Pearsall, 1998; Pearsall, Schwartz, & Russek, 2003; L. A. Sharp, 1995; Sylvia, with Novak, 1997). Hospital policies that mandate anonymity between organ donors and recipients make it difficult to study transplant cases, but the few that have come to light reveal intriguing similarities to the reincarnation cases that have been investigated by Stevenson and others.

Transplant recipients typically report feeling an alien presence within. Some recipients who have learned who their donors were and made contact with their families recognize people and behave toward them as their donors would have behaved. Some recipients develop phobias related to their donors' place or manner of death (Pearsall, 1998; Sylvia & Novak, 1997). Paul Pearsall (1998, pp. 123–24) described a "domino" transplant, with similar effects: A man underwent a successful heart-lung transplant, but his own heart was healthy enough to be given to another man. This man then took on personality traits of his donor, even calling his wife by the name of his donor's wife. Both the heart-lung and heart recipients were alive at the same time.

Similar effects have been reported with kidney and liver transplants (Chopra, 1993, p. 22; Pearsall, 1998, p. 83). Claire Sylvia, the only transplant recipient for whom long-term follow-up information has been published, says that it took three years for her to fully integrate the donor's personality but that she then became "a kind of third being that was neither the old Claire or the new Tim, but some combination of the two" (Sylvia, with Novak, 1997, pp. 208–9).

As yet there is no good explanation for transplant phenomena. Medical personnel who do not dismiss the cases as imaginary typically attribute them to "cellular memory" (Chopra, 1993; van Lommel, 2010; Pearsall, 1998), a hypothetical construct that some writers (Braude, 2003; Dossey, 2008) consider philosophically incoherent. Braude (2006) likened cellular memory to trace theories of memory because it suggests that memories are stored in the body. From the Whiteheadian perspective, cells are societies that enjoy streams of experience, but the cells' "memories" are of cellular activities and would not extend to the sorts of effects reported in transplant cases. Eric Weiss (2012, pp. 269–70) suggested that the "presiding personality" of an organ stayed with it when it was transplanted, but the same objection applies at this level. The effects are not specific to the transplanted organ, but belong to the organism as a whole, and therefore cannot be attributable to cell or organ memory.

Psychometry or token object reading (handling an object to facilitate psi) is another popular explanation for transplant cases. Most psychometry readings relate to people or places in which the token objects have been in contact, which would be true of transplanted organs, but the sort of clairvoyant impressions normally conveyed in psychometry are nothing like the reported transplant phenomena. Michael Tymn (2001) conjectured that the abruptness with which organs were removed from recently deceased bodies prevents spirits from detaching themselves in time to avoid being carried along with the extracted body parts. Spirits consequently "hovered" around the parts, then possessed the recipients' bodies when the parts were inserted into them. Tymn's explanation would not apply to transplants of multiple organs or to living donors. Moreover, although the organ recipient may sense the donor's presence within himself, and display its influence behaviorally, the recipient's personality is not displaced, even temporarily, as happens with ordinary cases of possession (Braude, 2003, pp. 242–44).

Perhaps transplant cases can be explained in terms of holography, in which a part contains a representation of the whole. Holography would be a natural way to conceptualize transplant phenomena, and it may not be beyond reason. Neurosurgeon Karl Pribram (1991, 2004, 2013) has argued for years that memory is best explained holonomically (his preferred term), which allows him to adhere to a brain-production theory of mind while acknowledging that memory is not contained in the brain. There is no evident reason that the subconscious mind could not be organized like a hologram, even if it were not generated by the brain. If memory is registered in the subconscious holographically and a mind is distributed over a body rather than being confined to a brain, then when an organ is transplanted it would carry with it all of the donor's memories, personality traits, and behavior patterns.

Whether or not we accept a holographic model of the subconscious, a similar process would seem to be involved in transplant cases, in concurrent reincarnation, and in continuous incarnation. In these cases, content from the subconscious of multiple consciousness streams appears to merge with the subconscious of a host without affecting the host's sense of self. Although we see behavioral influences in cases of these types, there are no episodic memories or complete identifications with the previous persons or organ donors. There are differences between individuals descended from the same spirit in multiple reincarnation, and we should expect to see differences in the experiences of recipients of different organs from the same donor, but these differences would not necessarily be due to different content conveyed to the different individuals. Different expressions of the same content might instead be attributable to differences in the way the subconscious minds of the individuals involved allow the content to be displayed physically and supraliminally.

If concurrent and multiple reincarnation, and continuous incarnation, occur, the processual soul theory will have to be adjusted to allow for them. The best way to achieve this may be to bring in a holographic conception of the subconscious, along with the possibility of a merger of consciousness streams at the subconscious level with a shared conscious awareness. I am not yet convinced that these phenomena do occur. The use of announcing dreams, birthmarks, and behaviors alone (without verified past-life memories) in making identifications means that social construction is a plausible interpretation of the Gitxsan and Tibetan accounts and cases presently in evidence. The transplant cases are intriguing, but so far none have been studied properly, and until they are, it would be a mistake to draw firm conclusions from them. Cases of these types have been widely reported, however, and there is hope of getting better descriptions of them in the future.

The processual soul theory can accommodate these unusual types of cases, and can do so without strain, in contrast to its rivals. Substance dualism can make no sense of transplant phenomena, any more than it can of concurrent and multiple reincarnation; rather than holding open the possibility of their occurrence, it rules them out at the start. I cannot see that subtle bodies and morphogenetic fields (as posited by Sheldrake, 1982, 1988, 2009, and Stevenson, 1997a, 2001) are any better prepared to deal with minds that divide or replicate postmortem or that merge at a subconscious level while embodied.

The answer to the question of whether there is evidence for reincarnation depends on how reincarnation is defined, but I believe an affirmative answer also requires an acceptable theory of the process. When I began writing the course lectures on which this book is based, I was not committed to reincarnation as the best interpretation of the case material. I maintained that although the evidence pointed in that direction, "we must be cautious in our conclusions, since it may turn out that our present ideas are not quite right and that another solution, which we cannot yet envision, is the correct one" (Matlock, 2011, pp. 808–9). It was in writing my lectures, wrestling with the implications of the data, that I conceived my processual soul theory. That theory provided the framework I needed to make sense of the data in relation to other scientific knowledge and I now feel no hesitancy in declaring that I believe reincarnation to be the only intellectually defensible interpretation of the data.

The processual soul theory is a theory of postmortem survival in general and, more broadly, of consciousness and its relation to the body. It conceives of consciousness as duplex, having subliminal and supraliminal strata, and portrays the subconscious as a non-physical information-bearing matrix with psychological dynamics sometimes attuned to, sometimes at odds with, conscious thoughts and motivations. When its physical body is no longer able to support the consciousness stream, the body dies, but the stream continues on and takes possession of another physical body at a later time.

The processual soul theory provides a framework that satisfies me. It is intentionally loose in some respects, but it does make some predictions. The theory does not have any expectations about the length of the intermission or of the relationships between the previous and present lives, but it denies the possibility of transmigrating across species lines and rules out external influences such as juridical and retributive karma, affirming only that there will be psychological continuity across lives. I believe the data support at least these generalizations, although we must be mindful that they derive from fewer than two thousand solved cases and doubtless there is much about reincarnation still hidden from our view.

Reincarnation as defined by the processual soul theory has considerable explanatory power, potentially clarifying a variety of matters, including otherwise inexplicable post-traumatic symptoms and gender dysphoria (Stevenson, 1977c, 2000a) and the etiology of many unusual birthmarks and birth defects (Stevenson, 1993, 1997a, 1997b). Reincarnation also brings new perspectives to issues of personality formation and memory. In the social sphere, it could help to explain the persistence of cultural traits in a given population or region over time. Among peoples like the Druze who have long recognized the reality of reincarnation, it is fundamental not only to social cohesion, but to group identity (Bennett, 2006; Halabi & Horenzyk, 2019).

Resistance to the idea in the modern Western world is largely cultural, born of Christian religious opposition and seemingly confirmed by an eighteenth-century reductionist mind-set now known to be in error. With no valid reasons for rejecting reincarnation a priori, the question of its occurrence should be settled by the evidence. Mainstream science still refuses to look at the relevant data, but as materialism continues its decline, we can expect more openness to research topics previously marginalized or dismissed, including postmortem survival and reincarnation. Admittedly, I am unable to provide a detailed account of the reincarnation process that is amenable to verification or falsification, as science requires. That account will have to be worked out in quantum biology and neuropsychology, fields beyond my expertise, and I must leave the theorizing and testing to later generations of thinkers and workers. By reviewing the evidence for reincarnation as it stands today and providing a theoretical model of the reincarnation process, I have tried to give my successors a start on this project.

Afterword

Implications of Reincarnation Cases for Biology

Michael Nahm

In this Afterword to James Matlock's meticulous study of what he calls "reincarnation cases" (his term for what Ian Stevenson called "cases of the reincarnation type"), I set out to show how these cases relate to biological concepts about life and the inheritance of morphological and cognitive traits of organisms. Although reincarnation cases cannot be accounted for within a strictly physicalist and mechanistic frame of thought, such as is promoted in current mainstream biology, I argue that they can well be accounted for within the frame of a more organismically oriented tradition of biological thought that has always run in parallel to physicalist and mechanistic conceptions of biology. Because reincarnation cases directly concern issues of inheritance, one focus of this Afterword rests on evolutionary biology. In the following pages, I expound on how much current mainstream biological thinking needs to be enhanced and deepened and then turn to discussing possible implications of reincarnation cases in this context.

First, however, let me state the position from which I am arguing. Like Matlock, I consider the compiled material on reincarnation cases sufficiently robust to acknowledge that there is something very interesting going on. Following an objective and open-minded assessment of the available material, it is in my opinion unavoidable to acknowledge that the strongest cases studied by Ian Stevenson, Erlendur Haraldsson, Jim Tucker, and others provide solid evidence that at least some fragments of a former and deceased person can resurface in another individual, and that the acquisition of many of the recounted memories cannot be explained by usual means of communication or the use of the normal senses. Similarly, this applies to certain behavioral traits of the subjects with past-life memories, or to bodily features such as birthmarks and birth defects of these subjects. Consequently, I will argue from the position of somebody who, as a general rule, assumes that the basic findings of reincarnation research as presented by Matlock are established facts. With regard to their interpretation, I concur with researchers like Stevenson, Haraldsson, Tucker, Antonia Mills, and Matlock, that regarding the strongest cases, a survivalist notion seems at present most convincing, as the existing alternative approaches face even more explanatory challenges (Nahm & Hassler, 2011).

In the Western world, ideas of reincarnation existed among early Greek philosophers such as Pythagoras, and in later centuries they received renewed attention especially through the writings of Franciscus Mercurius van Helmont (1614–1699) (Zander, 1999). Although different varieties of reincarnation beliefs persisted into later times (a noted example is the Spiritism of Allen Kardec; also, Arthur Schopenhauer discussed reincarnation in his philosophy), they generally received little attention from natural scientists and biologists, including evolution theorists.

The first significant theory of evolution was put forward by Jean-Baptiste de Lamarck (1809). It built to a considerable extent on the assumption that the desire-driven use and disuse of body parts would result in a gradual morphological adaption to the preferred modes of utilization. For example, by constantly stretching the neck to reach nutritious leaves of trees for generations, early giraffes with short necks might have slowly evolved into individuals with longer necks. In general, evolution along these lines would proceed through characteristics developed or acquainted by certain individuals that were transmitted to their offspring. However, this theory of the inheritance of acquired characteristics was soon to be replaced by another theory of evolution that was developed independently by Charles Darwin and Alfred Russel Wallace. Both men argued that the main driver of evolution consisted in the production of offspring that varied randomly in different respects and that a natural selection process would select the individuals best adapted to their environments (Darwin, 1859). Thus, certain variations of advantageous body traits, such as a slightly longer neck in environments in which rewarding food could be found on trees, would be selected in an ongoing process over many generations in Darwin's theory, and would thus also result in increasingly long necks, as in giraffes.

Indeed, there are several grave difficulties for the theory of the inheritance of acquired characteristics. For instance, Darwin noted that it cannot function in social insects that live in state-like communities, as numerous ant and bee species do, because their highly specialized and sterile worker castes cannot produce offspring, and thus cannot pass on any advantageous body traits they might acquire (Darwin, 1859). It is curious, however, that Darwin became increasingly skeptical of the explanatory power of his theory of variation and natural selection and resorted to the inheritance of acquired characteristics again in later works. To illustrate how it might work, he proposed the concept of "pangenesis": Little particles he called gemmules would be distributed in the bodies of organisms and aggregate in their "sexual elements." Thus, the gemmules would be able to transmit information about the status of the different body parts into the germline and cause the reemergence of characteristics that had been acquired by individuals in their offspring (Darwin, 1868, vol. 2, chap. 27).

Similarly, Wallace became increasingly convinced that variation and selection alone could not account for the vast diversity of life. In contrast to his friend Darwin, however, he postulated a "new cause or power" he termed "vitality" that would influence evolutionary developmental processes such as the origin of first living cells (Wallace, 1889, pp. 474–75). In doing so, Wallace assumed a position that is typically known as vitalism. It can be defined as the notion according to which the origin, evolution, and functioning of living beings cannot be attributed to physicochemical interactions of inanimate matter alone. Rather, according to vitalism, organisms are permeated by vital principles of organization, which govern their individual development (ontogenesis) and vital functions. This way of thinking has a long tradition in biology, beginning with Aristotle, and it included numerous important pioneers of biology such as Georg Ernst Stahl, Johannes Müller, Jakob von Uexküll, and Hans Driesch (for a history of older concepts of vitalism, see Driesch, 1922). Moreover, numerous biologists in addition to Wallace have argued that vitalistic principles were also involved in governing the development of increasingly complex taxa in the course of evolution (phylogenesis).

Summing up, the founders of evolution theories postulated three different factors that would drive developmental processes. Each of them exists in several variations, but in general, these are the basic types:

1. Evolution by means of inheritance of acquired characteristics (Lamarck, Darwin)
2. Evolution through random variation/mutation and subsequent natural selection (Darwin, Wallace)
3. Evolution by means of vital, non-mechanistic organizing principles (Wallace)

During several decades of the twentieth century, the Darwinian concept of variation and natural selection was combined with a wealth of other issues related to evolutionary biology, resulting in the formation of the so-called Modern Synthesis (Mayr & Provine, 1980). However, although several examples from domestication, experimentation, and also wildlife, still pointed toward the possibility of the inheritance of acquired characteristics (e.g., Kammerer, 1924), possible mechanisms according to which information from the body tissue could be transferred to the germline were not conceivable in the frame of the Modern Synthesis and thus Lamarckian approaches were discredited (e.g., Koestler, 1971; Mayr, 1982). Similarly, vitalistic concepts were rejected by mainstream biologists (Mayr, 1982), often with emotionally tinted disdain (e.g., Ditfurth, 1981).

Nevertheless, the theory-driven rejection of the inheritance of acquired characteristics proved to be premature. The observable facts were too persistent and in recent decades aspects of the inheritance of acquired characteristics have become fashionable again under the headings of "epigenetics" and "developmental plasticity" (e.g., Jablonka & Lamb, 1995, 2006; Jablonka & Raz, 2009; Moore, 2015; Vargas, Krabichler, & Guerrero-Bosagna, 2017; West-Eberhard, 2003). Similarly, the rejection of vitalistic concepts appears premature, as indicated by numerous insufficiencies of the mainstream biological approach, including its perspective on evolution. In a previous publication, I elaborated in detail why vitalistic approaches are still legitimate and in fact necessary to advance an adequate understanding of the functioning of living organisms (Nahm, 2007). In the following, I will recapitulate some of the lines of argumentation very briefly. But before that, I would like to illustrate on a more general level why mainstream biology needs to be freed from historically grown self-restrictions.

Modern physics provides a suitable starting point to recognize how little we know about the universe and about life. For instance, regarding the macrocosm, there are numerous unanswered cosmological questions that stretch all the way back to implications of the assumed Big Bang. It is still not fully understood why the space-time continuum behaves like it does and why movement in relation to an observer, for example, can influence the passage of time and also the mass of an object. Similarly, numerous aspects of the microcosm and quantum physics defy a fully understandable logical and monocausal explanation, including weird properties such as the unpredictability of particle decay, wave-particle duality, and that particles like photons can be entangled and react as one system when one of the photons is measured, even when they are separated from each other by large distances. The reaction of the second entanglement partner does not even take time and strictly speaking, is not even a reaction but an instantaneous co-affection. It is obvious that presently available theories concerning the properties of macrocosm and microcosm are rough anthropocentric approximations of reality designed by logical thinking and consequently are inevitably incomplete. Indeed, a "Theory of Everything" that could successfully link established theories about macrocosm and microcosm is not yet in sight in mainstream physics (for alternative approaches, see for example Heim, 1988, and Neppe & Close, 2012), and some physicists paint a rather pessimistic picture regarding the research progress of the last decades (e.g., Hossenfelder, 2018).

Hence, it is obvious that our senses and the functions of our brains are chiefly adapted to the environment that surrounds us. As soon as we are concerned with certain properties of macrocosm and microcosm, and therefore, also the foundations of reality and existence, the useful ability of thinking in monocausal and bottom-up terms of cause and effect loses its seemingly universal applicability. The familiar ambience is only one part of reality; it is the tip of an iceberg. When an organism is trying to fully understand itself, and metaphorically speaking is also the visible part of the iceberg above the water surface, it is certain that it will never be able to achieve this goal. Strangely, however, most academic biologists and also physicians (medicine can be regarded as a subdiscipline of biology) still rely on the axioms of classical physics—axioms that physicists themselves have long recognized as outdated. Popular conceptualizations of mainstream biology and the Modern Synthesis, such as that advocated for example by Richard Dawkins (2010, 2016), are concerned with only a small excerpt of biological existence and are thus too simplistic. Consequently, biologists who intend to be up-to-date with other science disciplines, and not only scratching on the surface of life, need to extend and deepen their research questions. As mentioned above, there are very good reasons for doing so, and I will now briefly outline some of the most important issues.

The first and foremost enigma of evolution concerns the origin of life. Although one might obtain a different impression from following discussions in the public media, it needs to be stressed that it is still entirely unknown how the first chain molecules like DNA and the first living cells came into existence. In a previous book (Nahm, 2007), I described twenty-four of the most important biochemical difficulties that need to be overcome both in theory and in practice before one can state with reasonable confidence that we might find a way to explain or understand the origins of life. Important examples concern the chirality of molecules and hydrolysis. Even fashionable concepts of self-organization and computer models such as the hypothetical "hypercycles" as developed by Manfred Eigen (1987) have hardly achieved applicable relevance in practical prebiotic research and thus do not change this situation. The current knowledge on the reaction behavior of simple organic molecules, based on more than six decades of practical and theoretical experience in pre-biotic chemistry since the landmark experiments of Miller (1953), speaks against an accidental formation of life—even if one takes the immense periods of time that come into question into account. Despite seemingly successful and optimistic reports about newer findings (e.g., Todisco et al., 2018; Yi et al., 2018), this appraisal remains valid on close examination of the methods applied and results achieved in such studies. Accordingly, and similar to physicists, leading experts in the field of probiotic chemistry have conceded a lack of progress and success in their research discipline (Nahm, 2007).

Still, despite all obstacles, life appeared on Earth. According to the standard theory of evolution, the first cells developed into increasingly complex organisms by random mutations in their genes and by subsequent selection of the best adapted individuals. Mutations demonstrably occur in organisms and can also be produced in large numbers by artificial means such as X-rays. Consequently, scientists have explored the creative potential of mutations in huge and extensive studies. Literally millions of random mutations were generated in numerous unicellular organisms as well as animal and plant species, for example, by exposing them to X-rays. Yet, the very few mutations that could be interpreted positively under certain circumstances always concerned the loss of previously existing traits or the modification of an already existing metabolism pathway.

Moreover, even supposedly positive mutations in the genome often have negative side effects, and quite importantly, the emergence of new selectable organs and structures that were accompanied by an increase in biological complexity has never been observed in this branch of mutation research. Despite enormous initial expectations, this research was quietly abandoned by disappointed biologists decades ago. The bottom line is this: It seems impossible to identify stable selectable mutations that occur randomly or "by chance" and lead to increasing complexity.

Like mutations, natural selection among living organisms does occur in nature. But does it explain evolution? Biologists disagree with regard to answers to this question and they have advanced several different hypotheses revolving around selection processes. On close examination, however, all of them lack a concrete and continuously available point of action that would explain the development of innumerable organismic characteristics, especially that of many macroscopic characteristics. The peacock is a prime example. Charles Darwin explained the development of its train and eyespots via sexual selection—that is, for generations, the peahen would have always selected the most magnificent males for mating. In that case, the peacock would illustrate how the result of supposed sexual selection can completely override an ideal body shape that would be useful in the purported continuous struggle for survival. If the peacock can survive with a severe handicap such as its train, then natural selection can only be regarded as a very tolerant judge of life and death, which is as at odds with the traditional neo-Darwinian view. And the peacock is only one example out of many in which the macroscopic appearance of an animal or plant species cannot be explained solely by merciless selection processes that eliminate all suboptimally adapted individuals. The amazing wealth of shapes and colors of the fruiting bodies of fungi provide more striking examples in which sexual selection does not occur: The macroscopic appearance of a given mushroom species has no bearing at all on its commonness or fitness. Without exception, specifications on the physiological level determine whether a fungus species is common or rare. This appraisal is also valid for numerous (but of course not all) plant and animal species. In short: Although selection processes in nature are at work, their ability to continuously influence the development of living beings in certain directions seems to be overestimated. At least in some cases, evolutionary developments seem to be driven by a momentum of their own that is largely decoupled from the direct influence of environmental conditions.

However, these are just a few general comments about the origin of life, mutations, and natural selection. There are many more problematical aspects regarding these pillars of neo-Darwinian evolution theory but space prohibits expounding them here (see Nahm, 2007). The take-away-message is: The development of many features of organisms in the course of evolution cannot be explained by chance interactions of molecules, random mutations, and selection processes alone. Rather, the development of life, and that of many macroscopic features of organisms, appears to include autonomous development dynamics. Numerous past biologists, but also paleontologists, have advanced evolutionary concepts along these lines of thought (to name only a few: Beurlen, 1937; Dacqué, 1935; Friederichs, 1955; Hardy, 1965; O. Kuhn, 1947; Randall, 1975; Reinke, 1899; Schindewolf, 1950; Schneider, 1911; Teilhard de Chardin, 1959; for an overview, see Nahm, 2007).

The need for an enhanced biological perspective is called for also by psi phenomena like telepathy, clairvoyance, and psychokinesis. They do not fit into current models of neo-Darwinian biology or any other strictly physicalist world view, yet, in my opinion, parapsychological research of the last two hundred years has shown convincingly that these phenomena (including those related to possible reincarnation and possession) exist and consequently an appropriate comprehension of the foundations of nature and life must build on a model of reality that can account for them. As a general frame, such a model of reality suggests that our environment, or rather, our perception of our environment, is only part of a larger structure of reality—many facets of which are usually hidden from direct experience and are not readily accessible with biological senses (Nahm, 2007). As shown earlier, this appraisal matches perfectly the concept of reality suggested by modern physics. On rare occasions, aspects of this background reality can enter our conscious awareness through, for example, psi phenomena, which thus are neither "supernatural" nor "paranormal." They are quite natural, albeit unusual. Moreover, there is considerable evidence that animals, also, possess psychic faculties, and thus, share the same rooting in this background reality (e.g., Bayless, 1970; Bozzano, 1905; Rhine & Feather, 1962; Sheldrake, 2011; for an overview of treatises on psi in animals, see Nahm, 2007; compare also Nahm, 2015, 2016). As a result, practically all biologists and researchers concerned with biology and its relation to parapsychology have come to the conclusion that the deeper layer of reality that mediates psi phenomena needs to feature or comprise psychic or mental qualities itself (be they conscious or unconscious; see E. F. Kelly et al., 2007; E. F. Kelly, Crabtree, & Marshall, 2015; Nahm, 2007). This, as a consequence, must relate to the biological organization of organisms, which extends into this background reality or has roots in it. Wallace, for example, was very interested in the phenomena of psychical research. He was convinced of their reality and held the view that certain evolutionary stages of progress, including the emergence of first living cells from inorganic matter and the emergence of consciousness, "point clearly to an unseen universe—to a world of spirit, to which the world of matter is altogether subordinate" (Wallace, 1889, p. 476). Advancing speculations along these lines further led authors to surmise that ultimately, all perception might effectively be a psychic act. The interposition of biological sense organs into the process of cognition might be a complicating detour (Driesch, 1938; Mattiesen, 1936–1939; compare also J. C. Carpenter, 2012; Griffin, 1997) that functions as a means to construct a reliable environment in the context of the various "filter" or "transmission" models of the mind (Grosso, 2015; E. F. Kelly & Presti, 2015).

Moreover, numerous authors have argued that when individual beings can be linked, or are linked, to each other on a usually hidden and largely psychic layer of reality, this might also apply to subconscious aspects of all individuals of a given organizational unit such as species. Concepts discussed in this context are the "collective unconscious" (Dacqué, 1926; Hardy, 1965; Jung conceived the collective unconscious differently, however; see Jung, 1969), "group souls" (Hardy, 1965), or other concepts of super-individuality (Becher, 1917; Carington, 1945; McDougall, 1961; Meyer-Abich, 1963; Schneider, 1911; Schopenhauer, 1969; von Hartmann, 1924; for an overview, see Nahm, 2007).

A representative example epitomizing this approach is provided by Sir Alister Hardy, a prominent Oxford biologist (Hardy, 1965).

My "vitalism" is a belief that there is a psychic side of the animal which, apart from inherited instinctive behaviour, may be independent from the DNA code that governs the form of the physical frame, but that it may interact with the physical system in the evolutionary process through organic selection. . . . The existence of such an unconscious telepathic communication between members of the same species of animals might at least help in developing and stabilizing common behavioural patterns. . . . Individual lives, animal "minds," would come and go—but the psychic stream of a shared behaviour pattern in the living population would flow on in time parallel to the flow of the physical DNA material. . . . And then again it might also be supposed that the "racial plan," linking all the members of the race, might gradually change as the character of the population became modified both by the changing environment's external selection and by the development of new behavioural patterns due to the exploring, exploitive, nature of animal life. (Hardy, 1965, pp. 254–59)

Hence, vitalistic models of evolution like these comprise all three basic types of biological development modes introduced above (inheritance of acquired characteristics, random variation/mutation and natural selection, and vital non-mechanistic organizing principles). However, evolution by means of inheritance of acquired characteristics is not mediated somatically via pangenesis or epigenetic factors in this case, but psychically via a collective sink of experiences in which individuals are rooted. Processes of random variation/ mutation and subsequent natural selection also occur, but are not assigned such an important role as in neo-Darwinian models. Obviously, the evolution by means of vital, non-mechanistic organizing principles, which often are attributed with subconscious properties, plays the decisive part. The fact that many authors who were concerned with the implications of psi phenomena for biology and evolution came to similar or sometimes identical answers lends legitimacy and considerable support for this model. For examples, see e.g., Arthur Schopenhauer (1889), who discussed modes of reincarnation in his philosophy (e.g., Schopenhauer, 1969, vol. 2, pp. 502-503, 601), and Eduard von Hartmann (1884), Karl Camillo Schneider (1911, 1926), Edgar Dacqué (1926), Hans Driesch (1931, 1933), Gustave Geley (1925), Oskar Kuhn (1947), Aloys Wenzl (1951), Karl Friederichs (1955), Henri Bergson (1911, 1914–1915), William McDougall (1961), Adolf Meyer-Abich (1963), Alister Hardy (1965), and John Randall (1975).

With regard to the reincarnation cases, it is obvious that the only viable conceptual frame that allows for them is the vitalistic perspective, as it includes a psychically driven variant of inheritance. In fact, the vitalistic theory of evolution and reincarnation cases legitimize each other—no matter if the latter are interpreted in terms of survival or super-psi (e.g., Keil, 2010b). Vitalistic theories of evolution such as that of Hardy (1965) were not developed with reincarnation cases in mind, and most were developed before academic reincarnation research began. Nevertheless, there is no need to develop a new biological framework to accommodate the reincarnation phenomena; it only takes a shift in perspective, in that biologists need to take psi and other facets of life that defy purely physicalist explanations seriously. In turn, reincarnation cases underscore the facticity of the psychic background of reality and justify vitalistic positions. They also offer opportunities to advance and broaden available knowledge of other biological intricacies such as the development of instincts, an issue not well understood (e.g., Fabre, 1950).

Furthermore, reincarnation cases underline that mainstream concepts about memory functioning are incomplete. Because memories of a past life can resurface in another individual at a later time and at a different location, they provide robust evidence supporting the notion that memories are not stored in the brain. Accordingly, Matlock suggests that memories are preserved in a typically subconscious non-physical information-bearing matrix. And, as he shows, there is considerable evidence from other areas of consciousness research that buttresses this notion, such as near-death experiences (e.g., Holden, 2009; Rivas, Dirven & Smit, 2016), terminal lucidity and other death-related phenomena (Nahm, 2011a, 2012; Nahm et al., 2012), and discrepancies between cerebral structures and cognitive functioning (Nahm, Rousseau, & Greyson, 2017). There are also philosophical considerations (e.g., Braude, 2006). Perhaps some remarkable faculties of certain savants can also be better understood in this context. For example, Kim Peek had memorized more than twelve thousand books verbatim by the end of his life—although he read each page only once within eight to ten seconds, and had a severely malformed brain (Treffert, 2010).

Intriguingly, many reincarnation case subjects also describe events that seemed to have occurred in the intermission periods between lives, and like several other elements of reincarnation cases, the supposed memories concerning this time interval contain culture-specific features. Such differences are to be expected from the perspective of the vitalistic theory of evolution. Given that all organisms evolved from simpler forms such as unicellular organisms into increasingly complex forms that also developed increasingly complex perceptional and cognitive faculties (such as primates, dolphins, corvids, etc.), one needs to assume that their subconscious aspects, or the psychic background reality in which these organisms are rooted, must have evolved as well. Accordingly, the subconscious and the dreams of a chimpanzee, and the assumed subconscious layer of the "group soul" of chimpanzees, are likely to differ from that of humans. Respective differences should also be present in different cultures, and even in individuals, as also exemplified by dreams. From dreams, there is a seeming continuum that runs from lucid dreams, through out-of-body experiences, to more drastic forms of mental life such as mystical experiences and NDEs, which also contain cross-culturally stable core elements that are nevertheless individually and culturally conditioned (e.g., Kelleher, 2009; Matlock, 2017; Shushan, 2018). Concordantly, aspects of NDEs seem to have evolved throughout centuries in a given geographic region (Nahm, 2009; Zaleski, 1987). Since reincarnation intermission memories share numerous similarities with NDEs (Matlock, 2017; Matlock & Giesler-Petersen, 2016; Sharma & Tucker, 2004) and relate to other death-related experiences (Nahm, 2011a) it seems warranted to assume that these experiences are ingrained in a common substrate.

Because both reincarnation intermission memories and NDEs can contain apparently veridical non-physical perceptions regarding the ordinary physical world that were gained via out-of-body experiences or from a "disembodied" state (Holden, 2009; Matlock & Giesler-Petersen, 2016; Rivas, Dirven, & Smit, 2016), but can also comprise meetings with deceased persons not known to be dead (Greyson, 2010b; Nahm, 2011a), the question arises whether the psychic matrix of the background reality that manifests as otherworldly realms in these cases possesses objective and verifiable properties (Matlock, 2017). Considering dreams again might provide a pathway to the answer (compare also Tucker, 2013).

It has long been known that among states that facilitate extrasensory perception such as telepathy and clairvoyance, dreams hold a prominent role, and dreams were used for an experimental test series on telepathy (Ullman, Krippner, & Vaughan, 2002; Van de Castle, 1995). In cases of shared dreams or clairvoyant dreams, the congruence between the experiences of two persons or with the event in the physical world is not always exact, and it can be symbolically vested. Thus, although objectively verifiable perceptions occur, and intersubjectivity in the dream world seems possible (e.g., Donahoe, 1979; Hart & Hart, 1932–1933; Magallòn, 1997), especially between closely related or even "entangled" individuals such as identical twins (e.g., Brusewitz et al., 2013; Playfair, 2012), that does not imply that the dream environment in which these experiences are made possesses an objective character as well. This is supposedly also valid for shared lucid dreams, a line of investigation that offers a wealth of tantalizing research options, but which is difficult to pursue and has received little attention up until the present (LaBerge, 1985; Waggoner, 2009). Yet, as shared lucid dream practices have allegedly been performed deliberately in mystical practices such as Sufism and Tibetan Buddhism (Bulkeley, 2008; Godwin, 1995; LaBerge, 1985; Norbu, 1999) as well as in some indigenous and shamanic traditions (e.g., Bulkeley, 2008; R. Moss, 2009; Sumegi, 2008), studies into their phenomenology do not seem impossible. They tie in neatly with other shared psi-experiences such as collective and reciprocal apparitions, out-of-body experiences, or shared NDEs and deathbed visions (e.g., Hart & Collaborators, 1956; Hart & Hart, 1932–1933; Moody & P. Perry, 2010; for further references, see Nahm, 2011a, 2012; compare also Stevenson, 1982). All these experiences occur predominantly in persons who are related or acquainted. Summing up this section, it appears that the psychic background aspect of reality, and an assumed collective subconscious of groups of individuals or species, does allow for intersubjectivity, but it is also ductile and shapeable by conscious and subconscious experiences of organisms. It thus evolves along with the evolution of the physical realm; and just as experiences of biological organisms shape the experience of this psychic realm, features of this realm might shape developmental processes in the biological realm.

Reincarnation cases involving birthmarks, birth defects, or other bodily characteristics related to the previous person provide striking examples of such influences. It is nevertheless difficult to find causal bottom-up explanations regarding how exactly such influences guide the shaping of body tissue in the frame of classical physics and modern mainstream biology. Numerous vitalists, especially Hans Driesch, emphasized that biological development processes comprise a different kind of causality in addition to the common *causa efficiens*. Driesch termed it "Ganzheitskausalität," what can be translated as "wholeness-causality." According to Driesch, wholeness-causality must not be regarded as a force, but, rather, as an organizing principle that does not primarily originate in our familiar space-time, although it extends into it. It bears similarity to Aristotle's *causa finalis*, and in Driesch's philosophy, it is the means by which entelechy as an organic guiding principle is realized and actualized (Driesch, 1928). Entelechy thus causes the coordinated generation of "whole" structures, including bodily modifications under hypnosis and the like, which can be elicited via subconscious ideas or impulses. Thus, entelechy, also, might possess unconscious but still "psychoid" qualities that are realized via processes guided by wholeness-causality. Similarly, Stevenson (1997a), Nahm & Hassler (2011), and also Matlock have argued that somatic peculiarities such as birthmarks might follow psychophysiological affectations based on mental images, impressions, or impulses, a concept that can be regarded as being tantamount to assuming that psychokinesis is at work. Driesch thus was convinced that parapsychological phenomena share the same psychic underpinning as entelechial developments in biology, and he considered parapsychology a bridge to vitalism—an issue that he often stressed (e.g., Driesch, 1926, 1933, 1939). In Driesch's time, there were hardly any good reincarnation cases available, but if he were convinced of their existence, he would certainly have argued that the ontogenesis of a reincarnation case subject was driven by a corresponding entelechy with a psychic and most likely subconscious root behind familiar space-time. Alternatively, or in addition, more recent concepts of entanglement correlations could also be considered to play a role in biological development processes and one might even regard mind and matter as correlated through entanglement, or dual aspects of a single unified principle, as discussed by Carl Gustav Jung and Wolfgang Pauli (Atmanspacher & Fach, 2015). Also in these concepts, traditional notions of linear upward causation or of self-organization of matter particles are dispensable and not applicable.

Nevertheless, because reincarnation cases unavoidably imply that memories or other personality traits continue to exist after the previous person died, and can resurface in children, it is inevitable to assume some kind of dualism on this level of biological organization. Still, as outlined by Matlock, that does not require adopting a classical variant of ontological substance-dualism as proposed by Descartes. Numerous vitalist biologists and philosophers held a dualistic position with regard to the functioning of organisms, but were at the same time convinced that the universe at large is a basically unified realm of existence (e.g., Schopenhauer, 1969; Driesch, 1938; Wallace, 1889, 1910). Hence, when conducting or discussing scientific research, it is crucial to always define the context and level of (biological) organization under examination, and to specify the appropriate nature-philosophical reference system. It becomes obvious, then, that dualistic and monistic positions do not exclude each other; they merely apply to different reference systems. At suitable intersections, these concepts could of course complement and enrich each other (Nahm, 2007).

1. At the level of the elucidation of linear biochemical reaction chains and connections, the appropriate reference system is the reductionist mechanism based on an understanding of usual causality as in classical physics.
2. On the level of research into the well-coordinated interplay of different biochemical reaction chains, cell structures, or organs, it takes a systems-orientated approach that includes processes of self-organization.
3. On the level of investigating the unfolding of organic life, organisms, consciousness, memory or psi phenomena, including reincarnation cases, it takes an at least partially dualistic vitalism.
4. Finally, when musing about the ultimate level of reality that underlies all being, the appropriate reference system might well be a kind of monistic holism in which organic and inorganic matter, but also mind and matter at large, are regarded as differently expressed aspects of a unified stratum of existence. It can also be conceived in such a way that all matter intrinsically possesses (proto-) mental aspects that become increasingly pronounced as the complexity and organizational structure of matter particles increases as in organisms.

This approach is quite consistent with evolutionary panpsychism and panexperientialism (Griffin, 1997) as favored also by Matlock in this book, and it seems a quite timely approach. Especially during the recent decade, theories of panpsychism have moved from a marginalized position to the center of philosophical debates concerning the mind-body problem, as physicalist and ontological dualist approaches have proven to be loaded with irresolvable difficulties (Brüntrup, 2018). It seems to be increasingly recognized among philosophers that panpsychist approaches offer advantages over these contenders, and while not disregarding intrinsic conceptual difficulties of panpsychism, some authors even developed models that include possibilities for higher-level forms of organization of exerting causal efficacy without violating the principle of physical causal closure on structurally lower levels (see for example the "emergent panpsychism" of Brüntrup, 2017, and Mørch, 2014). It is tempting to assign panpsychism a panentheist or idealist slant (E. F. Kelly, Crabtree, & Marshall, 2015; Meixner, 2017), especially when considering the research results of psychical research including reincarnation cases. However, with a few exceptions (e.g., Griffin, 1997), the discussions in philosophical academia settings probing the potentials of panpsychism are quite theory-centered (e.g., Brüntrup & Jaskolla, 2017) and ignore potentially decisive "rogue" phenomena (E. F. Kelly, 2015a) that must be taken into account when carving out the basic requirements for such theories. This unnecessary and unfortunate self-limitation of mainstream philosophy is similar to that found in biology.

As mentioned, reincarnation cases are among these rogue phenomena. They represent a very important piece in the puzzle of phenomena and experiences that outline possible pathways for developing future concepts for both biology and philosophy, which must of course be in mutual agreement to be of any value. And, although many aspects of reincarnation cases remain difficult to understand at present, a basic biological theoretical framework in which these exceptional phenomena could be allocated exists already. It even has a distinguished tradition in biological thinking, and the "processual soul" theory as outlined by Matlock with regard to possibilities of reincarnation and possession fits neatly into it. One hopes that one day, biologists, psychologists, and philosophers will recognize the enormous significance of reincarnation cases for conceptualizing a revitalized biology. It takes unusual but robust phenomena such as these to push the frontiers of established knowledge further into presently neglected territory and to elucidate little understood facets of human existence, and of life in general, in order to develop the next stages of a contemporary "Modern Synthesis" of biological thought (for possible directions, see E. F. Kelly, Crabtree, & Marshall, 2015; Nahm, 2007). However, in doing so, it is essential to always stay predominantly oriented toward empirical research results, and not toward preconceived hypotheses or theories, as exemplified by the curious ups and downs of the hypothesis of inheritance of acquired characteristics. Even though the significance of reincarnation (be it interpreted in survival or super-psi terms) as a means of evolution remains speculative at present, facets of the inheritance of acquired characteristics have in a sense finally been substantiated by reincarnation cases in a very curious turn of events that Lamarck and Darwin could never have foreseen. At the very least, reincarnation cases signify that regarding the ontogenesis of their subjects, there is a third factor at work that supplements genetics and environmental influence in the formation of human personality and physical features (Stevenson, 1997a, 1997b; Stevenson & Keil, 2005). This aspect alone has the potential to contribute to the necessary paradigm shift in biology.

Glossary of Specialized
and Technical Terms

The Glossary provides short definitions of specialized and technical terms used in this book. Terms whose definitions appear elsewhere in the Glossary are italicized.

account In contrast to a *case*, an uninvestigated story or anecdote of some unusual occurrence, for example, an *apparition*, or a claim to remember a *previous life*, about whose reliability we can say nothing.

acquaintance case A *reincarnation case* with an acquaintance relationship.

acquaintance relationship Denotes an acquaintance, but not a connection of blood or marriage, between the previous person and the parents of the subject in a reincarnation case.

actual occasion In the process metaphysics of Alfred North Whitehead, a fundamental event in the flow of conscious experience and in the subatomic processes that produce physical reality. Actual occasions are related through concrescence in a stream of experience or *stream of consciousness*.

adult case A *reincarnation case* in which the *subject* is ten years of age or older when he has his main memories of the *previous life*.

age regression *See past-life regression (PLR).*

agency The capacity of individuals to act independently and to make their own free choices. A discarnate *agent* (a *spirit*) possesses *discarnate agency*.

agent 1. An entity capable of thinking or acting on its own, expressing *agency*. 2. In parapsychology, the living person or *spirit* who apparently or ostensibly is the source of spontaneous *psi* experiences, such as *apparitions*.

Akashic field Term introduced by philosopher Ervin Laszlo for a sub-quantum information field that pervades the universe, similar to the *Akashic Records* of Theosophy.

Akashic Records In Theosophy, a chronicle of all cosmic and human activities since the dawn of time, indelibly impressed on a celestial ether. The term was derived from the Sanskrit *aksaha*, an etheric substance permeating the universe. The Akashic Records are thought to be accessible through *psi* and, since Edgar Cayce, have been proposed as a source of information about past lives.

anattā In Buddhism, the doctrine of "no-self" or "no-soul," which holds that the self is an illusion and that there is no enduring soul.

animism An empirically based worldview concerning *spirits* and their interaction with the living, characteristic of indigenous societies around the world.

announcing dream A dream, often a pregnancy dream, in which a woman or person related to her seems to see the *apparition* of a deceased person stating its intention to be reborn to her. Announcing dreams are a type of *rebirth announcement*.

anomalous-date case Stevenson's term for a case of *replacement reincarnation*, in which the *spirit* in *possession* of a body is supplanted by another spirit.

apparition Parapsychological term for what popularly is called a ghost. Apparitions are usually visual but may be auditory, olfactory, tactile, or, at least in principle, gustatory. Generally they appear in the waking state but they may present in dreams as well, e.g., in *announcing dreams* and *departure dreams*.

archetype In Jungian psychology, elements of the *collective unconscious* that are innately present in the minds all human beings, represented as common and recurring ideas, images, thought patterns, etc., that are interpreted differently by different cultural traditions.

assisted reincarnation In relation to the *selection problem*, help in deciding where to be reborn coming from another *spirit*, either human or nonhuman. When the assisting spirits are nonhuman, assisted reincarnation can be understood as a feature of the *theistic solution* to the selection problem.

astral body A term originating in Theosophy and now common in *New Age metaphysics*, denoting a quasi-physical *subtle body* aligned with the physical body during life. The astral body is said to separate from the physical body at death but to continue to support *consciousness*, personality, and memory, in a discarnate state until its union with a new physical body.

autobiographical impression An awareness of the personal context of *episodic* or other memories of a previous life, in contrast to the *autobiographical knowledge* that accompanies memories of the present life.

Autobiographical impressions are more limited in scope than is autobiographical knowledge. They may arise on their own, but usually accompany *declarative memories*.

autobiographical knowledge Memory researcher Martin Conway's term for abstract knowledge of personal histories which allows a rememberer to place memories in context. Full autobiographical knowledge is absent from most *past-life memory*, although it is compensated to some extent by *autobiographical impression*.

autobiographical memory In memory research, *declarative (explicit)* memory of one's life, consisting of *episodic memory, emotional memory,* and *autobiographical knowledge*. *Past-life memory* is a restricted form of autobiographical memory.

background consciousness An amorphous and undifferentiated *consciousness* that under *panpsychism* is presumed to represent the primordial state of the universe. This sort of consciousness is imagined still to lie in the background of the universe, but over time it has differentiated and evolved into many different forms.

behavioral memory In memory research, a category of *implicit memory* that includes *emotional memory* and *procedural memory*.

behavioral sign Any behavior or *behavioral memory* on the part of a case *subject* that is reminiscent of a *previous person* in a *reincarnation case*.

buried treasure In a *reincarnation case*, anything secreted by the *previous person* that the *subject* either locates or gives directions for finding.

case An account of some unusual occurrence or series of events that has been closely observed or investigated and documented by independent parties, often specifically a *reincarnation case*.

case of the reincarnation type (CORT) Stevenson's term for *reincarnation case*.

case subject See *subject*.

child case A *reincarnation case* in which the *subject* was under ten years old, and usually much younger, when he or she first starts to talk about remembering, or otherwise gives evidence of having lived, a *previous life*.

clairvoyance In parapsychology, a type of *extrasensory perception* that involves the acquisition of information directly from an object, place, external event, etc., without the involvement of another *mind*.

collective unconscious In the psychology of C. G. Jung, a deep level of mind that is shared by the entire human race, or by all members of a species. The collective unconscious is the realm of *archetypes* and is the source of *synchronicity*. It is contrasted with the *personal unconscious*.

concrescence In the process metaphysics of Alfred North Whitehead, the coalescence or growing together of *actual occasions* in an experiential stream, or *stream of consciousness.*

concurrent reincarnation The belief, found in some cultures, that more than one *spirit* may occupy a single body simultaneously.

conscious awareness Waking consciousness, associated with the *supraliminal mind*; in psychology and philosophy often simply called consciousness, but here contrasted with the *subconscious* processing associated with the *subliminal mind.* Conscious awareness and the subconscious are the two strata of a duplex *consciousness.*

consciousness In cognitive psychology and the philosophy of mind, often equated with *conscious awareness*, but in this book considered to be something larger and more expansive, having a duplex nature, encompassing the *subconscious* or *subliminal mind* as well as the *consciously aware supraliminal mind.* Consciousness is treated as fundamentally indistinct from mind, soul, spirit, and psyche and in a *process metaphysics* sense as a stream of experiential events, a *stream of consciousness.* Additionally, consciousness is understood in an *idealist* way, as the ground for material as well as mental reality, and in terms of an evolutionary *panpsychism* as having evolved and differentiated from an amorphous *background consciousness* in tandem with biological systems, so that each species of life is associated with its own specialized type of consciousness.

continuing business See *unfinished business.*

continuous incarnation Term introduced by anthropologist Lee Guemple to describe the Inuit belief in the possibility of a soul reincarnating before its body dies. Because the Inuit believe that a person may possess more than one soul simultaneously (*concurrent reincarnation*), continuous incarnation as described by Guemple is an example of both concurrent reincarnation and multiple reincarnation.

CORT Abbreviation for *case of the reincarnation type.*

crippling complexity Complications so dense and convoluted that they defy all plausibility. The concept and term were introduced by philosopher Stephen Braude to describe the convoluted nature of many *super-psi* explanations of the evidence for discarnate survival, including *reincarnation cases.*

cross-religion case See *interreligious case.*

cross-sex case See *sex-change case.*

cryptomnesia Also called source amnesia. An aberration of memory that concerns things that are read, heard, seen, etc., forgotten consciously, but retained in the subconscious and later presented to *conscious awareness* as if they are an *episodic* or *semantic* autobiographical memory.

deathbed vision A vision or *apparition* perceived by someone near death, often literally from the deathbed.

declarative (explicit) memory In memory research, types of memory, such as *episodic, emotional,* and *semantic memory,* that can be brought to *conscious awareness.* Declarative memory is contrasted with *implicit memory.*

departure dream A dream in which members of a deceased person's family dream that he (or occasionally a nonhuman *spirit*) tells them where he has been reborn.

diathanatic Term coined by Ian Stevenson, meaning "able to survive death," said of beliefs, behavioral dispositions, memories, etc.

discarnate agency The capacity of a discarnate agent (a *spirit*) to think and act independently, making its own free choices.

elective reincarnation Generally, the selection of its new parents by a spirit during the *intermission* period between lives, without input or assistance from other human or nonhuman spirits (*assisted reincarnation*). In *planned reincarnation*, the new parents are selected before death.

elective solution One of three solutions to the *selection problem.* The elective solution holds the individual directly responsible for choosing the parents of the new life, without the mediation of God (the *theistic solution*) or karma (the *karmic solution*).

emotional memory In memory research, a type of memory that is classified as *implicit* and unconscious, though it may be made conscious (brought to *conscious awareness*). Emotional memories may accompany *declarative memories,* although they may be independent of them as well.

enemy case A *reincarnation case* in which a member of a group killed in or near his enemy is reborn among them rather than among his own people.

entelechy In the *vitalism* of Hans Driesch, a non-physical organizational principle that governs the development of biological organisms, especially their somatic aspects. Driesch borrowed this term from the philosophy of Aristotle.

episodic memory In memory research, a type of *declarative memory* relating to personal experiences with events, people, and objects at particular times and places.

ESP See *extra-sensory perception.*

experimental birthmark A birthmark resulting from a mark made on a body, usually postmortem but sometimes (in Burma) shortly before death, with the intent of tracking a person's *spirit* into its next incarnation.

extrasensory perception (ESP) Also *psi* (ESP). Sometimes designated *psi (ESP).* In parapsychology, one of the two branches of *psi,* denoting acquisition of information about external (often distant) mental states or objects without use of the body's five senses. Types of ESP include *clairvoyance*, *telepathy*, *precognition*, and *retrocognition*.

false memory An apparent recollection of an event that did not actually occur.

family case Also, **same-family case**. A *reincarnation case* with a *family relationship*.

family relationship A connection through blood or marriage between the *subject* and the family of the *previous person* in a *reincarnation case*. In tribal societies, family relationships are expanded to include all members of a lineage or clan.

fantasy theory The assumption that all apparent *past-life memories* are fantasies. In a sense, the fantasy theory is a hypothesis derived from broader *materialist* theories of consciousness, perception, and memory as derivatives of cerebral activity.

FPL Acronym for "famous past life."

fruit of forgetfulness Generalized term denoting any substance offered to *spirits* during the *intermission*, thought to induce amnesia for their past embodied lives.

gandhabba (Pali) or **gandharva** (Sanskrit). In Buddhism, the complex formed of feelings, perceptions, predispositions, and consciousness (*conscious awareness*) that passes between lives and, under the guidance of *karma*, unites with a man's semen and a woman's menstrual blood or ovum to form the body and individuality of a new person.

genetic memory An emotional or behavioral disposition that is transferred across generations genetically, through epigenetic influences on gene expression. Genetic memory does not involve the transmission of *autobiographical memory*.

geographical factor In relation to the *selection problem*, any feature of geographic proximity between the death place of the *previous person* and the parents of a case *subject* that could have played a role in drawing a reincarnating *spirit* to its new family.

glossophobia Resistance to learning one's native language, sometimes seen with case *subjects* whose *previous persons* spoke a radically different language.

hypothesis A testable statement derived from a *theory*, used to evaluate that theory.

idealism In philosophy, the idea that the physical world is derived from or is fundamentally dependent upon the actions of mind or *consciousness*. Cf. *materialism*.

immediate reincarnation or **rebirth** The belief that rebirth occurs instantaneously upon death, as among the Druze, who hold that a *soul* passes from a dying person directly to the body of a newborn.

implicit memory In memory research, types of memory, such as *emotional memory* and *procedural memory*, that are acquired and processed unconsciously, even while they affect conscious thoughts and behaviors. Implicit memory is contrasted with *declarative (explicit) memory*.

induced past-life memory A past-life memory arising in an artificially induced altered state of consciousness, for example, under hypnosis or the influence of hallucinogenic drugs.

intercaste case An Indian *reincarnation case* in which the *subject* and *previous person* are of different castes.

interethnic case A *reincarnation case* in which the *subject* and *previous person* are of different ethnicities.

intermediate life In a *reincarnation case*, a claimed or verified life between the present life of the *subject* and the principal *previous life* recalled.

intermission or **intermission period** The interval between lives, from the death of *a previous person* to the birth of a case *subject*.

intermission distance The distance between the place the *previous person* died and the place the case *subject* was born.

intermission experience (IE) Experience of the *intermission* between lives, as recalled in *intermission memory*. The intermission experience may be broken down into five stages, not all of which are recalled by all rememberers. Stage 1 is the death of the *previous person*, Stage 2 is an indefinite period in a discarnate state, Stage 3 is the selection of parents for the next life, Stage 4 is intrauterine existence, and Stage 5 is birth of the case *subject*.

intermission length The length of time between the death of the *previous person* and the birth of the case *subject*.

intermission memory (IM) Claimed memory of the *intermission*.

international case A *reincarnation case* in which the *subject* was born in a country other than the one in which the *previous person* died.

interracial case A reincarnation case in which the *subject* and *previous person* are of different races.

interreligious case A reincarnation case in which the *subject* and *previous person* adhere to different religions.

involuntary memory A memory that surfaces in *conscious awareness* spontaneously, as in a spontaneous *reincarnation case*.

juridical (Indic) karma The classic Indic idea that where we are reborn, and what happens to us in life, is determined by an external, lawful force that is the product of the moral qualities of our actions and intentions in this and earlier lives. Compare *processual karma*; *retributive karma*.

karma See *juridical (Indic) karma, processual karma, retributive karma*.

karmic solution A solution to the *selection problem* in which one's *juridical* or *retributive karma* is said to determine where one is reborn.

life planning The idea that *spirits* decide on their goals or plan their lives in advance of rebirth.

long-distance case A *reincarnation case* in which the *previous person* died fifty or more kilometers (thirty-one miles) from where the *subject* was born.

manner of death or **mode of death** In a *reincarnation case*, the manner in which the *previous person* died, generally either natural or violent, with accidental deaths classified as violent.

materialism The philosophical position that material (physical) reality is primary and the mind or *consciousness* secondary to it.

maternal impression Physical impressions, such as birthmarks and congenital deformities, believed to be caused by the influence of a mother's thoughts and feelings on her baby in utero, generally as a result of her having seen something emotionally stressful.

matter In philosophy, the substance from which the physical world is derived. *Matter* is distinct from *mind*. In a materialist *property dualism*, mind and matter are considered properties of matter, whereas in an *idealist* property dualism mind and matter are considered properties of mind.

medium A type of *psychic practitioner* that specializes in exchanging information with or retrieving information from a discarnate *mind*. A trance medium enters an altered state of consciousness and allows a *spirit* to take temporary *possession* of her body, whereas a mental medium acquires information from discarnate minds through *extrasensory perception*.

mediumistic announcement A type of *rebirth announcement* in which a *spirit* proclaims through a *medium* its intention to be reborn to certain parents or in a certain situation.

mediumistic communication A message from a *spirit* passed through a *medium*, via *psi*.

memory Memory researchers classify memories as either *declarative* (*explicit*) or *implicit*. Most types of memory occur in *past-life memory*.

metaphysics The branch of philosophy concerned with existence, being, and the nature of reality.

metempsychosis Operarationalized as a rebirth cycle that includes one or more lives as a nonhuman animal (or other nonhuman entity) between human lives.

mind See *consciousness*.

multiple simultaneous reincarnation or **multiple reincarnation** The reincarnation of a *spirit* in more than one body simultaneously. In *animism*, the mechanism may be considered *soul replication*, but in *New Age metaphysics*, it is assumed to be *soul splitting*.

New Age metaphysics A loosely defined metaphysical system promoted by proponents of New Age spirituality.

obsession In parapsychology, an overshadowing influence on a living person by a *spirit*, short of *possession*.

panexperientialism In the philosophy of David Ray Griffin, a variety of *panpsychism* that emphasizes the importance of experience (the concrescence of actual occasions, in the terms of Whitehead's process metaphysics) and so grants *consciousness* (although not necessarily *conscious awareness*) only to those parts of an aggregate entity that enjoy experience.

panpsychism In philosophy, the idea that *consciousness* (although not necessarily *conscious awareness*) or feeling is inherent in all types of *matter*, inanimate as well as animate.

parakaya pravesh or *parakayapravesh* Hindi (orig. Sanskrit) term denoting the entry of a wandering spirit into a body, usually of someone just dead, thus bringing it back to life. It is usually glossed as *possession* in English but may be more accurately described as *replacement reincarnation*.

paramnesia In psychology, a distortion of memory in which fact and fantasy comingle. Paramnesia plays an important role in the *psychosocial theory* of *past-life memory* claims.

parapsychology The branch of psychology that deals with psychic phenomena, historically called psychical research. Parapsychology includes laboratory investigation of *psi* with living agents (experimental parapsychology) as well as the study of naturally occurring spontaneous cases of psi and phenomena such as *apparitions, mediumship,* and *reincarnation,* which suggest postmortem survival and the exercise of psi by discarnate *agents.*

parental guidance The idea that parents shape their children's thoughts and behaviors, used in the *psychosocial theory* as an explanation for *reincarnation cases.*

passive xenoglossy Subliminal awareness of an unlearned foreign language or regional or social dialect that affects one's speech performance or facility in reading and writing.

past life See *previous life.*

past-life memory *Autobiographical memory* of a *previous life* to which the rememberer often feels connected through a continuity of *self.* Past-life memory may be either *declarative* (*explicit*) or *implicit,* but it is often more restricted than memory of the present life, especially on the declarative side. It is largely *episodic memory,* with some *semantic memory* and little or no *autobiographical knowledge.* On the implicit side, both *emotional memories* and *procedural memories* are common.

past-life reading Reports by a *psychic practitioner* of the past lives of a client, sometimes felt to be retrieved from the client's mind, but more often from the *Akashic Records.*

past-life regression (PLR) The practice of age regressing subjects to what seem to be earlier lives under hypnosis, often simply "regression."

past-life therapy *Past-life regression* employed in a psychotherapy context, aimed at relieving clients of traumas derived from previous lives.

percipient In parapsychology, the receiver of a *psi* impression in an *apparition* or other psi-related *spontaneous case.*

person An embodied individual *consciousness.* A person is conceived to be composed of both body and mind. Persons are mortal but their *personalities* may survive their deaths, carried in the *subconscious* portion of their minds. See also *previous person.*

personality The characteristic patterns of thinking, feeling, and acting that help to define an individual *person* and to distinguish that person from other persons. A person's personality is constructed from dispositions, memories, emotions, etc., latent in his *subconscious* mind and is *diathanatic,* able to survive death.

personation Portrayal of someone else, as in acting. In a *reincarnation case,* the identification of a *subject* with a *previous person* through behaviors.

physical signs Physical features that link a *previous person* and a *subject* in a *reincarnation case.* Examples include birthmarks, birth defects, and other congenital abnormalities such as internal diseases, but also features like facial structure, eye form, skin color, body shape, and stature.

planned reincarnation A type of *elective reincarnation* in which the *previous person* states in advance of his death his intent to be reborn to particular parents, in a particular family, or in a particular place.

poltergeist German for "noisy ghost." In parapsychology, poltergeist activities include sounds such as knocks and other physical manifestations, produced by *psychokinesis,* by either embodied or discarnate *agents.*

possession The occupation of a body by a *spirit*. Possession may be transient or brief, as in *mediumistic* possession, or it may be long-term or permanent, as in *reincarnation*. Some writers use possession in the sense of *replacement reincarnation*.

postnatal reincarnation *Reincarnation* that occurs after the birth of the case *subject*. Most examples of postnatal reincarnation are also *replacement reincarnation*.

prebirth memories Memories of prenatal existence that do not involve memories of previous lives or deaths, covering Stages 2 through 4 of the *intermission experience*. The term is sometimes used more broadly, to include memories of death and birth (Stages 1 and 5 of the intermission experience) but is employed here in denote a distinct class of *intermission memories*.

precognition In parapsychology, *extrasensory perception* of future mental states or events.

preexistence (or **preexistence without prior incarnation**) The idea that a *soul* can come into existence and develop its own identity in a discarnate state before incarnating in a physical body.

premortem reincarnation *Reincarnation* that is initiated or accomplished before the death of the *previous person*.

previous life In a *reincarnation case*, an earlier life that the *subject* recalls or gives evidence of having lived.

previous person, often **previous personality (PP)** In *a reincarnation case*, the deceased person whose life the *subject* recalls or gives other evidence of having been.

principle of sufficient reason Physicist Henry Stapp's principle that, in a rationally coherent universe, nothing should happen without a sufficient reason for that particular thing to happen; nothing should happen by chance alone.

private case A *reincarnation case* that is not known beyond the family of the *subject*.

procedural memory In memory research, behavioral memory for the performance of certain actions, such as learned skills, repeated or practiced to the point that they are carried out without conscious direction or conscious involvement. Procedural memories are classified as *implicit memory* because they are acquired and performed unconsciously.

process metaphysics or **process philosophy** In philosophy, any metaphysics that considers the constituents of reality to be in continuous change or flux rather than static, as in *substance dualism*. In the thought of Alfred North Whitehead, the idea that the fundamental building blocks of reality are momentary events called actual occasions which follow one another in an experiential *stream of consciousness*.

processual karma The largely Western idea that what passes between lives are dispositional traits, emotional connections, psychological conflicts, and such. Processual karma is conceived of as a psychological force operating within an individual's mind or psyche, rather than externally to it. Compare *juridical karma*; *retributive karma*.

processual soul The soul, or *stream of consciousness*, regarded in process terms, as subject to psychological dynamics and change.

property dualism In philosophy, the idea that a single substance (see *substance monism*) has two different properties. In an *idealist* property dualism, *mind* and *matter* are the two basic properties of mind. Another type of idealist property dualism is the dualism of mind and body. Unlike *substance dualism*, which conceives of mind and body as composed of fundamentally different substances, an idealist property dualism holds that mind and body are composed of the same substance (*consciousness*), but the consciousness is of different type. Thus, a body is animated by an independent *stream of consciousness*.

psi In parapsychology, a term that embraces both *extrasensory perception (ESP)* and *psychokinesis (PK)*. These branches may be abbreviated *psi (ESP)* and *psi (PK)*. Psi transactions entail actions in a single step by a single mind or between two minds, in contrast to *super-psi*.

psi (ESP) See *extrasensory perception.*

psi (PK) See *psychokinesis.*

psyche A Greek word that may be translated as "mind," "soul," or "spirit," here considered to be synonymous with them and with *consciousness.*

psychic A type of *psychic practitioner* that specializes in retrieving information from other minds, written or physical materials, places, etc., through *extrasensory perception.*

psychical research Historically the name of the field now called *parapsychology.*

psychic identification The determination of past-life identities by shamans, mediums, or other *psychic practitioners.*

psychic practitioner A sensitive such as a *psychic*, *medium*, or *shaman* who interacts with the spirit world or retrieves information ostensibly from the minds of living persons or from the *Akashic Records.*

psychokinesis (PK) Sometimes designated *psi (PK)*. In parapsychology, a branch of *psi*; a property of *consciousness* that provides for direct action on physical and biological systems.

psychological or **psychic factor** In relation to the *selection problem*, family ties or bonds of affection or animosity between a *previous person* and the family of a *subject* that appear to have played a role in drawing a spirit to its new parents.

psychometry A practice (sometimes called token-object reading) whereby a *psychic practitioner* gains impressions from an item with which he or she is in physical contact.

psychophore Ian Stevenson's term for a subtle or *astral body* that would carry *consciousness*, behavior, and physical form between lives and serve as a template for a new physical body.

psychosocial theory A sophisticated version of the *fantasy theory* devised to account for *reincarnation cases* without presuming postmortem survival. According to the psychosocial theory, reincarnation cases are the products of a combination of psychological and social factors such as *parental guidance, social construction, subjective illusion of significance*, and memory distortions such *paramnesia* and *cryptomnesia* in accordance with a culturally mandated belief in rebirth.

rebirth The process by which the life force or *consciousness* associated with an entity leaves it, usually at death, and becomes associated with another entity, usually before birth. Rebirth denotes the common process of *reincarnation, transmigration* and *metempsychosis*, without making distinctions as to type.

rebirth announcement Expression of intention on the part of a discarnate *spirit* to be reborn to certain parents, made in an *announcing dream* or *mediumistic communication* or represented through an *apparition*.

rebirth syndrome The set of signs that co-occur in different combinations in an *account* or *case* of *reincarnation*.

recitative xenoglossy *Xenoglossy* that is rote, not comprehending the words spoken, in contrast to *responsive xenoglossy* and *passive xenoglossy*.

recognition memory A type of *declarative memory* that permits the remember to recognize places, objects, people, and so on.

recurrent birthmark or **birth defect** A birthmark or birth defect that recurs in successive reincarnations of the same individual.

regression See *past-life regression (PLR)*.

regression case An instance of *past-life regression* that has been studied and reported by its investigator.

reincarnation Operarationalized as the transfer of the life force or *consciousness* stream of a human being to the body of another human being. Variations include *concurrent reincarnation, continuous incarnation, multiple reincarnation*, and *replacement reincarnation*. In some cultures, it is thought possible for reincarnation to be initiated before death (*premortem reincarnation*).

reincarnation case A set of *signs of reincarnation* that has been investigated, in contrast to an *account*. A reincarnation case usually but not invariably includes *past-life memory*. Reincarnation cases may be *solved* or *unsolved*.

reincarnation signs See *signs of reincarnation.*

relationship status In a *reincarnation case*, the relationship between the *previous person* and the family of the case *subject*, classified as *family*, *acquaintance*, or *stranger*.

repeater child In West Africa, a child who returns to the same family again and again, only to die in infancy each time. Repeater children are thought to be members of a band who have taken an oath to die early, as a torment to their parents.

replacement reincarnation or **replacement case** A type of *postnatal reincarnation* in which the reincarnating *spirit* replaces the spirit originally in possession of a body without the body dying. Replacement reincarnation sometimes is referred to by the Sanskrit and Hindi term *parakaya pravesh*, as possession, or as an anomalous-date case. Unlike with what are popularly called *walk-ins*, there is a quick and complete substitution of the old personality with the new one, usually following an apparently fatal illness.

responsive xenoglossy A type of *xenoglossy* in which a case *subject* is able to comprehend and respond appropriately without having learned the language in question. Responsive xenoglossy has been reported in spontaneous *reincarnation cases*, in *regression cases*, and in *mediumship.*

retributive karma In Theosophy and in Asian popular conception, a variety of *juridical karma* that expects there to be direct, often physically apparent, consequences to actions, such as throat disease and loss of ability to speak related to having slit someone's throat in a previous life.

retrocognition In parapsychology, *extrasensory perception* of past mental states or events.

retroprehensive inclusion Philosopher David Ray Griffin's proposed variation of *super-psi* that involves reaching back *retrocognitively* to the lives of deceased people and incorporating their identities in one's own.

same-family case See *family case.*

selection problem The theoretical problem of how the new parents are chosen in *reincarnation* or, more generally, *rebirth*. The selection problem has been resolved in three ways by different thought traditions: there is a *karmic solution*, a *theistic solution*, and an *elective solution.*

self The "owner" or experiencer of a *stream of consciousness*, including both the *subconscious* and *conscious awareness*. The self has permanence and provides for continuity of identity over time, including over a succession of lives as different *persons.*

semantic memory In memory research, a type of *autobiographical memory* that includes general knowledge and facts about the world. Semantic memory is assumed to have originated in personal experience but to have lost contact with it.

sex-change case A *reincarnation case* in which the *previous person* and the *subject* are of opposite sexes.

shaman A type of *psychic practitioner*, common in indigenous societies around the world, that specializes in interactions with spirits, often out-of-body in a trance state. Shamans may also act as *psychics* to retrieve information from other *minds* through *extrasensory perception*.

signs of reincarnation Any phenomena taken to be indicative of reincarnation. The principal reincarnation signs that appear in *rebirth syndrome* and *reincarnation cases* may be grouped into three classes: *autobiographical memories* of *previous lives*, along with related *recognition memories* and *spatial memories*; *behavioral signs*, including *emotional memories* and *procedural memories*; and *physical signs* like birthmarks, birth defects, and other congenital abnormalities. Other common reincarnation signs are *announcing dreams*, *departure dreams*, and *pregnancy cravings* related to a *previous person*.

silent case A *reincarnation case* in which the *subject* makes no claim to remember a previous life.

skeptic As regards parapsychology, a critic who a priori rules out of hand the possibility of anything that contravenes the assumptions of *materialism*.

social construction The process by which members of a society employ cultural constructs to develop a consensus view of reality. Social construction is a central element of the *psychosocial theory*. As applied to *reincarnation cases*, it is the idea that members of a society with reincarnation beliefs interpret the world in terms of those beliefs and act to construct the cases in response to them. *Parental guidance* is a form of social construction.

solved case A *reincarnation case* with an identified *previous person*.

soul In this book, that which is regarded as the life force of an individual, synonymous with *mind*, *psyche*, *spirit*, or *stream of consciousness*, and, as such, open to continual change according to a *process metaphysics* rather than fixed and eternal as in *substance dualism*. When contrasted with *spirit*, an embodied rather than disembodied consciousness stream.

soul replication The replication of a *spirit* before *reincarnation*, thereby allowing for *multiple reincarnation* in some animistic cultures.

soul splitting The division of a *spirit* before *reincarnation*, proposed as a mechanism for multiple reincarnation in *New Age metaphysics*.

spatial memory A type of *declarative memory*, the recollection of spatial relations between places, items, et cetera. *Subjects* of *reincarnation cases* demonstrate spatial memory when they find their way around unfamiliar places known to them in their *previous lives*.

spirit 1. A disembodied soul, mind, psyche, or *stream of consciousness*. 2. Often plural, viz. spirits. An entity formed of spirit (sense 1). Spirits may be either human (previously incarnate) or nonhuman.

spontaneous case In parapsychology, a *case* with apparently paranormal experiences or events that arises naturally, in the waking state or dreams, rather than being produced in the laboratory or artificially induced, for example, under hypnosis.

stem soul A *stream of consciousness* that is not yet specialized to work with any particular species of biological organism or developed into a nonhuman *spirit*. Theoretically, there are two possibilities for the origin of stem souls. There might be an unlimited number available in the universe or they might be drawn from the *background consciousness* as required.

stranger case A *reincarnation case* with a *stranger relationship*.

stranger relationship In a *reincarnation case*, a situation in which the *previous person* and his family were unknown to the *subject* and his family when the subject began to speak of his memories of the *previous life*.

stream of consciousness A stream of experiential events that follow one after the other, as in the *process metaphysics* of Alfred North Whitehead; often simply termed *consciousness*. A stream of consciousness need not include *conscious awareness* but may be limited to varying degrees of a sensual *subconscious*. This is the case with *stem souls* and with the consciousness of inanimate objects and lower forms of biological life, consistent with an evolutionary *panpsychism*.

subconscious The stratum of a duplex *consciousness* associated with the *subliminal mind*. The subconscious is conceived as a non-physical matrix that records, stores, and manages information about activities, beliefs, emotions, behavioral and psychological dispositions, and so on, providing structure to the personality. The subconscious receives and processes *psi (ESP)* inputs before presenting these to *conscious awareness* and is the source of *psi (PK)* actions. The subconscious may be organized as a hologram and distributed over the entire body rather than being associated strictly with the brain. It appears to connect with the more primitive parts of the brain and is hypothesized to have been in existence before the development of *conscious awareness*. Some forms of consciousness, such as the *background consciousness* and *stem souls*, consist solely of subconscious elements.

subject or **case subject** In a *reincarnation case*, the person with *past-life* memor*ies or other *signs of reincarnation*.

subjective illusion of significance Term introduced by skeptical psychologist Leonard Angel for the tendency to see significant relationships or patterns where no more than chance is involved. The subjective illusion of significance is an important element of the *psychosocial theory*.

subliminal mind This term and the complementary *supraliminal mind* are borrowed from F. W. H. Myers. The subliminal mind is associated with the *subconscious* as opposed to *conscious awareness*.

substance In philosophy, an underlying or foundational essence, apart from its attributes. From the metaphysical perspective, there may be a single substance underlying reality (*substance monism*) or there may be two (*substance dualism*).

substance dualism In philosophy, the idea that physical and mental things (*matter* and *mind*) are separate *substances*. Physical things are localized and extended in space and do not possess thought. Mental things have thought at their core but are not localized or extended in space.

substance monism In philosophy, the idea that there is a single primary *substance* that is prior to all others. In *materialism*, *matter* is primary; in *idealism*, *mind* is primary.

super-psi In parapsychology, a hypothetical extrasensory ability that is either more extensive or more complex than regular *psi*. Because the limits of regular psi are unknown, it is impossible to rule out the possibly of an unusually extensive psi on theoretical grounds, but that is not true of complex super-psi, for which there is no evidence. In this book, super-psi denotes a hypothetical complex psi ability involving the acquisition of information in more than a single step, often requiring the integration of multiple sources, sometimes accompanied by psychokinetic (PK) actions on human bodies or on the material world in addition.

supraliminal mind This term and the complementary *subliminal mind* are borrowed from F. W. H. Myers. The supraliminal mind is the seat of *conscious awareness* and cognition as opposed to *subconscious* processing.

synchronicity Term introduced by C. G. Jung for the expression of contents of the collective unconscious in objective physical reality, sometimes described as "meaningful coincidence."

telepathy In *parapsychology*, a type of *extrasensory perception* that involves the transmission of thoughts or feelings from another mind.

terminal lucidity A sudden return of mental clarity and memory in seriously ill patients (some suffering organic brain disorders) shortly before they die.

theistic solution A solution to the *selection problem* which holds that God or a surrogate makes or shapes the decision about where to be reborn. There are three variants of the theistic solution. In one, God manages the application of karma; in the second, God or a spirit surrogate makes the decision directly; in the third, God or a spirit surrogate assists in the decision without making the final determination (a type of *assisted reincarnation*).

theory A construct or set of principles that explain something; a general statement about the working of some domain. A theory is confirmed or refuted by testing *hypotheses* derived from it.

thought bundle A proposal by Jürgen Keil to explain the transmission of information from a *previous person* to a child *subject* of a *reincarnation case*. Thought bundles would be emitted by a body in the last stages of life, remain attached to people, objects, localities, or situations, and attach themselves to pregnant women or young children who come into contact with them.

transmigration Operationalized as the transfer of the life force (mind or *stream of consciousness*) across species lines, for example, of a human being to the body of a nonhuman animal or of a nonhuman animal to the body of a human being.

unfinished business or **continuing business** In a *reincarnation case*, something left ongoing or incomplete by a *previous person* at death.

unsolved case A *reincarnation case* in which no *previous person* has been identified.

veridical Having basis in fact. In relation to a *reincarnation case*, having memories or other elements that have been confirmed to relate to a specific *previous life* or a *previous person*.

vitalism A nature-philosophical view according to which the functioning of living beings cannot be explained by the physicochemical laws of inanimate matter alone.

walk-in In *New Age metaphysics*, a type of *postnatal reincarnation* in which a *spirit* possesses an adult body, taking the place of a "walk-out" with the permission of the latter. There is said to be a gradual absorption of the new personality by the original one, but no loss of awareness of one's life or self-identification with the walk-in. Walk-ins typically are believed to be old souls coming to help with humankind's spiritual advancement. The walk-in phenomenon is sometimes confused with *replacement reincarnation*.

written-record case A *reincarnation case* with a record of a subject's statements (and sometimes behaviors, etc.) that was made in writing before the *previous person* was identified.

xenoglossy Language not learned in the present life. Xenoglossy may be responsive, involving an interactive use of the language; recitative, involving only a rote use of an unlearned language; or passive, involving a subliminal awareness of the language that nonetheless affects one's speech performance.

References

Akolkar, V. V. (1992). Search for Sharada: Summary of a case and its investigation. *Journal of the American Society for Psychical Research, 86*, 209–247.

Aksakof, A. (1875, Aug. 13). Researches on the historical origin of the reincarnation speculations of the French spiritualists. *The Spiritualist*, pp. 74–75.

Alderink, L. J. (1981). *Creation and salvation in ancient Orphism.* University Park, PA: American Philological Association.

Alexakis, A. (2001). Was there life beyond the life beyond? Byzantine ideas on reincarnation and final restoration. *Dumbarton Oaks Papers, 55*, 155–177.

Alexander, E. (2012). *Proof of Heaven: A neurosurgeon's journey into the afterlife.* New York, NY: Simon & Schuster.

Algeo, J. (1987). *Reincarnation explained.* Wheaton, IL: Theosophical Publishing House.

Allix, S. (2017). *Lorsque j'étais quelqu'un d'autre.* Paris: Mama Éditions.

Almeder, R. (1992). *Death and personal survival.* Lanham, MD: Rowman & Littlefield.

Almeder, R. (1996). Recent responses to survival research. *Journal of Scientific Exploration, 10*, 495–517.

Almeder, R. (1997). A critique of arguments offered against reincarnation. *Journal of Scientific Exploration, 11*, 499–526.

Almeder, R. (2001). On reincarnation: A reply to Hales. *Philosophia, 28*(1–4), 347–358.

Almeder, R. (2012). The major objections from reductive materialism against belief in the existence of Cartesian mind-brain dualism. In A. Moreira-Almeida & F. S. Santos (Eds.), *Exploring frontiers of the mind–brain relationship* (pp. 17–33). New York, NY: Springer.

Alvarado, C. S. (2003). The concept of survival of bodily death and the development of parapsychology. *Journal of the Society for Psychical Research, 67*, 65–95.

Anderson, R. (2012). *Pan Am Flight 759.* [Documentary film] Royd Anderson Productions.

Anderson, R. (2013, Aug. 20). Pan Am Flight 759 crash. *Know Louisiana: The Digital Encyclopedia of Louisiana and Home of Louisiana Cultural Vistas.* Retrieved from https://www.knowlouisiana.org/entry/pan-am-flight-759-crash

Andrade, H. G. (1988). *Reencarnação no Brasil: Oito casos que sugerem renascimento.* Matão, Brazil: Clarim.

Andrade, H. G. (2010a). A case suggestive of reincarnation. In *Science and spirit* (pp. 135–184). London, UK: Roundtable. (Originally published 1980 as *A case suggestive of reincarnation: Jacira and Ronaldo.* Monograph No. 3. São Paulo: Brazilian Institute for Psychobiophysical Research.)

Andrade, H. G. (2010b). *Reborn for love: A case suggestive of reincarnation.* London, UK: Roundtable.

Andrade, H. G. (2010c). The Ruytemberg Rocha case. In *Science and spirit* (pp. 77–134). London, UK: Roundtable.

Andrade, H. G. (2011). Psi matter. In G. L. Playfair, *The flying cow: Exploring the psychic world of Brazil* (pp. 227–237). Guildford, Surry, United Kingdom: White Crow Books.

Angel, L. (1994a). Empirical evidence of reincarnation? Examining Stevenson's "most impressive" case. *Skeptical Inquirer, 18,* 481–487.

Angel, L. (1994b). *Enlightenment East and West.* Albany, NY: State University of New York Press.

Angel, L. (2002). Reincarnation all over again: Backwards reasoning in Ian Stevenson's *Reincarnation and Biology. Skeptic, 9*(3), 86–90.

Angel, L. (2008). Reincarnation: Overview of the work of Ian Stevenson (1918–2007). *The Skeptic* (UK), *21*(1), 8–14.

Angel, L. (2015). Is there adequate empirical evidence for reincarnation? In M. Martin & K. Augustine (Eds.), *The myth of an afterlife: The case against life after death* (pp. 645–654). Lanham, MD: Rowman & Littlefield.

Anthony, D. W. (2007). *The horse, the wheel, and language: How Bronze-Age riders from the Eurasian steppes shaped the modern world.* Princeton, NJ: Princeton University Press.

Appleton, N. (2010). *Jātaka stories in Theravāda Buddhism: Narrating the Bodhisatta path.* Farnham, Surrey, England: Ashgate.

Appleton, N. (2014). *Narrating karma and rebirth: Buddhist and Jain multi-life stories.* Cambridge, UK: Cambridge University Press.

Ara, M. (2008). *Eschatology in the Indo-Iranian traditions: The genesis and transformation of a doctrine.* New York, NY: Peter Lang.

Arcangel, D. (2005). *Afterlife encounters.* Charlottesville, VA: Hampton Roads.

Atmanspacher, H. (2011). Quantum approaches to consciousness. *The Stanford Encyclopedia of Philosophy* (Summer 2011 Edition). Retrieved from http://plato.stanford.edu/archives/sum2011/entries/qt-consciousness/

Atmanspacher, H., & Fach, W. (2015). Mind-matter correlations in dual-aspect monism according to Pauli and Jung. In E. F. Kelly, A. Crabtree, & P. Marshall (Eds.), *Beyond physicalism: Toward a reconciliation of science and spirituality* (pp. 195–226). Lanham, MD: Rowman & Littlefield.

Augustine, K. (2015). Introduction. In M. Martin & K. Augustine (Eds.), *The myth of an afterlife: The case against life after death* (pp. 1–47). Lanham, MD: Rowman & Littlefield.

Augustine, K., & Fishman, Y. I. (2015). The dualist's dilemma: The high cost of reconciling neuroscience with a soul. In M. Martin & K. Augustine (Eds.), *The myth of an afterlife: The case against life after death* (pp. 203–292). Lanham, MD: Rowman & Littlefield.

Ayer, A. J. (1963). *The concept of a person and other essays*. London, UK: Macmillan.

Baars, B. J. (1997). *In the theater of consciousness: The workspace of the mind*. New York, NY: Oxford University Press.

Baird, R. D. (1986). Swami Bhaktivedanta: Karma, rebirth and the personal God. In R. W. Neufeldt (Ed.), *Karma and rebirth: Post classical developments* (pp. 277–300). Albany, NY: State University of New York Press.

Baker, R. A. (1982). The effect of suggestion on past-lives regression. *American Journal of Clinical Hypnosis, 25*, 71–76.

Baker, R. A. (1992). *Hidden memories: Voices and visions from within*. Buffalo, NY: Prometheus Books.

Barclay, C. R., & Wellman, H. M. (1986). Accuracies and inaccuracies in autobiographical memories. *Journal of Memory and Language, 25*, 93–103. Retrieved from http://deepblue.lib.umich.edu/bitstream/handle/2027.42/26271/0000356.pdf?sequence=1

Barker, D. R., & Pasricha, S. K. (1979). Reincarnation cases in Fatehabad: A systematic survey in north India. *Journal of Asian and African Studies, 14*, 231–240.

Barnes, W. (2000). *Thomas Andrews, voyage into history: Titanic secrets revealed through the eyes of her builder*. Gillette, NJ: Edin Books.

Barrett, W. (1926). *Death-bed visions: The psychical experience of dying*. London, UK: Rider.

Barrington, M. R. (2002). The case of Jenny Cockell: Towards a verification of an unusual "past life" report. *Journal of the Society for Psychical Research, 66*, 106–12.

Barrington, M. R. (2005). "The case of Iris Farczády—A stolen life": Correction. *Journal of the Society for Psychical Research, 69*, 232.

Barrington, M. R., Mulacz, P., & Rivas, T. (2005). The case of Iris Farczády—A stolen life. *Journal of the Society for Psychical Research, 69*, 49–77.

Barros, J. C. S. (2004, Jan. 10). Another look at the Imad Elawar case: A review of Leonard Angel's critique of this "past life memory case study." Last modified September 5, 2012. Retrieved from http://www.criticandokardec.com.br/imad_elawar_revisited.html

Baruš, I., & Mossbridge, J. (2017). *Transcendent mind: Rethinking the science of consciousness*. Washington, DC: American Psychological Association.

Bayless, R. (1970). *Animal ghosts*. New York, NY: University Books.

Beauregard, M. (2007). Mind does really matter: Evidence from neuroimaging studies of emotional self-regulation, psychotherapy, and placebo effect. *Progress in Neurobiology, 81*, 218–236.

Beauregard, M. (2012a). *Brain wars: The scientific battle over the existence of the mind and the proof that will change the way we live our lives.* New York, NY: HarperOne.

Beauregard, M. (2012b). Functional neuroimaging studies of emotional self-regulation and spiritual experiences. In A. Moreira-Alemeda & F. Santana Santos (Eds.), *Exploring the frontiers of the mind-brain relationship* (pp. 113–139). New York, NY: Springer.

Beauregard, M., & O'Leary, D. (2008). *The spiritual brain: A neuroscientist's case for the existence of the soul.* New York, NY: HarperCollins.

Becher, E. (1917). *Die fremddienliche Zweckmäßigkeit der Pflanzengallen und die Hypothese eines überindividuellen Seelischen.* Leipzig: Veit.

Beck, B. E. F. (1983). Karma and cursing in a local epic milieu. In C. F. Keyes & E. V. Daniel (Eds.), *Karma: An anthropological inquiry* (pp. 63–81). Berkeley, CA: University of California Press.

Beck, G. L. (1996). Recycling the Atman: Reflections on the doctrine of transmigration in classical Hinduism. In S. J. Kaplan (Ed.), *Concepts of transmigration: Perspectives on reincarnation* (pp. 87–117). Lewiston, NY: Edwin Mellen Press.

Becker, C. B. (1993a). *Breaking the circle: Death and the afterlife in Buddhism.* Carbondale, IL: Southern Illinois University Press.

Becker, C. B. (1993b). *Paranormal experience and survival of death.* Albany, NY: State University of New York Press.

ben Malka, O., & Shahar, Y. (2015). *A damaged mirror: A story of memory and redemption.* St. Paul, MN: Kasva Press.

Bennett, A. (2006). Reincarnation, sect unity, and identity among the Druze. *Ethnology, 45*(2), 87–104. doi: 10.2307/4617568

Bergson, H. (1911). *Creative evolution.* New York, NY: Henry Holt.

Bergson, H. (1914–1915). Presidential address (delivered on May 28, 1913). *Proceedings of the Society for Psychical Research, 27,* 157–175.

Bering, J. M. (2006a). The folk psychology of souls. *Behavioral and Brain Sciences, 29,* 453–498.

Bering, J. M. (2006b). The cognitive psychology of belief in the supernatural. In P. McNamara (Ed.), *Where God and science meet* (vol. 1, pp. 123–134). Westport, CT: Praeger.

Bering, J. M. (2012). *The belief instinct: The psychology of souls, destiny, and the meaning of life.* New York, NY: Norton.

Bernstein, M. (1956). *The search for Bridey Murphy.* Garden City, NY: Doubleday.

Bernstein, M. (1965). *The search for Bridey Murphy* (New ed.). Garden City, NY: Doubleday.

Berzin, A. (1996). Directing rebirth: The Tibetan tulku system. *The Berzin Archives: The Buddhist Archives of Dr. Alexander Berzin.* Retrieved from http://www.berzinarchives.com/web/en/archives/approaching_buddhism/teachers/spiritual_student/directing_rebith_tibetan_tulku_system.html

Besant, A. (1892). *Reincarnation* (Theosophical Manuals No. 2). London, UK: Theosophical Publishing Society.

Besterman, T. (1968a). Belief in rebirth among the natives of Africa (including Madagascar). *Collected papers on the paranormal* (pp. 22–59). New York, NY: Garrett Publications.

Besterman, T. (1968b). Belief in rebirth of the Druses and other Syrian sects. *Collected Papers on the Paranormal* (pp. 1–11). New York, NY: Garrett Publications.

Bettis, W. (1998). Researching reincarnation: Facts or subjective experience? *Journal of Regression Therapy*, *12*(1), 54–62.

Beurlen, K. (1937). *Die stammesgeschichtlichen Grundlagen der Abstammungslehre.* Jena: Gustav Fischer.

Bishai, D. (2000). Can population growth rule out reincarnation? A model of circular migration. *Journal of Scientific Exploration*, *14*, 411–420.

Blackman, W. S. (1927). *The Fellahin of Upper Egypt: Their social and industrial life today with special reference to survivals from ancient times.* London, UK: Harrap & Co.

Blavatsky, H. P. (1877). *Isis unveiled: A master-key to the mysteries of ancient and modern science and theology* (2 vols.). New York, NY: J. W. Bouton.

Blavatsky, H. P. (1886). Theories about reincarnation and spirits. *The Path 1*(8), 232–234. Retrieved from http:www.theosociety.org/pasadena/path/v01n08p232_theories-about-reincarnation-and-spirits.htm

Blavatsky, H. P. (1888a, June). Karmic visions. *Lucifer*, *3*(15). Reprinted in *Collected Writings*, vol. 9, pp. 318–319. Retrieved from http://www.ult.org/karmicvisions.pdf

Blavatsky, H. P. (1888b). *The secret doctrine: The synthesis of science, religion, and philosophy* (2 vols.). New York, NY: Theosophical Publishing Company.

Blavatsky, H. P. (1889a). *The key to Theosophy.* New York, NY: Theosophical Publishing Company.

Blavatsky, H. P. (1889b, April). Thoughts on karma and reincarnation. *Lucifer*, *4*(20), 89–99. Reprinted in H. P. Blavatsky, *Collected Writings*, vol. 11, pp. 136–146. Retrieved from http://www.katinkahesselink.net/blavatsky/articles/v11/y1889_020.htm

Bloch, M. (1982). Death, women and power. In M. Bloch & J. Parry (Eds.), *Death and the regeneration of life* (pp. 211–230). Cambridge, UK: Cambridge University Press.

Blythe, H. (1957). *The three lives of Naomi Henry.* New York, NY: Citadel.

Bolitho, H. (2002). Metempsychosis hijacked: The curious case of Katsugorō. *Harvard Journal of Asiatic Studies*, *62*(2), 389–414. doi: 10.2307/4126603

Bond, F. B. (1924). *The company of Avalon: A study of the script of Brother Symon, sub-prior of Winchester abbey in the time of King Stephen.* London, UK: Blackwell.

Bonwick, J. (1878). *Egyptian belief and modern thought.* London, UK: Kegan Paul.

Booth, R. (1998). The relationship between archetypal medicine and past life therapy: Interdisciplinary alternatives to reductionist practice. *International Journal of Transpersonal Studies*, *17*, 7–15.

Booth, R. (2007). Past life narratives as healing stories in psychotherapy. In S. Krippner, M. Bova, L. Gray, & A. Kay (Eds.), *Healing tales: The narrative arts in spiritual traditions* (pp. 33–51). Charlottesville, VA: Puente Publications.

Bowers, K. S., & Hilgard, E. R. (1988). Some complexities in understanding memory. In H. M. Pettinati (Ed.), *Hypnosis and memory* (pp. 3–18). New York, NY: Guilford.

Bowman, C. (1997). *Children's past lives: How past life memories affect your child.* New York, NY: Bantam Books.

Bowman, C. (2001). *Return from Heaven: Beloved relatives reincarnated within your family.* New York, NY: HarperCollins.

Boyce, M. (2001). *Zoroastrians: Their religious beliefs and practices* (2nd ed.). Boston, MA: Routledge.

Bozzano, E. (1905). Animals and psychic perceptions. *Annals of Psychical Science,* *2,* 79–120.

Brac de la Perrière, B. (2015). Possession and rebirth in Burma (Myanmar). *Contemporary Buddhism, 16*(1), 61–74. doi:10.1080/14639947.2015.1013000

Bradbury, R. E. (1965). Father and senior son in Edo mortuary ritual. In M. Fortes & G. Dieterlen (Eds.), *African systems of thought* (pp. 96–121). Oxford, UK: Oxford University Press for International African Institute.

Braud, W. (2003). *Distant mental influence: Its contributions to science, healing, and human interactions* (Studies in Consciousness). Charlottesville, VA: Hampton Roads.

Braude, S. E. (1979a). *ESP and psychokinesis: A philosophical examination.* (Philosophical Monographs, Third Annual Series). Philadelphia, PA: Temple University Press.

Braude, S. E. (1979b). Evaluating the super-psi hypothesis. In G. K. Zollschan, J. F. Schumaker, & G. F. Walsh (Eds.), *Exploring the paranormal: Perspectives on belief and experience* (pp. 25–28). Dorset, UK: Prism.

Braude, S. E. (1992). Survival or super-psi? *Journal of Scientific Exploration, 6,* 127–144.

Braude, S. E. (1995). Dissociation and survival: A reappraisal of the evidence. In L. Coly & J. D. S. McMahon (Eds.), *Parapsychology and thanatology: Proceedings of an international conference held in Boston, Massachusetts, November 6–7, 1993* (pp. 208–237). New York, NY: Parapsychology Foundation.

Braude, S. E. (2003). *Immortal remains: The evidence for life after death.* Lanham, MD: Rowman & Littlefield.

Braude, S. E. (2005). Personal identity and personal survival. *Social Philosophy and Policy 22*(2), 226–249.

Braude, S. E. (2006). Memory without a trace. *European Journal of Parapsychology, 21,* 182–202.

Braude, S. E. (2007). *The gold leaf lady and other parapsychological investigations.* Chicago, IL: University of Chicago Press.

Braude, S. E. (2009). Perspectival awareness and postmortem survival. *Journal of Scientific Exploration, 23,* 195–210.

Braude, S. E. (2013). The possibility of mediumship: Philosophical considerations. In A. J. Rock (Ed.), *The survival hypothesis: Essays on mediumship* (pp. 21–39). Jefferson, NC: McFarland.

Braude, S. E. (2017). Editorial. *Journal of Scientific Exploration, 31*(2), 153–158.

Broad, C. D. (1925/1949). *The mind and its place in nature.* London, UK: Routledge and Kegan Paul.

Broad, C. D. (1958/1976). Personal identity and survival. *Newsletter of the Parapsychology Foundation.* Reprinted in J. M. O. Wheatley & H. L. Edge (Eds.), *Philosophical dimensions of parapsychology* (pp. 348–365). Springfield, IL: Charles C Thomas.

Broad, C. D. (1962). Human personality, and the question of the possibility of its survival of bodily death. *Lectures on psychical research: Incorporating the Perrot Lectures given in Cambridge University in 1959 and 1960* (pp. 387–430). London, UK: Routledge & Kegan Paul.

Brody, E. B. (1979). Review of *Cases of the reincarnation type. Volume II: Ten cases in Sri Lanka* by I. Stevenson. *Journal of the American Society for Psychical Research, 73,* 71–81.

Broughton, R. S. (2006a). Memory, emotion and the receptive psi process. *Journal of Parapsychology, 70,* 255–274.

Broughton, R. S. (2006b). Why do ghosts wear clothes? Examining the role of memory and emotion in anomalous experiences. *European Journal of Parapsychology, 21,* 148–165.

Brown, R., & Kulik, J. (1982). Flashbulb memories. In U. Neisser (Ed.), *Memory observed: Remembering in natural contexts* (pp. 23–48). New York, NY: Freeman.

Brownell, G. B. (1949). *Reincarnation* (2nd ed.). Santa Barbara, CA: Aquarian Ministry.

Bruck, M., & Cesi, S. J. (1999). The suggestibility of children's memory. *Annual Review of Psychology, 50,* 419–439.

Brüntrup, G. (2017). Emergent panpsychism. In G. Brüntrup & L. Jaskolla (Eds.), *Panpsychism: Contemporary perspectives* (pp. 48–71). Oxford, UK: Oxford University Press.

Brüntrup, G. (2018). *Philosophie des Geistes. Eine Einführung in das Leib-Seele-Problem.* Stuttgart, Germany: Kohlhammer.

Brüntrup, G., & Jaskolla, L. (Eds.) (2017). *Panpsychism: Contemporary perspectives.* Oxford, UK: Oxford University Press.

Brusewitz, G., Cherkas, L., Harris, J., & Parker, A. (2013). Exceptional experiences amongst twins. *Journal of the Society for Psychical Research, 77,* 220–235.

Buchanan, T. W. (2008). Retrieval of emotional memories. *Psychological Bulletin, 133*(5), 761–779. doi:10.1037/0033-2909.133.5.761

Bulkeley, K. (2008). *Dreaming in the world's religions: A comparative history.* New York, NY: New York University Press.

Bulliet, R. W. (1976). Naw Bahār and the survival of Iranian Buddhism. *Iran, 14,* 140–145.

Burkert, W. (1972). *Lore and science in ancient Pythagoreanism.* Cambridge, MA: Harvard University Press.

Burley, M. (2016). *Rebirth and the stream of life: A philosophical study of reincarnation, karma and ethics.* London, UK: Bloomsbury Academic.

Byrd, C. (2017). *The boy who knew too much: An astounding true story of a young boy's past-life memories.* Carlsbad, CA: Hay House.

Calkowski, M. S. (2013, Aug.). Arriving ahead of time: The *Ma 'das sprul sku* and issues of *Sprul sku* personhood. *Journal of the International Association of Tibetan Studies,* Issue 7, pp. 340–364. Retrieved from http://www.thlib.org/static/reprints/jiats/07/pdfs/calkowskiJIATS_07_2013.pdf

Cannon, A. (1953). *The power within: The re-examination of certain psychological and philosophical concepts in the light of recent investigations and discoveries.* New York, NY: Dutton.

Cardeña, E. (2005). The phenomenology of deep hypnosis: Quiescent and physically active. *International Journal of Clinical and Experimental Hypnosis, 53,* 37–59.

Carington, W. (1945). *Telepathy: An outline of its facts, theory and implications.* London, UK: Methuen.

Carman, E. M., & Carman, N. J. (2013). *Cosmic cradle: Spiritual dimensions of life before birth* (Rev. ed.). Berkeley, CA: North Atlantic Books.

Carpenter, J. C. (2012). *First sight: ESP and parapsychology in everyday life.* Lanham, MD: Rowman & Littlefield.

Carpenter, S. (1995). *Past lives: True stories of reincarnation.* London, UK: Virgin Books.

Carter, C. (2012). *Science and the afterlife experience: Evidence for the immortality of consciousness.* Rochester, VT: Inner Traditions.

Cerminara, G. (1950). *Many mansions.* New York, NY: Sloane.

Cerminara, G. (1957). *The world within.* New York, NY: Sloane.

Chadha, N. K., & Stevenson, I. (1988). Two correlates of violent death in cases of the reincarnation type. *Journal of the Society for Psychical Research, 55,* 71–79.

Chadwick, H. (1984). *Early Christian thought and the classical tradition.* New York, NY: Oxford University Press.

Chalmers, D. J. (1996). *The conscious mind: In search of a fundamental theory.* Oxford, UK: Oxford University Press.

Chalmers, D. J. (2010). *The character of consciousness.* New York, NY: Oxford University Press.

Chari, C. T. K. (1967). Reincarnation: New light on an old doctrine. *International Journal of Parapsychology, 9,* 217–222.

Chari, C. T. K. (1987). Letter to the editor. *Journal of the Society for Psychical Research, 54,* 226–228.

Chau, L. (2011, September 8). Stories of "reincarnation" in Vietnam. *Talk Vietnam.* Retrieved from http://www.talkvietnam.com/2011/09/stories-of-reincarnation -in-vietnam/

Chopra, D. (1993). *Ageless body, timeless mind: The quantum alternative to growing old.* New York, NY: Harmony Books.

Churchill, C. H. (1853). *Mount Lebanon: A ten years' residence from 1842 to 1852* (Vol. 2) (3rd ed.). London, UK: Saunders and Otley.

Churchland, P. S. (1986). *Neurophilosophy: Toward a unified science of the mind-brain.* Cambridge, MA: MIT Press.

Cobbe, F. P. (1882). *The peak in Darien, with some other inquiries touching concerns of the soul and the body: An octave of essays.* Boston, MA: Ellis.

Cockell, J. (1994). *Across time and death: A mother's search for her past life children.* New York: Simon & Schuster.

Cockell, J. (2008). *Journeys through time: Uncovering my past lives.* London, UK: Piatkus.

Cockell, J. (2017). *Past lives eternal.* Scotts Valley, CA: CreateSpace Independent Publishing Platform.

Cohen, G., & Conway, M. A. (Eds.). (2008). *Memory in the real world* (3rd ed.). New York, NY: Psychology Press.

Cohn-Sherbok, D. (1991). Reincarnation in Judaism. In A. Berger & J. Berger (Eds.), *Reincarnation: Fact or fable?* (pp. 199–207). London, UK: Aquarian Press.

Coleman, M. R., & Owen, A. M. (2009). Disorders of consciousness. *Annals of the New York Academy of Sciences, 1157,* 81–89. doi: 10.1111/j.1749–6632.2008.04121.x C 2009 A

Collomb, H. (1973). The child who leaves and returns or the death of the same child. In E. S. Anthony (Ed.), *The child in his family. Vol. 2: The impact of disease and death* (pp. 439–463). New York, NY: Wiley.

Conway, M. A. (2005). Memory and the self. *Journal of Memory and Language, 53*(4), 594–628. doi:10.1016/j.jml.2005.08.005

Cook, E. W. (1994). The subliminal consciousness: F. W. H. Myers's approach to the problem of survival. *Journal of Parapsychology, 58,* 39–58.

Cook, E. W., Greyson, B., & Stevenson, I. (1998). Do any near-death experiences provide evidence for the survival of human personality after death? Relevant features and illustrative case reports. *Journal of Scientific Exploration, 12,* 377–406.

Cook, E. W., Pasricha, S., Samararatne, G., Maung, W., & Stevenson, I. (1983a). A review and analysis of "unsolved" cases of the reincarnation type. I: Introduction and illustrative case reports. *Journal of the American Society for Psychical Research, 77,* 45–62.

Cook, E. W., Pasricha, S., Samararatne, G., Maung, W., & Stevenson, I. (1983b). A review and analysis of "unsolved" cases of the reincarnation type. II: Comparison of features of solved and unsolved cases. *Journal of the American Society for Psychical Research, 77,* 115–135.

Cooper, I. S. (1920). *Reincarnation: The hope of the world.* Los Angeles, CA: Theosophical Publishing House.

Cousins, N. (1981). *Anatomy of an illness: As perceived by the patient.* Toronto, ON: Bantam Books.

Crabtree, A. (1985). *Multiple man: The enigma of possession and multiple personality.* New York, NY: HarperCollins

Cumont, F. (1922). *After life in Roman paganism.* New Haven, CT: Yale University Press.

Dacqué, E. (1926). *Natur und Seele.* München: Oldenbourg.

Dacqué, E. (1935). *Organische Morphologie und Paläontologie.* Berlin, Germany: Borntraeger.

Daie, N., Witztum, E., Mark, M., & Rabinowitz, S. (1992). The belief in the transmigration of souls: Psychotherapy of a Druze patient with severe anxiety reaction. *British Journal of Medical Psychology, 65*(2), 119–130.

Dalai Lama, H. H. the (1962). *My land and my people.* New York, NY: McGraw-Hill.

Dall, W. H. (1870). *Alaska and its resources.* Boston, MA: Lee and Shephard.

318   *References*

Darwin, C. (1859). *On the origin of species by means of natural selection*. London, UK: John Murray.

Darwin, C. (1868). *Variation of animals and plants under domestication* (2 vols.). London, UK: John Murray.

David-Neel, A. (1932/1965). *Magic and mystery in Tibet*. New Hyde Park, NY: University Books.

Davidson, J. R. T., Connor, K. M., & Lee, L.-C. (2005). Beliefs in karma and reincarnation among survivors of violent trauma: A community survey. *Social Psychiatry and Psychiatric Epistemology*, *40*(2), 120–125.

Davis, E. W. (2008). Between forests and families: A remembered past life. In A. Kent & D. P. Chandler (Eds.), *People of virtue: Reconfiguring religion, power and moral order in Cambodia today*. Copenhagen: Nordic Institute of Asian Studies.

Davis, E. W. (2015). Kinship beyond death: Ambiguous relations and autonomous children in Cambodian Buddhism. *Contemporary Buddhism*, *16*(1). doi:10.1080/14639947.2015.1008953

Davis, W. D. (1971). *Societal complexity and the nature of primitive man's conception of the supernatural* (Ph.D. dissertation). University of North Carolina, Chapel Hill. Ann Arbor, MI: University Microfilms.

Dawkins, R. (2010). *The greatest show on Earth: The evidence for evolution*. London, UK: Transworld Publishers.

Dawkins, R. (2016). *The selfish gene* (40th anniversary edition). Oxford, UK: Oxford University Press.

Dayal, P. (1988). A case of soul transference (parkaya pravesh). In *Proceedings of All India Conference on Reincarnation* (March 28–29, 1987). Allahabad: Foundation for Reincarnation and Spiritual Research.

De Groot, J. J. M. (1901). *The religious system of China*, Vol. 4. Leiden, the Netherlands: Brill.

de Laguna, F. (1972). *Under Mount Saint Elias: The history and culture of the Yakutat Tlingit*. (Smithsonian Contributions to Anthropology, Vol. 17.) Washington, DC: Smithsonian Institution.

DeConick, A. D. (2016). *The Gnostic new age: How a countercultural spirituality revolutionized religion from antiquity to today*. New York, NY: Columbia University Press.

Delanne, G. (1924). *Documents pour sevir a l'étude de la réincarnation*. Paris: Éditions de la B.P.S.

Delarrey, M. (1955). Une réincaranation annoncée et verificée. *Revue métapsychique*, *1*(2), 41–46.

DeMers, J. (1982, July 17). The final flight of Pan Am 759. UPI Archives. [Web post.] Retrieved from https://www.upi.com/Archives/1982/07/17/The-final-flight-of-Pan-Am-759/8033395726400/

Dennett, D. (1982). *Consciousness explained*. Boston, MA: Little, Brown & Co.

Descartes, R. (1641/2000). Meditations on first philosophy. In R. Ariew (Ed.), *René Descartes: Philosophical essays and correspondence* (pp. 97–141). Indianapolis, IN: Hackett.

Dethlefsen, T. (1977). *Voices from other lives: Reincarnation as a source of healing*. New York, NY: M. Evans.

Deutsch, E. (1973). *Advaita Vedānta: A philosophical reconstruction.* Honolulu, HI: University of Hawaii Press.

Dhiman, K. K. (2002, Jan. 12). Back from the land of no return. *The Tribune* (Chandigarh, India) online edition. Retrieved from https://www.tribuneindia. com/2002/20020112/windows/main1.htm

Dhiman, K. K. (2002, Dec. 28). Neetu's life after death. *The Tribune* (Chandigarh, India) online edition. Retrieved from http://www.tribuneindia.com/2002/20021228 /windows/main1.htm

Dias, B. G., & Ressler, K. J. (2014). Parental olfactory experience influences behavior and neural structure in subsequent generations. *Nature Neuroscience, 17*, 89–96.

Dillon, M., & Chadwick, N. K. (2003). *The Celtic realms: The history and the culture of the Celtic peoples from pre-history to the Norman invasion.* London, UK: Phoenix Press.

Dirix, C. E., Nijhuis, J. G., Jongsma, H. W., & Hornstra, G. (2009, July–Aug.). Aspects of fetal learning and memory. *Child Development, 80*, 1251–1258. doi:10.1111/j.1467–8624.2009.01329.x

Ditfurth, H. von (1981). *The origins of life: Evolution as creation.* San Francisco, CA: Harper & Row.

Doidge, N. (2006). *The brain that changes itself: Stories of personal triumph from the frontiers of brain science.* New York, NY: Viking Adult.

Donahoe, J. J. (1979). *Enigma: Psychology, the paranormal and self-transformation.* Oakland, CA: Bench Press.

Dossey, L. (2008, Sept.). Transplants, cellular memory, and reincarnation. *Explore, 4*(5), 285–293. doi:https://doi.org/10.1016/j.explore.2008.07.001

Driesch, H. (1922). *Geschichte des Vitalismus.* Leipzig: Ambrosius.

Driesch, H. (1926). Presidential address: Psychical research and established science. *Proceedings of the Society for Psychical Research, 36*, 171–186.

Driesch, H. (1928). *Philosophie des Organischen.* Leipzig: Quelle & Meyer.

Driesch, H. (1931). Das Wesen des Organismus. In H. Driesch & H. Woltereck (Eds.), *Das Lebensproblem* (pp. 384–450). Leipzig: Von Quelle & Meyer.

Driesch, H. (1933). *Psychical research: The science of the super-normal.* London, UK: Bell & Sons.

Driesch, H. (1938). *Alltagsrätsel des Seelenlebens.* Stuttgart, Germany: Deutsche Verlags-Anstalt.

Driesch, H. (1939). Vitalism as a bridge to psychical research. *Journal of the American Society for Psychical Research, 33*, 129–133.

Ducasse, C. J. (1961). *A critical examination of the belief in a life after death.* Springfield, IL: Charles C Thomas.

Durant, R. (Ed.) (1968). *Totality-man.* London, UK: Regency Press.

Durkheim, E. (1965 [1912]). *The elementary forms of the religious life.* New York: Free Press.

Dwairy, M. (2006). The psychosocial function of reincarnation among Druze in Israel. *Culture, Medicine and Psychiatry, 30*, 29–53.

Dwyan, J., & Bowers, K. (1983). The use of hypnosis to enhance recall. *Science, 222*, 184–185.

Dyer, W. W., & Garnes, D. (2015). *Memories of heaven: Children's astounding recollections of the time before they came to Earth*. Carlsbad, CA: Hay House.

East, J. N. (1960). *Eternal quest*. London, UK: Psychic Press.

Edelmann, J., & Bernet, W. (2007). Setting criteria for ideal reincarnation research. *Journal of Consciousness Studies, 14*, 92–101.

Edelstein, S. J. (1986). *The sickled cell: From myths to molecules*. Cambridge, MA: Harvard University Press.

Edwards, J., Peres, J., Monti, D. A., & Newburg, A. B. (2012). The neurobiological correlations of meditation and mindfulness. In A. Moreira-Almeida & F. S. Santos (Eds.), *Exploring frontiers of the mind-brain relationship* (pp. 97–112). New York, NY: Springer.

Edwards, P. (1996). *Reincarnation: A critical examination*. Amherst, NY: Prometheus Books.

Eichenbaum, H., & Cohen, N. J. (Eds.) (2001). *From conditioning to conscious recollection: Memory systems of the brain*. New York, NY: Oxford University Press.

Eigen, M. (1987). *Stufen zum Leben*. München: Piper.

Eisenbeiss, W., & Hassler, D. (2006). An assessment of ostensible communications with a grandmaster as evidence for survival. *Journal of the Society for Psychical Research, 70*(2), 129–147.

Ellenberger, H. (1970). *The discovery of the unconscious*. New York: Basic Books.

Ellis, D. (2003). A case suggestive of reincarnation of cats? *Paranormal Review, 28*, 23.

Ellis, P. (2011). *Panpsychism: The philosophy of the sensuous cosmos*. Alresford, Hants, UK: O-Books

Ellwood, G. F. (1971). *Psychic visits to the past: An exploration of retrocognition*. New York: New American Library.

Ellwood, R. S. (1996). Obligatory pilgrimage: Reincarnation in the Theosophical tradition. In S. J. Kaplan (Ed.), *Concepts of transmigration: Perspectives on reincarnation* (pp. 189–202). Lewiston, NY: Edwin Mellen Press.

Emmons, G. T. (1991). *The Tlingit Indians*. Edited with additions by Frederica de Laguna. Seattle, WA: University of Washington Press.

Empson, R. M. (2007). Enlivened memories: Recalling absence and loss in Mongolia. In J. Carsten (Ed.), *Ghosts of memory: Essays on remembrance and relatedness* (pp. 58–82). Malden, MA: Blackwell.

Empson, R. M. (2011). Housing others in rebirths. In *Harnessing fortune: Personhood, memory, and place in Mongolia* (pp. 205–232). New York, NY: Oxford University Press.

Epperson, M. (2004). *Quantum mechanics and the philosophy of Alfred North Whitehead* (American Philosophy, No. 14). New York, NY: Fordham University Press

Evans-Wentz, W. Y. (1911/2007). *The fairy-faith in Celtic countries*. London, UK: Forgotten Books.

Evans-Wentz, W. Y. (Ed.). (1957). *The Tibetan book of the dead* (3rd ed.). Oxford, UK: Oxford University Press.

Eylon, D. R. (2003). *Reincarnation in Jewish mysticism and gnosticism* (Jewish Studies Series, Vol. 25). Lewiston, NY: The Edwin Mellen Press.

References   321

Fabre, J. H. (1950). *Aus der Wunderwelt der Instinkte*. Meisenheim: Westkulturverlag Anton Hain.

Feather, S. R., with Schmicker, M. (2005). *The gift: ESP, the extraordinary experiences of ordinary people*. New York, NY: St. Martin's Press.

Fenwick, P., & Fenwick, E. (1999). *Past lives: An investigation into reincarnation memories*. New York: Berkeley Books.

Fielding[-Hall], H. (1898). *The soul of a people*. London, UK: Bentley and Son.

Fiore, E. (1978). *You have been here before: A psychologist looks at past lives*. New York, NY: Ballantine.

Flew, A. (1972/1976). Is there a case for disembodied survival? *Journal of the American Society for Psychical Research, 66*, 129–44. Reprinted in J. M. O. Wheatley & H. L. Edge (Eds.), *Philosophical dimensions of parapsychology* (pp. 330–347). Springfield, IL: Charles C Thomas.

Flournoy, T. (1963). *From India to the planet Mars: A study of a case of somnambulism with glossolalia* (New ed.). New Hyde Park, NY: University Books.

Foltz, R. (2010). *Religions of the Silk Road: Premodern patterns of globalization* (2nd ed.). New York, NY: Palgrave Macmillan.

Foster, M. (1992, July 12). Vacant lot is reminder of plane crash. Associated Press. Retrieved from http://articles.latimes.com/1992–07–12/news/mn–4128_1_vacant-lot

Fox, M. (2007, Feb. 18). Ian Stevenson dies at 88; studied claims of past lives [web post]. Retrieved from https://www.nytimes.com/2007/02/18/health/psychology/18stevenson.html

Freedman, T. B. (2002). *Soul echoes: The healing power of past-life therapy*. New York, NY: Citadel Press.

Friederichs, K. (1955). *Die Selbstgestaltung des Lebendigen*. München: Ernst Reinhardt.

Fürer-Haimendorf, C. von. (1953). The after-life in Indian tribal belief. *Journal of the Royal Anthropological Institute, 83*, 37–49.

Furst, J. (1971). *The return of Frances Willard: Her case for reincarnation*. New York, NY: Coward, McCann & Geoghegan.

Gadit, A. A. (2009). Myth of reincarnation: A challenge for the mental health profession. *Journal of Medical Ethics, 35*, 91.

Gamble, R. (2018). *Reincarnation in Tibetan Buddhism: The Third Karmapa and the invention of a tradition*. New York, NY: Oxford University Press.

Garrett, W. G. (2005). *Bad karma: Thinking twice about the social consequences of reincarnation theory*. Lanham, MD: University Press of America.

Gauld, A. (1961). The "super-ESP" hypothesis. *Proceedings of the Society for Psychical Research, 53*, 226–46.

Gauld, A. (1982). *Mediumship and survival: A century of investigations*. London, UK: Heinemann.

Gauld, A. (2007). Memory. In E. F. Kelly, E. W. Kelly, A. Crabtree, A. Gauld, M. Grosso, & B. Greyson, *Irreducible mind: Toward a psychology for the 21st century* (pp. 241–300). Lanham, MD: Rowman & Littlefield.

Geley, G. (1925). *From the unconscious to the conscious*. Glasgow, UK: Collins.

Geraerts E. (2012). Cognitive underpinnings of recovered memories of childhood abuse. In R. F. Belli (Ed.), *Memory and motivation: A reappraisal of the recovered/ false memory debate*. (Nebraska Symposium on Motivation, vol. 58, pp. 175–191). Lincoln, NE: University of Nebraska Press.

Gershom, Y. (1992). *Beyond the ashes: Cases of reincarnation from the Holocaust*. Virginia Beach, VA: A. R. E. Press.

Gershom, Y. (Ed.) (1996). *From ashes to healing: Mystical encounters with the Holocaust*. Virginia Beach, VA: A. R. E. Press.

Gershom, Y. (1999). Anne Frank returned? The case of Barbro Karlen. Retrieved from https://web.archive.org/web/20080218134906/http://www.pinenet.com/roos ter/karlen–1.html

Givens, T. L. (2010). *When souls had wings: Pre-mortal existence in Western thought*. New York, NY: Oxford University Press.

Göcke, B. P. (Ed.) (2012). *After physicalism*. Notre Dame, IN: University of Notre Dame Press.

Godwin, M. (1995). *The lucid dreamer*. Shaftesbury, UK: Element Books.

Goldberg, B. (1982). *Past lives, future lives: Accounts of regression and progression through hypnosis*. Rockville, MD: Borgo Press.

Goldberg, B. (1994). *The search for Grace: A documented case of murder and reincarnation*. Sedona, AZ: In Print Publishing.

Gorham, G. (2011). How Newton solved the mind-body problem. *History of Philosophy Quarterly*, *28*(1), 21–44.

Gottlieb, A. (2004). Spiritual Beng babies. *The afterlife is where we come from: The culture of infancy in West Africa* (pp. 87–104). Chicago, IL: University of Chicago Press.

Goulet, J-G. A. (1994). Reincarnation as a fact of life among the contemporary Dene Tha. In A. Mills & R. Slobodin (Eds.), *Amerindian rebirth: Reincarnation belief among North American Indians and Inuit* (pp. 156–176). Toronto, ON: University of Toronto Press.

Goulet, J-G. A. (1996). The "berdache"/"two-spirit": A comparison of anthropological and native constructions of gendered identities among the Northern Athapaskans. *Journal of the Royal Anthropological Institute*, *2*, 683–701.

Goulet, J-G. A. (1997). The Northern Athapaskan "berdache" reconsidered: On reading more than there is in the ethnographic record. In S.-E Jacobs, W. Thomas, & S. Lang (Eds.), *Two-spirit people: Native American gender identity, sexuality, and spirituality* (pp. 45–67). Urbana, IL: University of Illinois Press.

Goulet, J.-G. A. (1998). Searching for a womb. *Ways of knowing: Experience, knowledge and power among the Dene Tha* (pp. 167–192). Lincoln, NE: University of Nebraska Press.

Govinda, A. (1966). *The way of the white clouds: A Buddhist pilgrim in Tibet*. London, UK: Hutchinson.

Gravitz, M. (2002). The Search for Bridey Murphy: Implications for modern hypnosis. *American Journal of Clinical Hypnosis*, *45*, 3–10. doi:10.1080/00029157.200 2.10403492

Green, C., & McCreery, C. (1975). *Apparitions*. London, UK: Hamish Hamilton.

Greyson, B. (2000). Dissociation in people who have near-death experiences: Out of their bodies or out of their minds? *Lancet, 355*, 460–463.

Greyson, B. (2010a). Implications of near-death experiences for a postmaterialist psychology. *Psychology of Religion and Spirituality, 2*(1), 37–45.

Greyson, B. (2010b). Seeing dead persons not known to have died: "Peak in Darien" experiences. *Anthropology and Humanism, 35*, 159–171.

Griffin, D. R. (1997). *Parapsychology, philosophy, and spirituality: A postmodern exploration*. Albany, NY: State University of New York Press.

Griffin, D. R. (1998). *Unsnarling the world knot: Consciousness, freedom and the mind-body problem*. Berkeley, CA: University of California Press.

Grof, S. (1985). *Beyond the brain: Birth, death and transcendence in psychotherapy*. Albany, NY: State University of New York.

Grof, S. (2009). Evidence for the Akashic field from modern consciousness research. In E. Laszlo (Ed.), *The Akashic experience: Science and the cosmic memory field* (pp. 193–211). Rochester, VT: Inner Traditions.

Grosso, M. (2004). *Experiencing the next world now*. New York: Paraview Pocket Books.

Grosso, M. (2015). The "transmission" model of mind and body: A brief history. In E. F. Kelly, A. Crabtree, & P. Marshall (Eds.), *Beyond physicalism: Toward a reconciliation of science and spirituality* (pp. 79–113). Lanham, MD: Rowman & Littlefield.

Growse, F. W. (Trans.). (1937). *The Rámáyana of Tulsi Dás* (7th ed.). Allahabad: Ram Narain Lal.

Grubbs, A. (2006). *Chosen to believe*. Jonesboro, GA: Pink Elephant Press.

Guemple, L. (1994). Born again pagans: The Inuit cycle of spirits. In A. Mills & R. Slobodin (Eds.), *Amerindian rebirth: Reincarnation belief among North American Indians and Inuit* (pp. 107–122). Toronto, ON: University of Toronto Press.

Guirdham, A. (1970). *The Cathars and reincarnation*. Suffolk, UK: Neville Spearman.

Guirdham, A. (1974). *We are one another: A record of group reincarnation*. St. Helier, Jersey, United Kingdom: Neville Spearman.

Guirdham, A. (1976). *The lake and the castle*. Jersey, UK: Neville Spearman.

Gupta, L. D., Sharma, N. R., & Mathur, T. C. (1936). *An inquiry into the case of Shanti Devi*. New Delhi: International Aryan League.

Gurney, E., Myers, F. W. H., & Podmore, F. (1886). *Phantasms of the living* (2 vols). London, UK: Rooms of the Society for Psychical Research.

Halabi, R., & Horenczyk, G. (2019). Reincarnation beliefs among Israeli Druze and the construction of a hard primordial identity. *Death Studies*. doi: 10.1080/07481187.2019.1572674

Hales, S. D. (2001). Reincarnation redux. *Philosophia: Philosophical Quarterly of Israel, 28*, 359–367.

Hall, M. P. (1946). *Reincarnation: The cycle of necessity* (3rd ed.). Los Angeles, CA: Philosophical Research Society.

Hallett, E. (2002). *Soul trek: Meeting our children on the way to birth*. Hamilton, MT: Light Hearts Publishing.

Hamerton-Kelly, R. G. (1973). *Pre-existence, wisdom, and the Son of Man.* Cambridge, UK: Cambridge University Press.

Hammons, C. (2017). "The old me." In L. Kean, *Surviving death: A journalist investigates evidence for an afterlife* (pp. 54–66). New York, NY: Penguin Random House.

Haraldsson, E. (1991). Children claiming past life memories: Four cases in Sri Lanka. *Journal of Scientific Exploration, 5,* 233–262.

Haraldsson, E. (1995). Personality and abilities of children claiming previous-life memories. *Journal of Nervous and Mental Disease, 183,* 445–551.

Haraldsson, E. (1997). A psychological comparison between ordinary children and those who claim previous-life memories. *Journal of Scientific Exploration, 11,* 323–335.

Haraldsson, E. (2000a). Birthmarks and claims of previous-life memories: I. The case of Purnima Ekanayake. *Journal of the Society for Psychical Research, 64,* 16–25.

Haraldsson, E. (2000b). Birthmarks and claims of previous-life memories: II. The case of Chatura Karunaratne. *Journal of the Society for Psychical Research, 64,* 82–92.

Haraldsson, E. (2003). Children who speak of past-life experiences: Is there a psychological explanation? *Psychology and Psychotherapy, 76,* 55–67.

Haraldsson, E. (2008). Persistence of past-life memories: Study of adults who claimed in their childhood to remember a past life. *Journal of Scientific Exploration, 19,* 385–393.

Haraldsson, E. (2009). Alleged encounters with the dead: The importance of violent death in 335 new cases. *Journal of Parapsychology, 73,* 91–188.

Haraldsson, E. (2012a). Cases of the reincarnation type and the mind-brain relationship. In A. Moreira-Almeida & F. S. Santos (Eds.), *Exploring frontiers of the mind-brain relationship* (pp. 215–231). New York, NY: Springer.

Haraldsson, E. (2012b). *The departed among the living: An investigative study of afterlife encounters.* Guildford, Surrey, UK: White Crow Press.

Haraldsson, E., & Abu-Izzeddin, M. (2004). Three randomly selected Lebanese cases of children who claim memories of a previous life. *Journal of the Society for Psychical Research, 68*(2), 65–85.

Haraldsson, E., & Abu-Izzeddin, M. (2012). Persistence of "past-life" memories in adults who, in their childhood, claimed memories of a past life. *Journal of Nervous and Mental Disease, 200,* 985–989.

Haraldsson, E., Fowler, P. C., & Periyannanpillai, V. (2000). Psychological characteristics of children who speak of a previous life: A further field study in Sri Lanka. *Transcultural Psychiatry, 37,* 525–544.

Haraldsson, E., & Gissuarson, L. R. (2015). *Indridi Indridason: The Icelandic physical medium.* Hove, UK: White Crow Books.

Haraldsson, E., & Matlock, J. G. (2016). *I saw a light and came here: Children's experiences of reincarnation.* Hove, UK: White Crow Books.

Haraldsson, E., & Samararatne, G. (1999). Children who speak of a previous life as a Buddhist monk: Three new cases. *Journal of the Society for Psychical Research, 63,* 268–291.

Haraldsson, E., & Stevenson, I. (1975a). A communicator of the "drop-in" type in Iceland: The case of Gudni Magnusson. *Journal of the American Society for Psychical Research, 69,* 245–261.

Haraldsson, E., & Stevenson, I. (1975b). A communicator of the "drop-in" type in Iceland: The case of Runolfur Runolfsson. *Journal of the American Society for Psychical Research, 69,* 33–59.

Hardy, A. (1965). *The living stream: A restatement of evolution theory and its relation to the spirit of man.* London, UK: Collins.

Harris, M. (1986a). Are "past life" regressions evidence of reincarnation? *Free Inquiry, 6*(4), 18–24.

Harris, M. (1986b). *Investigating the unexplained.* Buffalo, NY: Prometheus Books.

Harrison, C. (1925). *Ancient warriors of the western Pacific.* London, UK: H. F. & G. Witherby.

Harrison, P., & Harrison, M. (1991). *The children that time forgot.* (First published 1983 as *Life before birth.*) New York, NY: Berkley Books.

Hart, H. (1959). *The enigma of survival: The case for and against an after life.* Springfield, IL: Charles C Thomas.

Hart, H., & Collaborators. (1956). Six theories about apparitions. *Proceedings of the Society for Psychical Research, 50,* 153–239.

Hart, H., & Hart, E. B. (1932–1933). Visions and apparitions collectively and reciprocally perceived. *Proceedings of the Society for Psychical Research, 41,* 205–249.

Hartmann, E. von. (1884). *Philosophy of the unconscious* (3 vols.). London, UK: Trübner.

Hartmann, E. von. (1924). *Philosophie des Schönen.* Berlin, Germany: Wegweiser-Verlag.

Hassler, D. (2013). A new European case of the reincarnation type. *Journal of the Society for Psychical Research, 77,* 19–31.

Hassler, D. (2015). *Geh' zurück in eine Zeit . . . Indizienbeweise für ein Leben nach dem Tod und die Wiedergeburt* (2 vols.). Aachen, Germany: Shaker Media.

Head, J., & Cranston, S. L. (1967). *Reincarnation in world thought.* New York, NY: Julian Press.

Heald, M. (1997). *Destiny: The true story of one man's journey through life, death and rebirth.* Shaftesbury, Dorset, UK: Element Books.

Hearn, L. (1897). *Gleanings in Buddha-fields: Studies of hand and soul in the Far East.* Boston, MA: Houghton Mifflin.

Heilman, K. M., & Valenstein, E. (2011). *Clinical neuropsychology* (5th ed). New York, NY: Oxford University Press.

Heim, B. (1988). *Postmortale Zustände? Die televariate Area integraler Weltstrukturen.* Innsbruck: Resch.

Hepper, P. G. (1996). Fetal memory: Does it exist? What does it do? *Acta Paediatrics, 416,* 16–20.

Herbert, N. (1993). *Elemental mind: Human consciousness and the new physics.* New York, NY: Dutton.

Hess, D. J. (1991). *Spirits and scientists: Ideology, Spiritism, and Brazilian culture.* University Park, PA: Pennsylvania State University Press.

Hess, D. J. (1994). *Samba in the night: Spiritism in Brazil.* New York, NY: Columbia University Press.

Hick, J. H. (1976). *Death and eternal life.* New York, NY: Harper & Row.

Hilgard, E. R. (1977). *Divided consciousness: Multiple controls in human thought and action.* New York, NY: Wiley.

Hill, J. A. (1929). Some reincarnationist automatic scripts. *Proceedings of the Society for Psychical Research, 38,* 375–387.

Hinze, S. (1995). *Coming from the light.* Springville, UT: Cedar Fort Publishing.

Hodgson, R., Netherclift, F. G., & Sidgwick, Mrs. H. (1885). Report of the committee appointed to investigate phenomena connected with the Theosophical Society. *Proceedings of the Society for Psychical Research, 3,* 201–400.

Holden, J. M. (2009). Veridical perception in near-death experiences. In J. M. Holden, B. Greyson, & D. James (Eds.), *The handbook of near-death experiences: Thirty years of investigation* (pp. 185–211). Santa Barbara, CA: ABC Clio.

Holland, A. C., & Kensinger, E. A. (2010). Emotion and autobiographical memory. *Physics of Life Reviews, 7*(1), 88–131.doi: 10.1016/j.plrev.2010.01.006

Hossenfelder, S. (2018). *Lost in math: How beauty leads physics astray.* New York, NY: Basic Books.

Hufford, D. J. (1982). *The terror that comes in the night: An experience-centered study of supernatural assault traditions.* Philadelphia, PA: University of Pennsylvania Press.

Hulme, A. J. H., & Wood, F. H. (1936). *Ancient Egypt speaks: A miracle of "tongues."* London, UK: Rider.

Hultkrantz, Å. (1953). *Conceptions of the soul among North American Indians: A study in religious ethnology.* Stockholm, Sweden: Ethnographical Museum of Sweden.

Hyman, I. E., Jr., & Loftus, E. F. (1998). Errors in autobiographical memory. *Clinical Psychology Review, 18,* 933–947.

Hyslop, J. H. (1909). A case of veridical hallucinations. *Proceedings of the American Society for Psychical Research, 3,* 1–469.

Iancu, I., Spivak, B., Mester, R., & Weizman, A. (1988). Belief in transmigration of the soul and psychopathology in Israeli Druze: A culture-sensitive psychotherapeutic approach. *Psychopathology, 31*(1), 52–58.

Ikegawa, A. (2005). Investigation by questionnaire regarding fetal/infant memory in the womb and/or at birth. *Journal of Prenatal and Perinatal Psychology and Health, 20*(2), 121–133.

In memory of Barbara Schultz. (2010, Nov. 21). Dignity Memorial [web site]. Retrieved from http://obits.dignitymemorial.com/dignity-memorial/obituary. aspx?n=Barbara-Schultz&lc=7863&pid=146777780&mid=4446008

Irwin, H. J., & Watt, C. A. (2007). *An introduction to parapsychology* (5th ed.). Jefferson, NC: McFarland.

Irwin, L. (2017a). Reincarnation in America: A brief history. *Religions, 8*(222). doi:10.3390/rel8100222

Irwin, L. (2017b). *Reincarnation in America: An esoteric history.* Lanham, MD: Lexington Books.

Iverson, J. (1976). *More lives than one? The evidence of the remarkable Bloxham Tapes.* London, UK: Souvenir Press.

Jablonka, E., & Lamb, M. J. (1995). *Epigenetic inheritance and evolution: The Lamarckian dimension.* Oxford, UK: Oxford University Press.

Jablonka, E., & Lamb, M. J. (2006). *Evolution in four dimensions.* Cambridge, MA: MIT Press.

Jablonka, E., & Raz, G. (2009). Transgenerational epigenetic inheritance: Prevalence, mechanisms, and implications for the study of heredity and evolution. *Quarterly Review of Biology, 84,* 131–176.

Jacobson, N. O. (1974). *Life without death? On parapsychology, mysticism and the question of survival.* New York, NY: Delacorte Press/Seymour Lawrence.

James, R. (1995). Verifiable past lives: Readily available? *Journal of Regression Therapy, 9*(1), 7–12.

James, W. (1898/1960). Human immortality: Two supposed objections to the doctrine. In G. Murphy & R. L. Ballou (Eds.), *William James on psychical research* (pp. 279–308). New York, NY: Viking.

Jay, C. E. (1977). *Gretchen, I am.* New York, NY: Wyden Books.

Jaymes, C. (2017). *A life by request: A walk-in soul's journey from Earth to Heaven, and back again.* East Greenwich, RI: Geronimo Publishing.

Jefferson, W. (2008). *Reincarnation beliefs of North American Indians: Soul journeys, metamorphoses and near-death experiences.* Summertown, TN: Native Voices.

Johnston, S. I. (2013). The myth of Dionysius. In F. Graf & S. I. Johnston (Eds.), *Ritual texts for the afterlife: Orpheus and the Bacchic gold tablets* (2nd ed.) (pp. 66–93). London, UK: Routledge.

Jones, L. F. (1914). *A Study of the Thlingets of Alaska.* New York, NY: Revell.

Joshi, S. (2011, Apr. 21). Memory transference in organ transplant recipients. *NAMAH: Journal of New Approaches to Medicine and Health, 19*(1). Retrieved from https://www.namahjournal.com/doc/Actual/Memory-transference-in-organ-transplant-recipients-vol–19-iss–1.html

Jung, C. G. (1959/1981). *The archetypes and the collective unconscious* (Collected Works of C. G. Jung, Vol. 9, Part 1) (2nd ed.). Translated by F. C. Hull. Princeton, NJ: Princeton University Press.

Jung, C. G. (1969). *The archetypes and the collective unconscious.* Princeton, NJ: Princeton University Press.

Jung, C. G. (1973). *Synchronicity: An acausal connecting principle.* (Collected Works of C. G. Jung, Vol. 8, Part 1) (2nd ed.). Translated by F. C. Hull. Princeton, NJ: Princeton University Press.

Kahn, C. H. (2001). *Pythagoras and the Pythagoreans.* Indianapolis, IN: Hackett.

Kammerer, P. (1924). *The inheritance of acquired characteristics.* New York, NY: Boni & Liveright.

Kampman, R. (1976). Hypnotically induced multiple personality: An experimental study. *International Journal of Clinical and Experimental Hypnosis, 24,* 215–227.

Kampman, R., & Hirvenoja, R. (1978). Dynamic relation of the secondary personality induced by hypnosis to the present personality. In F. H. Frankel & H. S. Zamansky (Eds.), *Hypnosis at its bicentennial* (pp. 183–188). New York, NY: Plenum.

Kan, S. (1989). *Symbolic immortality: The Tlingit potlatch of the nineteenth century* (Smithsonian Series in Ethnographic Inquiry). Washington, DC: Smithsonian Institution Press.

Kaplan, A. (1979). Introduction. In *The Bahir*, translated by A. Kaplan. York Beach, ME: Samuel Weiser.

Kardec, A. (1986). *The mediums' book*. Translated by A. Blackwell. Brasilia, Brazil: Federação Espírita Brasileira.

Kardec, A. (1996). *The spirits' book*. Translated by A. Blackwell. Brasilia, Brazil: Federação Espírita Brasileira.

Kardec, A. (2003). *Heaven and Hell: Divine justice validated in a plurality of existences* (New English ed.). Translated by A. Blackwell. New York: Spiritist Alliance for Books.

Karlén, B. (2000). *And the wolves howled: Fragments of two lifetimes*. London, UK: Clairview.

Kastrup, B. (2014). *Why materialism is baloney: How true skeptics know there is no death and fathom answers to life, the universe, and everything*. Winchester, UK: Iff Books.

Kastrup, B. (2015). *Brief peeks beyond: Critical essays on metaphysics, neuroscience, free will, skepticism and culture*. Alresford, UK: John Hunt Publishing.

Kean, L. (2017). *Surviving death: A journalist investigates evidence for an afterlife*. New York, NY: Penguin Random House.

Kear, L. (1999). *We're here: An investigation into gay reincarnation*. Atlanta, GA: Brookhaven.

Keene, J. J. (2003). *Someone else's yesterday: The Confederate general and Connecticut Yankee, a past life revealed*. Nevada City, CA: New Dolphin Publishing.

Keil, [H. H.] J. (1991). New cases in Burma, Thailand, and Turkey: A limited field study replication of some aspects of Ian Stevenson's research. *Journal of Scientific Exploration, 5*, 27–59.

Keil, [H. H.] J. (1996). Cases of the reincarnation type: An evaluation of some indirect evidence with examples of "silent" cases. *Journal of Scientific Exploration, 10*, 467–485.

Keil, [H. H.] J. (2010a). A case of the reincarnation type in Turkey suggesting strong paranormal information involvements. *Journal of Scientific Exploration, 24*, 71–77.

Keil, [H. H.] J. (2010b). Questions of the reincarnation type. *Journal of Scientific Exploration, 24*, 79–99.

Keil, [H. H.] J. (2011). Reply to the Nahm and Hassler commentary on Jürgen Keil's paper "Questions of the Reincarnation Type." *Journal of Scientific Exploration, 25*(2), 319–320.

Keil, [H. H.] J., & Stevenson, I. (1999). Do cases of the reincarnation type show similar features over many years? A study of Turkish cases a generation apart. *Journal of Scientific Exploration, 13*(2), 189–198.

Keil, H. H. J., & Tucker, J. B. (2005). Children who claim to remember previous lives: Cases with written records made before the previous personality was identified. *Journal of Scientific Exploration, 19*, 91–101.

Keil, H. H. J., & Tucker, J. B. (2010). Response to "How to improve the study and documentation of cases of the reincarnation type? A reappraisal of the case of Kemal Atasoy." *Journal of Scientific Exploration, 24*, 295–298.

Kellehear, A. (1996). *Experiences near death: Beyond medicine and religion.* New York, NY: Oxford University Press.

Kellehear, A. (2008). Census of non-Western near-death experiences to 2005: Overview of the current data. *Journal of Near-Death Studies, 26*, 249–265.

Kellehear, A. (2009). Census of non-Western near-death experiences to 2005: Observations and critical reflections. In J. M. Holden, B. Greyson, & D. James (Eds.), *The handbook of near-death experiences: Thirty years of investigation* (pp. 135–158). Santa Barbara, CA: ABC Clio.

Kelly, E. F. (2007). Toward a psychology for the 21st century. In E. F. Kelly, E. W. Kelly, A. Crabtree, A. Gauld, M. Grosso, & B. Greyson, *Irreducible mind: Toward a psychology for the 21st century* (pp. 577–643). Lanham, MD: Rowman & Littlefield.

Kelly, E. F. (2015a). Empirical challenges to theory construction. In E. F. Kelly, A. Crabtree, & P. Marshall (Eds.), *Beyond physicalism: Toward reconciliation of science and spirituality* (pp. 3–38). Lanham, MD: Rowman & Littlefield.

Kelly, E. F. (2015b). Toward a worldview grounded in science *and* spirituality. In E. F. Kelly, A. Crabtree, & P. Marshall (Eds.), *Beyond physicalism: Toward reconciliation of science and spirituality* (pp. 493–551). Lanham, MD: Rowman & Littlefield.

Kelly, E. F., Crabtree, A., & Marshall, P. (2015). *Beyond physicalism: Toward reconciliation of science and spirituality.* Lanham, MD: Rowman & Littlefield.

Kelly, E. F., Kelly, E. W., Crabtree, A., Gauld, A., Grosso, M., & Greyson, B. (2007). *Irreducible mind: Toward a psychology for the 21st century.* Lanham, MD: Rowman & Littlefield.

Kelly, E. F., & Locke, R. G. (2010). *Altered states of consciousness and psi: An historical survey and research prospectus* (Parapsychological Monograph Series No. 18). New York, NY: Parapsychology Foundation.

Kelly, E. F., & Presti, D. E. (2015). A psychobiological perspective on "transmission" models. In E. F. Kelly, A. Crabtree, & P. Marshall (Eds.), *Beyond physicalism: Toward a reconciliation of science and spirituality* (pp. 115–155). Lanham, MD: Rowman & Littlefield.

Kelly, E. W. (2001). Near-death experiences with reports of meeting deceased people. *Death Studies, 25*, 229–249.

Kelly, E. W. (2007a). F. W. H. Myers and the empirical study of the mind-body problem. In E. F. Kelly, E. W. Kelly, A. Crabtree, A. Gauld, M. Grosso, & B. Greyson, *Irreducible mind: Toward a psychology for the 21st century* (pp. 47–115). Lanham, MD: Rowman & Littlefield.

Kelly, E. W. (2007b). Psychophysiological influence. In E. F. Kelly, E. W. Kelly, A. Crabtree, A. Gauld, M. Grosso, & B. Greyson, *Irreducible mind: Toward a psychology for the 21st century* (pp. 117–239). Lanham, MD: Rowman & Littlefield.

Kelly, E. W. (Ed.) (2013). *Science, the self, and survival after death: Selected writings of Ian Stevenson.* Lanham, MD: Rowman & Littlefield.

Kelly, E. W., Greyson, B., & Kelly, E. F. (2007). Unusual experiences near death and related phenomena. In E. F. Kelly, E. W. Kelly, A. Crabtree, A. Gauld, M. Grosso, & B. Greyson, *Irreducible mind: Toward a psychology for the 21st century* (pp. 367–421). Lanham, MD: Rowman & Littlefield.

Kelsey, D., & Grant, J. (1967). *Many lifetimes.* Garden City, NY: Doubleday.

Kent, J. H. (2003). *Past life memories as a Confederate soldier.* Huntsville, AR: Ozark Mountain Publishers.

Keyes, C. F. (1983). Introduction: The study of popular ideas of karma. In C. F. Keyes & E. V. Daniel (Eds.), *Karma: An anthropological inquiry* (pp. 1–24). Berkeley, CA: University of California Press.

Keyes, C. F., & Daniel, E. V. (Eds.) (1983). *Karma: An anthropological inquiry.* Berkeley, CA: University of California Press.

Kim, J. (2015). What could pair a nonphysical soul to a physical body? In M. Martin & K. Augustine (Eds.), *The myth of an afterlife: The case against life after death* (pp. 335–347). Lanham, MD: Rowman & Littlefield.

Kingsley, P. (1995). *Ancient philosophy, mystery, and magic: Empedocles and Pythagorean tradition.* Oxford, UK: Clarendon Press.

Kingsley, P. (2010). *A story waiting to pierce you: Mongolia, Tibet, and the destiny of the Western world.* Point Reyes, CA: Golden Sufi Center.

Kiriyama, S. (2000). *You have been here before: Reincarnation.* Tokyo: Hirakawa Shuppan.

Kirk, G. S., Raven, J. E., & Schofield, M. (2007). *The Presocratic philosophers* (2nd ed.). Cambridge, UK: Cambridge University Press.

Kitamura, T., Ogawa, S. K., Roy, D. S., Okuyama, T., Morrissey, M. D., Smith, L. M, Redondo, R. K., & Tonegawa, S. (2017). Engrams and circuits crucial for systems consolidation of a memory. *Science, 356*(1663), 73–78. doi:10.1126/science.aam6808

Klausner, M. (1975). *Reincarnation.* Ramat-Gan, Israel: Massada.

Kline, M. V. (Ed.) (1956). *A scientific report on "The Search for Bridey Murphy."* New York, NY: Julian Press.

Klosin, A., Casas, E., Hidalgo-Carcedo, C., Vavouri, T., & Lehner, B. (2017). Transgenerational transmission of environmental information in *C. elegans. Science, 356*(5335), 320–323. doi: 10.1126/science.aah6412

Knight, Z. [G.] (1995). The healing power of the unconscious: How can we understand past life experiences in psychotherapy? *South African Journal of Psychology, 25*(2), 90–98.

Knight, Z. G. [1997]. *Healing stories of the unconscious: Past-life imagery in transpersonal psychotherapy.* (Ph.D. dissertation.) Grahamstown, South Africa: Rhodes University.

Koestler, A. (1971). *The case of the midwife toad.* London, UK: Hutchinson.

Koons, R. C., & Bealer, G. (Eds.) (2010). *The waning of materialism.* New York, NY: Oxford University Press.

Kripal, J. J. (2010). *Authors of the impossible: The paranormal and the sacred.* Chicago, IL: University of Chicago Press.

Krippner, S. (1987). Cross-cultural approaches to multiple personality disorder: Practices in Brazilian Spiritism. *Ethos, 15,* 273–295.

Krippner, S. (1991). The role of "past life" recall in Brazilian Spiritistic treatment for multiple personality disorders. In A. Berger & J. Berger (Eds.), *Reincarnation: Fact or fable?* (pp. 169–185). London, UK: Aquarian Press.

Krishan, Y. (1997). *The doctrine of karma: Its origin and development in Brahmanical, Buddhist and Jaina traditions*. Dehli, India: Motilil.

Krishnanand. (1968). *Reminiscences*. Bhadran, Gujarat, India: Krishnanand Shanti Ashram.

Kuhn, O. (1947). *Die Deszendenz-Theorie: Grundlagen der Ganzheitsbiologie*. Bamberg: Meisenbach.

Kuhn, T. S. (1962). *The structure of scientific revolutions*. Chicago, IL: University of Chicago Press.

Kurth-Voigt, L. E. (1999). *Continued existence, reincarnation, and the power of sympathy in classical Weimar*. Rochester, NY: Camden House.

LaBar, K. S., & Caveza, R. (2006). Cognitive neuroscience of emotional memory. *Nature Reviews Neuroscience, 7*(1), 51–54. doi:10.1038/nrn1825

LaBerge, S. (1985). *Lucid dreaming*. Los Angeles, CA: Jeremy Tarcher.

Lamarck, J.-B. de. (1809). *Philosophie zoologique*. Paris, France: Dentu.

Lancelin, C. [c. 1922]. *La vie posthume*. Paris, France: Henri Durville.

Langley, N. (1967). *Edgar Cayce on reincarnation*. New York, NY: Castle Books.

Lanza, R., with Berman, B. (2009). *Biocentrism: How life and consciousness are the keys to understanding the true nature of the universe*. Dallas, TX: BenBella Books.

Largest award yet in Pan Am crash. (1984, July 2). UPI Archives [web post]. Retrieved from https://www.upi.com/Archives/1984/07/02/Largest-award-yet-in -Pan-Am-crash/7899457588800/

Larrington, C. (Trans.) (2014). *The Poetic Edda* (2nd ed.). New York, NY: Oxford University Press.

Larsen, C. F. (2015). Conjuring up spirits in the improvisations of mediums. In M. Martin & K. Augustine (Eds.), *The myth of an afterlife: The case against life after death* (pp. 585–614). Lanham, MD: Rowman & Littlefield.

Laszlo, E. (2007). *Science and the Akashic field: An integral theory of everything* (2nd ed.). Rochester, VT: Inner Traditions.

Laszlo, E. (Ed.). (2009). *The Akashic experience: Science and the cosmic memory field*. Rochester, VT: Inner Traditions.

Laszlo, E., & Peake, A. (2014). *The immortal mind: Science and the continuity of consciousness beyond the brain*. Rochester, VT: Inner Traditions.

Layton, B. (1989). The significance of Basilides in ancient Christian thought. *Representations, 28*, 135–155.

Le Quang Hu'o'ng. (1972). Histoires vietnamiennes de réincarnation. *Message d'Extrême-Orient, 2*(7), 535–539.

Leadbeater, C. W. (1903a). *Clairvoyance* (2nd ed.). London, UK: Theosophical Publishing Society.

Leadbeater, C. W. (1903b). *The other side of death*. Chicago, IL: Theosophical Book Concern.

Leininger, B., & Leininger, A., with Gross, J. (2009). *Soul survivor: The reincarnation of a World War II fighter pilot*. New York, NY: Grand Central Publishing.

Lenz, F. (1979). *Lifetimes: True accounts of reincarnation.* Indianapolis, IN: Bobbs-Merrill.

Lester, D. (2005). *Is there life after death? An examination of the empirical evidence.* Jefferson, NC: McFarland.

Lester, D. (2015). Is there life after death? A review of the supporting evidence. In M. Martin & K. Augustine (Eds.), *The myth of an afterlife: The case against life after death* (pp. 631–649). Lanham, MD: Rowman & Littlefield.

Littlewood, R. (2001). Social institutions and psychological explanations: Druze reincarnation as a therapeutic resource. *British Journal of Medical Psychology, 74,* 213–222.

Llewelyn, K. (1991). *Flight into the ages.* Warriewood, New South Wales, Australia: Felspin.

Lock, M. (2002). *Twice dead: Organ transplants and the reinvention of death.* Berkeley, CA: University of California Press.

Locke, J. (1694/1975). Of identity and diversity. In J. Perry (Ed.), *Personal identity* (pp. 33–52). Reprinted from *An essay concerning human understanding* (2nd ed.), Chap. 27. Berkeley, CA: University of California Press.

Long, J. B. (1980). The concepts of human action and rebirth in the *Mahābhārata.* In W. D. O'Flaherty (Ed.), *Karma and rebirth in classical Indian traditions* (pp. 38–60). Berkeley, CA: University of California Press.

Long, J. B. (2005). Reincarnation. In L. Jones (Ed.), *Encyclopedia of religion* (2nd ed.) (vol. 11, pp. 7676–7681). New York, NY: Thomson Gale.

Long, J., & Perry, P. (2010). *Evidence of the afterlife: The science of near-death experiences.* New York, NY: HarperCollins.

Lönnerstrand, S. (1998). *I have lived before: The true story of the reincarnation of Shanti Devi.* Huntsville, AR: Ozark Mountain Publishers.

Loye, D. (2009). Return to Amalfi and the Akashic home. In E. Laszlo (Ed.), *The Akashic experience: Science and the cosmic memory field* (pp. 36–53). Rochester, VT: Inner Traditions.

Lucas, W. B. (Ed.). (2007). *Regression therapy: A handbook for professionals. Volume I: Past-life therapy.* Kill Devil Hills, NC: Transpersonal Publishing.

Lund, D. H. (2009). *Persons, souls and death: A philosophical investigation of an afterlife.* Jefferson, NC: McFarland.

Luria, Y. (2015). *Sha'ar hagilgulim—Gate of reincarnations: An English translation of the Arizal's work on reincarnation.* Translated by Pinchas Winston. Independently published.

Lynn, S. J., Lock, T. G., Myers, B., & Payne, D. G. (1997). Recalling the unrecallable: Should hypnosis be used to recover memories in psychotherapy? *Current Directions in Psychological Science, 6,* 79–83.

MacGregor, G. (1978). *Reincarnation in Christianity: A new vision of the role of rebirth in Christian thought.* Wheaton, IL: Theosophical Publishing House.

Mackenzie, V. (1988). *Reincarnation: The boy lama.* London, UK: Bloomsbury.

Mackenzie, V. (1996). *Reborn in the West: The reincarnation masters.* New York, NY: Marlowe.

Magallón, L. L. (1997). *Mutual dreaming.* New York, NY: Pocket Books.

Majeed, H. M. (2012). *An examination of the concept of reincarnation in African philosophy* (Ph.D. dissertation). University of South Africa. Retrieved from http:// uir.unisa.ac.za/bitstream/handle/10500/6414/thesis_majeed_h.pdf;jsessionid=83B 1EFD02199C339C357AA78453A3806?sequence=1

Marriot, J. (1984). Hypnotic regression and past lives therapy: Fantasy or reality? *Australian Journal of Clinical Hypnotherapy and Hypnosis, 5*(2), 65–72.

Marshall, P. (2015). Why we are conscious of so little: A neo-Leibnizian approach. In E. F. Kelly, A. Crabtree, & P. Marshall (Eds.), *Beyond physicalism: Toward a reconciliation of science and spirituality* (pp. 387–422). Lanham, MD: Rowman & Littlefield.

Martin, M., & Augustine, K. (Eds.). (2015). *The myth of an afterlife: The case against life after death.* Lanham, MD: Rowman & Littlefield.

Martin, R., & Barresi, J. (2006). *The rise and fall of soul and self: An intellectual history of personal identity.* New York, NY: Columbia University Press.

Matlock, J. G. (1986). Review of *The search for yesterday* by D. Scott Rogo. *Journal of the Society for Psychical Research, 53*(802), 229–232.

Matlock, J. G. (1988a). The decline of past life memory with subject's age in spontaneous reincarnation cases. In M. L. Albertson, D. S. Ward, & K. P. Freeman (Eds.), *Paranormal research* (pp. 388–401). Ft. Collins, CO: Rocky Mountain Research Institute.

Matlock, J. G. (1988b). Some further perspectives on reincarnation research: A rejoinder to D. Scott Rogo. *Journal of Religion and Psychical Research, 11*, 63–70.

Matlock, J. G. (1989). Age and stimulus in past life memory cases: A study of published cases. *Journal of the American Society for Psychical Research, 83*, 303–316.

Matlock, J. G. (1990a). Of names and signs: Reincarnation, inheritance and social structure on the Northwest Coast. *Anthropology of Consciousness, 1*(3–4), 9–18.

Matlock, J. G. (1990b). Past life memory case studies. In S. Krippner (Ed.), *Advances in parapsychological research 6* (pp. 184–267). Jefferson, NC: McFarland.

Matlock, J. G. (1992). Interpreting the case of Imad Elawar. *Journal of Religion and Psychical Research, 15*, 91–98.

Matlock, J. G. (1993). *A cross-cultural study of reincarnation ideologies and their social correlates* (M.A. thesis). Hunter College, City University of New York. Retrieved from http://jamesgmatlock.net/wp-content/uploads/2013/12/Reincarn ation-Ideologies-and-Social-Correlates.pdf

Matlock, J. G. (1994). Alternate generation equivalence and the recycling of souls: Amerindian rebirth in global perspective. In A. Mills & R. Slobodin (Eds.), *Amerindian rebirth* (pp. 263–283). Toronto, ON: University of Toronto Press.

Matlock, J. G. (1995). Death symbolism in matrilineal societies: A replication study. *Cross-Cultural Research, 29*, 158–177.

Matlock, J. G. (2011). Ian Stevenson's *Twenty cases suggestive of reincarnation*: An historical review and assessment. *Journal of Scientific Exploration, 25*, 789–820.

Matlock, J. G. (2015, Oct. 23). Evidence of past-life memory in a mildly autistic boy. Paper read at the Third Annual Meeting of the Lithuanian Society for the Study of

Religions, Vilnius, October 22–23, 2015. Retrieved from http://jamesgmatlock.net/wp-content/uploads/2015/11/Past-Life-Memory-in-a-Milldy-Autistic-Boy1.pdf

Matlock, J. G. (2016a). Review of Michael Sudduth, *A philosophical critique of empirical arguments for postmortem survival. Journal of Parapsychology*, 80, 107–110.

Matlock, J. G. (2016b). The myth of mortality: Comments on Martin and Augustine's *The myth of an afterlife*. In J. Palmer (Ed.), Special book review section: Do we survive death? A philosophical examination (pp. 190–203). *Journal of Parapsychology*, *80*, 169–264.

Matlock, J. G. (2016c). Whose prejudice? A response to the replies of Augustine, Smythe, and Larsen. In J. Palmer (Ed.), Special book review section: Do we survive death? A philosophical examination (pp. 235–50). *Journal of Parapsychology*, *80*, 169–264.

Matlock, J. G. (2017). Historical near-death and reincarnation-intermission experiences of the Tlingit Indians: Case studies and theoretical reflections. *Journal of Near-Death Studies*, *35*(4), 214–241.

Matlock, J. G. (2017, August). Xenoglossy in reincarnation cases. *Psi Encyclopedia*. Retrieved from https://psi-encyclopedia.spr.ac.uk/articles/xenoglossy-reincarnation-cases

Matlock, J. G. (2017, February). Patterns in reincarnation cases. *Psi Encyclopedia*. Retrieved from https://psi-encyclopedia.spr.ac.uk/articles/patterns-reincarnation-cases

Matlock, J. G. (2017, July). Reincarnation accounts pre-1900. *Psi Encyclopedia*. Last updated January, 2018. Retrieved from https://psi-encyclopedia.spr.ac.uk/articles/reincarnation-accounts-pre–1900

Matlock, J. G. (2017, June). Experimental birthmarks and birth defects. *Psi Encyclopedia*. Last updated, January, 2018. Retrieved from https://psi-encyclopedia.spr.ac.uk/articles/experimental-birthmarks-and-birth-defects

Matlock, J. G. (2017, March). Replacement reincarnation. *Psi Encyclopedia*. Last updated February 9, 2018. Retrieved from https://psi-encyclopedia.spr.ac.uk/articles/replacement-reincarnation

Matlock, J. G. (2017, May). Intermission memories. *Psi Encyclopedia*. Retrieved from https://psi-encyclopedia.spr.ac.uk/articles/intermission-memories

Matlock, J. G. (2017, October-a). Behavioural memories in reincarnation cases. *Psi Encyclopedia*. Retrieved from https://psi-encyclopedia.spr.ac.uk/articles/behavioural-memories-reincarnation-cases

Matlock, J. G. (2017, October-b). Buried treasure in reincarnation cases. *Psi Encyclopedia*. Retrieved from https://psi-encyclopedia.spr.ac.uk/articles/buried-treasure-reincarnation-cases

Matlock, J. G. (2018, August). Reincarnation. *Psi Encyclopedia*. Retrieved from https://psi-encyclopedia.spr.ac.uk/articles/reincarnation

Matlock, J. G. (2018, January). Announcing dreams and related experiences. *Psi Encyclopedia*. Retrieved from https://psi-encyclopedia.spr.ac.uk/articles/announcing-dreams-and-related-experiences

Matlock, J. G., & Giesler-Petersen, I. (2016). Asian versus Western intermission memories: Universal features and cultural variations. *Journal of Near-Death Studies, 35*(1), 3–29.

Matlock, J. G., & Mills, A. (1994). A trait index to North American Indian and Inuit reincarnation. In A. Mills & R. Slobodin (Eds.), *Amerindian rebirth: Reincarnation belief among North American Indians and Inuit* (pp. 299–356). Toronto, ON: University of Toronto Press.

Mattiesen, E. (1936–1939). *Das persönliche Überleben des Todes* (3 vols.). Berlin, Germany: Walter de Gruyter.

Mauskopf, S. H., & McVaugh, M. R. (1980). *The elusive science: Origins of experimental psychical research.* Baltimore, MD: Johns Hopkins University Press.

May, E. C., & Marwaha, S. B. (n.d.). An alternative hypothesis for the Géza Maróczy (via medium Rollans) vs. Viktor Korchnoi chess game. Retrieved from https://www.academia.edu/31084244/An_Alternative_Hypothesis_for_the_G%C3%A9za_Mar%C3%B3czy_via_medium_Rollans_vs._Viktor_Korchnoi_Chess_Game

Mayr, E. (1982). *The growth of biological thought: Diversity, evolution, and inheritance.* Cambridge, MA: Belknap Press.

Mayr, E., & Provine, W. B. (Eds.). (1980). *The evolutionary synthesis: Perspectives on the unification of biology.* Cambridge, MA: Harvard University Press.

Mbiti, J. S. (1989). *African religions and philosophy* (2nd ed). Oxford, UK: Heinemann.

McDermott, J. P. (1980). Karma and rebirth in early Buddhism. In W. D. O'Flaherty (Ed.), *Karma and rebirth in classical Indian traditions* (pp. 165–192). Berkeley, CA: University of California Press.

McDougall, W. (1961). *Body and mind: A history and a defense of animism.* Boston, MA: Beacon.

McEvilley, T. (2002). *The shape of ancient thought: Comparative studies in Greek and Indian philosophies.* New York, NY: Alsworth Press.

McFadden, J. (2002). *Quantum evolution: How physics' weirdest theory explains life's biggest mystery.* New York, NY: W. W. Norton.

McNally, R. J. (2012). Explaining "memories" of space alien abduction and past lives: An experimental psychopathology approach. *Journal of Experimental Psychopathology, 3,* 2–16.

McTaggart, J. M. E. (1906). *Some dogmas of religion.* London, UK: Edwin Arnold.

Meixner, U. (2017). Idealism and panpsychism. In G. Brüntrup & L. Jaskolla (Eds.), *Panpsychism: Contemporary perspectives* (pp. 387–405). Oxford, UK: Oxford University Press.

Melton, J. G. (1994). Edgar Cayce and reincarnation: Past life readings as religious symbology. *Syzygy: Journal of Alternative Religion and Culture, 3*(1–2). Retrieved from http://atlantisonline.smfforfree2.com/index.php?topic=6423.0;wap2

Meyer, M. (2008). *Same dog twice.* Independence, CA: Kearsarge Press.

Meyer-Abich, A. (1963). *Geistesgeschichtliche Grundlagen der Biologie.* Stuttgart, Germany: Fischer.

Meyersburg, C. A., Bodgan, R., Gallo, D. A., & McNally, R. J. (2009). False memory propensity in people reporting recovered memories of past lives. *Journal of Abnormal Psychology, 118*(2), 399–404.

Meyersburg, C. A., Carson, S. H., Mathis, M. B., & McNally, R. J. (2014). Creative histories: Memories of past lives and measures of creativity. *Psychology of Consciousness: Theory, Research, and Practice, 1*(1), 70–81. doi.org/10.1037/css0000004

Miller, S. L. (1953). A production of amino acids under possible primitive Earth conditions. *Science, 117*, 528–529.

Mills, A. (1988a). A comparison of Wet'suwet'en cases of the reincarnation type with Gitksan and Beaver. *Journal of Anthropological Research, 44*, 385–415.

Mills, A. (1988b). A preliminary investigation of reincarnation among the Beaver and Gitksan Indians. *Anthropologica, 30*, 23–59.

Mills, A. (1989). A replication study: Three cases of children in northern India who are said to remember a previous life. *Journal of Scientific Exploration, 3*, 133–184.

Mills, A. (1990). Muslim cases of the reincarnation type in Northern India: A test of the hypothesis of imposed identification (Parts 1 and 2). *Journal of Scientific Exploration, 4*, 171–202.

Mills, A. (1994a). Cultural contrast: The British Columbia Court's evaluation of the Gitksan-Wet'suwet'en and their own sense of self-worth as revealed in cases of reported reincarnation. *BC Studies*, no. 104, 149–172.

Mills, A. (1994b). Nightmares in Western children: An alternative interpretation suggested by data in three cases. *Journal of the American Society for Psychical Research, 88*, 309–325.

Mills, A. (1994c). Rebirth and identity: Three Gitksan cases of pierced-ear birthmarks. In A. Mills & R. Slobodin (Eds.), *Amerindian rebirth: Reincarnation belief among North American Indians and Inuit* (pp. 211–241). Toronto, ON: University of Toronto Press.

Mills, A. (2001). Sacred land and coming back: How Gitxsan and Witsuwit'en reincarnation stretches Western boundaries. *Canadian Journal of Native Studies, 21*, 309–331.

Mills, A. (2003). Are children with imaginary playmates and children said to remember previous lives cross-culturally comparable categories? *Transcultural Psychiatry, 40*, 63–91.

Mills, A. (2004). Inferences from the case of Ajendra Singh Chauhan: The effect of parental questioning, of meeting the "previous life" family, an aborted attempt to quantify probabilities, and the impact on his life as a young adult. *Journal of Scientific Exploration, 18*, 609–641.

Mills, A. (2006). Back from death: Young adults in northern India who as children were said to remember a previous life, with or without a shift in religion (Hindu to Muslim or vice versa). *Anthropology and Humanism Quarterly, 31*, 141–156.

Mills, A. (2010). Understanding the conundrum of rebirth experience of the Beaver, Gitxsan, and Witsuwit'en. *Anthropology and Humanism, 35*, 172–191.

Mills, A. (2014, March). Body/gender and mind fits and misfits in three cases: A preliminary exploration of the role of reincarnation in two-spirit people. Paper read at the annual meeting of the Society for the Anthropology of Consciousness Conference, University of California at Berkeley, March 24–28, 2014.

Mills, A., & Champion, L. (1996). Reincarnation as integration, adoption out as dissociation: Examples from First Nations northwest British Columbia. *Anthropology of Consciousness, 7*(3), 30–43.

Mills, A., & Dhiman, K. (2011). Shiva returned in the body of Sumitra: A posthumous longitudinal study of the significance of the Shiva/Sumitra case of the possession type. *Proceedings of the Society for Psychical Research, 59*(223), 145–193.

Mills, A., Haraldsson, E., & Keil, H. H. J. (1994). Replication studies of cases suggestive of reincarnation by three independent investigators. *Journal of the American Society for Psychical Research, 88*, 207–219.

Mills, A., Nyce, D., Nyce, E., Gosnell, J., Grandison, P., & Plante, L. (2011). The Nisga'a paradigm of rebirth. *Canadian Journal of Native Studies, 31*(2), 85–95.

Mills, A., & Slobodin, R. (Eds.). (1994). *Amerindian rebirth: Reincarnation belief among North American Indians and Inuit*. Toronto, ON: University of Toronto Press.

Mills, A., & Tucker, J. B. (2013). Past-life experiences. In E. Cardeña, S. J. Lynn, & S. Krippner (Eds.), *Varieties of anomalous experience: Examining the scientific evidence* (2nd ed.) (pp. 303–332). Washington, DC: American Psychological Association.

Mills, A., & Tucker, J. B. (2015). Reincarnation: Field studies and theoretical issues today. In E. Cardeña, J. Palmer, & D. Marcusson-Clavertz (Eds.), *Parapsychology: A handbook for the 21st century* (pp. 314–326). Jefferson, NC: McFarland.

Mishlove, J. (2000). *The PK man: A true story of mind over matter*. Charlottesville, VA: Hampton Roads.

Mishlove, J., & Engen, B. C. (2007). Archetypal synchronistic resonance: A new theory of paranormal experience. *Journal of Humanistic Psychology, 42*(2), 223–242.

Montgomery, R. (1979). *Strangers among us: Enlightened beings from a world to come*. New York, NY: Coward, McCann & Geohegan.

Monti, M. M., Vanhaudenhuyse, A., Coleman, M. R., Boly, M., Pickard, J. D., Tshibanda, L., Owen, A. M., & Laureys, S. (2010). Willful modulation of brain activity in disorders of consciousness. *New England Journal of Medicine, 362*, 579–589. doi:10.1056/NEJMoa0905370

Moody, R. A., Jr. (1975). *Life after life*. Atlanta, GA: Mockingbird Books.

Moody, R. [A.], Jr., & Perry, P. (2010). *Glimpses of eternity: Sharing a loved one's passage from this life to the next*. New York, NY: Guideposts.

Moore, D. S. (2015). *The developing genome: An introduction to behavioural epigenetics*. Oxford, UK: Oxford University Press.

Mørch, H. H. (2014). *Panpsychism and causation: A new argument and a solution to the combination problem* (Ph.D. dissertation). Oslo, Norway: University of Oslo. Retrieved from https://www.newdualism.org/papers/H.Morch/Morch-dissertation-Oslo2014.pdf

Moss, P., & Keeton, J. (1979). *Encounters with the past: How man can experience and relive history*. London, UK: Sidgwick & Jackson.

Moss, R. (2009). *The secret history of dreaming*. Novato, CA: New World Library.

Muller, K. E. (1970). *Reincarnation—based on facts*. London, UK: Psychic Press.

Murphy, G. (1967). Direct contacts with past and future: Retrocognition and precognition. *Journal of the American Society for Psychical Research, 61*, 3–23.

Murphy, G. (1973). A Caringtonian approach to Ian Stevenson's *Twenty Cases Suggestive of Reincarnation*. *Journal of the American Society for Psychical Research, 67*, 117–129.

Myers, F. W. H. (1903). *Human personality and its survival of bodily death* (2 vols.). London, UK: Longmans, Green and Co.

Nadeau, R., & Kafatos, M. (1999). Mind matters: Mega-narratives and the two-culture war. *The non-local universe: The new physics and matters of the mind* (pp. 147–175). New York, NY: Oxford University Press.

Nagel, T. (2012). *Mind and cosmos: Why the materialist neo-Darwinian conception of nature is almost certainly false*. New York, NY: Oxford University Press.

Nahm, M. (2007). *Evolution und Parapsychologie*. Norderstedt, Germany: Books on Demand.

Nahm, M. (2009). Four ostensible near-death experiences of Roman times with peculiar features: Mistake cases, correction cases, xenoglossy, and a prediction. *Journal of Near-Death Studies, 27*, 211–222.

Nahm, M. (2011a). Reflections on the context of near-death experiences. *Journal of Scientific Exploration, 25*, 453–478.

Nahm, M. (2011b). The *Tibetan Book of the Dead*: Its history and controversial aspects of its contents. *Journal of Near-Death Studies, 29*, 373–398.

Nahm, M. (2012). *Wenn die Dunkelheit ein Ende finde: Terminale Geistesklarheit und andere Phänomene in Todesnähe*. Amerang, Germany: Crotona.

Nahm, M. (2015). Mysterious ways: The riddle of the homing ability in dogs and other vertebrates. *Journal of the Society for Psychical Research, 79*, 140–155.

Nahm, M. (2016). The role of animals as co-percipients of apparitions in the work of Emil Mattiesen (1875–1939*). Journal of the Society for Psychical Research, 80*, 119–121.

Nahm, M., & Greyson, B. (2009). Terminal lucidity in patients with chronic schizophrenia and dementia: A survey of the literature. *Journal of Nervous and Mental Disease, 197*, 942–944. doi:10.1097/NMD.0b013e3181c22583

Nahm, M., Greyson, B., Kelly, E. W., & Haraldsson, E. (2012). Terminal lucidity: A review and a case collection. *Archives of Gerontology and Geriatrics, 55*, 138–142. doi:10.1016/j.archger.2011.06.031

Nahm, M., & Hassler, D. (2011). Thoughts about thought bundles: A commentary on Jürgen Keil's paper "Questions of the Reincarnation Type." *Journal of Scientific Exploration, 25*, 305–326.

Nahm, M., Navarini, A. A., & Kelly, E. W. (2013). *Canities subita*: A reappraisal of evidence based on 196 case reports published in the medical literature. *International Journal of Trichology, 5*(2), 63–68.

Nahm, M., Rousseau, D., & Greyson, B. (2017). Discrepancy between cerebral structure and cognitive functioning: A review. *Journal of Nervous and Mental Disease, 205*(12), 967–972.

Nanninga, R. (2008). Reïncarnatie onder hypnose: De Australische tv-documentaire van Peter Ramster. *Skepter, 21*(2). Retrieved 12/13/2014 from https://skepsis.nl/ramster-video/

Naranjo, C. (1973). *The healing.* New York, NY: Random House.

Nardi, D. (2011). *Neuroscience of personality: Brain savvy insights for all types of people.* Los Angeles, CA: Radiance House.

National Transportation Safety Board (NTSB). (1983). Aircraft accident report (NTSB/AAR–83/02). Springfield, VA: National Technical Information Service.

Nayak, G. C. (1976). Survival, reincarnation and the problem of personal identity. In J. M. O. Wheatley & H. L. Edge (Eds.), *Philosophical dimensions of parapsychology* (pp. 295–307). Springfield, IL: Charles C Thomas.

Neidhart, G. (1956). *Werden wir wieder geboren?* Munich, Germany: Gemeinschaft für Religiose und Geistige Erneuerung.

Neppe, V. M. (2007). A detailed analysis of an important chess game: Revisiting "Maróczy versus Korchnoi." *Journal of the Society for Psychical Research, 71*(3), 129–147.

Neppe, V. M., & Close, E. R. (2012). *Reality begins with consciousness: A paradigm shift that works.* [e-book]. Retrieved from http://www.brainvoyage.com

Netherton, M., & Shiffrin, N. (1978). *Past lives therapy.* New York, NY: William Morrow.

Neufeldt, R. W. (1986). In search of utopia: Karma and rebirth in the Theosophical movement. In R. W. Neufeldt (Ed.), *Karma and rebirth: Post classical developments* (pp. 233–255). Albany, NY: State University of New York Press.

Newton, I. (1687). *Philosophiæ naturalis principia mathematica.* London, UK: S. Pepys.

Newton, I. (1729). *Mathematical principles of natural philosophy* (2 vols.). Translated by Andrew Motte. London, UK: Benjamin Motte.

Newton, M. (1996). *Journey of souls: Case studies of life between lives* (5th rev. ed.). Woodbury, MN: Llewellyn.

Newton, M. (2000). *Destiny of souls: More case studies of life between lives.* Woodbury, MN: Llewellyn.

Nissanka, H. S. S. (2001). *The girl who was reborn: A case-study suggestive of reincarnation.* Colombo, Sri Lanka: S. Godage Brothers.

Noë, A. (2009). *Out of our heads: Why you are not your brain, and other lessons from the biology of consciousness.* New York, NY: Hill and Wang.

Norbu, N. (1986). *The crystal and the way of light.* London, UK: Routledge & Keagan Paul.

O'Flaherty, W. D. (1980a). Introduction. In W. D. O'Flaherty (Ed.), *Karma and rebirth in classical Indian traditions* (pp. ix–xxv). Berkeley, CA: University of California Press.

O'Flaherty, W. D. (1980b). Karma and rebirth in the Vedas and Purāṇas. In W. D. O'Flaherty (Ed.), *Karma and rebirth in classical Indian traditions* (pp. 3–37). Berkeley, CA: University of California Press.

O'Hara-Keeton, M. (1996). *I died on the Titanic.* [United Kingdom:] Pharaoh. (First published 1996 as *Hands off the "Titanic"! (and the "Californian")* by M. H. O'Hara. Merseyside, UK: Countyvise.)

Obeyesekere, G. (1980). The rebirth eschatology and its transformations: A contribution to the sociology of early Buddhism. In W. D. O'Flaherty (Ed.), *Karma and rebirth in classical Indian traditions* (pp. 237–164). Berkeley, CA: University of California Press.

Obeyesekere, G. (2002). *Imagining karma: Ethical transformation in Amerindian, Buddhist, and Greek rebirth.* Berkeley, CA: University of California Press.

Ogren, B. (2009). *Renaissance and rebirth: Reincarnation in early modern Italian Kabbalah* (Studies in Jewish History and Culture, vol. 24). Leiden, the Netherlands: Brill.

Ohkado, M. (2012). Children with "past-life memories": A case of a Japanese female child with "memories" as an Indian [In Japanese with abstract in English]. *Journal of Mind-Body Science, 21*(1), 17–25.

Ohkado, M. (2013). A case of a Japanese child with past life memories. *Journal of Scientific Exploration, 27,* 625–636.

Ohkado, M. (2014). Facial features of Burmese with past-life memories as Japanese soldiers. *Journal of Scientific Exploration, 28,* 597–603.

Ohkado, M. (2015). Children's birth, womb, prelife, and past-life memories: Results of an Internet-based survey. *Journal of Prenatal and Perinatal Psychology and Health, 30*(1), 3–16.

Ohkado, M. (2016). A same-family case of the reincarnation type in Japan. *Journal of Scientific Exploration, 30,* 524–536.

Ohkado, M. (2017). Same-family cases of the reincarnation type in Japan. *Journal of Scientific Exploration, 31,* 551–571.

Ohkado, M., & Ikegawa, A. (2014). Children with life-between-life memories. *Journal of Scientific Exploration, 28,* 477–490.

Ohkado, M., & Okamoto, S. (2014, February). A case of xenoglossy under hypnosis. *Edge Science* No. 17, pp. 7–12.

Onyewuenyi, I. C. (2009). *African belief in reincarnation: A philosophical reappraisal.* BookSurge Publishing. (Originally published 1982 as "A philosophical reappraisal of African belief in reincarnation" in *International Philosophical Quarterly, 22,* 157–168.)

Osborn, A. W. (1937). *The superphysical.* London, UK: Nicholson & Watson.

Osis, K. (1961). *Deathbed observations by physicians and nurses.* New York: Parapsychology Foundation.

Osis, K., & Haraldsson, E. (2012). *At the hour of death* (Rev. ed.). Guildford, Surrey, UK: White Crow Books.

O'Sullivan, M. (1998, Feb. 12). Making *Titanic* claims: Artist says he's reincarnation of muralist lost in 1912 disaster. *The Washington Post,* p. E07.

Owen, A. [M.] (2017). *Into the gray zone: A neuroscientist explores the border between life and death.* New York, NY: Scribner.

Owen, A. M., Coleman, M. R., Boly, M., Davis, M. H., Laureys, S. & Pickard, J. D. (2006). Detecting awareness in the vegetative state. *Science, 313,* 1402. doi:10.1126/science.1130197

Owens, J. E., Cook, E. W., & Stevenson, I. (1990). Features of "near-death experience" in relation to whether or not patients were near death. *The Lancet, 336,*
175–1177.

Parfit, D. (1984). *Reasons and persons.* Oxford, UK: Oxford University Press.

Parkin, R. (1988). Reincarnation and alternate generation equivalence in middle
India. *Journal of Anthropological Research, 44*(1), 1–20.

Parkin, R. (1992). *The Munda of central India: An account of their social organization.* Delhi, India: Oxford University Press.

Parnia, S. (2007). Do reports of consciousness during cardiac arrest hold the key to
discovering the nature of consciousness? *Medical Hypotheses, 69*(4), 933–937.
doi:10.1016/j.mehy.2007.01.076

Parnia, S. (2013). *Erasing death: The science that is rewriting the boundaries
between life and death.* New York, NY: HarperOne.

Pasricha, S. K. (1983). New information favoring a paranormal interpretation in the
case of Rakesh Gaur. *European Journal of Parapsychology, 5,* 77–85.

Pasricha, S. K. (1990a). *Claims of reincarnation: An empirical study of cases in
India.* New Delhi, India: Harman Publishing House.

Pasricha, S. [K.] (1990b). Three conjectured features of reincarnation type cases in
north India: Responses of persons unfamiliar with actual cases. *Journal of the
American Society for Psychical Research, 84,* 227–233.

Pasricha, S. [K.] (1992). Are reincarnation type cases shaped by parental guidance?
An empirical study concerning the limits of parents' influence on children. *Journal
of Scientific Exploration, 6,* 167–180.

Pasricha, S. [K.] (1993). A systematic survey of near-death experiences in South
India. *Journal of Scientific Exploration, 7,* 161–171.

Pasricha, S. K. (1998). Cases of the reincarnation type in northern India with birthmarks and birth defects. *Journal of Scientific Exploration, 12,* 259–293.

Pasricha, S. K. (2001a). Cases of the reincarnation type in South India: Why so few
reports? *Journal of Scientific Exploration, 15,* 211–221.

Pasricha, S. K. (2001b). Experience in rebirth research in India. In N. Senanay-
ake (Ed.), *Trends in rebirth research: Proceedings of an international seminar*
(pp. 37–55). Ratmalana, Sri Lanka: Sarvodaya Vishva Lekha.

Pasricha, S. K. (2008). *Can the mind survive beyond death? In pursuit of scientific
evidence* (2 vols.). New Delhi, India: Harman Publishing House.

Pasricha, S. K. (2011a). Do attitudes of families concerned influence features of children who claim to remember previous lives? *Indian Journal of Psychiatry, 53*(1),
21–24.

Pasricha, S. K. (2011b). Relevance of para-psychology in psychiatric practice.
Indian Journal of Psychiatry, 53(1), 4–8. PMCID: PMC3056186 doi: 10.4103/
0019-5545.75544

Pasricha, S. K., & Barker, D. R. (1981). A case of the reincarnation type in India: The
case of Rakesh Gaur. *European Journal of Parapsychology, 3,* 381–408.

Pasricha, S. K., Keil, [H. H.] J., Tucker, J. B., & Stevenson, I. (2005). Some bodily
malformations attributed to previous lives. *Journal of Scientific Exploration, 19,*
359–383.

Pasricha, S. K., Murthy, H. N., & Murthy, V. N. (1978). Examination of the claims of reincarnation in a psychotic condition. *Indian Journal of Clinical Psychology, 5,* 197–202.

Pasricha, S. [K.], & Stevenson, I. (1977). Three cases of the reincarnation type in India. *Indian Journal of Psychiatry, 19,* 36–42.

Pasricha, S. [K.], & Stevenson, I. (1979). A partly independent replication of investigations of cases suggestive of reincarnation. *European Journal of Parapsychology, 3,* 51–69.

Pasricha, S. [K.], & Stevenson, I. (1986). Near-death experiences in India: A preliminary report. *Journal of Nervous and Mental Disease, 174,* 165–170.

Pasricha, S. [K.], & Stevenson, I. (1987). Indian cases of the reincarnation type two generations apart. *Journal of the Society for Psychical Research, 54,* 239–246.

Paterson, R. W. K. (1995). *Philosophy and the belief in a life after death.* Basingstoke, UK: Palgrave Macmillan.

Patihis, L., Frenda, S. J., LePort, A. K. R., Petersen, N., Nichols, R. M., Stark, C. E. L., McGaugh, J. L., & Loftus, E. F. (2013). False memories in highly superior autobiographical memory individuals. *Proceedings of the National Academy of Sciences, 110*(52), 20947–20952. doi:10.1073/pnas.1314373110

Paton, L. B. (1921). *Spiritism and the cult of the dead in antiquity.* London, UK: Hodder & Stoughton.

Pearsall, P. (1998). *The heart's code: Tapping the wisdom and power of our heart energy.* New York, NY: Broadway Books.

Pearsall, P., Schwartz, G. E. R., & Russek, L. G. S. (2003). Changes in heart transplant recipients that parallel the personalities of their donors. *Journal of Near-Death Studies, 20*(3), 191–206.

Pehlivanova, M., Janke, M. J., Lee, J., & Tucker, J. B. (2018). Childhood gender nonconformity and children's past-life memories. *International Journal of Sexual Health.* doi:10.1080/19317611.2018.1523266

Penelhum, T. (1970). *Survival and disembodied existence.* London, UK: Routledge and Kegan Paul.

Peres, J. F. P., Mercante, J. P., & Nasello, A. G. (2005). Psychological dynamics affecting traumatic memories: Implications in psychotherapy. *Psychology and Psychotherapy, 78,* 431–447.

Peres, J. F. P., Moreira-Almeida, A., Nasello, A. G., & Koenig, H. G. (2007). Spirituality and resilience in trauma victims. *Journal of Religion and Health, 46,* 343–350.

Peres, J. F. P. (2012). Should psychotherapy consider reincarnation? *Journal of Nervous and Mental Disease, 200*(2, sup. 1, pt. 3), 174–179.

Perry, C. W., Laurence, J.-R., D'Eon, J., & Tallant, B. (1988). Hypnotic age regression techniques in the elicitation of memories: Applied uses and abuses. In H. M. Pettinati (Ed.), *Hypnosis and memory* (pp. 128–154). New York, NY: Guilford.

Perry, Y. (2013). *Walk-ins among us: Open your personal portal to cosmic awareness.* Nashville, TN: Write On! Publishing.

Phillips, M. L. (2003). Understanding the neurobiology of emotion perception: Implications for psychiatry. *British Journal of Psychiatry, 182,* 190–192. doi:10.1192/bjp.02.185

Pilgrim, R. B. (1999). Mahayana Buddhism. In S. J. Kaplan (Ed.), *Concepts of trans-migration: Perspectives on reincarnation* (pp. 119–132). Lewiston, NY: Edwin Mellen Press.

Pinson, D. (1999). *Reincarnation and Judaism: The journey of the soul.* Northvale, NJ: Jason Aronson.

Playfair, G. L. (2006). *New clothes for old souls: Worldwide evidence for reincarnation.* London, UK: Druze Heritage Foundation.

Playfair, G. L. (2011). *The flying cow: Exploring the psychic world of Brazil.* Guildford, Surrey, UK: White Crow Books.

Playfair, G. L. (2012). *Twin telepathy.* Guildford, Surrey, UK: White Crow Books.

Popper, K. R., & Eccles, J. C. (1977). *The self and its brain: An argument for inter-actionism.* Berlin, Germany: Springer Verlag.

Potter, K. H. (1980). The karma theory and its interpretation in some Indian philo-sophical systems. In W. D. O'Flaherty (Ed.), *Karma and rebirth in classical Indian traditions* (pp. 241–267). Berkeley, CA: University of California Press.

Prabhavananda. (1979). *The spiritual heritage of India.* Hollywood, CA: Vedanta Press.

Praed, Mrs. C. (1931). *Soul of Nyria.* London, UK: Rider.

Prasad, B. (1967). Harsh—A case suggestive of extra-cerebral memory. *Parapsychol-ogy, 7,* 23–31.

Prasad, M. N. (1999). *Karma and reincarnation: The Vedantic perspective.* (Contem-porary researches in Hindu philosophy & religion). Delhi, India: D.K. Printworld.

Premasiri, P. D. (1996). The Theravada Buddhist doctrine of survival after death. In S. J. Kaplan (Ed.), *Concepts of transmigration: Perspectives on reincarnation* (pp. 133–187). Lewiston, NY: Edwin Mellen Press.

Preuss, P. (1989). *Reincarnation: A philosophical and practical analysis.* Lewiston, NY: Edwin Mellen Press.

Pribram, K. [H.] (1991). *Brain and perception: Holonomy and structure in figural processing.* Hillsdale, NJ: Lawrence Erlbaum Associates.

Pribram, K. H. (2004). Consciousness reassessed. *Mind and Matter, 2,* 7–35.

Pribram, K. H. (2013). *The form within: My point of view.* New York, NY: Prospecta Press.

Price, H. H. (1995). Paranormal cognition and symbolism. In F. B. Dilley (Ed.), *Philosophical interactions with parapsychology: The major writings of H. H. Price on parapsychology and survival.* London, UK: Methuen.

Pyun, Y. D. (2015). Creating past-life identity in hypnotic regression. *International Journal of Clinical and Experimental Hypnosis, 63*(3), 365–372.

Pyun, Y. D., & Kim, T. J. (2009). Experimental production of past-life memories in hypnosis. *International Journal of Clinical and Experimental Hypnosis, 57,* 269–278.

Quinton, A. (1975). The soul. In J. Perry (Ed.), *Personal identity* (pp. 53–72). Berke-ley, CA: University of California Press.

Radin, D. [I.] (2006). *Entangled minds: Extrasensory experiences in a quantum real-ity.* New York, NY: Paraview Pocket Books.

Radin, D. [I.] (2009). *The conscious universe: The scientific truth of psychic phenomena* (Reprint ed.) New York: HarperOne.

Radin, D. I., & Nelson, R. D. (1989). Evidence for consciousness-related anomalies in random physical systems. *Foundations of Physics, 19,* 1499–1514.

Rahul, R. (1995). *The Dalai Lama: The institution.* New Delhi, India: Vikas.

Ramster, P. (1990). *The search for lives past.* Bowral, New South Wales, Australia: Somerset Film and Publishing.

Randall, J. (1975). *Parapsychology and the nature of life.* London, UK: Souvenir Press.

Ransom, C. (2015). A critique of Ian Stevenson's rebirth research. In M. Martin & K. Augustine (Eds.), *The myth of an afterlife: The case against life after death* (pp. 639–644). Lanham, MD: Rowman & Littlefield.

Ravaldini, G., Biondi, M, & Stevenson, I. (1990). The case of Giuseppe Riccardi: An unusual drop-in communicator in Italy. *Journal of the Society for Psychical Research, 56,* 257–265.

Rawat, K. S. (1979, July). A child is re-born. *Probe India,* pp. 93–96.

Rawat, K. S., & Rivas, T. (2005). The life beyond: Through the eyes of children who claim to remember previous lives. *Journal of Religion and Psychical Research, 28,* 126–136.

Rawat, K. S., & Rivas, T. (2007). *Reincarnation: The scientific evidence is building.* Vancouver, BC: Writers.

Reber, P. J. (2013). The neural basis of implicit learning and memory: A review of neuropsychological and neuroimaging research. *Neuropsychologia, 51,* 2026–2042.

Reichenbach, B. R. (1990). *The law of karma: A philosophical study.* Honolulu, HI: University of Hawaii Press.

Reid, C. R., Latty, T., Dussutour A., & Beekman, M. (2014). Slime mold uses an externalized spatial "memory" to navigate in complex environments. *Proceedings of the National Academy of Sciences of the United States, 109*(43), 17490–17494. doi:10.1073/pnas.1215037109

Reinke, J. (1899). *Die Welt als Tat.* Berlin, Germany: Paetel.

Rhine, J. B., & Feather, S. R. (1962). The study of cases of "psi-trailing" in animals. *Journal of Parapsychology, 16,* 1–22.

Rhine, L. E. (1966). Review of *Twenty cases suggestive of reincarnation* by I. Stevenson. *Journal of Parapsychology, 30,* 263–272.

Rhine, L. E. (1981). *The invisible picture: A study of psychic experiences.* Jefferson, NC: McFarland.

Richet, C. (1905–1907). Xénoglossie: L'écriture automatique en langues étrangères. *Proceedings of the Society for Psychical Research, 19,* 162–194.

Rieder, M. (1993). *Mission to Millboro.* Nevada City, CA: Blue Dolphin.

Rieder, M. (1996). *Return to Millboro: The reincarnation drama continues . . .* Nevada City, CA: Blue Dolphin.

Rinbochay, L., & Hopkins, J. (1980). *Death, intermediate state and rebirth in Tibetan Buddhism.* Boulder, CO: Snow Lion.

Rivas, T. (1991). Alfred Peacock? Reincarnation fantasies about the *Titanic. Journal of the Society for Psychical Research, 58,* 10–15.

Rivas, T. (1998). Memory and paramnesia: Early reincarnation research into spontaneous memories among adults and children in The Netherlands. Retrieved from http://txtxs.nl/artikel.asp?artid=642

Rivas, T. (2001). The case of S: Possible recollections of two previous lives and of intermediate states between incarnations. Papers of Athanasia, Issue 1. Retrieved from https://www.academia.edu/768154/The_case_of_S_Possible_recollections_ of_two_previous_lives_and_of_intermediate_states_between_incarnations

Rivas, T. (2003). Three cases of the reincarnation type in the Netherlands. *Journal of Scientific Exploration, 17,* 527–532.

Rivas, T. (2004). Six cases of the reincarnation type in the Netherlands. *Paranormal Review,* no. 29, 17–20.

Rivas, T. (2005). Rebirth and personal identity: Is reincarnation an intrinsically impersonal concept? *Journal of Religion and Psychical Research, 28,* 226–233.

Rivas, T. (2012). Amnesia: The universality of reincarnation and the preservation of psychological structure. Translated and condensed version of *Het geheugen en herinneringen aan vorigelevens: Neuro-psychologische en psychologische factoren, Spiegel der Parapsychologie, 37*(2–3), 81–104 (1999). Retrieved from https://www.academia.edu/768154/The_case_of_S_Possible_recollections_of_two_previous_lives_and_of_intermediate_states_between_incarnations

Rivas, T., Carman, E. M., Carman, N. J., & Dirven, A. (2015). Paranormal aspects of pre-existence memories in young children. *Journal of Near-Death Studies, 34*(2), 84–107.

Rivas, T., Dirven, A., & Smit, R. H. (2016). *The self does not die: Verified paranormal phenomena from near-death experiences.* Durham, NC: International Association for Near-Death Studies.

Robertson, T. J. (2013). *Things you can do when you're dead: True accounts of after death communication.* Guildford, Surrey, UK: White Crow Books.

Robertson, T. J. (2015). *More things you can do when you're dead: What can you truly believe?* Guildford, Surrey, UK: White Crow Books.

Rochas, A. de. (1896). *L'extériorisation de la motricité: Recueil d'expériences et d'observations.* Paris, France: Charmel.

Rochas, A. de. (1904). *Les états profonds de l'hypnose* (5th ed.). Paris, France: Bibliothèque Chacornac.

Rochas, A. de. (1911). *Les vies successives: Documents pour l'étude de cette question.* Paris, France: Bibliothèque Chacornac.

Roe, C. A., & Roxburgh, E. C. (2013). Non-parapsychological explanations of ostensible mediumship. In A. J. Rock (Ed.), *The survival hypothesis: Essays on mediumship* (pp. 65–78). Jefferson, NC: McFarland.

Rogo, D. S. (1985). *The search for yesterday: A critical examination of the evidence for reincarnation.* Englewood Cliffs, NJ: Prentice-Hall.

Rogo, D. S. (1986). Researching the reincarnation question: Some current perspectives. *Journal of Religion and Psychical Research, 9,* 128–137.

Rogo, D. S. (1991). State of consciousness factors in reincarnation cases. In A. Berger & J. Berger (Eds.), *Reincarnation: Fact or fable?* (pp. 15–30). London, UK: Aquarian Press.

Roll, W. G. (1972). *The poltergeist*. New York: Doubleday.

Roll, W. G. (1977). Where is Said Bouhamsy? *Theta, 5*(3), 1–4.

Roll, W. G. (1982). The changing perspective on life after death. In S. Krippner (Ed.), *Advances in parapsychological research 3* (pp. 147–291). New York, NY: Plenum.

Roll, W. G. (1983). Errata. In W. G. Roll, J. Belloff, & R. A. White (Eds.), *Research in parapsychology 1982* (p. 336). Metuchen, NJ: Scarecrow Press.

Roll, W. G. (1984). Rebirth memories and personal identity: The case of Imad Elawar. *Journal of the American Society for Psychical Research, 78*, 182–186.

Rosen, H. (1956). Introduction. In M. V. Kline (Ed.), *A scientific report on "The search for Bridey Murphy"* (pp. xv–xxxi). New York, NY: Julian Press.

Rosenblum, B., & Kuttner, F. (2011). *Quantum enigma: Physics encounters consciousness* (2nd ed). New York, NY: Oxford University Press.

Roth, C. (2008). *Becoming Tsimshian: The social life of names*. Seattle, WA: University of Washington Press.

Ryall, E. W. (1974). *Born twice: Total recall of a seventeenth-century life*. New York, NY: Harper and Row. (Originally published in 1974 as *Second time round*, London, UK: Neville Spearman.)

Saadia Gaon. (1989). *The book of beliefs and opinions* (Yale Judaica Series). Translated from Arabic and Hebrew by S. Rosenblatt. New Haven, CT: Yale University Press.

Sahay, K. K. N. [1927]. *Reincarnation: Verified cases of rebirth after death*. Bareilly, India: Gupta.

Sakellarios, S. (2011). *Mathew Franklin Whittier in his own words* (e-book). Last accessed January 31, 2018, from http://www.ial.goldthread.com/MFW.html

Salva, R. (2006). *Soul journey from Lincoln to Lindbergh: Revealing the mysteries of karma and rebirth*. San Jose, CA: Crystar Press.

Saunders, L. A. (2004). *Past-life recall: A phenomenological investigation of facilitated and nonfacilitated recall experiences and their contribution to psychospiritual development*. (Ph.D. dissertation.) Institute of Transpersonal Psychology.

Schibli, H. S. (1990). *Pherekydes of Syros*. New York, NY: Oxford University Press.

Schindewolf, O. (1950). *Grundfragen der Paläontologie*. Stuttgart, Germany: Schweizerbart.

Schlitz, M., & Braud, W. (1997). Distant intentionality and healing: Assessing the evidence. *Alternative Therapies in Health and Medicine, 3*(6), 62–73.

Schneider, K. C. (1911). *Einführung in die Deszendenztheorie*. Jena, Germany: Gustav Fischer.

Schneider, K. C. (1926). *Euvitalistische Biologie*. Munich, Germany: Bergmann.

Schopenhauer, A. (1889). *Two essays by Arthur Schopenhauer*. London, UK: Bell.

Schopenhauer, A. (1969). *The world as will and representation* (2 vols.). New York, NY: Dover Publications.

Schouten, S., & Stevenson, I. (1998). Does the socio-psychological hypothesis explain cases of the reincarnation type? *Journal of Nervous and Mental Disease, 186*, 504–506.

Schwartz, J. M., & Begley, S. (2002). *The mind and the brain: Neuroplasticity and the power of mental force*. New York: HarperCollins.

Schwartz, J. M., Gulliford, E. Z., Stier, J., & Thienemann, M. (2005). Mindful aware-ness and self-directed neuroplasticity: Integrating psychospiritual and biological approaches to mental health with a focus on obsessive compulsive disorder. In S. G. Mijares, & G. S. Khalsa (Eds.), *The psychospiritual clinician's handbook: Alternative methods for understanding and treating mental disorders.* Binghamton, NY: Haworth Reference Press.

Schwartz, J. M., Stapp, H. P., & Beauregard, M. (2004). The volitional influence of the mind on the brain, with special reference to emotional self-regulation. In M. Beauregard (Ed.), *Consciousness, emotional self-regulation, and the brain* (pp. 195–237). Philadelphia, PA: John Benjamins Publishing Company.

Schwartz, J. M., Stapp, H. P., & Beauregard, M. (2005). Quantum physics in neuro-science and psychology: A neurophysical model of mind–brain interaction. *Philo-sophical Transactions of the Royal Society B.* doi:10.1098/rstb.2004.1598

Schwartz, S. A. (1978). *The secret vaults of time: Psychic archaeology and the quest for man's beginnings.* New York, NY: Grosset & Dunlap.

Searle, J. R. (1997). *The mystery of consciousness.* New York, NY: New York Review of Books.

Semkiw, W. (2003). *Return of the revolutionaries: The case for reincarnation and soul groups reunited.* Charlottesville, VA: Hampton Roads.

Semkiw, W. (2011a). *Born again: Reincarnation cases involving evidence of past lives with xenoglossy cases researched by Ian Stevenson, MD* (expanded interna-tional ed.). N.p: Pluto Project.

Semkiw, W. (2011b). *Origin of the soul and the purpose of reincarnation, with past lives of Jesus: Expanded edition with past lives of Jesus.* N.p.: Pluto Project.

Semkiw, W. (n.d.-a). Past life story with a spirit being, raising of the dead & karma: Walk-In incarnation case of Sobha Ram / Jasbir Jat. Retrieved from http://www.iisis.net/index.php?page=reincarnation-walk-in-ian-stevenson-sobha-ram-jasbir-jat-walter-semkiw&

Semkiw, W. (n.d.-b). Split incarnation: When a soul inhabits more than one human body at a time (also known as parallel lives, twin souls & twin flames). Retrieved from http://www.iisis.net/index.php?page=semkiw-reincarnation-split-incarna tion-parallel-lives

Sharma, A. (1990). Karma and reincarnation in Advaita Vedānta. *Journal of Indian Philosophy, 18,* 219–236.

Sharma, I. C. (1975). *Cayce, karma and reincarnation.* Wheaton, IL: Theosophical Publishing House.

Sharma, P., & Tucker, J. B. (2004). Cases of the reincarnation type with memories from the intermission between lives. *Journal of Near-Death Studies, 23,* 101–118.

Sharp, L. A. (1995). Organ transplantation as a transformative experience: Anthropo-logical insights into the restructuring of the self. *Medical Anthropology Quarterly, 9*(3), 357–389. doi:10.1525/maq.1995.9.3.02a00050

Sharp, L. L. (2006). *Secular spirituality: Reincarnation and Spiritism in nineteenth-century France.* Lanham, MD: Lexington Books.

Sheldrake, R. (1982). *A new science of life: The hypothesis of formative causation.* Los Angeles, CA: J.P Tarcher

Sheldrake, R. (1988). *The presence of the past: Morphic resonance and the habits of nature.* New York: Times Books.

Sheldrake, R. (2009). *Morphic resonance: The nature of formative causation.* Rochester, VT: Park Street Press.

Sheldrake, R. (2011). *Dogs that know when their owners are coming home.* New York, NY: Three Rivers Press.

Shermer, M. (2018). *Heavens on Earth: The scientific search for the afterlife, immortality, and utopia.* New York, NY: Henry Holt.

Shirley, R. (1936). *The problem of rebirth: An enquiry into the basis of the reincarnationist hypothesis.* London, UK: Rider.

Shomrat, T, & Levin, M. (2013). An automated training paradigm reveals long-term memory in planaria and its persistence through head regeneration. *Journal of Experimental Biology, 216,* 3799–3810. doi:10.1242/jeb.087809

Shushan, G. (2009). *Conceptions of the afterlife in early civilizations: Universalism, constructivism, and near-death experience.* London, UK: Continuum.

Shushan, G. (2018). *Near-death experience in indigenous religions.* Oxford, UK: Oxford University Press.

Sidgwick, H., Sidgwick, E. M., & Johnson, A. (1894). Report on the Census of Hallucinations. *Proceedings of the Society for Psychical Research, 10,* 25–442.

Skeptico. (2005, July 7). Reincarnation all over again. Retrieved from: http://skeptico .blogs.com/skeptico/2005/07/reincarnation_a.html

Skilton, A. (2003). *A concise history of Buddhism.* New York, NY: Barnes & Noble.

Skrbina, D. (2005). *Panpsychism in the West.* Cambridge, MA: MIT Press.

Slobodin, R. (1994). Kutchin concepts of reincarnation. In A. Mills & R. Slobodin (Eds.), *Amerindian rebirth: Reincarnation belief among North American Indians and Inuit* (pp. 136–155). Toronto, ON: University of Toronto Press.

Smith, A. (1984). Did Porphyry reject the transmigration of human souls into animals? *Rheinisches Museum für Philologie* (Neue Folge), 127. Bd., H. 3/4, 276–284.

Smith, A. P. (2015a). *Lost teachings of the Cathars: Their beliefs and practices* (anniversary ed.). London, UK: Watkins Publishing.

Smith, A. P. (2015b). *The secret history of the Gnostics.* London, UK: Watkins Publishing.

Snow, R. L. (1999). *Looking for Carroll Beckwith: The true story of a detective's search for his past life.* Emmaus, PA: Rodale Books.

Somer, E., Klein-Sela, C., & Or-Chen, K. (2011). Beliefs in reincarnation and the power of fate and their association with emotional outcomes among bereaved parents of fallen soldiers. *Journal of Loss and Trauma, 16,* 459–475. doi:10.1080/15 325024.2011.575706

Somersan, S. (1981). *Death symbolism: A cross-cultural study* (Ph.D. dissertation). Ohio State University. Ann Arbor, MI: University Microfilms.

Somersan, S. (1984). Death symbolism in matrilineal societies. *Ethos, 12,* 151–164.

Sorabji, R. (2006). *Self: Ancient and modern insights about individuality, life, and death.* Chicago, IL: University of Chicago Press.

Sorensen, V. (1976). *Seneca: The humanist at the court of Nero.* Chicago, IL: University of Chicago Press.

Southern Weekly. (2015, July 13). Villagers cash in on reincarnation interest, gov't turns a blind eye. Downloaded from http://www.globaltimes.cn/content/931825.shtml

Southworth, F. C. (2005). *Linguistic archaeology of South Asia.* New York, NY: RoutledgeCurzon.

Spanos, N. P. (1996). *Multiple identities and false memories: A sociocognitive perspective.* Washington, DC: American Psychological Association.

Spanos, N. P., Menary, E., Gabora, N. J., DuBreuil, S. C., & Dewhirst, B. (1991). Secondary identity enactments during hypnotic past-life regression: A sociocognitive perspective. *Journal of Personality and Social Psychology, 61*(2), 308–320.

Sperry, R. W. (1980). Mind-brain interaction: Mentalism, yes; dualism, no. *Neuroscience, 5,* 195–206.

Spiro, M. E. (1982). *Buddhism and society: A great tradition and its Burmese vicissitudes* (2nd ed.). Berkeley, CA: University of California Press.

Spivak, B., Iancu, I., Daie, N., & Weizman, A. (1995). The belief in the transmigration of souls as a presenting symptom of generalized anxiety disorder in a military setting. *Psychopathology, 28,* 158–160.

Stapp, H. P. (1979). Whiteheadean approach to quantum theory and the generalized Bell's theorem. *Foundations of Physics, 9,* 1–25.

Stapp, H. P. (1999). Attention, intention, and will in quantum physics. *Journal of Consciousness Studies, 6*(8–9), 143–164.

Stapp, H. P. (2005). Quantum interactive dualism: An alternative to materialism. *Journal of Consciousness Studies, 19,* 43–58.

Stapp, H. P. [2009]. Compatibility of contemporary physical theory with personality survival. Retrieved from http://www-physics.lbl.gov/stapp/Compatibility.pdf

Stapp, H. P. (2011). *Mindful universe: Quantum mechanics and the participating observer* (2nd ed.). New York, NY: Springer.

Stapp, H. P. (2015). A quantum-mechanical theory of the mind/brain connection. In E. F. Kelly, A. Crabtree, & P. Marshall (Eds.), *Beyond physicalism: Toward reconciliation of science and spirituality* (pp. 157–193). Lanham, MD: Rowman & Littlefield.

Stearn, J. (1967). *Edgar Cayce, the sleeping prophet.* Garden City, NY: Doubleday.

Stearn, J. (1968). *The search for the girl with the blue eyes.* Garden City, NY: Doubleday.

Stearn, J. (1989). *Intimates through time: Edgar Cayce's mysteries of reincarnation.* New York, NY: Harper & Row.

Steiger, B., & Williams, L. G. (1976). *Other lives.* New York, NY: Hawthorn Books.

Stemman, R. (1998). Druze children who remember past lives: True or false. *Reincarnation International,* no. 15, pp. 19–21.

Stevens, E. W. (1887). *The Watseka wonder.* Chicago, IL: Religio-Philosophical Publishing House.

Stevenson, I. (1960a). The evidence for survival from claimed memories of former incarnations. Part I: Review of the data. *Journal of the American Society for Psychical Research, 54,* 51–71.

Stevenson, I. (1960b). The evidence for survival from claimed memories of former incarnations. Part II: Analysis of the data and suggestions for further investigations. *Journal of the American Society for Psychical Research, 54*, 95–117.

Stevenson, I. (1966a). Cultural patterns in cases suggestive of reincarnation among the Tlingit Indians of southeastern Alaska. *Journal of the American Society for Psychical Research, 60*, 229–243.

Stevenson, I. (1966b). Twenty cases suggestive of reincarnation. *Proceedings of the American Society for Psychical Research, 26*, 1–361.

Stevenson, I. (1970a). Characteristics of cases of the reincarnation type in Turkey and their comparison with cases of two other cultures. *International Journal of Comparative Sociology, 11*, 1–17.

Stevenson, I. (1970b). *Telepathic impressions: A review and report of thirty-five new cases*. Charlottesville, VA: University Press of Virginia.

Stevenson, I. (1971). The belief in reincarnation and related cases among the Eskimos of Alaska. In W. G. Roll, R. L. Morris, & J. D. Morris (Eds.), *Proceedings of the Parapsychological Association, Vol. 6, 1969* (pp. 53–55). Durham, NC: Parapsychological Association.

Stevenson, I. (1972). Are poltergeists living or are they dead? *Journal of the American Society for Psychical Research, 66*, 233–252.

Stevenson, I. (1973a). Carington's psychon theory as applied to cases of the reincarnation type: A reply to Gardner Murphy. *Journal of the American Society for Psychical Research, 67*, 130–145.

Stevenson, I. (1973b). Characteristics of cases of the reincarnation type in Ceylon. *Contributions to Asian Studies, 3*, 26–29.

Stevenson, I. (1974a). Some questions related to cases of the reincarnation type. *Journal of the American Society for Psychical Research, 68*, 395–416.

Stevenson, I. (1974b). *Twenty cases suggestive of reincarnation* (2nd ed., rev.). Charlottesville, VA: University Press of Virginia.

Stevenson, I. (1974c). *Xenoglossy: A review and report of a case*. Charlottesville, VA: University Press of Virginia.

Stevenson, I. (1975a). *Cases of the reincarnation type. Volume I: Ten cases in India.* Charlottesville, VA: University Press of Virginia.

Stevenson, I. (1975b). The belief and cases related to reincarnation among the Haida. *Journal of Anthropological Research, 31*, 364–375.

Stevenson, I. (1977a). *Cases of the reincarnation type. Volume II: Ten cases in Sri Lanka.* Charlottesville, VA: University Press of Virginia.

Stevenson, I. (1977b). The explanatory value of the idea of reincarnation. *Journal of Nervous and Mental Disease, 164*, 305–326.

Stevenson, I. (1977c). The southeast Asian interpretation of gender dysphoria: An illustrative case report. *Journal of Nervous and Mental Disease, 165*, 201–208.

Stevenson, I. (1980). *Cases of the reincarnation type. Vol. III: Twelve cases in Lebanon and Turkey.* Charlottesville, VA: University Press of Virginia.

Stevenson, I. (1982). The contribution of apparitions to the evidence for survival. *Journal of the American Society for Psychical Research, 76*, 341–358.

Stevenson, I. (1983a). American children who claim to remember previous lives. *Journal of Nervous and Mental Disease, 171*, 742–748.

Stevenson, I. (1983b). *Cases of the reincarnation type. Volume IV: Twelve cases in Thailand and Burma.* Charlottesville, VA: University Press of Virginia.

Stevenson, I. (1983c). Cryptomnesia and parapsychology. *Journal of the Society for Psychical Research, 52,* 1–30.

Stevenson, I. (1984). *Unlearned language: New studies in xenoglossy.* Charlottesville, VA: University Press of Virginia.

Stevenson, I. (1985). The belief in reincarnation among the Igbo of Nigeria. *Journal of Asian and African Studies, 20,* 13–30.

Stevenson, I. (1986a). Characteristics of cases of the reincarnation type among the Igbo of Nigeria. *Journal of Asian and African Studies, 21,* 204–216.

Stevenson, I. (1986b). Comments by Ian Stevenson. *Journal of the Society for Psychical Research, 53*(802), 232–239.

Stevenson, I. (1989). Some of my journeys in medicine. (The Flora Levy Lecture in the Humanities, 1989.) Edited by A. W. Fields. Lafayette, LA: University of Southwestern Louisiana. Retrieved from https://pdfs.semanticscholar.org/1aab/6f 3ee79ec8003b0e9ed370a4ae6c5e55297c.pdf

Stevenson, I. (1990). Phobias in children who claim to remember previous lives. *Journal of Scientific Exploration, 4,* 243–254.

Stevenson, I. (1992). A new look at maternal impressions: An analysis of 50 published cases and reports of two recent examples. *Journal of Scientific Exploration, 6,* 353–373.

Stevenson, I. (1993). Birthmarks and birth defects corresponding to wounds on deceased persons. *Journal of Scientific Exploration, 7,* 403–410.

Stevenson, I. (1994). Guest commentary: A case of the psychotherapist's fallacy: Hypnotic regression to "previous lives." *American Journal of Clinical Hypnosis, 36,* 188–193.

Stevenson, I. (1997a). *Reincarnation and biology: A contribution to the etiology of birthmarks and birth defects* (2 vols.). Westport, CT: Praeger.

Stevenson, I. (1997b). *Where reincarnation and biology intersect.* Westport, CT: Praeger.

Stevenson, I. (2000a). The phenomenon of claimed memories of previous lives: Possible interpretations and importance. *Medical Hypotheses, 54,* 652–659. doi:10.1054/mehy.1999.0920

Stevenson, I. (2000b). Unusual play in young children who claim to remember previous lives. *Journal of Scientific Exploration, 14,* 557–570.

Stevenson, I. (2001). *Children who remember previous lives: A question of reincarnation* (rev. ed.). Jefferson, NC: McFarland.

Stevenson, I. (2003). *European cases of the reincarnation type.* Jefferson, NC: McFarland.

Stevenson, I. (2006). Half a career with the paranormal. *Journal of Scientific Exploration, 20,* 13–21.

Stevenson, I., & Chadha, N. (1990). Can children be stopped from speaking about previous lives? Some further analyses of features in cases of the reincarnation type. *Journal of the Society for Psychical Research, 56,* 82–90.

Stevenson, I., Cook, E. W., & McClean-Rice, N. (1989–1990). Are persons reporting "near-death experiences" really near death? A study of medical records. *Omega: The Journal of Death and Dying, 20,* 45–54.

Stevenson, I., & Haraldsson, E. (2003). The similarity of features of reincarnation type cases over many years: A third study. *Journal of Scientific Exploration, 17,* 283–289.

Stevenson, I., & Keil, [H. H.] J. (2000). The stability of assessments of paranormal connections in reincarnation cases. *Journal of Scientific Exploration, 14,* 365–382.

Stevenson, I., & Keil, [H. H.] J. (2005). Children of Myanmar who behave like Japanese soldiers: A possible third element in personality. *Journal of Scientific Exploration, 19,* 172–183.

Stevenson, I., & Pasricha, S. [K.] (1979). A case of secondary personality with xenoglossy. *American Journal of Psychiatry, 136,* 1591–1592.

Stevenson, I., & Pasricha, S. [K.] (1980). A preliminary report of an unusual case of the reincarnation type with xenoglossy. *Journal of the American Society for Psychical Research, 74,* 331–348.

Stevenson, I., Pasricha, S. [K.], & McClean-Rice, N. (1989). A case of the possession type in India with evidence of paranormal knowledge. *Journal of Scientific Exploration, 3,* 81–101.

Stevenson, I., Pasricha, S. [K.], & Samararatne, G. (1988). Deception and self-deception in cases of the reincarnation type: Seven illustrative cases in Asia. *Journal of the American Society for Psychical Research, 82,* 1–31.

Stevenson, I., & Samararatne, G. (1988). Three new cases of the reincarnation type in Sri Lanka with written records made before verification. *Journal of Scientific Exploration, 2,* 217–238.

Stewart, A. J. (1978). *Died 1513, born 1929.* London, UK: Macmillan.

Stocking, G. W. (1971). Animism in theory and practice: E. B. Tylor's unpublished "Notes on spiritualism." *Man,* New Series *6*(1), 88–104.

Stokes, D. M. (2007). *The conscious mind and the material world: On psi, the soul and the self.* Jefferson, NC: McFarland.

Stokes, D. M. (2014). *Reimagining the soul: Afterlife in the age of matter.* Jefferson, NC: McFarland.

Story, F. (1975). *Rebirth as doctrine and experience: Essays and case studies.* Kandy, Sri Lanka: Buddhist Publishing Society.

Strieber, W., & Kripal, J. J. (2016). *The super natural: Why the unexplained is real.* New York, NY: Penguin Random House.

Sudduth, M. (2009). Super-psi and the survivalist interpretation of mediumship. *Journal of Scientific Exploration, 23,* 167–193.

Sudduth, M. (2013). Is postmortem survival the best explanation of the data of mediumship? In A. J. Rock (Ed.), *The survival hypothesis: Essays on mediumship* (pp. 40–64). Jefferson, NC: McFarland.

Sudduth, M. (2016). *A philosophical critique of empirical arguments for post-mortem survival.* Basingstoke, UK: Palgrave Macmillan.

Sudre, R. (1930). Re-incarnation and experience. *Journal of the American Society for Psychical Research, 23*, 215–220.

Sugrue, T. (1942). *There is a river: The story of Edgar Cayce.* New York, NY: Henry Holt.

Sumegi, A. (2008). *Dreamworlds of shamanism and Tibetan Buddhism.* Albany, NY: State University of New York.

Sunderlal, R. B. S. (1924). Cas apparents de réminescences de vies antériures. *Revue Métapsychique, 4*, 302–307.

Swanson, G. (1960). *The birth of the gods: The origin of primitive beliefs.* Ann Arbor, MI: University of Michigan Press.

Swanton, J. R. (1908). Social conditions, beliefs, and linguistic relationship of the Tlingit Indians. *Twenty-sixth annual report of the Bureau of American Ethnology* (pp. 395–485). Washington, DC: Smithsonian Institution.

Sylvia, C., with Novak, W. (1997). *A change of heart: A memoir.* Boston, MA: Little, Brown & Co.

Tabori, P. (1951). *My occult diary.* London: Rider.

Tarazi, L. (1990). An unusual case of hypnotic regression with some unexplained contents. *Journal of the American Society for Psychical Research, 84*, 309–344.

Tarazi, L. (1997). *Under the Inquisition: An experience relived.* Charlottesville, VA: Hampton Roads.

Tart, C. T. (2009). *The end of materialism: How evidence of the paranormal is bringing science and spirit together.* Oakland, CA: New Harbinger Publications and the Institute of Noetic Sciences.

Taylor, S. A. (2016). *The Akashic Records: Access the greatest source of information to empower your life.* Carlsbad, CA: Hay House.

Teilhard de Chardin, P. (1959). *The phenomenon of man.* New York, NY: Harper.

Temple, L. (1970). *The shining brother.* London, UK: Psychic Press.

TenDam, H. (1990). *Exploring reincarnation.* London, UK: Arkana.

Tenhaeff, W. H. C. (1972). *Telepathy and clairvoyance.* Springfield, IL: Charles C Thomas.

That Day in Kenner (n.d.). [web page]. Retrieved from http://media.nola.com/traffic/photo/graphic-panam–070812jpg-a057882d8912c02b.jpg

Thomason, S. G. (1984). Do you remember your past life's language in your present incarnation? *American Speech, 59*, 340–350.

Thomason, S. G. (1987, Summer). Past tongues remembered? *Skeptical Inquirer*, pp. 367–375.

Thomason, S. G. (1996). Xenoglossy. In G. Stein (Ed.), *The encyclopedia of the paranormal* (pp. 835–844). Amherst, NY: Prometheus Books.

Thompson, E. (2007). *Mind in life: Biology, phenomenology, and the sciences of mind.* Cambridge, MA: Harvard University Press.

Thompson, E. (2015). *Waking, dreaming, being: Self and consciousness in neuroscience, meditation, and philosophy.* New York, NY: Columbia University Press.

Thompson, G. [n.d]. Shamanism in the Ṛgveda and its Central Asian antecedents. Downloaded from http://www.people.fas.harvard.edu/witzel/Thompson.pdf

Thondup, T. (2005). *Peaceful death, joyful rebirth: A Tibetan Buddhist guidebook.* Boulder, CO: Shambhala.

Tigunait, R. (1997). *From death to birth: Understanding karma and reincarnation.* Honesdale, PA: Himalayan Institute.

Titchener, E. B. (1895). Affective memory. *Philosophical Review, 4*(1), 65–76.

Todisco, M., Fraccia, T. P., Smith, G. P., Corno A., Bethge, L., Klussmauu, S., Paraboschi, E. M., Asselta, R., Colombo, D., Zanchetta G., Clark, N. A., & Bellini, T. (2018). Nonenzymatic polymerization into long linear RNA templated by liquid crystal self-assembly. *ACS Nano, 12,* 9750–9762.

Tomlinson, A. (2006). *Healing the eternal soul: Insights from past-life and spiritual regression.* Alresford, UK: John Hunt Publishing.

Toynbee, A. (1959). *Hellenism: The history of a civilization.* London, UK: Oxford University Press.

Tramont, C. (2008). *From birth to rebirth: Gnostic healing in the 21st century.* Las Vegas, NV: Granite Publishing.

Treffert, D. A. (2010). *Islands of genius.* London, UK: Kingsley.

Trugman, A. A. (2008). *Return again: The dynamics of reincarnation.* New York: Devora Publishing.

Trumbower, J. A. (2016, Nov.). Closing the door on reincarnation in early Christianity: Limiting the options." Prepared for the Philo of Alexandria Seminar, Society of Biblical Literature Annual Meeting, San Antonio, Texas, November 2016. Downloaded from http://torreys.org/sblpapers2016/S20–345_Trumbower_Reincarnation2016.pdf

Tucker, J. B. (2000). A scale to measure the strength of children's claims of previous lives: Methodology and initial findings. *Journal of Scientific Exploration, 14,* 571–581.

Tucker, J. B. (2005). *Life before life: A scientific investigation of children's memories of a previous life.* New York: St. Martin's Press.

Tucker, J. B. (2013). *Return to life: Extraordinary cases of children who remember past lives.* New York, NY: St. Martin's Press.

Tucker, J. B. (2014, February). Thoughts on a shared dream model of reincarnation (and life). *Edge Science,* no. 17, pp. 13–17.

Tucker, J. B. (2016). The case of James Leininger: An American case of the reincarnation type. *Explore, 12*(3), 200–207.

Tucker, J. B., & Keil, H. H. J. (2001). Can cultural beliefs cause a gender identity disorder? *Journal of Psychology and Human Sexuality, 13,* 21–30.

Tucker, J. B., & Keil, H. H. J. (2013). Experimental birthmarks: New cases of an Asian practice. *Journal of Scientific Exploration, 27,* 269–282.

Tucker, J. B., & Nidiffer, F. D. (2014). Psychological evaluation of American children who report memories of previous lives. *Journal of Scientific Exploration, 28,* 583–594.

Tulving, E. (1972). Episodic and semantic memory. In E. Tulving & W. Donaldson (Eds.), *Organization of memory* (pp. 381–402). New York, NY: Academic Press.

Tulving, E. (1985). Memory and consciousness. *Canadian Psychology, 26,* 1–12.

Twenty worst aviation disasters involving U.S. carriers. [web post]. Retrieved from http://planecrashinfo.com/worstus.htm

Tylor, E. B. (1871). *Primitive culture: Researches into the development of mythology, philosophy, religion, language, art and custom* (2 vols.). London, UK: John Murray.

Tymn, M. E. (2001). Are organ transplants metaphysically contraindicated? *Journal of Religion and Psychical Research, 24,* 153–161.

Tyrrell, G. N. M. (1953/1973). *Apparitions.* London, UK: Society for Psychical Research.

Ullman, M., Krippner, S., & Vaughan, A. (2002). *Dream telepathy: Experiments in nocturnal extrasensory perception.* Charlottesville, VA: Hampton Roads.

Van de Castle, R. L. (1995). *Our dreaming mind.* New York, NY: Ballantine Books.

van Lommel, P. (2010). *Consciousness beyond life: The science of the near-death experience.* New York, NY: HarperCollins.

van Lommel, P., Wees, R. van, Meyers, V., & Elfferich, I. (2001). Near-death experience in survivors of cardiac arrest: A prospective study in the Netherlands. *Lancet, 358,* 2039–2045.

Vargas, A. O., Krabichler, Q., & Guerrero-Bosagna C. (2017). An epigenetic perspective on the midwife toad experiments of Paul Kammerer (1880–1926). *Journal of Experimental Zoology (Molecular and Developmental Evolution), 328B,* 179–192. doi:10.1002/jez.b.22708

Varela, F. J., Thompson, E., & Rosch, E. (2016). *The embodied mind: Cognitive science and human experience* (Rev. ed.). Cambridge, MA: MIT Press.

Veniaminov, I. (1840). *Zapiski ob Atkhinksikh Aleymakh i Koloshakh, sostably-ushie tratiyu chast Zapiski ob ostravakh Unalashkinshavo otdela [Notes on the Atkinksi Aleuts and Koloshes, constituting part three of Notes on the Islands of the Unalaska District].* St. Petersburg, Russia: Rosisko-Amerikanskaya Kompaniya.

Venn, J. (1986). Hypnosis and the reincarnation hypothesis: A critical review and intensive case study. *Journal of the American Society for Psychical Research, 80,* 409–425.

Visoni, V. M. (2010). How to improve the study and documentation of cases of the reincarnation type: A reappraisal of the case of Kemal Atasoy. *Journal of Scientific Exploration, 24,* 101–108.

Von Ward, P. (2008). *The soul genome: Science and reincarnation.* Tucson, AZ: Fenestra Books.

Wade, J. (1998). The phenomenology of near-death consciousness in past-life regression therapy: A pilot study. *Journal of Near-Death Studies, 17,* 31–53.

Waggoner, R. (2009). *Lucid dreaming.* Needham, MA: Moment Point.

Walker, E. D. (1888). *Reincarnation: A study of forgotten truth.* New York, NY: John W. Lovell.

Wallace, A. R. (1889). *Darwinism: An exposition of the theory of natural selection, with some of its applications.* London, UK: Macmillan.

Wallace, A. R. (1910). *The world of life: A manifestation of creative power, directive mind and ultimate purpose.* London, UK: Chapman & Hall.

Walter, T., & Waterhouse, H. (2001). Lives-long learning: The effects of reincarnation belief on everyday life in England. *Nova Religio: The Journal of Alternative and Emergent Religions, 5*(1), 85–101. doi.org/10.1525/nr.2001.5.1.85

Wambach, H. (1978). *Reliving past lives: The evidence under hypnosis*. New York, NY: Harper and Row.

Wangdu, K. S., Gould, B. J., & Richardson, H. E. (2000). *Discovery, recognition and enthronement of the 14th Dalai Lama: A collection of accounts*. Dharmsala, India: Library of Tibetan Work & Archives.

Wardle, E. (2009). *Death in the consulting room: Memories of the Holocaust and questions of "past-lives"* (MA thesis, Middlesex University, Group 11: 2007–2009).

Wardle, E. (2015). Memories of the Holocaust and questions of past lives. *Journal of Psychiatry, 18*(1). Retrieved from https://www.omicsonline.com/open-access/memories-of-the-holocaust-and-questions-of-past-lives-220.pdf

Wehrstein, K. M. (2019). An adult reincarnation case with multiple solved lives: Recalling Wilhelm Emmerich. *Journal of the Society for Psychical Research, 81*, 1–17.

Weird story from Burma: A reincarnated soul. (1907, Oct. 21). *The Advertiser* (Adelaide, South Australia), p. 8. Retrieved from http://trove.nla.gov.au/ndp/del/article/5100715

Weiss, B. L. (1988). *Many lives, many masters*. New York, NY: Simon & Schuster.

Weiss, E. M. (2012). *The long trajectory: The metaphysics of reincarnation and life after death*. Bloomington, IN: iUniverse.

Weiss, E. M. (2015). Mind beyond body: Transphysical process metaphysics. In E. F. Kelly, A. Crabtree, & P. Marshall (Eds.), *Beyond physicalism: Toward reconciliation of science and spirituality* (pp. 455–490). Lanham, MD: Rowman & Littlefield.

Wenzl, A. (1951). Drieschs Neuvitalismus und der Stand des Lebensproblems heute. In A. Wenzl (Ed.), *Hans Driesch: Persönlichkeit und Bedeutung für Biologie und Philosophie von heute* (pp. 65–179). Basel: Reinhardt.

Werblowsky, R. J. Z., & Bremmer, J. N. (2005). Transmigration. In L. Jones (Ed.), *Encyclopedia of religion* (2nd ed.) (vol. 13, pp. 9325–9331). New York, NY: Thomson Gale.

West, M. L. (1971). *Early Greek philosophy and the Orient*. Oxford, UK: Clarendon Press.

West-Eberhard, M.-J. (2003). *Developmental plasticity and evolution*. Oxford, UK: Oxford University Press.

Wetzel, L. J. (2009). *Akashic records: Case studies of past lives*. Houston, TX: Hot Pink Lotus Pod.

Wexelman, D. M. (1999). *The Jewish concept of reincarnation and creation: Based on the writings of Rabbi Chaim Vital*. Northvale, NJ: Aronson.

Wheatley, J. M. O. (1979). Reincarnation, "astral bodies," and "psi-components." *Journal of the American Society for Psychical Research, 79*, 109–122.

White, C. J. (2009). *Reasoning about personal identity: The case of reincarnation beliefs* (Ph.D. dissertation). Queens University, Belfast, Northern Ireland.

White, C. [J.]. (2015a). Cross-cultural similarities in reasoning about personal continuity in reincarnation: Evidence from South India. *Religion, Brain and Behavior, 6*(2), 130–153. doi.org/10.1080/2153599X.2015.1014061

White, C. [J.] (2015b). Establishing personal identity in reincarnation: Minds and bodies reconsidered. *Journal of Cognition and Culture, 15*(3–4), 402–429. doi: 10.1163/15685373–12342158

White, C. (2016). The cognitive foundations of reincarnation. *Method and Theory in the Study of Religion,* 1–23.

White, C. (2017). Who wants to live forever? Explaining the cross-cultural recurrence of reincarnation beliefs. *Journal of Cognition and Culture, 17,* 1–18.

White, C. [J.], Kelly, R., & Nichols, S. (2016). Remembering past lives. In H. De Cruz & R. Nichols (Eds.), *Advances in religion, cognitive science, and experimental philosophy.* New York, NY: Bloomsbury Academic.

Whitehead, A. N. (1978). *Process and reality: An essay in cosmology* (Corrected ed.). New York, NY: Free Press.

Whittier, B. (1996). The clock. In Y. Gershom (Ed.), *From ashes to healing: Mystical encounters with the Holocaust* (pp. 12–21). Virginia Beach, VA: A. R. E. Press.

Wick, R., & Byard, R. W. (2009). Electrocution and the autopsy. In M. Tsokos (Ed.), *Forensic pathology reviews 5* (pp. 53–66). Totowa, NJ: Humana Press.

Willerslev, R. (2007). *Soul hunters: Hunting, animism, and personhood among the Siberian Yukaghirs.* Berkeley, CA: University of California Press.

Willoughby-Meade, G. (1928). *Chinese ghouls and goblins.* London, UK: Constable.

Wilson, C. (1987). *Afterlife: An investigation of the evidence for life after death.* Garden City, NY: Doubleday.

Wilson, I. (1982). *All in the mind: Reincarnation, hypnotic regression, stigmata, multiple personality, and other little-understood powers of the mind.* New York: Doubleday. (Originally published 1981 as *Mind out of time? Reincarnation investigated.* London, UK: Victor Gollancz.)

Winkelman, M. J. (1992). *Shamans, priests and witches: A cross-cultural study of magico-religious practitioners.* (Anthropological Research Papers No. 44). Tucson, AZ: Arizona State University.

Winkler, G. (1996). Judaic perspectives on reincarnation. In S. J. Kaplan (Ed.), *Concepts of transmigration: Perspectives on reincarnation* (pp. 25–52). Lewiston, NY: Edwin Mellen Press.

Witnesses testify in Pan Am damage suits. (1984, Jan. 24). UPI Archives. Retrieved from

Witzel, M. (1999). Substrate languages in Old Indo-Aryan (Ṛgvedic, Middle and Late Vedic). *Electronic Journal of Vedic Studies, 5*(1), 1–67. doi.org/10.11588/ejvs.1999.1.828

Woods, K., & Baruša, I. (2004). Experimental test of possible psychological benefits of past-life regression. *Journal of Scientific Exploration, 18*(4), 597–608.

Woolger, R. J. (1987). *Other lives, other selves: A Jungian psychotherapist discovers past lives.* New York, NY: Doubleday.

Woollacott, M. H. (2015). *Infinite awareness: The awakening of a scientific mind.* Lanham, MD: Rowman & Littlefield.

Wortabet, J. (1860). *Researches into the religions of Syria.* London, UK: James Nisbet.

Wright, M. R. (Ed.) (1995). *Empedocles: The extant fragments.* London, UK: Bristol Classical Press.

Wynn, E., & White, D. (n.d.). Computing reincarnation beliefs across cultures. Retrieved from http://roninstitute.org/wp-content/uploads/2013/02/wynnwhite-final.pdf

Yarkoni, T. (2013). Neurobiological substrates of personality: A critical overview. In M Mikulincer, P. R. Shaver, M. L. Cooper, & R. J. Larsen (Eds.) (2015). *APA handbook of personality and social psychology, Volume 4: Personality processes and individual differences* (pp. 61–83). Washington, DC: American Psychological Association.

Yeats-Brown, F. (1936). *Lancer at large.* London, UK: V. Gollancz.

Yi, R., Hongo Y., Yoda, I., Adam, Z. R., & Fahrenbach, A. C. (2018). Radiolytic synthesis of cyanogen chloride, cyanamide and simple sugar precursors. *Chemistry Select, 3,* 10169–104174.

Yli-Karjanmaa, S. (2015). *Reincarnation in Philo of Alexandria* (Studia Philonica Monographs). Atlanta, GA: SBL Press.

Yogananda, P. (1998). *Autobiography of a yogi* (13th ed.). Los Angeles, CA: Self-Realization Fellowship.

Zaleski, C. (1987). *Otherworld journeys: Accounts of near-death experience in Medieval and modern times.* New York, NY: Oxford University Press.

Zander, H. (1999). *Geschichte der Seelenwanderung in Europa.* Darmstadt, Germany: Wissenschaftliche Buchgesellschaft.

Zivkovic, T. (2014). *Death and reincarnation in Tibetan Buddhism: In-between bodies.* Abingdon, Oxon, UK: Routledge.

Zolik, E. S. (1958). An experimental investigation of the psychodynamic implications of the hypnotic "previous existence" fantasy. *Journal of Clinical Psychology, 14,* 178–183.

Zolik, E. S. (1962). "Reincarnation" phenomena in hypnotic states. *International Journal of Parapsychology, 4,* 66–75.

Index

Following convention, case subjects are indexed by first name rather than surname. Titles and honorifics (e.g., Ma, Maung, Ven. in Burmese names) are ignored in the ordering of entries. Page references for figures and tables are italicized.

Abu-Izzeddin, Majd, 195, 196
acquaintance relationship/acquaintance
   case. *See* relationship status
adults, past-life memories of, xiv,
   101, 118, 229, 230, 289; déjà vu
   and, 96; developmental factors in
   transition from childhood forms,
   201–13; persistence from childhood,
   102, 145, 192, 194, 195, 195–96,
   198, 223; precursors in childhood,
   204–5, 211; spontaneous versus
   induced under hypnosis, 45, 222.
   See also past-life regression; Will,
   reincarnation case of
Africa: mediumship in, 227–28;
   reincarnation beliefs in, 187, 226,
   266; repeater children in, 155, 302.
   See also Igbo
age regression. *See* past-life regression
   (PLR); past-life therapy
Ahtun Re, xii, xiii, 232
A. J. Stewart, reincarnation case of, 102,
   204
Akashic field, 222, 227, 290
Akashic Records, 117, 222, 227, 267,
   290, 298, 300; and Cayce, 83, 230;
   and Theosophy, 83
Aksakof, Alexander, 84

Alan Gamble, reincarnation case of,
   149, 151, 202
alcohol intoxication, possible inhibitor
   of physical signs, 208
Alevi, 109, 113; features of
   reincarnation cases among,
   110, 165, 174, 180, *180*, *181*,
   182, 183, 188; reincarnation
   beliefs of, 71, 188, 262–63;
   reincarnation cases among, 99,
   107, 108, 113, 142–43, 165, 188,
   263, 266
Alexakis, Alexander, 39, 74
Alexandrina Samona, reincarnation
   case of, 94–95, 97, 124,
   144, 155, 163–64, 167, 264
Almeder, Robert, 52, 177, 211
American reincarnation beliefs,
   accounts, and cases. *See* United
   States
amnesia, source. *See* cryptomnesia
amnesia for events from previous lives,
   256, 259; and fruit of forgetfulness,
   170, 196–97, 294
Ampan Petcherat, reincarnation case of,
   170, 195
Anderson, Royd, 8, 9, 11, 14, 16, 18,
   21, *22*, 31, 49, 50

Andrade, Hernani G., 100, 142, 157, 166, 172, 173, 177, 186
Angel, Leonard, 103–6, 149, 211, 233, 305
Angela Grubbs, reincarnation case of, 204, 209
animism, 40–41, 111, 163, 184, 235, 257, 290; reincarnation concepts in, 39, 40, 41–42, 263–67, 297; spirit concepts in, 34–36, 37–38, 170, 303
announcing dreams, 48, 62, 87, 94, 178, 211, 223, 290, 301, 303; aids to past-life identification, 55, 58, 59, 60, 224, 250, 266; and belief in reincarnation, 39, 42, 62, 164; case subjects remember "sending," 166; cross-cultural variation in, 164–65, 188; cultural impacts on, 165, 178, 184, 185, 188; versus departure dreams, 165; and discarnate agency, 124, 163–77, 243, 250, 259; mis- / overinterpretation of, 87, 113, 269
Apken, Lauri, 16, 17, *22*
apparitions, 40, 41, 237, 248, 249, 289, 290, 297; after-effects of sighting, 216; demonstrate memory and purpose, 241; predominately male, 241, 245; and psi, 248–49, 256, 259, 298; and rebirth announcements, 55, 85, 165–66, 241, 301; sensory modes of, 166; study of, 87, 99, 110; suggest discarnate agency, 40, 116, 166, 172, 246, 248, 256, 259, 290; suggest survival of less than intact personality, 248; and unfinished business, 241, 245; and violent death, 241, 245
apparitions, types of: collectively perceived, 241; crisis, 241; deathbed, 239–40, 241, 293; reciprocal, 166, 255–56, 259
Appleton, Naomi, 76
Ara, Mitra, 40, 63
Archetypal Synchronistic Resonance (ASR), xii, xiv–xv, 233

archetypes, xv, 222–23, 290, 291
Aristotle, 64, 275, 284, 293
Ashok Kumar Shakya, reincarnation case of, 143, 148
'Askadut, reincarnation account of, 54–55
ASR. *See* Archetypal Synchronistic Resonance
assisted reincarnation, 170, 171, 172–73, 290, 293, 306
astral body, 78, 110, 158, 253, 290, 301
attacks of adulthood, 138–39
Augustine, Keith, 51, 239, 246
Aurangzeb, Emperor, 89, 90
autobiographical impression, 133, 290–91
autobiographical knowledge, 133, 252, 255, 291; absent from past-life memory, 133
autobiographical memory, 127, 133, 200, 291. *See also* memory (of present life); past-life memory, episodic
Autobiography of a Yogi, 38
Ayer, A. J., 250

Bahir, 73
Barbro Karlén, past-life memories of, 102
Barker, David R., 48, 49, 114–15
Barresi, John, 41
Barrington, Mary Rose, 100, 101
Barros, Julio, 105, 106
Barušs, Imants, 216
Basilides, 74
Baye, Lisa, 2, 8, *27*, 50
Bayer, Reşat, 100, 188
Bayesian analysis, of mind/brain identity thesis versus mind/brain independence, 246
B. B. Saxena, reincarnation case of, 139–40, 141, 157, 187
Beauregard, Mario, 158, 238, 244
Beaver Indians, 100, 177; features of reincarnation cases of, *180*, 181, *181*,

182, *182*, 185, 224; reincarnation beliefs and related customs of, 60, 166

Beck, Brenda, 81

Beck, G. W., 69

Becker, Carl B., 77

Begley, Sharon, 238

behavioral signs of reincarnation xiv, xv, 39, 61, 100, 109, 145, 149, 178, 196, 273, 291; in absence of conscious memories, 2–3, 32, 51, 190, 199, 208–9, 251; and age of case subject, 202, 203, 204; aids to past life identification, 55, 58, 59, 60, 62, 136–37, 266; and belief in reincarnation, 40; carried by psychophore, 158; carried in subconscious, 44, 159, 189, 247, 304; conveyed by psychokinesis, 147–48, 159, 252, 259; and differences of caste, ethnicity, religion, 137–40; explanations for alternative to reincarnation, 47, 112–13, 116, 117–18, 140, 146–47, 190; and monozygotic twins, 143–44; outlast episodic memories, 145; over-interpreted as signs of reincarnation, 87; precede episodic memories, 48, 136, 145, 208–9; responses to previous family, 144–45; and replacement reincarnation, 176; in sex-change cases, 139, 195, 270. *See also* past-life memory, emotional; past-life memory, procedural

behavioral signs of reincarnation, expressed in: children's play, 137, 139, 140, 197, 229; habitual behavior patterns (behavioral identification), 32, 136–48; phobias, 2–3, 95, 136, 139, 163, 193–94, 207, 211; post-traumatic symptoms, 2–3, 32, 51, 190–93; unlearned language and other skills, 140–43, 145, 146, 213

Beng, 59, 263

Bengal and Bengali, 140, 141, 211, 212, 213

Bergson, Henri, 281

Bering, Jesse M., 45

Bernet, William, 109–10

Bernstein, Morey, ix, 97, 214, 215

Besant, Annie, 110

Bhagavad-Gita, 80–81, 82

Bhaktivedanta, Swami, 81–82

biology, conventional, and reincarnation, 42, 44, 52, 121

biology, evolutionary, 273–87; and reincarnation cases, 281–87. *See also* evolution, biological

biology, quantum, and reincarnation, 43, 121, 236, 271

birth defects, 148

birth defects in reincarnation cases, 32, 152, 273–74, 284, 298, 303; aids to past life identification, 55; close correspondence to wounds, 150, 151; experimental, 155; and intermission length, 153; and maternal impression, 120, 150, 158; planned before death, 154; produced by reincarnating mind, 158–59, 284; recurrent in successive lives, 154, 301; and retributive karma, 159–60

birthmarks: causes of, 148; types of, 150

birthmarks in reincarnation cases, 61, 150, 178, 232, 270–71, 303; aids to past life identification, 40, 48, 55, 58, 60, 85, 91, 194, 224, 250, 298; announced through mediums, 225–26; appearance of, 150–51; corresponding to wounds documented in medical and police records, 149, 151–52; and entelechy, 284; experimental, 88, 154–55, 293; in prenatal replacement case, 176; incidence of, 152–53; location of, in relation to wounds, 104–5, 149; mis-/over-interpretation of, 85, 113, 158, 269; and monozygotic twins, 157;

multiple, 104–5, 149–50; phantom
pain at site of, 157, 210; phobias
associated with, 194; recurrent in
successive lives, 153–54, 154–55,
299; source of belief in reincarnation,
42, 53, 62, 148
birthmarks in reincarnation cases,
explanations for, xiv, 118, 152,
273–74; conveyed by psychophore,
158, 253; produced by maternal
impression, 120, 150, 296;
reincarnating mind responsible
for, 158–59, 252, 284; super-psi
interpretations of, 120
birthmarks in reincarnation cases,
factors related to appearance of:
alcohol intoxication at death, 208;
cadaver marking (experimental
birthmarks), 154, 158, 293;
intermediate lives, 153; intermission
length, 153; postmortem injuries,
152; premortem planning, 57, 85,
154; state of consciousness at death,
152; violent death, 32, 152, 153
Bishen Chand Kapoor, reincarnation
case of, 140, 143, 202–3, 208
Björnsson, Hafsteinn, 242
Blackman, Winifred S., 63–64
Blavatsky, H. P., 78–80, 82, 83, 96, 110
Bloxham, Arnall, 217
Blythe, Henry, 218
Bobby Hodges, reincarnation case of,
170
Bond, Frederick Bligh, 226
Bongkuch Promsin, reincarnation case
of, 138–39, 142, 143, 167
Bonwick, James, 64
Bourgeois, Theresa, 16, 17, *22*
Bowers, Kenneth, 217
Bowman, Carol, 101, 134, 170
brain, 45, 245, 277, 304; consciousness
evolved in tandem with, 258;
memory systems of, 121, 133, 147,
243, 250; neuroplasticity of, 238;
and personality, 245, 246, 249–50;

and quantum biology, 236. *See also*
mind/brain identity thesis; mind/
brain interaction; memory (of present
life)
Brassette, Natalie, 15, 17
Braude, Stephen E., 177, 247, 252; and
crippling complexity, 117, 292; and
family dynamics in reincarnation
cases, 190, 192, 212–13; qualified
survivalist position of, 117; and
super-psi, 116, 117, 120, 146, 248;
and trace theories of memory, 134,
268
Brazil: features of reincarnation cases
in, 177, *180*, 181, *181*, *182*, 225;
reincarnation cases in, 98, 140, 142,
157, 166, 186–87; Spiritism in, 84,
226, 231, 252. *See also* Andrade,
Hernani
Bremmer, Jan N., 33–34
Brihadaranyaka Upanishad, 69
Broad, C. D., 250, 253, 260
Brody, Eugene B., 47, 51, 120, 190, 192
Brownell, George B., 96, 142, 174, 219
Bruce Peck, reincarnation case of, 153,
154
Bruce Whittier, regression experiences
of, 220
Buddhism, 34, 98; anattā (no-self)
doctrine in, 37, 290; gandhabba
concept in, 76–77, 294; history of,
69–70; karma doctrine in, 34, 38–39,
69, 75–78, 80; rebirth beliefs and
related customs in, 33, 33–34, 37–38,
39, 173–74, 208; rebirth beliefs
versus reincarnation case data, 261.
See also Burma (Mynanmar); Sri
Lanka; Thailand
Buddhism (branches of): Mahayana, 70,
77, 80; Theravada, 34, 70, 77, 80,
169, 184, 261; Vajrayana (Tibetan),
36, 70, 76, 78, 261, 265, 283
"buried treasure," 92, 94, 115, 203, 207,
208, 291
Burkert, Walter, 39

Burma (Myanmar), 99, 100, 225, 266;
announcing dreams in, 165, 188;
Buddhism in, 69–70; experimental
birthmarks in, 154, 293; features
of reincarnation cases in, 131, *180*,
181, 182, *182*, 184, 188; intermission
memories in, 168, 171; reincarnation
cases in, 91, 97, 145, 152, 153,
155–56, 157, 160, 167, 264. *See also*
Ma Tin Aung Myo, reincarnation
case of
Buryat, reincarnation beliefs and
customs among, 60
Bush Negroes, 61

cadaver marking. *See* experimental
birthmarks
Calkowski, Marcia S., 265, 266
Cambodia, reincarnation accounts in,
169, 171, 196
Cannon, Sir Alexander, 214
Carington, Whately, 119
Carl Edon, past-life memories of, 112
Carlson, Chester, 98–99
Carpocrates, 74
Cathars, 74, 209
Cayce, Edgar, 82–83, 96–97, 229–30,
290
Celal Kapan, reincarnation case of, 127
cellular memory, 268
Celts, reincarnation beliefs of, 63
Central Thai, reincarnation beliefs of, 61
Cerminara, Gina, 229–30
Cevriye Bayrı, reincarnation case of,
264
Chadha, Narender K., 49, 177, 179, 196,
197
Chadwick, Nora K., 63
Chalmers, David J., 247
Chanai Choomalaiwong, reincarnation
case of, 104, 199
Chandogya Upanishad, 69, 75
Ven. Chaokhun Rajsuthajarn,
reincarnation case of, 175, 197, 208
Chari, C. T. K., 116, 190

Child Behavior Checklist, 190, 191,
192, 193
Child Dissociative Checklist, 192
childhood gender nonconformity, 139,
195. *See also* gender dysphoria
child prodigies, 96, 102, 140–41
Children's Apperception Test, 192
China, 226; Buddhism in, 69, 70, 77;
reincarnation beliefs and related
practices in, 196–97; reincarnation
accounts from, 88–89, 97, 154,
163–64, 166, 171, 175
Christian Haupt, reincarnation case of,
102, 140
Christianity, 54, 64, 74; and
reincarnation, 74–75
Churchill, Col. Charles Henry, 92
Cicero, 70
clairvoyance. *See* extrasensory
perception (ESP)
Clement of Alexandria, 74
Cobbe, Frances Power, 239
cognitive psychology, 45, 244, 247–48,
292
cognitive science, 45
cognitive science of religion, 45–46
cognitive unconscious, 134, 145, 148,
247–48, 295
collective unconscious, 117, 222–23,
233, 280, 290, 291, 305
concurrent reincarnation, 35–36, 265,
267, 269, 270, 292, 301
conscious awareness, of discarnate
actors. *See* discarnate agency
conscious awareness, of embodied
actors, 292, 293, 302, 304;
behavioral signs in absence of,
2–3, 32, 51, 190, 199, 208–9, 251;
and brain impairment, 237, 239,
240, 245, 282, 305; and Buddhism,
37–38, 76, 77, 246, 261, 294; and
Cartesian substance dualism, 255;
and deathbed visions, 239; and
memory distortions, 217, 292; part
of a duplex consciousness, 38, 124,

247–48, 259–60, 292, 305; phobias
    in absence of, 194; physical signs
    in absence of, 152, 159, 226; and
    present-life memory, 132, 145, 148,
    293, 295; process view of, 254,
    292, 297, 304; and psi impressions,
    248–49, 256, 280, 304; reset at each
    embodiment, 252, 255, 259, 260;
    shared, in multiple reincarnation
    and transplant cases, 265, 269; and
    synchronicity, 232–33. *See also*
    intersubjectivity; past-life memory,
    episodic
conscious awareness, of nonhuman
    spirits, 35
consciousness, 292, 294; acausal
    properties of, xii, 232–33; duplex
    nature of, 38, 44, 124, 189, 247,
    259, 261, 292; evolution and
    adaptation of, 258–59, 280–81,
    285; of nonhuman spirits, 41;
    philosophical (Cartesian, idealist,
    panpsychist, process) views of,
    254–57, 291, 294, 296, 297, 300,
    304; processual soul view of,
    256–57, 265, 269–70, 300; psi
    intrinsic property of, 227, 300;
    and quantum mechanics, 43, 123,
    236, 244, 247; synonymous with
    soul, spirit, mind, and psyche,
    37, 41, 124, 247, 292. *See also*
    conscious awareness; discarnate
    agency; mind/brain identity
    thesis; mind/brain independence;
    subconscious
consciousness, altered states of, and
    past-life memory, 127, 202, 206–7;
    dissociative states, 191, 192, 193,
    207, 208, 211–13; drug induced
    states, 97, 207, 219; meditation, 77,
    196, 206, 212, 130. *See also* dreams
    and past-life memory; past-life
    regression (PLR)
consciousness, postmortem survival of.
    See discarnate agency

consciousness, product of cerebral
    activity. *See* mind/brain identity
    thesis
Consolatio ad Apollonium, 70–71
Constantine the Great, 74
continuous incarnation, 36, 265, 267,
    269, 292, 301
Conway, Martin A., 133, 200, 209, 291
Cook, Emily W., 174; features of solved
    versus unsolved cases, 131–32, 152,
    177, 179, 185, 194, 195. *See also*
    Kelly, Emily W.
Cooper, Irving S., 82, 110
Cordelia Ekouroume, reincarnation case
    of, 189
Corliss Chotkin, Jr., reincarnation case
    of, 140, 154
Cousins, Norman, 237
crisis apparitions, 241
Cristina Matlock: intermission
    memories of, 164, 167; episodic
    past-life memories of, xxi, 125–28,
    131, 195–96, 199
cross-cultural patterns in reincarnation
    cases: intermission length, 180–81,
    180; intermission memories, 168,
    169; relationship status, 181–82, *181*;
    sex change, 182–83, *182*; solved
    versus unsolved cases, 131–32,
    152, 179, 185, 192–93, 194, 195;
    universal and near-universal features,
    178–80, 195; violent death, x, 128,
    131, 152–53, 179–80, 193, 194
cross-cultural studies of reincarnation
    beliefs, xviii, xx, 34, 60–63, 260
cross-historical patterns in reincarnation
    cases, 183
Cruz Moscinski, reincarnation case of,
    186
cryptomnesia (source amnesia), 141,
    217–18, 292, 301
Cumont, Franz, 65

Dacqué, Edgar, 281
Dalai Lama, 69, 225, 266

Daniel, E. Valentine., 81
Darwin, Charles, 274–75, 278–79, 287
David Loye, regression experiences of, 222
Davidson, J. R. T., 199
Davis, E. W., 169, 197
Davis, W. D., 61
deathbed visions, 239–40, 283, 293
De Bello Gallico (Gallic Wars), 63
De Groot, J. J. M., 88, 97, 154, 163, 262
déjà vu experiences, 96, 204
de Laguna, Frederica, 54, 56–57, 265
DG, reincarnation case of, 156
Delanne, Gabriel, 96
Delarrey, Maurice, 225–26
Dene Tha (Slavey), reincarnation cases of, 60, 166, 182
departure dreams, 165, 166, 171, 173, 290, 293, 303
Derek Pitnov, reincarnation case of, 194
Descartes, René, 235, 254, 255, 285
Dethlefsen, Thorwald, xvii, 215
Deutsch, Eliot, 161
developmental factors in past-life memory, 127, 130, 201–13, 222
Dhiman, Kuldip Kumar, 100, 176, 262
Dianne Seaman, past-life memories of, 102
Dillon, Myles, 63
Diogenes Laertius, 65
direct mental action on living systems (DMILS), 147–48
discarnate agency, 163–77, 245, 255–56, 289, 293; and choice of rebirth parents, 170–71, 172; contravenes karma, 173; influenced by beliefs carried into death, 187–89, 261; in international cases and, 171, 178–79; and psi, 227, 248; and suicide cases, 171, 179. *See also* announcing dreams; apparitions; departure dreams; mediumistic communicators and communications; poltergeist activity

dissociation: and adult past-life memory, 207–8, 211–13; and childhood past-life memory, 191, 192, 193, 207. *See also* MPD/DID
Dissociative Identity Disorder (DID). *See* MPD/DID
Ditta Larusdottir, reincarnation case of, 186
Division of Perceptual Studies (DOPS), 99, 100; reincarnation case database of, 167, 178, 179, 180, 186, 252
Doidge, Norman, 238
Dolon Champa Mitra, reincarnation case of, 197
DOPS. *See* Division of Perceptual Studies (DOPS)
Dream Questionnaire, 191
dreams and dreaming, 18, 241, 248, 256, 282, 283; in animism, 35, 40, 41, 53, 55, 61, 164. *See also* announcing dreams; departure dreams
dreams and past-life memory, xiv, 79, 97, 127, 206–7, 209, 211, 223; distortions in, 209–10; in relation to past-life readings by sensitives, 228, 230–31; in relation to regression experiences, 214, 219, 220; Rylann O'Bannion's, 13–14, *23, 25, 26, 29*
Driesch, Hans, 275, 281, 284, 293
Druze, 71, 199; reincarnation beliefs of, 34, 39, 48, 71–72, 262, 271; reincarnation beliefs of versus cases among, 48, 174, 185, 187, 262–63
Druze reincarnation accounts and cases, 110, 111–12, 114, 266; age at death in, 179–80; announcing dreams in, 165, 185; cross-historical studies of, 183; international connections in, 263; intermission length in, 48, 174, 180, *180*, 185, 187, 262–63, 295; investigated after 1960, 142, 172, 208, 266–67; psychological studies of, 191; relationship status in, *181*, 185; recorded before 1960, 92, 97,

132; sex change absent in, *182*, 185,
262; solved versus unsolved cases
in, 185; violent death in, 179–80.
See also Imad Elawar, reincarnation
case of
Ducasse, C. J., 230
Duminda Ratnayake, reincarnation case
of, 263
Durkheim, Émile, 40, 41, 63
Dwairy, Marwan, 114

Eastern Kutchin (Gwich'in):
reincarnation beliefs and related
customs of, 60; reincarnation cases
of, 177, *180*, *181*, 182–83, *182*, 185
Edelmann, Jonathan, 109–10
Edward Ryall, past life memories of,
209, 219
Edwards, Jesse, 238
Edwards, Paul, 106, 110, 161
Egypt, ancient, xii, 39, 41, 68, 82, 83,
88, 230; rebirth beliefs in, 63–65
Egypt, modern: reincarnation beliefs of
Fellahin, 63–64
Eigen, Manfred, 277
elective reincarnation, 170–71, 172,
173, 255, 293, 298–99. *See also*
planned reincarnation
elective solution to selection problem.
See selection problem
Empedocles, 67
Empson, Rebecca M., 154
Engen, Brendan, 233
entelechy, 284, 293
Eskimo, 36, 224. *See also* Inuit
Essenes, 72
European reincarnation beliefs,
accounts, and cases. *See* Western
countries
evolution, biological, 273–87; and
cognitive science of religion, 45;
and panpsychism, 258, 264, 285–86;
and psi, 279–81, 283–84; and
reincarnation, 258, 281–83, 284–85,
286–87; and Theosophy, 36, 78, 111

experimental birth defects, 155
experimental birthmarks, 88, 154–55,
293
extrasensory perception (ESP), 293–94,
300, 305; and altered states of
consciousness, 283; of case subjects,
8–9, 50, 115–16, 135; of discarnate
minds, 77, 236–37; processed
in subconscious, 248. *See also*
precognition; psi; retrocognition
Eylon, Dina Ripsman, 72

facial similarity, between previous
person and case subject, 155, 156,
157, 298; Semkiw on, xii, 102, 232,
264
fading of past-life memory. *See* past-life
memory, episodic
family relationship/family cases. *See*
relationship status
famous past life (FPL) reports, 210–11,
231
fantasy theory, 44–45, 46, 294, 301
Fellahin, reincarnation beliefs and
related customs of, 63–64
Fenwick, Peter and Elizabeth, 101
Fielding-Hall, Harold, 91, 96, 264
Fiore, Edith, 215
Fishman, Yonatan, 51, 239, 246
Flammarion, Camille, 226
flatworms, planarian, learning/memory
of, 133
Flew, Antony, 253
fMRI. *See* functional magnetic
resonance imaging (fMRI)
France, 82, 217; reincarnation beliefs
of Celtic peoples in, 63, 84;
reincarnation cases in, 97, 206;
Spiritism in, 84
fraud and deception, 96, 111–12,
115–16
Freedman, Thelma B., 220–21
Freud, Sigmund, 38, 98, 222, 243, 248
Friederichs, Karl, 281
fruit of forgetfulness, 170, 294

functional magnetic resonance imaging (fMRI), 237–38

Gadit, A. A., 199
Gauls, reincarnation beliefs of, 84
Geley, Gustave, 281
gender dysphoria (gender identity disorder), 139, 195, 270. *See also* childhood gender nonconformity
genetic memory, 118, 294
George Field, regression experiences of, 219
George Neidhart, reincarnation case of, 204, 206
Geraerts, Elke, 216–17
Gershom, Yonassan, 138, 206
Ghost Inside My Child (*GIMC*), 5, 7–8; Cindy O'Bannion's contacts with producers of, 7, 8, 9, 11, *25*, *26*, *27*, 49; episode featuring Rylann O'Bannion, xix, 7, 9–10, 11, 18, *27*, *28*
Giesler, Iris, 13, 14, 168–69, 170, 173, 208
Gillian and Jennifer Pollock, reincarnation cases of, 143–44, 157
Gitxsan, 100, 177; features of reincarnation cases of, *180*, 181, *181*, 182, *182*, 185; reincarnation cases of, 154, 266, 269; reincarnation beliefs and related customs of, 58, 152, 224, 267
glossophobia, 142, 294
Gnanatilleka Baddewithana, reincarnation case of, 132, 135, 195
Gnosticism, 72, 74
Goldberg, Bruce, 220, 222
Goldkamp, Toni, 11, 14, *28*
Gopal Gupta, reincarnation case of, 138, 144
Goulet, Jean-Guy, 166
Govinda, Anagarika, 143
Greece, ancient, reincarnation beliefs in, 39–40, 64–68, 70

Gretchen, responsive xenoglossy case of, 218–19
Greyson, Bruce, 174, 239
Griffin, David Ray, 51, 212–13, 251, 253, 257–58; panexperientialism of, 257, 297; retroprehensive inclusion of, 117–18, 146, 302
Grof, Stanslav, 222
group soul, 280, 282
Gudjonsson Suggestibility Scale, 190
Guemple, Lee, 292
Giuseppe Costa, reincarnation case of, 204
Maung Gyi and Maung Ngè, reincarnation cases of, 264

Haida, 58; features of reincarnation cases of, 174, 180, *180*, *181*, *182*, 185, 187, 224, 263; reincarnation beliefs and related customs of, 58; reincarnation cases of, 153, 224
Hales, Stephen D., 51
Hall, Manly Palmer, 93, 96
Haraldsson, Erlendur, xix, 239, 273–74; cross-historical studies, 177–78, 183; reincarnation case investigations, 100, 149, 179–80; studies of past-life memory retention, 195–96; studies of psychology of children with past-life memories, 190–91, 192–93; survival-related case investigations, 110, 242
Hardy, Alister, 280–81
Harris, Melvin, 217
Harrison, Peter and Mary, 101, 146, 171
Harsh Vardham, reincarnation case of, 166
Hartmann, Eduard von, 281
Hassler, Dieter, 167, 172, 177, 214, 216, 221
Hearn, Lafcadio, 90–91
Hélène Smith, past-life memory claims of, 229
Heraclides of Pontus, 65, 66
Herodotus, 39, 64–65, 67
Hick, John H., 119

hidden treasure. *See* "buried treasure"
Hill, J. A., 229
Hinduism, 257; God in, 80–82; history
  of, 68–69; karma doctrine in, 34,
  38–39, 69, 75, 81–82; rebirth beliefs
  and related customs in, 34, 37,
  38, 39, 85; rebirth beliefs versus
  reincarnation case data, 183–84, 208,
  261–62. *See also* India
Hirvenoja, Reijo, 218
Holland, A. C., 208
HRAF. *See* Human Relations Area Files
Hufford, David J., 46
Hultkrantz, Åke, 35
Human Relations Area Files (HRAF),
  60, 62

Iamblichus, 65, 71
Igbo, 99, 177; features of reincarnation
  cases of, 165, 180–81, *180*, 181–82,
  181, *182*, 183, 185; reincarnation
  accounts and cases of, 152, 189;
  reincarnation beliefs and related
  customs of, 58, 59–60, 155, 224–25,
  266
Iliad, 65
Imad Elawar, reincarnation case of, 115,
  130, 143; Angel on, 105–6; Roll on,
  266–67
implicit learning, 247
implicit memory, 145, 247, 291, 293,
  295, 299
India, 42, 78, 111–12, 199; features of
  reincarnation cases in, 131, 165, 169,
  179–80, *180*, 181, *181*, *182*, 183–84,
  186; post-1960 adult reincarnation
  cases in, 206–7, *207*, 211–13; post-
  1960 child reincarnation cases in,
  128–29, 130, 137–38, 140, 142, 143,
  151, 166, 167, 175, 225; post-1960
  interreligious child reincarnation
  cases in, 48–49, 138, 157, 178, 187;
  pre-1960 reincarnation accounts
  and cases in, xxi, 48, 49, 89–90,
  92–94, 97, 108, 113; psychological

characteristics of reincarnation
  case subjects in, 191–92, 194, 196;
  reincarnation beliefs and related
  customs in, 37, 38, 39–40, 42,
  68–69, 81, 81–82, 154, 187;
  reincarnation case investigations in,
  92–94, 98, 100, 109, 111; responses
  of parents to reincarnation cases in,
  48–49, 196, 197; study of deathbed
  visions in, 239; study of near-
  death experiences in, 110. *See also*
  Hinduism
Indika and Kakshappa Ishwara,
  reincarnation cases of, 144, 157
Indus Valley Civilization, 68
inheritance, biological, 273–87
inheritance, of property, and
  reincarnation, 57–58, 62–63
interethnic cases, 139–40, 156, 188,
  232, 263, 295; versus international
  cases, 139–40; xenoglossy in, 142
intermediate lives, 48, 129, 130, 140,
  153, 295
intermission, nature of: Buddhist ideas
  about, 77–78; Michael Newton's
  portrayal of, 85–86, 172, 263;
  Theosophical ideas about, 79, 110
intermission distance, 186, 295
intermission experience, structure of,
  167–69, 295
intermission length, 183, 211, 230,
  265, 295; according to Buddhism,
  76, 173–74, 184, 261; according to
  Theosophy, 79, 82, 263; cultural
  impacts on, 188; cultural variations
  in, 174, 180–81, *180*, 183, 184,
  185, 186–87, 262–63; and manner
  of death, 179; and replacement
  reincarnation, 175, 176; and past-life
  regressions, 216, 217; and population
  increase, 111; and physical signs,
  153
intermission memories, 5, *24*, 54, 89,
  120, 133, 163, 164, 167–70, 250,
  264, 282, 283, 295; and assisted

reincarnation, 170, 171, 172–73, 290, 293, 306; cultural impacts on, 169–70, 256; and elective reincarnation, 170–71, 172, 173, 255, 293, 298–99; and fruit of forgetfulness, 170, 294; versus karmic solution to selection problem, 173; versus prebirth memories, 243; versus theistic solution to selection problem, 173; with veridical actions or observations, 166, 167, 168, 170, 245, 259
internal diseases in reincarnation cases, 155–56
international cases, 139–40, 142, 171, 182, 186–87, 188, 263, 295; versus interethnic cases, 139–40; motive in, 178–79
interreligious cases, 138, 295
intersubjectivity, 164, 166, 173, 239, 241, 283–84
Inuit: reincarnation beliefs and related customs of, 36, 265, 292; reincarnation cases of, 224. *See also* Eskimo
Iris Farczády, reincarnation case of, 175, 176
Isis Unveiled, 78, 83
Islam, Shia: reincarnation beliefs and cases in, 34, 71–72, 73, 83. *See also* Alevi; Druze
Islam, Sunni: reincarnation beliefs absent from, 71, 187; and reincarnation cases, 48–49, 138, 157, 178, 183, 199
İsmail Aktınkılıç, reincarnation case of, 264
Israel, 34, 71; reincarnation beliefs, accounts, and cases in, 112, 114, 199
Italy, reincarnation cases in. *See* Alexandrina Samona, reincarnation case of

Jacobson, Nils O., 205
Jainism, 34, 38, 69

James, William, 243; purported past-life identity of Jeffrey Mishlove, xii–xiii, 233
James Leininger, reincarnation case of, 101, 124–25, 130, 134–35, 139, 170, 186, 194
Japan: Buddhism in, 69, 70, 77; experimental birthmarks in, 154; features of reincarnation cases in, 182; past-life identifications in, 226; prebirth memories in, 243, 263; reincarnation cases in, 143, 146, 154, 167, 179; responsive xenoglossy in, 218–19. *See also* Katsugoro, reincarnation case of
Japanese soldiers killed in Burma, reincarnation cases of, 157, 171, 188. *See also* Ma Tin Aung Myo, reincarnation case of
Jasbir Jat, replacement reincarnation case of, 138, 175, 176
Jean Slade, multiple reincarnations of, 266
Jeffery, reincarnation case of, 223–24
Jeffrey Keene, reincarnation case of, 102, 204, 229, 230–31, 232
Jenny Cockell: past-life memories of Charles Savage, 204, 219, 230; past-life memories of Mary Sutton, 101, 204, 230
Jensen, responsive xenoglossy case of, 218, 219
John Rhodes, intermission memories of, 171
Josephus, 72
Judaism, reincarnation beliefs in, 34, 64, 72–73
judgment, of soul after death, 39, 68, 69, 72, 73
Julius Caesar, 63
Jung, Carl Gustav, xi–xii, xv, 222–23, 280, 285. *See also* archetypes; collective unconscious; synchronicity
Justin Martyr, 74
Juta, reincarnation case of, 175

Kabbalah, 73
Kampman, Reima, 218
Karaite movement, 72
Kardec, Allan, 83–84, 96. *See also*
  Spiritism
Karen, reincarnation case of, 166
karma, juridical, 69–70, 75–78, 189,
  261, 263, 295, 295–96; absent
  from or crudely developed in non-
  Indic belief systems, 42, 70, 71,
  262, 265; common denominator
  of Indic belief systems, 34, 38; as
  coping mechanism, 199; and God,
  81–82, 82, 83, 85, 184; no good
  evidence for, 173, 184; not logically
  associated with reincarnation, 38;
  originated in India, 42, 69; versus
  processual karma, 39, 86, 300; versus
  retributive karma, 80, 110, 159–60,
  300, 302
karma, processual, 39, 86, 189, 200,
  296, 300
karma, retributive, 79–80, 86, 230, 265,
  270, 296, 300, 302; reincarnation
  cases inconsistent with, 159–61, 173,
  263
karmic solution to selection problem.
  See selection problem
Katsugoro, reincarnation case of, 90–91,
  97, 132, 169, 182
Kees, intermission memories of, 171
Keeton, Joe, 217
Keil, H. H. Jürgen, 100, 177; cross-
  historical studies, 49, 177, 183;
  questions about and alternative
  interpretations of reincarnation cases,
  116, 119–20, 146–77, 177, 179, 306;
  reincarnation case investigations in
  Burma and Thailand, 144, 152, 197;
  reincarnation case investigations in
  Turkey, 108–9, 113, 142–43
Kelly, Edward F., 246, 257
Kelly, Emily W., 158, 237–38, 239. *See
  also* Cook, Emily W.
Kelsey, Denys, 215

Kemal Atasoy, reincarnation case of,
  108, 147, 188
Ken Llewelyn, reincarnation case of,
  227–28
Kensinger, E. A., 208
Keyes, Charles F., 81
Ma Khin Ma Gi, reincarnation case of,
  160
Ma Khin Nyein, reincarnation case of,
  153, 155
Khulusat-ut-Tawarikh, 89
Kim, T. J., 216
Kingsley, Peter, 40, 65, 66
Kiriyama, Seiya, 226
Korchnoi, Victor, 241–42
Kripal, Jeffrey J., 46
Krishan, Yuvraj, 82
Krishnanand, 207, 208, 211
Kuhn, Oskar, 281
Kumkum Verma, reincarnation case of,
  142

Lalitha Abeyawardena, reincarnation
  case of, 127
Lamarck, Jean-Baptiste de, 274, 275,
  287
Lancelin, Charles, 94–95
language skills in reincarnation cases.
  See xenoglossy
Lapps, reincarnation beliefs among, 61
Laszlo, Ervin, 117, 222, 290
Laure Reynaud, reincarnation case of,
  204
Leadbeater, C. W., 83, 166
Lebanon, 263; reincarnation research
  in, 98, 100, 126, 131, 190, 192, 193,
  196. *See also* Druze
Lekh Pal Jatav, reincarnation case of,
  150
Lenz, Frederick, 205–6
Lester, David, 167
Levin, Michael, 153
life force, 36, 37. *See also*
  consciousness
life planning, 85–86, 172, 221, 263, 296

Littlewood, Roland, 199
living agent psi, 117, 260. *See also* psi;
   super-psi
Locke, John, 250
Long, J. Bruce, 33, 82
Lönnerstrand, Sture, 93
LSD and, past-life memory, 207
Luria, Yitzchak (Isaac), 36, 73, 111
Lynn, Stephen J., 217

Mackenzie, Vicki, 101, 225
Mahābhārata, 80, 81, 82
Mallika Aroumougam, reincarnation
   case of, 108, 203
Maróczy, Géza, mediumistic
   communications from, 241–42, 250
Marta Lorenz, reincarnation case of,
   135, 155, 225
Martin, Raymond, 41
materialism, 45, 46, 198, 235, 245, 271,
   294, 296, 303, 305; case data pose
   threat to, 46–47, 102–3, 239, 240–41,
   243; versus idealism, 43, 254,
   294, 296; and mind/brain identity
   thesis, 42, 133, 238, 239, 243, 244,
   245; promissory, 236; questions
   about, 51, 52, 239, 246; rules out
   possibility of postmortem survival
   and reincarnation, 42, 51
maternal impression, 120, 150, 158, 296
Maung, U Win, 131
M. C., reincarnation case of, 147
McDougall, William, 281
McEvilley, Thomas, 39
McFadden, Johnjoe, 258
meditation, 169: neurobiological
   correlates of, 238; past-life memories
   during, 77, 196, 206, 212, 230;
   previous person experienced in, 153,
   208, 252
mediumistic communicators and
   communications, 119, 133, 163,
   224, 259; demonstrate memory
   and purpose, 241–42, 256; drop-
   in, 242, 250; identification of, 242,

249–50; localized in space, 255;
   preponderance of male, 245; psi of,
   226–27, 227, 242, 248, 259, 296;
   rebirth announcements made by, 94,
   96, 124, 165–66, 225–26, 264, 301;
   reliability of, 229; and Spiritism,
   83–84; and super-psi, 116, 117; and
   violent death, 242
mediumship, physical, 244
Mehmet Arikdal, reincarnation case of,
   142
Melton, J. Gordon, 82
memory and purpose, postmortem
   persistence of, 241–42, 246, 256, 290
memory (of present life), 121; brain
   structures related to, 147, 243; and
   cognitive unconscious, 200, 247;
   declarative (explicit), 132, 147, 148,
   291, 293, 296, 301, 303; distortions
   of, 45, 107, 292, 297, 301; fallibility
   of, 99, 129; false, 65, 294; implicit,
   145, 146, 147, 148, 295, 296, 299;
   and personal identity, 249–50,
   250–51; Pribram's holonomic model
   of, 269; registration of, during
   NDEs, 133, 241, 282; storage of,
   in brain (trace theory of), 44–45,
   133, 134, 268, 294; storage of, in
   subconscious, 133–34, 148, 256,
   269, 282; and terminal lucidity,
   239, 282, 305; and vitalism, 285;
   Whiteheadian process view of, 254,
   257, 268. *See also* cellular memory;
   genetic memory
memory, past-life. *See* past-life memory
memory, prebirth. *See* prebirth
   memories
Meno, 66
metempsychosis, 44, 61, 78; belief
   in, 36–37, 61, 64–65, 71, 73, 262;
   operational definition of, 36–37, 297,
   301; and processual soul theory, 262
Meyer-Abich, Adolf, 281
Michael Wright, reincarnation case of,
   186

Miller, S. L., 277
Mills, Antonia, 100, 274; on dreams and
    nightmares, 127, 194; on imaginary
    playmates, 191–92; on Hindu/
    Muslim interreligious cases, 48, 138;
    on multiple reincarnation among
    Gitxsan, 266; other reincarnation
    case investigations among Canadian
    first nations, 58, 100, 152, 166,
    177, 182, 185, 223, 224; other
    reincarnation case investigations in
    India, 100, 109, 113–14, 132, 133,
    145, 148, 176; psychological testing
    of case subjects, 192, 196
mind. *See* consciousness
mind, subliminal. *See* subconscious
mind, supraliminal. *See* conscious
    awareness
mind/brain identity thesis, 45, 46, 236,
    239, 245–46, 254, 269; problems
    with, 246
mind/brain interaction, 43, 148, 235–
    39, 243–46, 257, 305; reset at each
    embodiment, 252, 255, 256, 259, 260
Ma Min Myint, reincarnation case of,
    188
Minucius Felix, Marcus, 74
Mishlove, Jeffrey, 233
Mongolia, 40, 60, 65, 66; experimental
    birthmarks in, 154
Monica O'Hara-Keeton, regression
    experiences of, 220
Montgomery, Ruth, 176
Moody, R. A., Jr., 205
mortuary practices and reincarnation,
    53, 54, 59–60, 61
Moss, Peter, 217
Mounzer Haïdar, reincarnation case of,
    107
MPD/DID, 255; Brazilian Spiritist
    therapy and, 226, 231; versus
    reincarnation and past-life memory,
    190, 193, 212, 251, 252, 265
Müller, Karl E., 140, 166, 183, 205–6,
    228

multiple past lives, memories of, 66,
    173, 210, 230, 231
Multiple Personality Disorder (MPD).
    See MPD/DID
multiple simultaneous reincarnation
    (multiple reincarnation), 297, 301,
    303; among animistic peoples, 35,
    36, 265, 266, 292; in Tibet, 36,
    57, 58, 265, 266; processual soul
    theory and, 265–67, 269–70; versus
    transplant cases, 267, 269;
Murphy, Gardner, 119
Murvet Dissiz, reincarnation case of,
    142
Myanmar. *See* Burma (Myanmar)
Myers, Frederic W. H., 38, 124, 243,
    248, 254, 260, 261, 305
Myth of Er, 68, 70, 170

Nadine Mann, reincarnation case of, 202
Nagel, Thomas, 258
Nahm, Michael, 177, 239; on
    evolutionary biology, 273–87
Nai Chook, reincarnation case of,
    188–89
naming practices and reincarnation,
    57–59
Nanninga, Rob, 218
Naranjo, Claudio, 219
natural death in reincarnation cases,
    131, 179–80, 193, 194, 208, 296
Nawal Daw, reincarnation case of, 142
near-death experiences (NDEs), 99, 110,
    174, 237; findings of research on,
    193, 205, 216, 240–41; implications
    of for postmortem survival, 40,
    237, 241, 266; versus intermission
    memories, 168, 169, 217, 282–83;
    memory registration during, 133,
    241, 282; veridical perceptions
    during, 168, 282, 283
Nehunia ben HaKana, 73
Neppe, Vernon. M., 242
Netherton, Morris, 215
neuroplasticity, 238, 244

New Age metaphysics, 75, 83, 86, 158, 230, 235, 264, 290, 297, 303, 306
New Age reincarnation mythos, 84, 85, 172, 221, 263–64
Newton, Sir Isaac, 235
Newton, Michael, 85–86, 172, 221
Newtonian (classical) mechanics, versus quantum mechanics, 42–43, 235–36
Nidiffer, F. Don, 192
Nisga'a, reincarnation case of, 154
Nissanka, H. H. S., 132
Noë, Alva, 246
Norman Despers, reincarnation case of, 155
Nosairi, reincarnation beliefs of, 71
Nyria, regression case of, 218

O'Bannion, Cindy, 1–33, *22–30*, 49–51, 118, 125
O'Bannion, Lane, 5, 6, 7, 8, 13, *25*, *26*, *29*
O'Bannion, Lonny, 2, 4, 7, 8, 9, *22*, *29*
Obeyesekere, Gananath, 71
obsession, psychic, 159, 191, 297
obsessive-compulsive disorder (OCD), neuroplasticity and, 238
Ohkado, Masayuki, xx, 100, 177; on prebirth memories, 243, 263; on reincarnation cases, 143, 146, 154, 167, 172, 179, 182, 264; on responsive xenoglossy, 218–19
Ojibwa, reincarnation signs among, 61
Onyewuenyi, I. C., 152
organ transplants. *See* transplant cases
Origen, 74
Orphism, 64
Osborn, Arthur W., 96
Ovid, 66
Owen, A. M., 238

panentheism, 257
panexperientialism, 257, 285–86, 297
panpsychism, 235, 257, 285–86, 292, 297, 304

parakaya pravesh, 37, 80, 174, 297, 302. *See also* replacement reincarnation
parental guidance, 47, 48–49, 51, 112–13, 114, 163, 190, 297, 301, 303
Parfit, Derek, 250
Parmod Sharma, reincarnation case of, 207
Parnia, Sam, 239
Pasricha, Satwant K., 100, 131; cross-historical studies, 93, 177, 183; NDE studies, 110; reincarnation case investigations, 143, 144, 149, 151, 206–7; studies of parental attitudes, 48, 197, 200; survey of reincarnation cases in India, 48, 49. *See also* Rakesh Gaur, reincarnation case of
passive xenoglossy, 141, 142–43, 298, 301
past-life identifications, by psychic practitioners, 185, 201, 223–30, 300; versus past-life readings, 230–31. *See also* Ahtun Re; Semkiw, Walter
past-life memory, behavioral. *See* behavioral signs of reincarnation
past-life memory, emotional, 146, 147, 199, 291; mediating role of, in memory retrieval, 148; persistence of, into adulthood, 145, 198
past-life memory, episodic, 65, 80, 87, 98, 200, 291, 298; of adults versus children (developmental factors in), 201–13; autobiographical knowledge absent from, 133; errors and distortions in, 31, 129–30, 209–10; fading versus retention of, 56, 90, 131–32, 148, 193, 195–96; of famous people, 210–11, 231; fragmentary nature of, 190, 211; meet psychological needs, 200, 207, 208–9, 213, 231, 253; versus MPD/DID, 190, 231; of multiple lives, 66, 173, 210, 230, 231; versus past-life regression, 45, 216, 218, 219, 221, 221–22, 223; versus psi and super-psi, 76, 135–36, 233;

psychological impacts of, 189–200; recency effect in,128, 136; recorded before 1960, 66, 87–98; reincarnation without (silent cases), 152, 194, 226, 250, 251; reminiscence bump in, 128; self-deception regarding, 103, 211, 233, 301, 304–5; versus spirit possession, 118; suppression of, by parents, 49, 196–97, 198. *See also* past-life memory retrieval; past-life memory storage

past-life memory, procedural, 145–46, 147, 200, 203, 291, 298, 299; in replacement reincarnation cases, 176; conveyance to new body in reincarnation, 147–48, 164. *See also* behavioral signs of reincarnation; skills in reincarnation cases

past-life memory, recognition, 132–33, 136

past-life memory, semantic, 132, 298

past-life memory, spatial. 132, 136, 303–4

past-life memory retrieval: cues to, 11, 12, 124–25, 127, 136, 202, 209; developmental factors in, 127, 130, 201–13, 222; factors on side of previous person, 207–9, 212–13; during meditation, 77, 196, 206, 212, 130; psychic blocks to, 200, 251, 259; state of consciousness factors in, 79, 202, 206–7, 208, 211–13. *See also* consciousness, altered states of, and past-life memory; dreams and past-life memory

past-life memory storage, 121; in "spiritual ego," 79; in subconscious, 38, 147–48, 189, 212, 227, 231, 247, 248, 251

past-life readings, 117, 224, 230–31, 233, 298; of Edgar Cayce, 96–97, 230

past-life regression (PLR), ix–x, xii–xiii, xiv, 96, 117, 213–23, 298, 301; distortions in, 201, 217–18,

264; versus involuntary past-life memory, 216, 220–22, 223; versus past-life readings, 224, 228, 231; and responsive xenoglossy 141, 182, 218–19; veridical, 218–19, 219–21

past-life therapy, 215–16, 298

Paterson, R. W. K., 249

patterns in reincarnation cases: cross-historical, 183; universal and near-universal, 178–80; culture-linked, 180–83, *180, 181, 182,* 183–89

Patrick Christenson, reincarnation case of, 186

Pauli, Wolfgang, xi–xii, xv, 285

Paulo Lorenz, reincarnation case of, 140, 195

Peabody Picture Vocabulary Test, 190

Peak in Darien experiences, 239

Peek, Kim, 282

Penelhum, Terence, 249

Penney Peirce, psychic identification of, 267

Peres, Julio, 199

person, versus personality, 46–47, 249

personal identity, postmortem survival, and reincarnation, 246–59; denied by Buddhism, 33–34, 111, 255, 261; and memory, 249, 250–51

personality, 39, 265, 271, 287; carried in subconscious, 38, 44, 189, 247–48, 248–49, 251, 259; merger of different constellations of, 265, 269; neurobiological influences on, 245, 246, 250, 260; versus person, 46–47, 249; postmortem developmental change in, 249–50; postmortem fragmentation of, 119, 248; postmortem persistence of, 33–34, 42, 99, 241, 246, 255, 285; postmortem transfer of to another spirit, 118; and processual karma, 39, 86; reappearance of in reincarnation cases, 17, 32, 120, 136, 206, 251–53, 256, 261, 285; reappearance of in transplant cases, 267–68, 269. *See also* MPD/DID

Phaedo, 111

Phaedrus, 111

Pharisees, 72

Pherecydes of Syros, 64, 66

Philo of Alexandria, 72

philosophy of organism (Whitehead), 254

phobias: in past-life therapy, 220; in reincarnation cases, xiv, 2–3, 95, 139, 163, 193–94, 207, 211; in transplant cases, 267–68

Phoh, Sergeant, reincarnation case of, 152

physical signs of reincarnation, 148–61; expressed in aspects of core identity, 156–57; expressed in internal diseases, 155–56. *See also* birth defects in reincarnation cases; birthmarks in reincarnation cases; facial similarity, between previous person and case subject

Pindar, 66–67

Piper, Leonora, 242

placebo effect, 148, 237, 238, 260

Planck, Max, 43

planned reincarnation, 55, 84–85, 88, 154, 172, 266, 293, 298

Plato, 41, 66, 67–68, 70, 71, 84, 111. *See also* Myth of Er

play, children's: behavioral sign in reincarnation cases, 137, 139, 140, 197, 229

Plotinus, 71

Plutarch, 70–71

poltergeist activity, 85, 124, 167, 172, 244, 298

population growth, reincarnation theory and, 111

Porphyry, 66, 71

possession: defined as occupation of a body by a spirit, 174, 299; reincarnation as long term, 159, 174; transient (mediumistic) or short term,

118, 174, 211, 212, 296; vitalism and, 279, 286; versus psychic obsession, 159; versus replacement reincarnation, 37, 174, 290, 297, 302; versus transplant cases, 268

Pourciau, Ethel Koscho, xxi, 15, 18, 24, 29

Pourciau, Evelyn: friend of Jennifer Schultz, 1–2, 8, 9–10, 17; house of, 14, 15, 21; witness in case of Rylann O'Bannion, xxi, 14, 16, 17, 18, 19, 21, 22, 24, 27, 29, 30, 32, 33, 50

Pourciau, Ruth, 14, 15, 15, 19

The Power Within, 214

Prasad, Jamuna, 100

Pratomwan Inthanu, reincarnation case of, 206, 230

prayer and past-life memory, 206

prebirth memories, 237, 243, 263, 299

precognition, 9, 50, 294, 299

preexistence without prior incarnation, 72, 73, 74, 111, 243, 259, 299

pregnancy cravings, 167, 303

pregnancy dreams. *See* announcing dreams

previous personality, versus previous person, 46–47, 249

previous persons in reincarnation cases, 46–47, 299; age at death of, 127, 179–80; case subjects' identification with, 55, 116, 126–27, 136–48; manner of death of, 179; mental qualities of, 152, 208; needs of expressed by case subjects, 200, 207–8; place of death of in relation to case subjects' birthplace, 171–72, 178–79, 186–87, 294, 296; and premortem planning of reincarnation, 55, 84–85, 88, 154, 172, 266, 293, 298; psi abilities of, 135; sex of, 178, 182–83, 182; unfinished business of, 178, 180, 207–8, 209, 212, 245, 306. *See also* interethnic cases; interreligious cases; international cases; relationship status, between

case subject and previous person;
sex-change cases
Pribram, Karl H., 269
processual karma, 39, 86, 189, 200, 300
processual soul theory, 235, 257–58,
259–60, 260–61, 270–71;
versus Buddhism, 261; versus
Cartesian substance dualism,
255–56; and concurrent and multiple
reincarnation, 265–67, 269–70;
versus New Age reincarnation
mythos, 263–64; and spiritual
advancement, 264; and transplant
cases 267–70; and transmigration,
262; versus Tucker, 256; versus
Weiss, 256
psi, 134, 268, 300; of children
with past-life memories, 50–51,
115, 135; of discarnate minds,
227, 248, 253, 255, 259; and
evolutionary biology, 279–80, 281,
282, 285; experimental detection
of, 96, 200, 244, 297; and mind/
brain interaction, 257, 258; of
nonhuman animals, 280; versus
past-life memory, 50–51, 116,
135–36; and past-life regression,
219, 222; of psychic practitioners,
226–27, 242, 296; and quantum
mechanics, 236–37; of reincarnating
mind, 147–48, 159, 253, 260, 284;
and retrieval of information from
Akashic Records/Akashic field,
222, 290; spontaneous cases of,
200, 289, 297, 298; subconscious
processing of, 248–49, 256, 304;
versus super-psi, 116, 136, 248.
See also extrasensory perception
(ESP); precognition; psychokinesis;
retrocognition; super-psi
Ψ-component (psi-component),
253
psi (ESP). *See* extrasensory perception
(ESP)
psi (PK). *See* psychokinesis (PK)
psychic identifications, 223–31, 300

psychics: past-life identifications of, xx,
201, 228; past-life readings of, 117,
224, 228
psychokinesis (PK), 50, 116, 279,
300; of discarnate agents, 167, 248,
259; initiated in subconscious, 244,
248; in lab tests, 116; in physical
mediumship, 244; in psychic healing,
147–48, 244; of reincarnating mind,
147–48, 159, 253, 260, 284. *See
also* maternal impression; poltergeist
activity
psychophore, 158, 159, 174, 253, 256,
301
psychoplasm, 253
psychosocial theory, 51, 88, 147;
assumptions of, 47, 114, 150, 178,
183, 301; challenges to, 123, 134,
143, 163, 187, 194; evaluation
of tenets of, 48–49, 190–92;
parapsychological extensions of,
115–18, 200. *See also* parental
guidance; social construction;
subjective illusion of significance
Pythagoras, 64–66, 111; past-
life memories of, 65–66, 88;
reincarnation teachings of, 41,
64–65, 274
Pyun, Y. D., 216

quantum biology, 236; and
reincarnation, 121, 271
quantum mechanics, 44, 52, 236,
276–77; and consciousness, 42–43,
123, 244, 247, 254; and process
metaphysics, 254, 257; and psi,
236–37, 258, 279–80; and survival/
reincarnation, 43, 121

Rakesh Gaur, reincarnation case of,
114–15, 130, 132–33, 135
Ramster, Peter, 218
Randall, John, 281
Rani Saxena, reincarnation case of, 124
Ransom, Champe, 106–7
Raven Progressive Matrices, 190

Ravi Shankar Gupta, reincarnation case
of, 151, 194
Rawat, K. S., 89, 93, 100, 115
Reber, Paul J., 148
rebirth: cross-cultural studies of
beliefs in, 60–63; history of beliefs
in, 63–75; operational definition
of, 37, 301; origin of belief in,
39–41, 42; variety of beliefs in
and about, 34–39, 53–63, 75–86.
See also animism; Buddhism;
Christianity; Hinduism; Judaism;
metempsychosis; reincarnation; Shia
Islam; transmigration
rebirth announcements, 166, 301;
through waking apparitions,
166, 172; through mediumistic
communications, 165, 172, 225, 296.
See also announcing dreams
rebirth syndrome, 91, 92, 95–96, 101,
117, 148, 152, 166, 178, 301, 303;
provides challenge to sociocultural
theory, 87–88, 123
recency effect, 128; in life series, 230–
31; in past-life memory, 128, 136
recitative xenoglossy, 141, 142, 218,
301, 307
Reena Kulshreshtha, reincarnation case
of, 135, 144–45, 199
Reichenbach, Bruce R., 75, 82
Reid, Chris, 133
reincarnation: criticisms of research on,
47–48, 49, 51, 103–10; evolutionary
biology and, 258, 281–83, 284–85,
286; operational definition of, 36,
301; origin of belief in signs of,
40–41, 42, 63, 148, 164;
philosophical ideas about, 246–59;
research on, xviii, 48–49, 92–94,
97–98, 98–101; versus possession,
174; versus transmigration, 36
Reincarnation and Biology, 104–5, 149,
151, 152, 158, 174, 187
relationship status, between case subject
and previous person, 100, 302;
acquaintance, 181, *181*, 182, 184,

185, 186, 289; family, 47, 56, 97,
165, 171, 179, 181–82, *181*, 184,
185, 186, 192, 294; stranger, 48,
97, 181, *181*, 184, 185, 186,
304
reminiscence bump, in past-life
memory, 128
repeater children, 155, 302
replacement reincarnation, 180, 251,
267, 290, 299, 301, 302, 306;
cases of, 175–77; in Hinduism and
Tibetan Buddhism, 37, 183, 297;
versus walk-ins, 176–77, 302
Republic, 68, 84, 170
responsive xenoglossy, 141,
142, 218–19, 302, 307
resurrection, bodily, 40, 63–64, 71, 72,
74
retention of past-life memory. *See*
past-life memory, episodic
retrocognition, 76, 118, 134, 136, 294,
302
retroprehensive inclusion, 117–18, 146,
213, 302
Rhine, J. B, 96
Rhine, L. E., 116
Richet, Charles, 141, 214
Rieder, Marge, 218, 264
Rig Veda, 68
Rivas, Titus, 89, 100, 112, 255
Robert Snow, regression case of, 219
Rochas, Albert de, 96, 214
Rogerio, reincarnation case of, 157
Rogo, D. Scott, 96, 106, 107–8, 119,
219; on adult past-life memories,
202, 205, 207
Roll, W. G., 119, 266–67
Rome, ancient, reincarnation beliefs in,
70–71
Rosemary, mediumistic case of, 226
Rossman, Martin, xiii
Rousseau, David, 239
Runki Runolfsson, mediumistic
communicator, 242, 250
Ruprecht Schulz, reincarnation case of,
175, 204, 207

Ryan Hammons, reincarnation case of, 130–31, 132, 135, 186, 203, 209
Ryerson, Kevin, xii, xiii–xiv, 102, 228, 231–32
Rylann O'Bannion: conflation of images, past and present, 12, 25, 31, 130; intermission memories of, 5, 164, 167, 169; behavioral memories of, 2, 22, 32, 136, 146; episodic past-life memories of, x, 1–33, 49–51, 101, 118, 127, 132, 186, 196; post-traumatic reactions of, 2–3, 6, 20–11, *22–23*, 32, 190, 193–94, 199; psi of, 8–9, 135

Saadia, 73
Sadducees, 72
Sahay, K. K. N., 93, 97, 99, 171–72, 202–3
Sakellarios, Stephen, 220, 228
Sakte Lal, reincarnation case of, 113–14, 115, 130, 132
Salva, Richard, 232, 233
Samararatne, Godwin, 100, 112, 131, 200
Santosh Sukla, reincarnation case of, 170
Saunders, Lyn A., 216, 220
Ven. Sayadaw U Sobhana, reincarnation case of, 171, 173
Schneider, Karl Camillo, 281
Schopenhauer, Arthur, 274
Schouten, Sybo, 49, 130
Schultz, Barbara, 2, 8, 11, 16, 18, 19, *26*
Schultz, Christopher, 16, *24*
Schultz, Jennifer, x, xi, xxi, 2, 6, 8–33
Schultz, Rachael, 2, 8, 11, 16, 19, *27, 28*
Schwartz, Jeffrey M., 238, 244
Schwartz, Stephan A., 230
Schwinger, Julian, 236
The Search for Bridey Murphy, ix, 97, 214–15
selection problem, 75, 164, 290, 294, 300–301, 302; elective solution to, 84–86, 164, 172, 293; karmic

solution to, xx, 75–80, 86, 164, 173, 184, 261–62, 296; theistic solution to, 80–84, 86, 164, 172–73, 305–6
self, 209; continuity of in reincarnation, 298; denied by Buddhism, 33, 111, 255, 290; "owner" of consciousness stream, 38, 302
Semïh Tutşmuş, reincarnation case of, 150
Semkiw, Walter, xii, xiii, 102, 231–33, 264, 267
Seneca, Lucius Annaeus, xiii–xiv, 233
Senegal, repeater children in, 155
Serer, repeater children among, 155
sex-change cases, 160; beliefs about possibility of, 184, 185, 188, 262, 303; cultural variance in incidence of, 182–83, *182*; gender nonconformity and dysphoria in, 194–95; physical signs and, 156; sex of subjects of, 178. *See also* Ma Tin Aung Myo, reincarnation case of
shamans, xiv, 41, 64, 65, 283; psychic identifications of, 185, 201, 223–24, 300
Shamlinie Prema, reincarnation case of, 135, 202
Sharada. *See* Uttara Huddar, reincarnation case of
shared experience. *See* intersubjectivity
Sharma, Poonam, 167–68, 177
Shealy, Norm, 102
Sheldrake, Rupert, 117, 270
Shermer, Michael, 103, 110, 134–35, 161
Shiffrin, Nancy, 215
Shirley, Ralph, 94, 96
Shomrat, Tal, 133
Shushan, Gregory, 41, 46
"silent" reincarnation cases, 152, 194, 226, 250, 251, 303
Simon, Christy, 16, *17*
Sinhalese, 131, 184, 195. *See also* Sri Lanka

Sivanthie and Sheromie Hettiaratchi, reincarnation cases of, 264
skills, language. *See* xenoglossy
skills in reincarnation cases, 42, 116, 140–43, 145, 299; and neural pathways, 147–48, 252; and super-psi, 146, 213
Skinner, B. F., 244
slime mold, learning/memory of, 133
Slobodin, Richard, 177, *180, 181*, 182, *182*, 183
Mrs. Smith, past-life memories of, 209, 219
social construction, reincarnation cases and, 47–48, 113–16, 135, 269, 301, 303; difficulties facing hypothesis of, 88, 140, 146, 158. *See also* parental guidance
solved reincarnation cases, 46–47, 302, 303; child versus adult, 209–10; versus solved regression experiences, 221; versus unsolved reincarnation cases, 128, 130, 131–32, 152, 179, 185, 192–93, 194, 195, 200; with written records made before verifications, 1–33, 105–6, 107, 130, 202–3
Som Pit Honcharoen, reincarnation case of, 210
Somer, Eli, 199
Somersan, Semra, 61
soul: denied in Buddhism, 37, 290; pre-existence of, 72, 73, 74, 111, 118, 243, 259, 299; splitting/ replication of, 35, 266–67, 297, 303; synonymous with life force, consciousness, mind, psyche, spirit, 37, 41, 124, 247, 292; treated as mental construct by social sciences, 40, 60–61
soul groups, 172, 263–64
soul mates, 263–64
soul splitting and replication, 35, 266, 267, 297, 303
Spanos, Nicholas P., 216, 217

spirit guides, xii, xiii, 85
Spiritism, 187, 274; Brazilian, 83–84, 226, 231, 252; French, 35, 83–84, 96
spirits, human, 39, 60, 304; animistic concepts of, 35, 41, 46, 85, 185, 290; considered mental constructs, 40, 45, 61; interact with living persons, 54, 85, 164, 166–67, 239–40; interact with living persons through mediums, 83, 124, 167, 171, 224, 225, 226, 229; interact with nonhuman spirits, 54–55, 77; interact with nonhuman spirits during the intermission, 54–55, 164, 168–69, 171; interact with nonhuman spirits in near-death experiences, 168, 240, 241; and New Age metaphysics, 85–86; and organ transplants, 268; and possession, 118; postmortem division or replication of, 35, 60, 111, 265. *See also* discarnate agency
spirits, nature, in animism, 35
spirits, nonhuman, 290, 293, 304; animistic concepts of, 35, 36, 37, 40, 41, 290; in announcing and departure dreams, 171, 173; and assisted reincarnation, 170, 171, 172–73, 290, 293, 306; as God's surrogates and underlings, 80, 172–73, 305–6; in intermission memories, 54–55, 164, 168–69, 169–70, 171, 172–73; in near-death experiences, 168, 240, 241; ontological status of, 170, 172; and repeater children, 155; and stem souls, 258, 304
spiritual advancement, 79, 85, 263, 306
Spiritualism, Anglo-American, 35, 40–41, 84, 96
Sri Lanka (formerly Ceylon), 112; Buddhism in, 69, 70; features of reincarnation cases in, 126, 130, 131, 153, 165, 178, *180*, 181, *181, 182*, 184, 195; psychological studies of case subjects in, 190–91, 192–93; reincarnation cases in, 98, 100, 132,

141, 144, 157, 160, 172, 230, 263,
264
Stanford-Binet Intelligence Scale, 192
Stapp, Henry P., 43, 120, 123, 158,
236–37, 244, 257, 260, 299
Stearn, Jess, 218
stem souls, 258–59
Stephen Stein, reincarnation case of,
143
Stevenson, Ian, life and work of, x,
xiv, 31, 209, 220; case collection of,
126, 128, 130, 131; colleagues and
successors of, 100–101; critics and
criticisms of, 45, 47, 103–8, 119,
121, 232; early life and career of,
98–99; field research methods of,
98–100; review of pre-1960 cases,
87, 97–98, 148, 225; terminology of,
46–47, 139, 141, 142, 174, 249, 290,
291, 293, 301;
Stevenson, Ian, writings and opinions
of, 48, 49, 131, 136, 146, 252,
262; on announcing and departure
dreams, 55, 163, 165, 166; on
anomalous-date cases, 174; on
beliefs of Shia Islamic sects, 48, 49,
71–72, 174–80; on birthmarks and
physical signs, 55, 149–58; on case
subjects' identification with previous
persons, 126–27; on children's play,
137; on cross-cultural patterns,
177–83, 183–87, 203; on cross-
historical patterns, 183; on deception
and self-deception, 111–12; on
ESP plus personation, 116, 146;
on geographical and psychological
factors, 171–72; on multiple-
reincarnation beliefs among the Igbo,
266; on parental guidance, 49, 113,
200; on past-life regressions, 217;
on phobias in reincarnation cases,
194; on postmortem influence of
premortem beliefs and expectations,
187–89; on previous persons
in natural-death cases, 208; on

psychophore, 158, 174, 253, 256;
on responsive xenoglossy, 141,
218; on retributive karma, 80,
160; on suppression attempts, 49,
196, 197; on twin pairs, 171; on
unfinished business, 180, 207–8;
on violent versus natural death,
179–80. *See also Reincarnation and
Biology; Twenty Cases Suggestive of
Reincarnation*
stigmata, 158, 237
Stokes, Douglas M., 246
Story, Francis, 100, 262
stranger relationship/stranger cases. *See*
relationship status
Strieber, Whitely, 46
Subashini Gunasekera, reincarnation
case of, 142
subconscious, 38, 159, 244, 246, 249,
304, 305; absent from Cartesian
substance dualism and Buddhism,
255, 261; blocks past-life memory
from reaching conscious awareness,
201, 228, 251, 259; versus cognitive
unconscious (implicit learning
and memory), 145, 148, 247–48,
295; collective/shared, 280, 284;
versus consciousness awareness,
38, 124, 247, 260, 292, 304; content
from influences behavior without
conscious awareness, 259; ensures
continuity of identity and self over
successive lives, 255; and entelechy/
vitalism, 281, 284; Freudian concept
of, 247, 248; holographic conception
of, 269; and memory distortions,
292; and memory storage, 133–34,
147, 227, 269, 282; merger of
multiple consciousness streams in,
269, 270; and multiple personality,
212, 228; Myers' concept of, 124,
243, 248; of nonhuman animals,
282; non-physical information-
bearing matrix , 256, 270, 282;
and past-life memory, 38, 147–48,

212, 227, 231, 251; and past-life readings, 227, 228; and past-life regression/therapy, 216, 217, 222; process view of, 254; and psi, 159, 248–49, 256; repository of behavioral dispositions, personality, etc., 124, 189, 231, 247, 248, 249, 251–52

subjective illusion of significance, 47, 103, 211, 301, 305

subjects of reincarnation cases: age at fading of past-life memories, 56, 90, 131–32, 148, 193, 195–96; age at first speaking of previous life, 48, 97, 125, 126, 203; age at replacement in replacement reincarnation, 175; differences from previous person in ethnicity, religion, or economic status, 137–40, 142–43, 184, 186–87, 188; differences of sex from previous person, 182–83, *182*; later development of, 100, 196; physical resemblance to previous person, 95, 155, 156, 157, 232; psi of, 8–9, 50, 115, 135; psychological evaluation of, 190–93; sex of, 97, 178. *See also* relationship status, between case subject and previous person

subliminal stratum of mind. *See* subconscious

substance dualism, Cartesian, 235, 253, 254, 299, 305; versus processual soul theory, 255, 257, 265, 267, 269–70, 285, 303

substance monism, 254, 300, 305

subtle body, 34, 247, 253, 254, 256. *See also* astral body; psychophore

successive lives, 65, 67, 255; physical signs in, 153–55

Sudduth, Michael, 43, 51–52, 116, 117, 213, 246, 248, 260

Sudhakar Misra, reincarnation case of, 175

suicide, and reincarnation cases, 153, 156, 171, 179, 226

Sujith Lakmal Jayaratne, reincarnation case of, 124, 127, 130, 137, 139

Suleyman Andary, reincarnation case of, 203–4

Süleyman Zeytun, reincarnation case of, 160–61

Sumitra Singh, reincarnation case of, 175, 176

Sunder Lal, reincarnation case of, 93, 171–72

Sunderlal, R. B. S., 92–93, 97

super-psi, 200, 212, 213, 248, 281, 292, 305; and behavioral signs, 136, 146, 147, 213; and maternal impression, 120, 150, 158; and mediumship, 226, 242; and psychic practitioners, 226–27, 242; versus regular psi, 116, 136, 248; and reincarnation cases, 116–17, 119, 136, 286–87. *See also* retroprehensive inclusion

suppression measures, enacted by parents, 49, 196–97

supraliminal stratum of mind. *See* conscious awareness

survival after death. *See* discarnate agency

Susan Eastland, reincarnation case of, 186

Swanton, John R., 54, 56

Swaran Lata, reincarnation case of, 137–38

Swarnlata Mishra, reincarnation case of, 128–29, 132, 135, 138, 147, 230; intermediate-life memories of, 129, 130, 140, 141

Sylvia, Claire, 268

synchronicity, xi–xiv, 232–33, 264, 291, 305; and Archetypal Synchronistic Resonance (ASR), xii, xiv–xv, 233

Syria, 34, 71; reincarnation accounts in, 92, 97

Tali Sowaid, reincarnation case of, 105, 156

Tarazi, Linda, 218

telepathy. *See* extrasensory perception (ESP)

Tellegen Absorption Scale, 192

terminal lucidity, 237, 239, 282, 305

Tertullian, 74, 110–11

Thailand, 99, 100; Buddhism in, 69, 70; experimental birthmarks in, 154; features of reincarnation cases in, 131, *180, 181, 182,* 185; reincarnation beliefs in, 61; reincarnation cases in, 138–39, 143, 144, 152, 175, 188–89, 197, 206, 225; transmigration account in, 262

theistic solution to selection problem. *See* selection problem

Theophilus of Antioch, 74

Theosophy, 78, 96, 98; and Akashic Records, 83, 117, 290; and astral body, 158, 253, 290; and karma, 38, 75, 78, 79–80, 302; and reincarnation, 78–79, 82, 110, 111, 173–74, 187, 235, 263; and transmigration, 36, 78

Thomason, Sarah G., 213, 218

Thompson, Evan, 45, 109, 247

thought bundles, 119–20, 146–47, 306

Thusitha Silva, reincarnation case of, 172

Tibet: Buddhism in, 36, 69–70, 76, 77; rebirth beliefs in, 37, 40, 63, 65, 66, 76, 78, 169, 261; reincarnation of adepts from, 85, 101; reincarnation accounts in, 225, 265, 266; tantric practices in, 266

Timaeus, 67, 68

Ma Tin Aung Myo, reincarnation case of, 139, 142, 157, 160; gender dysphoria and homosexuality in, 139, 195; geographical and psychological factors in, 171–72; mother's announcing dreams in, 164–65, 188

Maung Tinn Sein, reincarnation case of, 167

Tlingit, 53, 58, 148; features of reincarnation cases of, 163, 165, *180,*

181, 182, *182,* 185; reincarnation accounts and cases of, 54–55, 84–85, 149, 154, 194, 265; reincarnation beliefs and related customs of, 53–58, 60, 62, 136–37

Tomo, reincarnation case of, 140, 187

Tomonaga, Shinichiro, 236

Toradja, signs of reincarnation among, 61

Toran (Titu) Singh, reincarnation case of, 176

Toynbee, Arnold, 39–40

Tramont, Charles, xii–xiii

transmigration, 33, 44, 61; accounts of, 262; beliefs in, 61, 68, 71, 73, 78, 262, 265; operational definition of, 36, 37, 301, 306; and processual soul theory, 262

Transpersonal Process Metaphysics, 256

transplant cases, 267–70

Trobrianders, reincarnation beliefs of, 61

Trugman, Avraham, 73

Tucker, Jim B., 100, 108, 149, 151, 165, 178, 202, 256, 262, 273, 274; on intermission memories, 167–68, 177; on psychology of case subjects, 192; Asian reincarnation case investigations of, 176, 197; Western reincarnation case investigations of, 100, 101, 102, 125, 134–35, 140, 186

Tulving, Endel, 127, 145

Turkey, reincarnation beliefs and case investigations in. *See* Alevi

Twenty Cases Suggestive of Reincarnation, 54, 55, 98, 99, 100, 105, 106, 107, 132, 149, 174

twins, 81, 111, 170, 283

twins with past-life memories, 94–95, 171, 264; monozygotic, 143–44, 157–58

Tylor, Sir Edward Burnett, 34–35, 40–41, 42, 46, 60, 63, 148, 164

Tymn, Michael E., 268

unconscious: cognitive, 145, 148,
247–48, 295; collective, 117,
222–23, 233, 280, 290, 291, 305;
psychoanalytic conception of, 38, 47,
216, 248. *See also* subconscious
unconscious perception, 247
unfinished business: and apparitions,
241, 245; and mediumistic
communicators, 242, 245; and
reincarnation cases, 178, 180, 207–8,
209, 212, 245, 306
United States, 99, 100, 239, 243, 263;
features of nontribal reincarnation
cases in, 100, 126, 131, *180*, 181,
181, *182*, 183, 185–86, 199, 205–6;
nontribal reincarnation accounts and
cases in, 97, 101, 127, 138, 156, 166,
170, 194; psychological study of
case subjects in, 191–92, *192*, 193;
reincarnation beliefs in, 75, 78–80,
82–83, 85–86, 96, 195, 263–64.
See also Cristina Matlock; Rylann
O'Bannion; Will, reincarnation case
of
unsolved cases, 101, 128, 136, 182, 187,
188, 192, 194, 218, 306; with adult
subjects, 205, 221–31; behavioral
and physical signs in, 138, 139, 140,
142, 151, 156; features of, versus
solved cases, 131–32, 152, 179,
192–93, 194, 195, 200; and past-life
regression, 218, 219; and psychic
identifications, 226; veridical content
in, 231; xenoglossy in, 142, 182
Uttara Huddar, reincarnation case of,
211–13, 219, 231, 252

Valentinus, 74
van Helmont, Franciscus Mercurius, 274
Veer Singh, reincarnation case of, 138,
167, 168, 170
Veniaminov, Iouann (Ivan), 54
Venn, Jonathan, 217
Vietnam, reincarnation account in, 170,
175

Vineland Adaptive Behavior Scales, 192
violent death: and apparitions, 241, 245;
and mediumistic communicators,
242, 245
violent death in reincarnation cases,
x, 128, 179, 193, 241, 242, 245,
296; and age at death, 179–80;
and age at first speaking about
previous life, 179; cross-cultural
patterns in, 128, 131, 179–80, 193,
194; and intermission length, 179;
and memory errors, 131, 136; and
physical signs, 32, 152, 153; and
phobias, 2, 194; and post-traumatic
symptoms, 3, 32, 51, 193; in
unsolved versus solved cases, 131,
152, 179. *See also* suicide
Virgil, 70
Virginia Tighe, regression case of, 97,
214, 218, 219
Visoni, V. M., 108–9
Vital, Chaim, 73
vitalism, 275, 280–81, 284, 285, 293,
306
von Neumann, John, 236
Von Ward, Paul, 210, 253

walk-ins, versus replacement
reincarnation, 176–77, 302
Wallace, Alfred Russel, 274–75, 280
Wambach, Helen, 215
Wardle, Elise, 223
Warnasiri Adikari, reincarnation case of,
230, 262
The Wars of the Jews (The Jewish War),
74
Watson, John, 243–44
Weems, E. V., 1, 18
Wehrstein, K. R., 205, 230, 231
Weiss, Eric. M., 253, 256, 268
Wenzl, Aloys, 281
Werblowsky, R. J. Z., 33
West, M. L., 39
Western countries: features of
reincarnation cases in, 168, 169,

183, 186–87, 197–98; prebirth
memories in, 243; reincarnation
accounts and cases in, 48, 94–96,
100, 101–2; reincarnation beliefs in,
38–39, 63–68, 75, 78–80, 82–86,
200, 230, 263, 274, 300; resistance
to reincarnation belief in, 42, 102–3,
121, 271. *See also* United States
Wet'suwet'en, 100, 177; features of
reincarnation cases of, *180*, 181,
181, 182, *182*, 185; reincarnation
case of, 223; reincarnation beliefs
and related customs of, 58, 224
Wheatley, J. M. O., 253
White, Claire J., 45–46
Whitehead, Alfred North, 253,
254–55, 256, 257, 258, 260, 268,
289, 292, 297, 299–300, 304;
on the postmortem survival of
consciousness, 255, 257; and
quantum mechanics, 257
Wijeratne, reincarnation case of, 153,
160, 193
Will, reincarnation case of, 195, 205,
220, 230, 231
Willerslev, Rane, 59
William George, Jr., reincarnation case
of, 84–85

Williams, John, 14, 16, 19, *20*, 21, *22*
Willoughby-Mead, Gerald, 88–89, 97,
164, 166, 171
Wilson, Colin, 219–20
Wilson, Ian, 108, 184, 190, 216, 217
Ma Win Myint reincarnation case of,
139–40
Woods, Kellye, 216
Woolger, Roger J., 215, 216, 223
Wortabet, John, 92, 132
written records made before
verifications, solved reincarnation
cases with. *See* solved reincarnation
cases

xenoglossy, 141–43, 218–19, 298, 301,
302, 307

Maung Yin Maung, 155–56, 166
Yogananda, 38
Yukaghir, 59

Zohar, 73
Zolik, E. S., 215, 218
Zouheir Chaar, reincarnation case of,
172

About the Author and Contributors

James G. Matlock is coauthor with Erlendur Haraldsson of *I Saw a Light and Came Here: Children's Experiences of Reincarnation* (2016). He received a BA in English from Emory University in 1977; a master's in library science from the University of Maryland, College Park, in 1986; and PhD in anthropology from the University of Southern Illinois at Carbondale in 2002. He has worked at the American Society for Psychical Research in New York City and at the Rhine Research Center in Durham, North Carolina. He is presently affiliated with the Parapsychology Foundation as a Research Fellow. His chief research interests are reincarnation, near-death experiences, and other phenomena suggestive of postmortem survival, the anthropology of religion, and the history of parapsychology. In addition to *I Saw a Light and Came Here*, he has published numerous journal papers and book chapters in parapsychology and anthropology and has contributed articles on reincarnation to the Internet-based *Psi Encyclopedia*. Since 2014, he has taught an online seminar course on reincarnation research and theory, the basis of a series of twelve video conversations with Jeffrey Mishlove for his *New Thinking Allowed* YouTube channel, and for this book.

Jeffrey Mishlove received his PhD in parapsychology from the University of California, Berkeley, in 1980, the only doctoral diploma in "parapsychology" ever awarded by an accredited university. Dr. Mishlove is a past vice president of the Association for Humanistic Psychology and the recipient of its Pathfinder Award for his contributions to the field of consciousness exploration. He is also past president of the nonprofit Intuition Network, an organization dedicated to creating a world in which all people are encouraged to cultivate and apply their inner, intuitive abilities. His books include *The Roots of Consciousness* (1975, with an updated edition in 1997), *Psi Development*

Systems (1983), and *The PK Man* (2000). Between 1986 and 2002, he coproduced and hosted a public television series called *Thinking Allowed*, which in 2015 he revived on YouTube as *New Thinking Allowed: Conversations on the Leading Edge of Knowledge and Discovery*.

Michael Nahm studied zoology, botany, genetics, and paleontology and received his PhD in forestry from the Albert-Ludwigs-University of Freiburg, Germany, in 2006. In recent years he has initiated and coordinated national and international research projects on agroforestry. He is also a research associate at the Institute for Frontier Areas of Psychology and Mental Health (IGPP) in Freiburg. His parapsychology-related research interests include enigmas of evolution, unusual phenomena in near-death states, physical mediumship, and the history of parapsychology. He is a member of the Parapsychological Association, the Society for Psychical Research, and the Society of Scientific Exploration. He has authored or coauthored more than one hundred publications in scientific journals and other research outlets and published two books in German: *Evolution und Parapsychologie* (2007) and *Wenn die Dunkelheit ein Ende findet* (2012).